D1476601

Basic Technical Japanese

Basic Technical Japanese

Edward E. Daub

University of Wisconsin-Madison

R. Byron Bird

University of Wisconsin-Madison

Nobuo Inoue

Science University of Tokyo

The University of Wisconsin Press

University of Tokyo Press

The University of Wisconsin Press
114 North Murray Street
Madison, Wisconsin 53715, USA

3 Henrietta Street
London WC2E 8LU, England

University of Tokyo Press
7-3-1 Hongo, Bunkyo-ku
Tokyo 113, Japan

Library of Congress Cataloging-in-Publication Data
Daub, Edward E.
   Basic Technical Japanese / Edward E. Daub, R. Byron Bird, Nobuo Inoue.
   664 pp.   21.6 x 28 cm.
   Includes index.
   1. Japanese language—Textbooks for foreign speakers—English.
2. Japanese language—Technical Japanese—Translating into English.
I. Inoue, Nobuo, 1919-   . II. Bird, R. Byron (Robert Byron), 1924-
III. Title.
PL539.5.E5D38   1990
495.6'82421'0245—dc20   90-50082
ISBN 0-299-12730-3   CIP

ISBN 0-299-12730-3 (Wisconsin)
Territory: worldwide except for Japan and Oceania

ISBN 4-13-087051-3; 0-86008-467-1 (Tokyo)
Territory: Japan and Oceania

Contents

Preface

The purpose of this book is to teach scientists and engineers with no previous background in Japanese how to make accurate English translations of Japanese technical abstracts, research publications, and reference works. The main topics we include are the Japanese writing system, the elements of Japanese grammar, the development of a scientific vocabulary, and the use of dictionaries and other reference works.

The book is designed to serve as a text for self or group study as well as for formal courses in Japanese. If you are using the book for self-study, there are several features that you will find especially helpful: (1) the book is wholly self-contained — no additional material is necessary; (2) every grammatical point is illustrated with example sentences in Japanese, accompanied by translations; (3) English translations are provided for portions of the Japanese exercises that conclude the chapters on grammar; (4) in addition to the grammar chapters there are other chapters that contain actual Japanese technical texts from several fields, with notes and complete translations. Thus, at all stages you will be able to gauge your progress and assess your mastery of the writing system, grammar, and scientific vocabulary.

In studying the Japanese writing system you will learn the 46 KATAKANA (phonetic symbols used for transcribing foreign words), the 46 HIRAGANA (phonetic symbols used for certain Japanese words and all inflectional endings), and 365 of the 2000 or so KANJI used in modern Japanese (ideographs used primarily for writing nouns, verb stems, and adjective stems). The 365 KANJI that you learn in this book are high-frequency characters, their frequencies having been established by analysis of physics, chemistry, and biology textbooks. By emphasizing this carefully selected group of 365 KANJI we can assure you that right from the start you are learning the most important characters needed for technical translations. This is an enormous advantage, since mastery of the KANJI is the most difficult part of learning to read Japanese, and you will want to use your valuable time efficiently. If you learn the 365 required KANJI in this book, we estimate that you will recognize about 80% of the

KANJI in a typical technical text; your character recognition can be further enhanced by learning the supplementary list of 135 KANJI in Appendix C. If later you learn another 100 or so characters frequently used in your own specialty, you will be well on the road to reading within your major field of interest with little need to consult a KANJI dictionary.

Although the Japanese writing system is a major hurdle, the grammar is easier than that of most European languages: no gender, number, or case for nouns; only four irregular verbs; no verb inflection within a tense; in adjectives, no changes with number, gender, or case of the modified nouns. In this book you will learn only those elements of grammar and those inflected forms needed for technical reading. By not burdening you with many topics required for spoken and literary Japanese, we enable you to focus on learning how to read and comprehend technical Japanese. As a result you will be able to read about neutrons, halides, integrals, and computers, but you will not be able to buy a train ticket, ask about the nearest noodle shop, or savor the subtleties of Japanese poetry. After mastering technical Japanese, some readers will, we hope, decide to go further and study the spoken language. You will have nothing to unlearn, but you will have to master many other KANJI and some additional inflectional forms; you will also have to learn honorific forms, names for family members, verbs of giving and receiving, women's language, telling time, and colloquial expressions.

This book emphasizes the Japanese writing system from the outset. After the discussion of pronunciation in Chapter 2 and the introduction of the Japanese syllabaries in Chapters 3 and 4, romanized Japanese is purposely avoided. Our refraining from romanized spelling will enable you to focus on the standard Japanese orthography. In sample sentences, tabulations, and vocabulary lists, pronunciations are given in KATAKANA or HIRAGANA. Our emphasis on Japanese orthography will prepare you well for using dictionaries and other reference works that Japanese scientists and engineers themselves regularly consult.

For illustrative sentences in the grammatical discussions, we have made every effort to provide you with examples that are similar to those that you might encounter in actual technical reading. However, in the early chapters, because of the limited vocabulary and grammatical constructions available, some sentences may be somewhat oversimplified, compared to actual technical texts. Nonetheless, they always emphasize the high-frequency KANJI of technical Japanese.

After the early chapters, the example sentences become increasingly representative of actual texts, and in fact paragraphs from such texts begin to enter the exercises. Toward the end of the book, excerpts from essays by Japanese scientists and from authoritative reference works will provide you with an excellent test of your mastery of technical Japanese. Technical Japanese, you will find, abounds in long, involved sentences, and we have tried from Chapter 7 on to emphasize compound sentences and the techniques for coping with them.

This book incorporates several features that allow for periodic review and ready reference. The KANJI charts at the beginning of Chapters 5-20 can be used for reviewing readings and meanings. The large KANJI charts at the end of the book give you stroke counts and can be used to make KANJI cards. Appendices A and B will be helpful for reviewing verb and adjective endings that you may have forgotten. The subject index, KANJI lists, and vocabulary lists at the back of the book will also enable you to find information in the main body of the book quickly.

We do not regard this book as a "quick fix" for learning technical Japanese. We estimate that you will need at least a year to master the material by self-study and somewhat less with an instructor. Don't try to rush through the material too quickly; you will need a lot of time to become thoroughly familiar with the writing system and grammatical ideas, and you will also have to spend some time reviewing the contents of previous chapters.

This book is consistent with a long tradition in science and engineering education: universities have long provided courses on applied mathematics for engineers and scientists to enable them to learn how to use mathematical techniques without rigorous mathematical theorems and proofs. Many textbooks for such courses were written by scientists and engineers who themselves had garnered much experience in using mathematics as a tool. Thus a book on Japanese for scientists and engineers who want to be able to use Japanese without mastering irrelevant aspects of grammar, phonetics, and vocabulary is similarly appropriate. Perhaps because few linguists have recognized this need and even fewer have the necessary background in science and engineering to meet it, the lot of writing a textbook on technical Japanese translation has fallen on the three of us. We are scientists and engineers by training, who share a strong interest in both technical English and technical Japanese. All three of us have had extensive experience in technical translation and in lecturing in foreign languages. In writing here for our science and engineering colleagues, we have tried to keep grammatical and linguistic jargon to a minimum; wherever possible we have used terms that may be familiar from study of English grammar or the grammar of other European languages, even though the terminology may not be optimal from a linguistic point of view.

This book is the basis for a two-course sequence that is double-listed in the Department of East Asian Languages and Literature and in the College of Engineering at the University of Wisconsin, where one of us (EED) has been teaching technical Japanese for many years, using our previous book *Comprehending Technical Japanese* (University of Wisconsin Press and University of Tokyo Press, 1975, 4th Printing, 1987; Chinese Edition, 1985). Most of the material in the present book has been class tested, and we are very grateful to the students who, having no previous background in Japanese, labored many hours to master the material and offered many suggestions for improving the manuscript: John Banerian, Joan-Carles Casas, Timothy A. Cooper, Jonathan C. Dorofi, Donald L. Gaymon, Ching-Gang Peng, Byron J. Peterson, Joan Redwing, George W. Rodrigues, and I-Teh Tong.

We also wish to thank several people who helped us in preparing that manuscript and in improving it in various ways: Dr. Sigmund Floyd of Rohm and Haas, a bilingual chemical engineer with degrees from Tokyo Insitute of Technology and the University of Wisconsin, who read early drafts of most of the chapters and made extensive comments and helpful additions; Professor James L. Davis, our first student of technical Japanese, who went on to do his UW doctoral research at Kyoto University in the Faculty of Wood Science and Technology, who worked through all the exercises and evaluated them for relevance and suitability; Mr. Masami Yamaguchi, Supervisor of International Affairs at the University of Tokyo Press, who read the entire manuscript with great care, and suggested several vital revisions; Ms. Elizabeth Steinberg, Assistant Director at the University of Wisconsin Press, for her gracious cooperation and helpful advice in producing this book.

The two of us at Madison (EED and RBB) also wish to thank Professor Akira Miura, who heads the Japanese-language program at the University of Wisconsin, to whom we often turned for help on puzzling aspects of Japanese grammar. We must also thank the many professors and students from Japan whom we badgered from time to time through the years with all sorts of questions about Japanese grammar, usage, and vocabulary. They have been an invaluable on-the-spot source of information as only native speakers can be for the two of us who are not.

Special thanks go to Mr. Ken R. Lunde, a doctoral candidate in the Department of Linguistics with a minor in Japanese, who designed the gothic-style KANJI for teaching stroke order, offered ideas on KANJI usage and meanings, and served as the typographer of the final manuscript. We deeply appreciate the quality of his workmanship and the spirit with which he has met our many requests. Accuracy, thoroughness, dependability, good humor, dedication, and enthusiasm have marked his every effort.

Finally, EED wishes to acknowledge financial support from the University of Wisconsin, in the form of a sabbatical semester, for work on the manuscript for this book. In addition, RBB wishes to acknowledge funds made available from a Vilas Research Professorship and a John D. MacArthur Professorship, some of which were used for the preparation of the manuscript. We are very grateful for this assistance, without which the completion of this book would not have been possible.

July 1990   Edward E. Daub
Madison, Wisconsin   R. Byron Bird
Tokyo, Japan   Nobuo Inoue

Conventions and Notation

We have adopted a number of notational conventions in this book. These are summarized here for reference.

1. In English explanations, Japanese terms, particularly those with no satisfactory English equivalent, are written in capital letters: KANJI (Chinese characters), KATA-KANA (syllabary used mainly for writing loan words), HIRAGANA (syllabary used primarily for writing particles, adverbs, and endings).

2. In writing Japanese in roman letters in Chapters 1 and 2, ON readings of KANJI are written in capital letters and KUN readings of KANJI in lower-case letters. Words and endings that are written with HIRAGANA in Japanese are transcribed with lower-case letters, and those written with KATAKANA with underlined lower-case letters.

3. We use the letter 'x' followed by a vowel to mean "any syllable in the KANA syllabary ending with that vowel." Thus 'xa' stands for a, ka, sa, ta, na, ha, ma, ya, ra, wa, ga, za, da, ba, pa; 'xi' stands for i, ki, shi, chi, ni, hi, mi, ri, gi, ji, bi, pi; and so on.

4. In the KANJI tables that begin each chapter from Chapter 5 on, the ON readings are given first and then the KUN readings: the ON are written in KATAKANA, the KUN in HIRAGANA, as is customary in most Japanese reference works. If a verb's readings include a pair of verbs, one transitive (*v.t.*) and one intransitive (*v.i.*), the transitive verb is always given first. In giving the readings for verbs and other words that include OKURIGANA, the OKURIGANA are enclosed in parentheses. For example:

上	ジョウ	over, up, above, on
	うえ	upper part, top
	あ(げる)	to raise, elevate
	あ(がる)	to rise, go up

5. In presenting example sentences in the grammatical discussions, we first give the sentence as you may expect it to appear in standard technical Japanese writing. Immediately below, the same sentence is repeated entirely in KANA to show the pronunciation. Below that we give an English translation.

Example:
この溶液をビーカーに注ぐ。
このヨウエキをビーカーにそそぐ。
We pour this liquid into the beaker.

In the original Japanese sentence the underlining of a KANJI indicates that this is a KANJI you have not yet learned. We have tried to keep such not-yet-learned KANJI to a minimum in the earlier chapters of the book, but occasionally it was necessary to use such KANJI in order to emphasize some grammatical point or to make an appropriate scientific sentence. In the KANA version of the sentence, underlined KATAKANA give the ON readings of the KANJI, and underlined HIRAGANA give their KUN readings.

6. Brackets and braces are used in several ways.

(a)   In the text and in some tabular summaries, pronunciations in KANA are included between brackets: 注ぐ [そそぐ].
(b)   In vocabulary lists and some tables, when Japanese words are written in HIRAGANA, thick brackets will be used to indicate that it is also possible to write the word using KANJI: および【及び】.
(c)   In vocabulary lists braces are used for giving explanatory information, such as field of study or part of speech: 両性- amphoteric {chem}.
(d)   In an English translation of a Japanese sentence, if we wish to emphasize that some word not explicit in the text has to be supplied, that word is enclosed in brackets: 注ぐ [we] pour; 一定である [it] is constant. Generally we do not put the articles "a," "an," and "the" in brackets because they always have to be supplied in the English translation; the same comment holds for relative pronouns.

7. In addition to the use of parentheses for OKURIGANA in the KANJI tables, as mentioned in 4, parentheses are also used in several other ways.

(a) 一定で(は)ない means that in some situations 一定でない is used and in others 一定ではない is used.

(b) (非)線形 [(ヒ)センケイ] "(non)linear" means that 線形 is "linear" and 非線形 is "nonlinear"; this is done in vocabulary lists.

(c) (方程)式 [(ホウテイ)シキ] "equation" means that "equation" is sometimes written as 方程式 and sometimes simply as 式; this is done in vocabulary lists.

Also, in vocabulary lists, a not-yet-learned KANJI is underlined: 規則 [キソク] "rule."

8. Hyphens are used to indicate KANJI or JUKUGO that are used as standard prefixes or suffixes: 非- non-, un-; 外部- external; -中 within, during.

9. In the exercises at the ends of chapters, for KANJI compounds (JUKUGO) that contain one or more not-yet-learned KANJI, the Japanese pronunciation in KANA and the English meaning are immediately given within brackets. For verbs with not-yet-learned KANJI, the dictionary form is given. For example:

規格化[キカクカ = normalization]
保存された[from ホゾンする = to conserve]

When a JUKUGO containing a not-yet-learned KANJI appears a second time, often the pronunciation is given but not the meaning; in all further appearances of the KANJI, it will be underlined.

10. In tables of inflected forms an exclamation point (!) is used to call attention to irregular forms.

KANJI for Basic Technical Japanese

Mastering KANJI is critical in learning to read Japanese. The current JOOYOO KANJI list promulgated by the Japanese government for general use contains 1945 characters, but in this book we restrict our attention to 500 that are important for technical Japanese reading:

365	High-frequency KANJI	Chapters 5-20
135	Less-high-frequency KANJI	Appendix C

In selecting 365 KANJI for mastery (just one a day for a year!), we have been guided by frequency counts in physics, chemistry, and biology done in connection with the preparation of *Comprehending Technical Japanese* (CTJ), the general-use frequency list prepared by the National Language Research Institute (NLRI) in Japan, the GAKUSHUU KANJI (GK) list for Japanese elementary-school students, and some less official lists dealing with Japanese technical vocabulary. Our 365 KANJI include

(a)   339 of the 500 KANJI in the CTJ list (including the top 200);
(b)   230 of the top 500 of the NLRI list (including 124 of the top 200);
(c)   309 of the GK list of 996 KANJI (including 77 of the top 221 — the KANJI learned in the first two grades of elementary school).

These figures suggest several points. We have emphasized the KANJI that are frequent in technical terms; all of the top 200 of the *Comprehending Technical Japanese* list are included in our 365. Of our list of 365 KANJI, 85% are on the KYOOIKU KANJI list for elementary-school students in Japan and hence are quite important in other types of Japanese reading; however, 15% are not on the elementary-school list, yet they arise in many technical terms of importance in science and engineering. Clearly, two-thirds of the KANJI in the GK list are not of primary importance in technical reading, and the same is true of about half of the top 500 of the NLRI list.

We provide a supplementary list of 135 KANJI for those who want to continue their vocabulary building. We have included in this list KANJI that arise in common words that are not specific to any particular field of science. In selecting these words we have been guided by the frequency lists and also to some extent by our own experience and intuition.

We feel confident that the list of 500 KANJI can provide technical personnel with a firm foundation on which to build their own technical vocabulary. Equally important is our selection of JUKUGO (KANJI compounds), which is almost exclusively aimed at scientific and engineering terms. The student using this book will develop an extensive technical vocabulary that would not be learned in a general first-year course.

Basic Technical Japanese

CHAPTER 1 第一章 [ダイイッショウ]

Introduction

This chapter will give you an overview of major features of the Japanese language, especially those relevant to learning technical Japanese. Below is a sample technical sentence that you will be able to translate when you have finished this book.

太陽のまわりを運動する一惑星については、角運動量が一定値をとるだけではなく、力学的エネルギー、すなわち位置エネルギーと運動エネルギーとの和、もまた保存される。

We will use this sentence to discuss the most important features of the Japanese language. In Sections 1.1 through 1.3 we tell you about the three kinds of symbols used in this sentence. In Sections 1.4 and 1.5 we give a brief explanation of how sentences are put together and how nouns are "marked" with "particles" to indicate their functions within the sentence. In Section 1.6 we give a brief discussion of the inflected forms you will encounter, and in Section 1.7 we comment further on Japanese orthography. The last two sections, 1.8 and 1.9, give some hints on how to study technical Japanese and some information on reference works.

Consider this chapter as it is intended, to provide you with a first perspective on the language, and not as material that you should now commit to memory. All the points in this chapter will be presented in more detail later.

1.1 KANJI

You probably noticed right away in the Japanese sentence above that no spaces occur between the symbols; the words are simply run together. You may wonder how you will know where one word ends and another word begins. You will find that the beginnings and ends of words can be inferred from the three kinds of symbols used in a Japanese sentence and from the "particles" that serve as "markers" in the sentence. In this and the following sections we discuss these clues.

You can gain the first clue by looking carefully at the symbols. Some are more complex than others and appear in clusters. Look again at the sentence with these more complex symbols enclosed in brackets; note that only one of these more complex symbols appears singly.

[太陽]のまわりを[運動]する[一惑星]については、[角運動量]が[一定値]をとるだけではなく、[力学的]エネルギー、すなわち[位置]エネルギーと[運動]エネルギーとの[和]、もまた[保存]される。

The individual symbols within the brackets are called KANJI. KAN means "China"; JI, "character": thus, "Chinese character." The Japanese did not write their language until they adopted Chinese writing in the fifth and sixth centuries A.D. and adapted it to their language. Not only did they take over the Chinese characters along with their meanings, they also introduced into their language the Chinese method of forming complex words by joining several characters together. These words — words formed by combining several KANJI and pronounced with sounds adopted from China — are called KANGO (KAN being an abbreviation for KANJI, GO meaning "word"). Pronunciations adopted from China are called ON readings.

Below we give the KANGO and the one lone KANJI as they appear in the sample sentence above, together with their pronunciations and their meanings. We have bracketed those parts of the meaning that are necessary in English but not stated in the Japanese: here, the definite and indefinite articles, which do not exist in Japanese.

太陽	TAIYOO	[the] sun
運動	UNDOO	motion
一惑星	ICHI-WAKUSEI	[a] single planet
角運動量	KAKU-UNDOO-RYOO	angular momentum
一定値	ITTEI-CHI	constant value
力学的	RIKIGAKU-TEKI	mechanical
位置	ICHI	position
和	WA	sum
保存	HOZON	conservation

(Pronounce the consonants approximately as in English; the vowels roughly as in the Spanish words *amigo* and *Venezuela*. Double vowels and double consonants indicate a doubling of the length of the vowels and consonants. Details of pronunciation are given in Chapter 2, but be sure to pronounce DOO as "dough.") Some of these KANGO entered the language when Japan adopted Chinese writing, e.g., TAIYOO, "[the] sun." Others originated with the introduction of Western science, e.g., KAKU-UNDOO-RYOO, "angular momentum."

The meanings of the individual KANJI combine to give the more complex meaning of a KANGO. TAIYOO combines TAI, meaning "fat and burly," and YOO, the positive principle of activity and brightness in Chinese philosophy: thus, "sun." The next word, UNDOO, combines UN, "to transport," and DOO, "to move": thus, "motion." WAKU means "to wander," and SEI means "star": thus, "planet" or "planets." (Japanese nouns do not have singular and plural forms.)

The hyphenated words show how KANJI can be added to KANGO as prefixes and suffixes. ICHI-WAKUSEI adds the prefix ICHI to WAKUSEI. The prefix ICHI adds the KANJI for "one": thus, "[a] single planet" or simply "a planet."

KAKU-UNDOO-RYOO involves both a prefix and a suffix. KAKU means "angle," so KAKU-UNDOO means "angular motion." The suffix RYOO, meaning "quantity," added to UNDOO gives "quantity of motion": thus, "momentum." KAKU-UNDOO-RYOO, therefore, is "angular momentum." ITTEI-CHI follows the same pattern: it adds the suffix CHI to ITTEI. ITTEI combines two KANJI: ITSU, meaning "one and the same," and TEI, meaning "fixed, determined": thus, "constant." CHI means "value": thus, ITTEI-CHI means "constant value." (Note that the combination ITSU plus TEI becomes ITTEI. This change in pronunciation is discussed in Sections 2.5 and 5.4.)

TEKI, in contrast to these suffixes that add meaning, plays a grammatical role. It converts the preceding noun into an adjective. RIKIGAKU, combining RIKI, "force," and GAKU, "study, learning," means the field of study known as "mechanics." The addition of TEKI transforms RIKIGAKU from the noun "mechanics" to the adjective "mechanical." We will discuss the remaining KANGO when we further analyze this sentence in the next few sections.

We want to stress, however, that learning KANJI is the key to learning to read Japanese, and that concentration on those KANJI that are frequent in technical Japanese is the key to learning to read technical Japanese. Thus, as indicated in the Preface, we emphasize a very carefully selected group of 365 KANJI, and we can assure you that they are the most important KANJI in technical Japanese.

From the discussion of KANGO above, it should be clear that the Japanese language has a highly developed word-building scheme. You will often be able to guess the meaning of a KANGO from knowledge of the individual KANJI. The number of KANGO that can be formed goes up approximately as the 1.4 power of the number of KANJI, so learning 365 KANJI will give you access to over three thousand KANGO.

In the sample Japanese sentence the symbols that are not KANJI are KANA; they represent basic syllables of spoken Japanese and comprise two parallel but quite distinct sets of phonetic symbols: KATAKANA and HIRAGANA. The first set is angular in its strokes, the second cursive. In the next two sections we discuss these phonetic symbols, but first a brief comment on their origins.

After the Japanese adopted KANJI, they developed KANA in order to provide a simple way to write native Japanese words not written with KANJI and to write endings for the verbs and adjectives whose stems were written in KANJI. At first the Japanese chose rather simple KANJI to represent the basic Japanese sounds; to write the sound 'ka', they used the simple KANJI 加 that was pronounced 'ka'; to write the sound 'u', the simple KANJI 宇 that was pronounced 'u'.

To simplify these phonetic symbols, two strategies developed. In one strategy, a small part of the character was chosen to represent the sound. Thus, in this strategy 加 became カ; 宇 became ウ. This strategy apparently developed among Buddhist monks in order to speed their writing.

The second strategy developed among the ladies of the imperial court when they composed poetry. They gradually transformed the original phonetic KANJI when they wrote them with rapid and continuous brush strokes. In this strategy, 加 became か; 宇 became う. Thus, two independent sets of symbols for syllables evolved: angular KATAKANA and cursive HIRAGANA.

1.2 KATAKANA

In technical Japanese you will encounter KATAKANA symbols primarily as words that transliterate Western scientific terms and the names of Western scientists into words having Japanese pronunciations, roughly similar to the original pronunciations. These clusters of KATAKANA symbols provide another way to identify the beginnings and endings of words in the continuum of KANJI and KANA within a Japanese sentence.

Only one KATAKANA word appears in the sample sentence above; you may be able to spot it because it appears three times in quick succession. To help you find it we highlight it below by putting its symbols in brackets.

...力学的[エネルギー]、すなわち位置[エネルギー]と運動[エネルギー]...

The word is エネルギー, enerugii, "energy." It follows each of three KANGO, forming a compound word with each. If you check the list of KANGO, you will find that the three words mean "mechanical," "position," and "motion." The addition of enerugii to these meanings gives the terms "mechanical energy," "potential energy," and "kinetic energy."

Words such as enerugii written in KATAKANA need not be attached to a KANGO; enerugii can stand alone. Such words that transliterate Western words and are written in KATAKANA are called GAIRAIGO, literally, words that have come from outside: GAI, "outside"; RAI, "come"; and GO, "word." In most cases you will be able to recognize GAIRAIGO in your own field from the pronunciations.

1-4

GAIRAIGO are not limited to technical terms; there are countless Western words imported into everyday Japanese. For example, gorufu is "golf," tenisu is "tennis," and biiru is "beer." Many such words are abbreviated almost beyond recognition: waapuro, short for waado-purosessa, is "word processor"; pasokon, short for paasonaru-konpyuuta, is "personal computer."

1.3 HIRAGANA

The remaining symbols in the sentence consist of HIRAGANA symbols, and they represent nouns, verbs, phrases, and particles. Particles are so important in Japanese grammar that we will devote the entire next section to them. Here are the words and phrases written in HIRAGANA.

まわり	mawari	surroundings, circuit
...について	ni-tsuite	with regard to ...
する	suru	do(es), perform(s)
とる	toru	take(s) on
...だけではなく	dake-de-wa-naku	not only ...
すなわち	sunawachi	that is (to say)
また	mata	in addition
される	sareru	is (are) done

The verb 'suru' merits special attention. It means "do(es)" or "perform(s)." However, when it is attached to a KANGO noun, it changes that preceding KANGO noun into a verb. Thus, when 'suru' is attached to UNDOO, "motion," the combination means "[it] executes motion," i.e., "[it] moves [along]." When it is attached to HOZON, "conservation," the combination means "perform(s) conservation," i.e., "conserve(s)." 'Sareru' is the passive form of 'suru', so HOZON-sareru means "is conserved." Such KANGO-suru verbs are common in technical Japanese.

1.4 Particles

We have now introduced all the words and phrases in the sentence except for the particles. Written with HIRAGANA symbols, particles appear between words and phrases and knit these words and phrases into longer phrases and clauses. The particles in our sentence are all single HIRAGANA symbols; there are others written with two or more HIRAGANA.

The particles that appear in the sample sentence are の (no), を (o), は (wa), が (ga), と (to), and も (mo); we highlight them with brackets.

太陽[の]まわり[を]運動する一惑星について[は]、角運動量[が]一定値[を]とるだけではなく、力学的エネルギー、すなわち位置エネルギー[と]運動エネルギー[と][の]和、[も]また保存される。

To show you the functions performed by these particles we excerpt the pertinent phrases in the sentence, bracketing the particles.

太陽[の]まわり	TAIYOO-[no] mawari	circuit around [the] sun
まわり[を]運動する	mawari-[o] UNDOO-suru	moves on [its] circuit
一惑星について[は]	ICHI-WAKUSEI-ni-tsuite-[wa]	with regard to a planet
角運動量[が]	KAKU-UNDOO-RYOO-[ga]	[the] angular momentum
一定値[を]とる	ITTEI-CHI-[o] toru	takes on a constant value
位置エネルギー[と] 　運動エネルギー 　[と][の]和	ICHI-enerugii-[to] UNDOO- 　enerugii-[to]-[no]-WA	[the] sum of [the] potential and [the] 　kinetic energies
力学的エネルギー[も]	RIKIGAKU-TEKI-enerugii-[mo]	also [the] mechanical energy

Let us now show how particles function as signposts or markers.

a. Particles after Nouns; Postpositions: 'no' (の) and 'to' (と)

The next-to-last entry in the foregoing paragraph has two nouns in succession, each followed by 'to'. This construction joins the two nouns as the word "and" does in English. Thus, ICHI-enerugii-to UNDOO-enerugii-to means "potential and kinetic energy" (the second 'to' may be omitted).

The particle 'no' is most often translated by "of" as in enerugii no WA, "the sum of the energies." Another example, which does not appear in the sample sentence, is WAKUSEI no UNDOO-enerugii, "[the] kinetic energy of [the] planet." In both of these examples the noun followed by 'no' is equivalent to the possessive form in English. Sometimes, however, the particle 'no' indicates some other kind of relationship between the two nouns; thus, in the sample sentence, TAIYOO-no mawari corresponds in English to "circuit around [the] sun." There is no one-to-one correspondence between Japanese postpositions and English prepositions.

The other important postpositions, which do not appear in the sample sentence, are 'ni' and 'de'. The particle 'ni' following a noun indicates the place where something is, whereas 'de' indicates where some action is taking place. For example, TAIYOO-ni indicates that something is "in the sun"; TAIYOO-de shows that something is happening "in the sun" or "at the sun." Not all postpositional particles correspond to prepositions in English, as you will see next.

b. Particles after Topics or Subjects: 'wa' (は), 'ga' (が), and 'mo' (も)

Two particles in the sample sentence play roles in Japanese that are not found in English. They are postpositional, i.e., they follow the words to which they refer, but they do not correspond to prepositions in English. They indicate that the previous word or phrase is a topic or a subject of a sentence or a clause. The particle 'wa' follows ICHI-WAKUSEI-ni-tsuite to indicate that the previous phrase is the topic of the sentence. The particle 'ga' follows KAKU-UNDOO-RYOO, indicating that KAKU-UNDOO-RYOO is the subject of the verb HOZON-sareru. These particles are not translated in English.

1-6

They simply serve as markers that guide the reader through the sentence. However, when the particle 'mo' is the subject marker, as in the phrase RIKIGAKU-TEKI-enerugii ... mo, 'mo' has to be translated because it means "also."

c. The Particle after the Object of the Forthcoming Verb: 'o' (を)

As the particle 'ga' indicates the subject of a clause, the particle 'o' indicates the object of the verb in the clause. This particle appears immediately after the noun that is the object of a verb. It joins the two, the object of the verb coming first. Thus, we have ITTEI-CHI-o toru: "takes on a constant value." With verbs of motion, the particle 'o' following the noun identifies the region through which the motion occurs; hence TAIYOO-no-mawari-o UNDOO-suru means "move(s) on [its] circuit around [the] sun."

1.5 Sentence Structure

In contrast to English, where the normal word order is subject-verb-object, Japanese is one of the subject-object-verb languages. Linguists also refer to these languages as left-branching because their modifying clauses precede the nouns that they modify and thus appear to the left of the noun modified.

Our sentence has one left-branching modifying clause: TAIYOO-no mawari-o UNDOO-suru, which means "move(s) on [its] circuit around [the] sun." It modifies the noun ICHI-WAKUSEI, "a planet," which comes after the clause ending with the verb "suru." Thus, the noun plus its modifying clause means "a planet that moves on its circuit around the sun."

Developing the ability to understand left-branching modifying clauses is perhaps the most critical step in learning to comprehend technical Japanese because you meet these modifying clauses before you know what they modify.

We can now join the pieces of information in the sample sentence. We will write it first in KANJI, KATAKANA, and HIRAGANA, and next in romanized form. The vocabulary list and the English translation of the sentence follow. Note how our romanization indicates the three kinds of writing in the Japanese sentence. KANGO are written in capital letters; KATAKANA words in lower case with underlining; HIRA-GANA in lower case with no underlining. Thus, the three styles of romanization should help you to observe the three kinds of Japanese writing that occur in the sentence. In the romanized sample sentence, we use hyphens to connect words and particles that form units of information.

太陽のまわりを運動する一惑星については、角運動量が一定値をとるだけではなく、力学的エネルギー、すなわち位置エネルギーと運動エネルギーとの和、もまた保存される。

TAIYOO-no-mawari-o UNDOO-suru ICHI-WAKUSEI-ni-tsuite-wa KAKU-UNDOO-RYOO-ga ITTEI-CHI-o toru dake-de-wa-naku, RIKIGAKU-TEKI-enerugii, sunawachi ICHI-enerugii-to UNDOO-enerugii-to-no-WA, mo mata HOZON-sareru.

太陽のまわりを	TAIYOO-no-mawari-o	on [its] circuit around [the] sun
運動する	UNDOO-suru	moves
一惑星	ICHI-WAKUSEI	[a] single planet
については	ni-tsuite-wa	with regard to {topic}
角運動量が	KAKU-UNDOO-RYOO-ga	[the] angular momentum {subject}
一定値をとる	ITTEI-CHI-o toru	takes on a constant value
だけではなく	dake-de-wa-naku	not only that [but]
力学的エネルギー	RIKIGAKU-TEKI-enerugii	[the] mechanical energy
すなわち	sunawachi	that is to say
位置エネルギーと運動 エネルギーとの	ICHI-enerugii-to UNDOO- enerugii-to-no	of [the] potential and [the] kinetic energies
和	WA	[the] sum
も	mo	also
また	mata	in addition
保存される	HOZON-sareru	conservation is done

With regard to a planet moving on its circuit around the sun, not only does the angular momentum take on a constant value, but (in addition) the mechanical energy, that is to say, the sum of the potential and kinetic energies, is also conserved.

You may already have noticed this feature of Japanese sentence structure: verbs appear at the ends of modifying clauses and sentences. They are therefore not difficult to pick out. However, what is difficult is the fact that until you reach the verb, you will not know whether it will be affirmative or negative. Add to this uncertainty that of left-branching clauses — where you read without knowing whether you are reading a dependent modifying clause or the main clause of the sentence — and you see that some challenges lie ahead.

The pieces of information in a Japanese sentence come in patterns different from those in English sentences, and only practice will give you the skill to process the pieces in Japanese and to fit them into English sentence patterns. But take heart — Japanese is in some respects simpler and more regular than English and other Western languages, and we now introduce some of these simpler characteristics of nouns, verbs, and adjectives.

1.6 Nouns, Verbs, and Adjectives

A common misconception is that Japanese grammar is very complicated. The fact is, however, that the grammatical rules and the inflectional forms are considerably easier than in Western languages.

Japanese nouns have no gender, number, or case, and no definite or indefinite articles are used. (Compare that with *der*, *die*, and *das* of German and the declensions of nouns in German and Russian.) When you have learned nouns like

エネルギー	enerugii	energy	力学	RIKI-GAKU	mechanics
運動	UNDOO	motion	化学	KA-GAKU	chemistry
太陽	TAIYOO	sun	物理学	BUTSURI-GAKU	physics

there really is nothing more to learn about them.

Almost all Japanese verbs are regular (only four are irregular)! (Compare that with the myriad of irregular verbs in French, Spanish, or Russian.) Furthermore, within one Japanese "tense," there are no inflections: "suru" means "I do," "you do," "he/she does," etc. (Compare this with French: *je fais, tu fais, il fait, nous faisons, vous faîtes, ils font.*) Japanese verbs, however, are inflected by the addition of endings to the stem to indicate various tenses and meanings.

		PRESENT	
Affirmative	示す	shimesu	[we] show
Negative	示さない	shimesanai	[we] do not show

		PAST	
Affirmative	示した	shimeshita	[we] showed
Negative	示さなかった	shimesanakatta	[we] did not show

		PROVISIONAL	
Affirmative	示せば	shimeseba	if [we] show
Negative	示さなければ	shimesanakereba	if [we] do not show

		DESIDERATIVE	
Affirmative	示したい	shimeshitai	[we] want to show
Negative	示したくない	shimeshitakunai	[we] do not want to show

		PRESENT PASSIVE	
Affirmative	示される	shimesareru	[it] is shown
Negative	示されない	shimesarenai	[it] is not shown

These and other verb forms can all be obtained by using clear sets of rules. Note that the stem of the verb ('shime') is written in KANJI (示) and the endings in HIRA-GANA. Whereas "not" in English indicates negation, there are separate endings in Japanese for affirmative and negative.

Japanese adjectives behave more like verbs than like English adjectives. For example, instead of resembling the English adjective "white," the Japanese adjective, 'shiroi' (白い), is like a verb, "to be white."

		PRESENT	
Affirmative	白い	shiroi	[it] is white
Negative	白くない	shirokunai	[it] is not white

		PAST	
Affirmative	白かった	shirokatta	[it] was white
Negative	白くなかった	shirokunakatta	[it] was not white

| Affirmative | 白ければ | shirokereba | if [it] is white |
| Negative | 白くなければ | shirokunakereba | if [it] is not white |

There are many more endings, but not so many as for verbs. 'Shiroi' is an example of an i-adjective (so called because the present affirmative ends in 'i'), and all i-adjectives have exactly the same endings. Another group of adjectives, called the na- and no-adjectives, are also regular and can be inflected.

Thus, Japanese nouns and inflected forms will not be as difficult to master as you may have been led to believe. The major hurdle will be learning to read Japanese writing, KANJI and KANA.

1.7 Further Comments on the Writing System

As we pointed out in Section 1.3, the Japanese language is written using three kinds of characters.

KANJI: These Chinese characters are used for writing most nouns, most adjective stems, most verb stems, and some adverbs.

HIRAGANA: These phonetic symbols are used to write endings on verbs and adjectives; some nouns, verbs, and adjectives; and conjunctions, particles, pronouns, and demonstratives.

KATAKANA: These phonetic symbols are used chiefly in transliteration of GAI-RAIGO.

The HIRAGANA and KATAKANA tables are made up of syllables; each table contains 46 basic characters. These phonetic symbols are introduced along with exercises for learning to write and read them in Chapters 3 and 4. They must be learned thoroughly before going on to Chapter 5 and beyond.

KANJI number in the thousands, but the Japanese government has tried to restrict the use of these characters to about 2000. For reading technical Japanese, knowing our 365 high-frequency KANJI should enable you to recognize about 80% of the KANJI encountered in the fields of physics, chemistry, and biology. But whatever the number, learning to recognize KANJI is a major undertaking, and locating KANJI in a KANJI dictionary is time-consuming and often frustrating.

But this brings us to an even more frustrating feature of KANJI. They have multiple readings: one or more "ON readings" to represent their pronunciations in KANGO, and often one or more "KUN readings" to represent pronunciations in native Japanese words. When you encounter a KANJI, you have the difficult task of deciding which reading to use.

For example, consider the KANJI 力 that appeared in the sample sentence. It means "force" or "power." It has two ON readings, RIKI and RYOKU. Thus, it is read

RIKI in 力学, RIKIGAKU, but RYOKU in 電力, DENRYOKU, which means "electrical power." If it appears alone, it is read 'chikara', the Japanese word for "force." Or, consider its companion in RIKIGAKU, 学, which we have already told you means "study, learning." Fortunately, it has only one ON reading, GAKU. When it appears alone, however, it takes on its KUN reading, 学ぶ, 'manabu', the verb meaning "study (studies)." Not only does its pronunciation change, but it also requires HIRAGANA appended to its stem reading ('mana') to indicate the various inflections, as you already saw in the inflections for the verb 'shimesu'.

Beginners are often troubled because the orthography of Japanese is not completely standardized. For example, the verb 'manabu' is sometimes written with KANJI and HIRAGANA 学ぶ (as was done above) and sometimes in HIRAGANA まなぶ. In fact, the same author may use these different "spellings" on the same page, both of which clearly represent the verb 'manabu'. Since both are understandable, you should be able to cope with this lack of standardization in Japanese writing.

In contrast to these difficulties with KANJI and HIRAGANA, you will find most GAIRAIGO written in KATAKANA simple and straightforward.

エンジン	enjin	engine	ピストン	pisuton	piston
エネルギー	enerugii	energy	ベンゼン	benzen	benzene
エントロピー	entoropii	entropy	ニュートン	nyuuton	Newton

Some may cause trouble until you become accustomed to the limitations of Japanese sounds for expressing English pronunciations.

ビーカー	biikaa	beaker	レーザー	reezaa	laser
アルコール	arukooru	alcohol	オルト	oruto	ortho-
レンズ	renzu	lens	ベクトル	bekutoru	vector

Some may be less obvious because they originated in other Western languages, for example, German names of elements that came via Dutch chemistry books:

| カリウム | kariumu | potassium | ナトリウム | natoriumu | sodium |

or names of French scientists:

| ラウール | rauuru | Raoult | ラグランジュ | raguranju | Lagrange |

Once learned, however, they are not difficult to recognize when encountered a second time.

1.8 How to Study This Book

In the next four chapters we will lay the groundwork for reading Japanese writing. Chapter 2 will introduce romanization, the representation of Japanese with the roman alphabet, and pronunciation. You have already encountered romanization of

Japanese words in this chapter, and you probably sounded the syllables correctly in many cases. Chapter 2 will give you a more detailed understanding of how Japanese sounds and of how it is represented in the two major systems of romanization: the modified Hepburn system, which is used in this book; and the KUNREI system, which is used in the technical dictionaries compiled by the Japanese Ministry of Education, Science, and Culture.

Chapter 3 will focus on KATAKANA and GAIRAIGO and will provide you with copious exercises to work through in order to develop writing and reading skills. You will simply have to memorize these symbols and how they are used to construct words. Chapter 4 will do the same with HIRAGANA. You will have to master both KATAKANA and HIRAGANA before moving on to Chapter 5.

In Chapter 5 you will be introduced to KANJI, their stroke orders and stroke counts, the system of classifying them by radicals — special sub-parts of the KANJI — and looking them up in dictionaries; the difference between ON and KUN readings; and the formation of KANGO. In Chapter 5 you will also begin to memorize KANJI at the rate at which they will be introduced in succeeding chapters, usually 20 or 25 per chapter. By the end of this book, you will know the 365 KANJI most frequent in the sciences.

After you have mastered the fundamentals of Japanese writing, you will be able to begin the study of Japanese grammar that follows in Chapters 6 through 13. In addition to the grammar explanations and the new KANJI plus vocabulary in each chapter, there will be readings to help you master the grammar, the KANJI, and the vocabulary. Chapters 6 through 13 contain those elements of Japanese grammar needed for technical translation. Chapters 14 and 15 introduce you to some of the special features of Japanese mathematical and chemical terminology and nomenclature. Then in Chapters 16 through 20 we give you some additional reading practice with no additional grammar study, but again with new KANJI in each chapter.

Chapters 6 through 13 are organized as follows:

- A table that lists the KANJI introduced in the chapter, together with the ON and KUN readings and fundamental meanings
- A vocabulary list that gives technical terms using the above KANJI
- A grammatical discussion along with example sentences and English translations
- Exercises emphasizing KANJI, vocabulary, and grammar, with some English translations

First familiarize yourself with the new KANJI and JUKUGO and additional vocabulary. Then read the grammar discussions, paying particular attention to the sample sentences, which you should read and re-read until you understand them thoroughly. At this point go back and study the new KANJI and vocabulary to make sure you have thoroughly mastered them. Then proceed to the exercises and readings. These may include additional vocabulary items, but you need not memorize them.

In technical translation you need only be able to recognize the KANJI. However, you will find it helpful to practice writing the KANJI so that you become more familiar with the structure, especially with the radicals by which they are organized in most KANJI dictionaries. Furthermore, writing the KANJI will help you learn how to count the number of strokes, and stroke counts are also necessary for looking up KANJI in a dictionary. KANJI charts in the back of the book will be your guide.

Some students find it helpful to make flash cards, with the KANJI on one side and the ON and KUN readings on the other. They can then review the KANJI by going through the cards frequently. An additional tactic is to add JUKUGO that include the KANJI on the card to promote facility in reading. In addition you might decorate your room or your office with KANJI and JUKUGO so that you see these characters often as you go about your daily activities. In any event, you must get well acquainted with KANJI so that they cease to be foreign — so that they become familiar and friendly.

1.9 Reference Works

In order to do effective technical translation you will need to have some reference works. Above all you will need a KANJI dictionary. The following are now available:

A. N. Nelson, *The Modern Reader's Japanese-English Character Dictionary*, Tuttle, Rutland, Vt. (1974), 2nd (Revised) Edition.

M. Spahn and W. Hadamitzky, *Japanese Character Dictionary with Compound Lookup via any Kanji*, Nichigai Associates, Tokyo (1989).

Osaka University of Foreign Studies Staff, *A New Dictionary of Kanji Usage*, Gakken Co. Ltd., Tokyo (1982).

P. G. O'Neill, *Essential Kanji*, Weatherhill, New York (1973).

K. G. Henshall, *A Guide to Remembering Japanese Characters*, Tuttle, Rutland, Vt. (1988).

Table 1.1 gives some information about these dictionaries. Clearly the first two are the most extensive, and any serious translator must have one of these two. For beginners the other three dictionaries may be useful because they teach the reader how to write KANJI and how to count strokes. In the Gakken dictionary the JUKUGO (compounds) are grouped together to emphasize the various meanings of the KANJI, and this is particularly helpful for beginners. The O'Neill dictionary contains the Chinese (Mandarin) pronunciations, which may be helpful to those who have studied Chinese.

It is also important to have a large Japanese-English dictionary with romanized entries available, and on occasion to have the companion English-Japanese dictionary as well. The Kenkyusha dictionaries are the best (though the Japanese entries in the English-Japanese volume are given only in KANJI and related HIRAGANA, thus giving no indication of the pronunciation). The Japanese-English Kenkyusha Dictionary offers a remarkable coverage of many scientific terms.

Table 1.1 KANJI Dictionaries

| | no. of KANJI | WAYS TO LOOK UP KANJI | | | | KANJI COMPOUNDS | | stroke order |
		by radicals	by strokes	by ON-KUN	by meaning	how many?	with KANJI not appearing first in compound	
Nelson	4775	yes	no	yes	no	very many	no	no
S & H	5906	yes	no	yes	no	very many	yes	no
Gakken	2000	no	yes	yes	yes	many	yes	yes
O'Neill	2000	no	yes	yes	no	2-3	yes	yes
Henshall	1945	no	yes	yes	no	3	yes	no

Science dictionaries are also important. The Japanese Ministry of Education, Science, and Culture (Monbusho) has arranged for a series of small dictionaries to be prepared for various fields: mathematics, astronomy, physics, meteorology, optics, chemistry, zoology, botany, geology, genetics, mechanical engineering, electrical engineering, instrumentation technology, nuclear engineering, civil engineering, metallurgy, geography, logic, dentistry, construction, seismology, and aeronautical engineering. The romanization in these dictionaries is KUNREI, and their publishers are varied. The dictionary in your own field from this series would be well worth having for accurate technical terms.

The most comprehensive science dictionary is the set published by Interpress, *Kagaku Gijutsu Nijuugoman-go*, 2 volumes, Japanese-English and English-Japanese, Tokyo (1983). Literally translated, the title means "Two hundred and fifty thousand words in science and technology." Only a professional translator need have these volumes at hand, but they have become the standard reference work.

What you should finally acquire is a technical dictionary that is used for reference by Japanese scientists and engineers. In the physical sciences, *Rikagaku Jiten*, published by Iwanami, is indispensable. The index lists English, German, French, and Russian technical terms in the physical sciences and engineering, and every entry corresponding to these terms gives the Japanese technical term plus an excellent discussion of its meaning. There is no better way to expand your knowledge of technical Japanese than to read about key concepts in your discipline in *Rikagaku Jiten*. Iwanami has a companion volume for the life sciences, *Seibutsugaku Jiten*.

For additional grammar information you may find the following books helpful. The best in romanized texts are

A. Alfonso, *Japanese Language Patterns*, Sophia University Center of Applied Linguistics, Tokyo (1971), 2 volumes. Written with a wealth of illustrative sentences and very comprehensive, it is also easy to use for self-study.

S. E. Martin, *A Reference Grammar of Japanese*, Yale University Press, New Haven (1975). Though not particularly easy to read, it is a gold-mine of information that includes many obscure points of grammar not to be found in other grammar books.

Books somewhat less extensive in scope that include Japanese writing are

O. Mizutani and N. Mizutani, *An Introduction to Modern Japanese*, The Japan Times, Ltd., Tokyo (1977).

Y. Yoshida et al., *Japanese for Today*, Gakken Co., Ltd., Tokyo (1973).

M. Soga and N. Matsumoto, *Foundations of Japanese Language*, Taishukan Publishing Co., Tokyo (1978).

All three books focus on the spoken language and give basic vocabulary for daily life in Japan. They include copious exercises for self-study. The first two use both romanized and Japanese text; the third, very little romanized text.

A helpful, easy reference grammar for use in translation is

Y. M. McClain, *Handbook of Modern Japanese Grammar*, Hokuseido Press, Ltd., Tokyo (1981).

All entries are in romanized text, and the book has an excellent set of indexes.

Another important reference grammar is

S. Makino and M. Tsutsui, *A Dictionary of Basic Japanese Grammar*, The Japan Times, Ltd., Tokyo (1986).

It contains much useful information about the usage of particles and verb forms and the nuances among closely related expressions.

CHAPTER 2 第二章 [ダイニショウ]

2 Pronunciation and Romanization

In this chapter you will learn the sounds of Japanese and how to read Japanese words written in roman letters (rooma-JI). Even though you do not need to know how to speak Japanese in order to do technical translations, it is a good idea to learn correct pronunciation at the outset. The explanations given in this chapter will supply minimal information on pronunciation; the best method of acquiring good pronunciation habits is to listen to a native speaker or to tapes.

Roman letters are very helpful as an initial step for learning how to pronounce Japanese words. However, the most important reason for learning how to read romanized Japanese is that many Japanese-English dictionaries and KANJI dictionaries use romanization. In addition, roman letters can be used for entering Japanese phonetically into word processors and electronic dictionaries.

Unfortunately there is not one system of romanization, but several. The two most important ones are the modified Hepburn (or hebon-SHIKI) romanization, named after a 19th-century Presbyterian medical missionary, and the KUNREI-SHIKI romanization, which is the official system adopted by the Japanese government. Both systems are encountered in reference works needed for technical Japanese translation.

To illustrate the pronunciations of the various roman letters, for the most part we use GAIRAIGO that will appear again in Chapter 3; these will be written in lower-case letters and underlined. In a few places we illustrate pronunciations with KANGO that occur in Chapter 5 or shortly thereafter; these will be written in capital letters.

2.1 Vowels

The five vowels of Japanese are given in Table 2.1 in the order in which they appear in the Japanese syllabary, along with their approximate pronunciations. It is important to remember that these vowels must be pronounced crisply and quickly; they are not slurred into diphthongs as in English. Examples of GAIRAIGO that contain the five vowels are

antena	antenna	ozon	ozone
uran	uranium	amin	amine
benzen	benzene	okutan	octane
giga	giga {prefix used in SI units}		

Table 2.1 The Vowels

Symbol	Approximate Pronunciation	Additional Comments
a	*a* in father	
i	*i* in police	throat muscles much tighter than in English
u	*u* in rhubarb	make the 'u' sound with the throat muscles but leave the lips and facial muscles relaxed
e	*e* in bet	
o	*o* in open	between the 'o' in "open" and the 'ou' in "fought"
Note: All of these vowels must be pronounced quickly and crisply.		

The vowels 'i' and 'u' are sometimes nearly inaudible when they occur between the voiceless consonant sounds 'k', 's', 'f', 'sh', 't', 'ch', 'p', and 'h'. Hence supin (spin) is pronounced like s'pin, and hekisan (hexane) sounds like hek'san. Even though the vowels are nearly inaudible, the syllables in which they occur still must have the same length as all other syllables. When a 'u' at the end of a word follows a voiceless consonant, both in Japanese words and in GAIRAIGO, it is nearly inaudible. For example, wakkusu (wax) is pronounced wakk's'.

The vowels 'i' and 'u' do not disappear when they occur in an accented syllable in GAIRAIGO. For example, the prefix "cyclo-" in "cyclohexane" is shikuro in Japanese. Because the first syllable is accented in English, the 'i' is clearly heard in Japanese and the word is not pronounced sh'kuro.

No system of romanization is perfect, and we now point out one important irregularity. The combination 'iu' is often pronounced as 'yuu,' where the doubled vowel indicates a vowel of doubled length. This is particularly true of the verb 'iu' (say(s)) and the ending -iumu for many metals.

neputsuniumu	(pronounced nep'tsunyuumu)	neptunium
kadomiumu	(pronounced kadomyuumu)	cadmium

A few books actually use the 'yuu' spelling in their romanization.

When two or more vowels appear in succession, each vowel in the sequence is given equal length.

sain	sine	ion	ion
kosain	cosine	sofutouea	software

When you pronounce these words, be sure that each vowel gets one "beat" in an almost metronome-like timing. The last word above should be pronounced so-fu-to-u-e-a in six distinct "beats" of equal length.

2.2 Doubled Vowels

Japanese contains five "doubled vowels," that is, vowels that are two "beats" in length; these are sometimes referred to as "long vowels." These double-beat vowels are shown in Table 2.2.

Table 2.2 Doubled Vowels

Symbol	Approximate Pronunciation	Additional Comments
aa *	*a* in calm	
ii *	*i* in machine	
uu	*u* in plume	
ee **	*ei* in reign	should not be a diphthong as in English
ei **	*ei* in reign	
oo	*o* in bone	should be a lengthened 'o' sound of Table 2.1, and not a diphthong as in English
* 'aa' and 'ii' never occur in ON readings.		
** 'ee' is used only in GAIRAIGO, and 'ei' is used in the ON readings of KANJI.		

The doubled vowels are indicated by repeating the vowel, the only exception being the use of 'ei' in ON readings of KANJI. Some examples of words containing doubled vowels are

enerugii	energy	KEISO	silicon
biikaa	beaker	REI	example
oomu	ohm	KANKEI	relation
paasento	percent	TEISUU	constant
ameeba	amoeba		
eeteru	ether		
etanooru	ethanol		
kondensaa	condenser		
kuuron	coulomb		

It is extremely important to give double vowels their full two syllable length. For example, NODO means "throat," NOODO, "concentration (in a solution)," and NOO-DOO, "an agricultural road."

2.3 Consonants

The consonants are shown on the left side of Table 2.3. These include one consonant cluster ('ts') and two semivowels ('y' and 'w'). Most of these sounds present no particular problem, since they are sounds familiar to you in English. The only ones that deserve special attention are 'f', 'r', and 'n'.

Table 2.3 Consonants and Palatalized Consonants

Consonants			Palatalized Consonants	
Symbol	Approximate Pronunciation		Symbol	Approximate Pronunciation[5]
k	*k* in kit	(voiceless)	ky	*k y* in took you
g	*g* in get[1]	(voiced)	gy	*g y* in beg you
s	*s* in sat	(voiceless)	sh	*s y* in bless you
z	*z* in zip[2]	(voiced)		
t	*t* in top	(voiceless)	ch	*t y* in let you
d	*d* in dot	(voiced)	j	*d y* in did you
p	*p* in pit	(voiceless)	py	*p y* in keep you
b	*b* in bit	(voiced)	by	*b y* in rob you
h	*h* in hot[3]		hy	(no English equivalent)
f	*f* in foot[4]			
m	*m* in met		my	*m y* in from you
n	*n, m, ng* in net, met, and sing[4]		ny	*n y* in upon you
r	*r* in pero (Spanish)[4]		ry	(no English equivalent)
y	*y* in yet			
w	*w* in wasp			
ts	*ts* in puts			
1 Sometimes pronounced like 'ng' in "sing" in the middle of words and in the particle 'ga.'				
2 In 'za' and 'zu' some speakers pronounce 'z' as 'dz.'				
3 The 'h' in the syllable 'hi' is almost like the 'ch' in German *ich*.				
4 For more detailed explanation see text.				
5 Pronounced as in normal conversation.				

If you pronounce 'f' as in "foot," you will be understood by the Japanese. But if you listen closely, you will note that the Japanese 'f' sound is more like the 'wh' in "when" but with the lips almost pressed together as if to form the 'p' sound. Some Japanese technical words using 'f' are

fureon	Freon	furufuraaru	furfural
furanji	flange	firamento	filament

The consonant 'f' is always followed by the vowel 'u' in Japanese words and in KANGO, but in GAIRAIGO other vowels may follow.

The sound that we represent by 'r' is not at all like the 'r' in English. It is really just one "roll" of a trilled 'r'. If you roll an 'r' you will note that your tongue just barely touches the gum right behind your upper teeth. The Japanese 'r' is made with a quick flap of the tongue against the gum. Practice the 'r' sound in the following:

rajio	radio	rajian	radian
ruumen	lumen	purazuma	plasma
renzu	lens	purizumu	prism

By now you will have realized that since there is no 'l' in Japanese, the 'r' is used instead. The 'r' sound and the 'd' sound may easily be confused. In making the 'r' sound the tongue touches the roof of the mouth about one centimeter behind the teeth, whereas in making the 'd' sound the tongue touches the back side of the teeth. Try pronouncing 'doro-doro' (the Japanese word for "muddy") just for practice.

The symbol 'n' serves several functions: (a) When it precedes a vowel in the syllables 'na', 'ni', 'nu', 'ne', 'no', it is pronounced as the 'n' in "net." (b) When it is at the end of a word, it is pronounced like a nasal sound (as in French) similar to the 'ng' in "sing" but without the tip of the tongue touching the roof of the mouth. Examples are

| seren | selenium | pasokon | personal computer |
| chitan | titanium | moribuden | molybdenum |

The 'n' in these words is a syllable by itself and has a full "beat." It is sometimes called a "syllabic -n." (c) When a "syllabic -n" precedes a consonant, its pronunciation depends on the consonant that follows:

When followed by	Pronounce '-n' as
b, m, p	*m* in "them"
k, g	*ng* in "sing"
other consonants	*n* as in "hen" or a nasal sound as in (b) above

Examples are

ganma	gamma	moomento	moment
anpea	ampere	tangusuten	tungsten
inpiidansu	impedance	tanku	tank

(d) When a "syllabic -n" is followed by a vowel or a syllable beginning with a 'y', we separate the '-n' and the following letter by an apostrophe, and the '-n' is pronounced as a nasal sound as in (b) above. This "syllabic -n" occurs only in KANGO, and some examples are

NIN'I	arbitrary	BUN'ATSU	partial pressure
TAN'I	unit	DEN'ATSU	voltage
GEN'IN	cause	EN'UNDOO	circular motion
TEN'I	transition	KAN'YOO	common usage
GEN'ON	fundamental tone	TAN'YOO	simple leaf

You have to be meticulous in pronouncing these words. For example, TAN'I is three "beats" long and means "unit," but TANI is two beats long and means "valley." After the apostrophe, the vowels becomes somewhat distorted: 'i' is pronounced like 'yi', 'e' like 'ye', and 'o' like 'wo', approximately.

2.4 Palatalized Consonants

A consonant immediately followed by the 'y' sound in "yet" is called a "palatalized" consonant. The romanized spelling of the palatalized consonants is shown on the right side of Table 2.3. Most of them are represented by putting a 'y' to the right of the consonant. However, the palatalized 's', 't', and 'd' are represented by 'sh', 'ch', and 'j' respectively in the Hepburn system, because these are familiar to English speakers as the 'sh' in "sheep," the 'ch' in "cheap," and the 'j' in "jeep." The pronunciations in Table 2.3 are somewhat more accurate, however.

You will note from Table 2.3 that all but two of these palatalized consonants occur in English. The pronunciation of the palatalized 'h', written as 'hy', is similar to the 'h' in "huge," particularly as pronounced in England. The palatalized 'r', designated by 'ry', is the most difficult sound for English-speaking people to master. It requires making the single-flapped 'r' followed quickly by the 'y' in "yet."

Some GAIRAIGO and KANGO in which palatalized consonants appear are

kyurii	curie	RYUUTAI	fluid
nyuuton	newton	RYOOSHI	quantum
hyuuzu	fuse	NYUURYOKU	input
konpyuuta	computer	HYOOMEN	surface
juuteriumu	deuterium		
byuretto	burette		

In connection with the word konpyuuta, we should point out that some writers use 'aa' in lieu of 'a' in words like this which end in "-er" in English.

2.5 Doubled Consonants

Just at the end of the foregoing section we gave the word byuretto. This word has four "beats": byu-re-t-to. The 't' preceding the syllable 'to' is a "syllabic consonant" and the result is a doubling of the consonant 't'. The two t's are not pronounced separately. Instead, when you place your tongue behind your teeth to form the syllabic '-t', you maintain the tongue in that position for one full beat and then proceed to pronounce the final syllable. Notice carefully that the 'tt' is not pronounced like the 'tt' in "cattle," where, in fact, the length of the 'tt' is no different from the 't' in "cat." On the other hand, the 'tt' in "cat tail" requires the kind of lengthened consonant that one encounters in Japanese.

Table 2.4 Doubled Consonants

Symbol	Approximate Pronunciation	Do NOT pronounce as
kk	*k k* in bookkeeper	*ck* in ticking
ss	*s s* in bus siren	*ss* in bussing
tt	*t t* in cat tail	*tt* in cutting
pp	*p p* in top point	*pp* in topping
nn	*n n* in ten nets	*nn* in tennis
nm	*m m* in drum major	*mm* in drummer
ssh	*s sh* in bus show	*sh* in bashing
tch	*t ch* in hot chocolate	*tch* in itching
tts	*tt s* in watt second	*tz* in pretzel
gg	*g g* in big gate	*gg* in bigger
dd	*d d* in bad dog	*dd* in bidder
bb	*b b* in tub bath	*bb* in rubbing
jj	*d j* in bad job	*dg* in badger

The various possible "doubled consonants" (also called "long consonants") are shown in Table 2.4. The last four entries in the table involve the voiced consonants and occur only in GAIRAIGO. Some examples of doubled consonants in GAIRAIGO are

<u>watto</u>	watt	<u>tonneru</u>	tunnel {as in "tunnel effect"}
<u>suitchi</u>	switch	<u>nikkeru</u>	nickel
<u>anmonia</u>	ammonia	<u>pipetto</u>	pipette
<u>burijji</u>	bridge	<u>Raipunittsu</u>	Leibniz

It is very important to distinguish between single and doubled consonants. For example, JIKKEN (experiment) has four "beats": JI-K-KE-N; on the other hand, JIKEN (event) has three "beats": JI-KE-N.

2.6 The Syllabary: Modified Hepburn Romanization

The Japanese do not think of the sounds in their language in terms of vowels and consonants, but rather in terms of syllables. A syllable can be any of the following:

- a. A vowel
- b. The first or second half of a doubled vowel
- c. A consonant plus a vowel
- d. A palatalized consonant plus a vowel
- e. The syllabic '-n'
- f. The syllabic consonants '-k', '-s', '-t', '-p', etc.

In Table 2.5 we give the syllables of Japanese in the form of a "syllabary." In the center of the table, outlined by a heavy line, you will find a 5×10 matrix of squares, most of which contain entries. This is a familiar array to all Japanese, since they regard this as their list of "basic" syllables. In the top row (the "a-row") you see the five vowels arranged in the traditional Japanese order a-i-u-e-o. In the "a-column" you see the ten rhyming syllables a-ka-sa-ta-na-ha-ma-ya-ra-wa. It is essential that you memorize these two sequences, since these specify the order in which entries are to be found in dictionaries and other listings based on the traditional syllabary. Every Japanese can rattle off these two sequences just as English speakers can recite their ABC's. There are a few blank squares in the 5×10 matrix; these syllables are missing in modern Japanese. Each of the syllables in the table can be written by one KANA symbol, as will be described in Chapters 3 and 4.

Directly below the basic 5×10 matrix is an additional 5×5 matrix of syllables. Although these are written separately, they are related to certain of the entries in the basic table. The first three syllables in the a-column of the lower table are 'ga', 'za', and 'da', which contain voiced consonants; they correspond to the entries 'ka', 'sa', and 'ta', which contain the corresponding voiceless consonants. Then we find 'ba' containing a voiced consonant, and 'pa' with the corresponding voiceless consonant. The Japanese regard 'ba' and 'pa' as being related to 'ha' in the basic table. In certain word formations, phonetic changes occur in which syllables in the basic table are replaced by modified syllables.

NIHYAKU	two hundred	NISEN	two thousand
SANBYAKU	three hundred	SANZEN	three thousand
ROPPYAKU	six hundred		

In Chapters 3 and 4 you will see that the KANA used to write the syllables in the lower auxiliary table are obtained simply by adding diacritical marks to the KANA in the basic table.

Note that several of the entries in Table 2.5 are irregular. Where we expect to find 'si', 'ti', and 'di' — all nonexistent syllables in Japanese — we find that the consonants have been palatalized, so that 'shi', 'chi', and 'ji' appear instead. Similarly, where we expect 'tu' and 'hu', we find 'tsu' and 'fu'. In addition, where we expect to see 'wo' we find 'o', so that the sound 'o' appears twice in the table. Finally, where we expect to see the voiced analogs of 'shi' and 'tsu' (which do not exist in modern spoken Japanese), we find 'ji' and 'zu' instead (enclosed in braces), thus duplicating syllables from an adjacent row; the duplication of these two syllables is discussed further in Chapters 3 and 4.

In the right-most three columns of the table we have two more auxiliary tables. In the top 3×9 matrix we have the syllables formed from the palatalized consonants and the vowels 'a', 'o', and 'u'. Then below, in a 3×5 matrix, we find the same kinds of

Table 2.5 The Syllabary: Modified Hepburn Romanization

Basic Syllables

a	i	u	e	o
ka	ki	ku	ke	ko
sa	shi	su	se	so
ta	chi	tsu	te	to
na	ni	nu	ne	no
ha	hi	fu	he	ho
ma	mi	mu	me	mo
ya		yu		yo
ra	ri	ru	re	ro
wa				o

Syllabic Consonants

| -k |
| -s |
| -t |
| |
| -h, -f |
| |
| |
| |
| |

| -n |

| -g |
| |
| -d, -j |
| -b |
| -p |

Palatalized

kya	kyu	kyo
sha	shu	sho
cha	chu	cho
nya	nyu	nyo
hya	hyu	hyo
mya	myu	myo
rya	ryu	ryo

Modified

ga	gi	gu	ge	go
za	{ji}	zu	ze	zo
da	ji	{zu}	de	do
ba	bi	bu	be	bo
pa	pi	pu	pe	po

Modified and Palatalized

gya	gyu	gyo
{ja}	{ju}	{jo}
ja	ju	jo
bya	byu	byo
pya	pyu	pyo

Vowel Doubling

+	+	+	+	+
a	i	u	e, i	o

+	+	+
a	u	o

combinations corresponding to the consonants 'g', 'z', 'd', 'b', and 'h' of the lower table at the left.

In the left-most column we indicate the various syllabic consonants. The dash before the consonant serves as a reminder that the consonant is always preceded by a syllable ending in a vowel. By combining these syllabic consonants with the consonants of the syllables in the same row, we get 'kk', 'ss', 'ssh', 'tt', 'tch', 'tts', and 'pp', which are just the doubled consonants discussed earlier. The syllabic '-n' can precede any syllable to the right of it in the table and therefore occupies a special position. The syllabic '-h', '-g', '-d', '-j', and '-b' occur only in GAIRAIGO.

At the very bottom of the table we indicate how the vowels in the various syllables can be lengthened by adding an additional vowel. Usually this is done by doubling the vowel, but 'e' is lengthened by adding an 'i' in ON readings of KANJI.

Table 2.5 is an important summary of the sounds of the Japanese language, arranged in terms of the syllables that occur in the language. Whereas Westerners think in terms of sounds and letters, the Japanese think in terms of syllables and KANA. In the next two chapters you will learn how to read and write the KANA that correspond exactly to the entries in Table 2.5.

2.7 The Syllabary: KUNREI-SHIKI Romanization

In Table 2.6 we show the KUNREI-SHIKI table of syllables. The basic difference between the modified Hepburn system and the KUNREI system is in the symbols assigned to the consonants. In the Hepburn system the consonant symbols within a given row are changed to reflect the changes in pronunciation, whereas in the KUNREI system the same symbol is used throughout, and one has to assign different phonetic values to the consonant symbols depending on which vowel follows. The KUNREI table looks neater because of the greater consistency. For example, in the ta-row, we have ta-ti-tu-te-to, which looks nice, but one has to remember that the 't' in these syllables has three different pronunciations.

This consistency is particularly clear if we compare the syllables containing palatalized consonants.

Hepburn	ya	yu	yo
shi	sha	shu	sho
chi	cha	chu	cho
ji	ja	ju	jo

KUNREI	ya	yu	yo
si	sya	syu	syo
ti	tya	tyu	tyo
zi	zya	zyu	zyo

In the KUNREI system, the 'ya', 'yu', and 'yo' appear in all syllables with palatalized consonants, whereas the Hepburn system contains irregularities. Also, the doubled consonants appear to be simpler in the KUNREI system, since one finds simply 'ssi', 'tti', and 'ttu' appearing with the consonant symbols doubled.

Table 2.6 The Syllabary: KUNREI-SHIKI Romanization
{Underlined syllables differ from those in the Hepburn System}

Basic Syllables

Syllabic Consonants

	a	i	u	e	o
	a	i	u	e	o
-k	ka	ki	ku	ke	ko
-s	sa	si	su	se	so
-t	ta	ti	tu	te	to
	na	ni	nu	ne	no
-h	ha	hi	hu	he	ho
	ma	mi	mu	me	mo
	ya		yu		yo
	ra	ri	ru	re	ro
	wa				o

-n

Palatalized

kya	kyu	kyo
sya	syu	syo
tya	tyu	tyo
nya	nyu	nyo
hya	hyu	hyo
mya	myu	myo
rya	ryu	ryo

Modified

-g	ga	gi	gu	ge	go
	za	{zi}	zu	ze	zo
-d, -z	da	zi	{zu}	de	do
-b	ba	bi	bu	be	bo
-p	pa	pi	pu	pe	po

Modified and Palatalized

gya	gyu	gyo
{zya}	{zyu}	{zyo}
zya	zyu	zyo
bya	byu	byo
pya	pyu	pyo

Vowel Doubling

+	+	+	+	+
a	i	u	e, i	o

+	+	+
a	u	o

2-11

We feel that the KUNREI system is not particularly suitable for introducing English-speaking people to Japanese pronunciation, and hence we do not use it in this book. Nonetheless, you must become familiar with it in order to use certain reference works.

2.8 Romanization Used in Reference Works

In almost all dictionaries that give the Japanese entries in roman letters, the doubled vowels represented in this book by 'aa', 'ii', 'uu', 'ee', and 'oo' are written 'ā', 'ī', 'ū', 'ē', 'ō' in the modified Hepburn system and 'â', 'î', 'û', 'ê', 'ô' in the KUNREI system. The principal exception to this rule is that 'ii' in KUN readings is not denoted by use of a mark over the symbol; in GAIRAIGO the doubled 'i' is written as 'ī' (or 'î') in some books but as 'ii' in others. In alphabetical lists an entry containing a vowel with a mark over it appears immediately following the entry with the corresponding short vowel.

In some dictionaries and reference works using the Hepburn system (notably Nelson's *Japanese-English Character Dictionary*), '-n' appearing before 'm', 'p', or 'b' is written as 'm' to designate its pronunciation.

You will encounter both the modified Hepburn system and the KUNREI system in standard reference works. If you are familiar with these two systems and the differences between them, you should experience no difficulty. Here are some examples to illustrate the kinds of romanized spellings you may come across:

	This book	Kenkyusha	Nelson	Monbusho Dictionaries
big	ookii	ōkii	ōkii	ôkii
small	chiisai	chiisai	chiisai	tiisai
beaker	biikaa	bīkā	...	biikâ
amplitude	SHINPUKU	shinpuku	shimpuku	sinpuku
experiment	JIKKEN	jikken	jikken	zikken
resin	JUSHI	jushi	jushi	zyushi
nitric acid	SHOOSAN	shōsan	shōsan	syôsan
neutron	CHUUSEI-SHI	chūseishi	chūseishi	tyûseisi

VOCABULARY FOR EXERCISES

Note: Henceforth we follow the common practice of giving the infinitive of an English verb along with the dictionary form of the Japanese verb (even though the latter is the present-tense form). Similarly we give the English adjective along with the dictionary form of the Japanese adjective (even though the latter is a verb in present-tense form).

wa	{particle indicating topic of a sentence}
ga	{particle indicating subject of a verb}
o	{particle indicating object of a verb}
ni	in, on, to, into
to	with, and
mo	also, too
no	of
KITAI	gas
EKITAI	liquid
RYUUSHI	particle
GENSHI	atom
BUNSHI	molecule
UNDOO	motion
UNDOO-RYOO	momentum
KAKU-UNDOO-RYOO	angular momentum
SHITSURYOO	mass
CHISSO	nitrogen
HOZON	conservation
ITTEI	constant
enerugii	energy
biikaa	beaker
heriumu	helium
benzen	benzene
mizu	water
sosogu	to pour
fukumu	to contain
aru	to be {in a place}
suru	to do
sareru	to be done {passive of 'suru'}
ookii	large
chiisai	small
kono	this, these {demonstrative adjectives}
sono	that, those {demonstrative adjectives}
korerano	these {demonstrative adjective}
A-o B-to suru	We let A be (designated by the symbol) B
A-o B-to iu	A we call B; A is called B
A-wa B-de-aru	A is B

2-13

EXERCISES

Note: The main purpose of these exercises is to familiarize you with the sounds of the Japanese language. By giving you some simple sentences we hope that at the same time you will begin to get a feeling for the structure of Japanese sentences. The grammatical rules will be given later, but in these elementary sentences you may be able to infer some of these rules. Words in brackets in the English translation are not given explicitly in Japanese.

Ex 2.1 Sentence build-ups

Ookii.	[It] is big.
Biikaa-ga ookii.	The beaker is big.
Kono-biikaa-wa ookii.	This beaker is big.
Chiisai.	[They] are small.
BUNSHI-wa chiisai.	Molecules are small.
Korerano-BUNSHI-wa chiisai.	These molecules are small.
Sosogu.	[We] pour.
EKITAI-o sosogu.	[We] pour the liquid(s).
Kono-EKITAI-o sosogu.	[We] pour this liquid.
Kono-EKITAI-o biikaa-ni sosogu.	[We] pour this liquid into a beaker.
Fukumu.	[They] contain.
GENSHI-o fukumu.	[They] contain atoms.
BUNSHI-wa GENSHI-o fukumu.	Molecules contain atoms.
Aru.	[It] exists {in a place}. There is.
Benzen-ga aru.	There is benzene.
Biikaa-ni benzen-ga aru.	There is benzene in the beaker.
Kono-biikaa-ni benzen-ga aru.	There is benzene in this beaker.
Aru.	[It] exists. There is.
Mizu-mo aru.	There is also water.
Biikaa-ni mizu-mo aru.	There is also water in the beaker.
Biikaa-ni-mo mizu-ga aru.	There is water in the beaker, too.
KITAI-de-aru.	[It] is a gas.
Heriumu-wa KITAI-de-aru.	Helium is a gas.
CHISSO-mo KITAI-de-aru.	Nitrogen is also a gas.
Heriumu-to CHISSO-to wa KITAI-de-aru.	Helium and nitrogen are gases.
Heriumu-mo CHISSO-mo KITAI-de-aru.	Both helium and nitrogen are gases.
SHITSURYOO-o m-to suru.	[We] let the mass be m.
RYUUSHI-no SHITSURYOO-o m-to suru.	[We] let the mass of the particle be m.

2-14

HOZON.	Conservation.
HOZON-suru.	[We] conserve.
HOZON-sareru.	[It] is conserved.
Enerugii-ga HOZON-sareru.	The energy is conserved.
Enerugii-to SHITSURYOO-to-ga HOZON-sareru.	The energy and mass are conserved.
UNDOO.	Motion.
UNDOO-suru.	[They] move.
RYUUSHI-ga UNDOO-suru.	The particles move.
Korerano-RYUUSHI-ga UNDOO-suru.	These particles move.
ITTEI.	Constant.
ITTEI-de-aru.	[It] is constant.
SHITSURYOO-ga ITTEI-de-aru.	The mass is constant.
SHITSURYOO-ga ITTEI-de-aru-koto.	The fact that the mass is constant.
SHITSURYOO-ga ITTEI-de-aru-koto-o SHITSURYOO-HOZON-to iu.	The fact that the mass is constant is called "conservation of mass."

Ex 2.2 Substitution drills

Translate the sentence. Then replace the word in brackets by each of the words in the parentheses in turn, and translate the resulting sentences.

1. [RYUUSHI]-no SHITSURYOO-o m-to suru.
   (GENSHI, mizu, BUNSHI, biikaa)
2. [Enerugii]-ga HOZON-sareru.
   (KAKU-UNDOO-RYOO, SHITSURYOO, UNDOO-RYOO)
3. [EKITAI]-o sosogu.
   (Mizu, benzen, EKITAI-CHISSO)
4. Kono-KITAI-wa [heriumu]-o fukumu.
   (CHISSO)
5. Kono-biikaa-wa [ookii].
   (chiisai)
6. Kono-biikaa-ni [EKITAI-CHISSO]-ga aru.
   (mizu, benzen)
7. [Benzen]-wa EKITAI-de-aru.
   (mizu)
8. [RYUUSHI]-ga UNDOO-suru.
   (EKITAI, KITAI)
9. [Enerugii]-ga ITTEI-de-aru-koto-o [enerugii]-HOZON-to iu.
   (UNDOO-RYOO)

2-15

Ex 2.3 Fill-in-the-blanks exercise

Insert a word in the blank to make a scientifically meaningful sentence.

1. Mizu-wa _____-de-aru.
2. _____-wa KITAI-de-aru.
3. _____-wa chiisai.
4. _____-o sosogu.
5. Biikaa-ni _____-ga aru.
6. KITAI-ga _____-o fukumu.
7. _____ biikaa-ni-mo benzen-ga aru.

Ex 2.4 Conversion from KUNREI romanization to Hepburn romanization

The following GAIRAIGO are written in the KUNREI system. Rewrite them in the Hepburn system, and then identify each with the number for the corresponding English word listed below.

hurukutôsu	syasii	tiamin	zyasumin
buriizingu	tiizu	sirika-geru	zyô-kurassya
isobutiren	tyanneru	sisutin	zyurarumin
ôtokurêbu	tyûingamu	purasuto-gurahu	zirukoniumu
patti	turiumu	pâzi	ziguzagu

(1) autoclave, (2) bleeding, (3) channel, (4) chassis, (5) cheese, (6) chewing gum, (7) cystine, (8) duraluminum, (9) fructose, (10) isobutylene, (11) jasmine, (12) jaw crusher, (13) patch, (14) plastograph, (15) purge, (16) silica gel, (17) thiamine, (18) thulium, (19) zig-zag, (20) zirconium

Ex 2.5 Conversion from Hepburn romanization to KUNREI romanization

Rewrite the following words in the KUNREI system:

stroboscope	sutorobosukoopu	cavitation	kyabiteeshon
alkali	arukari	chronometer	kuronomeetaa
detonation	detoneeshon	methane	metan
gasoline	gasorin	ethylene	echiren
agglutination	aguruchineeshon	acetylene	asechiren
ethane	etan	gyroscope	jairosukoopu
decantation	dekanteeshon	alkaloid	arukaroido
glycerine	guriserin	piezometer	piezomeetaa

2-16

CHAPTER 3　　第三章　　[ダイサンショウ]

3 KATAKANA

In this chapter you will learn the KATAKANA syllabary. It is used extensively in technical Japanese to write thousands of scientific and engineering words that have been borrowed from English and other Western European languages. You must master the KATAKANA symbols before going further in this book.

3.1 The Basic KATAKANA Table

In Table 3.1, we show the 46 basic symbols; each of these represents a syllable (see the upper left section of Table 2.5). There are five vowels: 'a' (ア), 'i' (イ), 'u' (ウ), 'e' (エ), 'o' (オ); these are followed by the various consonant-vowel combinations: 'ka' (カ), 'ki' (キ), 'ku' (ク), 'ke' (ケ), 'ko' (コ), and so on. Finally, the syllabic nasal '-n' (ン) is given. The symbol ヲ in the wa-row has the same pronunciation as オ in the a-row (ヲ is almost never encountered in technical Japanese, and hence you need not learn it). After you have done the exercises at the end of the chapter, you should be able to reproduce the table from memory. In writing the KATAKANA be sure that you follow the proper stroke order shown in the tables in the exercises. Be very careful to distinguish between ン (-n) and ソ (so), between ソ (so) and リ (ri), between シ (shi) and ツ (tsu), and between ク (ku) and ワ (wa). (*Note:* Table 3.1 is often called the GOJUUON Table (GOJUU = "fifty," ON = "sound"), since in former times there were entries in *all* the spaces in the 5×10 matrix, each representing a basic "sound" in Japanese.)

Table 3.1 The Basic KATAKANA Table

	...	a	i	u	e	o
...		ア a	イ i	ウ u	エ e	オ o
k		カ ka	キ ki	ク ku	ケ ke	コ ko
s		サ sa	シ shi	ス su	セ se	ソ so
t		タ ta	チ chi	ツ tsu	テ te	ト to
n		ナ na	ニ ni	ヌ nu	ネ ne	ノ no
h		ハ ha	ヒ hi	フ fu	ヘ he	ホ ho
m		マ ma	ミ mi	ム mu	メ me	モ mo
y		ヤ ya		ユ yu		ヨ yo
r		ラ ra	リ ri	ル ru	レ re	ロ ro
w		ワ wa				ヲ (w)o
-n	ン -n					

To illustrate the use of the symbols in Table 3.1 we give the names of some chemical elements (for a complete listing of the chemical elements, see Chapter 15).

ネオン	neon	neon	アルミニウム	aruminiumu	aluminum
キセノン	kisenon	xenon	チタン	chitan	titanium
タンタル	tantaru	tantalum	ウラン	uran	uranium
ナトリウム	natoriumu	sodium	クロム	kuromu	chromium
セシウム	seshiumu	cesium			

As we mentioned in Chapter 2, the ending -iumu which appears in many of the elements is pronounced -yuumu. Since Japanese has no 'l' sound, the KATAKANA symbols in the ra-row have to be used. Also, Japanese pronunciation does not include the juxtaposition of pairs of consonants as in Western languages, and hence extra vowels have to be interposed, as in kuromu and kisenon. Since some scientific words were taken from languages other than English, such as chitan, uran, and kuromu (cf. German "Titan," "Uran," and "Chrom"), these KATAKANA words may not be immediately recognized by speakers of English.

Occasionally KATAKANA are used for writing words that formerly were written with KANJI. For example, 蛋白 "albumen" is now usually written as タンパク (tanpaku). One even finds words in which one of the KANJI is replaced by KATAKANA. An example of this is 燐酸 "phosphoric acid," which is now commonly written as リン酸 (rinsan).

3.2 The Modified KATAKANA

In Table 3.2 (which has the same structure as Table 2.5) we see the basic KATAKANA of Table 3.1 enclosed within heavy lines. Along the bottom and right side additional syllables are added. First we note that the ka-, sa-, ta-, and ha-rows can be transformed into the ga-, za-, da-, and ba-rows by the addition of two accent marks, called NIGORI, to the KATAKANA symbols. In addition, the ha-row is transformed into the pa-row by addition of a small circle, called a MARU. These "modified" KATAKANA are shown in a 5×5 matrix in the lower part of Table 3.2. Now we can write the names of some more elements, thus:

カドミウム	kadomiumu	cadmium	プルトニウム	purutoniumu	plutonium
ニオブ	niobu	niobium	ネプツニウム	neputsunium	neptunium
アルゴン	arugon	argon	タングステン	tangusuten	tungsten

Once you have learned the カ, サ, タ, and ハ rows, you will find that you can read the ガ, ザ, ダ, バ, and パ rows easily.

Note that in the da-row チ and ツ are enclosed in braces. Although they are pronounced 'ji' and 'zu', in GAIRAIGO the syllable 'ji' is always written as ジ and not as チ, and the syllable 'zu' is written as ズ and not as ツ (cf. Table 2.5).

3.3 The Palatalized Consonants in KATAKANA Syllables

Next we look at the syllables in the last three columns of Table 3.2. These are formed by adding "subscripted" ヤ (ya), ユ (yu), and ヨ (yo) to the KATAKANA and modified KATAKANA in the i-column. This produces the syllables キャ (kya), キュ (kyu), and キョ (kyo); シャ (sha), シュ (shu), ショ (sho); and so on (see Table 2.5). Some examples of words containing palatalized consonants are

キュリウム	kyuriumu	curium
ジャイロコンパス	jairokonpasu	gyrocompass
ジョセフソン	josefuson	Josephson

Remember that キヤ (kiya) contains two syllables, キャ (kya) but one.

3.4 The Doubled Vowels

In writing GAIRAIGO in KATAKANA, a double-length vowel is indicated quite simply by a dash following the KATAKANA symbol. For example, to lengthen the vowels in オ (o), ド (do), メ (me), キャ (kya), and ジュ (ju), we write オー (oo), ドー (doo), メー (mee), キャー (kyaa), and ジュー (juu). Examples of words containing doubled vowels are the names of the following elements:

ノーベリウム	nooberiumu	nobelium	ユーロピウム	yuuropiumu	europium
バークリウム	baakuriumu	berkelium	ジューテリウム	juuteriumu	deuterium

3-3

Table 3.2 The KATAKANA Syllabary

	Syllabic Consonants	a	i	u	e	o	Palatalized		
		ア	イ	ウ	エ	オ			
k	ッ	カ	キ	ク	ケ	コ	キャ	キュ	キョ
s	ッ	サ	シ	ス	セ	ソ	シャ	シュ	ショ
t	ッ	タ	チ	ツ	テ	ト	チャ	チュ	チョ
n		ナ	ニ	ヌ	ネ	ノ	ニャ	ニュ	ニョ
h	ッ	ハ	ヒ	フ	ヘ	ホ	ヒャ	ヒュ	ヒョ
m		マ	ミ	ム	メ	モ	ミャ	ミュ	ミョ
y		ヤ		ユ		ヨ			
r		ラ	リ	ル	レ	ロ	リャ	リュ	リョ
w		ワ				ヲ			
-n	ン								

	Syllabic Consonants	Modified					Modified and Palatalized		
g	ッ	ガ	ギ	グ	ゲ	ゴ	ギャ	ギュ	ギョ
z	ッ	ザ	ジ	ズ	ゼ	ゾ	ジャ	ジュ	ジョ
d	ッ	ダ	{ヂ}	{ヅ}	デ	ド			
b	ッ	バ	ビ	ブ	ベ	ボ	ビャ	ビュ	ビョ
p	ッ	パ	ピ	プ	ペ	ポ	ピャ	ピュ	ピョ
**		+	+	+	+	+	+	+	+
Vowel Doubling		―	―	―	―	―	―	―	―
				ウ	イ	ウ		ウ	ウ

*

Notes for Table 3.2

* The symbol ― is used for vowel doubling in GAIRAIGO, whereas the symbols in the last line are used for doubled vowels in ON readings of KANJI.

** The subscripted ッ, placed in front of any syllable to its right in the same row, indicates doubling of the consonant in the syllable, the consonant that identifies the row.

3-4

In writing the doubled vowels for the ON readings of KANJI, a different method is used: KATAKANA in the u- and o-columns have their vowels lengthened by adding ウ, and KATAKANA in the e-column have their vowels lengthened by adding イ. Hence スウ, メイ, and ゴウ are SUU, MEI, and GOO in ON readings. For example:

| ケイ素 | KEISO | silicon | ヨウ素 | YOOSO | iodine |
| ホウ素 | HOOSO | boron | | | |

Here the KATAKANA parts of these words are used in lieu of ON readings of KANJI no longer officially in use, as mentioned at the end of Section 3.1. The KANJI 素 (SO) is a suffix appearing in the names of eleven of the elements.

3.5 The Doubled Consonants

A "subscripted" ツ appearing before a KATAKANA symbol indicates the doubling of the consonant of the KATAKANA. Thus the combination ツカ stands for '-kka', ップ stands for '-ppu', and ツキョ stands for '-kkyo'. Some examples of the use of ツ are

| ニッケル | nikkeru | nickel | フッ素 | FUSSO | fluorine |
| イットリウム | ittoriumu | yttrium | | | |

Here フッ replaces the KANJI 弗 (FUTSU), which is no longer officially used.

A double 'n' is written by placing ン just before a syllable in the n-row.

| チャンネル | channeru | channel |
| トンネルダイオード | tonnerudaioodo | tunnel diode |

In Table 3.2 the small ツ is placed in the left-most column of those rows whose syllables can undergo consonant doubling.

3.6 Supplement to the KATAKANA Syllabary

In addition to the syllables given in Table 3.2 there are other combinations that are in widespread use; these are displayed in Table 3.3. A few names of prominent scientists are

ファーレンハイト	faarenhaito	Fahrenheit
ディラック	dirakku	Dirac
ジェフリーズ	jefuriizu	Jeffreys
ヴァイヤシュトラス	vaiyashutorasu	Weierstrass
ウィーグナー	wiigunaa	Wigner

As indicated in the table, many of these supplementary syllables can be preceded by ツ to double the consonant immediately following.

Table 3.3 KATAKANA Syllable Supplement

		a	i	u	e	o	yu
y					イェ ye		
w			ウィ wi		ウェ we	ウォ wo	
kw		クァ kwa				クォ kwo	
sh	ッ				シェ she		
ch	ッ				チェ che		
ts	ッ	ツァ tsa			ツェ tse	ツォ tso	
t	ッ		ティ ti	トゥ tu			テュ tyu
f	ッ	ファ fa	フィ fi		フェ fe	フォ fo	フュ fyu
gw	ッ	グァ gwa					
j	ッ				ジェ je		
d	ッ		ディ di	ドゥ du			デュ dyu
v	ッ	ヴァ va	ヴィ vi	ヴ vu	ヴェ ve	ヴォ vo	ヴュ vyu

3.7 Guidelines for Reading GAIRAIGO Written in KATAKANA

Some of the GAIRAIGO written in KATAKANA that you have seen thus far may have been difficult to decipher. The following rules may be helpful to get the feel of how the transliteration works.

(a)   Since Japanese does not allow for the juxtaposition of all pairs of consonants found in Western languages, superfluous vowels often appear in GAIRAIGO.

レントゲン	rentogen	Roentgen
タングステン	tangusuten	tungsten
シクロヘキサン	shikurohekisan	cyclohexane
アルゴン	arugon	argon

(b)   Since Japanese words do not end in consonants (other than '-n'), a superfluous vowel often appears at the end of GAIRAIGO.

フラスコ	furasuko	flask	ピペット	pipetto	pipette
ポンプ	ponpu	pump	スイッチ	suitchi	switch

(c)   A ッ often appears before the KATAKANA symbol containing a superfluous vowel in order to double the consonant and thereby shift the emphasis in the pronunciation from the vowel to the consonant.

ジェット	jetto	jet
ワックス	wakkusu	wax
ビュレット	byuretto	burette
ホイートストーンブリッジ	hoiitosutoonburijji	Wheatstone bridge

3-6

(d)   When the Japanese want a vowel to sound long, a superfluous doubled vowel often appears. This is particularly true in some words ending in a vowel plus 'r', where they imitate the British pronunciation.

エタノール	etanooru	ethanol	セルロース	seruroosu	cellulose
パーセント	paasento	per cent	エーテル	eeteru	ether
ポリマー	porimaa	polymer	コンピューター	konpyuutaa	computer

Sometimes such vowel doubling for words ending in "-er" in English is eliminated; hence you will encounter コンピュータ as well as コンピューター. The shorter form occurs in compound words such as コンピュータグラフィックス (computer graphics).

(e)   The ra-row is used for writing words containing both 'r' and 'l'.

| レンズ | renzu | lens | レイリー | reirii | Rayleigh |
| レオロジー | reorojii | rheology | | | |

(f)   The sa- and ta-rows are usually used for the voiceless 'th' sound, and the za-row for the voiced 'th' sound.

| サーモスタット | saamosutatto | thermostat | チキソトロピー | chikisotoropii | thixotropy |
| カラザーズ | karazaazu | Carothers | トリウム | toriumu | thorium |

(g)   The ba-row is often used for words containing the 'v' sound.

| ビニル | biniru | vinyl | バナジウム | banajiumu | vanadium |
| ベクトル | bekutoru | vector | バルブ | barubu | valve (or bulb) |

(h)   Many terms, particularly in organic chemistry, are transliterated into KATA-KANA according to the German, French, or Dutch pronunciation.

ベンゼン	benzen	benzene	プロパン	puropan	propane
イソブタン	isobutan	isobutane	エネルギー	enerugii	energy
グリニャール	gurinyaaru	Grignard			

(i)   The English syllables 'si', 'ti', 'di', and 'zi' are transliterated by シ, チ, ジ, and ジ, respectively.

シリカ	shirika	silica	シアナミド	shianamido	cyanamide
チンキ	chinki	tincture	チタン	chitan	titanium
ジエン	jien	diene	ジエチル	jiechiru	diethyl
ジルコニウム	jirukoniumu	zirconium			

3-7

(j)   The English syllables 'ca' and 'ga', as in "cap and "gap," often become キャ and ギャ in KATAKANA.

キャリヤー	kyariyaa	carrier	ギャップ	gyappu	gap
キャビテーション	kyabiteeshon	cavitation	ギャラクシー	gyarakushii	galaxy

Although the KATAKANA transcriptions of most scientific words are rather well standardized, some variations may be encountered; for example, "volt" is written both as ボルト and ヴォルト. In addition, some words are drastically abbreviated: パソコン (personal computer); ワープロ (word processor).

3.8 Indexing Entries in Listings Based on KANA

In dictionaries and other lists based on KATAKANA (or HIRAGANA), entries are arranged in "GOJUUON order" (based on the GOJUUON arrangement in Table 3.1); the following rules are used:

(a)   The entries are arranged in the order of the syllables in the KANA tables: a-i-u-e-o-ka-ki-ku-ke-ko-sa-shi-etc. Thus スズカゴウブツ, "tin compounds," precedes スズサン, "stannic acid," and this in turn precedes スチルベン, "stilbene."

(b)   Modified KATAKANA (marked with the diacritical marks ゛ and ゜) follow the unmodified KATAKANA. Thus タイスウカンスウ, "logarithmic function," precedes ダイスウカンスウ, "algebraic function." Similarly コウフン, "excitation," precedes コウブンシ, "macromolecule." Also, トウホウセイ, "isotropic," comes before トウポテンシャル, "equipotential." Note that ハ is followed by バ, which in turn is followed by パ.

(c)   The "subscripted" アイウエオヤユヨツ follow the normal アイウエオヤユヨツ. For example, ジユウスイ, "free water," precedes ジュウスイ, "heavy water."

(d)   Roman letters used in technical abbreviations, such as UHF (ultra high frequency), are alphabetized according to the Japanese pronunciation of the letters; there is no standard way to do this, but here is one scheme that is used (taken from KOOJIEN, Iwanami, 1983).

A	エー	B	ビー	C	シー	D	ディー	E	イー
F	エフ	G	ジー	H	エッチ	I	アイ	J	ジェー
K	ケー	L	エル	M	エム	N	エヌ	O	オー
P	ピー	Q	キュー	R	アール	S	エス	T	ティー
U	ユー	V	ブイ	W	ダブリュー	X	エックス	Y	ワイ
Z	ゼット, ゼッド								

In saying the names of letters in mathematical formulas, the Japanese pronounce them as shown above. Note that 'Z' is not pronounced ジー as might be expected from the American pronunciation of this letter.

3.9 The KATAKANA Syllabary in Common GAIRAIGO

The following words contain all of the 46 basic KATAKANA symbols at least once. Many are high-frequency words that you will encounter in subsequent chapters and should be learned now.

1. スカラー　　　scalar　　　　　ベクトル　　　vector
    サイン　　　　sine　　　　　　コサイン　　　cosine
    タンジェント　tangent　　　　　ランダム　　　random

2. メートル　　　meter {unit}　　ミクロン　　　micron {unit}
    ニュートン　　newton {unit}　　オーム　　　　ohm {unit}
    ワット　　　　watt {unit}

3. ヘリウム　　　helium　　　　　ネオン　　　　neon
    ナトリウム　　sodium　　　　　カリウム　　　potassium
    アルミニウム　aluminum　　　　ニッケル　　　nickel

4. プロパン　　　propane　　　　ベンゼン　　　benzene
    アルコール　　alcohol　　　　モノマー　　　monomer
    ポリマー　　　polymer　　　　レーヨン　　　rayon
    ナイロン　　　nylon

5. ヌクレオシド　nucleoside　　　ヌクレオチド　nucleotide
    ホルモン　　　hormone　　　　アメーバ　　　amoeba

6. ビーカー　　　beaker　　　　　ダイヤル　　　dial
    ソレノイド　　solenoid　　　　バルブ　　　　valve; bulb
    ワイヤ　　　　wire　　　　　　ケーブル　　　cable
    スイッチ　　　switch　　　　　テープ　　　　tape
    ギヤ　　　　　gear　　　　　　ソケット　　　socket
    セメント　　　cement

7. エネルギー　　energy　　　　　エントロピー　entropy
    データ　　　　data　　　　　　サイクル　　　cycle

These exercises will present KATAKANA in several rows at a time to help you master them. On the next page you will find a KATAKANA table different from the standard one found in Table 3.2. This table brings voiceless and voiced consonants together in adjoining rows (although technically ジ is not the voiced form of シ) because the two sets of sounds use the same basic symbols, for example, カキクケ コ, 'ka ki ku ke ko', and ガギグゲゴ, 'ga gi gu ge go', as you have learned in this chapter. In the exercises you will be introduced first to voiceless rows and then to the corresponding voiced rows.

Before beginning the exercises we recommend that you become familiar with the table for future reference. The left part gives the syllables of the individual KATA-KANA; the right part the syllables with palatalized consonants. The left part lists the romanized consonants in the far left column, and the romanized vowels in the top row. (You know, of course, that in Hepburn romanization these consonants sometimes change within a row.) At the bottom of the table we give the KATAKANA symbol ン for the syllabic '-n'.

The right part gives all of the syllables with palatalized consonants. In the left column of the table you will find the KATAKANA symbols: キギシジチニヒビピ ミリ. Their combinations with ヤユヨ are indicated in the respective columns. At the bottom of the table we give the small KATAKANA symbol ッ for doubling the consonant that follows it, and the bar symbol ― used for doubling a vowel in GAIRAIGO.

Preceding the exercises that introduce new KATAKANA symbols, you will find the basic KATAKANA symbols as they appear at successive strokes of a pen. Note that most strokes have a single direction: left to right, or top to bottom. However, some strokes change direction; we call them "hooks."

Each of the first six exercises has two parts, **EXAMPLES** and **MATCHING EXERCISES**. The **EXAMPLES** give columns of GAIRAIGO that introduce the KATAKANA in the order that they appear in a table at the head of the exercise. In addition, you will find their Hepburn readings and English meanings. If the GAIRAIGO is part of a compound word, the additional English word is given in parentheses. If the English term may not be familiar, additional information appears in braces.

In the **MATCHING EXERCISES** you will encounter a second column of GAIRAIGO with no romanization. You should select the English word that corresponds to each GAIRAIGO by comparing the KATAKANA pronunciation with the various English words and choosing the right match.

After completing these six exercises, you will find an additional KATAKANA pronunciation table to remind you of how sounds that are not natural in the Japanese language are written in KATAKANA, as discussed in Section 3.6 and in the exercise. You will find again **EXAMPLES** and a **MATCHING EXERCISE** in which names of various Western scientists and other GAIRAIGO written in this notation are given.

The exercises end with two lists of technical terms in KATAKANA and in English: a list of computer terms and one of chemical elements. You are to match them. We give a full discussion of the names of the chemical elements in Chapter 15. Here we give you only those names that are derived from Western languages.

カタカナ一覧表[イチランヒョウ]

	a	i	u	e	o
	ア	イ	ウ	エ	オ
k	カ	キ	ク	ケ	コ
g	ガ	ギ	グ	ゲ	ゴ
s	サ	シ	ス	セ	ソ
z	ザ	ジ	ズ	ゼ	ゾ
t	タ	チ	ツ	テ	ト
d	ダ			デ	ド
n	ナ	ニ	ヌ	ネ	ノ
h	ハ	ヒ	フ	ヘ	ホ
b	バ	ビ	ブ	ベ	ボ
p	パ	ピ	プ	ペ	ポ
m	マ	ミ	ム	メ	モ
y	ヤ		ユ		ヨ
r	ラ	リ	ル	レ	ロ
w	ワ				
-n	ン				

i	Palatalized Consonants		
	ya	yu	yo
キ	キャ	キュ	キョ
ギ	ギャ	ギュ	ギョ
シ	シャ	シュ	ショ
ジ	ジャ	ジュ	ジョ
チ	チャ	チュ	チョ
ニ	ニャ	ニュ	ニョ
ヒ	ヒャ	ヒュ	ヒョ
ビ	ビャ	ビュ	ビョ
ピ	ピャ	ピュ	ピョ
ミ	ミャ	ミュ	ミョ
リ	リャ	リュ	リョ
ツ	doubles the following consonant		
ー	doubles the preceding vowel		

カタカナ第一表[ダイイッピョウ]

	STEP 1	STEP 2	STEP 3	STEP 4	
a	ア				
i	イ				
u	ウ				
e	エ				
o	オ				

	STEP 1	STEP 2	STEP 3	STEP 4	
ka	カ				
ki	キ				
ku	ク				
ke	ケ				
ko	コ				

	STEP 1	STEP 2	STEP 3	STEP 4	
sa	サ				
shi	シ				
su	ス				
se	セ				
so	ソ				

	STEP 1	STEP 2	STEP 3	STEP 4
-n	ン			

Example of writing NIGORI

	STEP 1	STEP 2	STEP 3	STEP 4
zu	ズ			

Ex 3.1 The a-row, ka-row, sa-row, and syllabic -n

ア	a	アー	aa
イ	i	イー	ii
ウ	u	ウー	uu
エ	e	エー	ee
オ	o	オー	oo

カ	ka	カー	kaa
キ	ki	キー	kii
ク	ku	クー	kuu
ケ	ke	ケー	kee
コ	ko	コー	koo

サ	sa	サー	saa
シ	shi	シー	shii
ス	su	スー	suu
セ	se	セー	see
ソ	so	ソー	soo

ン	-n

EXAMPLES

アイ	ai	eye (camera)
ウエア	uea	(soft)ware
イオン	ion	ion
アンカ	anka	anchor (chain)
キー	kii	key
アーク	aaku	arc (weld)
ケーキ	keeki	(filter) cake
コーキン	kookin	calking
サイン	sain	sine
オキシ	okishi	oxy (salt)
エクス	ekusu	x-(ray)
アクセス	akusesu	access (time)
ケーソン	keeson	caisson

MATCHING EXERCISE

1. シス	( ) aqua (complex)
2. ウイスキー	( ) Sequoia {tree}
3. コサイン	( ) earth {British}, ground {American}
4. コカイン	( ) K (scope, truss)
5. ケイ	( ) kink
6. エーカー	( ) cis (form)
7. イソシアン	( ) echo (machine)
8. アクア	( ) whiskey
9. エコー	( ) cosine
10. アース	( ) cocaine
11. キンク	( ) acre
12. オンコース	( ) on course
13. セコイア	( ) isocyanic (acid)

Ex 3.2 The ga-row and za-row

ガ	ga	ガー	gaa		ザ	za	ザー	zaa
ギ	gi	ギー	gii		ジ	ji	ジー	jii
グ	gu	グー	guu		ズ	zu	ズー	zuu
ゲ	ge	ゲー	gee		ゼ	ze	ゼー	zee
ゴ	go	ゴー	goo		ゾ	zo	ゾー	zoo

EXAMPLES

ガス	gasu	gas/gases
ギガ	giga	giga {unit}
コーキング	kookingu	calking
ジエン	jien	diene
ゲージ	geeji	gage
インジゴ	injigo	indigo
カイザー	kaizaa	kayser {unit}
ジーンズ	jiinzu	(Sir James) Jeans
カゼイン	kazein	casein
オゾン	ozon	ozone

MATCHING EXERCISE

1.	アガシ	( ) Geiger
2.	ガウス	( ) Gauss
3.	オーガ	( ) Agassiz
4.	ガイガー	( ) Edison
5.	アジソン	( ) ageing (lamp)
6.	エージング	( ) Addison
7.	アゾ	( ) keying
8.	オンサーガー	( ) azo (compound)
9.	エジソン	( ) Onsager
10.	キーイング	( ) auger

カタカナ第二表[ダイニヒョウ]

	STEP 1	STEP 2	STEP 3	STEP 4			STEP 1	STEP 2	STEP 3	STEP 4
ta	タ	ノ	グ	タ		na	ナ	ニ	ナ	
chi	チ	ノ	ニ	チ		ni	ニ	コ	ニ	
tsu	ツ	ツ	ツ	ツ		nu	ヌ	フ	ヌ	
te	テ	コ	ニ	テ		ne	ネ	ヽ	ヲ	ネ	ネ
to	ト	ト	ド			no	ノ	ノ	

	STEP 1	STEP 2	STEP 3	STEP 4
ha	ハ	ノ	バ	
hi	ヒ	ク	ヒ	
fu	フ	フ		
he	ヘ	ヘ		
ho	ホ	ニ	ナ	オ	ホ

Example of writing MARU

	STEP 1	STEP 2	STEP 3	STEP 4
pi	ピ	ク	ヒ	ピ	

Ex 3.3 The ta-row, na-row, and ha-row

タ	ta	ター	taa		ナ	na	ナー	naa		ハ	ha	ハー	haa
チ	chi	チー	chii		ニ	ni	ニー	nii		ヒ	hi	ヒー	hii
ツ	tsu	ツー	tsuu		ヌ	nu	ヌー	nuu		フ	fu	フー	fuu
テ	te	テー	tee		ネ	ne	ネー	nee		ヘ	he	ヘー	hee
ト	to	トー	too		ノ	no	ノー	noo		ホ	ho	ホー	hoo

EXAMPLES

タンク	tanku	tank
ツイスタ	tsuisuta	twister
スイッチ	suitchi	switch
テンキー	tenkii	ten-key
ソケット	soketto	socket
ソーナ	soona	sonar
ニコチン	nikochin	nicotine
エヌシー	enushii	NC {= numerical control}
ネオン	neon	neon
ノッキング	nokkingu	knocking
ハーフトーン	haafutoon	half-tone
ヒスト	hisuto	histo(gram)
ヘキソース	hekisoosu	hexose
ホスゲン	hosugen	phosgene

MATCHING EXERCISE

1. コンタクト	( ) horn (antenna)
2. アンチノック	( ) toxin
3. アンテナ	( ) anion
4. トキシン	( ) hexane
5. アニオン	( ) antenna
6. ネオンサイン	( ) software
7. オキシケトン	( ) anti-knock
8. ソハイオ	( ) oxyketone
9. ヒータ	( ) heater
10. ソフトウエア	( ) neon sign
11. ヘキサン	( ) off-set
12. ホーン	( ) (air) ejector
13. ノッチング	( ) contact
14. エゼクタ	( ) Sohio (process)
15. オフセット	( ) nano (seconds)
16. ナノ	( ) notching (relay)

Ex 3.4 The da-row, ba-row, and pa-row

ダ	da	ダー	daa	バ	ba	バー	baa	パ	pa	パー	paa
				ビ	bi	ビー	bii	ピ	pi	ピー	pii
				ブ	bu	ブー	buu	プ	pu	プー	puu
デ	de	デー	dee	ベ	be	ベー	bee	ペ	pe	ペー	pee
ド	do	ドー	doo	ボ	bo	ボー	boo	ポ	po	ポー	poo

EXAMPLES

アダプタ	adaputa	adapter
データ	deeta	data
ドナー	donaa	donor
バイアス	baiasu	bias (method)
ビット	bitto	bit
イソブタン	isobutan	isobutane
ベース	beesu	base (load)
サーボ	saabo	servo (brake)
ダンパ	danpa	damper
スピン	supin	spin
イソプレン	isopuren	isoprene
ピペット	pipetto	pipette
エポキシド	epokishido	epoxide

MATCHING EXERCISE

1. インピーダンス   ( ) videotape
2. アンペア   ( ) dubbing
3. アノードアーク   ( ) converter
4. コンバータ   ( ) anode arc
5. コードバー   ( ) peak (load)
6. ベースタービン   ( ) impedance
7. デテクトバー   ( ) pipe
8. ドットパターン   ( ) ampere
9. ダビング   ( ) doping
10. ピーク   ( ) code bar
11. ドーピング   ( ) dot pattern
12. ビデオテープ   ( ) base turbine
13. パイプ   ( ) detector bar

カタカナ第三表[ダイサンヒョウ]

		STEP 1	STEP 2	STEP 3	STEP 4
ma	マ	⇗	マ		
mi	ミ	⇁	⇌	≡	
mu	ム	↙	ム		
me	メ	ノ	メ		
mo	モ	⇁	⇌	モ	

		STEP 1	STEP 2	STEP 3	STEP 4
ya	ヤ	⇗	ヤ		

		STEP 1	STEP 2	STEP 3	STEP 4
yu	ユ	⇗	ユ		

		STEP 1	STEP 2	STEP 3	STEP 4
yo	ヨ	⇗	ヨ	ヨ	

		STEP 1	STEP 2	STEP 3	STEP 4
ra	ラ	⇁	ラ		
ri	リ	↓	リ		
ru	ル	ノ	ル		
re	レ	↓↗			
ro	ロ	↓	⇗	ロ	

		STEP 1	STEP 2	STEP 3	STEP 4
wa	ワ	↓	⇗		

Ex 3.5 The ma-row, ya-row, ra-row, and wa-row

マ	ma	マー	maa
ミ	mi	ミー	mii
ム	mu	ムー	muu
メ	me	メー	mee
モ	mo	モー	moo

ヤ	ya	ヤー	yaa
ユ	yu	ユー	yuu
ヨ	yo	ヨー	yoo

ラ	ra	ラー	raa
リ	ri	リー	rii
ル	ru	ルー	ruu
レ	re	レー	ree
ロ	ro	ロー	roo

ワ	wa	ワー	waa

EXAMPLES

ガンマ	ganma	gamma
アミン	amin	amine
オーム	oomu	ohm
アメーバ	ameeba	amoeba
モーメント	moomento	moment
タイヤ	taiya	tire
ユニオン	yunion	union
ヨーク	yooku	yoke
グラフ	gurafu	graph
レオロジー	reorojii	rheology
マトリックス	matorikkusu	matrix
ダイヤル	daiyaru	dial
ワット	watto	watt

MATCHING EXERCISE

1.	ロータリー	( )	minimum (pause)
2.	ワープロ	( )	monotropy
3.	ヌクレオ	( )	rim drive
4.	ルーメン	( )	random (access)
5.	リレー	( )	unitary (space)
6.	ランダム	( )	lumen
7.	ユニタリー	( )	reset
8.	モノトロピー	( )	rotary (kiln)
9.	メタロイド	( )	nucleo(side)
10.	リセット	( )	microphone
11.	マイクロホン	( )	metalloid
12.	ミニマム	( )	relay
13.	リムドライブ	( )	word processor

Ex 3.6 Palatalized consonants, such as in

キャ kya	キュ kyu	キョ kyo

EXAMPLES

キャリヤー	kyariyaa	carrier (gas)
ギャラクシー	gyarakushii	galaxy
ポテンシャル	potensharu	potential
ジャイロ	jairo	gyro(scope)
チャンネル	channeru	channel
フライアッシュ	furaiasshu	fly ash
チューブミル	chuubumiru	tube mill
ニュートリノ	nyuutorino	neutrino
ヒューズ	hyuuzu	fuse
ビューレット	byuuretto	burette
コンピュータ	konpyuuta	computer
シミュレータ	shimyureeta	simulator
コアレーショ	koareesho	core ratio
チョーク	chooku	choke (coil)
テレビジョン	terebijon	television

MATCHING EXERCISE

1. ジュール	( ) curie {unit}
2. チョッパ	( ) overshoot
3. プランジャ	( ) newton {unit}
4. キュリー	( ) shutter
5. ニュートン	( ) messenger
6. ジャック	( ) joule {unit}
7. スキャッタ	( ) scatter
8. ギャップ	( ) chopper
9. メッセンジャ	( ) gap
10. シュリーレン	( ) plunger
11. オーバシュート	( ) jack
12. グリニャール	( ) Schottky (effect)
13. ルシャトリエ	( ) Grignard's (reagent)
14. ショットキー	( ) Schlieren (method)
15. シャッタ	( ) Le Chatelier's (rule)

Ex 3.7 Reading and writing foreign names and GAIRAIGO

The following table is given to help you choose the correct way to write non-Japanese sounds in foreign names. The left-hand column gives the romanized consonant sounds, the top row the vowels.

Table for Reading and Writing Foreign Names

	a	i	u	e	o
ch				che チェ	
d		di ディ	du ドゥ		
dy			dyu デュ		
f	fa ファ	fi フィ		fe フェ	fo フォ
fy			fyu フュ		
j				je ジェ	
sh				she シェ	
t		ti ティ	tu トゥ		
ts	tsa ツァ			tse ツェ	tso ツォ
v	va ヴァ	vi ヴィ	vu ヴュ	ve ヴェ	vo ヴォ
w		wi ウィ		we ウェ	wo ウォ

The table below gives the KATAKANA combinations used for GAIRAIGO in *Kenkyusha's Japanese-English Dictionary*, Tokyo (1974), 4th Edition. The left column of KATAKANA gives the first KATAKANA in the combination and the top row gives the second smaller one that appears as a subscript. Using this as a matrix, you can easily find any such combination and confirm its pronunciation. Remember that you should read the consonants in the romanized equivalents as you would normally do.

Supplementary Table for Reading and Writing GAIRAIGO

	ア	イ	ウ・ユ	エ	オ
ウ		ウィ wi		ウェ we	ウォ wo
ヴ	ヴァ va	ヴィ vi	ヴュ vu	ヴェ ve	ヴォ vo
シ				シェ she	
ジ				ジェ je	
チ				チェ che	
ツ	ツァ tsa			ツェ tse	ツォ tso
テ		ティ ti			
デ		ディ di	デュ du		
ト			トゥ tu		
ド			ドゥ du		
フ	ファ fa	フィ fi	フュ fyu	フェ fe	フォ fo

EXAMPLES

ヴァールブルク	vaaruburuku	Warburg (manometer)
ウィルスン	wirusun	Wilson (cloud chamber)
ヴィッカース	vikkaasu	Vickers (hardness)
ヴィーン	viin	Wien (effect)
ウェーハ	weeha	wafer
ウェストン	wesuton	Weston (cell)
ヴェーバー	veebaa	Weber (number)
ウォームギヤ	woomugiya	worm gear
ヴォルタ	voruta	Volta (effect)
シェージング	sheejingu	shading
ジェイ	jei	J (signal)
ツァイゼ	tsaize	Zeise's (salt)
ツァイゼル	tsaizeru	Zeisel's (method)
ティセリウス	tiseriusu	Tiselius (apparatus)
トゥンベリ	tunberi	Thunberg (tube)
チェックイン	chekkuin	check-in (signal)
チェックアウト	chekkuauto	check-out (signal)
ディジタル	dijitaru	digital (computer)
ディフラクトメーター	difurakutomeetaa	diffractometer
ドゥブローイー	duburooii	De Broglie (wave)
デュマ	dyuma	Dumas (method)
ファイバー	faibaa	fiber (optics)
フィッション	fisshon	fission (chamber)
フェナジン	fenajin	phenazine
フォトダイオード	fotodaioodo	photodiode

MATCHING EXERCISE

1. ウィンチ	( ) Zeuner (valve diagram)
2. ウェーク	( ) folding machine
3. ジェットエンジン	( ) winch
4. チェーンコンベヤ	( ) ferroaluminum
5. チェッカー	( ) fan casing
6. ツェリータービン	( ) checker (brick)
7. ツォイナー	( ) jet engine
8. ディスロケーション	( ) wake
9. ファンケーシング	( ) Zoelly turbine
10. フィニッシャビリチ	( ) dislocation
11. フェロアルミニウム	( ) chain conveyor
12. フォルディングマシン	( ) finishability {concrete}

Ex 3.8 Computer terms in KATAKANA

アクセッシング　　　コンピュータアニメーション　ドキュメンテーション
アセンブラ　　　　　コンピュータビジョン　　　トランスレータ
アナログ　　　　　　シーケンシャル　　　　　　チャネルインタフェイス
アルゴリズム　　　　ジェネレータ　　　　　　　バーチャルメモリ
アレイプロセッサ　　シミュレータプログラム　　ハードウエア
インクワイアリシステム　スケジューリング　　　パートプログラム
インタプリタ　　　　スタックオートマトン　　　ファイル
インタリービング　　スーパバイザリシステム　　プッシュアップ
エミュレーション　　スループット　　　　　　　プッシュダウン
オートマトン　　　　ソーティング　　　　　　　プログラミング
オフライン　　　　　ソフトウエア　　　　　　　プログラムスキーム
オペレーティングシステム　ターンアラウンド　　　プログラムパッケージ
オンライン　　　　　ダイナミックモデル　　　　プログラムメンテナンス
ガーベジコレクション　タブレット　　　　　　　マイクロプロセッサ
キャッシュメモリ　　タンデムシステム　　　　　ミニコンピュータ
ゲーミングシミュレーション　データベース　　　ユーティリティプログラム
コーディング　　　　ディジタイザ　　　　　　　ライトペン
コマンドアンドコントロール　テキスト　　　　　ワードプロセッサ
コンパイラ　　　　　デバッギング

accessing	file	push down
algorithm	gaming simulation	push up
analog	garbage collection	scheduling
array processor	generator	sequential
assembler	hardware	simulator program
automaton	inquiry system	software
cache memory	interleaving	sorting
channel interface	interpreter	stack automaton
coding	light pen	supervisory system
command and control	microprocessor	tablet
compiler	minicomputer	tandem system
computer animation	off-line	text
computer vision	on-line	throughput
data base	operating system	translator
debugging	part program	turn around
digitizer	program maintenance	utility program
documentation	programming	virtual memory
dynamic model	program package	word processor
emulation	program scheme	

Ex 3.9 Chemical elements in KATAKANA

アインスタイニウム Es
アクチニウム Ac
アスタチン At
アメリシウム Am
アルゴン Ar
アルミニウム Al
アンチモン Sb
イッテルビウム Yb
イットリウム Y
イリジウム Ir
インジウム In
ウラン U
エルビウム Er
オスミウム Os
カドミウム Cd
ガドリニウム Gd
カリウム K
ガリウム Ga
カリホルニウム Cf
カルシウム Ca
キセノン Xe
キュリウム Cm
クリプトン Kr
クロミウム Cr
ゲルマニウム Ge
コバルト Co

サマリウム Sm
ジスプロシウム Dy
ジルコニウム Zr
スカンジウム Sc
ストロンチウム Sr
セシウム Cs
セリウム Ce
セレン Se
タリウム Tl
タングステン W
タンタル Ta
チタン Ti
ツリウム Tm
テクネチウム Tc
テルビウム Tb
テルル Te
トリウム Th
ナトリウム Na
ニオブ Nb
ニッケル Ni
ネオジム Nd
ネオン Ne
ネプツニウム Np
ノーベリウム No
バークリウム Bk
ハフニウム Hf

パラジウム Pd
バリウム Ba
ビスマス Bi
フェルミウム Fm
フランシウム Fr
プラセオジム Pr
プルトニウム Pu
プロタクチニウム Pa
プロメチウム Pm
ヘリウム He
ベリリウム Be
ホルミウム Ho
ポロニウム Po
マグネシウム Mg
マンガン Mn
メンデレビウム Md
ユーロピウム Eu
ラジウム Ra
ラドン Rn
ランタン La
リチウム Li
ルテチウム Lu
ルテニウム Ru
ルビジウム Rb
レニウム Re
ローレンシウム Lr
ロジウム Rh

actinium Ac
aluminum Al
americium Am
antimony Sb
argon Ar
astatine At
barium Ba
berkelium Bk
beryllium Be
bismuth Bi
cadmium Cd
calcium Ca
californium Cf
cerium Ce
cesium Cs
chromium Cr
cobalt Co
curium Cm
dysprosium Dy
einsteinium Es
erbium Er
europium Eu
fermium Fm
francium Fr
gadolinium Gd
gallium Ga

germanium Ge
hafnium Hf
helium He
holmium Ho
indium In
iridium Ir
krypton Kr
lanthanum La
lawrencium Lr
lithium Li
lutetium Lu
magnesium Mg
manganese Mn
mendelevium Md
neodymium Nd
neon Ne
neptunium Np
nickel Ni
niobium Nb
nobelium No
osmium Os
palladium Pd
plutonium Pu
polonium Po
potassium K [Kalium]
praseodymium Pr

promethium Pm
protactinium Pa
radium Ra
radon Rn
rhenium Re
rhodium Rh
rubidium Rb
ruthenium Ru
samarium Sm
scandium Sc
selenium Se
sodium Na [Natrium]
strontium Sr
tantalum Ta
technetium Tc
tellurium Te
terbium Tb
thallium Tl
thorium Th
thulium Tm
titanium Ti
tungsten W
uranium U
xenon Xe
ytterbium Yb
yttrium Y
zirconium Zr

　　第四章　　[ダイよんショウ]

4 HIRAGANA

In this chapter you will learn the HIRAGANA syllabary. It is used for writing particles, adverbs, and conjunctions, as well as some words for which KANJI are no longer used. HIRAGANA symbols are always used for writing the endings of verbs and adjectives. You must master the HIRAGANA before going further in this book.

4.1 The Basic HIRAGANA Table

In Table 4.1 we show the 46 basic HIRAGANA symbols. They correspond to the 46 KATAKANA symbols of Table 3.1 and have exactly the same pronunciation. After you have done the exercises at the end of this chapter, you should be able to reproduce the table from memory. In writing the HIRAGANA be sure that you follow the proper stroke order shown in the tables in the exercises. The following pairs of HIRAGANA are somewhat similar in appearance, and writing them will require special attention: い (i) and り (ri); う (u) and ら (ra); た (ta) and な (na); ぬ (nu) and ね (ne); ね (ne) and れ (re); れ (re) and わ (wa); る (ru) and ろ (ro).

Since the HIRAGANA are phonetic symbols, words written with them are easy to pronounce. Here are some high-frequency words that often appear at the beginnings of sentences.

すなわち	【即ち】	sunawachi	that is (to say)
いま	【今】	ima	now
しかし		shikashi	however
そして		soshite	and, then
さらに	【更に】	sara-ni	further(more), again

なお	【尚】	nao	further
また	【又】	mata	moreover, and (in addition)

Some of these words are occasionally written with KANJI, but the trend is to use HIRAGANA for words of this sort.

Three of the HIRAGANA symbols have irregular readings when they are used as postpositions.

は　(the symbol for 'ha') is pronounced as 'wa' when used as a postposition to denote the topic of a sentence.

へ　(the symbol for 'he') is pronounced as 'e' when used as a postposition meaning "to" or "toward."

を　(the symbol in the 'wo' position) is always pronounced as 'o' and is used only as a postposition to designate the object of a verb.

More will be said about these particles in Chapter 6. (In using roman letters to input HIRAGANA on a word processor, these three particles are always entered as 'ha', 'he', and 'wo', regardless of their pronunciation.)

Table 4.1 The Basic HIRAGANA Table

	...	a	i	u	e	o
...		あ a	い i	う u	え e	お o
k		か ka	き ki	く ku	け ke	こ ko
s		さ sa	し shi	す su	せ se	そ so
t		た ta	ち chi	つ tsu	て te	と to
n		な na	に ni	ぬ nu	ね ne	の no
h		は ha	ひ hi	ふ fu	へ he	ほ ho
m		ま ma	み mi	む mu	め me	も mo
y		や ya		ゆ yu		よ yo
r		ら ra	り ri	る ru	れ re	ろ ro
w		わ wa				を (w)o
-n	ん -n					

4.2 The Modified HIRAGANA

In Table 4.2 we see the full display of HIRAGANA syllables, including the basic HIRAGANA enclosed within the heavy lines. This table corresponds to Table 3.2 for KATAKANA. Below the basic symbols, in a 5×5 matrix, we find the symbols that are modified by the addition of NIGORI (the ga-, da-, za-, and ba-rows) and those that are modified by the addition of MARU (the pa-row). With these modified symbols some more high-frequency, sentence-initial expressions can be written.

Table 4.2 The HIRAGANA Syllabary

	a	i	u	e	o
	あ	い	う	え	お
k	か	き	く	け	こ
s	さ	し	す	せ	そ
t	た	ち	つ	て	と
n	な	に	ぬ	ね	の
h	は	ひ	ふ	へ	ほ
m	ま	み	む	め	も
y	や		ゆ		よ
r	ら	り	る	れ	ろ
w	わ				を

Syllabic Consonants

k	っ
s	っ
t	っ
n	
h	
m	
y	
r	
w	

-n	ん

g	
z	
d	
b	
p	っ

**

Palatalized

きゃ	きゅ	きょ
しゃ	しゅ	しょ
ちゃ	ちゅ	ちょ
にゃ	にゅ	にょ
ひゃ	ひゅ	ひょ
みゃ	みゅ	みょ
りゃ	りゅ	りょ

Modified

が	ぎ	ぐ	げ	ご
ざ	じ	ず	ぜ	ぞ
だ	ぢ	づ	で	ど
ば	び	ぶ	べ	ぼ
ぱ	ぴ	ぷ	ぺ	ぽ

Modified and Palatalized

ぎゃ	ぎゅ	ぎょ
じゃ	じゅ	じょ
びゃ	びゅ	びょ
ぴゃ	ぴゅ	ぴょ

Vowel Doubling

+	+	+	+	+
あ	い	う	え	お
		う	い	う

*

+	+	+
あ	う	う

Notes for Table 4.2

*   The HIRAGANA in the top row occur primarily in KUN readings, whereas those in the bottom row appear primarily in ON readings.

**   The subscript っ, placed in front of any syllable to its right in the same row, indicates doubling of the consonant in the syllable, the consonant that identifies the row.

たとえば	【例えば】	tatoeba	for example
つぎに	【次に】	tsugi-ni	next
まず	【先ず】	mazu	first (of all)
すでに	【既に】	sude-ni	previously
なぜ	【何故】	naze	why

As we noted in the KATAKANA discussion, the sounds 'ji' and 'zu' are duplicated in the table. Normally one uses じ for 'ji' and ず for 'zu'. However, when giving the KUN reading of KANJI, it is customary to write the sound 'ji' as ぢ in the special combination "chiji," and to represent the sound 'zu' by づ in the special combination "tsuzu." Hence we write

ちぢまない	【縮まない】	chijimanai	incompressible
つづける	【続ける】	tsuzukeru	to continue

In reduplicatives we also find the symbols ぢ and づ used.

ちかぢか	【近々】	chika-jika	in the near future
つねづね	【常々】	tsune-zune	usually

Here the symbol 々 indicates that the preceding KANJI is repeated, something like ditto marks in English.

Also, when a syllable is modified in the formation of a JUKUGO, the symbols ぢ and づ are used in giving pronunciation for words in KANJI dictionaries. For example:

はな	【鼻】	hana	nose
ち	【血】	chi	blood
はなぢ	【鼻血】	hanaji	nosebleed
て	【手】	te	hand
つくる	【作る】	tsukuru	to make
てづくり	【手作り】	tezukuri	hand-made

However, in modern Japanese dictionaries in which words are listed by pronunciation in HIRAGANA, the symbols じ and ず are used.

4.3 The Palatalized Consonants in HIRAGANA Syllables

Next we look at the syllables in the last three columns of Table 4.2. These are formed by adding "subscripted" や (ya), ゆ (yu), and よ (yo) to the HIRAGANA and modified HIRAGANA in the i-column. This gives the syllables きゃ (kya), きゅ (kyu), きょ (kyo), しゃ (sha), しゅ (shu), しょ (sho), and so on; compare this with the last three columns of Table 3.2. These syllables, written in HIRAGANA, are rarely encountered in Japanese. The reason for this is that palatalized consonants do not arise in native Japanese words and hence do not appear in HIRAGANA words or in the KUN readings of KANJI. You will occasionally encounter syllables with palatalized consonants when HIRAGANA symbols are used to write the ON readings of KANJI that are no longer in current use: for example, ひょう (hail) and しょうのう (camphor). You will also come upon these syllables in indexes and listings where all entries, including GAIRAIGO and KANGO, are written in HIRAGANA.

4.4 The Doubled Vowels

To double the short vowels in the syllables in the a-, i-, u-, and e-columns, we simply add あ, い, う, and え to the entries in the table. Some examples are

ばあい	【場合】	baai	case, situation
もちいる	【用いる】	mochiiru	to use
すう	【吸う】	suu	to breathe, suck
ひとしい	【等しい】	hitoshii	equal
ちいさい	【小さい】	chiisai	small

These doubled vowels, written with HIRAGANA, occur relatively infrequently in Japanese.

To double the o-column vowels, a HIRAGANA う is added.

こう		koo	in this way
そう		soo	in that way
どう		doo	in what way
もう		moo	already
もうける	【設ける】	mookeru	to equip, establish

In indicating KUN readings of KANJI, the o-column vowels are sometimes lengthened by adding お instead.

おおきい	【大きい】	ookii	large
おおい	【多い】	ooi	many
とおい	【遠い】	tooi	far
とおり	【通り】	toori	way, manner

This method of doubling the o-column vowels has to be kept in mind in using dictionaries and in inputting words in word processing.

4.5 The Doubled Consonants

A subscripted つ before a HIRAGANA symbol serves to double the consonant in the next syllable. This is exactly analogous to the use of the subscripted ツ in KATAKANA. The つ in the left-most column of Table 4.2 indicates that the syllables to the right of it in that row can undergo consonant doubling. In dictionaries and listings where all entries (including GAIRAIGO and KANGO) are written in HIRAGANA, the symbol つ may appear before syllables in rows other than those shown in Table 4.2, such as the ba-, ga-, and da-rows; this is illustrated in some of the exercises at the end of the chapter.

A few high-frequency sentence-initial words containing doubled consonants are

したがって	【従って】	shitagatte	therefore
よって		yotte	consequently, therefore
いっぱんに	【一般に】	ippan-ni	generally, in general

In this chapter you have seen several groups of high-frequency words that occur at the beginnings of sentences. A more complete list of sentence-initial words and expressions is given in Table 4.3. Most are nearly always written in HIRAGANA in modern scientific texts. Some are often written with KANJI. You should practice reading and writing these words in HIRAGANA so that you can readily use this table as a reference when you study later chapters.

Table 4.3 Sentence-Initial Words and Phrases in GOJUUON Order

*	あるいは	【或は】	or
	いいかえれば		in other words
	いうまでもなく		needless to say
	いずれにしても		in either case
	いっぱんに	【一般に】	in general, generally
**	いっぽう	【一方】	however, on the one hand
	いま	【今】	now
	かつ	【且つ】	moreover
	くわしくいえば	【詳しく言えば】	strictly speaking
	こうして		by doing this
	このため	【この為】	because of this
	このとき	【この時】	for this situation
	このばあい	【この場合】	in this case
	このように		thus, in this way
	このようにして		by doing this
	これにはんし(て)	【これに反し(て)】	in contrast to this
#	さて		well, now
	さらに	【更に】	further(more), again
	しかし(ながら)		however
	しかも		furthermore
	したがって	【従って】	therefore
	すでに	【既に】	previously
	すなわち	【即ち】	that is (to say), in other words
	すると		if so
	せいかくにいえば	【正確に言えば】	if we state it (more) precisely
*	ぜんたいでは	【全体では】	on the whole
	そうしたら		if so, then
	そうして		and
	そうすると		if so, then
	そうすれば		if we do that
	そうでないと		if that is not true
	そこで		thereupon, accordingly

	そして		and, then
	そのあいだ	【その間】	during that time (interval)
	そのうえ	【その上】	moreover
	そのけっか	【その結果】	as a result
	そのさい	【その際】	in that situation
	そのため	【その為】	because of that
	それから		and then
	それだから		therefore, accordingly
	それで		thereupon, then
*	それでは		well then
	それでも		but, be that as it may
	それとも		or
	それなのに		in spite of that, nevertheless
	それなら		if so
*	それにしては		considering that
	それにしても		even so, admitting that
	それにはんして	【それに反して】	in contrast to that
	それにもかかわらず		in spite of that, nevertheless
	それゆえ	【それ故】	consequently, therefore
	たしかに	【確かに】	to be sure, undoubtedly
##	ただし		provided that
	たとえば	【例えば】	for example
	つぎに	【次に】	next
	つまり	【詰まり】	in other words, put simply
	とくに	【特に】	in particular
	ところが		but, however
	ところで		incidentally, by the way
	なお	【尚】	further
	なぜ	【何故】	why
	なぜかといえば	【何故かと言えば】	the reason is
	なぜなら(ば)	【何故なら(ば)】	the reason is
	なんとなれば	【何となれば】	the reason is
	ばあいによって	【場合によって】	depending on the situation
	はじめに	【初めに】	first, at the start
	まず	【先ず】	first (of all)
	また	【又】	moreover, and (in addition)
*	または	【又は】	or
	もし		if
	もちろん	【勿論】	of course
	もともと	【元々】	originally, in the past
	やはり		after all, still
	ゆえに	【故に】	therefore
	よって		consequently, therefore

* Here は is pronounced 'wa'.

** When 一方 appears alone, it can be translated as "however." The construction 一方[イッボウ] ... 他方[タホウ] ... corresponds to "on the one hand ... on the other hand ...."

\# さて is a very weak connective and is often best left untranslated.

\#\# The word ただし indicates that what follows is an elaboration on the immediately preceding statement. Specifically, after chemical or mathematical equations ただし is usually best translated simply as "here," or "in this equation."

EXERCISES

You will learn to read HIRAGANA with the same exercises with which you learned KATAKANA, by reading GAIRAIGO. Although GAIRAIGO are written in KATAKANA in technical texts, in Japanese technical dictionaries where entries are given in HIRAGANA, even GAIRAIGO are written in HIRAGANA and in the same style as in KATAKANA, namely, with a bar (ー) to indicate a doubled vowel.

Exercise 4.7 will remind you of how entries are ordered in Japanese technical dictionaries, as discussed in Section 3.8. The exercise is based on the electronic dictionary, *Denki Yoogo Jiten*, Corona Publishing, Tokyo (1982), which uses English letters to signify technical concepts, e.g., ABC for "automatic boiler control."

Exercises 4.8 and 4.9 are preceded by a vocabulary list needed for understanding the Japanese sentences in Exercise 4.8 and for translating the sentences in Exercise 4.9. Exercise 4.8 introduces you to sentences in which the HIRAGANA symbols for particles appear: を for 'o', は for 'wa', and へ for 'e'. These exercises repeat some of the simple sentences that you read in Hepburn romanization in Chapter 2. However, now they are written in HIRAGANA and KATAKANA. After giving the Japanese sentence, we show how the sentence can be built up from a very simple sentence by successively adding more phrases. Exercise 4.9 gives you some very simple Japanese sentences to translate.

Exercises 4.10 and 4.11 repeat the final exercises in Chapter 3, giving the same computer terms and names of chemical elements but now in HIRAGANA.

ひらがな一覧表[いちらんひょう]

	a	i	u	e	o
	あ	い	う	え	お
k	か	き	く	け	こ
g	が	ぎ	ぐ	げ	ご
s	さ	し	す	せ	そ
z	ざ	じ	ず	ぜ	ぞ
t	た	ち	つ	て	と
d	だ	ぢ	づ	で	ど
n	な	に	ぬ	ね	の
h	は	ひ	ふ	へ	ほ
b	ば	び	ぶ	べ	ぼ
p	ぱ	ぴ	ぷ	ぺ	ぽ
m	ま	み	む	め	も
y	や		ゆ		よ
r	ら	り	る	れ	ろ
w	わ				を
-n	ん				

i	Palatalized Consonants		
	ya	yu	yo
き	きゃ	きゅ	きょ
ぎ	ぎゃ	ぎゅ	ぎょ
し	しゃ	しゅ	しょ
じ	じゃ	じゅ	じょ
ち	ちゃ	ちゅ	ちょ
に	にゃ	にゅ	にょ
ひ	ひゃ	ひゅ	ひょ
び	びゃ	びゅ	びょ
ぴ	ぴゃ	ぴゅ	ぴょ
み	みゃ	みゅ	みょ
り	りゃ	りゅ	りょ
っ	doubles the following consonant		
ー	doubles the preceding vowel		

ひらがな第一表[だいいっぴょう]

	STEP 1	STEP 2	STEP 3	STEP 4
a	あ			
i	い			
u	う			
e	え			
o	お			

	STEP 1	STEP 2	STEP 3	STEP 4
ka	か			
ki	き			
ku	く			
ke	け			
ko	こ			

	STEP 1	STEP 2	STEP 3	STEP 4
sa	さ			
shi	し			
su	す			
se	せ			
so	そ			

	STEP 1	STEP 2	STEP 3	STEP 4
-n	ん			

Example of writing NIGORI

	STEP 1	STEP 2	STEP 3	STEP 4
zu	ず			

4-10

Ex 4.1 The a-row, ka-row, sa-row, and syllabic -n

あ	a	あー	aa		か	ka	かー	kaa		さ	sa	さー	saa
い	i	いー	ii		き	ki	きー	kii		し	shi	しー	shii
う	u	うー	uu		く	ku	くー	kuu		す	su	すー	suu
え	e	えー	ee		け	ke	けー	kee		せ	se	せー	see
お	o	おー	oo		こ	ko	こー	koo		そ	so	そー	soo

ん	-n

EXAMPLES

あい	ai	eye (camera)
うえあ	uea	(soft)ware
いおん	ion	ion
あんか	anka	anchor (chain)
きー	kii	key
あーく	aaku	arc (weld)
けーき	keeki	(filter) cake
こーきん	kookin	calking
さいん	sain	sine
おきし	okishi	oxy (salt)
えくす	ekusu	x-(ray)
あくせす	akusesu	access (time)
けーそん	keeson	caisson

MATCHING EXERCISE

1. しす	( ) aqua (complex)
2. ういすきー	( ) Sequoia {tree}
3. こさいん	( ) earth {British}, ground {American}
4. こかいん	( ) K (scope, truss)
5. けい	( ) kink
6. えーかー	( ) cis (form)
7. いそしあん	( ) echo (machine)
8. あくあ	( ) whiskey
9. えこー	( ) cosine
10. あーす	( ) cocaine
11. きんく	( ) acre
12. おんこーす	( ) on course
13. せこいあ	( ) isocyanic (acid)

Ex 4.2 The ga-row and za-row

が	ga	がー	gaa	ざ	za	ざー	zaa
ぎ	gi	ぎー	gii	じ	ji	じー	jii
ぐ	gu	ぐー	guu	ず	zu	ずー	zuu
げ	ge	げー	gee	ぜ	ze	ぜー	zee
ご	go	ごー	goo	ぞ	zo	ぞー	zoo

EXAMPLES

がす	gasu	gas/gases
ぎが	giga	giga {unit}
こーきんぐ	kookingu	calking
じえん	jien	diene
げーじ	geeji	gage
いんじご	injigo	indigo
かいざー	kaizaa	kayser {unit}
じーんず	jiinzu	(Sir James) Jeans
かぜいん	kazein	casein
おぞん	ozon	ozone

MATCHING EXERCISE

1. あがし	( ) Geiger
2. がうす	( ) Gauss
3. おーが	( ) Agassiz
4. がいがー	( ) Edison
5. あじそん	( ) ageing (lamp)
6. えーじんぐ	( ) Addison
7. あぞ	( ) keying
8. おんさーがー	( ) azo (compound)
9. えじそん	( ) Onsager
10. きーいんぐ	( ) auger

4-12

ひらがな第二表[だいにひょう]

		STEP 1	STEP 2	STEP 3	STEP 4
ta	た	こ	た	だ	た
chi	ち	こ	ち		
tsu	つ	う			
te	て	て			
to	と	゛	と		

		STEP 1	STEP 2	STEP 3	STEP 4
na	な	こ	た	だ	な
ni	に	⺊	⻣	に	
nu	ぬ	い	ぬ		
ne	ね	⺉	ね		
no	の	の			

		STEP 1	STEP 2	STEP 3	STEP 4
ha	は	⺉	に	は	
hi	ひ	ひ			
fu	ふ	゛	ふ	ふ	ぶ
he	へ	へ			
ho	ほ	⺉	に	に	ほ

Example of writing MARU

		STEP 1	STEP 2	STEP 3	STEP 4
pi	ぴ	ひ	ぴ		

4-13

Ex 4.3 The ta-row, na-row, and ha-row

た	ta	たー	taa	な	na	なー	naa	は	ha	はー	haa
ち	chi	ちー	chii	に	ni	にー	nii	ひ	hi	ひー	hii
つ	tsu	つー	tsuu	ぬ	nu	ぬー	nuu	ふ	fu	ふー	fuu
て	te	てー	tee	ね	ne	ねー	nee	へ	he	へー	hee
と	to	とー	too	の	no	のー	noo	ほ	ho	ほー	hoo

EXAMPLES

たんく	tanku	tank
ついすた	tsuisuta	twister
すいっち	suitchi	switch
てんきー	tenkii	ten-key
そけっと	soketto	socket
そーな	soona	sonar
にこちん	nikochin	nicotine
えぬしー	enushii	NC {= numerical control}
ねおん	neon	neon
のっきんぐ	nokkingu	knocking
はーふとーん	haafutoon	half-tone
ひすと	hisuto	histo(gram)
へきそーす	hekisoosu	hexose
ほすげん	hosugen	phosgene

MATCHING EXERCISE

1. こんたくと	( ) horn (antenna)
2. あんちのっく	( ) toxin
3. あんてな	( ) anion
4. ときしん	( ) hexane
5. あにおん	( ) antenna
6. ねおんさいん	( ) software
7. おきしけとん	( ) anti-knock
8. そはいお	( ) oxyketone
9. ひーた	( ) heater
10. そふとうえあ	( ) neon sign
11. へきさん	( ) off-set
12. ほーん	( ) (air) ejector
13. のっちんぐ	( ) contact
14. えぜくた	( ) Sohio (process)
15. おふせっと	( ) nano (seconds)
16. なの	( ) notching (relay)

Ex 4.4 The da-row, ba-row, and pa-row

だ	da	だー	daa
で	de	でー	dee
ど	do	どー	doo

ば	ba	ばー	baa
び	bi	びー	bii
ぶ	bu	ぶー	buu
べ	be	べー	bee
ぼ	bo	ぼー	boo

ぱ	pa	ぱー	paa
ぴ	pi	ぴー	pii
ぷ	pu	ぷー	puu
ぺ	pe	ぺー	pee
ぽ	po	ぽー	poo

EXAMPLES

あだぷた	adaputa	adapter
でーた	deeta	data
どなー	donaa	donor
ばいあす	baiasu	bias (method)
びっと	bitto	bit
いそぶたん	isobutan	isobutane
べーす	beesu	base (load)
さーぼ	saabo	servo (brake)
だんぱ	danpa	damper
すぴん	supin	spin
いそぷれん	isopuren	isoprene
ぴぺっと	pipetto	pipette
えぽきしど	epokishido	epoxide

MATCHING EXERCISE

1. いんぴーだんす	( ) videotape
2. あんぺあ	( ) dubbing
3. あのーどあーく	( ) converter
4. こんばーた	( ) anode arc
5. こーどばー	( ) peak (load)
6. べーすたーびん	( ) impedance
7. でてくとばー	( ) pipe
8. どっとぱたーん	( ) ampere
9. だびんぐ	( ) doping
10. ぴーく	( ) code bar
11. どーぴんぐ	( ) dot pattern
12. びでおてーぷ	( ) base turbine
13. ぱいぷ	( ) detector bar

ひらがな第三表[だいさんひょう]

		STEP 1	STEP 2	STEP 3	STEP 4
ma	ま	ニ	三	ま	
mi	み	及	み		
mu	む	二	む	む	
me	め	い	め		
mo	も	し	も	も	

		STEP 1	STEP 2	STEP 3	STEP 4
ya	や	ら	ら	や	

		STEP 1	STEP 2	STEP 3	STEP 4
yu	ゆ	ゆ	ゆ		

		STEP 1	STEP 2	STEP 3	STEP 4
yo	よ	二	よ		

		STEP 1	STEP 2	STEP 3	STEP 4
ra	ら	ゝ	ら		
ri	り	り	り		
ru	る	る			
re	れ	り	れ		
ro	ろ	ろ			

		STEP 1	STEP 2	STEP 3	STEP 4
wa	わ	り	わ		
wo	を	二	六	を	

Ex 4.5 The ma-row, ya-row, ra-row, and wa-row

ま	ma	まー	maa
み	mi	みー	mii
む	mu	むー	muu
め	me	めー	mee
も	mo	もー	moo

や	ya	やー	yaa
ゆ	yu	ゆー	yuu
よ	yo	よー	yoo

ら	ra	らー	raa
り	ri	りー	rii
る	ru	るー	ruu
れ	re	れー	ree
ろ	ro	ろー	roo

わ	wa	わー	waa

EXAMPLES

がんま	ganma	gamma
あみん	amin	amine
おーむ	oomu	ohm
あめーば	ameeba	amoeba
もーめんと	moomento	moment
たいや	taiya	tire
ゆにおん	yunion	union
よーく	yooku	yoke
ぐらふ	gurafu	graph
れおろじー	reorojii	rheology
まとりっくす	matorikkusu	matrix
だいやる	daiyaru	dial
わっと	watto	watt

MATCHING EXERCISE

1. ろーたりー	( ) minimum (pause)
2. わーぷろ	( ) monotropy
3. ぬくれお	( ) rim drive
4. るーめん	( ) random (access)
5. りれー	( ) unitary (space)
6. らんだむ	( ) lumen
7. ゆにたりー	( ) reset
8. ものとろぴー	( ) rotary (kiln)
9. めたろいど	( ) nucleo(side)
10. りせっと	( ) microphone
11. まいくろほん	( ) metalloid
12. みにまむ	( ) relay
13. りむどらいぶ	( ) word processor

Ex 4.6 Palatalized consonants, such as in

| きゃ kya | きゅ kyu | きょ kyo |

EXAMPLES

きゃりやー	kyariyaa	carrier (gas)
ぎゃらくしー	gyarakushii	galaxy
ぽてんしゃる	potensharu	potential
じゃいろ	jairo	gyro(scope)
ちゃんねる	channeru	channel
ふらいあっしゅ	furaiasshu	fly ash
ちゅーぶみる	chuubumiru	tube mill
にゅーとりの	nyuutorino	neutrino
ひゅーず	hyuuzu	fuse
びゅーれっと	byuuretto	burette
こんぴゅーた	konpyuuta	computer
しみゅれーた	shimyureeta	simulator
こあれーしょ	koareesho	core ratio
ちょーく	chooku	choke (coil)
てれびじょん	terebijon	television

MATCHING EXERCISE

1. じゅーる	( ) curie {unit}
2. ちょっぱ	( ) overshoot
3. ぷらんじゃ	( ) newton {unit}
4. きゅりー	( ) shutter
5. にゅーとん	( ) messenger
6. じゃっく	( ) joule {unit}
7. すきゃった	( ) scatter
8. ぎゃっぷ	( ) chopper
9. めっせんじゃ	( ) gap
10. しゅりーれん	( ) plunger
11. おーばしゅーと	( ) jack
12. ぐりにゃーる	( ) Schottky (effect)
13. るしゃとりえ	( ) Grignard's (reagent)
14. しょっときー	( ) Schlieren (method)
15. しゃった	( ) Le Chatelier's (rule)

Ex 4.7 The pronunciation of the ABC's written in HIRAGANA

A	えい	B	びー	C	しー	D	でぃー	E	いー
F	えふ	G	じー	H	えいち	I	あい	J	じぇい
K	けい	L	える	M	えむ	N	えぬ	O	おう
P	ぴー	Q	きゅー	R	あーる	S	えす	T	てぃー
U	ゆー	V	ぶぃー	W	だぶりゅー	X	えくす	Y	わい
Z	ぜっど								

Source: Denki Yoogo Jiten, Corona Publishing, Tokyo (1982).

Verify that the following abbreviations appearing in this Japanese technical dictionary are in the 五十音[ゴジュウオン] order. For example, ASR is written and pronounced えいえすあーる and hence precedes ASC えいえすしー.

1. IFR   instrument flight rules
2. ILS   instrument landing system
3. IC   integrated circuit
4. EHF   extremely high frequency
5. ELF   extremely low frequency
6. ASR   airport surveillance radar
7. ASC   automatic selectivity control
8. AFC   automatic frequency control
9. ACC   automatic combustion control
10. APL   average picture level
11. ABC   automatic boiler control
12. APC   automatic phase control
13. AVR   automatic voltage regulator
14. SWR   standing-wave ratio
15. STC   sensitivity time control
16. OCR   optical character reader
17. OWF   optimum working frequency
18. ODR   omnidirectional radio range
19. PRF   pulse repetition frequency
20. PAM   pulse-amplitude modulation

ベンゼン	benzene
アルコール	alcohol
ビーカー	beaker
フラスコ	flask
リサーチ	research
センター	center
ウイルス	virus
サンプル	sample
ラボ	lab(oratory)
バイオテク	biotech
ヨードチンキ	tincture of iodine
そそぐ	to pour
まぜる	to mix
ある	to be {for locating inanimate things}
ながれる	to flow
いく	to go
おくる	to send
これ	this {pronoun}
それ	that {pronoun}
この	this {adjective}
その	that {adjective}
は {pronounced 'wa'}	{postposition}
を {pronounced 'o'}	{postposition}
が	{postposition}
へ {pronounced 'e'}	to, toward {postposition}
に	in, into {postposition}
で	in, at {postposition}
も	also {postposition}
の	of {postposition}
と	and {postposition}
から	from {postposition}
AとB(と)	A and B
AはBである。	A is B.

Ex 4.8 The particles は, を, **and** へ

1.　　　　　　これはベンゼンである 。

　　　　ベンゼンである。　　　[It] is benzene.
　　　これはベンゼンである。　　This is benzene.

2.　　　　　　それはアルコールである 。

　　　　アルコールである。　　　[It] is alcohol.
　　　それはアルコールである。　That is alcohol.

3.　　　　　　これはビーカーである 。

　　　　ビーカーである。　　　[It] is a beaker.
　　　これはビーカーである。　This is a beaker.

4.　　　　　　それもビーカーである 。

　　　　ビーカーである。　　　[It] is a beaker.
　　　それもビーカーである。　That also is a beaker.

5.　　　　ベンゼンをこのビーカーにそそぐ 。

　　　　　　そそぐ。　　　　　[We] pour.
　　　このビーカーにそそぐ。　　[We] pour into this beaker.
　ベンゼンをこのビーカーにそそぐ。　[We] pour the benzene into this beaker.

6.　　　　アルコールをそのビーカーにそそぐ 。

　　　　　　そそぐ。　　　　　[We] pour.
　　　そのビーカーにそそぐ。　　[We] pour into that beaker.
　アルコールをそのビーカーにそそぐ。　[We] pour the alcohol into that beaker.

7.　　　　ベンゼンをフラスコにそそぐ 。

　　　　　　そそぐ。　　　　　[We] pour.
　　　フラスコにそそぐ。　　　[We] pour into a flask.
　ベンゼンをフラスコにそそぐ。　　[We] pour the benzene into a flask.

8.　　　　アルコールもフラスコにそそぐ 。

　　　　　　そそぐ。　　　　　[We] pour.
　　　フラスコにそそぐ。　　　[We] pour into the flask.
　アルコールもフラスコにそそぐ。　[We] also pour the alcohol into the flask.

9.　　　　アルコールもフラスコにある 。

　　　　　　ある。　　　　　[It] is.
　　　フラスコにある。　　　[It] is in the flask.
　アルコールもフラスコにある。　The alcohol also is in the flask.

10.　　　　　フラスコでベンゼンとアルコールとをまぜる 。

まぜる。	[We] mix.
ベンゼンとアルコールとをまぜる。	[We] mix the benzene and the alcohol.
フラスコでベンゼンとアルコールとを まぜる。	[We] mix the benzene and the alcohol in the flask.

11.　　　　　ガスがAからBへながれる 。

ながれる。	[It] flows.
Bへながれる。	[It] flows to B.
AからBへながれる。	[It] flows from A to B.
ガスがAからBへながれる。	The gases flow from A to B.

12.　　　　　ソニーのリサーチセンターへいく 。

いく。	[We] go.
リサーチセンターへいく。	[We] go to the research center.
ソニーのリサーチセンターへいく。	[We] go to Sony's research center.

13.　　　　　ウイルスのサンプルをバイオテクのラボへおくる 。

おくる。	[We] send.
ラボへおくる。	[We] send to the lab.
バイオテクのラボへおくる。	[We] send to the biotech lab.
サンプルをバイオテクのラボへおくる。	[We] send samples to the biotech lab.
ウイルスのサンプルをバイオテクのラ ボへおくる。	[We] send the virus samples to the biotech lab.

Ex 4.9 Translate the following sentences

1. tはスカラーである。
2. vはベクトルである。
3. Eはガスのエネルギーである。
4. このガスはベンゼンである。
5. そのガスはヘリウムである。
6. ヨードチンキをこのビーカーにそそぐ。
7. ヨードチンキをこのフラスコにもそそぐ。
8. ポリマーはAからBへながれる。
9. フラスコでモノマーとポリマーをまぜる。
10. このフラスコにセッケンがある。
11. これはアメーバである。それもアメーバである。
12. バイオテクのラボへいく。
13. ソレノイドをリサーチラボへおくる。

Ex 4.10 KATAKANA computer terms in HIRAGANA

あくせっしんぐ　　　　　　こんぴゅーたあにめーしょん　どきゅめんてーしょん
あせんぶら　　　　　　　　こんぴゅーたびじょん　　　　とらんすれーた
あなろぐ　　　　　　　　　しーけんしゃる　　　　　　　ちゃねるいんたふぇいす
あるごりずむ　　　　　　　じぇねれーた　　　　　　　　ばーちゃるめもり
あれいぷろせっさ　　　　　しみゅれーたぷろぐらむ　　　はーどうえあ
いんくわいありしすてむ　　すけじゅーりんぐ　　　　　　ぱーとぷろぐらむ
いんたぷりた　　　　　　　すたっくおーとまとん　　　　ふぁいる
いんたりーびんぐ　　　　　すーぱばいざりしすてむ　　　ぷっしゅあっぷ
えみゅれーしょん　　　　　するーぷっと　　　　　　　　ぷっしゅだうん
おーとまとん　　　　　　　そーてぃんぐ　　　　　　　　ぷろぐらみんぐ
おふらいん　　　　　　　　そふとうえあ　　　　　　　　ぷろぐらむすきーむ
おぺれーてぃんぐしすてむ　たーんあらうんど　　　　　　ぷろぐらむぱっけーじ
おんらいん　　　　　　　　だいなみっくもでる　　　　　ぷろぐらむめんてなんす
がーべじこれくしょん　　　たぶれっと　　　　　　　　　まいくろぷろせっさ
きゃっしゅめもり　　　　　たんでむしすてむ　　　　　　みにこんぴゅーた
げーみんぐしみゅれーしょん　でーたべーす　　　　　　　ゆーてぃりてぃぷろぐらむ
こーでぃんぐ　　　　　　　でぃじたいざ　　　　　　　　らいとぺん
こまんどあんどこんとろーる　てきすと　　　　　　　　　わーどぷろせっさ
こんぱいら　　　　　　　　でばっぎんぐ

accessing	file	push down
algorithm	gaming simulation	push up
analog	garbage collection	scheduling
array processor	generator	sequential
assembler	hardware	simulator program
automaton	inquiry system	software
cache memory	interleaving	sorting
channel interface	interpreter	stack automaton
coding	light pen	supervisory system
command and control	microprocessor	tablet
compiler	minicomputer	tandem system
computer animation	off-line	text
computer vision	on-line	throughput
data base	operating system	translator
debugging	part program	turn around
digitizer	program maintenance	utility program
documentation	programming	virtual memory
dynamic model	program package	word processor
emulation	program scheme	

Ex 4.11 KATAKANA chemical elements in HIRAGANA

あいんすたいにうむ Es
あくちにうむ Ac
あすたちん At
あめりしうむ Am
あるごん Ar
あるみにうむ Al
あんちもん Sb
いってるびうむ Yb
いっとりうむ Y
いりじうむ Ir
いんじうむ In
うらん U
えるびうむ Er
おすみうむ Os
かどみうむ Cd
がどりにうむ Gd
かりうむ K
がりうむ Ga
かりほるにうむ Cf
かるしうむ Ca
きせのん Xe
きゅりうむ Cm
くりぷとん Kr
くろみうむ Cr
げるまにうむ Ge
こばると Co

さまりうむ Sm
じすぷろしうむ Dy
じるこにうむ Zr
すかんじうむ Sc
すとろんちうむ Sr
せしうむ Cs
せりうむ Ce
せれん Se
たりうむ Tl
たんぐすてん W
たんたる Ta
ちたん Ti
つりうむ Tm
てくねちうむ Tc
てるびうむ Tb
てるる Te
とりうむ Th
なとりうむ Na
におぶ Nb
にっける Ni
ねおじむ Nd
ねおん Ne
ねぷつにうむ Np
のーべりうむ No
ばーくりうむ Bk
はふにうむ Hf

ぱらじうむ Pd
ばりうむ Ba
びすます Bi
ふぇるみうむ Fm
ふらんしうむ Fr
ぷらせおじむ Pr
ぷるとにうむ Pu
ぷろたくちにうむ Pa
ぷろめちうむ Pm
へりうむ He
べりりうむ Be
ほるみうむ Ho
ぽろにうむ Po
まぐねしうむ Mg
まんがん Mn
めんでれびうむ Md
ゆーろぴうむ Eu
らじうむ Ra
らどん Rn
らんたん La
りちうむ Li
るてちうむ Lu
るてにうむ Ru
るびじうむ Rb
れにうむ Re
ろーれんしうむ Lr
ろじうむ Rh

actinium Ac
aluminum Al
americium Am
antimony Sb
argon Ar
astatine At
barium Ba
berkelium Bk
beryllium Be
bismuth Bi
cadmium Cd
calcium Ca
californium Cf
cerium Ce
cesium Cs
chromium Cr
cobalt Co
curium Cm
dysprosium Dy
einsteinium Es
erbium Er
europium Eu
fermium Fm
francium Fr
gadolinium Gd
gallium Ga

germanium Ge
hafnium Hf
helium He
holmium Ho
indium In
iridium Ir
krypton Kr
lanthanum La
lawrencium Lr
lithium Li
lutetium Lu
magnesium Mg
manganese Mn
mendelevium Md
neodymium Nd
neon Ne
neptunium Np
nickel Ni
niobium Nb
nobelium No
osmium Os
palladium Pd
plutonium Pu
polonium Po
potassium K [Kalium]
praseodymium Pr

promethium Pm
protactinium Pa
radium Ra
radon Rn
rhenium Re
rhodium Rh
rubidium Rb
ruthenium Ru
samarium Sm
scandium Sc
selenium Se
sodium Na [Natrium]
strontium Sr
tantalum Ta
technetium Tc
tellurium Te
terbium Tb
thallium Tl
thorium Th
thulium Tm
titanium Ti
tungsten W
uranium U
xenon Xe
ytterbium Yb
yttrium Y
zirconium Zr

CHAPTER 5　第五章　[ダイゴショウ]

一	イチ	one
	イツ	one; same
	ひと(つ)	one

| 人 | ジン; ニン | person, people |
| | ひと | person, people |

行	ギョウ	line; row
	コウ	acting
	おこな(う)	to do, perform
	い(く); ゆ(く)	to go

| 水 | スイ | water |
| | みず | water |

| 金 | キン | gold; metal |
| | かね | money; metal |

大	タイ; ダイ	large
	おお(きい)	large
	おお(きな)	large
	おお(きさ)	magnitude

見	ケン	seeing, viewing
	み(る)	to see
	み(える)	to be visible
	み(なす)	to regard ... as

| 二 | ニ | two |
| | ふた(つ) | two |

高	コウ	tall, high
	たか(い)	tall
	たか(さ)	height

入	ニュウ	entering
	い(れる)	to insert
	はい(る) {xu}	to enter
	-い(る) {xu}	to enter

子	シ	child
	-シ	small entity
	こ	child

| 方 | ホウ | side, direction |
| | -かた | way, style |

| 示 | シ; ジ | indication |
| | しめ(す) | to show, indicate |

面	メン	surface, plane
	-メン	aspect(s) of
	おもて	surface

| 石 | シャク; セキ | rock, stone |
| | いし | stone(s) |

用	ヨウ	use, utility
	-ヨウ	for use in
	もち(いる)	to use

小	ショウ	small
	こ-	small
	ちい(さい)	small
	ちい(さな)	small

| 力 | リキ; リョク | force, power |
| | ちから | force |

生	ショウ; セイ	life, existence
	う(む)	to give birth
	い(かす)	to give life, enliven
	い(きる)	to live

立	リツ	standing upright
	た(てる)	to set up, erect
	た(つ)	to stand

5-1

一

一見する	イッケンする	to glance
一方	イッポウ	one side, way
一人	ひとり {N.B. irreg. rdg. り for 人}	one person

行

マトリックスの行	マトリックスのギョウ	row of a matrix

金

金メッキ	キンメッキ	gold plate

見

見方	みかた	point of view
一見する	イッケンする	to glance

高

高大な	コウダイな	grand, impressive

子

原子	ゲンシ	atom
原子力	ゲンシリョク	atomic power
分子	ブンシ	molecule
高分子	コウブンシ	macromolecule

示

示力図	ジリョクズ	force diagram

石

石ケン	セッケン	soap
石ケン水	セッケンスイ	soapy water

小

大小	ダイショウ	size

生

水生の	スイセイの	aquatic
生ずる	ショウずる {N.B. ショウ not セイ}	to arise, be generated
生じる	ショウじる {N.B. ショウ not セイ}	to arise, be generated

人
人力の	ジンリョクの	manual
一人	ひとり {N.B. irreg. rdg. り for 人}	one person
二人	ふたり {N.B. irreg. rdg. り for 人}	two people

水
水力	スイリョク	water power
-用水	ヨウスイ	water for use in
大水	おおみず	flooding

大
高大な	コイダイな	grand, impressive

二
二原子-	ニゲンシ	diatomic
二人	ふたり {N.B. irreg. rdg. り for 人}	two people

入
入力する	ニュウリョクする	to input

方
見方	みかた	point of view
立方-	リッポウ	cubic
方々	ホウボウ	all directions

面
水面	スイメン	water surface
方面	ホウメン	field {e.g., of study}

用
-用水	ヨウスイ	water for use in

力
入力する	ニュウリョクする	to input
人力の	ジンリョクの	manual
水力	スイリョク	water power
力学	リキガク	mechanics

立
立方-	リッポウ	cubic

5   KANJI

You have already learned that KANJI came to Japan from China; that they have ON and KUN readings — the ON from China and the KUN from native Japanese words whose meanings correspond to those of the KANJI; and that they most frequently appear in clusters to form KANGO, words that are pronounced with the ON readings and which express meanings that combine the meanings of the individual KANJI.

The first Chinese characters, apparently engraved on bones and tortoise shells, pictured fundamental things such as human beings, birds, fire, and flowing water. Later these elementary pictures became simplified and stylized in an effort to make writing easier.

Later the characters depicting fundamental things were grouped together so as to form new characters whose meanings depended on the combination of the elementary ideas. For example, two characters introduced in this lesson, 人 for "person" and 立 for the verb "to stand," were joined to form the new character 位 to express the idea of "a person's rank in the court." In technical Japanese this character appears in the KANGO 単位[タンイ], meaning "unit" (the KANJI 単 means "single" or "simple").

As the characters increased in number and complexity, it became necessary to have a method to classify them. The method adopted was to classify them on the basis of one of the simpler characters of which they were composed. These parts for classifying the characters are called "radicals" in English, and these radicals are

5-4

arranged in a KANJI dictionary according to their number of strokes, i.e., the number of strokes that must be made when the radical is written alone as a KANJI with a brush and charcoal ink. There are 214 radicals.

In this chapter we give you all the information about KANJI that you need to study this book. We first discuss stroke order and stroke count. We then discuss radicals so that you can use a KANJI dictionary; ON and KUN readings so that you can understand the dictionary readings for the KANJI; JUKUGO so that you can find your way among the vocabulary entries; and then specifically Nelson's KANJI dictionary. We then explain the format of the charts that open this chapter and Chapters 6-20 and give some suggestions for learning KANJI.

5.1 Writing KANJI: Stroke Order and Stroke Count

Because radicals are classified according to number of strokes, you must learn how to count strokes in order to locate a radical easily in the list of 214. Moreover, because under each radical, the KANJI are classified according to the number of strokes in the remainder of the character, here again you have to know how to count strokes. Finally, if for some reason you cannot locate a KANJI under its radical, you may need to look it up in a table in the dictionary that lists KANJI according to total stroke count. This, you will find, is a last and desperate measure. In any event, you need to learn how to count strokes in order to use a KANJI dictionary.

You have already learned something about stroke order and stroke count in writing KATAKANA and HIRAGANA in Chapters 3 and 4. Your model for learning these features of KANJI should be KATAKANA, where strokes are clear and definite, because KANJI dictionaries are based on KATAKANA-type strokes.

Below we will show you the stroke order and stroke count for several of the KANJI in this lesson in order to call your attention to certain principles for writing KANJI. One is to write the left part first, the right part second. This is well illustrated by the KANJI 行.

STEP 1	STEP 2	STEP 3	STEP 4	STEP 5	STEP 6
彳	彳	彳	彳	行	行

A second principle is to write from the top down. This is already illustrated in the stroke order above for the left and the right parts of 行. It is especially evident with KANJI such as 立.

STEP 1	STEP 2	STEP 3	STEP 4	STEP 5
亠	亠	产	立	立

5-5

A third principle is to complete the top and sides of an enclosure before writing what it encloses. This is well illustrated by the KANJI 用.

STEP 1	STEP 2	STEP 3	STEP 4	STEP 5
丿	冂	月	月	用

There are other principles, but the above three principles plus the stroke orders and stroke counts that we give for each KANJI in every chapter should be sufficient for your needs. Below you will find the KANJI in this lesson in the order of their total stroke counts.

1	一	6	行
2	二人入力	7	見
3	大子小	8	金
4	方水	9	面
5	生用石示立	10	高

Confirm these counts, remembering that small rectangles and rectangles that enclose other strokes count three strokes because they include one "hook." In addition, three other KANJI have "hooks": 力 written in the same order and stroke pattern as the KATAKANA カ; 水 where the first stroke is the vertical and the second is the "hook" on the left of the vertical, just like the KATAKANA フ; and 子 where the first stroke is the same as the first stroke in the KATAKANA マ.

5.2 Radicals

All the KANJI introduced in this lesson are radicals. In Table 5.1 you will find examples of KANJI in this book classified under these radicals in Nelson's dictionary, *The Modern Reader's Japanese-English Character Dictionary*, Tuttle, Rutland, Vt. (1974), 2nd (Revised) Edition. In looking at the table you should note these points:

(a)   The first column gives the KANJI of this chapter; all are radicals.

(b)   The second column gives the number that Nelson assigns to these radicals.

(c)   The third column gives the number of strokes in the KANJI of Column 1.

(d)   The fourth column shows how the radicals actually appear in KANJI. Some of the radicals (e.g., the radical 人) have different shapes depending on where they are located in the KANJI; they may also even have a different number of strokes than the KANJI in Column 1 from which they are derived (e.g., the radicals 水 and 示). In tables of radicals, you will find 水 listed under 4 strokes, and also its three-stroke variant under 3 strokes.

(e)   The fifth column gives many of the KANJI included in this book that are classified under the radical or one of its variants. These are listed in order of increas-

Table 5.1 Examples of KANJI Classified by Radicals in Nelson

KANJI	NUMBER	STROKES	RADICAL	CLASSIFICATIONS OF KANJI IN THIS BOOK
一	1	1	一	与三下互天不可平正両再亜
二	7	2	二	[互] 元 [亜]
人	9	2	人	以
			亻	化他仕付代件伝位体低作価例使係信倍値個
			𠆢	合全含
入	11	2	入	[内] [全]
力	19	2	力	加
			力	[励] 効動
大	37	3	大	[天] 太
子	39	3	子	存学
小	42	3	⺌	光当常
方	70	4	方	放族
水	85	4	氵	波注油法活消流液混測温減溶濃
生	100	5	生	[産]
用	101	5	用	
石	112	5	石	研硫硝磁確
示	113	5	礻	神
立	117	5	立	端
			産	産
行	144	6	行	
見	147	7	見	[視] 規観
金	167	8	釒	鉛鉱鉄銅銀錯鋼
面	176	9	面	
高	189	10	高	

ing number of additional strokes needed to complete the KANJI after writing the radical; for example, for the seven KANJI listed after 金, the numbers of additional strokes are 5, 5, 5, 6, 6, 8, and 8. Some radicals have very few KANJI classified under them; in Nelson, no KANJI are classified under 用, 面, 高, and 行.

(f)　　The brackets around a KANJI indicate that the KANJI has traditionally been classified under the given radical, but that Nelson classifies it differently.

5.3 ON and KUN Readings

In KANJI dictionaries prepared by Japanese for Japanese, ON readings are given in KATAKANA, KUN readings in HIRAGANA. We follow this standard practice in the KANJI table at the beginning of each chapter in this book. Verb and adjective endings, called OKURIGANA, are written in HIRAGANA and enclosed in parentheses. In KANJI dictionaries prepared for non-Japanese it is customary to put ON readings in capital letters and KUN readings in lower-case letters, with verb and adjective endings in parentheses.

Several KANJI have multiple ON readings; for example, in this lesson, the eight KANJI 一, 人, 力, 大, 生, 石, 示, and 行. When a KANJI has several ON readings, we do not necessarily give all these readings in the table that heads the chapter. We give only those ON readings that occur frequently in technical Japanese. For example, the ON readings of 金 are キン and コン, but we omit コン because it does not appear in technical Japanese.

KUN readings occur in nouns, adjectives, and verbs. Nouns are the simplest. When KANJI that represent nouns appear singly, they are usually given their KUN readings.

人	ひと	子	こ	石	いし
力	ちから	水	みず	面	おもて

One exception in this chapter is 金, which most often will be given its ON reading キン in technical writing, meaning "gold." Another is the character 方, which is given the ON reading in such expressions as この方[このホウ], "this direction," and その方 [そのホウ], "that direction." Nouns which are derived from adjectives, such as 高さ [たか(さ)], "height," and from verbs, such as 行い[おこな(い)], "action," are given the KUN readings, however, since adjectives and verbs are inflected.

Next we look at the KUN readings of the i-adjectives, which, as you saw in Section 1.6, are written with a KANJI followed by HIRAGANA. In this chapter we have 大きい[おお(きい)], 小さい[ちい(さい)], and 高い[たか(い)]. These are the "dictionary forms" of the i-adjectives; the HIRAGANA that follow the KANJI in the dictionary form or in various inflected forms are called OKURIGANA. There are no rules that govern how much of the adjective is written with OKURIGANA. With some KANJI for adjectives there are two different meanings, and these are distinguished only by the differing OKURIGANA. For example, in Chapter 9 you will learn the KANJI

細. As 細い[ほそ(い)] it means "thin, slender," as 細かい[こま(かい)] it means "finely divided."

Next we turn to verbs, which are also written with KANJI followed by HIRAGANA, as you saw in Section 1.6. Here again, the HIRAGANA in the dictionary and inflected forms are called OKURIGANA, and you have no way of knowing a priori how much of the verb is to be written with OKURIGANA without consulting a dictionary.

Some verbs in this chapter have only a single transitive form: 用いる[もち(いる)], "to use," and 示す[しめ(す)], "to show, indicate"; others a single intransitive form 生じる[ショウ(じる)], "to arise, be generated." Still others have two related forms, one "transitive," the other "intransitive": for example, 立てる[た(てる)], "to set up, erect"; 立つ[た(つ)], "to stand (up)."

Another pair in this chapter shows a further complication that may arise with KUN readings of some verbs: 入れる[い(れる)], "to insert"; 入る[はい(る)], "to enter." Here the KANJI 入 is read as い in the transitive verb and as はい in the intransitive verb. In addition, 入る can also occur in combination with another verb, in which case 入 is read い: for example, 立ち入る[た(ち)い(る)], "to trespass."

Finally, occasionally one KANJI serves for writing two verbs not related as a transitive-intransitive pair. For example, in this chapter 行 represents both the verb 行く[い(く)] or [ゆ(く)] "to go," and the verb 行う[おこな(う)], "to do, perform."

As we pointed out above, KANJI that appear singly, i.e., KANJI that are not immediately followed by another KANJI, take on their KUN readings. One very important exception must be made to this general rule. Some single KANJI form verbs with the addition of する (or one of its variants, ずる or じる), and in those cases the KANJI takes its ON reading. For example, the KANJI 生 in this lesson forms the very important verb 生ずる, or 生じる, meaning "to emerge, arise, be generated." It has the readings ショウ(ずる) and ショウ(じる) respectively.

5.4 JUKUGO

JUKUGO are Japanese words that contain two or more KANJI. There are several classes of JUKUGO.

a. Both KANJI Have ON Readings

Most JUKUGO are read in this way, and, as mentioned in Chapter 1, they are called KANGO. In this chapter 水力[スイリョク], meaning "water power," is an example of a JUKUGO in which ON readings are used. Because of the importance of KANGO, you must make the memorization of ON readings a priority. Knowing the ON readings, you can easily look up JUKUGO directly in a Japanese-English dictionary. If you do not know the ON readings, then you will have to resort to a KANJI dictionary, which is much more cumbersome.

b. Both KANJI Have KUN Readings

A very small number of JUKUGO fall into this category. In this chapter we encounter 大水[おおみず], meaning "flood." For this word there is no way you can tell a priori that KUN readings are required. On the other hand, when you see 用い方 [もち(い)かた], meaning "way of using," the appearance of the OKURIGANA suggests that the KUN readings are appropriate. In some cases, however, the OKURIGANA are omitted; for example, you may see 立ち入り, 立入り, or 立入, all of which are read たちいり.

c. Mixed ON and KUN Readings

Two other types of readings occasionally occur. They consist of mixed readings of ON and KUN: ジュウばこよみ, in which the first KANJI has an ON reading and the second a KUN reading; and ゆトウよみ, in which the first KANJI has a KUN reading and the second an ON reading. The common suffix よみ means "reading." The words that identify these two types of readings are simply well-known words that illustrate the respective types: 重箱[ジュウばこ] refers to a set of tiered lacquered boxes to serve individual meals; 湯桶[ゆトウ] to a small wooden bucket for dipping hot water at a Japanese bath.

d. Irregular Readings

Some JUKUGO have irregular readings that are not related to the readings of the individual KANJI contained in them. For example, the word for "adult" is written as 大人, but read おとな.

e. Both ON and KUN Readings Possible

Occasionally there are JUKUGO that can be read in two ways. For example, the JUKUGO 小人, meaning "child," is read as ショウジン, whereas 小人, meaning "pygmy, dwarf," is read as こびと.

Of the above five classes of JUKUGO, the first is the most common, and therefore your first choice should be to assume ON readings. If your technical dictionary does not have a word listed with that pronunciation, you will have to consult a KANJI dictionary and its listing of JUKUGO under the first KANJI in the JUKUGO. The KANJI dictionary will list the JUKUGO under a given KANJI in the order of the number of strokes in the second KANJI, another reason to become familiar with counting strokes. Thus, the entry for 大小 will come before 大水 in the listing of JUKUGO under the first KANJI 大.

KANJI dictionaries also give the pronunciations of JUKUGO. Occasionally the ON and KUN readings change their sounds in JUKUGO, for example, from voiceless to voiced consonants or from single to doubled consonants:

小[こ] combines with 人[ひと] to give 小人[こびと].

Here the voiceless ひ changes to the voiced び. Consonant doubling occurs in KANGO when the first KANJI has a reading ending in ツ.

立[リツ] combines with 方[ホウ] to give 立方[リッポウ].
一[イツ] combines with 見[ケン] to give 一見[イッケン].

Note also the change from ホ to ポ in the first case. Consonant doubling also occurs when the first KANJI ends in 'i' or 'u' preceded by a voiceless consonant, and the second KANJI begins with the same voiceless consonant.

石[セキ] combines with ケン to give 石ケン[セッケン].
学[ガク] combines with 会[カイ] to give 学会[ガッカイ].

The word 学会 stands for "a (learned) society," from 学, "to learn, and 会, "to meet."

In the word 石ケン, "soap," above, the second part is written in KATAKANA because ケン stands for a KANJI no longer used. In the next chapter you will find the word ロート, "funnel." It is not a GAIRAIGO as you might expect; it is written in KATAKANA because it was originally written with two KANJI no longer used. Using KATAKANA to write KANJI no longer in use has been the usual practice, but it does not seem to be standard. Thus, the word for "protein" is often written in KANA rather than KANJI, and you will find it written both as タンパク and as たんぱく.

5.5 Nelson's KANJI Dictionary

There are many KANJI dictionaries for Japanese (KANWA-JITEN) and a few for English-speaking people (KAN'EI-JITEN). In all of these the main idea is to look up a KANJI in order to find its meaning, its readings, and its JUKUGO and their readings and meanings. The procedures for finding a KANJI vary from book to book. We choose here to discuss Nelson's *The Modern Reader's Japanese-English Character Dictionary*, which has been the standard reference work for several decades. This dictionary uses a classification scheme that is fairly standard and uses the traditional method of grouping the characters under the 214 "classical radicals." Once you know the method used in Nelson's dictionary, you will find it easy to use others. Also, the same method is used in electronic dictionaries.

Let us now see how we look up a given KANJI. First of all, if it is one of the 214 classical radicals, then you can find it at once; this presupposes a good familiarity with the 214 radicals. You will find 高 as radical 189 and not listed under radical 8 (亠). Similarly, you will find 用 as radical 101, and not listed under radical 13 (冂).

To understand strategies for classifying KANJI, you should become familiar with the seven basic structural patterns of KANJI and an eighth structure unique to Nelson, shown schematically below.

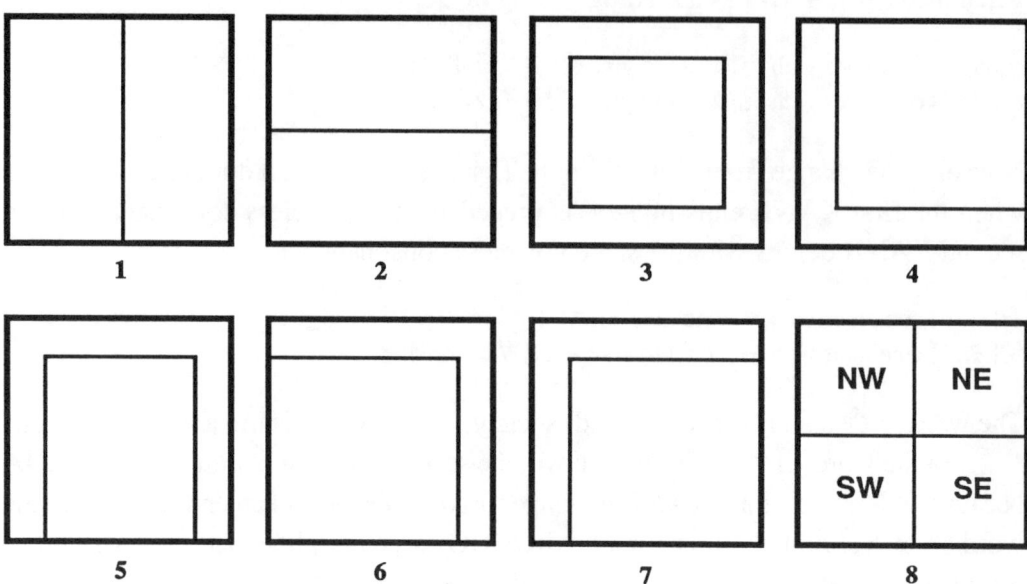

Pattern 1 is divided into left and right; an example of this pattern is a KANJI mentioned earlier, 位. In classifying KANJI having this pattern, Nelson gives preference to the left side. Thus, if the left side is a radical, he classifies under that radical: 位 is classified under radical 9 (人) and not under radical 117 (立). If the left side is not a radical and the right side is, Nelson classifies the KANJI under the right radical: for example, 動 under radical 19 (力).

Pattern 2 is divided into top and bottom; an example is the KANJI for "charcoal" 炭. In classifying KANJI having this pattern, Nelson gives preference to the top. Thus, 炭 is classified under radical 46 (山) "mountain." If the top is not a radical and the bottom is, he classifies under the bottom radical, for example, 素 for "element(s)" is classified under radical 120 (糸) "thread." These two KANJI form the KANGO 炭素 [タンソ] "carbon."

Types 3 through 7 involve enclosures. Examples in this book for these types are the five KANJI 図, 速, 同, 気, and 度, under radicals 31 (囗), 162 (辶), 13 (冂), 84 (气), and 53 (广). Here his rule for classifying is that radicals that are enclosures take precedence over all others. Adopting these strategies, Nelson seems guided by the rules for writing KANJI given earlier: priority to the left before the right, the rule to write first on the left and then on the right; priority to the top before the bottom, the rule to write first at the top and then at the bottom; priority to an enclosure, the rule to write top and sides first. Radical 162 (辶), however, though an enclosure, is written last.

With characters of type 8 Nelson adopts a procedure of dividing the KANJI into quadrants. The four quadrants are treated as part of a map: northwest (NW), northeast (NE), southeast (SE), and southwest (SW). The procedure is to look first for a radical in the NW corner, then following clockwise to NE, SE, and finally SW in choosing the radical for classifying the KANJI. It is not necessary for the KANJI to have all four quadrants. For example, Nelson classifies 題 under radical 72 (日).

5.6 How We Present KANJI In Each Chapter

We introduce new KANJI in each chapter (usually 20 or 25), in the order of their ON readings, in a table like the one you found at the beginning of this chapter. Next to these entries you will find boxes that give the ON and KUN readings and the meanings of the KANJI. Consider first an entry for a noun, 人. It has two ON readings, ジン and ニン, with the meaning "person" or "people." As a noun, its KUN reading has no OKURIGANA: 人 is read ひと. It also means "person" or "people." For KUN readings of adjectives and verbs that include OKURIGANA, the OKURIGANA are enclosed in parentheses.

For an adjective, consider 大. It too has two ON readings, タイ and ダイ, with the meaning "large." As an adjective, its KUN reading includes OKURIGANA: 大き い is read おお(きい), the OKURIGANA きい in parentheses indicating that the KUN reading of the KANJI itself is おお.

For a verb, consider the entry 生. It has the transitive verb 生む[う(む)], "to give birth," as well as the transitive-intransitive verb pair 生かす[い(かす)], "to give life, enliven," and 生きる[い(きる)], "to live." In presenting transitive-intransitive pairs we always list the transitive verb first. With regard to the verb 入る[はい(る)], you will notice the notation {xu} in the table. The significance of designating this as an xu-verb will be made clear in Chapter 7.

In later chapters there will be some KANJI that have no KUN readings. Occasionally a KANJI will have a KUN reading that arises only in connection with other KANJI in a JUKUGO. One example is 方, which has the KUN reading かた in combinations with verbs and their KUN readings. In our table we indicate that fact by putting a hyphen before the KUN reading: -かた. Similarly, 小 has the KUN reading こ when it is a prefix to another KANJI, and we indicate that in a similar fashion by putting the hyphen after the KUN reading: こ-.

Some KANJI are frequently used as suffixes with their ON readings. For example, from this chapter, 子[シ] is a suffix to indicate "small things," 面[メン] to indicate "aspect(s)" of the meaning that precedes it, and 用[ヨウ] to indicate "for use in" what precedes it. To show this use of a KANJI as a suffix, we repeat the ON reading in the chart and place a hyphen before the second reading. Thus, in the table for this chapter, シ and -シ, メン and -メン, and ヨウ and -ヨウ.

In the KANJI CHARTS, we list the KANJI for each chapter in a large bold style known as ゴシック体[ゴシックタイ] (for "gothic-style") and include numbers that indicate both the stroke order and direction of the strokes, the numbers being positioned at the end of the stroke or at the "corner" for "hooks." For example, consider the KANJI 子 in this chapter:

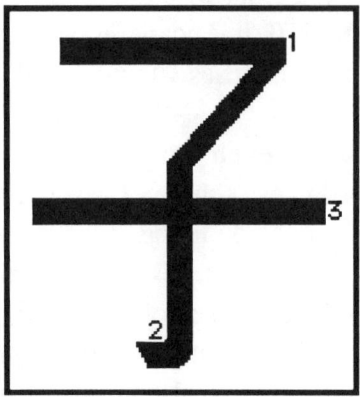

The first stroke for 子 is a hook, the second a downward stroke from the bottom of the hook, and the third a horizontal stroke from left to right just below the bottom of the hook.

Finally, we give you a vocabulary list, important JUKUGO for each new KANJI that include KANJI you have already learned in previous chapters and other new KANJI in the present chapter.

5.7 How to Learn KANJI

It will help you in learning a KANJI to keep in mind the fact that (a) the radical often contributes to its meaning, and (b) the remainder of the KANJI sometimes suggests the ON reading. Let us comment on these two points briefly.

a. The Radical and Its Meaning

Some of the radicals upon which we focused attention in this chapter are especially significant in this regard. Thus, any KANJI containing 金 will be related to metals: 銅 (copper), 鉛 (lead), 銀 (silver), and 鉱 (ore). KANJI with the abbreviated form of water 水 on the left refer often to liquids and actions with liquids: 液 (liquid), 注 (to pour), 混 (to mix). Sometimes the association of meaning may be more abstract. Thus, although 石 in the KANJI 硝 (saltpeter) connotes its literal meaning of "stone," in the KANJI 確 (to confirm or establish truth), it supplies the connotation of "being certain, on a solid foundation." Many radicals are not themselves used as individual KANJI, and yet they somehow make a clear contribution to the meaning. For example, the enclosure that is common to the following KANJI indicates motion: 速 (to be fast), 送 (to send), and 運 (to carry).

Here are some KANJI not required in this text that are radicals for KANJI you will be learning and which impart meaning to them.

木 (tree)	植 (plants)
火 (fire)	炉 (furnace)
	熱 (heat [the lower part is a variant of 火])
	燃 (combustion)
土 (earth)	地 (the earth)
	場 (place)
糸 (thread)	線 (line, wire)
	続 (continuation)
手 (hand)	抗 (opposition)
	抵 (resistance)
肉 (flesh)	脂 (fat)
	胞 (sac)

Be careful not to confuse the radical 肉 (radical 130), which appears as 月 in a KANJI, with the look-alike radical (radical 74) that is far less common and represents "moon," 月. The only two KANJI important in technical Japanese that you should associate with the radical for moon are 明 (brightness) and 期 (a time period).

b. The Remainder and the ON Reading

In addition to associating the parts of a KANJI with its meaning, you may also often help yourself remember the ON reading of a KANJI by noting that a reading sometimes originates from a part of the KANJI, usually the right-hand part. Thus, among the KANJI taught in this book, you will find the following similarities in ON readings: 低 and 抵 are both read テイ, 同 and 銅 are both ドウ, 及 and 吸 are キュウ, 径 and 経 are ケイ, 作 and 酢 are サク, 植 and 殖 are ショク, 生 and 性 are セイ, 容 and 溶 are ヨウ, 流 and 硫 are リュウ, and 列 and 裂 are レツ. Thus, in learning the ON readings of KANJI, try to be alert to ways that you can tie together the reading of a new KANJI with that of one you have already learned.

These helpful hints will not always be relevant, and we recommend that you approach the KANJI introduced in each chapter in the following way. First, study the new KANJI a few at a time, not trying to master all at once. Second, practice writing the KANJI to become familiar with them and their component parts; remember the conventions: numbers are placed at the end of the stroke or at the bend in a hook. Third, make KANJI cards for each new KANJI, being sure to record their ON and KUN readings and their JUKUGO, and keep them current by adding JUKUGO for that KANJI as they come up in later chapters.

JUKUGO build rapidly, and we do not repeat the English meanings of JUKUGO when they appear again in future chapters. We do give a KANJI vocabulary list at the back of the book for each KANJI and every JUKUGO where that KANJI begins the JUKUGO, plus chapter numbers. This enables you to check back to the KANJI tables in the pertinent chapters. We also recommend that you use this vocabulary list from time to time for periodically reviewing the JUKUGO for a given KANJI. This will strengthen your grasp of its meanings and the roles that it plays in technical Japanese.

Finally, remember Euclid's supposed answer to the king who sought a short cut to learning geometry: *There is no royal road to geometry.* Similarly, there is no short cut to learning KANJI. You must be able to recognize them, to remember their ON and KUN readings, and to understand how they contribute meaning to the JUKUGO in which they appear. Mastering these essentials will not solve all your problems in learning to read technical Japanese, but without them you will not be able to solve any.

ADDITIONAL VOCABULARY FOR EXERCISES

たす		to add
なる		to become
それで		thereupon
しかし		however
ブレーキ		brake
ポンプ		pump
かんがい		irrigation
...のとき		at the time of ...
あがる		to rise
まで		up (down) to
あらゆる		all, every
すなわち		that is, in other words
ふくむ		to contain
もの		thing
10^6	ジュウのロクジョウ	
あわ		bubble

EXERCISES

In these exercises we introduce a format to show both the information bits in a Japanese sentence and the pronunciation of KANJI. After the original sentence with KANJI, we rewrite it as follows. Each information bit is followed by a space; each KANJI is replaced by KATAKANA or HIRAGANA, for ON and KUN readings respectively, and these replacements are underlined.

Practice reading the sentence build-ups and then the sentences as a whole. Do not worry about the grammar or the different verb forms, some of which are in past tense and some even in the passive voice. The main point of these exercises is to show you how KANJI appear in sentences and how Japanese sentences build up. We hope that you will begin to develop a feel for Japanese sentence structure, even before learning any of the formal rules.

Ex 5.1 Sentence build-ups using each of the KANJI in this chapter

一

一に一をたす。
<u>イチ</u> に <u>イチ</u>を　たす。

たす。	[We] add.
一をたす。	[We] add one.
一に一をたす。	[We] add one to one.

二

それで二になる。
それで　<u>二</u>に　なる。

なる。	[It] becomes.
二になる。	[It] becomes two.
それで二になる。	Thereupon [it] becomes two.

力

力はベクトルである。
<u>ちから</u>は　ベクトルである。

ベクトルである。	[They] are vectors.
力はベクトルである。	Forces are vectors.

大

しかし力の大きさはスカラーである。
しかし　<u>ちから</u>の　<u>おお</u>きさは　スカラーである。

スカラーである。	[They] are scalars.
大きさはスカラーである。	Magnitudes are scalars.
力の大きさはスカラーである。	Magnitudes of forces are scalars.
しかし力の大きさはスカラーである。	However, magnitudes of forces are scalars.

入 コンピュータにデータを入力する。
コンピュータに　データを　ニュウリョクする。

入力する。 [We] input.
データを入力する。 [We] input data.
コンピュータにデータを入力する。 [We] input data into the computer.

人 このタクシーに人力ブレーキがある。
このタクシーに　ジンリョク　ブレーキが　ある。

ある。 [There] are.
ブレーキがある。 There are brakes.
人力ブレーキがある。 There are manual brakes.
このタクシーに人力ブレーキがある。 In this taxi there are manual brakes.

水 Hydraulic Ramは水力ポンプの　一つである。
Hydraulic Ramは　スイリョク　ポンプの　ひとつである。

一つである。 [It] is one.
ポンプの一つである。 [It] is one of the pumps.
水力ポンプの一つである。 [It] is one of the water-powered pumps.
Hydraulic Ramは 水力ポンプの一つで A hydraulic ram is one of the water-powered
ある。 pumps.

用 カリフォルニアでかんがい用水を 用いる。
カリフォルニアで　かんがいヨウスイを　もちいる。

用いる。 [They] use.
かんがい用水を用いる。 [They] use irrigation water.
カリフォルニアでかんがい用水を用い In California [they] use irrigation water.
る。

面 大水のとき、かんがい用水の水面が あがった。
おおみずのとき、　かんがいヨウスイの　スイメンが　あがった。

あがった。 [It] rose.
水面があがった。 The water surface rose.
かんがい用水の水面があがった。 The surface of the irrigation waters rose.
大水のとき、かんがい用水の水面があ At the time of flooding, the surface of the
がった。 irrigation waters rose.

高 　　　　　10メートルの高さまであがった。
　　　　　10メートルの　たかさまで　あがった。

　　　　　　　　あがった。　　　　[It] rose.
　　　　　　高さまであがった。　　[It] rose up to a height.
　　　　10メートルの高さまであがった。　[It] rose up to a height of 10 meters.

方　テクノロジーのあらゆる方面でコンピュータが用いられている。
　　テクノロジーの　あらゆるホウメンで　コンピュータが
　　　　　　　　　もちいられている。

　　　　　　　用いられている。　　　　　[They] are being used.
　　　　コンピュータが用いられている。　Computers are being used.
　　あらゆる方面でコンピュータが用いら　In every field computers are being used.
　　　　　　　　　れている。
　　テクノロジーのあらゆる方面でコン　In every field of technology computers are
　　ピュータが用いられている。　　　　being used.

見　　　　　アインシュタインの見方は高大である。
　　　　　アインシュタインの　みかたは　コウダイである。

　　　　　　　　高大である 。　　　[It] is impressive.
　　　　　　見方は高大である 。　　[The] point of view is impressive.
　　アインシュタインの見方は高大である 。　Einstein's point of view is impressive.

金　　　　　一見して金メッキか金かわからなかった。
　　　　　イッケンして　キンメッキか　キンか　わからなかった。

　　　　　　わからなかった。　　　　[We] did not know.
　　　　　金かわからなかった。　　　[We] did not know whether it was gold.
　　　金メッキか金かわからなかった。　[We] did not know whether it was gold plate or
　　　　　　　　　　　　　　　　　　gold.
　一見して金メッキか金かわからなかっ　At a glance [we] did not know whether it was
　　　　　　　た。　　　　　　　　　gold plate or gold.

示　　　　　　　示力図で力を示す。
　　　　　　ジリョクズで　ちからを　しめす。

　　　　　　　示す。　　　[We] show.
　　　　　力を示す。　　　[We] show forces.
　　示力図で力を示す。　　[We] show forces by means of a force diagram.

小 　　　　　　　　　力には大小がある。
　　　　　　ちからには　ダイショウが　ある。

　　　　　　　　　　ある。　　　　　　[There] are.
　　　　　　　　大小がある。　　　　There are sizes.
　　　　　　力には大小がある。　　Among forces there are sizes.

　　　　すなわち大きい力と小さい力とがある。
　　　　すなわち　おおきいちからとちいさいちからとが　ある。

　　　　　　　　　　ある。　　　　　　　　　　[There] are.
　　　　大きい力と小さい力とがある。　　　There are large forces and small forces.
　　すなわち大きい力と小さい力とがある。　That is, there are large forces and small forces.

子 　　　　　　　　原子は電子をふくむ。
　　　　　　　ゲンシは　デンシを　ふくむ。

　　　　　　　　　ふくむ。　　　　　[They] contain [them].
　　　　　　電子をふくむ。　　　　[They] contain electrons.
　　　　原子は電子をふくむ。　　Atoms contain electrons.

生 　　　　　はじめに生きていたものは水生であった。
　　　　はじめに　いきていたものは　スイセイであった。

　　　　　　　　水生であった。　　　　　　　[They] were aquatic.
　　　　生きていたものは水生であった。　　The things that lived were aquatic.
　　はじめに生きていたものは水生であっ　　The things that lived in the beginning were
　　　　　　　　　　　た。　　　　　　　　　aquatic.

立 　　　　一立方メートルは10⁶立方センチメートルである。
　　　　イチリッポウメートルは　10⁶リッポウセンチメートルである。

　　　10⁶立方 センチメートルである。　　　[It] is 10^6 cubic centimeters.
　　一立方メートルは10⁶立方センチメート　　One cubic meter is 10^6 cubic centimeters.
　　　　　　　　ルである。

石 　　　　　　　石ケン水はあわが立つ。
　　　　　セッケンスイは　あわが　たつ。

　　　　　　　　　立つ。　　　　　　[It] stands.
　　　　　　あわが立つ。　　　　　Bubbles stand.
　　　　石ケン水はあわが立つ。　　Soapy water is frothy.

行 　　　　　　　　　マトリックスのi行に入れる。
　　　　　　　　マトリックスの　iギョウに　いれる。

入れる。	[We] insert [it].
i行に入れる。	[We] insert [it] into the i-th row.
マトリックスのi行に入れる。	[We] insert it into the i-th row of the matrix.

　　　　　　　もとは水力で行われた。
　　　　　　もとは　スイリョクで　おこなわれた。

行われた。	[It] was done.
水力で行われた。	[It] was done by water power.
もとは水力で行われた。	In the past [it] was done by water power.

　　　　　　いまは原子力で行われている。
　　　　　いまは　ゲンシリョクで　おこなわれている。

行われている。	[It] is being done.
原子力で行われている。	[It] is being done by atomic power.
いまは原子力で行われている。	Now [it] is being done by atomic power.

Ex 5.2 Translate the following sentences

1. 高さはスカラーである。大きさもスカラーである。
2. コンピュータに力の大きさを入力する。
3. この二つのビーカーに水がある。
4. このラボに一つのポンプを用いる。
5. 大きなコンピュータを用いる。
6. あわを見る。
7. これは金である。
8. この力は小さい。その力は大きい。
9. 力はベクトルである。
10. 力の大きさはスカラーである。

液	エキ	liquid

温	オン	warmth, heat

下	カ; ゲ	below; down
	した	lower part, bottom
	さ(げる)	to hang, lower
	さ(がる)	to sag, go lower

化	カ	conversion, transformation
	-カ	-ization, -cation, -tion

学	ガク	learning
	-ガク	science (of)
	まな(ぶ)	to learn, study

間	カン	interval, space, between
	あいだ	interval, space, between

気	キ	air, gas

原	ゲン	original, proto-
	はら	field

固	コ	solid; firm
	かた(める)	to harden
	かた(まる)	to harden

上	ジョウ	over, up, above, on
	うえ	upper part, top
	あ(げる)	to raise, elevate
	あ(がる)	to rise, go up

体	タイ	(the) body; object
	からだ	(the) body

中	チュウ	center, middle
	-チュウ	within; during
	なか	inside

定	テイ	fixed, constant
	さだ(める)	to determine
	さだ(まる)	to be determined

度	ド	degree, measure (of)

動	ドウ	motion
	うご(かす)	to move
	うご(く)	to move

比	ヒ	ratio; comparison
	ヒ-	specific
	くら(べる)	to compare

物	ブツ	thing, object
	もの	thing, object

分	フン	minute (of time)
	ブン	dividing; fraction (of)
	わ(ける)	to divide (in parts)
	わ(かる)	to understand, know

変	ヘン	change
	ヘン(な)	strange
	か(える)	to change
	か(わる)	to be changed

例	レイ	example
	たと(えば)	for example

液

液体	エキタイ	liquid
液面	エキメン	liquid surface
液化	エキカ	liquefaction
分液ロート	ブンエキロート	separatory funnel

温

体温	タイオン	body temperature
温度	オンド	temperature
高温	コウオン	high temperature
一定温度	イッテイオンド	constant temperature

下

下(で)	もと(で)	under, at {e.g., at 1 atm}
下(で)	した(で)	beneath, underneath
下る	くだる	to go down
上下	ジョウゲ	up and down

化

変化	ヘンカ	change
水化物	スイカブツ	hydrate
気化	キカ	vaporization
液化	エキカ	liquefaction
固化	コカ	solidification

学

化学	カガク	chemistry
生化学	セイカガク	biochemistry
立体化学	リッタイカガク	stereochemistry
生物学	セイブツガク	biology
動物学	ドウブツガク	zoology
力学	リキガク	mechanics
生体力学	セイタイリキガク	biomechanics
動力学	ドウリキガク	dynamics
水力学	スイリキガク	hydraulics
変分学	ヘンブンガク	calculus of variations

間

中間子	チュウカンシ	meson
一分間	イップンカン	one minute

中間体	チュウカンタイ	(an) intermediate {chem}
分子間力	ブンシカンリョク	intermolecular forces
人間	ニンゲン {N.B. ゲン}	human being(s)

気

気体	キタイ	gas
大気	タイキ	atmosphere
気化	キカ	vaporization

原

原子	ゲンシ	atom
原子(動)力	ゲンシ(ドウ)リョク	atomic power
二原子-	ニゲンシ	diatomic
原生動物	ゲンセイドウブツ	protozoan

固

固体	コタイ	solid
固化	コカ	solidification
固定-	コテイ	fixed
固定子	コテイシ	stator {elect engr}

上

上(に)	うえ(に)	above
-上	ジョウ	from view point of; on {a line, surface}
化学上	カガクジョウ	from the chemical point of view
上下	ジョウゲ	up and down
見かけ上の	みかけジョウの	apparent

体

大体	ダイタイ	generally
立方体	リッポウタイ	cube
体温	タイオン	body temperature
生体	セイタイ	organism
気体	キタイ	gas
液体	エキタイ	liquid
固体	コタイ	solid
物体	ブッタイ	body; object

中

中間体	チュウカンタイ	(an) intermediate {chem}
中間子	チュウカンシ	meson
中立面	チュウリツメン	neutral plane

定

一定の	イッテイの	constant
一定温度	イッテイオンド	constant temperature
定温-	テイオン	constant temperature
定比例	テイヒレイ	fixed proportion

度

温度	オンド	temperature
一度	イチド	one degree; one time
二度	ニド	two degrees; two times

動

動物	ドウブツ	animal
原生動物	ゲンセイドウブツ	protozoan
行動	コウドウ	behavior
変動	ヘンドウ	fluctuation, variation
動力	ドウリョク	power

比

比例	ヒレイ	proportion
定比例	テイヒレイ	fixed proportion

物

物体	ブッタイ	body; object
動物	ドウブツ	animal
生物	セイブツ	living thing, creature

分

水分	スイブン	moisture
分力	ブンリョク	component of force
分液ロート	ブンエキロート	separatory funnel
分子	ブンシ	molecule
高分子	コウブンシ	macromolecule
分子間力	ブンシカンリョク	intermolecular force
二原子分子	ニゲンシブンシ	diatomic molecule

変

変動	ヘンドウ	fluctuation, variation
変化	ヘンカ	change

例

比例	ヒレイ	proportion
定比例	テイヒレイ	fixed proportion

6 Elementary Sentence Structure; Basic Verbs

In this chapter you will learn how to read some simple sentences using the grammar presented here and the KANJI of this and the preceding chapter. After a few comments on nouns and pronouns, you will encounter in a table the こ, そ, あ, and ど words, a small group of demonstrative and interrogative words that are closely related. Then you will learn more about the "particles" that you have already met in earlier chapters. You will also be introduced to the verbs ある, いる, する, なる, and いう. These are very high-frequency verbs with a wide variety of uses.

6.1 Nouns and Pronouns

Japanese has no articles, such as "a," "an," and "the" in English. Furthermore, most Japanese nouns do not have a plural form. Therefore 分子[ブンシ] may be translated as "a molecule," "molecule(s)," or "the molecule(s)." In addition, Japanese nouns have no gender or case.

When you desire to be specific as to singular versus plural, additional words can be used, such as "one," "two," "several," "many," and so on.

一つの力	[ひとつのちから]	one force, a force
二つの温度	[ふたつのおんど]	two temperatures
たくさんの液体	[たくさんのエキタイ]	many liquids
おのおのの気体	[おのおのキタイ]	each gas

| いろいろな固体 | [いろいろなコタイ] | various solids |
| すべての分子 | [すべてのブンシ] | all (the) molecules |

More will be said in Section 7.3 about adjectives that require の and な. A few nouns form plurals by "reduplication."

| 人々 | [ひとびと] | persons, people |
| 方々 | [ホウボウ] | all directions; everywhere |

Here the symbol 々 indicates a repetition of the preceding KANJI, often with a phonetic change (shown by NIGORI in the KANA transcription).

Personal pronouns are not used much in Japanese, and in technical Japanese they are rarely encountered. Occasionally you will come across the first-person plural pronoun われわれ (we) in technical books. Second-person pronouns (you) never occur. Third-person pronouns (he, she, they) are normally not used. Once persons are mentioned by name, in subsequent sentences they are usually the implied subject and not explicitly indicated with third-person pronouns.

In lieu of the third-person pronouns (it, they) for things and actions, the demonstratives are frequently used. For example, それ (that) can be translated as "it," and それら (those) can be translated as "they." The reason for the infrequent use of pronouns is that Japanese verbs do not require an explicit subject. For example, consider the following pair of sentences:

これは固体である。プラスチックである。
これはコタイである。プラスチックである。
This is a solid. [This solid] is a plastic. (or: [It] is a plastic.)

In the English translation of the second sentence it is necessary to supply the subject of the verb. Sometimes it may be difficult to decide what subject is implied in Japanese.

The fact that the subject of the verb may be omitted in Japanese is related to another difference between Japanese and English. In technical English liberal use is made of the passive voice. In Japanese the passive voice may be used, but frequently you will find the active voice with the subject unspecified.

気体を液化する。
キタイをエキカする。
[One] liquefies the gas. (or: The gas is liquefied.)

When no specific subject is implied in the Japanese, using the passive voice in the English translation is often appropriate.

6.2 The こ・そ・あ・ど Words

Next we take up a group of demonstrative and interrogative words and expressions. These can be arranged in a table (see Table 6.1) that shows you how these

Japanese words are formed systematically, by combining the syllables こ, そ, あ, or ど (listed along the top of the table) with the endings given in the second column. Only two entries are irregular, and both occur in the あ column. The entries in this column seldom, if ever, arise in technical Japanese and hence you need not learn them now; they are included for completeness. The same may be said of the row of entries ending with んな, which are fairly colloquial.

In ordinary usage the words beginning with こ refer to what is near the speaker (or writer) in space, time, or context. Those beginning with そ refer to what is near the listener (or reader) in space, time, or context. The あ words refer to what is remote from both the speaker and the listener.

In technical writing it is primarily the contextual use of these words that is important, and generally the uses of the こ and そ words correspond to those given in English in Table 6.1. The そ words appear most frequently in their role as substitutes for third-person pronouns, as noted in the foregoing section. The interrogative words, beginning with ど, occur occasionally in rhetorical questions, and in addition they are used in constructions to be learned later, in Section 12.4. Here are a few examples of how the demonstratives are used:

ここでTは温度である。
ここでTはオンドである。
Here T is the temperature.

その場合には化学変化がおこる。
そのばあいにはカガクヘンカがおこる。
In that case a chemical reaction occurs.

これらの力は大きい。
これらのちからはおおきい。
These forces are large.

その液体をそそぐ。
そのエキタイをそそぐ。
[We] pour that liquid (or: those liquids).

Remember that それ is often just a third-person pronoun and can be translated simply as "it," and その as "its" or "of it."

Note that the words ending in の may have two different meanings, depending on the context.

| この例 | [このレイ] | this example; an example of this |
| これらの高さ | [これらのたかさ] | these heights; the heights of these |

The following constructions occur quite often and are worth noting:

この中に	[このなかに]	inside of this
その上に	[そのうえに]	on top of it
その下に	[そのしたに]	underneath that; beneath it

The table entries ending in のような are adjectives.

そのような液面	[そのようなエキメン]	that kind of liquid surface
どのような高分子	[どのようなコウブンシ]	what kinds of macromolecules
このような二原子分子	[このようなニゲンシブンシ]	this kind of diatomic molecule

Table 6.1 The こ・そ・あ・ど Words

Function	Suffix	こ-	そ-	あ-	ど-
Noun	-こ	ここ this place	そこ that place	あそこ！ that place	どこ which place
Pronoun	-れ	これ this (one)	それ that (one)	あれ that (one)	どれ which (one)
Pronoun	-れら	これら these	それら those	あれら those	
Adjective	-の	この this	その that, it	あの that	どの which
Adjective	-れらの	これらの these	それらの those	あれらの those	
Adjective	-んな	こんな this kind of	そんな that kind of	あんな that kind of	どんな which kind of
Adjective	-のような	このような this kind of	そのような that kind of	あのような that kind of	どのような which kind of
Adverb	-う	こう in this way	そう in that way	ああ！ in that way	どう in which way
Adverb	-のように	このように in this way	そのように in that way	あのように in that way	どのように in which way
Adverb	-こに	ここに here	そこに there	あそこに！ there	どこに where
Note: The exclamation points (!) call attention to irregularities					

Note also the adverbial expressions このように "in this way, thus," そのように "in that way," and どのように "in what way, how." When このように occurs at the beginning of a sentence, it should usually be translated as "thus."

6.3 Particles

In Chapter 1 you were introduced to "particles," the small but important HIRAGANA words that serve as markers within a sentence. They play various roles: as postpositions following nouns they explain the function of the nouns in the sentence; at the end of a clause they serve as conjunctions; and the particle か at the end of a sentence makes the sentence interrogative. In the exercises of Chapters 2, 4, and 5 you read sentences containing particles used as postpositions. In this section we give further illustrations of the use of particles. In Chapter 7 you will see how particles are used as conjunctions between clauses.

a. Postpositions in Japanese That Correspond to Prepositions in English

　　　The following Japanese postpositions (which follow nouns) function very much like English prepositions (which precede nouns):

の	of	へ [e]	to, toward
に	in, on, at	から	from
で	in, at; by means of	まで	(up) to, as far as
と	and; with		

It is not possible to give an exact English equivalent for every Japanese postposition; the above should be regarded as an attempt to give you translations that will usually be reasonable. Examples of the use of postpositions are

液体の(高さ)	[エキタイの(たかさ)]	(the height) of the liquid
液面で	[エキメンで]	at the liquid surface
分液ロートで	[ブンエキロートで]	by means of the separatory funnel
大学へ	[ダイガクへ]	to(ward) the university
AからBまで		from A to B
ビーカーに		in the beaker

The same particles are often used with verbs and adjectives in an idiomatic way.

物体にはたらく。	[ブッタイにはたらく]	[It] acts on the body.
力に比例する。	[ちからにヒレイする]	[It] is proportional to the force.
固体になる。	[コタイになる]	[It] becomes a solid.
原子から成る。	[ゲンシからなる]	[It] is made up of atoms.
液体とちがう。	[エキタイとちがう]	[It] differs from a liquid.

You will learn these usages by practice. Occasionally the particle の will appear between a noun and the pronoun それ. Here それ refers back to another noun that previously appeared as the topic. For example:

気体の温度は液体のそれとちがう。
キタイのオンドはエキタイのそれとちがう。
The temperature of the gas differs from that of the liquid.

b. Postpositions in Japanese That Have No Counterpart in English

　　　As you learned in Chapter 1, three important postpositions have no English equivalents.

は [wa]	{Denotes the topic of a sentence}
が	{Denotes the subject of a verb}
を [o]	{Denotes the object of a verb}

6-9

The particle が simply marks the subject of a clause, and the particle を usually marks the object of a transitive verb; they are not translated into English.

その学生が動物学を学ぶ。
そのガクセイがドウブツガクをまなぶ。
That student studies zoology.

Sometimes the particle を does not mark the object of a transitive verb. When the verb is a verb of motion, the word marked by を indicates the region in, on, or through which the motion is occurring.

液体はパイプをながれる。
エキタイはパイプをながれる。
The liquid flows through the pipe.

The particle は [wa] marks the "topic" of a sentence. The topic is the object, action, or idea about which the sentence gives information. As a crude approximation you can take it to mean "as for." A sentence starting with 分子間力は means "as for the intermolecular force ..."; 分液ロートには means "as for [what is] in the separatory funnel." When the topic is a noun it may turn out to be the subject of the corresponding English sentence, or it may be the object of the verb at the end of the sentence. The topic may, however, be a prepositional phrase, or even a whole clause. The following sentences illustrate the use of は; in each case we give a crude translation using "as for," and then an idiomatically correct translation.

その液体はベンゼンである。
そのエキタイはベンゼンである。
As for that liquid — [it] is benzene. = That liquid is benzene.

二つの分子の間の力は分子間力という。
ふたつのブンシのあいだのちからはブンシカンリョクという。
As for the force between two molecules — [we] call [it] the intermolecular force. = The force between two molecules is called the intermolecular force.

液面にはあわがある。
エキメンにはあわがある。
As for [what is] at the liquid surface — there is a bubble. = There is a bubble at the liquid surface.

固体は温度が高い。
コタイはオンドがたかい。
As for the solid — [its] temperature is high. = The temperature of the solid is high.

This last sentence is particularly important, since it contains both a topic (marked with は) and a subject (marked with が). This ...は...が construction is very common in Japanese.

Usually the particle は poses no problem in translating from Japanese into English, and it never appears explicitly in an idiomatic English translation. Learning how to use は and が properly in writing and speaking Japanese is a major problem for non-Japanese, well outside the scope of this book. For more information you should consult the grammar books by Alfonso, Martin, and Makino and Tsutsui (see references in Section 1.9).

Here are some additional examples of the use of particles as postpositions in simple sentences:

ここでTは液体の温度を示す。
ここでTはエキタイのオンドをしめす。
Here T indicates the temperature of the liquid.

われわれは大学で生化学を学ぶ。
われわれはダイガクでセイカガクをまなぶ。
We study biochemistry at the university.

大学へ行く。
ダイガクへいく。
[We] go to(ward) the university.

物体はAからBまで動く。
ブッタイはAからBまでうごく。
The body moves from A to B.

ヨードベンゼンの分子は液面上にある。
ヨードベンゼンのブンシはエキメンジョウにある。
The iodobenzene molecules are at the liquid surface.

力が物体にはたらく。
ちからがブッタイにはたらく。
A force acts on the body.

Aの温度とBの温度を比べる。
AのオンドとBのオンドをくらべる。
[We] compare the temperature of A and the temperature of B. = The temperature of A is compared with that of B.

c. Double Particles and Compound Postpositional Phrases
Occasionally two particles appear one after the other.

大気での化学変化を学ぶ。
タイキでのカガクヘンカをまなぶ。
[They] study chemical changes in the atmosphere.

これは立体化学への応用である。
これはリッタイカガクへのオウヨウである。
This is an application to stereochemistry.

The double particles での and への are used because two nouns cannot be linked together with で or へ.

    Particles also appear in some frequently used "compound postpositional phrases" such as

...の中に	[のなかに]	inside of ...
...の上に	[のうえに]	above ..., on top of ...
...の下に	[のしたに]	below ..., underneath ...
...の間に	[のあいだに]	(in) between ...
...のまわりに		around ...

If an action is taking place at the location, に is replaced by で. Note that the KANJI in these phrases are all given their KUN readings. Some additional postpositional phrases are

...のほかに	beside ..., in addition to ...
...のように	like ..., as ...
...とともに	(along) with ...

Here are some sentences containing these compound postpositional phrases:

分液ロートの中には二つの液体がある。
ブンエキロートのなかにはふたつのエキタイがある。
There are two liquids in the separatory funnel.

ベンゼンの分子は液面の下にある。
ベンゼンのブンシはエキメンのしたにある。
The benzene molecules are beneath the liquid surface.

yはtとともに変化する。
yはtとともにヘンカする。
y changes with t.

Note also the following parallel constructions:

気体の中の分子は動く。	気体中の分子は動く。
キタイのなかのブンシはうごく。	キタイチュウのブンシはうごく。

Both sentences mean "The molecules in the gas are moving." In technical writing the second construction is quite common. Note that it uses the ON reading of 中, whereas the first construction uses the KUN reading.

d. The Particle も

The particle も means "also"; the construction ...も...も "both ... and ...."

温度も変化する。
オンドもヘンカする。
The temperature also changes.

われわれは生化学も生物学も学ぶ。
われわれはセイカガクもセイブツガクもまなぶ。
We study both biochemistry and biology.

Note that in these example sentences も replaces が, は, or を. With other particles, such as に, で, and へ, it follows them. For example:

液面でも化学変化がおこる。
エキメンでもカガクヘンカがおこる。
A chemical change occurs also at the liquid surface.

e. The Particles と, や, とか, か, and など

We now look at some particles that are used in listing things.

と	and	とか	and
や	and, or	など	etc., and so on
か	or		

The particles と and や both mean "and." A listing of nouns joined by と is understood to be all-inclusive; the use of や implies an incomplete listing.

生化学と生物学と動物学(と)を学ぶ。
セイカガクとセイブツガクとドウブツガク(と)をまなぶ。
[They] study biochemistry, biology, and zoology [and nothing else].

水力学や化学を学ぶ。
スイリキガクやカガクをまなぶ。
[They] study hydraulics and chemistry [among other things].

Note that と is sometimes repeated after the last item of the listing. The particle など after a noun implies an incomplete listing and means "such things as"; it often corresponds to "etc." In technical writing, instead of using と or や, listed items are often connected with centered dots (·) or commas (、); if など is used with such listings, it implies that the listing is incomplete.

The particle か between two nouns means "or." (Sometimes や between two nouns also has this meaning.) By far the most important use of か is as the marker that is added at the end of a declarative sentence to transform it into a question.

この生物は動く。　　　　　　　　　この生物は動くか。
このセイブツはうごく。　　　　　　このセイブツはうごくか。
This organism moves.　　　　　　　　Does this organism move?

That is, か functions as a spoken question mark.

The phrase かどうか means "whether or not." Compare the following two sentences:

金かわからなかった。　　　　　　　金かどうかわからなかった。
We did not know whether it was gold.　We did not not know whether or not it was gold.

You encountered the first of these sentences in Exercise 5.1.

In technical writing you will often encounter ways of joining two nouns other than by using と and か. The following are much-used expressions:

および	【及び】	and
ならびに	【並びに】	and
または	【又は】	or
あるいは	【或いは】	or

These expressions are also used between the last two nouns in a series. The KANJI shown (except for 及び) are not required in this book, but we cite them because some authors do use them. Note that は in または and あるいは is pronounced like わ.

f. Some Other Particles

The following particles, used as postpositions overlap to some degree, and the first two occur frequently in technical writing:

のみ	only
だけ	only, just; exactly {after numbers}
しか	only {when the verb is negative}

6.4 The Verbs ある and いる

There are two verbs "to be" in Japanese: ある and いる. Their present-tense affirmative and negative forms are

ある	is, are		ない	is not, are not
いる	is, are		いない	is not, are not

Let us now discuss several ways in which these verbs are used.

First we consider two pairs of sentences, in which ある and いる are used in the meaning of "exists" or "is located"; ある is used when the subject is inanimate and いる when the subject is animate (i.e., a human being or other animal).

フラスコには液体がある。
フラスコにはエキタイがある。
There is a liquid in the flask.

ビーカーには液体がない。
ビーカーにはエキタイがない。
There is no liquid in the beaker.

このカエルは水の中にいる。
このカエルはみずのなかにいる。
This frog is in the water.

そのミミズは水の中にいない。
そのミミズはみずのなかにいない。
That earthworm is not in the water.

In technical Japanese the ...がある and ...はある constructionas are much more prevalent than the ...がいる and ...はいる constructions.

Next we discuss the ...である construction (note that there is no ...でいる construction). We give here two pairs of sentences containing ...である — one affirmative and one negative.

これは分液ロートである。
これはブンエキロートである。
This is a separatory funnel.

そのロートは分液ロートで(は)ない。
そのロートはブンエキロートで(は)ない。
That funnel is not a separatory funnel.

アメーバは原生動物である。
アメーバはゲンセイドウブツである。
An amoeba is a protozoan.

その原生動物はアメーバで(は)ない。
そのゲンセイドウブツはアメーバで(は)ない。
That protozoan is not an amoeba.

In the upper pair of sentences である means "equals," whereas in the lower pair である means something like "is a member of the set of." With either meaning である is translated as "is." The grouping である is a grammatical unit called the "copula," because it couples two nouns together. In this type of sentence, AはBである, the subject A may be either animate or inanimate. More often than not, the negative でない is replaced by ではない [de-wa-nai] with almost no difference in meaning.

The verbs ある and いる can both be used as auxiliary verbs, as you will see in Section 9.3.

6.5 The Verb する

The present-tense affirmative and negative forms of the verb する are as follows:

する   do, does   しない   do not, does not

This verb is without doubt the most widely used verb in Japanese. You already learned one standard expression involving the verb する in Chapter 2.

温度をTとする。
オンドをTとする。
We let the temperature be T.

Because する has the basic meaning of "to do," it is often used together with a noun to form a verb that indicates the action implied by the noun.

6-15

Noun			Verb	
変化 [ヘンカ]	change		変化する	to change
上下 [ジョウゲ]	up and down		上下する	to move up and down
比例 [ヒレイ]	proportionality		比例する	to be proportional to
液化 [エキカ]	liquefaction		液化する	to liquefy, be liquefied
気化 [キカ]	vaporization		気化する	to vaporize, be vaporized
固定 [コテイ]	fixing {in a place}		固定する	to fix {in a place}

Here are a few sentences using some of these verbs.

気体の温度は変化しない。
キタイのオンドはヘンカしない。
The temperature of the gas does not change.

アルゴンを液化する。
アルゴンをエキカする。
[They] liquefy the argon.

YはXに比例しない。
YはXにヒレイしない。
Y is not proportional to X.

As you continue your study of Japanese you will encounter hundreds of these verbs formed by adding する to a noun.

In all of the examples above a KANGO is combined with する. Sometimes, as was noted in Chapter 5, a single KANJI is used with する to make a verb. In such verbs する may appear in one of the modified forms: ずる and じる; the two voiced forms (with NIGORI) have a negative form, じない. The only verb of this type that you have learned up to this point is

生じる	[ショウじる]	arise(s), is (are) generated
生ずる	[ショウずる]	arise(s), is (are) generated
生じない	[ショウじない]	do(es) not arise, is (are) not generated

KANJI whose ON readings end in ツ undergo a consonant doubling with する, as illustrated with the KANJI 熱[ネ ツ] "heat," which is introduced in the next chapter.

熱する	[ネッする]	heat(s)
熱しない	[ネッしない]	do(es) not heat

A few verbs have さない in the negative; for the KANJI 属[ゾク]"family," which occurs in a later chapter, we have the verb

属する	[ゾクする]	belong(s)
属さない	[ゾクさない]	do(es) not belong

6-16

These minor variations on the main theme should cause you no trouble if you remember the comments given here.

6.6 The Verb なる

The present-tense affirmative and negative of the verb なる are

なる   become(s)   ならない   do(es) not become

This is a high-frequency verb in Japanese with a wide variety of uses and meanings. Here we consider only the construction ...になる (or sometimes ...となる) meaning "become(s) ..." or "turn(s) out to be."

0°Cで水は固体になる。
0°Cでみずはコタイになる。
At 0°C water becomes a solid.

高い温度ではベンゼンは気体になる。
たかいオンドではベンゼンはキタイになる。
At high temperatures benzene becomes a gas.

The above two sentences illustrate the construction "become(s)" followed by a noun. Similarly, some adjectives have the same kind of construction.

xはランダムになる。
x becomes random.

この場合温度の変化は大切にならない。
このばあいオンドのヘンカはタイセツにならない。
In this case the change in the temperature does not turn out to be important.

Not all adjectives take this construction, as you will learn when an adjective followed by なる is discussed in Chapter 9. Occasionally the translation of ...になる or ...となる as "become(s) ..." will sound strange in English; in such cases "is/are ..." may be appropriate. You will usually know from the context.

One reason that we have juxtaposed the discussions of する and なる is that these two verbs often occur in similar constructions.

xはランダムになる。   xをランダムにする。
x becomes random.   [We] make x random.

力の大きさが一定になる。   力の大きさを一定にする。
ちからのおおきさがイッテイになる。   ちからのおおきさをイッテイにする。
The magnitude of the force becomes constant.   [We] set the magnitude of the force constant.

More examples of parallel constructions with する and なる will appear later.

It is important to note that the construction ...からなる means "consist(s) of." The verb なる in this construction is often written as 成る, which uses a KANJI introduced in Chapter 8. Preferred usage is that なる with the meaning of "become(s)" is written with HIRAGANA; on the other hand, in the construction ...から成る the verb stem is usually written in KANJI.

分子は原子から成る。
ブンシはゲンシからなる。
Molecules consist of atoms.

高分子も原子から成る。
コウブンシもゲンシからなる。
Macromolecules also consist of atoms.

6.7 The Verb いう

The present affirmative and present negative of the verb いう are

いう　say(s)

いわない　do(es) not say

Once again we remind you that いう is pronounced as if it were written ゆう. In ordinary usage という following a clause indicates what someone else says; the particle と is equivalent to "that."

この力はランダムであるという。
このちからはランダムであるという。
[They] say that this force is random.

This sentence illustrates the verb いう with the basic meaning of "say(s)."

Many kinds of constructions in technical Japanese use the verb いう, and we mention several of them here. The first of these appeared in several example sentences in Chapter 2, where it was pointed out that AをBという means "A we call B," or "A is [called] B."

これを液化という。
これをエキカという。
This is called liquefaction.

それを固化とはいわない。
それをコカとはいわない。
That is not called solidification.

二つの分子の間の力を分子間力という。
ふたつのブンシのあいだのちからをブンシカンリョクという。
The force between two molecules is called the intermolecular force.

アメーバ、ゾーリムシを原生動物という。
アメーバ、ゾーリムシをゲンセイドウブツという。
Amoebae and paramecia are called protozoans. {The word for "paramecium" is made up of ゾーリ "slipper" and ムシ "bug."}

Note that the negative of ...という is ...と(は)いわない.

A second use of いう is in the phrase ...というのは meaning literally "the thing we call ..."; here の is a noun meaning "thing." This phrase follows a noun (or even a clause) and functions as a topic marker very much as は does.

アメーバというのは原生動物である。
アメーバというのは<u>ゲンセイドウブツ</u>である。
An amoeba is a protozoan.

Sometimes というのは is shortened to とは. The important thing to keep in mind is that というのは, とは, and は just mark the topic of the sentence; they do not appear in the English translation. In giving the definition of a concept, a sentence usually begins with the term to be defined followed by というのは or とは.

A third use of いう occurs in the following expressions used before nouns:

こういう	or	こういうような	this kind of
そういう	or	そういうような	that kind of
どういう	or	どういうような	what kind of

These are synonymous with このような, そのような, and どのような in Table 6.1.

ADDITIONAL VOCABULARY FOR EXERCISES

...学では	ガクでは	in the field of ...
「...」		{the equivalent of quotation marks in English}
まっすぐ		straight ahead
いくら		how much, how many
かたまり		a clump, piece
ほとんど動かない	ほとんどうごかない	hardly move
おおよそ		roughly, approximately

EXERCISES

Ex 6.1 Matching Japanese and English technical terms

(a) Fields of study

動力学（ ）　1. biology
生化学（ ）　2. dynamics
生物学（ ）　3. biodynamics
立体化学（ ）4. hydraulics
水力学（ ）　5. stereochemistry
生体力学（ ）6. biochemistry

(b) Various technical terms

中間体（ ）　1. one minute
一度（ ）　　2. neutral plane
中立面（ ）　3. body; object
原子力（ ）　4. one degree
立方体（ ）　5. cube
一分間（ ）　6. intermediate
物体（ ）　　7. power winch
動力ウィンチ（ ）8. atomic power

Ex 6.2 True or false statements

T F　1. 固定子は動く。
T F　2. 体温は大体一定温度である。
T F　3. 生体は生物である。
T F　4. 大気中には中間子がある。
T F　5. アルコールには原生動物がいる。
T F　6. 原生動物学では大きい動物の行動を学ぶ。
T F　7. 分子間力は原子と原子との間ではたらく。
T F　8. 力学では力を分力に分ける。
T F　9. 化学では水化物中の水分を定める。
T F 10. 一定の比は定比例という。
T F 11. 二原子分子は高分子ともいう。
T F 12. 気体も固体も液化する。
T F 13. 金は高温で気化する。
T F 14. 水は0[レイ]度で固化しない。
T F 15. 液面変動では液面が上下する。
T F 16. 「化学上」とは「化学からの見方」である。
T F 17. 液体は分液ロートで分ける。

Ex 6.3 Translate the following sentences

1. メタンは気体である。エタンも気体である。メタンもエタンも気体である。

2. 水は液体である。アルコールも液体である。水もアルコールも液体である。

3. 金は固体である。セラミックスも固体である。金もセラミックスも固体である。
4. ビーカーやフラスコは立方体ではない。
5. 大気中にはいろいろの気体がある。
6. 水中にアメーバがいる。
7. ビーカーには水がある。金もビーカーにある。金は水面の下にある。
8. ネオンの分子は二原子分子ではない。
9. カエル[frog]の体温は高温ではない。またそれは変化する。
10. 人間の体温も高温ではない。しかしこれは一定である。
11. 水面の下では力がはたらく。その力は水の高さに比例する。またそれは方々にはたらく。
12. ポンプが水の高さを一定にする。したがって水面の下での力も一定になる。
13. 化学には生化学がある。生化学でホルモンや生体高分子などを学ぶ。

Ex 6.4 Read the following essays for comprehension

1. ここに物体がある。これをAという。そこにも物体がある。それをBという。AとBの間は6[ロク]メートルである。またその間に小さい動物がいる。この動物とAとの間は3[サン]メートルである。Bとの間も3メートルである。いま動物がまっすぐ3メートル動く。それでAとの間の距離[キョリ＝distance]は変化しない。Bとの間の距離[キョリ]をxメートルとする。xはいくらであるか。

2. ここにビーカーがある。このビーカーの中には水がある。水の力がビーカーの下面にはたらく。いまビーカーに金の立方体を入れる。水面の高さが変化する。そしてビーカーの下面での水の力も変化する。

3. コンピュータにはハードウエアがある。ハードウエアの中にメモリがある。そしてメモリの中にデータベースがある。コンピュータのキーボードからデータを入力する。そのデータがデータベースに入る。このようにデータベースが変化する。

Ex 6.5 Translate the following essay

大きい石の上にどのような物が見えるか。金の小さいかたまりが見える。このかたまりは固体である。固体の中の原子はほとんど動かない。その温度を上げる。固体の中では変化が生じる。金の固体は液化する。液化の温度は一定である。またそれは高い。この液化の温度はおおよそ原子間力に比例する。金の原子間力は大きい。

ビーカーの中には水がある。その温度を下げる。水は固化する。水の固化の温度は0度である。この固化の温度はおおよそ分子間力に比例する。水の分子間力は小さい。水の温度を0度から100[ヒャク]度まで上げる。水は気化する。これらの変化は化学変化ではない。

TRANSLATIONS

Ex 6.3 Sentences

1. Methane is a gas. Ethane also is a gas. Both methane and ethane are gases.
2. Water is a liquid. Alcohol also is a liquid. Both water and alcohol are liquids.
3. Gold is a solid. Ceramics also are solids. Both gold and ceramics are solids.
4. Beakers and flasks are not cubes.
5. There are various gases in the atmosphere.
6. There are amoebas in the water.
7. Water is in the beaker. Gold also is in the beaker. The gold is below the water surface.
8. Neon molecules are not diatomic molecules.
9. The body temperature of frogs is not a high temperature. Moreover, it changes.
10. The body temperature of human beings is also not a high temperature. However, this [temperature] is constant.
11. Below the surface of water forces act. Those forces are proportional to the height of the water. Moreover, they act in all directions.
12. A pump keeps the height of the water constant. Therefore, the forces at [places] below the surface of the water are also constant.
13. Within chemistry there is biochemistry. In biochemistry [one] studies [such chemicals as] hormones and biomacromolecules.

Ex 6.5 Essay

What kind of object can be seen on the top of the large stone? A small piece of gold can be seen. The piece is a solid. The atoms within the solid hardly move. [One] raises its temperature. Changes arise within the solid. The gold solid melts. The melting temperature is constant. Moreover, it is high. The melting temperature is approximately proportional to the interatomic forces. The interatomic forces of gold are large.

There is water in the beaker. [One] lowers its temperature. The water solidifies. The freezing temperature of the water is 0 degrees. This freezing temperature is approximately proportional to the intermolecular forces. The intermolecular forces of water are small. [One] raises the temperature from 0 degrees to 100 degrees. The water vaporizes. These changes are not chemical.

関	カン	connection

含	ガン	containing
	ふく(む)	to contain, include

係	ケイ	connection

酸	サン	acid; oxygen
	す(っぱい)	sour

重	ジュウ	heavy; layered
	おも(い)	heavy
	かさ(ねる)	to pile up, layer
	かさ(なる)	to be piled up

少	ショウ	few; small amount
	すく(ない)	few
	すこ(し)	a little; slightly

素	ソ	element; basic part

多	タ	many; large amount
	タ-	poly-, multiple
	おお(い)	many; frequent

炭	タン	carbon
	すみ	charcoal

注	チュウ	injection; pouring
	チュウ	annotations; notes
	そそ(ぐ)	to pour

的	テキ	target
	-テキ(な)	{adjectival suffix}

等	トウ	grade; equal
	ひと(しい)	equal
	など	etc.
	-ら	et al.

同	ドウ	same, identical
	おな(じ)	the same

熱	ネツ	heat
	ネツ-	thermal, thermo-
	ネッ(する)	to heat (up)
	あつ(い)	hot

必	ヒツ	certainty; necessity
	かなら(ず)	necessarily
	かなら(ずしも)	not necessarily
	+negative	

表	ヒョウ	expressing, showing; table
	-ヒョウ	table of ...
	あらわ(す)	to express, show

無	ム	non-existence
	ム-	{negative prefix}
	な(い)	is not; are none

有	ユウ	possession
	あ(る)	to be, exist; to have

要	ヨウ	necessity
	い(る) {xu}	to need, require

流	リュウ	flowing; current
	なが(れ)	flow
	なが(す)	to let flow; to flush
	なが(れる)	to flow

関

関係	カンケイ	relation
無関係の	ムカンケイの	unrelated

含

含有する	ガンユウする	to contain
含水の	ガンスイの	hydrated, hydrous

係

関係	カンケイ	relation
無関係の	ムカンケイの	unrelated

酸

酸素	サンソ	oxygen
酸化	サンカ	oxidation
酸化物	サンカブツ	oxide
一酸化炭素	イッサンカタンソ	carbon monoxide
二酸化炭素	ニサンカタンソ	carbon dioxide
二酸化イオウ	ニサンカイオウ	sulfur dioxide
二酸化ケイ素	ニサンカケイソ	silicon dioxide
水酸化物	スイサンカブツ	hydroxide
水酸化ナトリウム	スイサンカナトリウム	sodium hydroxide
リン酸	リンサン	phosphoric acid

重

重力	ジュウリョク	gravity
比重	ヒジュウ	specific gravity
重水	ジュウスイ	heavy water
重水素	ジュウスイソ	deuterium
多重の	タジュウの	multiple
重要な	ジュウヨウな	important
二重らせん	ニジュウらせん	double helix

少

多少の	タショウの	some

素

酸素	サンソ	oxygen
水素	スイソ	hydrogen
重水素	ジュウスイソ	deuterium

水素化物	スイソカブツ	hydride
炭素	タンソ	carbon
ホウ素	ホウソ	boron
フッ素	フッソ	fluorine
ヒ素	ヒソ	arsenic
ヨウ素	ヨウソ	iodine
ケイ素	ケイソ	silicon
元素	ゲンソ	element {chem}
(電子)素子	(デンシ)ソシ	(electronic) element

多

多重の	タジュウの	multiple
多少の	タショウの	some
多原子-	タゲンシ	polyatomic
多面体	タメンタイ	polyhedron

炭

炭素	タンソ	carbon
炭酸	タンサン	carbonic acid
炭化	タンカ	carbonization
炭化物	タンカブツ	carbide
炭化水素	タンカスイソ	hydrocarbon
炭水化物	タンスイカブツ	carbohydrate
一酸化炭素	イッサンカタンソ	carbon monoxide
二酸化炭素	ニサンカタンソ	carbon dioxide
石炭	セキタン	coal
石炭酸	セキタンサン	phenol, carbolic acid

注

注入する	チュウニュウする	to pour into

的

力学的な	リキガクテキな	mechanical
熱力学的な	ネツリキガクテキな	thermodynamic
化学的な	カガクテキな	chemical

等

等分する	トウブンする	to divide equally
同等の	ドウトウの	equal
等温-	トウオン	isothermal
等ポテンシャル面	トウポテンシャルメン	equipotential surface

同

同一の	ドウイツの	identical
同等の	ドウトウの	equal
同素体	ドウソタイ	allotrope
同定	ドウテイ	identification

熱

比熱	ヒネツ	specific heat
熱力学	ネツリキガク	thermodynamics
高熱	コウネツ	high fever
高熱-	コウネツ	pyro-

必

必要な	ヒツヨウな	necessary

表

表面	ヒョウメン	surface
表示する	ヒョウジする	to indicate, display

無

無用の	ムヨウの	useless
無水の	ムスイの	anhydrous
無水物	ムスイブツ	anhydride

有

有用な	ユウヨウな	useful
固有-	コユウ	characteristic, eigen-

要

必要な	ヒツヨウな	necessary
重要な	ジュウヨウな	important

流

流体	リュウタイ	fluid
流体力学	リュウタイリキガク	fluid mechanics
水流ポンプ	スイリュウポンプ	aspirator

7 Present-Tense Forms; Complex Sentence Structure

In Chapter 6, you learned about the present-tense forms of the verbs ある, いる, する, なる, and いう, in both the affirmative and negative forms. In Sections 7.1 to 7.3 we discuss the present-tense forms for all verbs and adjectives. This requires the introduction of schemes for classifying verbs and adjectives into groups, each of which follows a distinct set of rules. Once these rules are understood, learning the inflected forms for verbs and adjectives is fairly straightforward.

In Sections 7.4 and 7.5 we show how compound sentences can be constructed by joining two independent clauses by conjunctions and by the use of modifying clauses. By the end of this chapter you will be able to translate sentences that are structurally much more complicated than those in Chapter 6.

This chapter concludes with a very short section dealing with verbs that do not take a direct object.

7.1 The Present Tense of Verbs (う)

A rather complete summary of the inflectional forms of verbs is given in Appendix A. In Chapters 7 through 13 we take up various verb inflections, and as we do so you will find it useful to see how these forms fit into the table in Appendix A. Then by the time you finish Chapter 13, Appendix A will be a useful reference. The table given there shows how to start with the "dictionary form" of the verb (the affirmative present-tense form) and obtain the "stem" of the verb; then it shows how to generate various "bases" by adding syllables to the stem. To these bases "endings" are added in order to get the various inflected forms; the endings are given at the bottom of the table, and they are the same for *all* verbs.

Japanese verbs are divided into two main categories:

The xu-verbs
The dictionary forms of these verbs end in 'xu', where 'xu' stands for a syllable in the う column of the HIRAGANA table; the syllables that actually occur as verb endings are う, く, す, つ, ぬ, む, る, ぐ, and ぶ. (There is only one verb in Japanese ending in ぬ, namely 死ぬ[しぬ] "to die.") Two xu-verbs, ある and 行く, are irregular in one base only.

The ru-verbs
The dictionary forms of these verbs end in 'ru' (る), with a syllable from the い column or え column of the HIRAGANA table immediately preceding る (that is, in romanization these verbs end in 'xeru' or 'xiru'). There are a few xeru- and xiru-verbs that are conjugated like xu-verbs; the most important of these for technical Japanese are listed in Appendix A. Two verbs, する and くる, are irregular ru-verbs, since they have variable stems.

In order to know how to conjugate a verb, you have to know which class it belongs to. If the dictionary form does not end in る, you know at once that it is an xu-verb. If it ends in る, but is immediately preceded by a syllable from the あ, お, or う column, then you know definitely that it is an xu-verb. If it ends in る and is immediately preceded by a syllable from the い or え columns, then you know that it is probably an ru-verb. Up to this point the only exceptions to this last rule are the xu-verbs 入る [はいる] and 要る[いる].

Now we are ready to consider the present tense of verbs. The affirmative of the present tense is, as we have mentioned, just the form given in the dictionary. The negative of the present tense is formed by adding ない to the xa-base of the xu-verbs and to the stem of the ru-verbs; this is done as follows:

The xa-base of xu-verbs
Change the ending 'xu' to 'xa', which is the corresponding HIRAGANA entry in the a-column (that is, change く to か, change つ to た, etc.); there is one exception: verbs ending in う have an xa-base ending of わ.

The stem of ru-verbs
Remove the ending る.

Here are some present-tense forms, both affirmative and negative, for verbs you can now write with the KANJI of Chapters 5 through 7.

xu-verbs

示す	[しめす]	shows
示さない	[しめさない]	does not show
いう	{pronounced ゆう}	says
いわない	{N.B. わ}	does not say
要る	[いる]	is needed
要らない	[いらない]	is not needed
重なる	[かさなる]	is piled up
重ならない	[かさならない]	is not piled up
立つ	[たつ]	stands
立たない	[たたない]	does not stand
動く	[うごく]	moves
動かない	[うごかない]	does not move
注ぐ	[そそぐ]	pours
注がない	[そそがない]	does not pour
学ぶ	[まなぶ]	learns
学ばない	[まなばない]	does not learn
含む	[ふくむ]	contains
含まない	[ふくまない]	does not contain

ru-verbs

見る	[みる]	sees
見ない	[みない]	does not see
用いる	[もちいる]	uses
用いない	[もちいない]	does not use
流れる	[ながれる]	flows
流れない	[ながれない]	does not flow
いる		is
いない		is not
できる		is possible
できない		is not possible

Irregular verbs

行く	[いく]	goes
行かない	[いかない] {regular}	does not go
ある		is
ない	{irregular}	is not
する		does
しない	{irregular}	does not
くる		comes
こない	{irregular}	does not come

7-7

The ru-verb できる in the preceding list means not only "to be possible," but also "to be finished" and "to be made"; when it has the last meaning, the material from which something is made is marked with the particle で. It may also indicate that a state or condition has developed.

The present tense in technical Japanese is used in very nearly the same way as in English, namely to describe current, habitual, or future actions. As an example of the future-action use, we can cite the English expression "Next we discuss the periodic table," in which "discuss" has a future meaning and is equivalent to "shall discuss." Some examples of the use of the present tense in sentences are

つぎに流体を注ぐ。
つぎにリュウタイをそそぐ。
Next we pour the fluid.

この関係は要らない。
このカンケイはいらない。
We don't need this relation. {*Note:* は in lieu of を}

二酸化炭素は水素を含まない。
ニサンカタンソはスイソをふくまない。
Carbon dioxide does not contain hydrogen.

ポリマー液体はニュートン流体と同じようには流れない。
ポリマーエキタイはニュートンリュウタイとおなじようにはながれない。
Polymeric liquids do not flow in the same way as Newtonian fluids.

その学生は熱力学を学ばない。
そのガクセイはネツリキガクをまなばない。
That student does not study thermodynamics.

重水は重水素を含む。
ジュウスイはジュウスイソをふくむ。
Heavy water contains deuterium.

固体では原子はあまり動かない。
コタイではゲンシはあまりうごかない。
In solids the atoms do not move very much.

固体では比熱は温度によらない。
コタイではヒネツはオンドによらない。
For solids the specific heat does not depend on the temperature.

In dictionaries it is common practice to give the Japanese verb in the present tense (i.e., the dictionary form) along with the infinitive of the corresponding English verb: 含む "to contain." We follow that practice in this book.

7.2 The Present Tense of i-Adjectives (い)

A summary of the endings for adjectives is given in Appendix B. In this and the following chapters we discuss various adjective inflections, and in reading these discussions you may want to consult Appendix B in order to see how these forms fit into the table given in the appendix. In looking at the table you will see that Japanese adjectives are divided into two major classes: the i-adjectives, and the na- and no-adjectives. In this section we discuss the present tense of i-adjectives, and in the next section that of na- and no-adjectives.

The i-adjective is so called because its dictionary form (i.e., the present-tense affirmative form) ends with い; the ending い is always preceded by a syllable from the あ, い, う, or お column of the HIRAGANA table, and never by a syllable from the え column. The negative form of the present tense is obtained as follows: first remove the い of the dictionary form to get the "stem"; then add the syllable く; and to that add the negative ending ない. Examples of i-adjectives you can write with KANJI that you now know are

高い	[たかい]	is tall
高くない	[たかくない]	is not tall
等しい	[ひとしい]	is equal
等しくない	[ひとしくない]	is not equal
熱い	[あつい]	is hot
熱くない	[あつくない]	is not hot
重い	[おもい]	is heavy
重くない	[おもくない]	is not heavy
大きい	[おおきい]	is big
大きくない	[おおきくない]	is not big
小さい	[ちいさい]	is small
小さくない	[ちいさくない]	is not small
少ない	[すくない]	are few
少なくない	[すくなくない]	are not few
多い	[おおい]	are numerous
多くない	[おおくない]	are not numerous

Sometimes in the negative present-tense form は is inserted between く and ない with virtually no difference in meaning. Hence you may occasionally see 高くはない instead of 高くない. In the listing above we have written "is tall," and "is equal," to emphasize the verbal nature of these adjectives; in dictionaries and vocabulary lists, however, it is customary to omit "is" or "are."

Most i-adjectives are native Japanese words, written as a KANJI plus the ending い. All adjectives ending in しい have this ending as OKURIGANA. The adjectives 大きい, 小さい, 少ない, and a number of others are also written with two or more

OKURIGANA. In a few instances, different OKURIGANA have to be used to distinguish between two adjectives written with the same KANJI; in Chapter 5 we cited an example of this: 細い[ほそい] "slender, narrow," and 細かい[こまかい] "finely divided."

Here are some examples to show how the i-adjectives are used at the end of a sentence:

このびんの中の流体は重い。
このびんのなかのリュウタイはおもい。
The fluid in this bottle is heavy.

ポンプの中の二酸化炭素は熱い。
ポンプのなかのニサンカタンソはあつい。
The carbon dioxide in the pump is hot.

ピストンの温度は気体の温度に等しい。
ピストンのオンドはキタイのオンドにひとしい。
The temperature of the piston is equal to the temperature of the gas.

炭化水素は熱くない。
タンカスイソはあつくない。
The hydrocarbons are not hot.

液面はあまり高くない。
エキメンはあまりたかくない。
The liquid surface is not very high.

このような炭水化物は少なくない。
このようなタンスイカブツはすくなくない。
These kinds of carbohydrates are not few [in number].

このようなばあいが多い。
このようなばあいがおおい。
There are many cases of this kind.

The i-adjectives can also be placed directly before nouns as modifiers (that is, they can be used "attributively").

びんには熱い液体がある。
びんにはあついエキタイがある。
In the bottle there is a hot liquid.

分液ロートの中には二つの熱くない液体がある。
ブンエキロートのなかにはふたつのあつくないエキタイがある。
In the separatory funnel there are two liquids [that] are not hot.

7-10

AとBとは等しくないベクトルである。
AとBとはひとしくないベクトルである。
A and B are vectors [that] are not equal.

Note that the affirmative adjectives appearing before nouns are translated as adjectives in English. If we wanted to bring out the verbal nature of the Japanese adjectives we could translate them by relative clauses. For example, the first sentence above could be rendered as "In the bottle there is a liquid [that] is hot." When negative adjectives appear directly before nouns, a relative clause is an appropriate translation. The word "that" does not appear in Japanese relative clauses. The main thing to remember about i-adjectives is that they function very much like verbs. In fact, they are sometimes called "verbal adjectives."

One point needs to be emphasized: the present-negative form of verbs, which ends in ない, is in fact an i-adjective and is inflected as such. This will become apparent in the next few chapters when other tenses are discussed.

The adjectives can be preceded by adverbs, very much as in English. Here are some examples:

高い	is high	かなり高い	is fairly high
重い	is heavy	大変重い	is very heavy
大きい	is large	きわめて大きい	is extremely large
小さい	is small	ごく小さい	is exceedingly small
熱くない	is not hot	あまり熱くない	is not very hot

The adverb あまり is frequently used with negative adjectives to mean "not very"; when used with affirmative adjectives, it means "too."

7.3 The Present Tense of na- and no-Adjectives (な・の)

We now turn to the na- and no-adjectives, which behave very much like nouns, and which are sometimes called "noun adjectives" (the term "quasi-adjectives" has also been used). The following na- and no-adjectives can be written with the KANJI that you know thus far:

na-adjectives

有用な	[ユウヨウな]	useful
必要な	[ヒツヨウな]	necessary
重要な	[ジュウヨウな]	important
化学的な	[カガクテキな]	chemical
等方的な	[トウホウテキな]	isotropic
あいまいな		vague
ランダムな		random
モダンな		modern

no-adjectives

無用の	[ムヨウの]	useless
一定の	[イッテイの]	constant
二重の	[ニジュウの]	double
中間の	[チュウカンの]	intermediate, interim

Here we have given the "dictionary forms." They are usually KANGO, or occasionally single KANJI (such as 変な[ヘンな] "strange") or GAIRAIGO. The adjective あいまいな is written in HIRAGANA, because the KANJI used to write the KANGO are no longer in common use. There is no way to know whether an adjective will occur with な or with の, but this information is always given in dictionaries. Most adjectives ending in 的 (which often corresponds to the endings "-ic" and "-ical" in English) are na-adjectives. Most adjectives with the prefix 無 are no-adjectives.

Earlier you learned the sentence patterns AはBである and AはBで(は)ない, in which A and B are nouns. The same patterns are followed if B is a na- or no-adjective. To use a na- or no-adjective at the end of a sentence, we drop the な or の to get the stem, and add である in the affirmative or で(は)ない[de-(wa)-nai] in the negative.

これらの流体は等方的である。
これらのリュウタイはトウホウテキである。
These fluids are isotropic.

酸素は重要である。
サンソはジュウヨウである。
Oxygen is important.

表2は必要で(は)ない。
ヒョウ2はヒツヨウで(は)ない。
Table 2 is not necessary.

When na- and no-adjectives are used to modify nouns (that is, attributively), the following constructions are used:

等方的な流体	[トウホウテキなリュウタイ]	an isotropic fluid
等方的でない流体	[トウホウテキでないリュウタイ]	a fluid [that] is not isotropic
有用な関係	[ユウヨウなカンケイ]	a useful relation
有用でない関係	[ユウヨウでないカンケイ]	a relation [that] is not useful
一定の温度	[イッテイのオンド]	a fixed temperature
一定でない温度	[イッテイでないオンド]	a temperature [that] is not fixed

As the above shows, an adjective followed by でない can appear directly in front of a noun. However, an adjective followed by the copula である cannot. In this case, the copula である is replaced by one of its alternative forms, な or の. Keep in mind that some adjective+noun combinations in English correspond to a single compound noun in Japanese: 化学変化 (chemical change), ランダムコイル (random coil). In such cases, な and の are omitted.

Some na- and no-adjectives are normally used only attributively in technical writing. The following are particularly important:

いろいろな	【色々な】	various
さまざまな	【様々な】	various
おのおのの	【各々の】	each
もろもろの		various, all
それぞれの		several, each

The word それぞれ (without の) is an adverb meaning "respectively."

We now conclude this section with a few minor points. There are four adjectives dealing with size and quantity that exhibit some peculiarities. For 大きい and 小さい there are corresponding na-adjectives which are used only attributively.

大きいポンプ	=	大きなポンプ	a large pump
小さいギヤ	=	小さなギヤ	a small gear

In fact, in technical writing there seems to be a preference for the na-adjectives when the adjective modifies a noun.

The i-adjectives 多い and 少ない cannot be used before a noun (unless they are at the end of a modifying clause which precedes a noun as described in Section 7.4); for 多い, a related no-adjective is used, but no such construction is available for 少ない.

多くの分子
おおくのブンシ
many molecules

大気中に多い酸素分子
タイキチュウにおおいサンソブンシ
oxygen molecules, [which] are numerous in the atmosphere

The adjective 同じ is anomalous in that it requires neither な nor の when modifying a noun.

AはBと同じである。
AはBとおなじである。
A is the same as B.

いま同じ流体を用いる。
いまおなじリュウタイをもちいる。
Now we use the same liquid.

Finally, there are a few words used as noun modifiers that require no endings of any sort.

わが国	[わがくに]	our country {i.e., Japan}
いわゆるニュートン流体	[いわゆるニュートンリュウタイ]	so-called Newtonian fluids
ある動物	[あるドウブツ]	certain animals, some animals
あらゆる液体	[あらゆるエキタイ]	all liquids
いかなるばあいにも		in any case

These five words わが (our), いわゆる (so-called), ある (certain, some), あらゆる (all), and いかなる...も (any) occur frequently in technical writing.

7.4 Modifying Clauses

In the two foregoing sections you learned that affirmative or negative adjectives placed before a noun can be translated into English as short relative clauses. Actually, an entire adjective clause can be placed before a noun, resulting in a complex sentence, as we now illustrate. We can classify the types of complex sentences according to the role that the modified noun of the complex sentence plays in the simple sentence implied by the modifying clause. In each illustration below we give first a simple sentence, ending with an adjective, and then a complex sentence that incorporates the simple sentence as a modifying clause. Boxes are drawn around phrases common to both sentences; in the second sentence of each pair the noun following the box is the "modified noun."

i. The modified noun is followed by は or が in the simple sentence.

液体は あまり熱くない 。
エキタイはあまりあつくない。
The liquid is not very hot.

ビーカーには あまり熱くない 液体がある。
ビーカーにはあまりあつくないエキタイがある。
In the beaker there is a liquid [which] is not very hot.

固体は 温度が高い 。
コタイはオンドがたかい。
As for the solid — [its] temperature is high. = The temperature of the solid is high.

温度が高い 固体のばあいには、石原らの関係を用いない。
オンドがたかいコタイのばあいには、いしはららのカンケイをもちいない。
In the case of a solid [whose] temperature is high, we do not use the relation of Ishihara et al.

The ら (et al.) following the proper name 石原 is sometimes written with the KANJI 等, which you learned in this chapter.

7-14

ii. The modified noun is followed by some other particle in the simple sentence.

水に|アメーバが多い|。
みずにアメーバがおおい。
In the water amoebae are numerous. = There are many amoebae in the water.

このフラスコには|アメーバが多い|水がある。
このフラスコにはアメーバがおおいみずがある。
In this flask there is water [in which] there are many amoebae.

iii. The modified noun does not appear in the simple sentence.

|流体力学的な関係が必要である|。
リュウタイリキガクテキなカンケイがヒツヨウである。
The fluid dynamical relation is necessary.

|流体力学的な関係が必要な|例は少ない。
リュウタイリキガクテキなカンケイがヒツヨウなレイはすくない。
There are few examples [in which] the fluid dynamical relation is necessary.

Note that the na-adjective is followed by である at the end of the simple sentence, but has the な ending in the complex sentence. The notion that な and の may be considered as alternate forms of the copula である has already been discussed in Section 7.3.

Until you become familiar with modifying clauses that end in na-adjectives, you may make the mistake of thinking that the na-adjective modifies the noun that follows it and thus miss the true modifier of the noun, the whole modifying clause. For example, in the sentence above you might at a glance think that 必要な modifies 例, interpreting 必要な例 to mean "a necessary example." The fact that this expression is preceded by 関係が, a noun plus the subject marker が, should alert you to the correct interpretation: the copula である at the end of the simple sentence is replaced by な in the complex sentence (another type of replacement of である by な is discussed at the end of Section 8.6).

|分子の運動エネルぎーが同一である|。
ブンシのウンドウエネルギーがドウイツである。
The molecular kinetic energies are identical.

|分子の運動エネルギーが同一の|ガスの温度は等しい。
ブンシのウンドウエネルギーがドウイツのガスのオンドはひとしい。
The temperatures of gases whose molecular kinetic energies are identical are equal.

Here you might at first glance interpret 同一のガスの温度 to mean "the temperatures of identical gases," but again the fact that this expression is preceded by a noun plus the subject marker が should alert you to the correct interpretation: the copula である at the end of the simple sentence is replaced by の in the complex sentence.

Note that in English you have to supply the relative pronoun as well as the preposition — in the above sentences "which," "in which," and "whose" (= of which). In Japanese these various relationships are not made explicit and must be supplied by the reader.

Thus far all the modifying clauses have ended with adjectives. A very similar discussion can be given for modifying clauses that end with verbs.

i. The modified noun is followed by は or が in the simple sentence.

酸化は 大気中で生じる 。
サンカは タイキチュウでショウ じる。
Oxidations occur in the atmosphere.

大気中で生じる 酸化が多い。
タイキチュウでショウ じるサンカが おおい。
Oxidations [that] occur in the atmosphere are numerous. = There are many oxidations [that] occur in the atmosphere.

ii. The modified noun is followed by を in the simple sentence.

流体を フラスコに注入する 。
リュウタイをフラスコに チュウニュウ する。
[We] pour the fluid into the flask.

フラスコに注入する 流体はあわ立つ。
フラスコに チュウニュウ するリュウタイはあわだつ。
The fluid [that] [we] pour into the flask foams.

石炭酸は パイプを 流れる 。
セキタンサンはパイプをながれる。
The carbolic acid flows through the pipe.

石炭酸が流れる パイプをスクラッバーに固定する。
セキタンサンがながれるパイプをスクラッバーに コテイ する。
[We] fix the pipe, [through which] the carbolic acid flows, to the scrubber.

iii. The modified noun is followed by a particle other than は, が, or を in the simple sentence.

液面に 大気の力がはたらく 。
エキメンにタイキのちからがはたらく。
The force of the atmosphere acts on the liquid surface.

大気の力がはたらく 液面は上下する。
タイキのちからがはたらくエキメンはジョウゲする。
The surface [on which] the force of the atmosphere acts moves up and down.

7-16

酸素は石炭の上を流れる。
サンソはセキタンのうえをながれる。
The oxygen flows over the coal.

酸素が上を流れる石炭は高い温度でもえる。
サンソがうえをながれるセキタンはたかいオンドでもえる。
The coal, [over which] the oxygen flows, burns at a high temperature.

Note that the topic marker は follows 酸素 in the simple sentence; in the modifying clause in the complex sentence 酸素 is marked with が. The particle は seldom occurs in a modifying clause.

iv. The modified noun does not appear in the simple sentence.

温度は一定である。
オンドはイッテイである。
The temperature is constant.

温度が一定である化学変化はあまり多くない。
オンドがイッテイであるカガクヘンカはあまりおおくない。
There are not many chemical reactions [in which] the temperature is constant.

Here again, note the switch from は to が.

In the above illustrations the subject of the verb in the modifying clause is always marked with が. Sometimes this が may be replaced by the particle の. An example of this is

例外のない規則はない。　　　　　{例外 = exception; 規則 = rule}
レイガイのないキソクはない。
There are no rules [that] have no exceptions. = There are no rules without exceptions.

Sometimes short modifying clauses that end in an i-adjective may easily mislead you if you do not recognize that の replaces が; you might mistakenly think that the の, because it follows a noun, modifies the next noun. For example, a sentence might begin 重さの小さい物体, which identifies the topic, "a body that has a small weight." However, if you were to think mistakenly of the の as the particle の that indicates a noun modifying a noun, then you would make the further mistake of thinking that 小さい modifies 物体. To make matters worse, you might then even forget that word order is often reversed in Japanese as compared with English and interpret the expression to mean "the weight of a small body." Such short modifying clauses, noun followed by の, followed by i-adjective, followed by another noun, occur with some

7-17

frequency in technical Japanese, so be alert to the replacement of が with の in the modifying clause.

It is very important that you be able to recognize modifying clauses and translate sentences containing them. Keep the following rules in mind: (1) the particle は seldom occurs in a modifying clause; (2) a noun marked with が always goes with the next verb that appears; (3) が may sometimes be replaced by の in modifying clauses; and (4) relative pronouns and associated prepositions usually have to be supplied in English translations.

7.5 Conjunctions and Compound Sentences

Suppose that we have in Japanese two independent clauses, A and B, and that we want to indicate some relation between these clauses. This can be done in two ways.

(1) | Clause A. | | Introductory words | | Clause B. |
(2) | Clause A | | conjunction, | | Clause B. |

In the first pattern there are two separate sentences, the second of which starts with some sort of introductory words to indicate the relation to the first. In the second pattern a conjunction is placed between the two clauses to form a compound sentence; note that the conjunction is followed by a comma to indicate the location of the pause in reading. We use the word "conjunction" here rather loosely. By this term we sometimes mean a particle, and sometimes a noun or a noun followed by a particle. The point is that these words function more or less as conjunctions do in English.

We now illustrate both patterns for six different types of clausal relationships. Later on, as you acquire additional vocabulary, you will be able to translate other compound sentences similar to those presented here.

a. Contrast

To indicate a simple contrast the introductory word しかし "however" can be used at the beginning of Clause B. Alternatively the particle が may be used at the end of Clause A in a compound sentence.

流体は動かない。しかしその中のあわは動く。
リュウタイはうごかない。しかしそのなかのあわはうごく。
The liquid does not move. However, the bubbles in it do move.

流体は動かないが、その中のあわは動く。
リュウタイはうごかないが、そのなかのあわはうごく。
The liquid does not move, but the bubbles in it do [move].

7-18

b. Cause and Effect; Reason and Result

To indicate that Clause B is the consequence of Clause A in the first pattern, we can introduce the second clause by any of the following: したがって【従って】 "therefore, consequently"; それゆえ "because of that"; その結果[そのケッカ] "as a result"; だから "therefore." In the second pattern the conjunctions から "because" or ので "because" are used; sometimes ため(に) is used with the meaning of "because." (Caution: ため(に) also has the meaning "in order to.") Alternatively the first clause may end with the noun 結果[ケッカ] "as a result of the fact that." The KANJI in 結果 are introduced in Chapters 9 and 10.

流体の温度は変化する。 したがって その中のあわの大きさも変化する。
リュウタイのオンドはヘンカする。したがってそのなかのあわのおおきさもヘンカする。
The temperature of the fluid changes. Therefore, the size of the bubbles in it changes too.

流体の温度が変化する ので から ため 結果 、 その中のあわの大きさも変化する。
Because the temperature of the fluid changes, the size of the bubbles in it changes too.

The "because" clause in a technical Japanese sentence is often long and complicated. Therefore, we recommend that you break such sentences into two parts: Clause A. Therefore, Clause B.

c. Temporal Relations

To indicate that Clause B takes place at the same time as Clause A, the second clause can be introduced by そのとき【その時】 "at that time, then," or by その間 [そのあいだ] "during that time." Alternatively the first clause may be followed by とき(に)【時(に)】 "when," or by 間(に)[あいだ(に)] "during the time that, while." Occasionally the first clause will end with 場合[ばあい] meaning something like "on the occasion that, when" or ところ meaning "at the point in time that, when."

炭化水素はもえる。 そのとき 酸素が必要である。
タンカスイソはもえる。そのときサンソがヒツヨウである。
Hydrocarbons burn. At that time oxygen is necessary.

炭化水素がもえる とき 、 酸素が必要である。
When hydrocarbons burn, oxygen is necessary.

化学変化がおこる。 その間 温度が上がる。
カガクヘンカがおこる。そのあいだオンドがあがる。
A chemical change occurs. During that time the temperature increases.

化学変化がおこる 間 、 温度が上がる。
While a chemical change occurs, the temperature increases.

Note: Since 時, 間, 場合, and ところ are nouns, the clauses immediately before them are modifying clauses. As a consequence the subject marker が in these clauses can be replaced by の.

d. Purpose

To specify the purpose of an action in Clause A, Clause B can be preceded by そのために "in order to do that." Alternatively a compound sentence may be generated with Clause A ending in のに, には, or ために(は) "in order to."

液体を熱する必要がある。 そのために バーナーが要る。
エキタイをネッするヒツヨウがある。そのためにバーナーがいる。
It is necessary to heat the liquid. In order to do that we need a burner.

液体を熱する | には / のに / ために(は) | 、バーナーが要る。
In order to heat the liquid, we need a burner.

Although のに usually means "in order to" in technical Japanese, occasionally it means "in spite of the fact that."

e. Conditional Relation

To indicate that the action in Clause B will not occur without the action in Clause A, Clause B can be preceded by その場合[ばあい] "in that event, in that case." Alternatively a compound sentence may be formed with Clause A ending in と "if, whenever." Sometimes the conditional clause may end in 場合(に)[ばあい(に)] "in the event that" or 時[とき] "at the time when"; these two expressions have a wide range of meanings overlapping the temporal and conditional ideas.

一酸化炭素が酸化する。 そのばあい それが二酸化炭素に変わる。
イッサンカタンソがサンカする。そのばあいそれがニサンカタンソにかわる。
Carbon monoxide is oxidized. In that event it changes into carbon dioxide.

一酸化炭素が酸化する | と / ばあい | 、それが二酸化炭素に変わる。
If carbon monoxide is oxidized, it changes into carbon dioxide.

f. Augmentation with Cause and Effect

To augment the idea in Clause A with information in Clause B, one can introduce the latter with the word また 【又】, "besides, moreover." Alternatively the two clauses may be joined by the particle し, "and besides, and in addition." More than two clauses may be joined by using this particle. These clauses frequently serve to introduce the cause of an effect, or the reason for a result, and therefore often appear in constructions of type *b* above.

7-20

メタンは気体である。また炭化水素でもある。したがってそれがもえるとき、大変熱い。
メタンはキタイである。またタンカスイソでもある。したがってそれがもえるとき、タイ
　　ヘンあつい。
Methane is a gas. Furthermore it is also a hydrocarbon. Therefore when it burns, it is very hot.

メタンは気体であるし、炭化水素であるから、それがもえるとき、大変熱い。
Methane is a gas and [in addition] it is a hydrocarbon; therefore when it burns, it is very hot.

In Chapters 9 and 10 you will learn other ways of joining two clauses by the use of various verb forms such as the connective, the conjunctive, the provisional, and the conditional.

7.6 Verbs That Do Not Have Objects

Here we consider several verbs that do not have objects marked with the particle を.

要る	[いる]	to be needed	or	to need
見える	[みえる]	to be visible	or	to be able to see
できる		to be possible, be "do-able"	or	to be able to do
わかる		to be understood	or	to understand

We have purposely given a passive and an active translation for each verb because both are possible. We give a pair of sentences below for each of the above verbs. The first is simple, with the verb being given a passive translation in English. The second contains the ...は...が construction, in which the noun marked by は corresponds to the subject, and the noun marked by が corresponds to the object, in a free English translation; here the verb is given its active translation.

酸素が要る。
サンソがいる。
Oxygen is needed.

動物は酸素が要る。
ドウブツはサンソがいる。
As for animals — oxygen is needed.
　　= Animals need oxygen.

分子は見えない。
ブンシはみえない。
Molecules are not visible.

人は分子が見えない。
ひとはブンシがみえない。
As for people — molecules are not visible.
　　= People cannot see molecules.

力学ができる。
リキガクができる。
Mechanics is "do-able."

大学生は力学ができる。
ダイガクセイはリキガクができる。
As for university students — mechanics is "do-able."
　　= University students can do mechanics.

7-21

酸化反応がわかる。　　　　　　　　　化学を学ぶ人は酸化反応がわかる。
サンカハンノウがわかる。　　　　　　カガクをまなぶひとはサンカハンノウがわかる。
Oxidation reactions are understood.　As for people who study chemistry — oxidation reactions
　　　　　　　　　　　　　　　　　　　　　are understood. = People who study chemistry
　　　　　　　　　　　　　　　　　　　　　understand oxidation reactions.

For the second sentence of each pair, you will always want to choose the free translation
with the active verb in English. The literal translation, however, may be useful because
it is consistent with the usual functions of は and が. You will find that this same kind
of ...は...が construction arises in connection with potential verbs (Section 11.2) and
desiderative adjectives (Section 13.2).

ADDITIONAL VOCABULARY FOR EXERCISES

つくる		to make
ゲームをやる		to play games
注ぎ入れる	そそぎいれる	to pour into
...からのもの		a thing (made) from ...
...ばあいでも	【場合でも】	even when ...
...からである		it is because ...
下方	カホウ	lower region
上方	ジョウホウ	upper region
これと同じ	これとおなじ	the same as this
...当たり	あたり	per ...
...と同じような...	とおなじような	... the same as ...
高度に熱する	コウドにネッする	to heat to a high degree
重さ	おもさ	weight

EXERCISES

Ex 7.1 Matching Japanese and English technical terms

(a) Chemical elements

ケイ素( )	1. arsenic
酸素( )	2. boron
重水素( )	3. carbon
水素( )	4. deuterium
炭素( )	5. fluorine
ヒ素( )	6. hydrogen
フッ素( )	7. iodine
ホウ素( )	8. oxygen
ヨウ素( )	9. silicon

(b) Chemical compounds

General

酸化物( )	1. anhydride
水酸化物( )	2. carbide
水素化物( )	3. carbohydrate
炭化水素( )	4. hydride
炭化物( )	5. hydrocarbon
炭水化物( )	6. hydroxide
無水物( )	7. oxide

Specific

一酸化炭素( )	1. carbolic acid
水酸化ナトリウム( )	2. carbonic acid
石炭酸( )	3. carbon dioxide
炭酸( )	4. carbon monoxide
二酸化イオウ( )	5. phosphoric acid
二酸化ケイ素( )	6. silicon dioxide
二酸化炭素( )	7. sodium hydroxide
リン酸( )	8. sulfur dioxide

Ex 7.2 True or false statements

T F　1. ダイヤモンド[diamond]は炭素の同素体の一つである。
T F　2. 炭化物をつくるために、炭素が必要である。
T F　3. 炭化物をつくるのに、ダイヤモンドを用いる。
T F　4. ガラスをつくるとき、二酸化ケイ素が要る。
T F　5. 一酸化炭素を酸化すると、二酸化炭素が生じる。
T F　6. 石炭を熱すると、多少の石炭酸が生じる。
T F　7. 炭水化物は炭素を含む水酸化物である。
T F　8. 分子の<u>運動</u>[ウンドウ = motion]をかんがえるとき、その<u>運動</u>[ウンドウ]と温度との関係は重要である。
T F　9. 石炭酸はフェノールともいう。
T F 10. 化学的な見方には重力は無関係である。

Ex 7.3 Sentences with the same verb in the affirmative and the negative

Supply the negative forms of the verbs where indicated in the following sentences, and then translate.

1. このテストを行うが、行＿ ＿ ＿ときもある。
2. 動物は動く生物であるが、動＿ ＿ ＿生物もある。
3. ビーカーから液体を注ぐが、ビーカーから注＿ ＿ ＿液体もある。
4. データを表で表すが、表で表＿ ＿ ＿データをグラフで表す。
5. 固体は立つが、流体は立＿ ＿ ＿。
6. 力学では化学変化を学＿ ＿ ＿が、化学熱力学では学ぶ。
7. 水和物[スイワブツ＝hydrate]は水を含むが、無水物は水を含＿ ＿ ＿。
8. 物体を上げるのに力が要るが、それを下げるために力は要＿ ＿ ＿。
9. データを表すのに表を用いるとき、グラフを用＿ ＿ ＿。
10. 流体は流れるが、ゼラチン[gelatin]は流＿ ＿ ＿。

Ex 7.4 Sentences with the same adjective in the affirmative and the negative

Supply the negative forms of the adjectives where indicated in the following sentences, and then translate.

1. 大気中には二原子分子は多いが、一原子分子は多＿ ＿ ＿。
2. 大気中にはオゾンの分子は少ないが、スモッグ[smog]には
   少＿ ＿ ＿ ＿。
3. 100[ヒャク]キログラムの物体は重いが、1キログラムの物体は
   重＿ ＿ ＿。
4. 高温は熱いが、体温は熱＿ ＿ ＿。
5. すべての人間の体温は等しいが、すべての動物の体温は
   等＿ ＿ ＿ ＿。
6. 100度C[シー]と212[ニヒャクジュウニ]度F[エフ]の温度は同じであるが、
   1インチと2センチメートルは同じ＿ ＿ ＿。
7. 酸化的な化学変化を要するとき、酸素が必要であるが、炭化的な化学変化を要するとき、それは必要＿ ＿ ＿。
8. ワープロはコンピュータの有用な用い方の一つであるが、ゲームをやる用い方はあまり有用＿ ＿ ＿。

Ex 7.5 Sentences with modifying clauses

In this exercise you will be translating for the first time sentences that have modifying clauses. We suggest the following approach: (1) identify the noun and the modifying clause; (2) begin to build up your translation from the noun in a way similar to the sentence build-ups in preceding chapters. You can identify a modifying clause and the noun it modifies by seeing that a verb precedes that noun. For example, in a sentence that begins 体の中で酸化する炭水化物は, you recognize that the topic is the noun 炭水化物 because it is followed by the particle は. You may also recognize that it has a modifying clause because it is preceded by the verb 酸化する. Now you can work back from the noun until you have all the parts of the modifying clause.

炭水化物は	carbohydrates
酸化する炭水化物は	carbohydrates that [one] oxidizes
体の中で酸化する炭水化物は	carbohydrates that are oxidized in the body

Consider another example: 石炭酸が流れるパイプは.

パイプは	pipe
流れるパイプは	the pipe [in which something] flows
石炭酸が流れるパイプは	the pipe in which carbolic acid flows

As you become more familiar with the structure of Japanese modifying clauses, you will be able to interpret such clauses without such an explicit build-up. However, for the present we recommend that you use this method. Note that in the first case given above, the translation is in the passive voice because there is no agent of the oxidation. You should carefully compare your translations with those given at the close of the exercises.

1. 体の中で酸化する炭水化物は二酸化炭素と水に変わる。
2. 炭水化物を酸化するのに必要な酸素は炭水化物が含む炭素を酸化する<u>量</u>[リョウ = quantity]である。
3. パイプから流れる石炭酸は熱い。
4. 石炭酸が流れるパイプは重い。
5. 重水素を酸化するとき生じる水は重水という。
6. 炭化水素を注ぎ入れるビンは炭化水素と<u>反応</u>[ハンノウ = reaction]しないセラミックスからのものである。

Ex 7.6 Read the following essays for comprehension

1. 多重プロセッサは多重のCPU[シーピーユー]を有するコンピュータシステムである。このシステムに多重のCPUがあるから、一つのCPUがはたらかないばあいでも、その一つのCPUと無関係にシステムがはたらく。

2. 熱力学的な変化で温度が一定であると、それは等温変化である。その一例は気体が液化するときである。しかし、固体を熱すると、温度は一定でない。温度が上がるから、この変化は等温ではない。

3. 酸素は動物に必要である。酸素が少ないと、動物は動かない。動物が動くのに、酸素が要るからである。オゾンは酸素の同素体であるが、動物に

はスモッグと同じようである。そのため大気の下方ではオゾンをスモッグと同じように見なす。しかし、大気の上方ではオゾンは重要な物質である。

4．炭化水素は炭素と水素を含有する。メタンやエタンがその例である。セルロースも炭素と水素を含むが、酸素を含む。セルロースは炭水化物の一つである。炭水化物の分子は多原子分子である。その分子の中の水素原子と酸素原子の比は水の分子の中の水素原子と酸素原子の比と同一である。

5．ある流体は0℃[レイドシー]では流れないが、これを少し熱すると、流れる。しかし、1セコンド当たり[あたり]に流れる重さは小さい。高度に熱すると、1セコンドに流れる重さは大きい。固体にもこれと同じような例がある。もちろん固体は流れないが、高度に熱すると、それは液化した固体が流れる。例えば、液化した金を立方のイガタ[mold]に注入する。

Ex 7.7 Translate the following essay

　動物が生きるためには酸素が必要である。酸素がないとき動物はしぬ。大気中には酸素が多いが、水も多少の酸素を含有する。水中の動物はこの酸素を用いる。大気中で炭素を熱すると、一酸化炭素を生じる。温度が高いとこれが二酸化炭素に変化する。これらの変化は化学的である。
　二酸化炭素中の酸素の重さと炭素の重さとの間には一定の関係がある。すなわち、同じ重さを有する二つのサンプルを比べると、酸素の重さも炭素の重さもそれぞれ同一である。
　二酸化炭素は重い気体である。大気中にあるアルゴンも重い気体である。このような重い気体をビンから物体の上に注ぐと、これらの気体は物体の表面上を流れる。

Ex 7.8 Japanese names
　　　With the KANJI you have learned, you can already read a number of Japanese family names. Japanese family names are usually given KUN readings. They precede the given name. Given name often have irregular readings and are not as readily deciphered as family names. An excellent dictionary is *Japanese Names* by P. G. O'Neill, Weatherhill, New York (1972). Practice reading the following names:

大原 [おおはら]	大石 [おおいし]	石原 [いしはら]
高原 [たかはら]	高見 [たかみ]	上原 [うえはら]
小方 [おがた]	金子 [かねこ]	中原 [なかはら]

Ex 7.3 Sentences with the same verb in the affirmative and the negative

1. We [will] do this test, but there also are times when we do not.
2. Animals are creatures that move, but there also are creatures that do not (move).
3. [One] pours liquids from beakers, but there are also liquids [one] does not pour from beakers.
4. [We] express the data in tables, and data that [we] do not express in tables [we] show by means of graphs.
5. A solid stands up, but a liquid does not (stand up).
6. [One] does not study chemical changes in mechanics; one studies those in chemical thermodynamics.
7. Hydrates contain water, anhydrides do not (contain water).
8. In order to lift a body a force is necessary, but in order to lower it a force is not necessary.
9. When [one] uses a table to express data, [one] does not use a graph.
10. Fluids flow, but gelatin does not (flow).

Ex 7.4 Sentences with the same adjective in the affirmative and the negative

1. There are many diatomic molecules in the atmosphere, but there are not many monatomic molecules.
2. There are few ozone molecules in the atmosphere, but there are not (just) a few in smog.
3. A 100 kilogram body is heavy, but a 1 kilogram body is not (heavy).
4. High temperatures are hot; body temperatures are not (hot).
5. The body temperatures of all human beings are the same, but the body temperatures of all animals are not the same.
6. The temperatures 100°C and 212°F are the same, but 1 inch and 2 centimeters are not (the same).
7. When [one] needs an oxidizing chemical change, oxygen is necessary, but when [one] needs a carburizing chemical change, [it] is not (necessary).
8. A word processor is one of the useful ways of using a computer, but (the way of) using [it] to play games is not very useful.

Ex 7.5 Sentences with modifying clauses

1. Carbohydrates that are oxidized in the body change into carbon dioxide and water.
2. The oxygen necessary to oxidize a carbohydrate is the amount to oxidize the carbon that the carbohydrate contains.

3. The carbolic acid flowing from the pipe is hot.
4. The pipe in which the carbolic acid flows is heavy.
5. The water generated when deuterium is oxidized is called heavy water.
6. The bottle [into which] [we] pour the hydrocarbon is [made] from a ceramic that does not react with hydrocarbons.

Ex 7.7 Essay

In order to live, animals need oxygen. When there is no oxygen, animals die. Oxygen is plentiful in the atmosphere, and water also contains some oxygen. Animals [living] in water use this oxygen. If we heat carbon in the atmosphere, [it] generates carbon monoxide. If the temperature is high, this changes to carbon dioxide. These changes are chemical.

There is a constant relation between the weight of carbon and the weight of oxygen in carbon dioxide. That is, if we compare two samples that have the same weight, the weights of oxygen and the weights of carbon are respectively identical.

Carbon dioxide is a heavy gas. Argon, which is in the atmosphere, is also a heavy gas. If we pour these kinds of heavy gases from a bottle onto the top of an object, these gases flow over the surface of the object.

圧	アツ	pressure

違	イ	difference
	ちが(い)	difference
	ちが(う)	to differ, vary

| 応 | オウ | responding |

| 験 | ケン | testing |

| 元 | ゲン | source, origin |
| | もと | source, origin |

合	ゴウ	agreement; joining
	あ(わせる)	to put together
	あ(う)	to meet; to combine

式	シキ	formula; equation
	-シキ	formula; equation
	-シキ	style, type, mode

| 質 | シツ | substance; quality; essence |

| 実 | ジツ | true, real; fruit |
| | み | fruit |

数	スウ	number
	かず	number
	かぞ(える)	to count

| 性 | セイ | property, characteristic |

| 成 | セイ | consisting of; turning into |
| | な(る) | to consist of; to turn into |

| 積 | セキ | accumulation; product {math} |
| | つ(もる) | to accumulate |

速	ソク	speed
	はや(い)	fast, rapid
	すみ(やかに)	quickly; immediately

| 対 | タイ | contrasting, opposite |
| | ツイ | pair, couple |

| 電 | デン | electricity |

| 発 | ハツ | emerging; emanating |

| 反 | ハン | opposite |

| 法 | ホウ | law; method |
| | -ホウ | method, method of |

| 量 | リョウ | quantity (of) |
| | はか(る) | to measure |

圧

圧力	アツリョク	pressure
圧電-	アツデン	piezoelectric
電圧	デンアツ	voltage
分圧	ブンアツ	partial pressure
高圧	コウアツ	high pressure
水圧	スイアツ	water pressure
等圧-	トウアツ	isobaric
等圧変化	トウアツヘンカ	isobaric change
大気圧	タイキアツ	atmospheric pressure
一気圧	イチキアツ	one atmosphere

違

間違い	まちがい {N.B. ま}	mistake, error
違法キャラクタ	イホウキャラクタ	illegal character {comp sci}

応

応じる	オウじる	to respond (to)
応用力学	オウヨウリキガク	applied mechanics
反応	ハンノウ {N.B. ノウ}	chemical reaction
反応速度	ハンノウソクド	rate of reaction
反応物	ハンノウブツ	reactants
(に)対応する	(に)タイオウする	to correspond (to)
応力	オウリョク	stress
熱応力	ネツオウリョク	thermal stress

験

実験	ジッケン	experiment
実験式	ジッケンシキ	empirical formula {chem}

元

元素	ゲンソ	element {chem}

合

合成	ゴウセイ	synthesis
合力	ゴウリョク	resultant force
合金	ゴウキン	alloy
化合物	カゴウブツ	chemical compound
重合体	ジュウゴウタイ	polymer
重ね合わせ	かさねあわせ	superposition

式

化学式	カガクシキ	chemical formula
反応式	ハンノウシキ	reaction equation
分子式	ブンシシキ	molecular formula
等式	トウシキ	equality
方式	ホウシキ	method, mode, system
実験式	ジッケンシキ	empirical formula
定式化する	テイシキカする	to formalize

質

質量	シツリョウ	mass
質量数	シツリョウスウ	mass number
性質	セイシツ	property
物質	ブッシツ	substance(s)
タンパク質	タンパクシツ	protein

実

実数	ジッスウ	real number
実験	ジッケン	experiment
実験式	ジッケンシキ	empirical formula {chem}
実用性	ジツヨウセイ	practicality

数

数学	スウガク	mathematics
数表	スウヒョウ	numerical table
数量的な	スウリョウテキな	quantitative, numerical
数度	スウド	several times
数係数	スウケイスウ	numerical coefficient
定数	テイスウ	constant
係数	ケイスウ	coefficient
実数	ジッスウ	real number
変数	ヘンスウ	variable
対数	タイスウ	logarithm
素数	ソスウ	prime number
関数	カンスウ	function
応用数学	オウヨウスウガク	applied mathematics
量子数	リョウシスウ	quantum number
質量数	シツリョウスウ	mass number
数々の	かずかずの	several, numerous

性

中性の	チュウセイの	neutral
中性子	チュウセイシ	neutron
実用性	ジツヨウセイ	practicality
定性的な	テイセイテキな	qualitative
等方性の	トウホウセイの	isotropic
酸性の	サンセイの	acidic
性質	セイシツ	property

成

成り立つ	なりたつ	to be valid; to consist of
成立する	セイリツする	to be valid, hold true
成分	セイブン	component(s) {not meaning "part(s)"}
生成する	セイセイする	to generate
生成物	セイセイブツ	(reaction) products
合成	ゴウセイ	synthesis
合成化学	ゴウセイカガク	synthetic chemistry

積

積分	セキブン	integral
積分学	セキブンガク	integral calculus
二重積分	ニジュウセキブン	double integral
定積分	テイセキブン	definite integral
面積	メンセキ	area
体積	タイセキ	volume
ベクトル積	ベクトルセキ	vector product

速

速度	ソクド	velocity
高速度	コウソクド	high velocity
等速度	トウソクド	uniform velocity
流速	リュウソク	flow velocity

対

対物レンズ	タイブツレンズ	objective lens
(に)対応する	(に)タイオウする	to correspond (to)
対数	タイスウ	logarithm
対流	タイリュウ	convection current
一対	イッツイ	(a) pair, couple
電子対	デンシツイ	electron pair
熱電対	ネッデンツイ	thermocouple

電

電圧	デンアツ	voltage
電動-	デンドウ	electrically driven
電動式	デンドウシキ	electrically driven type
電子	デンシ	electron
電子素子	デンシソシ	electronic element
電流	デンリュウ	electric current
電気	デンキ	electricity
電気化学	デンキカガク	electrochemistry
電力	デンリョク	electric power
発電	ハツデン	generation of electricity
熱電対	ネツデンツイ	thermocouple

発

発見	ハッケン	discovery
発熱反応	ハツネツハンノウ	exothermic reaction
発電	ハツデン	generation of electricity
発生する	ハッセイする	to arise, emerge
発生学	ハッセイガク	embryology
発電子	ハツデンシ	armature
反発力	ハンパツリョク	repulsive force

反

反応	ハンノウ {N.B. ノウ}	chemical reaction
反応式	ハンノウシキ	reaction equation
反応性	ハンノウセイ	reactivity
反応熱	ハンノウネツ	heat of reaction
反応物	ハンノウブツ	reactants
反応速度	ハンノウソクド	rate of reaction
反対	ハンタイ	opposite
反対力	ハンタイリョク	counterforce, opposing force
反発力	ハンパツリョク	repulsive force
反比例	ハンピレイ	inverse proportion

法

方法	ホウホウ	method
変分法	ヘンブンホウ	calculus of variations
積分法	セキブンホウ	integration
炭水素定量法	タンスイソテイリョウホウ	method of determining C and H

量

質量	シツリョウ	mass
重量	ジュウリョウ	weight
少量	ショウリョウ	small amount
多量	タリョウ	large amount
原子量	ゲンシリョウ	atomic weight
分子量	ブンシリョウ	molecular weight
定量的な	テイリョウテキな	quantitative
流量	リュウリョウ	flow
含水量	ガンスイリョウ	water content
量子力学	リョウシリキガク	quantum mechanics
量子化する	リョウシカする	to quantize

8   Past-Tense Forms; Noun- and Verb-Following Expressions

In this chapter we discuss the past-tense forms of verbs and adjectives. You will learn how to obtain these forms from the dictionary forms and how the past tense is used in Japanese. Then we conclude the chapter with some "noun-following expressions" and some "verb-following expressions." These are standard constructions that allow you to augment considerably the range of sentences that you can translate.

8.1 The Past Tense of Verbs (た)

For ru-verbs the past tense is formed by adding た to the stem of the verb (obtained by dropping the る of the dictionary form). For xu-verbs the past tense is formed by adding た, or its voiced analog だ, to the modified xi-base; this base and the voicing of the past-tense ending depend on the terminal syllable of the dictionary form.

Final syllable of dictionary form (i.e., 'xu')	Modified xi-base is formed by replacing 'xu' by	Past-tense ending to be added to the modified xi-base	
す	し	た	
つ	っ {small subscripted つ}	た	
る	っ {small subscripted つ}	た	
う	っ {small subscripted つ}	た	
く	い	た	
ぐ	い		だ
ぶ	ん		だ
む	ん		だ
ぬ	ん		だ

Of all the bases the modified xi-base is the only one that is difficult to learn. It is essential that you master the rules for its formation, since it is the base for several other verb forms: connective (Chapter 9), conjunctive (Chapter 9), conditional (Chapter 10), and representative (Chapter 13).

In Chapter 7 you learned that the negative of the present tense of verbs ends in ない, which is further inflected as an i-adjective. The negative of the past tense for *all* verbs is formed by changing the い of the present-negative ending to かった; as you will see in the next section, this is the rule for making the past tense of i-adjectives.

	Present Affirmative	Past Affirmative	Present Negative	Past Negative
ru-verbs				
to use	用いる	用いた	用いない	用いなかった
to count	数える	数えた	数えない	数えなかった
xu-verbs				
to show	表す	表した	表さない	表さなかった
to consist of	成り立つ	成り立った	成り立たない	成り立たなかった
to go up	上がる	上がった	上がらない	上がらなかった
to differ	違う	違った	違わない	違わなかった
to move	動く	動いた	動かない	動かなかった
to pour	注ぐ	注いだ	注がない	注がなかった
to study	学ぶ	学んだ	学ばない	学ばなかった
to contain	含む	含んだ	含まない	含まなかった
Irregular verbs				
to go	行く	行った！	行かない	行かなかった
to be	ある	あった	ない！	なかった
to do	する	した！	しない！	しなかった
to come	くる	きた！	こない！	こなかった

The past tense of verbs in Japanese is translated by various past-tense forms in English. For example, 動いた[うごいた] may be translated as "did move," "moved," or "has moved." Occasionally a past-tense form before a noun is most conveniently translated as an adjective; for example, 違った方法[ちがったホウホウ] "a different method; another method." Phrases ending with a past-tense form may immediately precede a noun as a modifying clause; the construction is exactly the same as that discussed in Section 7.4, where present-tense forms were used. The following sentences illustrate the use of the past tense:

AとBの間に成り立った関係はCとDの間にも成り立つ。
AとBのあいだになりたったカンケイはCとDのあいだにもなりたつ。
The relation that was valid between A and B is also valid between C and D.

中原らが発見した方法を用いた。
なかはららがハッケンしたホウホウをもちいた。
They used the method discovered by Nakahara et al.

すでに学んだように、温度が一定のとき、気体の圧力はその体積に反比例する。
すでにまなんだように、<u>オンド</u>が<u>イッテイ</u>のとき、<u>キタイ</u>の<u>アツリョク</u>はその<u>タイセキ</u>に
<u>ハンピレイ</u>する。
As we have already learned, when the temperature is constant, the pressure of a gas is inversely
proportional to its volume.

水素イオンを含んだ液体をびんに注いだ。
<u>スイソ</u>イオンを<u>ふくんだ</u><u>エキタイ</u>をびんに<u>そそいだ</u>。
We poured the liquid that contained hydrogen ions into the bottle.

石原はアメリカへ行ったとき、ウィスコンシン大学のバイオトロンで重大な実験を行った。
<u>いしはら</u>はアメリカへ<u>いった</u>とき、ウィスコンシン<u>ダイガク</u>のバイオトロンで<u>ジュウダイ</u>
な<u>ジッケン</u>を<u>おこなった</u>。
When Ishihara went to America, he carried out important experiments at the University of Wisconsin
Biotron.

上の式で表面素をdS、体積素をdVとした。
<u>うえ</u>の<u>しき</u>で<u>ヒョウメンソ</u>をdS、<u>タイセキソ</u>をdVとした。
In the above equation we have let the surface element be dS and the volume element be dV.

tの関数を積分したのち、積分定数を定めた。
tの<u>カンスウ</u>を<u>セキブン</u>したのち、<u>セキブンテイスウ</u>を<u>さだめた</u>。
After we integrated the function of t, we determined the constant of integration.

温度が100℃まで上がったとき、一気圧でも化学反応がおこった。
<u>オンド</u>が100℃まで<u>あがった</u>とき、<u>イチキアツ</u>でも<u>カガクハンノウ</u>がおこった。
When the temperature rose to 100°C, a chemical reaction took place even at one atmosphere pressure.

8.2 The Past Tense of i-Adjectives (かった)

The past tense of *all* i-adjectives, affirmative and negative, is obtained by
replacing the ending い by the ending かった. (For an overview of the adjective
endings see Appendix B.) Here are some examples of the i-adjective forms:

	Present Affirmative	Past Affirmative	Present Negative	Past Negative
fast	速い	速かった	速くない	速くなかった
heavy	重い	重かった	重くない	重くなかった
equal	等しい	等しかった	等しくない	等しくなかった
hot	熱い	熱かった	熱くない	熱くなかった
large	大きい	大きかった	大きくない	大きくなかった
small	小さい	小さかった	小さくない	小さくなかった
many	多い	多かった	多くない	多くなかった
few	少ない	少なかった	少なくない	少なくなかった

The translation of the past-tense forms is straightforward; thus 速かった means "was
fast (or quick)" and 速くなかった means "was not fast." All the forms displayed
above usually appear at the end of a clause or sentence; in addition, they may

occasionally appear before nouns to modify them. Here are some illustrations of their use.

この化学反応は速くなかった。
このカガクハンノウははやくなかった。
This chemical reaction was not fast.

この実験では気体の圧力が大変高かった。
このジッケンではキタイのアツリョクがタイヘンたかかった。
In this experiment the gas pressure was very high.

合原らは流体が大変熱かったばあい、温度を熱電対ではかった。
あいばららはリュウタイがタイヘンあつかったばあい、オンドをネツデンツイではかった。
When the fluids were very hot, Aibara et al. measured temperatures by means of thermocouples.

8.3 The Past Tense of na- and no-Adjectives

We saw in Section 7.3 that the na- and no-adjectives have two forms in the present affirmative — one for use before nouns (attributive form) and one for use at the ends of sentences or clauses (terminal form). In all other respects these adjectives are conjugated just like noun+である.

	Present Affirmative	Past Affirmative	Present Negative	Past Negative
necessary	必要である 必要な	必要であった	必要で(は)ない	必要で(は)なかった
constant	一定である 一定の	一定であった	一定で(は)ない	一定で(は)なかった

In the "Present Affirmative" column the first entry is the "terminal form," and the second entry is the "attributive form" or "dictionary form." The following sentences illustrate their use:

この実験を行うのに、ビュレットが必要であった。
このジッケンをおこなうのに、ビュレットがヒツヨウであった。
In order to perform this experiment a burette was necessary.

そのばあいには、重合体は等方的ではなかった。
そのばあいには、ジュウゴウタイはトウホウテキではなかった。
In that case the polymer was not isotropic.

これらの電気化学的(な)実験では一定の電圧が必要であった。
これらのデンキカガクテキ(な)ジッケンではイッテイのデンアツがヒツヨウであった。
In these electrochemical experiments a fixed voltage was necessary.

8-10

8.4 Noun-Following Expressions

In Chapter 6 you learned that a number of particles can be used as postpositions: に, で, へ, まで, etc. You also learned a handful of compound postpositional phrases such as の上に, の間に, and の下に. These are all "noun-following expressions." In this section we give you some noun-following expressions that differ from those given earlier in that they contain verb forms. There are well over a hundred of these noun-following expressions in common use, and on almost any page of scientific writing you may expect to encounter five to ten of them. Here we give you some of the most important ones.

...に関して	about, as regards, with respect to	...に関する
...に対して	for, in, against	...に対する
...において	in, at, on, as for	...における
...によって	by (means of), on the basis of, due to	...による
...に応じて	in response to	...に応じる
...に対応して	corresponding to	...に対応する
...に反して	in contrast to, contrary to	...に反する
...に比べて	as compared to	...に比べる
...にわたって	(extending) over	...にわたる
...につれて	in accordance with, as	...につれる
...と違って	unlike, differing from	...と違う
...について	as for, as regards, with respect to	
...として	(considered) as	

The expressions on the left consist of a particle (に or と) and the て form of the verb (obtained by replacing the た of the past tense by て); these expressions function very much like postpositional particles and appear in English translation as prepositional phrases or as adverbial expressions. These expressions can also be followed by の, in which case they act as noun modifiers.

The expressions on the right are also noun-following expressions; in contrast to their counterparts on the left, they end in the present-tense form of the verb. The first three expressions always precede a noun and modify it; the other expressions often do.

We now illustrate the use of the above noun-following expressions.

定積分に関していろいろな例を学んだ。
テイセキブンにカンしていろいろなレイをまなんだ。
With regard to definite integrals we studied various examples.

xに関する積分において、aは電圧による定数である。
xにカンするセキブンにおいて、aはデンアツによるテイスウである。
In the integral with respect to x, a is a constant that depends on the voltage.

力に応じて物体が動く。
ちからにオウじてブッタイがうごく。
The body moves in response to the force.

式(1)において、Bは式(2)における定数Aに対応する定数である。
シキ(1)において、Bはシキ(2)におけるテイスウAにタイオウするテイスウである。
In Eq. (1) B is the constant that corresponds to the constant A in Eq. (2).

分子の大きさによって、分子間力が違う。
ブンシのおおきさによって、ブンシカンリョクがちがう。
Intermolecular forces differ depending on the size of the molecules.

ここでaおよびbはt＝0における速度によって定まる定数である。
ここでaおよびbはt＝0におけるソクドによってさだまるテイスウである。
Here a and b are constants that are determined by the velocities at t＝0.

電流による力をFとする。
デンリュウによるちからをFとする。
We let F be the force due to the electric current.

ここで速度vに対しては、式(2.6)を用いた。
ここでソクドvにタイしては、シキ(2.6)をもちいた。
Here we used Eq. (2.6) for the velocity v.

体積素dVにおける質量が体積素dV'における質量に対して力をおよぼす。
タイセキソdVにおけるシツリョウがタイセキソdV'におけるシツリョウにタイしてちからを
　　およぼす。
The mass in volume element dV exerts a force on the mass in volume element dV'. {Note that V' is
　　　　pronounced ブイダッシュ (bui-dasshu) in Japanese.}

その実験において液体の酸性度を変えた。
そのジッケンにおいてエキタイのサンセイドをかえた。
In that experiment we changed the acidity of the liquids.

固体の表面において、化学反応が生じた。
コタイのヒョウメンにおいて、カガクハンノウがショウじた。
On the surface of the solid a chemical reaction took place.

Aにおける電流をIとする。
AにおけるデンリュウをIとする。
We let the electric current at A be I.

物体の表面にわたって積分した。
ブッタイのヒョウメンにわたってセキブンした。
We integrated over the surface of the body.

したがって、重力によって動く物体の力学的エネルギーは一定である。
したがって、ジュウリョクによってうごくブッタイのリキガクテキエネルギーはイッテイ
　　である。
Therefore, the mechanical energy of a body moving due to gravity is constant.

気体と違って、水のような液体はちぢまない流体と見なす。
キタイとちがって、みずのようなエキタイはちぢまないリュウタイとみなす。
We regard liquids such as water, unlike gases, as incompressible.

炭素原子および酸素原子に比べて、高分子はずいぶん大きい。
タンソゲンシおよびサンソゲンシにくらべて、コウブンシはずいぶんおおきい。
Macromolecules are extremely large in comparison with carbon and oxygen atoms.

アミノ酸の例として、バリンおよびロイシンについてのべた。
アミノサンのレイとして、バリンおよびロイシンについてのべた。
As examples of amino acids we discussed valine and leucine.

8.5 The Nouns こと, の, and もの

In this section we discuss three nouns all of which can be translated roughly as "thing." Usually こと and の refer to intangible things, such as facts, matters, and subjects, whereas もの generally refers to things that are tangible or visible.

a. The Noun こと

The noun こと has many meanings, such as "matter, affair, subject, fact," depending on the context.

このことがわかる。
[We] understand this fact. = This is evident.

このことをのべた。
[I] discussed this subject.

そのようなことから分子間力の大きさを定めた。
そのようなことからブンシカンリョクのおおきさをさだめた。
From those kinds of facts [they] determined the magnitude of the intermolecular forces.

A very important use of こと is as a "nominalizer." Any verb or adjective can be converted into a noun simply by adding こと to the dictionary form. In such instances こと is often translated as "act" or "fact."

示すこと	[しめすこと]	(the act of) showing
数えること	[かぞえること]	(the act of) counting
反対すること	[ハンタイすること]	(the act of) opposing
重なり合うこと	[かさなりあうこと]	(the fact of) being superposed
違うこと	[ちがうこと]	(the fact of) being different
多いこと	[おおいこと]	(the fact) that there are many

In English we have two special verb forms that function as nouns: the gerund (ending in "-ing") and the infinitive (the verb preceded by "to"). In the sentence "Counting from 1 to 10 is easy," a gerund is used, whereas in the sentence "To count from 1000 to 1

backwards is difficult," an infinitive is used. Both "counting" and "to count" are 数え
ること in Japanese.

The use of こと as a nominalizer is not restricted to the dictionary forms of verbs
and adjectives, as is illustrated here.

間違わないこと	[まちがわないこと]	(the act of) not making an error
注いだこと	[そそいだこと]	(the act of) having poured
定めなかったこと	[さだめなかったこと]	(the fact of) not having determined
流れなかったこと	[ながれなかったこと]	(the fact of) not having flowed
少なかったこと	[すくなかったこと]	(the fact) that there were few
多くなかったこと	[おおくなかったこと]	(the fact) that there were not many

In Japanese dictionaries JUKUGO are often defined by giving the corresponding verb
followed by こと; for example, 変化 is defined as 変わること. Also in laboratories
you may see something like しめないこと! "Do not shut!" or あけないこと! "Do
not open!" Here こと imparts a strong imperative meaning.

Any clause ending with a sentence-terminal verb or adjective form followed by
こと becomes a noun and can function as such in a sentence. That is, it can be followed
by が, は, を, に, or other particles. Here are some examples:

このような関数を積分することはむずかしい。
このようなカンスウをセキブンすることはむずかしい。
To integrate this kind of function is difficult.

AとB(と)の間に関係がないことを発見した。
AとB(と)のあいだにカンケイがないことをハッケンした。
We discovered that there is no connection between A and B.

Van der Waals式によって気体の圧力を定めることについて学んだ。
Van der Waalsシキによってキタイのアツリョクをさだめることについてまなんだ。
We studied about determining the pressure of gases by the van der Waals equation.

b. The Noun の

Often, instead of こと the noun の can be used, as in the construction just
discussed for こと, provided that の is followed by が, は, or を. Usually the part of
the sentence following のが, のは, or のを is quite short, as in the sentences given
here.

表面における熱流量をもとめるのはあまりむずかしくない。
ヒョウメンにおけるネツリュウリョウをもとめるのはあまりむずかしくない。
It is not very difficult to obtain the heat flow at the surface.

この場合にサスペンションが流れないのを見つけた。
このばあいにサスペンションがながれないのをみつけた。
They found that in this case the suspensions do not flow.

When an adjective is followed by の it is often translated as "one."

どのフィルターを用いたか。大きいのを用いた。
どのフィルターを<u>もち</u>いたか。<u>おおき</u>いのを<u>もち</u>いた。
Which filter did they use? They used the large one.

In this construction こと is not used.

     Up to this point you have learned a number of uses for の and it may prove helpful to summarize them along with the appropriate section numbers: (a) the particle の that is used between two nouns to indicate some kind of relationship between them (most often translated as "of" in English) (6.3); (b) the particle の that replaces が as the subject marker in a modifying clause (7.4, 8.6); (c) the noun の that replaces こと to nominalize a clause (8.5c); (d) the noun の, following an adjective, that can be translated as "one" (8.5c); (e) the particle の that appears in ので ("because") and in のに ("in order to") (7.5b, d); (f) the の that is an alternative form of the copula である (7.4).

c. The Noun もの
     The noun もの, when referring to concrete objects or specific topics, can be translated as "object" or "item" or by some other word appropriate in the context.

これは動物には見えないものである。
これは<u>ドウブツ</u>には<u>み</u>えないものである。
This is a thing that is not seen by animals.

応用としては、プラズマ・スプレー・ベンチュリーメーターに関するものなどがある。
<u>オウヨウ</u>としては、プラズマ・スプレー・ベンチュリーメーターに<u>カン</u>するものなどがある。
Among the applications are those related to plasmas, sprays, and Venturi meters.

このようにvan der Waals式においてaおよびbは分子間力によるものである。
このようにvan der Waals<u>シキ</u>においてaおよびbは<u>ブンシカンリョク</u>によるものである。
Thus, the a and b in the van der Waals equation are quantities that depend on the intermolecular forces.

Finally we mention one other use of もの. When そのもの follows a noun it means something like "itself" or "of itself." For example, 熱力学そのもの means "thermodynamics (of) itself."

8.6 Verb-Following Expressions
     A verb in its present or past form can be followed by a number of "verb-following expressions." In this section we discuss some of these that involve the nouns こと and の discussed in the foregoing section.

Now that you know how to nominalize a verb by adding こと, you are in a position to appreciate verb-following expressions that use こと; the most important of these are

...ことができる	... is possible; is able to ...; can ...
...ことがわかる	... is clear; we understand that ...
...ことがある	sometimes (it happens that) ...
...ことが多い	there are many times when ...; often ...
...ことである	the fact is that ...
...ことになる	it turns out that ...
...ことにする	we decide that ...
...ことによる	depends on ...; is accomplished by ...

The particle が in these expressions may be replaced by の if the expression occurs in a modifying clause, and it may be replaced by も with the meaning of "also" when appropriate. In the corresponding negative expressions は may appear; for example, ...ことはできない, "cannot ...." The verb or adjective before or after こと may be in the present or past tense and may be affirmative or negative. As a result, quite a few combinations are possible. Most of the time you can figure out appropriate translations for these expressions. Note that 変わったことはない means "It has never changed."

The word こと cannot be replaced by the particle の in any of the above expressions. Here are some examples of how these expressions are used:

重合体の中には原子が多いことがわかる。
ジュウゴウタイのなかにはゲンシがおおいことがわかる。
We know that there are many atoms in polymers.

その化学反応の速さを定める必要はないことになった。
そのカガクハンノウのはやさをさだめるヒツヨウはないことになった。
It turned out that there was no need to determine the speed of that chemical reaction.

中性子の質量を定めることもできた。
チュウセイシのシツリョウをさだめることもできた。
They were also able to determine the mass of the neutron.

元生らはアミノ酸を合成することにした。
もといきらはアミノサンをゴウセイすることにした。
Motoiki et al. decided to synthesize the amino acids.

固体の比熱をはかるのはあまりむずかしくないことである。
コタイのヒネツをはかるのはあまりむずかしくないことである。
The fact is that it is not too difficult to measure the specific heat of solids.

この実験式を用いることがある。
このジッケンシキをもちいることがある。
Sometimes we use this empirical equation.

違った方法を用いることが多い。
ちがったホウホウをもちいることがおおい。
Often different methods are used.

The expression noun+することができる is occasionally abbreviated as noun+でき
る. Thus 発見できる means "(he is) able to discover" or "can be discovered."

      The expression ...のである often follows the terminal verb of a sentence. This
can mean "It is a fact that ...," but in most cases it does not need to be translated into
English. Adding ...のである sometimes adds emphasis or just provides some stylistic
variation. Here are some examples: •

上にのべたように、グリセリンをニュートン流体と見なすのである
うえにのべたように、グリセリンをニュートンリュウタイとみなすのである。
As discussed above, (it is a fact that) we regard glycerine as a Newtonian fluid.

高原はこのような化合物を発見したのである。
たかはらはこのようなカゴウブツをハッケンしたのである。
Takahara discovered this kind of chemical compound.

      If のである is added to a clause that ends in である, the である in the original
clause is replaced by the alternative form of the copula な, as seen in the following
sentence:

アルコールはニュートン流体なのであるが、ポリエチレンはニュートン流体ではない。
アルコールはニュートンリュウタイなのであるが、ポリエチレンはニュートンリュウタ
    イではない。
Alcohol is a Newtonian fluid, but polyethylene is not a Newtonian fluid.

動物が生きるのに、酸素は必要なのである。
ドウブツがいきるのに、サンソはヒツヨウなのである。
In order for animals to live [they] need oxygen.

つける		to attach
うしなう		to lose
10,000以上	イチマンイジョウ	more than 10,000; 10,000 or more
つなぐ		to connect {wires}
一つずつ	ひとつずつ	one by one
一度も...ない	イチドも...ない	even once
例としてあげる	レイとしてあげる	offer as an example
つぎの	【次の】	the next ...
つぎに	【次に】	next
...だけで		only by (means of) ...
それをしるために	【それを知るために】	in order to get to know that
はじめ(に)		first
...からとる		to take from ...
...からである		it is because ...
同じころ		in the same period
間違っていた	まちがっていた	was erroneous
無くなった	なくなった	disappeared
...をもとにして		with ... as a basis
わかるようになった		came to be understood

EXERCISES

Ex 8.1 Matching Japanese and English technical terms

(a) Fields of study

応用化学( ) 1. applied chemistry
応用数学( ) 2. applied mathematics
応用力学( ) 3. applied mechanics
合成化学( ) 4. calculus of variations
積分学( )　5. integral calculus
変分法( )　6. quantum mechanics
量子力学( ) 7. synthetic chemistry

(b) Suffixes 数 and 式

化学式( )　　1. chemical formula
関数( )　　　2. coefficient
係数( )　　　3. constant
実験式( )　　4. empirical formula
実数( )　　　5. equality
質量数( )　　6. function
素数( )　　　7. logarithm
対数( )　　　8. mass number
定数( )　　　9. method
等式( )　　　10. molecular formula
反応式( )　　11. prime number
分子式( )　　12. quantum number
変数( )　　　13. reaction formula
方式( )　　　14. real number
量子数( )　　15. variable

(c) Various words with common KANJI

生成物( )　　1. acidic
化合物( )　　2. atmospheric pressure
熱応力( )　　3. atomic weight
圧力( )　　　4. chemical compound
反発力( )　　5. convection current
発電( )　　　6. electric current
中性子( )　　7. electron pair
中性の( )　　8. mass
酸性の( )　　9. molecular weight
対流( )　　　10. neutral
電流( )　　　11. neutron
電子対( )　　12. power generation
熱電対( )　　13. pressure
原子量( )　　14. reaction products
含水量( )　　15. repulsive force
質量( )　　　16. thermal stress
重量( )　　　17. thermocouple
分子量( )　　18. water content
大気圧( )　　19. water pressure
水圧( )　　　20. weight

Ex 8.2 Matching concepts and definitions

　　In defining a concept, an English technical dictionary often gives a short definition that is not a complete sentence. For example, it might give the following definition of gram-molecule: "The molecular weight of a compound expressed in grams." The definition is written as though it were the completion of a sentence beginning with "A gram-molecule is ...," and thus is not itself a complete sentence.

　　A Japanese technical dictionary often does the same. For example, for the Japanese word for gram-molecule グラム分子, it may give the following:分子量にグラムをつけたもの, "the quantity that has [the units of] grams attached to the molecular weight." As in this example, the general noun もの or こと is often used rather than a more appropriate specific noun, e.g., here the noun 量.

In this exercise you will find a list of technical concepts in English and a list of Japanese definitions that use the general nouns もの or こと. Match each concept with its appropriate definition.

1. acetylene polymer
2. Avogadro's law
3. denaturation (of alcohol)
4. fructification
5. melting

6. gel
7. gram formula weight
8. hoverplane
9. hydrogen ion
10. macromolecular compound

( )　アルコールを変性アルコールにすること。
( )　式量にグラムをつけたもの。
( )　実をむすぶこと。
( )　水素原子が一つの電子をうしなったもの。
( )　アセチレンの重合したもの。
( )　分子量が10,000以上[イチマンイジョウ]のもの。
( )　同じ温度と同じ圧力で同じ体積の気体は同数の分子を含むということ。
( )　ヘリコプタのこと。
( )　ゾルが流動性をうしなったもの。
( )　固体が液体に変わること。

Ex 8.3 Verbs and adjectives in their affirmative and negative forms

Each of the following sentences ends in a verb or adjective in the present-affirmative form. Read each sentence aloud and then translate. For each sentence create three new sentences by changing the verb or adjective into (1) the present-negative form, (2) the past-affirmative form, and (3) the past-negative form. Again read each sentence aloud and then translate.

1. この実験では電圧は小さい。小さ＿＿＿。小さ＿＿＿。
   小さ＿＿＿＿＿。
2. これらのベクトルは等しい。等し＿＿＿。等し＿＿＿。
   等し＿＿＿＿＿。
3. そのコンピュータは重い。重＿＿＿。重＿＿＿。重＿＿＿＿＿。
4. この例は重要である。で＿＿。で＿＿＿。で＿＿＿＿。
5. 同じ数表を用いる。用い＿＿。用い＿。用い＿＿＿＿。
6. 体積は温度とともに変化する。変化＿＿＿。変化＿＿。
   変化＿＿＿＿＿。
7. 中性子の質量を定める。定め＿＿。定め＿。定め＿＿＿＿。
8. 式2は成り立つ。成り立＿＿＿。成り立＿＿。成り立＿＿＿＿＿。

9. 二つの針金[はりがね = wires]をつなぐ。つな＿＿＿。つな＿＿。
   つな＿＿＿＿＿。
10. Bは速度の対数と同一である。で＿＿。で＿＿＿。で＿＿＿＿＿。
11. 発生学と積分学を学ぶ。学＿＿＿。学＿＿。学＿＿＿＿＿。
12. フラスコの中の流体は水素イオンを含む。含＿＿＿。含＿＿。
    含＿＿＿＿＿。
13. ビーカーの中の液体は石炭酸と違う。違＿＿＿。違＿＿。
    違＿＿＿＿＿。
14. 違った重合体を発見する。発見＿＿＿。発見＿＿。
    発見＿＿＿＿＿。
15. アメーバは動く。動＿＿＿。動＿＿。動＿＿＿＿＿。
16. この重合体は流れる。流れ＿＿。流れ＿。流れ＿＿＿＿。
17. 電気化学反応では電圧と反応速度との間に関係がある。＿＿。
    ＿＿＿。＿＿＿＿＿。
18. 高温の固体は大変熱い。熱＿＿＿。熱＿＿＿。熱＿＿＿＿＿。
19. フッ素のような元素は少ない。少な＿＿＿。少な＿＿＿。
    少な＿＿＿＿＿。
20. 熱電対が要る。要＿＿＿。要＿＿。要＿＿＿＿＿。
21. 水に動物がいる。い＿＿。い＿。い＿＿＿＿。
22. 動物が水の方へ行く。行＿＿＿。行＿＿。行＿＿＿＿＿。
23. 実験で発見したことをいう。い＿＿＿。い＿＿。い＿＿＿＿＿。

Ex 8.4 Translate the following sentences

1. そろばんを用いたときには、コンピュータを用いなかった。
2. 分子数を数えたが、それらを一つずつ数えなかった。
3. 大きな動物が動いたから、小さな動物は動かなかった。
4. この実験では水を注いだが、その実験では注がなかった。
5. 実験データを図[ズ = diagram]で表したが、表でそれを表さなかった。
6. 高温ではこの関係が成り立ったが、高圧では成り立たなかった。
7. 力学で力のことを学んだが、化学反応のことを学ばなかった。
8. 高圧の実験ではこの炭水化物が水を含んだが、高温の実験では水を含まなかった。
9. 速度が速いとき、その関係が成立したが、速くないとき、成立しなかった。
10. 分子量が大きかった化合物は流れなかったが、それが大きくなかった化合物が流れた。
11. 流体の性質が流れることである。これに反して、流れないことは固体の性質の一つである。
12. サインカーブ[sine curve]の下の面積を定めるのに、そのサインカーブを表す式を積分することが一つの方法である。

13. 熱によって発電することは有用である。それに対して熱発電によって生じる酸性雨[サンセイウ = acid rain]は有害[ユウガイ = harmful]である。
14. 化学反応において化合物が変化する。これに反して、その化合物が成り立つ元素は変わらない。
15. データは違ったが、使った[from つかう = to use]方法は違わなかった。

8.5 Read the following essays for comprehension

1. 化合物の分子を表示するためには分子式を用いる。例えば水を例としてあげると、分子式はH_2Oである。水の分子式を定めるために、つぎの方法を用いた。一定量の水では酸素の量と水素の量とは一定である。実験によって、酸素と水素との重量比がわかる。それは水素11.19%[パーセント]、酸素88.81%である。これらの数とそれぞれの元素の原子量との比は11.10と5.55である。これらの数は水の分子中のそれぞれの原子数に比例する。そのため、これらの数の比は水素原子と酸素原子との数の比に等しい。この比は2:1[ニタイイチ]であるから、それで水の分子式をH_2Oにすることができるか。このデータだけではできない。これがいわゆる実験式である。水の分子式がH_2OであるかH_4O_2であるか、このデータだけではわからない。それをしるためには水の分子量をしる必要がある。水を気化する実験によって、水の分子量が18であることがわかる。それで水の分子式は水の実験式と同じであることがわかる。

2. $ab = c$の式において数cは数aと数bの積である。この積を定めるために対数を用いることができるが、そのためには対数表が要る。はじめに数aと数bのそれぞれの対数を表からとる。つぎにそれらをたす。$\log ab$は$\log a + \log b$に等しいから、aの対数とbの対数とをたした数がcの対数と同一である。そこで対数表からこの対数に対応する真数[シンスウ = anti-logarithm]をとる。これが数aと数bの積cである。

3. 力学においては力がはたらくことを学ぶ。力を表示するのにベクトルを用いる。そのベクトルを成分に分ける。二つの力がはたらくとき、それらの成分をたすことによって、その合力がわかる。物体が動くとき、その速度が変化すると、力がはたらいたことになる。物体が動かないときでも、力がはたらくことがある。そのときはたらく力の合力が0であるから、物体が動かない。例えば、物体には必ず重力がはたらく。物体が動かないのは、物体に重力に反対する力がはたらくからである。重力は物体の質量に比例してはたらくから、物体が動かないとき、その重力に反対する力の大きさがわかる。それは物体の重さに等しいが、向き[むき = direction]が反対の力である。

8-22

4．化学反応によって物質の性質が変化する。例えば化合物はその成分元素と違った性質をもつ[tohave]。化学反応を表示するのに、反応式を用いる。反応式では反応物と生成物を分ける。反応物を左[ひだり＝left]の方に、生成物を右[みぎ＝right]の方に表す。反応には発熱反応が多い。発熱反応においては熱が発生するから、生成物の温度が上がる。生成物が気体であるばあい、気体の圧力が温度に比例するから、圧力も上がる。発生する熱が大きいとき、体積が小さいと、圧力が高圧になる。等温においては圧力が体積に反比例するからである。

5．発電とは電圧と電流とを発生することである。電流が電圧に応じて流れる。電流は流体と違う。流体は物質から成るものである。これに反して、電流は多くの高速度で動く電子から成り立つものである。熱によって発電することが多いが、電気化学反応によって電気を発生することもできる。しかし、発生した電気の電圧は高くない。電力を用いるのに、高い電圧が要る。このため、電気化学反応による発電の実用性は高くない。

Ex 8.6 Translate the following essay

　J.J.Thomsonは電子を発見したが、電子の電気量とその質量の比を実験的に定めた。同じころ、R.A.Millikanは電子の質量を定めたので、これら二つの量の積として電子の電気量がわかった。その数は量子力学が成り立つために必要である。はじめMillikanの実験方法は少し間違っていた。それで、速度の定め方を変えた。このため間違いは無くなった。これらの実験をもとにして、原子や分子の反応に対する数式が量子力学的にわかるようになった。高圧下の化合もよくわかるようになった。

TRANSLATIONS

Ex 8.4 Sentences

1. When an abacus was used, a computer was not used.
2. [We] counted the number of molecules, but [we] did not count them one by one.
3. The large animal moved; therefore, the small animals did not (move).
4. In this experiment we poured water, but in that experiment we did not (pour [it]).
5. [We] showed the experimental data in a diagram, but not in a table.
6. At high temperatures this relation was valid, but at high pressures it was not (valid).
7. In mechanics we studied about forces, but [we] did not study about chemical reactions.

8. In experiments at high pressure this carbohydrate contained water, but in experiments at high temperature [it] did not (contain water).

9. When the velocity was high, this relation held, but when [it] was not, [it] did not hold.

10. The compounds having large molecular weights did not flow, but the compounds which did not have large [molecular weights] did (flow).

11. To flow is the property of a fluid. In contrast, not to flow is one of the properties of a solid.

12. In order to determine the area under a sine curve, one method is to integrate the equation that expresses the sine curve.

13. Generating electric power by means of heat is useful. [But] in relation to this, the acid rain generated in thermal power generation is harmful.

14. Chemical compounds change in chemical reactions. In contrast, the elements from which the compounds are made do not change.

15. The data differed, but the method used did not differ.

Ex 8.6 Essay

J. J. Thomson discovered the electron, and he determined experimentally the ratio of the quantity of electricity to the mass of the electron. In the same period, R. A. Millikan determined the mass of the electron. Therefore, [physicists] found the quantity of electricity of the electron by taking the product of these two quantities. That number is necessary in order for establishing quantum mechanics. At first Millikan's experimental method was slightly erroneous. Then, he changed [his] way of determining the velocity. Because of this [change] the error disappeared. With these experiments as a basis, the (mathematical) equations for the reactions of atoms and molecules came to be understood quantum mechanically. Chemical combination under high pressure also came to be well understood.

CHAPTER 9 第九章

位	イ	rank; place; position
	くらい	approximately

時	ジ	time; hour
	とき	time; occasion

運	ウン	transporting
	はこ(ぶ)	to carry

色	シキ; ショク	color
	いろ	color

解	カイ	dismantling; analysis
	と(く)	to untie; to solve

出	シュツ	sending out, going out
	だ(す)	to send out, take out
	で(る)	to emerge, go out (from)

管	カン	governing; tube, pipe
	くだ	pipe

心	シン	heart; mind
	こころ	heart

機	キ	machine

全	ゼン	all
	まった(く)	entirely
	すべ(て)(の)	all (of something)

計	ケイ	plan; measure
	-ケイ	meter
	はか(る)	to measure

則	ソク	rule, law

結	ケツ	binding; concluding
	むす(び)	conclusion
	むす(ぶ)	to tie, bind; to conclude

単	タン	simple; single
	タン-	mono-, single

向	コウ	direction
	む(き)	direction
	む(く)	to turn toward *(v.i.)*
	む(かう)	to face toward *(v.i.)*

部	ブ	part
	-ブ	department (of)

細	サイ	slender, fine
	ほそ(い)	slender, narrow
	こま(かい)	detailed, fine

溶	ヨウ	melting; dissolving
	と(かす)	to melt; to dissolve
	と(ける)	to melt; to dissolve

使	シ	use
	つか(う)	to use

理	リ	principle; reason

位

単位	タンイ	unit
同位体	ドウイタイ	isotope
電位	デンイ	electric potential
変位	ヘンイ	displacement

運

運動	ウンドウ	motion
運動量	ウンドウリョウ	momentum
等速運動	トウソクウンドウ	uniform motion
運び出す	はこびだす	to carry out

解

分解	ブンカイ	decomposition
溶解する	ヨウカイする	to dissolve
溶解度	ヨウカイド	solubility
溶解熱	ヨウカイネツ	heat of solution
電解質	デンカイシツ	electrolyte
解重合	カイジュウゴウ	depolymerization
理解する	リカイする	to understand

管

ガラス管	ガラスカン	glass tubing
ゴム管	ゴムカン	rubber tubing
管理	カンリ	management, control
電子管	デンシカン	electron tube
血管	ケッカン	blood vessel

機

有機的な	ユウキテキな	organic
無機的な	ムキテキな	inorganic
機関	キカン	engine
熱機関	ネツキカン	heat engine

計

流量計	リュウリョウケイ	flow meter
時計	とケイ {N.B. irreg. rdg. of 時}	clock, watch
圧力計	アツリョクケイ	pressure meter
気圧計	キアツケイ	barometer
温度計	オンドケイ	thermometer

高度計	コウドケイ	altimeter
速度計	ソクドケイ	speedometer
合計	ゴウケイ	sum, total

結

結合	ケツゴウ	bond {chem}
結合水	ケツゴウスイ	bound water
結合性電子	ケツゴウセイデンシ	bonding electron
二重結合	ニジュウケツゴウ	double bond

向

上向き	うわむき {N.B. reading of 上}	upward
反対向き	ハンタイむき	opposite direction
下向き	したむき	downward
方向	ホウコウ	direction
向上	コウジョウ	improvement
対向流	タイコウリュウ	countercurrent flow

細

細分する	サイブンする	to subdivide
細部	サイブ	detail

使

使い方	つかいかた	way of using
使用する	シヨウする	to use
使用法	シヨウホウ	(directions for) how to use
使用-	シヨウ	working
使用温度	シヨウオンド	working temperature

時

時間	ジカン	time
時計	とケイ {N.B. と}	clock, watch
同時の	ドウジの	simultaneous
時々	ときどき	sometimes
時定数	ジテイスウ	time constant

色

単色の	タンショクの	monochromatic
無色の	ムショクの	colorless, achromatic
色素	シキソ	pigment
原色	ゲンショク	primary color
色々な	いろいろな	various

出

見出す	みいだす {N.B. いだす}	to discover, find
出入りする	でいりする	to go in and out
溶出液	ヨウシュツエキ	effluent
出力	シュツリョク	output
流れ出る	ながれでる	to flow out

心

向心力	コウシンリョク	centripetal force
関心を持つ	カンシンをもつ	to have concern
中心力	チュウシンリョク	central force
重心	ジュウシン	center of gravity
心理学	シンリガク	psychology

全

全部(の)	ゼンブ(の)	all (of)
全体の	ゼンタイの	all of
全色性の	ゼンショクセイの	panchromatic

則

法則	ホウソク	law
原則	ゲンソク	principle

単

単一	タンイツ	single-
単体	タンタイ	simple substance
単位	タンイ	unit
有理化単位	ユウリカタンイ	rationalized units
単原子分子	タンゲンシブンシ	monatomic molecule
単動式	タンドウシキ	single action type
単色の	タンショクの	monochromatic
単量体	タンリョウタイ	monomer

部

全部(の)	ゼンブ(の)	all (of)
部分	ブブン	part
大部分	ダイブブン	the greater part
-学部	ガクブ	college of {e.g., engineering}
一部	イチブ	one part
部分積分	ブブンセキブン	integration by parts
部分モル量	ブブンモルリョウ	partial molar quantity

溶

溶出	ヨウシュツ	elution
溶出液	ヨウシュツエキ	effluent
溶液	ヨウエキ	solution
溶質	ヨウシツ	solute
溶解する	ヨウカイする	to dissolve
溶解度積	ヨウカイドセキ	solubility product
溶原性の	ヨウゲンセイの	lysogenic

理

生理学	セイリガク	physiology
合理的な	ゴウリテキな	rational
原理	ゲンリ	principle
定理	テイリ	theorem
理解する	リカイする	to understand
物理学	ブツリガク	physics
物理化学	ブツリカガク	physical chemistry
理化学	リカガク	the physical sciences
管理	カンリ	management, control

9

Connective and Conjunctive Forms

In this chapter you will learn about the connective and conjunctive forms of verbs and adjectives. The principal use of these forms is to connect two clauses, but they serve other functions as well. The connective form may be combined with any of seven auxiliary verbs to provide a number of new types of expressions, and the conjunctive form may be joined to other verbs to create "compound verbs." The connective forms are widely used in both written and spoken Japanese, whereas the conjunctive forms occur primarily in writing.

In many books on Japanese grammar the connective form is referred to as the "gerund" or the "gerundive." The conjunctive form is frequently called the "infinitive." We prefer to use the nonstandard terms "connective" and "conjunctive" because they describe the principal functions of these two forms, namely, to join verbs, adjectives, and clauses.

9.1 The Connective Form of Verbs (て)

In the foregoing chapter you learned how to form the past-tense (た) forms of verbs. The connective forms of the verbs are obtained just by replacing the た or だ of the past tense by て or で respectively. There are no exceptions to this rule, which applies to ru-verbs, xu-verbs, and irregular verbs. The negative of the connective is formed by replacing the い of the present-negative ending by くて for all verbs. In the following list we show the connective forms for verbs of each class, including some of the verbs introduced for the first time in this chapter.

	Present Affirmative	Past Affirmative	Connective Affirmative	Present Negative	Connective Negative
ru-verbs					
go out	出る	出た	出て	出ない	出なくて
to see	見る	見た	見て	見ない	見なくて
xu-verbs					
to dissolve	溶かす	溶かした	溶かして	溶かさない	溶かさなくて
to stand	立つ	立った	立って	立たない	立たなくて
to measure	計る	計った	計って	計らない	計らなくて
to use	使う	使った	使って	使わない	使わなくて
to solve	解く	解いた	解いて	解かない	解かなくて
to connect	つなぐ	つないだ	つないで	つながない	つながなくて
to tie	結ぶ	結んだ	結んで	結ばない	結ばなくて
to contain	含む	含んだ	含んで	含まない	含まなくて
Irregular verbs					
to go	行く	行った!	行って	行かない	行かなくて
to be	ある	あった	あって	ない!	なくて
to do	する	した!	して	しない!	しなくて
to come	くる	きた!	きて	こない!	こなくて

Verbs formed from KANJI followed by する, ずる, **or** じる

to heat	熱する	熱した!	熱して	熱しない	熱しなくて
to arise	生じる	生じた	生じて	生じない	生じなくて
	or 生ずる				

Now that you know how the connective forms are derived, we can proceed to the discussion of the uses of the connective.

a. The ...てから Construction

　　　We learned earlier that the particle から has the meaning of "because" or "since" when it follows a present- or past-tense form of the verb or adjective. When から follows the て form, it means "after." We give now two pairs of sentences, one with the ...てから construction and one with the ...たから construction.

ポリマーを炭化水素に溶かしてから、それを溶液として流すことができた。
ポリマーをタンカスイソにとかしてから、それをヨウエキとしてながすことができた。
After [they] dissolved the polymer in a hydrocarbon, [they] were able to make it flow as a solution.

ポリマーを炭化水素に溶かしたから、それを溶液として流すことができた。
ポリマーをタンカスイソにとかしたから、それをヨウエキとしてながすことができた。
Because [they] dissolved the polymer in a hydrocarbon, [they] were able to make it flow as a solution.

水に電解質を|溶かしてから|、それに電流を流すことができる。
みずにデンカイシツをとかしてから、それにデンリュウをながすことができる。
After [we] dissolve the electrolyte in water, [we] can pass an electric current through it.

水に電解質を|溶かしたから|、それに電流を流すことができた。
みずにデンカイシツをとかしたから、それにデンリュウをながすことができた。
Because [we] dissolved the electrolyte in water, [we] were able to pass an electric current through it.

In the second and fourth sentences above, one would probably be more apt to encounter ので rather than から in technical writing.

b. The ...ても Construction

When a connective is followed by も, it means "even if" or "even though."

溶液を熱しても、化合物は溶けなかった。
ヨウエキをネッしても、カゴウブツはとけなかった。
Even though we heated the solution, the compound did not dissolve.

この実験ではガラス管を使わなくても、定量的なデータをもとめることができる。
このジッケンではガラスカンをつかわなくても、テイリョウテキなデータをもとめることができる。
Even if we do not use a glass tube in this experiment, we can obtain quantitative data.

A more emphatic construction is ...にもかかわらず following the present or past forms: 熱したにもかかわらず means "in spite of the fact that we heated ...."

c. Expressions of Obligation and Permission

There are several closely related constructions associated with obligation and permission that are formed with the connective.

...てもよい	is permitted, may	...なくてもよい	is not required, need not
...てはならない	is not permitted, must not	...なくてはならない	is required, must
...てはいけない	is not permitted, must not	...なくてはいけない	is required, must

この場合には熱い水酸化ナトリウム溶液を使ってはならない。
このばあいにはあついスイサンカナトリウムヨウエキをつかってはならない。
In this case you must not use a hot NaOH solution.

この関数f(x)はlog(x)を含むにもかかわらず、0から1まで積分してもよい。
このカンスウf(x)はlog(x)をふくむにもかかわらず、0[ゼロ]から1までセキブンしてもよい。
In spite of the fact that this function f(x) contains log(x), we may integrate it from 0 to 1.

理学部の学生は物理学を学ばなくてはならない。
リガクブのガクセイはブツリガクをまなばなくてはならない。
College of Science students must study physics.

この積分定数は定めなくてもよい。
このセキブンテイスウはさだめなくてもよい。
We need not determine this constant of integration.

These expressions of obligation and permission are often used in technical Japanese, particularly in describing details of experimental procedures, where advice is given regarding what must or may or must not be done.

d. The Joining of Two Clauses

Two entire clauses can be joined together by putting the first verb in the connective form and the second verb in the present or past form. When this is done the connective form assumes the same tense as the final verb, and the two clauses are joined in English by "and." As you become more skillful you may sometimes find that in a polished translation the two clauses may be joined by expressions like "and then," "and as a result," or "and in this way." The subjects of the first and second clauses may be the same or different. More than two clauses may be joined in the same way. The following sentences illustrate the use of the connective forms:

水に炭酸水素ナトリウムを溶かして、溶液を熱する。
みずにタンサンスイソナトリウムをとかして、ヨウエキをネッする。
[We] dissolve the sodium bicarbonate in water and [then] heat the solution.

時原らは水酸化ナトリウムを用いて、ほかの水酸化物を合成した。
ときはららはスイサンカナトリウムをもちいて、ほかのスイサンカブツをゴウセイした。
Tokihara et al. used sodium hydroxide and synthesized other hydroxides.

LDVの実験で無色の流体の速度と流れの方向を定めて、定量的なデータをもとめることができた。
LDVのジッケンでムショクのリュウタイのソクドとながれのホウコウをさだめて、テイリョウテキなデータをもとめることができた。
In the LDV (laser-doppler velocimetry) experiment [they] determined the velocity of the colorless fluids and the direction of the flow, and were able to obtain quantitative data.

ボイル・シャルルの法則によると、気体の体積は温度に比例して、圧力に反比例する。
ボイル・シャルルのホウソクによると、キタイのタイセキはオンドにヒレイして、アツリョクにハンピレイする。
According to the laws of Boyle and Charles, the volume of a gas is proportional to the temperature and inversely proportional to the pressure.

石原等は反応生成物の量の時間に関する変化をもとめて、高見等は反応速度定数を定めた。
いしはららはハンノウセイセイブツのリョウのジカンにカンするヘンカをもとめて、たかみらはハンノウソクドテイスウをさだめた。
Ishihara et al. obtained the change of the amount of reaction products with time, and Takami et al. determined the reaction rate constants.

e. The Negative Connective Form Ending in ないで

We learned above that the negative of the connective is obtained by replacing the ending い of the present negative by くて. A second negative connective form is obtained by adding で to the ない of the present negative. This form is usually translated by "without ...ing." For example, 使わなくて means "does not use, and ...," whereas 使わないで means "without using."

ガラス管を使わないで、フラスコをつないだ。
ガラスカンをつかわないで、フラスコをつないだ。
We connected the flasks without using glass tubing.

We also note that the て form and the ないで form can be followed by 下さい[くだ さい] to make the sort of polite requests that you will encounter in reading instruction manuals: つないで下さい "please connect," and 使わないで下さい "please do not use."

温度の高いとき使わないでください。
オンドのたかいときつかわないでください。
Please do not use when the temperature is high.

9.2 The Connective Form of Adjectives (くて)

The connective form of i-adjectives is obtained by replacing the い ending of the dictionary form by the ending くて. The negative connective is obtained by replacing the い of the present negative by the ending くて. For the な and の adjectives, the な or の is replaced by で(あって) for the affirmative form and で(は)なくて for the negative form.

	Present Affirmative	Connective Affirmative	Present Negative	Connective Negative
i-adjectives				
good	よい	よくて	よくない	よくなくて
thin, slender	細い	細くて	細くない	細くなくて
finely divided	細かい	細かくて	細かくない	細かくなくて
hot	熱い	熱くて	熱くない	熱くなくて
equal	等しい	等しくて	等しくない	等しくなくて
na- and no-adjectives				
inorganic	無機的である	無機的で(あって)	無機的でない	無機的でなくて
soluble	溶性である	溶性で(あって)	溶性でない	溶性でなくて
same	同じである	同じで(あって)	同じでない	同じでなくて

Adjectives follow the same patterns as described in *b* and *d* of the foregoing section. First we illustrate the ...ても construction.

温度が高くても、溶かした気体は溶液から出てこない。
オンドがたかくても、とかしたキタイはヨウエキからでてこない。
Even though the temperature is high, the dissolved gases do not come out of solution.

定数AとBが等しくなくても、この式を解くことができる。
テイスウAとBがひとしくなくても、このシキをとくことができる。
Even though the two constants A and B are not equal, we can solve this equation.

Next we illustrate the joining together of two clauses involving adjectives.

ウラン原子は大きくて重い。
ウランゲンシはおおきくておもい。
The uranium atom is large and heavy.

このようなコンピュータは小さくて使いやすい。
このようなコンピュータはちいさくてつかいやすい。
This kind of computer is small and easy to use.

これらのベクトルは向きが反対で大きさが等しい。
これらのベクトルはむきがハンタイでおおきさがひとしい。
These vectors are opposite in direction and equal in magnitude.

9.3 Constructions Made from the て Form plus Auxiliary Verbs

In Section 9.1 we showed how the て form is used to join two verbs or two clauses together. There are several standard combinations of て forms with other verbs that function as auxiliary verbs. The most common constructions of this type in technical Japanese are

Auxiliary Verb	Idea Expressed by て Form plus Auxiliary Verb
いる	Continuing action, or a state resulting from an action
ある	State brought about by someone that is not specified
おく	Action performed with the idea of subsequent action or use
くる	Action involving motion toward the speaker; inception of an action that continues to the current time
いく (or ゆく)	Action involving motion away from the speaker; continuation of an action after the current time
みる	Action performed with the idea of seeing what the consequences will be
しまう	Action that has been completed

These verbs, when used as auxiliary verbs, are almost never written using KANJI, even though several of them normally are written with KANJI when used as ordinary verbs: 行く[いく or ゆく], 見る[みる], 置く[おく], 来る[くる]. Let us now examine these constructions one by one.

The …ている construction can be translated by the progressive form in English: "is …ing." When the verb is intransitive, however, the …ている construction may indicate the result of an action that has already occurred.

9-11

電圧計と電流計を使っている。
デンアツケイとデンリュウケイをつかっている。
We are using a voltmeter and an ammeter.

溶液の温度をはかるのに、はじめは温度計を使っていた。
ヨウエキのオンドをはかるのに、はじめはオンドケイをつかっていた。
At first we were using a thermometer to determine the temperature of the solution.

いま水にヨウ化ナトリウムを溶かしている。
いまみずにヨウカナトリウムをとかしている。
We are now dissolving sodium iodide in water.

ビーカーの中でヨウ化カリウムが水に溶けている。
ビーカーのなかでヨウカカリウムがみずにとけている。
In the beaker potassium iodide is dissolved in water.

モノマーが反応してから重合体はベンゼンに溶けていた。
モノマーがハンノウしてからジュウゴウタイはベンゼンにとけていた。
After the monomer reacted, the polymer was dissolved in benzene.

Note that the ...ている construction is not restricted to living beings as the ...にいる construction for specification of location is.

The ...てある construction indicates that an action has been carried out by some person, although that "someone" is not specified. This construction occurs only with transitive verbs.

炭酸水素ナトリウムは水に溶かしてある。
タンサンスイソナトリウムはみずにとかしてある。
The sodium bicarbonate has been dissolved in water [by someone].

The ...てくる construction indicates motion toward the speaker, but the ...ていく construction indicates motion away from the speaker.

ガラス管が細かったので、ポリマー溶液は流れ出てこなかった。
ガラスカンがほそかったので、ポリマーヨウエキはながれでてこなかった。
Because the glass tube was narrow, the polymer solution did not come [flowing] out of the glass tube.

ボンベの中から無色の気体が流れていった。
ボンベのなかからムショクのキタイがながれていった。
The colorless gas went [flowing] out of the [gas] cylinder.

Sometimes these constructions imply the idea of gradualness. Hence 流れていった might in some instances be translated best as "gradually flowed out."

More often than not the ...てくる and ...ていく constructions indicate temporal ideas. For example, the ...てくる construction means something like "It comes about that ...," often with the understanding that the action continues into the present time, possibly with increasing intensity. The ...ていく construction means "keeps on ...ing" or "continues to ...," with the action extending into the future.

上原等はこの実験に対して見方を変えてきた。
うえはらららはこのジッケンにタイしてみかたをかえてきた。
Uehara et al. came to change their viewpoint regarding this experiment.

溶液のアルカリ性を示すためにフェノールフタレインを使ってきた。
ヨウエキのアルカリセイをしめすためにフェノールフタレインをつかってきた。
To indicate the alkalinity of a solution, phenolphthalein has come to be [increasingly] used [and continues to be used].

気体のあわが水とともに流れていく。
キタイのあわがみずとともにながれていく。
The gas bubbles flow along with the water [and will continue to do so].

溶液を熱すると、炭酸ナトリウムが溶けていく。
ヨウエキをネッすると、タンサンナトリウムがとけていく。
When we heat the solution, the sodium carbonate gradually dissolves.

酸とアルカリの反応においては、pHが変わっていく。
サンとアルカリのハンノウにおいては、pHがかわっていく。
In an acid-base reaction, the pH continually changes.

In the ...ておく construction the main idea is that some action is being performed or something is being set aside, either permanently or with the idea of future use or planned action. Normally such ideas are not made explicit in English and hence it is often appropriate to omit ...ておく in translation.

水に炭酸水素カリウムを溶かしておく。
みずにタンサンスイソカリウムをとかしておく。
We dissolve the potassium bicarbonate in the water [for later use].

In the ...てみる construction, it is implied that some action is attempted with the idea of seeing what happens next. Here again it may not be necessary to translate this into English, since this idea is often not expressed explicitly in our language. "To try ...ing" is sometimes an appropriate translation.

つぎに高圧で溶液を熱してみた。
つぎにコウアツでヨウエキをネッしてみた。
Next we tried heating the solution at high pressure.

In the ...てしまう construction, the emphasis is on the fact that an action is completed. Once more, explicit translation into English may not be called for.

水酸化ナトリウムを全部使ってしまった。
スイサンカナトリウムをゼンブつかってしまった。
[We] used [up] all the sodium hydroxide.

9.4 The Conjunctive Form of Verbs

For ru-verbs the conjunctive is identical to the stem of the verb (obtained by dropping the る ending of the dictionary form). For xu-verbs the conjunctive is identical to the xi-base (obtained by replacing the 'xu' of the dictionary form by 'xi'). The negative conjunctive for all verbs is obtained by replacing the い of the present negative by く. There is a second negative conjunctive form — generally regarded as a literary form — which is obtained by replacing the ない of the present negative by ず. Here are examples of the conjunctive forms:

	Present Affirmative	Conjunctive Affirmative	Present Negative	Conjunctive なく-Form	Negative ず-Form
ru-verbs					
to determine	定める	定め	定めない	定めなく	定めず
to use	用いる	用い	用いない	用いなく	用いず
xu-verbs					
to take out	出す	出し	出さない	出さなく	出さず
to possess	もつ	もち	もたない	もたなく	もたず
to become	なる	なり	ならない	ならなく	ならず
to perform	行う	行い	行わない	行わなく	行わず
to move	動く	動き	動かない	動かなく	動かず
to carry	運ぶ	運び	運ばない	運ばなく	運ばず
to pile up	積む	積み	積まない	積まなく	積まず
Irregular verbs					
to go	行く	行き	行かない	行かなく	行かず
to be	ある	あり	ない!	なく	あらず!
to do	する	し!	しない!	しなく	せず!
to come	くる	き!	こない!	こなく	こず
Verbs formed from KANJI followed by する, ずる, or じる					
to heat	熱する	熱し!	熱しない!	熱しなく	熱せず!
to arise	生じる or 生ずる	生じ	生じない	生じなく	生ぜず!

Note that 生じる, which is sometimes written as 生ずる, is an example of a verb that is in a state of transition. In some of its forms it behaves like an ru-verb (with forms like 生じない, 生じた, and 生じ), but in a few forms it behaves like a する verb with DAKUON (as in 生ぜず).

We should now point out one further irregularity of a different sort. The verb いる has the affirmative conjunctive form い. Because this form is so short, it is replaced by おり, which is the affirmative conjunctive form of the more formal verb おる "to be."

Now that you know how the conjunctive forms are obtained, we can proceed to the explanation of the various uses of these forms.

a. The Joining of Two Clauses

One of the main uses of the conjunctive form is to join two clauses with "and" in the same way that the connective form is used. This is particularly common in the written language. For example:

炭酸水素カリウムを溶かし、溶液を熱する。
タンサンスイソカリウムをとかし、ヨウエキをネッする。
[We] dissolve the potassium bicarbonate in water and heat the solution.

この法則によると、気体の圧力は温度に比例し、体積に反比例する。
このホウソクによると、キタイのアツリョクはオンドにヒレイし、タイセキにハンピレイ
　　する。
According to this law the pressure of a gas is proportional to the temperature and inversely proportional to the volume.

このばあいには物体Aは運動せず、同時に物体Bは運動する。
このばあいにはブッタイAはウンドウせず、ドウジにブッタイBはウンドウする。
In this case body A does not move, and at the same time body B does.

アルゴンは無色の気体であり、フッ素は無色ではない。
アルゴンはムショクのキタイであり、フッソはムショクではない。
Argon is a colorless gas; fluorine is not [colorless].

Here again, as you become more expert at translating, you may in some instances find that "and" may be replaced by some more appropriate linking phrase such as "and next," "and as a result," or "and in this way."

The construction ...ずに is very similar in meaning to ...ないで, and can be translated as "without ...ing": 使わずに ＝使わないで (without using), 分解せずに ＝分解しないで (without decomposing), 溶けずに ＝溶けないで (without dissolving).

スラリー反応では固体は液体に溶けずに反応する。
スラリーハンノウではコタイはエキタイにとけずにハンノウする。
In a slurry reaction the solid reacts without dissolving in the liquid.

There is another verb form closely related to the ず form that is borrowed from the literary language. For all verbs it is formed by replacing ず by ざる; for example from せず we get せざる. We mention this form here solely because of its use in the phrase ...せざるを得ない[...せざるをえない] which means "cannot avoid doing ...," "is compelled to do ...," "has to do."

9-15

b. Formation of Compound Verbs

The second main use of the conjunctive form is to join together two verbs to make a "compound verb." There are many compound verbs that are formed from the conjunctive form of one verb followed by the dictionary form of a second verb. The resulting compound verb is then conjugated according to the endings that one would expect for the second verb. Some examples of compound verbs are

成る	+	立つ	=	成り立つ	to consist of; to be valid
できる	+	上がる	=	でき上がる	to be completed
流れる	+	出る	=	流れ出る	to flow out

実験装置ができ上がった。
ジッケンソウチができあがった。
The experimental apparatus has been completed.

A detailed discussion of compound verbs is given in Section 9.6.

c. Formation of Adjectives (with やすい and にくい)

By affixing やすい or にくい to the conjunctive forms we get adjectives with the meaning of "easy to ..." or "difficult to ...." For example:

このワープロは使いにくくて、間違いをしやすい。
このワープロはつかいにくくて、まちがいをしやすい。
This word processor is difficult to use, and it is easy to make errors [with it].

見ただけでこの関数は積分しやすくないことがわかる。
みただけでこのカンスウはセキブンしやすくないことがわかる。
Just by looking at it we see that this function is not easy to integrate.

d. The Conjunctive Used as a Noun

The conjunctive forms of some verbs are used as nouns. The following are examples of nouns made from verbs that you know:

はたらく	to work	はたらき	work(ing), action
動く	to move	動き	movement, motion
向く	to face, turn toward	向き	direction
違う	to differ	違い	difference
流れる	to flow	流れ	flow, current, stream
行う	to perform, do	行い	performance, action

You will encounter many more examples of conjunctives used as nouns in later chapters. In large dictionaries you will find entries for both the verb and the derived noun.

9.5 The Conjunctive Form of Adjectives (く)

For i-adjectives the conjunctive is obtained by replacing the い of the dictionary form by く. The negative conjunctive is made by replacing the い of the present-negative ending by く. For na- and no-adjectives the affirmative and negative conjunctives are obtained by replacing the な or の of the dictionary form by であり or でなく respectively.

We now illustrate the formation of the conjunctive forms of adjectives.

	Present Affirmative	Conjunctive Affirmative	Present Negative	Conjunctive Negative
i-adjectives				
difficult	むずかしい	むずかしく	むずかしくない	むずかしくなく
finely divided	細かい	細かく	細かくない	細かくなく
thin, slender	細い	細く	細くない	細くなく
hot	熱い	熱く	熱くない	熱くなく
good	よい	よく	よくない	よくなく
few	少ない	少なく	少なくない	少なくなく
na- and no-adjectives				
necessary	必要である	必要であり	必要でない	必要でなく
colorless	無色である	無色であり	無色でない	無色でなく
same	同じである	同じであり	同じでない	同じでなく
		or 同じく！		

The irregular conjunctive form 同じく is widely used. We now turn to a discussion of the use of the conjunctive forms of adjectives.

a. The Joining of Two Clauses

The conjunctive form is used to join two clauses together in the same way that the connective forms て and なくて are used.

これらのベクトルは大きさが等しく、向きが反対である。
これらのベクトルはおおきさがひとしく、むきがハンタイである。
These vectors have equal magnitude and are opposite in direction.

この有機化合物はアルコールに溶けにくく、ベンゼンに溶けやすい。
このユウキカゴウブツはアルコールにとけにくく、ベンゼンにとけやすい。
This organic compound dissolves with difficulty in alcohol, but it dissolves easily in benzene.

運動量の単位はエネルギーの単位と同じでなく、kg·m/sである。
ウンドウリョウのタンイはエネルギーのタンイとおなじでなく、kg·m/sである。
The units of momentum are not the same as the units of energy; they are kg·m/s.

h. The Conjunctive Form with する *and* なる

The conjunctive form of i-adjectives (and also the negative conjunctive forms of verbs ending in なく) can be followed by the verbs なる (to become, to turn out to be) and する (to make, to bring about) as these examples show:

熱くなる	to become hot
熱くする	to heat, to make hot
できなくなる	to become impossible
流れなくする	to arrange it so that something will not flow

For the na- and no-adjectives the な or の is replaced by に before adding する or なる. Therefore we have

重要になる	to become important
一定にする	to make constant
同じになる	to become the same, to turn out to be the same

Let us now look at some sentences in which these constructions appear.

はりがねは熱くなり、まわりの気体は熱くならない。
はりがねは<u>あつ</u>くなり、まわりの<u>キタイ</u>はあつくならない。
The wire becomes hot, [whereas] the surrounding gas does not.

これらの流速ベクトルは等しくなっていく。
これらの<u>リュウソク</u>ベクトルは<u>ひと</u>しくなっていく。
These flow-velocity vectors [gradually] become equal.

温度が高くなると、この重合体は溶かしやすくなる。
<u>オンド</u>がたかくなると、この<u>ジュウゴウタイ</u>はとかしやすくなる。
If the temperature becomes higher, this polymer becomes easier to dissolve.

<u>東京理科大学</u>の石原らが重合体の流れるガラス管を細くした時、実験データは大分よくなった。
<u>トウキョウリカダイガク</u>のいしはららが<u>ジュウゴウタイ</u>の<u>なが</u>れる<u>ガラスカン</u>を<u>ほそ</u>くした<u>とき</u>、<u>ジッケン</u>データは<u>ダイブ</u>よくなった。
When Ishihara et al. of Science University of Tokyo narrowed the glass tubes through which the polymer flowed, the experimental data improved considerably.

液体が流れなくなったとき、圧力と温度をはかった。
<u>エキタイ</u>が<u>なが</u>れなくなったとき、<u>アツリョク</u>と<u>オンド</u>をはかった。
When the liquid stopped flowing, [they] measured the pressure and temperature.

温度が上がると分子の運動が速くなる。
<u>オンド</u>が<u>あ</u>がると<u>ブンシ</u>の<u>ウンドウ</u>が<u>はや</u>くなる。
If the temperature increases, the molecular motion becomes faster.

9-18

ポリマー溶液の流れをかんがえる場合には、ポリマー分子量が重要になる。
ポリマーヨウエキのながれをかんがえるばあいには、ポリマーブンシリョウがジュウヨウ
　　　になる。
When we consider the flow of polymer solutions, molecular weight becomes important.

c. The Adverbial Use of the Conjunctive

The conjunctive form of an i-adjective can be used before any verb, and in this combination the adjective is translated as an adverb in English. For na- and no-adjectives, the adverbial form is obtained by replacing な or の by に.

バルブをあけたとき、水が速く出てきた。
バルブをあけたとき、みずがはやくでてきた。
When we opened the valve, the water came out rapidly.

大石らは実験により流れのパターンをよく理解した。
おおいしらはジッケンによりながれのパターンをよくリカイした。
Ooishi et al. well understood the flow patterns from the experiments.

大気中で酸化反応がよく生じることは理解しやすい。
タイキチュウでサンカハンノウがよくショウじることはリカイしやすい。
It is easy to understand the fact that oxidation reactions often occur in the atmosphere.

Note that the conjunctive of よい (good), which is よく, may mean "well" or "often, frequently."

d. The Conjunctive Used as a Noun

For a very small number of i-adjectives the conjunctive form can be used as a noun. In technical Japanese two of these are important.

近い	[ちかい]	near	近く	[ちかく]	vicinity, proximity
遠い	[とおい]	far, distant	遠く	[とおく]	a distant place

e. The Literary Negative Conjunctive

We conclude this section by mentioning that i-adjectives may also form a literary negative conjunctive by dropping the terminal い of the dictionary form and adding か らず. For example, from 少ない we get少なからず, which is synonymous with 少 なくなく.

9.6 Compound Verbs

In Section 9.4 we mentioned that adding other verbs to the xi-base of an xu-verb or the stem of an ru-verb can create a wide variety of compound verbs. Here we explore that point further, in order to assist you in vocabulary building and word recognition as you proceed with your study of Japanese.

Three problems arise with regard to compound verbs. First of all, you will discover that not all compound verbs can be found in dictionaries — even comprehensive ones. However, you will usually be able to figure out the meaning from the component parts. Second, sometimes the OKURIGANA of the first verb may be omitted so that 組み合わせる[くみあわせる] (to join together) is also written 組合わせる[くみあわせる]. And third, you may find one or both of the verbs in the compound written entirely with HIRAGANA. It just depends on the whim of the author. For example, 及ぼし合う[およぼしあう] (to exert on one another) may be written as 及ぼしあう, およぼし合う, or およぼしあう. When you have trouble deciphering such a compound, remember that the first verb is the xi-base (for xu-verbs) or the stem (for ru-verbs) and that the second will have some familiar inflectional ending.

Here we give a short list of compound verbs that arise in technical Japanese, arranging them by groups according to the second verb in the compound. The list includes some KANJI unfamiliar to you.

Verbs compounded with 合う have a "reciprocal" meaning:

及ぼし合う	[およぼしあう]	to exert on each other	[exert+meet]
強め合う	[つよめあう]	to reinforce each other	[strengthen+meet]
反発し合う	[ハンパツしあう]	to repel one another	[repel+meet]
重なり合う	[かさなりあう]	to overlap one another	[pile up+meet]

Verbs compounded with 合わせる usually contain the idea of "together":

組み合わせる	[くみあわせる]	to join together	[assemble+unite]
重ね合わせる	[かさねあわせる]	to superpose	[pile up+unite]
加え合わせる	[くわえあわせる]	to add together	[add+unite]

Verbs compounded with 出す have an "egressive" meaning:

作り出す	[つくりだす]	to produce	[make+put out]
流し出す	[ながしだす]	to rinse out	[flow+put out]
送り出す	[おくりだす]	to send forth	[send+put out]
導き出す	[みちびきだす]	to derive (an equation)	[lead+put out]
溶かし出す	[とかしだす]	to elute	[dissolve+put out]

Verbs compounded with 入れる or 込む[こむ] contain an "ingressive" idea:

押し入れる	[おしいれる]	to push in	[push+insert]
流れ込む	[ながれこむ]	to flow in	[flow+enter]

Verbs compounded with 回す[まわす] or 回る[まわる] often imply motion within a confined region of space or rotatory motion:

振り回す	[ふりまわす]	to swing around	[move back and forth +rotate]
動き回る	[うごきまわる]	to move around	[move+rotate]

Some other compound verbs:

書き表す	[かきあらわす]	to express {in writing}	[write+show]
言い表す	[いいあらわす]	to express {in speech}	[say+show]
結び付ける	[むすびつける]	to tie up, connect	[tie+attach]
書き直す	[かきなおす]	to rewrite	[write+correct]
押し縮める	[おしちぢめる]	to compress	[push+shrink]
押し当てる	[おしあてる]	to push against	[push+strike]

There are a few verbs that frequently appear as the second component of a compound verb and that have a very well-defined meaning. Some of these are

すぎる	【過ぎる】	to do something to excess, to overdo
なおす	【直す】	to redo and correct something
はじめる	【始める】	to begin doing something
つづける	【続ける】	to continue doing something
うる	【得る】	to be able to do something
つくす	【尽くす】	to do something exhaustively

As the second component of a compound verb these verbs are now generally written in HIRAGANA.

Here are some examples of compound verbs formed with these second components:

使いすぎる	[つかいすぎる]	to overuse
作りなおす	[つくりなおす]	to remake, rebuild
動きはじめる	[うごきはじめる]	to start moving
流れつづける	[ながれつづける]	to keep on flowing
解きうる	[ときうる]	to be able to solve

The verb 得る requires a special comment. When used as the independent verb "to obtain" it is pronounced える. When it appears as the second component of a compound verb, meaning "to be able," it is pronounced うる in the affirmative, but えない in the negative.

つくり出す	【作り出す】	to produce
みちびく	【導く】	to conduct
かける		to apply (pressure, voltage)
もつ		to have
結びつける	むすびつける	to connect
二分の一	ニブンのイチ	one-half
示量変数	ジリョウヘンスウ	extensive variable
下等な	カトウな	lower (plant, animal)
おちる		fall
水時計	みずどケイ	water clock
あな		hole
原理にする	ゲンリにする	take as a principle
いうまでもない		it goes without saying
時計方向	とケイホウコウ	clockwise direction
用いられている	もちいられている	is being used
しぼり流量計	しぼりリュウリョウケイ	orifice flowmeter
しぼる		to narrow, contract in area
計れない	はかれない	cannot measure
見えるようにする	みえるようにする	to make something visible
...が...しないようにする		so that ... does not ...
ます		a container (for measuring)

EXERCISES

Ex 9.1 Matching Japanese and English technical terms

(a) Simple JUKUGO

管理( )	1. all
結合( )	2. bond
原色( )	3. center of gravity
原則( )	4. colorless
向上( )	5. decomposition
細部( )	6. detail
重心( )	7. displacement
出力( )	8. improvement
全部( )	9. input
単位( )	10. law
単色の( )	11. management
定理( )	12. monochromatic
電位( )	13. output
入力( )	14. part
部分( )	15. potential
分解( )	16. primary color
変位( )	17. principle
法則( )	18. rational
無色の( )	19. theorem
有理( )	20. unit

(b) JUKUGO with prefixes and suffixes

結合水( )	1. bound water
使用法( )	2. directions for use
全色性の( )	3. effluent
電子管( )	4. electron tube
熱機関( )	5. heat engine
有理化( )	6. heat of solution
溶解度積( )	7. lysogenic
溶解熱( )	8. panchromatic
溶原性の( )	9. rationalized
溶出液( )	10. solubility product

(c) Measuring devices

圧力計( )	1. altimeter
温度計( )	2. barometer
気圧計( )	3. flowmeter
高度計( )	4. pressure gauge
速度計( )	5. speedometer
時計( )	6. thermometer
流量計( )	7. watch

Ex 9.2 Matching Japanese technical terms and definitions

You began this kind of exercise in Chapter 8 and became familiar with the use of もの and こと. You will continue to have such exercises throughout the book in order to become familiar with modifying clauses. Remember to work back from the noun. For example, in 一点[イッテン = a single point]に向かってはたらく力, work back from 力.

力	forces
はたらく力	forces that act
一点[イッテン]に向かってはたらく力	forces that act toward a single point

However, when a series of clauses precede the noun modified, you may have to jump back to the first clause. This is especially true when one of the clauses ends in で, where で is the conjunctive form of である. For example, in 原子番号[バンゴウ = number]が同じで原子量が違う元素, you should do so.

元素　elements
原子番号[バンゴウ]が同じ元素　elements having the same atomic number
原子番号が同じで原子量が違う元素　elements having the same atomic number and differing atomic weights

圧力計(　)　1. 物理学的、化学的方法を用いて生物体をまなぶこと。
運動量(　)　2. 細菌[サイキン＝bacteria]がバクテリオファージをつくり
解重合(　)　　出すこと。
向流(　)　3. 一原子からなる分子。
時定数(　)　4. 単一元素からなる物質。
生理学(　)　5. 一点に向かってはたらく力。
単体(　)　6. 流体の流量を計るもの。
単原子分子(　)　7. 原子番号が同じで原子量が違う元素。
中心力(　)　8. 二流体間で熱や物質の移動[イドウ＝transport]を行うと
電解質(　)　　き、二流体が反対方向に流れること。
同位体(　)　9. 気体または流体の圧力を計るもの。
等速度運動(　)　10. 液体と固体からなる溶液では固体のこと。
溶原性(　)　11. 水溶液にしたときイオン化して電流をみちびく化合物。
溶質(　)　12. 一定の電位差[サ＝difference]をかけてから定常[テイジョ
溶出(　)　　ウ＝steady]電流の(1－1/e)倍[バイ＝times]になるまでの時
流量計(　)　　間。
　　13. 重合体から単量体になる反応。
　　14. クロマトグラフィーで成分を固定相[ソウ＝phase]から溶
　　　かし出すこと。
　　15. 速度が一定の運動。
　　16. 物質の質量と速度との積。

Ex 9.3 True or false statements

T F　1. 水素と酸素は無色の気体ではない。
T F　2. メタンは有機化合物である。
T F　3. セコンドは速度の単位である。
T F　4. 運動は動くことである。
T F　5. 二酸化炭素の分子は単原子分子ではない。
T F　6. 溶けている物質は溶質という。
T F　7. 方向と大きさをもつ量はベクトル量という。
T F　8. 化学の実験でゴム管もガラス管もよく使う。
T F　9. 量子力学によって化学結合を理解することができる。
T F 10. 高度計を使用して時間を計ることができる。
T F 11. ボイルの法則を固体に応用してもよい。
T F 12. 熱力学は物理学の一部である。

ＴＦ 13. 一定の圧力差[サ]でいろいろのガラス管の中を流体が流れている実験において、細いガラス管を使う時には流量が大きくなる。
ＴＦ 14. dx/dt = 1/t という式の解は x = lnt + C である。
ＴＦ 15. 溶液の一部を熱していくと、溶液全部が熱くなる。
ＴＦ 16. 出力があると入力もある。
ＴＦ 17. 立方体の重心はその中心ではない。
ＴＦ 18. 気圧計は圧力計の一つである。

Ex 9.4 Translate the following sentences

1. 実験を行ってからコンピュータを使ってデータベースに実験データを入力した。
2. 動物が水の方に向かってからその方向へ動いた。
3. 水酸化ナトリウムの上に水を注いでから、それを溶かして、水酸化ナトリウムの水溶液ができた。
4. 水酸化カルシウムを水に溶かしてみたが、全部が溶けなかった。
5. ビーカーの中に水を流し、溶けなかった水酸化カルシウムを流し出した。
6. このガラス管は細くて高分子流体が流れにくい。
7. ストップウォッチを使用すると、時間が計りやすく反応速度が定めやすくなる。
8. スモッグにおいてのオゾンと有機化合物との反応は結びつけにくく、それらの関係は解きやすくはない。
9. 二酸化炭素は有機化合物ではなく、無機化合物である。
10. フェノールフタレイン[phenolphthalein]はアルカリ性の水溶液においては無色ではなく、ピンク色である。
11. 円運動[エンウンドウ = circular motion]で動いている物体に向心力がはたらくとき、物体の動いている方向でなく必ずその運動の中心に向かってはたらく。
12. 実験をしないで、定理と原理だけによって法則を立ててみることは必ずしも合理的ではない。
13. ボルトは電流の単位でなく、電位の単位である。アンペアが電流の単位である。
14. 化学反応の全部が発熱反応ではないが、その大部分がそうである。

Ex 9.5 Read the following essays for comprehension

1. 物体の質量mと速度vとの積を運動量という。力学においてベクトルを使って運動量を表す時、その向きは速度ベクトルの向きと同じく、大きさは速度ベクトルの大きさのm倍[バイ = times]である。物体の運動のエネルギーを表すとき、運動エネルギーを用いるが、それは運動量と速度とのスカラー積の二分の一と同一である。

2. 水に電位差[サ = difference]をかけても電流は流れない。それはイオン化している水の分子数が少ないからである。電流が流れるためには水の中に電気を運んでいくものがなくてはならない。いま、水に水酸化ナトリウムのような無機化合物を溶かすと、電流が流れるようになる。それは無機化合物は電解質で、水に溶解したときイオンに分解してそのイオンが電気を運んでいくからである。

3. 化学熱力学において部分モル量は溶液の性質を理解するために重要な物理化学的な量である。溶液において成分の量をそれぞれ $n_1, n_2, ...$ モルとし、示量変数の一つ(体積 V、エンタルピー H など)を X とするとき、$(\partial X/\partial n_i)$ を部分モル量という。

4. 下等な動物では酸素の物理的溶解のみで生きることができるが、大部分の動物は大量の酸素を必要とするので、化学的溶解を用いる。このために血液[ケツエキ = blood]色素[hemochrome]を有する。血液[ケツエキ]色素は酸素の分圧が高い体の部分で酸素と結合して、血管[ケッカン = blood vessels]の細かい毛細管[モウサイカン = capillaries]まで結合酸素を運んでいき、そこで酸素の分圧が高くない体の部分に酸素を出す。

5. 物理学において物体の運動に関する法則を定めるために、時間を計ることが必要である。例えば、ガリレオはおちる物体の速度と時間との関係を定めるのに、水時計を使った。水時計では水が一定の速度であなから流れ出て、その量を量ることができる。この量が時間に比例することを原理にして、ガリレオはおちる物体の速度と時間との関係を見いだした。ガリレオの時から時計が向上してきたことはいうまでもない。例えばいまはクォーツ[quartz]の時計を使用する。クォーツの時計の中にはいわゆるディジタル時計があり、その表示はいわゆる時計方向を示していない。

6. 同じ元素からなる分子は必ずしも全部が同じではない。ある元素には同位体がある。同位体は同じ化学的性質をもっている。しかし違った原子量をもつ原子である。例えば、ふつうの酸素中には質量数16[ジュウロク]、17[ジュウシチ]、および18[ジュウハチ]をもつ原子がある。同位体は同素体とは違う。同素体というのは同一の元素の異なる[ことなる = to differ]単体である。例えば、オゾンは大気中の酸素二原子分子が原子に分解して、その一原子が酸素二原子分子と結合して生ずる酸素の同素体である。またオゾンの化学的性質は酸素二原子分子のそれと大分違う。

Ex 9.6 Translate the following essay

　水力発電で発電機を動かす時には水の流量を計ることが必要である。管中を流れる流体の流量を計るために流量計を使用する。多く用いられてい

中を流れる流体の流量を計るために流量計を使用する。多く用いられているしぼり流量計では、管の一部の面積を小さくしぼっておいて、流体がこの細くしぼった部分を流れる時の圧力変化を計り、ベルヌーイの定理に質量一定の法則を結び合わせて解いて、流量や管の中心部における流速を定める。流れが速くて流管が時間的に変動するときにはよく計れないので、色素をとかして流管の運動が見えるようにし、流速を下げて流管が変動しないようにして計る。体積流量計では単位時間に管中を流れる流体を全部ますに向かって流出させその体積を計る。

TRANSLATIONS

Ex 9.4 Sentences

1. After doing the experiments, we used a computer and inputted the experimental data into a data base.
2. The animal, after facing toward the water, moved in that direction.
3. After water was poured on the sodium hydroxide, it was dissolved, and an aqueous solution of sodium hydroxide resulted.
4. We tried dissolving calcium hydroxide in water, but it did not all dissolve.
5. We flushed the inside of the beaker with water and flushed out the undissolved calcium hydroxide.
6. This glass tube is narrow, and the macromolecular fluid does not flow easily [through it].
7. If a stopwatch is used, time is easily measured and the reaction velocity is readily determined.
8. It is difficult to connect the reactions of ozone with organic compounds in smog, and it is not easy to resolve their relationships.
9. Carbon dioxide is not an organic compound; it is an inorganic compound.
10. In an alkaline aqueous solution phenolphthalein is not colorless; it is pink.
11. When a centripetal force acts on a moving body in circular motion, it always acts toward the center of motion, not in the direction in which the body is moving.
12. It is not necessarily rational to try to set up laws based only on theorems and principles, without performing experiments.
13. Volts are not units of electric current; they are units of [electric] potential. Amperes are the units of electric current.
14. Not all chemical reactions are exothermic [reactions], but the greater part [of them] are [such].

When electric generators are driven in hydroelectric power generation, it is necessary to measure the amount of water flowing. In measuring the amount of fluid flowing through a pipe, a flow meter is used. With the orifice flow meters widely used, the area in one part of the pipe is contracted to a small [size], and the pressure change when the fluid flows through the narrowly contracted part is measured; then, combining the law of constant mass flow with Bernoulli's theorem and solving, we determine the flow and the flow rate in the central part of the pipe. When the flow is rapid and the flow tubes fluctuate with time, [we] cannot measure [the flow rate] well; therefore, we dissolve a pigment in the fluid, making the flow tubes visible, lower the flow velocity so that the motions of the flow tubes do not fluctuate, and then measure [the rate]. With a volumetric flow meter, we direct the [flow] toward a container and make all of the fluid that flows through the pipe in unit time flow [out] [into it] , and then measure its volume.

| 塩 | エン | salt |
| | しお | salt |

| 果 | カ | fruit |
| | は(たす) | to accomplish |

加	カ	addition, increase
	くわ(える)	to add, include
	くわ(わる)	to increase

起	キ	occurring; initiation
	お(こす)	to generate, initiate
	お(こる)	to happen, occur

| 交 | コウ | intersecting; exchanging |
| | まじ(わる) | to intersect |

光	コウ	light
	ひかり	light
	ひか(る)	to shine, glitter

| 考 | コウ | thought, consideration |
| | かんが(える) | to think, consider |

| 作 | サ; サク | making, building |
| | つく(る) | to make, build |

次	ジ	order; next
	つぎ(の)	next, the following
	つ(ぐ)	to come after, follow

場	ジョウ	place
	ば	place; occasion
	-ば	field {electric; force}

| 振 | シン | vibration |
| | ふ(る) | to swing, vibrate |

| 線 | セン | line; wire |

| 相 | ソウ | phase |
| | あい- | each other |

増	ゾウ	increase
	ふ(やす)	to increase
	ふ(える)	to increase
	ま(す)	to increase

| 測 | ソク | measurement |
| | はか(る) | to measure |

| 置 | チ | place, location |
| | お(く) | to put, place |

長	チョウ	length
	-チョウ	head (of)
	なが(い)	long
	なが(さ)	length

直	チョク	straight; direct
	なお(す)	to mend; to correct
	なお(る)	to get well

| 点 | テン | point; dot |

平	ヘイ	horizontal; flat
	たい(ら)(な)	horizontal; flat
	ひら(たい)	flat

塩

塩素	エンソ	chlorine
塩素化	エンソカ	chlorination
塩素水	エンソスイ	chlorine water
塩化ナトリウム	エンカナトリウム	sodium chloride
塩酸	エンサン	hydrochloric acid
塩化水素	エンカスイソ	hydrogen chloride
塩化物	エンカブツ	chloride
塩素酸塩	エンソサンエン	chlorate
リン酸塩	リンサンエン	phosphate
ホウ酸塩	ホウサンエン	borate

果

結果	ケッカ	result
果実	カジツ	fruit
果実学	カジツガク	carpology

加

加圧する	カアツする	to pressurize
加熱する	カネツする	to heat
加工する	カコウする	to process, treat, work upon
加速度	カソクド	acceleration
加速電圧	カソクデンアツ	accelerating voltage
加水分解	カスイブンカイ	hydrolysis

起

起電力	キデンリョク	electromotive force
起振力	キシンリョク	vibromotive force
起重機	キジュウキ	crane
起動力	キドウリョク	motive power

交

交流	コウリュウ	alternating current
交点	コウテン	point of intersection, node
直交する	チョッコウする	to intersect at right angles
相交わる	あいまじわる	to intersect each other

光

光電気	コウデンキ	photoelectricity
光電子	コウデンシ	photoelectron

10-2

光電管	コウデンカン	photoelectric tube
光子	コウシ	photon
光学的高温計	コウガクテキコウオンケイ	optical pyrometer
光高温計	ひかりコウオンケイ	optical pyrometer
光速度	コウソクド	velocity of light
光起電力	コウキデンリョク	photoelectromotive force
光化学的な	コウカガクテキな	photochemical
光分解	コウブンカイ	photolysis
光線	コウセン	light ray
光合成	コウゴウセイ	photosynthesis
光学	コウガク	optics
光度	コウド	luminous intensity

考

考えに入れる	かんがえにいれる	to take into consideration
考え方	かんがえかた	way of thinking
考え直す	かんがえなおす	to rethink

作

作動-	サドウ	working
作用-	サヨウ	working
動作-	ドウサ	working
作動シリンダ	サドウシリンダ	working cylinder
作用高さ	サヨウたかさ	working depth
動作時間	ドウサジカン	working time
動作流体	ドウサリュウタイ	working fluid
動作電流	ドウサデンリュウ	working (operating) current
作動させる	サドウさせる	to run, operate
作用	サヨウ	action
反作用	ハンサヨウ	reaction
作物	サクモツ {N.B. モツ, not ブツ}	crops
作り直す	つくりなおす	to remake, rebuild

次

次元	ジゲン	dimension
無次元	ムジゲン	dimensionless
二次電子	ニジデンシ	secondary electron
二次反応	ニジハンノウ	second-order reaction

場

場合	ばあい	case, occasion
立場	たちば	standpoint

電場	デンば	electric field
力場	リキば	force field
ベクトル場	ベクトルば	vector field

振

単振り子	タンふりこ	simple pendulum
振動	シンドウ	oscillation, vibration
振動子	シンドウシ	oscillator
振動数	シンドウスウ	frequency
振動量子数	シンドウリョウシスウ	vibrational quantum number
起振力	キシンリョク	vibromotive force

線

直線	チョクセン	straight line
線積分	センセキブン	line integral
線分	センブン	line segment
電線	デンセン	electric wire
電線管	デンセンカン	(electrical) conduit
流線	リュウセン	streamline
法線応力	ホウセンオウリョク	normal stress

相

気相	キソウ	vapor phase
液相	エキソウ	liquid phase
固相	コソウ	solid phase
二相流	ニソウリュウ	two-phase flow
位相速度	イソウソクド	phase velocity
相同の	ソウドウの	homologous
相違	ソウイ	difference
相違点	ソウイテン	points of difference
相関関係	ソウカンカンケイ	correlation
相対性原理	ソウタイセイゲンリ	principle of relativity
相対運動	ソウタイウンドウ	relative motion
相等しい	あいひとしい	to equal each other

増

増大	ゾウダイ	increase
増加	ゾウカ	increase

測

測定	ソクテイ	measurement
測光単位	ソッコウタンイ	photometric unit

測面法	ソクメンホウ		planimetry
測面計	ソクメンケイ		planimeter
測色計	ソクショクケイ		colorimeter
測量学	ソクリョウガク		surveying
比重測定法	ヒジュウソクテイホウ		method for measuring specific gravity

置

位置	イチ	location
位置エネルギー	イチエネルギー	potential energy
位置ベクトル	イチベクトル	position vector

長

長時間	チョウジカン	long time
成長する	セイチョウする	to grow
部長	ブチョウ	department head; dean
細長い	ほそながい	long and slender

直

直線	チョクセン	straight line
直流	チョクリュウ	direct current
直結する	チョッケツする	to connect directly
直交する	チョッコウする	to intersect at right angles
考え直す	かんがえなおす	to rethink
作り直す	つくりなおす	to remake, rebuild

点

相違点	ソウイテン	points of difference
原点	ゲンテン	origin (of coordinates)
中点	チュウテン	mid-point
交点	コウテン	point of intersection, node
点線	テンセン	dotted line

平

1平方キロ	イチヘイホウキロ	one square kilometer
平行な	ヘイコウな	parallel
平行線	ヘイコウセン	parallel lines
平面	ヘイメン	plane surface
水平面	スイヘイメン	horizontal plane

10

Provisional and Conditional Forms

This chapter is primarily concerned with clauses that begin with the word "if" in English. There are four main ways that "if" clauses are expressed in Japanese: use of the particle と as discussed in Section 7.5e; use of the "provisional" form, ending in ば for verbs and ければ for adjectives; use of なら(ば) after the present or past forms; and use of the "conditional" form, ending in たら for verbs and かったら for adjectives. In technical writing the use of the particle と and the use of the provisional form are by far the most important. Furthermore, the provisional is used in several common expressions. The material in the first three sections should be mastered thoroughly; the next two sections are included for completeness. You will find that the provisional and conditional forms are especially easy to learn.

A final section on transitive-intransitive pairs is appended for help in vocabulary building and word recognition.

10.1 The Provisional Form of Verbs (ば)

The provisional is formed by adding the ending ば to the xe-base of an xu-verb and to the re-base of an ru-verb. In both classes (and also for irregular verbs) the required base is formed by replacing the last syllable of the dictionary form by the corresponding syllable in the え column of the HIRAGANA table. The provisional negative is obtained by replacing the い of the present-negative ending by ければ.

	Present Affirmative	Provisional Affirmative	Present Negative	Provisional Negative
ru-verbs				
to consider	考える	考えれば	考えない	考えなければ
to use	用いる	用いれば	用いない	用いなければ
xu-verbs				
to increase	増す	増せば	増さない	増さなければ
to be valid	成り立つ	成り立てば	成り立たない	成り立たなければ
to make	作る	作れば	作らない	作らなければ
to be in error	間違う	間違えば	間違わない	間違わなければ
to place	置く	置けば	置かない	置かなければ
to smell (*v.t.*)	かぐ	かげば	かがない	かがなければ
to tie	結ぶ	結べば	結ばない	結ばなければ
to contain	含む	含めば	含まない	含まなければ
Irregular verbs				
to go	行く	行けば	行かない	行かなければ
to be	ある	あれば	ない！	なければ
to do	する	すれば	しない！	しなければ
to come	くる	くれば	こない！	こなければ

A clause ending in the provisional is translated by "if."

気相の温度が高くなれば、反応速度が増加する。
キソウのオンドがたかくなれば、ハンノウソクドがゾウカする。
If the temperature of the gas phase becomes higher, the reaction velocity increases.

物体が原点から上向きに動けば、その位置エネルギーは増加する。
ブッタイがゲンテンからうわむきにうごけば、そのイチエネルギーはゾウカする。
If the body moves upward from the origin, its potential energy increases.

細長いガラス管を使わなければ、流量計でその液体の速度を測定することはできない。
ほそながいガラスカンをつかわなければ、リュウリョウケイでそのエキタイのソクドをソ
　　クテイすることはできない。
You cannot measure the velocity of that liquid by means of a flow meter if you do not use a long, thin
　　glass tube.

10.2 The Provisional Form of Adjectives (ければ)

For i-adjectives the provisional is formed by replacing the terminal い of the dictionary form by ければ. For na- and no-adjectives the な or の of the dictionary form is replaced by であれば to get the provisional. The provisional negative is obtained by replacing the い of the present-negative ending by ければ.

	Present Affirmative	Provisional Affirmative	Present Negative	Provisional Negative
i-adjectives				
long	長い	長ければ	長くない	長くなければ
equal	等しい	等しければ	等しくない	等しくなければ
heavy	重い	重ければ	重くない	重くなければ
hot	熱い	熱ければ	熱くない	熱くなければ
na- and no-adjectives				
parallel	平行である	平行であれば	平行でない	平行でなければ
horizontal	水平である	水平であれば	水平でない	水平でなければ
organic	有機である	有機であれば	有機でない	有機でなければ
inorganic	無機である	無機であれば	無機でない	無機でなければ
same	同じである	同じであれば	同じでない	同じでなければ

Just as for verbs, the provisional forms of adjectives are translated by an "if clause" in English. The following sentences illustrate their use:

圧力が高くなければ、ガラスのリアクターを使ってもよい。
アツリョクがたかくなければ、ガラスのリアクターをつかってもよい。
If the pressure is not high, we may use a glass reactor.

この化合物の分子量があまり大きければ、次にのべる実験でそのエンタルピーを測定する
　　ことができない。
このカゴウブツのブンシリョウがあまりおおきければ、つぎにのべるジッケンでそのエン
　　タルピーをソクテイすることができない。
If the molecular weights of these compounds are too high, their enthalpies cannot be measured in the
　　experiment we discuss next.

In the first sentence 高くなければ may also be replaced by the expression 高くない
かぎり. The word かぎり【限り】 literally means "limit." Following an affirmative
verb it means "insofar as," and after a negative verb it means "unless+affirmative verb."
Hence われわれのしっているかぎり means "insofar as we know," and 液体を加
熱しないかぎり means "unless we heat the liquid," or "as long as we do not heat the
liquid."

10.3 Constructions Made with the Provisional
　　　Several common constructions are made with the provisional. In the first one the
provisional negative of verbs is followed by ならない (or, less commonly, いけな
い) to mean "must." Sometimes ...なければならない is shortened to ...ねばなら
ない.

この場合には応力テンソルの成分を定めなければならない。
このばあいにはオウリョクテンソルのセイブンをさだめなければならない。
In this case we must determine the components of the stress tensor.

この場合には分子間力を考えに入れなければならない。
この<u>ばあい</u>には<u>ブンシカンリョク</u>を<u>かんが</u>えに<u>い</u>れなければならない。
In this case we have to take into account the intermolecular forces.

In the next construction the provisional is followed by よい (meaning literally "It is good"). This conveys the idea of "It is best to ..." or "We (only) have to ..." or "All we (have to) do is ...."

物体にはたらく力を定めるには、物体上の応力をその全表面にわたって積分すればよい。
<u>ブッタイ</u>にはたらく<u>ちから</u>を<u>さだ</u>めるには、<u>ブッタイジョウ</u>の<u>オウリョク</u>をその<u>ゼンヒョウメン</u>にわたって<u>セキブン</u>すればよい。
To determine the force acting on the body, we only have to integrate the stress on the body over its entire surface.

この場合Sの二つの表面にはたらく圧力のつりあいだけを考えればよく、これらは相等しい。
この<u>ばあい</u>Sの<u>ふた</u>つの<u>ヒョウメン</u>にはたらく<u>アツリョク</u>のつりあいだけを<u>かんが</u>えればよく、これらは<u>あいひと</u>しい。
In this case we have to consider only the balancing of the pressures acting on the two surfaces of S, and these are equal to each other.

この式を解くには、次のように考えればよい。
この<u>シキ</u>を<u>と</u>くには、<u>つぎ</u>のように<u>かんが</u>えればよい。
To solve this equation it is best to think in the following way.

Another use for the provisional is in expressions that correspond to "the more ... the more ..." in English. This makes use of the noun ほど meaning "extent."

長ければ長いほどよい。
<u>なが</u>ければ<u>なが</u>いほどよい。
The longer it is, the better. {Lit.: If it is long, to the extent that it is long, it is good.}

溶液を加熱すればするほど、反応速度が増加していく。
<u>ヨウエキ</u>を<u>カネツ</u>すればするほど、<u>ハンノウソクド</u>が<u>ゾウカ</u>していく。
The more one heats the solution, the more the reaction velocity increases.

Among scientific writers there are two common constructions: noun+と+すれば (if we let ...) and verb+と+すれば (if we suppose that ...).

いま電子が電場の中で動いているとすれば、それにはたらく力を次のように定めることができる。
いま<u>デンシ</u>が<u>デン</u>ばの<u>なか</u>で<u>うご</u>いているとすれば、それにはたらく<u>ちから</u>を<u>つぎ</u>のように<u>さだ</u>めることができる。
Now if we suppose that the electron is moving in an electric field, we can determine the force acting on it as follows.

一直線上を速度vで運動している質量mの物体に力Fが作用して時間tの間に速度がuに変わっ
たとすれば、F＝maという式は次のようにかき表し得る: [m(u-v)]/t＝F。
<u>イッチョクセンジョウ</u>を<u>ソクド</u>vで<u>ウンドウ</u>している<u>シツリョウ</u>mの<u>ブッタイ</u>に<u>ちから</u>Fが
<u>サヨウ</u>して<u>ジカン</u>tのあいだに<u>ソクド</u>がuに<u>かわ</u>ったとすれば、F＝maという<u>シキ</u>は
<u>つぎ</u>のようにかき<u>あらわ</u>し<u>う</u>る: [m(u-v)]/t＝F。
If we suppose that a force F acts on a body of mass m, moving on a straight line with velocity v, and
as a result its velocity has changed to u during a time interval t, then we can express the equation
F = ma in the following way: [m(u-v)]/t = F.

一モルの気体については、その分子数をNとすれば、pV＝NkT＝RTとなる。この式でRは
ガス定数という。
<u>イチモル</u>の<u>キタイ</u>については、その<u>ブンシスウ</u>をNとすれば、pV＝NkT＝RTとなる。この
<u>シキ</u>でRは<u>ガステイスウ</u>という。
If we let N be the number of molecules in one mole of gas, then pV = NkT = RT. In this equation R
is (called) the gas constant.

There are some standard phrases involving the provisional that occur now and then in
technical writing. You might want to glance at these for future reference; some of them
use KANJI that you have not yet had. In the left column we give the form which you
are most apt to encounter.

いいかえれば...	【<u>言</u>い<u>換</u>えれば】	in other words ...
速度をvとすれば...	[ソクドをvとすれば]	if we let v be the velocity ...
簡単にいえば...	[カンタンにいえば]	in short ...
この結果によれば...	[このけっかによれば]	from these results ...
例えば...	[たとえば]	for example ...
なんとなれば...からである。	【<u>何</u>となれば...からである】	that is because ...

10.4 The Use of なら(ば)

In Chapter 8 you learned that the expression のである is often added at the end
of a sentence, meaning "it is a fact that" (or sometimes just to add some stylistic
variation). The provisional of this expression is のであれば, which means "if it is a
fact that," or simply "if." This phrase is now sometimes shortened to ならば or even
なら. When なら(ば) follows a verb or adjective, it can be translated simply as "if."
When なら(ば) follows a noun, it means "if it is" or "if they are." Here are some
examples of the use of なら(ば):

単振り子の振動があまり大きくならないならば、式(7)を用いてもよい。
<u>タン</u>ふりこの<u>シンドウ</u>があまり<u>おお</u>きくならないならば、<u>シキ</u>(7)を<u>もち</u>いてもよい。
If the oscillations of the simple pendulum do not become too large, we may use Eq. (7).

物体の運動が等速直線運動ならば、その変位xは時間tに比例するのである。

ブッタイのウンドウがトウソクチョクセンウンドウならば、そのヘンイxはジカンtにヒレ
　　　　イするのである。

If the motion of a body is uniform linear motion, its displacement x is proportional to the time t.

Do not confuse ならば ("if") with なれば ("if it becomes"); the latter is the provisional form of the verb なる.

The following sentences illustrate two idiomatic uses of なら that occur occasionally:

必要なら塩化カリウムのかわりに塩化ナトリウムを使ってもよい。

ヒツヨウならエンカカリウムのかわりにエンカナトリウムをつかってもよい。

If necessary you may use sodium chloride instead of potassium chloride.

なぜなら(ば)塩化ナトリウムも溶解度が高いからである。

なぜなら(ば)エンカナトリウムもヨウカイドがたかいからである。

That is because the solubility of sodium chloride is also high.

This last construction, なぜなら(ば)...からである is often used to add an explanation to the preceding sentence. This can be translated as "If [you ask] why, it's because ...." There are two other constructions with the same meaning: なんとなれば...からである and なぜかというと...からである. Even simpler is それは...からである. As an example we give

流体の中のあわの大きさは変化した。それは流体の温度が変化したからである。

リュウタイのなかのあわのおおきさはヘンカした。それはリュウタイのオンドがヘンカし
　　　　たからである。

The size of the bubbles in the fluid changed; that's because the fluid temperature changed.

Note that the first sentence gives the "result" and the second sentence gives the "reason." This order is the inverse of that encountered in Section 7.5b.

10.5 The Conditional Form of Verbs (たら) and Adjectives (かったら)

The conditional forms of all verbs and all adjectives, without exception, are made by adding ら to the past-tense forms, both the affirmative and the negative. A few examples for verbs and adjectives of the several categories will suffice:

	Present Affirmative	Past Affirmative	Conditional Affirmative	Past Negative	Conditional Negative
ru-verbs					
to add	加える	加えた	加えたら	加えなかった	加えなかったら
xu-verbs					
to shine	光る	光った	光ったら	光らなかった	光らなかったら
to correct	直す	直した	直したら	直さなかった	直さなかったら
Irregular verbs					
to do	する	した	したら	しなかった	しなかったら
to come	くる	きた	きたら	こなかった	こなかったら
to be	ある	あった	あったら	なかった	なかったら
i-adjectives					
long	長い	長かった	長かったら	長くなかった	長くなかったら
slender	細い	細かった	細かったら	細くなかった	細くなかったら
few	少ない	少なかった	少なかったら	少なくなかった	少なくなかったら
na-adjectives					
necessary	変な	変であった	変であったら	変でなかった	変でなかったら

In technical writing the meaning of the conditional and that of the provisional are very nearly the same, so that clauses ending with a verb in the conditional can be translated by "if" clauses in English. Sometimes the conditional may express a bit more doubt than the provisional, and the conditional is normally used when expressing "if" clauses in the past. In the spoken language the conditional is used much more than the provisional, but in technical writing it is just the opposite. In fact, you will rarely encounter the conditional; when you do, it will be easy to recognize and easy to translate. In the spoken language the conditional has some uses other than "if" clauses, but they need not concern you here.

気体が出なくなったら、圧力を増さなければならない。
キタイがでなくなったら、アツリョクをまさなければならない。
If the gas stops coming out, you must increase the pressure.

You may occasionally come across the ...たら+よい construction, which is similar in meaning to provisional+よい. The conditional+よい construction may occur followed by か in rhetorical questions with the translation "What is the best way to ...?"

二原子分子の分子間ポテンシャルはどう考えたらよいか。
ニゲンシブンシのブンシカンポテンシャルはどうかんがえたらよいか。
What is the best way to think about the intermolecular potential for diatomic molecules?

To summarize, up to this point you have learned several types of clauses that can be translated as clauses beginning with "if" in English:

(1) Clauses ending with a verb or adjective plus と. Here と may sometimes mean "if" in the sense of "when(ever)."

(2) Clauses ending with a verb or adjective in the provisional form (ば). Here "if" may sometimes be replaced by "provided that."

(3) Clauses ending with a verb, adjective, or noun followed by なら(ば). Here ならば may mean "if it is true that" (after verbs and adjectives) or "if we focus our attention on" (before nouns).

(4) Clauses ending with a verb or adjective in the conditional form (たら).

Sometimes the last three types of clauses are introduced by the word もし. This word emphasizes the conditional meaning of the clause and alerts you to the "if" construction coming at the end of the clause.

10.6 Transitive-Intransitive Verb Pairs

You already know that one KANJI often serves as the stem for two related verbs: one transitive, the other intransitive. You also know that transitive verbs can take an object marked with を, and that they can occur in the ...てある construction discussed in Section 9.3.

In Japanese, transitive verbs are called 他動詞[タドウシ], and intransitive verbs are called 自動詞[ジドウシ]. In dictionaries, the abbreviations 他 and 自 are often used.

About one-third of the transitive-intransitive verb pairs have the following endings:

他 -xeru	自 -xaru

Here, 'xe' is any syllable from the え column of the KANA table, and 'xa' is the syllable in the あ column of the same row. Examples of transitive-intransitive pairs of this type are

定める	to determine	定まる	to be determined
上げる	to raise	上がる	to rise
変える	to change (something)	変わる	to change, become different

Note the (not altogether unexpected) irregular appearance of わ in the last pair. In the above listing the -xeru verb is always transitive and the -xaru verb is intransitive.

Another third of the transitive-intransitive pairs have the ending す for the transitive verb with some other ending for the intransitive verb. The following kinds of pairs will be encountered, as well as a few more:

他 -su	自 -ru or -reru
他 -xosu	自 -xu or -xiru
他 -xasu	自 -xu or -xiru or -xeru

Some specific examples of these verb pairs are

動かす	to move (something)	動く	to move
出す	to put out, take out	出る	to come out, appear
流す	to make (something) flow	流れる	to flow
直す	to correct	直る	to be mended, get well

Many of the remaining third of the transitive-intransitive verb pairs have this form:

他	-xeru	自	-xu
他	-xu	自	-xeru

Among these are

入れる	to insert	入る[いる]	to enter {as a suffix}
向ける	to turn (something) towards	向く	to turn towards
立てる	to erect	立つ	to stand up
くだく	to crush	くだける	to be crushed

We omit other, less frequently occurring combinations.

Normally these verb pairs do not present much of a problem, inasmuch as both members of the pair are generally given in the dictionary along with their meanings. In puzzling out some complicated verb endings, however, you will have to be careful to choose the correct member of the verb pair.

With regard to verbs formed by a KANGO followed by する, there is no way to know a priori whether the verb is transitive or intransitive. For example, the verb 運動する (to move) is intransitive, but 測定する (to measure) is transitive. Some verbs may be both: 液化する may be either intransitive (to become liquefied) or transitive (to liquefy [something]). Note that the intransitive KANGO+する verbs take させる when used transitively.

させる{causative of する}		to cause (an action)
作動させる	サドウさせる	to operate
なんの動きもない	なんのうごきもない	there is no motion whatever
どこかで		at some place
したがう		to obey (an equation); to follow (a method)
およぼす	【及ぼす】	to exert (a force)
およぼしかえす		exert (a force) in return
セシウム		cesium
アンチモン		antimony
きまる		to be determined
間違いない	まちがいない	to (certainly) not be wrong
もう一人	もうひとり	another person
もとにする		to take as a basis
くりかえす		to repeat
あとは{ato-wa}		after that
つるす		to suspend {e.g., from a hook}
ばね		spring
おもり		a (plumb) weight
結びつける	むすびつける	to (tie and) attach
変位させる	ヘンイさせる	to displace
はなす		to release
ロッシェル塩	ロッシェルエン	Rochelle salt
振動させる	シンドウさせる	to cause to oscillate
あらわれる	【現われる】	to appear, to become manifest

EXERCISES

Ex 10.1 Matching Japanese and English technical terms

(a) Force-related terms

加速電圧( )　1. acceleration voltage
起振力( )　　2. action
起電力( )　　3. electric field
起動力( )　　4. electromotive force
光起電力( )　5. force field
作用( )　　　6. motive force
電場( )　　　7. normal stress
反作用( )　　8. photoelectromotive force
法線応力( )　9. reaction
力場( )　　　10. vibromotive force

(b) Equipment-related terms

起重機( )　　　1. colorimeter
光学的高温計( )2. conduit
光電管( )　　　3. crane
振動子( )　　　4. electric wire
測色計( )　　　5. optical pyrometer
測面計( )　　　6. oscillator
単振り子( )　　7. photoelectric tube
電線( )　　　　8. planimeter
電線管( )　　　9. simple pendulum
動作流体( )　　10. working fluid

(c) Motion-related terms

位相速度( )　1. acceleration
加速度( )　　2. alternating current
光線( )　　　3. direct current
光速度( )　　4. frequency
交流( )　　　5. light ray
振動数( )　　6. phase velocity
相対運動( )　7. relative motion
直流( )　　　8. stream line
二相流( )　　9. two phase flow
流線( )　　　10. velocity of light

(d) Mathematics-related terms

位置ベクトル( )1. intersection, node
原点( )　　　2. line integral
交点( )　　　3. line segment
線積分( )　　4. mid-point
線分( )　　　5. origin
測面法( )　　6. parallel lines
測量学( )　　7. planimetry
中点( )　　　8. position vector
直線( )　　　9. straight line
平行線( )　　10. surveying

(e) Physics-related terms		(f) Chemistry-related terms	
液相( )	1. dimensionless	塩化水素( )	1. chlorate
気相( )	2. horizontal plane	塩化物( )	2. chloride
光学( )	3. liquid phase	塩酸( )	3. chlorination
光電気( )	4. luminous intensity	塩素( )	4. chlorine
光度( )	5. optics	塩素化( )	5. chlorine water
固相( )	6. photoelectricity	塩素酸塩( )	6. hydrochloric acid
水平面( )	7. photometric unit	塩素水( )	7. hydrogen chloride
相対性原理( )	8. principle of relativity	加水分解( )	8. hydrolysis
測光単位( )	9. solid phase	光合成( )	9. photolysis
比重( )	10. specific gravity	光子( )	10. photon
無次元( )	11. vapor phase	光分解( )	11. photosynthesis

Ex 10.2 Pronunciations and meanings of verbs and adjectives

Match the following verbs and adjectives with their English meanings and write the Japanese words in KANA. Use HIRAGANA for KUN readings and KATAKANA for ON readings.

相交わる	＿＿＿＿＿＿＿ ( )	1.	to connect directly with
相等しい	＿＿＿＿＿＿＿ ( )	2.	to decompose
加圧する	＿＿＿＿＿ ( )	3.	to be equal to each other
加熱する	＿＿＿＿ ( )	4.	to grow
考えに入れる	＿＿＿＿＿＿＿＿ ( )	5.	to heat
考え直す	＿＿＿＿＿＿ ( )	6.	to increase
作動させる	＿＿＿＿＿＿ ( )	7.	to intersect
測定する	＿＿＿＿＿＿ ( )	8.	to intersect at right angles
増加する	＿＿＿＿ ( )	9.	to measure
振動する	＿＿＿＿＿ ( )	10.	to operate, run
成長する	＿＿＿＿＿＿＿ ( )	11.	to pressurize
直結する	＿＿＿＿＿＿＿ ( )	12.	to remake
直交する	＿＿＿＿＿＿＿ ( )	13.	to rethink
作り直す	＿＿＿＿＿ ( )	14.	to take into consideration
分解する	＿＿＿＿＿ ( )	15.	to vibrate, oscillate

Ex 10.3 Verb and adjective forms

(a) Give the provisional affirmative and the provisional negative forms of the following verbs and adjectives.

1. 測る　　　　測＿＿　　　　　　　　測＿＿＿＿＿＿
2. 起こす　　　起＿＿＿＿　　　　　　起＿＿＿＿＿＿
3. 光る　　　　光＿＿　　　　　　　　光＿＿＿＿＿＿
4. 見る　　　　見＿＿　　　　　　　　見＿＿＿＿＿
5. ある　　　　あ＿＿　　　　　　　　＿＿＿＿＿
6. 測定する　　測定＿＿＿　　　　　　測定＿＿＿＿＿＿
7. 長い　　　　長＿＿＿　　　　　　　長＿＿＿＿＿＿
8. 少ない　　　少＿＿＿＿　　　　　　少＿＿＿＿＿＿＿
9. 小さい　　　小＿＿＿＿　　　　　　小＿＿＿＿＿＿＿
10. 同じ　　　　同＿＿＿＿＿＿　　　　同＿＿＿＿＿＿＿

(b) For each of the following verbs, write the forms corresponding to "need not" do ... and "must" do ....

1. 置く　　　　置かなくてもよい　　　　置かなければならない
2. 注ぐ　　　　注＿＿＿＿＿＿＿＿　　　注＿＿＿＿＿＿＿＿＿＿
3. 考える　　　考＿＿＿＿＿＿＿＿　　　考＿＿＿＿＿＿＿＿＿＿
4. 運動する　　運動＿＿＿＿＿＿＿＿　　運動＿＿＿＿＿＿＿＿＿＿
5. 出る　　　　出＿＿＿＿＿＿　　　　　出＿＿＿＿＿＿＿＿
6. 直す　　　　直＿＿＿＿＿＿＿　　　　直＿＿＿＿＿＿＿＿＿
7. 結ぶ　　　　結＿＿＿＿＿＿＿　　　　結＿＿＿＿＿＿＿＿＿

(c) For each of the verbs below, make the three other "if" forms as shown.

1. 光ると　　　光れば　　　　　　光るならば　　　　光ったら
2. 置くと　　　置＿＿　　　　　　置＿＿＿＿　　　　置＿＿＿
3. 測定すると　測定＿＿＿　　　　測定＿＿＿＿＿＿　測定＿＿＿
4. 考えると　　考＿＿＿　　　　　考＿＿＿＿＿　　　考＿＿＿
5. 出てくると　出＿＿＿＿　　　　出＿＿＿＿＿＿＿　出＿＿＿＿
6. 間違うと　　間違＿＿　　　　　間違＿＿＿＿　　　間違＿＿＿
7. 含むと　　　含＿＿　　　　　　含＿＿＿＿　　　　含＿＿＿

Ex 10.4 Translate the following sentences

1. 物体をその質量中心でナイフエッジの上に置けばモーメントは0である
から、なんの動きも起こることはない。
2. 単振り子が振動する場合振動する角度[カクド=angle]が大きくなけれ
ば振動数が一定で、等時性を示す。
3. カルノーサイクルにおいて、作動物質を理想[リソウ=ideal]気体と考え
れば熱量と温度との関係は $q = RT \log V_2/V_1$ という式によって定めるこ
とができる。
4. 液体を一定の圧力で加熱する場合、温度が増加してから一定になったと
すれば、気相もできてきたと考えることができる。
5. 同一物質の液相と気相ができているとき圧力は温度だけの関数である。
したがって、温度さえ測定すれば圧力は測定しなくてもそれをしること
ができる。
6. 一平面において二つの平行でない直線はどこか一点で相交わらなければ
ならない。
7. ある点における電場はその点に単位電気量を置いたときにその電気量に
はたらく力であり、ベクトル量である。
8. 点Aと点Bとの間で光速度を測定する場合には、点Aと点Bとの間の距離
[キョリ=distance]が長ければ長いほど結果がよい。

Ex 10.5 Read the following essays for comprehension

1. 塩素を水に溶かすと、塩素水ができる。この溶液において、塩素の一部
は次の反応式にしたがって水と作用する。$H_2O + Cl_2 \rightarrow HCl + HClO$。HClO
は次亜塩素酸[ジアエンソサン=hypochlorous acid]といい、塩酸と酸素に分
解しやすいので、塩素水ができてから時間が長ければ長いほど次亜塩素酸
[ジアエンソサン]の量は少なくなる。

2. ニュートンの法則によれば物体Aが物体Bに力をおよぼすとき、BはAに
必ず力をおよぼしかえす。これら二つの力は大きさが等しく、向きが反対
である。およぼす力は作用の力、およぼしかえす力を反作用の力とよび、
この法則を作用・反作用の法則とよぶことも多い。

3. 光電子は光によって起動する電子である。電子管に光電子を使用すれば、
これを光電管とよぶ。ある光電管にはセシウムとアンチモンの合金光電面
を用いる。光電子を起こす力は光起電力という。

4. 発電機には交流用と直流用の二つがあるが高電圧発電の場合は水力発電
でない限り[かぎり]交流であると考えれば間違いない。交流発電の場合起電

力の向きと大きさはサイン関数的に変わる。発電機にコイルを増すことによって、多相電流を作ることができる。

5．物体の運動はニュートンの運動法則、すなわち(質量m)×(加速度a) = 力によって定まる。したがって力のはたらいていない物体では、加速度は0でなければならない。そして加速度は0であるから、速度は一定でなければならない。

6．二人の人が物体の速度を同時に測る場合、その一人がもう一人に対して等速直線運動をしているとすれば、二人のそれぞれの測定の結果は違った大きさになる。しかし光速度を測る場合にはこれと違って二人のそれぞれの測定の結果は同一でなければならない。なぜかというと、アインシュタインの相対性原理によれば光速度を測定した結果はそれを測定した人の速度によらず一定でなければならないからである。これをアインシュタインの光速度一定の原理とよぶ。これはニュートン力学の考え方に対する大きな相違点である。

7．三角[サンカク = triangle]測量は次のように行う。平らな表面に二つの点AとBを定め、その間の距離[キョリ]を測る。次にAに立って∠CABを、Bに立って∠CBAを測れば一辺[イッペン = one side]と二角[カク = angle]がわかるから、ABに対するCの位置がきまる。次にACをもとにして、同じ方法で点Dの位置をきめる。この方法をくりかえせばABの距離を測るだけで、あとは角度[カクド]を測ることによってすべての点の位置、また点と点との間の距離が次々にきまっていく。

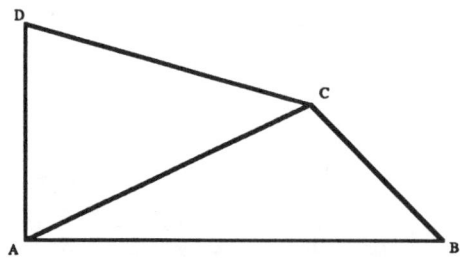

Ex 10.6 Translate the following essay

　重力場で固定点からつるした直線ばねにおもりを結びつけ、おもりに力を加えて下方に少し変位させてはなすと運動が起きる。この運動を振動という。振動の式を作るためには、時間と位置を測定する必要がある。位置測定、すなわち長さの測定には光学的方法を用いて、細かい長さも大きくして測り、実験結果の間違いを小さくする。固定点に加わる力はロッシェル塩等[など]を用いた圧電式圧力計で測ればよい。

おもりの質量を増せば振動数が小さくなり、ばねが上下に振動する時間は長くなる。これはおもりの質量が大きいと、バネの力の大きさは同じであっても、おもりを動かすのに長い時間を要するからである。次に、おもりの振動中、固定点を水平方向に振動させたと考えれば、おもりは直交する二つの方向の振動を合成した振動を行い、位相の違いに応じて色々の振動があらわれる。そして実験によってその色々の振動を表すことができる。

TRANSLATIONS

Ex 10.4 Sentences

1. If a body is placed on a knife edge at its center of mass, then because the moments are zero, no motion whatever occurs.
2. When a simple pendulum oscillates, if the angle [through which] it oscillates is not large, then the frequency is constant, and [it] displays isochronism.
3. In the Carnot cycle, if we consider the working substance to be an ideal gas, then the relation between the quantity of heat and the temperature can be determined by the equation $q = RT \log V_2/V_1$.
4. When heating a liquid at constant pressure, if we suppose that the temperature, after increasing, becomes constant, then we can consider that the vapor phase has (come to be) formed.
5. When liquid and gas phases of one and the same substance have been formed, the pressure is a function only of temperature. Consequently, if we measure only the temperature, we (can) know the pressure (even) without measuring it.
6. Two lines that are not parallel, [lying] in a single plane, must intersect at a point (somewhere).
7. The electrical field at a (certain) point is a vector quantity; it is the force that acts on a unit quantity of electricity when that amount of electricity is placed at that point.
8. When the velocity of light is measured between point A and point B, the longer the distance between point A and point B, the better the results.

Ex 10.6 Essay

If we attach a weight to a linear spring hanging from a fixed point in a gravitational field, then apply a force to the weight, displace it downwards and release it, motion occurs. This motion is called vibration. In order to construct an equation for [this] vibration, it is necessary to measure times and positions. For the measurement of position, that is, for measuring the length [of the spring], [we] measure [it] using an optical method, magnify even minute lengths, and [thus] reduce the errors in the experimental results. The force acting on the fixed point is best measured with a piezoelectric-type pressure gauge which uses a Rochelle salt (or some other similar substance).

If [we] increase the mass of the weight, the frequency becomes smaller, and the time [interval] during which the spring vibrates up and down becomes longer. The reason is [as follows]: if the mass of the weight is large, then even if the magnitude of the force of the spring is the same, it requires a longer time to move the weight. If next we suppose that we make the fixed point oscillate horizontally during the weight's vibration, the weight will execute vibrations as the resultant of two orthogonal vibrations. Various vibrations [can] appear in response to differences in their phases, and we can show these various vibrations by means of experiments.

CHAPTER 11　　第十一章　[ダイジュウイッショウ]

以	イ	from; than

外	ガイ	outer, external
	そと	outside, exterior
	ほか(の)	another, different
	(の)ほか(に)	other than

器	キ	instrument; container

期	キ	period, term

強	キョウ	strength
	つよ(い)	strong
	つよ(さ)	strength

近	キン	near, close
	ちか(い)	near, close
	(の)ちか(く)(に)	near, close

後	ゴ; コウ	behind; after
	あと(で)	after
	のち(に)	after
	うし(ろ)	behind

最	サイ	most, maximum
	もっと(も)	most

周	シュウ	circuit, circumference
	まわ(り)	circumference; surroundings

状	ジョウ	condition, state
	-ジョウ	-shape(d)

蒸	ジョウ	vapor; steam
	む(す)	to steam

正	セイ	positive {+}; correct
	ただ(しい)	correct

赤	セキ	red
	あか(い)	red

前	ゼン	front; before
	まえ	front; before

態	タイ	condition, appearance

程	テイ	extent
	ほど	extent

得	トク	benefit, profit
	え(る)	to get, obtain, gain
	-う(る)	to be able to
	-え(ない)	not to be able to

内	ナイ	inner, internal
	うち	inside; among

白	ハク	white
	しろ(い)	white

不	フ-	{negative prefix}

以

(これ)以前	(これ)イゼン	before (this)
(これ)以後	(これ)イゴ	after (this)
(これ)以内	(これ)イナイ	within (this)
(これ)以外	(これ)イガイ	other than (this)
(これ)以上	(これ)イジョウ	equal to or more than (this); abov
(これ)以下	(これ)イカ	equal to or less than (this); below

外

(これ)以外	(これ)イガイ	other than (this)
外力	ガイリョク	external force
外積	ガイセキ	outer product, vector product
外部-	ガイブ	external
外面	ガイメン	outer surface
外圧	ガイアツ	external pressure

器

電圧変成器	デンアツヘンセイキ	voltage transformer
計数器	ケイスウキ	counter
加速器	カソクキ	accelerator
分光器	ブンコウキ	spectroscope

期

期間	キカン	period of time
周期	シュウキ	cycle, period
周期運動	シュウキウンドウ	periodic motion
周期関数	シュウキカンスウ	periodic function
周期(律)表	シュウキ(リツ)ヒョウ	periodic table

強

強酸	キョウサン	strong acid
強電解質	キョウデンカイシツ	strong electrolyte
強度	キョウド	strength
比強度	ヒキョウド	specific strength

近

最近	サイキン	recently
近赤外線	キンセキガイセン	near infrared rays

後

(これ)以後	(これ)イゴ	after (this)
後部	コウブ	back (part)
後面	コウメン	rear face
後流	コウリュウ	backwash, wake
直後に	チョクゴに	immediately after
前後に動く	ゼンゴにうごく	to move back and forth
...の前後に	のゼンゴに	before and after ...

最

最小の	サイショウの	minimum
最大の	サイダイの	maximum
最高の	サイコウの	highest
最後の	サイゴの	last, final
最近	サイキン	recently

周

周期	シュウキ	cycle, period
周期的な	シュウキテキな	periodic
周期運動	シュウキウンドウ	periodic motion
周期関数	シュウキカンスウ	periodic function
周期(律)表	シュウキ(リツ)ヒョウ	periodic table

状

状態	ジョウタイ	state
状態(方程)式	ジョウタイ(ホウテイ)シキ	equation of state
状態変化	ジョウタイヘンカ	change of state
管状の	カンジョウの	tubular
管状反応器	カンジョウハンノウキ	tubular reactor

蒸

蒸発	ジョウハツ	vaporization
蒸発熱	ジョウハツネツ	heat of vaporization
蒸発器	ジョウハツキ	evaporator, vaporizer
蒸気圧	ジョウキアツ	vapor pressure
蒸気機関	ジョウキキカン	steam engine
蒸気管	ジョウキカン	steam pipe
水蒸気	スイジョウキ	steam, water vapor

正

正数	セイスウ	a positive number
正比例	セイヒレイ	direct proportion

正反対の	セイハンタイの	directly opposite
正多面体	セイタメンタイ	regular polyhedron
正の電気	セイのデンキ	positive electricity

赤

赤外線	セキガイセン	infrared rays
赤色光	セキショクコウ	red light
赤熱	セキネツ	red heat

前

(これ)以前	(これ)イゼン	before (this)
前後に動く	ゼンゴにうごく	to move back and forth
...の前後に	のゼンゴに	before and after ...
前部	ゼンブ	front (part)
前面	ゼンメン	front face
前線	ゼンセン	(weather) front
直前に	チョクゼンに	immediately before

態

状態	ジョウタイ	state
状態(方程)式	ジョウタイ(ホウテイ)シキ	equation of state
状態量	ジョウタイリョウ	state quantity
生態学	セイタイガク	ecology
生態的地位	セイタイテキチイ	ecological niche

程

程度	テイド	degree, extent
行程	コウテイ	stroke {of a piston}
方程式	ホウテイシキ	equation

得

結果を得る	ケッカをえる	to obtain results
電子を得る	デンシをえる	to gain an electron

内

(これ)以内	(これ)イナイ	within (this)
内積	ナイセキ	inner product, scalar product
内部-	ナイブ	internal
内面	ナイメン	inner surface
内圧	ナイアツ	internal pressure
内量子数	ナイリョウシスウ	inner quantum number
内部エネルギー	ナイブエネルギー	internal energy
内部応力	ナイブオウリョク	internal stress

白

白金	ハッキン	platinum
白色光	ハクショクコウ	white light
白熱	ハクネツ	white heat, incandescence
白熱光	ハクネツコウ	incandescent light

不

不必要な	フヒツヨウな	unnecessary
不変の	フヘンの	unchangeable, constant
不等式	フトウシキ	inequality
不合理な	フゴウリな	illogical
不対電子	フツイデンシ	unpaired electron

Passive, Causative, and Potential Verbs; More on Adjectives

In this chapter you will learn how to make three "derived" verbs from a given "dictionary" verb. For example, from the verb 使う (to use), which you will find in a Japanese dictionary, you can derive three other verbs, which you normally will not find in the dictionary:

Passive Verb:	使われる	is used
Potential Verb:	使える	can be used
Causative Verb:	使わせる	causes (someone or something) to use

These three "derived" verbs are ru-verbs and have their own conjugations with past, provisional, connective, and conditional forms, both affirmative and negative. On just about every page of technical Japanese you will encounter passive verb forms, but less frequently the causative and potential.

We also include in this chapter additional information about adjectives, particularly regarding various constructions that correspond to comparatives and superlatives in English. In addition, we discuss the way in which some adjectives are related to other parts of speech.

11.1 The Passive Verbs

The passive verb is obtained from the "dictionary" verb by adding れる to the xa-base of an xu-verb, or to the ra-base of an ru-verb. For both classes of verbs the base is obtained by replacing the last syllable of the dictionary verb (a syllable from the う column of the HIRAGANA table) by the corresponding syllable from the あ column. Some illustrations of forming passive verbs are

	"Dictionary" Verb Present Affirmative	Passive Verb Present Affirmative	Passive Verb Present Negative
ru-verbs			
to use	用いる	用いられる	用いられない
to determine	定める	定められる	定められない
xu-verbs			
to use	使う	使われる {N.B. わ}	使われない
to show	示す	示される	示されない
to measure	測る	測られる	測られない
to hold	もつ	もたれる	もたれない
to solve	解く	解かれる	解かれない
to pour	注ぐ	注がれる	注がれない
to tie	結ぶ	結ばれる	結ばれない
to surround	囲む[かこむ]	囲まれる	囲まれない
Irregular verbs			
to do	する	される！	されない
to come	くる	こられる！	こられない
Verbs formed with する			
to heat	加熱する	加熱される！	加熱されない
to heat	熱する	熱せられる！	熱せられない

The passive verbs derived from する and くる are irregular. You will probably never encounter the passive of くる in technical writing; it is just included here for completeness, inasmuch as it can arise in the spoken language. Note also that the verbs formed from a single KANJI followed by する are slightly different from verbs formed from KANGO followed by する. Verbs formed with KANJI followed by ずる, such as 生ずる, can be inflected in the same manner as 熱する but with the appropriate NIGORI; nowadays it seems to be more common to use the corresponding verb with KANJI followed by じる (such as 生じる), which is inflected as an ru-verb. Hence the passive verb corresponding to 生じる is 生じられる.

The passive verbs are, as we have already mentioned, ru-verbs. They can be conjugated further, as we show here by giving a few of the grammatically possible inflected forms for the verb 注がれる.

	Affirmative		Negative	
Present	注がれる	is poured	注がれない	is not poured
Past	注がれた	was poured	注がれなかった	was not poured
Provisional	注がれれば	if it is poured	注がれなければ	if it is not poured
Connnective	注がれて	is poured and ...	注がれなくて	is not poured and ...
Conjunctive	注がれ	is poured and ...	注がれず	is not poured and ...

The present and past forms occur frequently, but the other forms are less common. The passive verb forms are often combined with various auxiliary verbs to form more complicated verbal expressions such as 注がれていれば (if it is being poured), 注がれなければならない (it must be poured), etc.

In spoken Japanese the passive verbs are used in several ways, but in technical writing their principal use is virtually identical with that of the passive voice in English, as is indicated in the tabulation given above. When it is necessary to specify the agent of the action (that is, who is doing the pouring in the above listing) the agent is followed by によって, により, に, or から, any of which are translated as "by." The following sentences containing passive verbs will show you how these verbs are used in technical writing; in the first two sentences the particle に does not indicate the agent but serves other functions that you have already learned.

光電管はテレビカメラなどに用いられている。
コウデンカンはテレビカメラなどにもちいられている。
Photoelectric tubes are used in television cameras and other devices.

この方程式においてはMKS単位が用いられる。
このホウテイシキにおいてはMKSタンイがもちいられる。
In this equation MKS units are used.

酸素はスウェーデンのシェーレによって発見された。
サンソはスウェーデンのシェーレによってハッケンされた。
Oxygen was discovered by Scheele of Sweden.

この実験では振動の周期は測定されなかった。
このジッケンではシンドウのシュウキはソクテイされなかった。
In this experiment the period of the oscillation was not measured.

この方法を用いれば、次の方程式が得られる。
このホウホウをもちいれば、つぎのホウテイシキがえられる。
If we use this method, the following equations are obtained.

$S = k \ln W$はBoltzmannの原理とよばれ、熱力学の第2法則にあたらしい見方をあたえた。
$S = k \ln W$はBoltzmannのゲンリとよばれ、ネツリキガクのダイ2ホウソクにあたらしいみかたをあたえた。
$S = k \ln W$ is called Boltzmann's principle, and it has given a new way of looking at the second law of thermodynamics.

式2.2はBoltzmann式とよばれている。
シキ2.2はBoltzmannシキとよばれている。
Equation 2.2 is called Boltzmann's equation.

$dS > dQ/T$という式はClausiusの不等式としてしられている。
$dS > dQ/T$というシキはClausiusのフトウシキとしてしられている。
The formula $dS > dQ/T$ is known as the Clausius inequality.

11-8

In addition to the principal use of the passive verb illustrated above, there are other uses. The passive verb may in some instances have a "potential" meaning, as described in the next section. In addition the passive verb may be used — primarily in the spoken language — in an "honorific" sense; here the passive verb has the same meaning as the corresponding active verb but is considered to be more polite. Compare the passive verbs in the following two sentences: in the first the passive verb is translated as the passive voice in English; in the second the passive verb is used in the honorific sense and is translated as the active voice in English.

相対性原理はアインシュタインによって発見された。
ソウタイセイゲンリはアインシュタインによってハッケンされた。
The principle of relativity was discovered by Einstein.

アインシュタイン博士が相対性原理を発見された。{Honorific style}
アインシュタインハクシがソウタイセイゲンリをハッケンされた。
Dr. Einstein discovered the principle of relativity.

In normal scientific prose, the second sentence would end in 発見した, but in certain formal situations (such as a eulogy) the use of the passive verb adds politeness to the sentence. You will encounter this polite style only rarely in technical Japanese.

Finally, we make a few comments regarding the verbs formed by KANGO followed by する. Those which are intransitive, such as 上下する[ジョウゲする] (to go up and down) and 運動する[ウンドウする] (to move), do not have a corresponding passive verb in technical Japanese (formed by changing する to される). On the other hand, those that are transitive, such as 加熱する[カネツする] (to heat) and 測定する[ソクテイする] (to measure), can be made into passive verbs by replacing する with される. Therefore you will find with forms like

測定された   was measured   加熱されない   is not heated

11.2 The Potential Verbs

In previous chapters you learned two ways that the "potential" idea can be expressed — that is, ways of indicating that some action "is possible" or "can be done."

この方程式を解くことができる。   See Section 8.6.
この方程式は解き得る。   See Section 9.6.

Both of these sentences mean "This equation can be solved." As was pointed out in Section 9.6, 解き得る is pronounced ときうる, whereas the negative form 解き得ない is read ときえない.

In this section you will learn a third way to express the potential idea, namely, by means of the potential verb. The potential verb is derived by adding る to the xe-base of xu-verbs. This is the same base to which the ば ending is added to get the provisional.

11-9

For the ru-verbs the potential verb is identical to the passive verb. Here are some examples that illustrate the formation of the potential verbs:

	"Dictionary" Verb Present Affirmative	Potential Verb Present Affirmative	Potential Verb Present Negative
ru-verbs			
to use	用いる	用いられる	用いられない
to consider	考える	考えられる	考えられない
xu-verbs			
to show	示す	示せる	示せない
to use	使う	使える	使えない
to make	作る	作れる	作れない
to hold	もつ	もてる	もてない
to move	動く	動ける	動けない
to pour	注ぐ	注げる	注げない
to tie	結ぶ	結べる	結べない
to contain	含む	含める	含めない
Irregular verbs			
to do	する	される	されない
to come	くる	こられる	こられない

The irregularly formed potential of する, namely される, is generally not used. Instead, the verb できる is used. As a result 加熱される is never used in the potential sense; instead one uses 加熱(することが)できる "[we] can heat."

The verbs 見る[みる] "to see" and 聞く[きく] "to hear" have in addition to the usual potential verbs 見(ら)れる and 聞ける the additional passive potential verbs 見える[みえる] "can be seen, is visible" and 聞こえる[きこえる] "can be heard, is audible."

The potential verbs are ru-verbs and can be conjugated as such. For the verb 使う we give a few of the grammatically possible inflected forms.

	Affirmative		Negative	
Present	使える	can be used	使えない	cannot be used
Past	使えた	could be used	使えなかった	could not be used
Provisional	使えれば	if it can be used	使えなければ	if it cannot be used
Connective	使えて	can be used and ...	使えなくて	cannot be used and ...
Conjunctive	使え	can be used and ...	使えなく	cannot be used and ...

For the ru-verbs the potential and passive verbs have the same form, and hence there may be some ambiguity as to the meaning. For example, the sentence 次の式が得られる may mean "The following equation is obtained" or "The following equation can be obtained." Even for the xu-verbs the corresponding passive verb may sometimes have a potential connotation; for instance, 使われる usually means "is used," but occasionally it may mean "can be used." When it is necessary to be sure that the "potential" idea be expressed, the unambiguous ...ことができる construction is used; and when it is necessary that the "passive" idea be expressed, the ...(xa)れている construction is used.

Here are several sentences containing potential verbs. The first two contain a potential verb formed from an xu-verb, the third contains a potential verb formed from an ru-verb, and the fourth contains a passive verb formed from an xu-verb with a potential meaning.

ホイヘンスの原理は次のようにいい表せる。
ホイヘンスのゲンリはつぎのようにいいあらわせる。
The principle of Huygens can be expressed in the following way.

つまり t が小さいときには、式 (2) が使える。
つまり t がちいさいときには、シキ (2) がつかえる。
That is, when t is small, equation (2) can be used.

水素原子のエネルギーは次の式であたえられている。
スイソゲンシのエネルギーはつぎのシキであたえられている。
The energy of the hydrogen atom is given by the following equation.

内部エネルギーをUとすると、熱力学の第1法則はdU＝dQ－dWと表される。
ナイブエネルギーをUとすると、ネツリキガクのダイ1ホウソクはdU＝dQ－dWとあらわされる。
If we let the internal energy be U, the first law of thermodynamics is expressed (or: "can be expressed") as dU＝dQ－dW.

Certain commonly used expressions contain negative verb forms that are derived from potential verbs. For example, the いけない that you learned in expressions like 注いではいけない "you must not pour" (in Section 9.1a) is the present negative of the potential verb いける derived from the verb いく "to go." Also, in the standard phrase sometimes added at the end of a sentence, かも知れない[かもしれない], the verb 知れない is the present negative of the potential verb 知れる, which in turn is derived from 知る "to know." Adding this phrase has the same effect as using words like "may," "maybe," or "perhaps" in the corresponding English sentence. For example, この原理はその前に発見されたかも知れない can be translated "This principle may have been discovered before then." The character 知 will be learned in Chapter 13.

Finally, one word of caution regarding the potential verbs: quite a few potential verbs have developed into independent verbs in their own right, with special meanings different from the expected potential meanings. For example, you will find the following verbs listed separately in dictionaries:

知れる	to become known	違える	to change
含める	to include	間違える	to make a mistake

11-11

You will know whether or not the verb is the potential verb from the context.

11.3 The Causative Verbs

The causative verbs are formed by adding the ending せる to the xa-base of xu-verbs (that is, replacing 'xu' by 'xa') and to the sa-base of ru-verbs (that is, replacing る by さ). Here are some examples of causative verbs:

	"Dictionary" Verb Present Affirmative	Causative Verb Present Affirmative	Causative Verb Present Negative
ru-verbs			
to obtain	得る	得させる	得させない
to consider	考える	考えさせる	考えさせない
xu-verbs			
to dissolve	溶かす	溶かさせる	溶かさせない
to meet	合う	合わせる {N.B. わ}	合わせない
to make	作る	作らせる	作らせない
to hold	もつ	もたせる	もたせない
to move	動く	動かせる	動かせない
to join	つなぐ	つながせる	つながせない
to tie	結ぶ	結ばせる	結ばせない
to contain	含む	含ませる	含ませない
Irregular verbs			
to do	する	させる!	させない
to come	くる	こさせる!	こさせない

Note that the causative verbs derived from する and くる are irregular; the causative of くる will arise very seldom if at all in technical writing.

The causative verbs are ru-verbs and can be conjugated as such. For example, a few of the grammatically possible inflected forms for the verb 考えさせる are

	Affirmative		Negative
Present	考えさせる	causes ... to consider	考えさせない
Past	考えさせた	caused ... to consider	考えさせなかった
Provisional	考えさせれば	if it causes ... to consider	考えさせなければ
Connective	考えさせて	causes ... to consider and ...	考えさせなくて
Conjunctive	考えさせ	causes ... to consider and ...	考えさせず

The meaning of the causative is "to cause someone (or something) to perform an action," as indicated above. The causative can be combined with the passive voice. Thus はたらかせられなかった means "was not made to act." It is the past negative of はたらかせられる, which is the passive verb derived from the causative verb はたらかせる, which is in turn derived from the verb はたらく "to act, to do work." This gives you an idea of the amazing range of the Japanese verbal system and the enormous number of verb forms that can arise from a single verb.

We now give several sample sentences to illustrate the use of the causative verbs:

固定されていない物体に力をはたらかせると、物体が加速する。
<u>コテイ</u>されていない<u>ブッタイ</u>に<u>ちから</u>をはたらかせると、<u>ブッタイ</u>が<u>カソク</u>する。
If we cause a force to act on a body that is not fixed, the body accelerates.

流体が運動している場合でも、pに圧力という意味をもたせることにする。
<u>リュウタイ</u>が<u>ウンドウ</u>しているばあいでも、pに<u>アツリョク</u>という<u>イミ</u>をもたせることにする。
Even when the fluid is moving, we may ascribe to p the meaning of pressure. {Lit.: we may decide to make p have the meaning ...}

In conclusion we mention that the causative verbs formed from KANGO＋する can be derived by changing する to させる as would be expected. Hence, for typical intransitive verbs the causative forms are

運動する	[ウンドウする]	to move {intransitive}
運動させる	[ウンドウさせる]	to cause [something] to move
振動する	[シンドウする]	to oscillate {intransitive}
振動させる	[シンドウさせる]	to cause [something] to oscillate

The causative verbs corresponding to transitive KANGO＋する verbs are not common in technical Japanese.

点Qで固定されたばねに質量mの質点Pをとりつけ、水平面上でx方向に運動させる。
<u>テン</u>Qで<u>コテイ</u>されたばねに<u>シツリョウ</u>mの<u>シッテン</u>Pをとりつけ、<u>スイヘイメンジョウ</u>でx<u>ホウコウ</u>に<u>ウンドウ</u>させる。
We attach a mass point P with mass m to a spring that has been fixed at point Q, and we cause it [i.e., the mass point P] to move in the x-direction in a horizontal plane.

単振り子を振動させれば、その周期を測定することができる。
<u>タン</u>ふりこを<u>シンドウ</u>させれば、その<u>シュウキ</u>を<u>ソクテイ</u>することができる。
If we cause a simple pendulum to oscillate, we can measure its period.

11.4 Comparative and Superlative Adjective Expressions

In English we form the comparative and superlative forms of adjectives by using the endings "-er" and "-est," or words like "more," "most," "less," "least." In Japanese the way of expressing comparison is quite different.

a. Positive Comparisons

The standard construction for making positive comparisons is AはBより＋ adjective, although many variations on this basic construction occur. Here より is translated as "than." An example of this standard construction is

ケイ素原子は水素原子より大きい。
ケイソゲンシはスイソゲンシよりおおきい。
The silicon atom is larger than the hydrogen atom.

Note that there is no ending on the Japanese adjective that corresponds to the ending "-er" in English. Often より is followed by the particle は or the particle も (sometimes implying a slight emphasis).

Now we turn to some of the variations on the pattern AはBより+adjective. If A and B are nouns, one or both of them may be followed by の方 (where 方 is pronounced ホウ). Thus the sentence above could be written in the following two forms:

ケイ素原子の方が水素原子より大きい。

水素原子よりはケイ素原子の方が大きい。

In some cases the two objects being compared may be clear from the context so that it is not necessary to mention both. For example, in the sentences given above it may be possible to shorten the sentences and write

ケイ素原子の方が大きい。
The silicon atom is larger.

If A and B are sentences, one or both of them may be followed by 方. Some illustrative sentences follow.

この場合には二酸化炭素を使うよりも水蒸気を使った方がよい。
このばあいにはニサンカタンソをつかうよりもスイジョウキをつかったホウがよい。
In this situation it would be better to use steam than to use carbon dioxide. {...使うほうがよい = "it is better to use ..."}

このような不定積分を定めるには、部分積分法を用いる方が速い。
このようなフテイセキブンをさだめるには、ブブンセキブンホウをもちいるホウがはやい。
To determine this kind of indefinite integral, it is faster to use the method of integration by parts.

In the last sentence, the "Bより" part of the construction is omitted.

After the sentence AはBより近い (A is nearer than B), you could add しかしCはさらに近い (but C is even nearer), the word さらに (or もっと) indicating a further comparison. Sometimes a noun is modified by an adjective that is preceded by より, for example, より近い位置[よりちかいイチ], meaning "a closer position."

Interrogative words followed by よりも take on more general meanings: なによりも "... than anything else," どこよりも "... than anywhere else." For example:

オスミウムの比重はどの元素よりも大きい。
オスミウムのヒジュウはどのゲンソよりもおおきい。
The specific gravity of osmium is larger than that of any other element.

11-14

Note also the use of より in the following sentence:

振動の周期はおもったより長かった。
シンドウのシュウキはおもったよりながかった。
The period of the oscillation was longer than we had expected.

You must, however, always keep in mind the fact that より does not always mean "than." Sometimes より is used in lieu of から in the sense of "from" as in the following sentence:

物体が原点より上向きに運動する。
ブッタイがゲンテンよりうわむきにウンドウする。
The body moves upward from the origin.

b. Negative Comparisons

In making negative comparisons the word ほど is used. This word is a noun meaning "extent" or "degree." Nowadays it is usually written with HIRAGANA in expressions of comparison, although you will occasionally see it written with the KANJI 程 introduced in this lesson. The standard pattern for negative comparisons is AはBほど+negative adjective. Here are some sample sentences:

この状態式はpV＝RTという式ほど使いやすくないが、より正しい結果をあたえる。
このジョウタイシキはpV＝RTというシキほどつかいやすくないが、よりただしいケッカをあたえる。
This equation of state is not as easy to use as (the one called) pV = RT, but it gives more accurate results.

白石らが使った圧力計は前原らが使ったものほど重くない。
しらいしらがつかったアツリョクケイはまえばらららがつかったものほどおもくない。
The pressure gauge that Shiraishi et al. used is not as heavy as that used by Maebara et al.

c. Words Implying a Comparison

There are some words formed with the KANJI 以 that indicate or imply that a comparison is being made. These words are

以上	[イジョウ]	more than, above; ... or more
以下	[イカ]	less than, below, inferior to; ... or less
以外	[イガイ]	other than, outside of
以内	[イナイ]	within, inside of
以前	[イゼン]	earlier than, before
以後	[イゴ]	later than, after

Some illustrations of the uses of these words follow:

水酸化ナトリウムをこれ以上使わない方がよい。
スイサンカナトリウムをこれイジョウつかわないホウがよい。
It is better not to use more sodium hydroxide than this.

11-15

このフラスコの重さは500g以下である。
このフラスコの<u>おも</u>さは500g<u>イカ</u>である。
The weight of this flask is 500 grams or less.

ベックマン温度計以外のものを使ってはいけない。
ベックマン<u>オンドケイイガイ</u>のものを<u>つか</u>ってはいけない。
You must not use any thermometer other than the Beckmann.

化学反応が3s以内に起こることがわかる。
<u>カガクハンノウ</u>が3s<u>イナイ</u>に<u>おこ</u>ることがわかる。
We know that the chemical reaction occurs within three seconds.

それ以前コンピュータはあまり使われなかったのである。
それ<u>イゼン</u>コンピュータはあまり<u>つか</u>われなかったのである。
Prior to that time computers were not used very much.

d. Superlative Expressions

The simplest way to form the superlative in Japanese, corresponding to the "-est" ending in English, is to place 最も[もっとも] or 一番[イチバン] immediately in front of the adjective or modifying clause (もっとも is far more common in technical writing).

pV＝RTはもっともよく使われている状態式である。
pV＝RTはもっともよく<u>つか</u>われている<u>ジョウタイシキ</u>である。
pV＝RT is the equation of state that is most often used.

これらのモノマーの内、エチレンが最も反応性が高い。
これらのモノマーの<u>うち</u>、エチレンが<u>もっとも</u><u>ハンノウセイ</u>が<u>たか</u>い。
Among these monomers, ethylene has the highest reactivity.

In technical Japanese the prefix 最[サイ] also serves to indicate a superlative, as in the following:

最大の	[サイダイの]	the largest
最小の	[サイショウの]	the smallest
最長の	[サイチョウの]	the longest
最近の	[サイキンの]	the most recent
最多数の	[サイタスウの]	the most numerous

Sometimes the particle の is omitted.

最高点	[サイコウテン]	the highest point, the maximum
最小作用	[サイショウサヨウ]	the least action
最大電流	[サイダイデンリュウ]	the maximum current

11-16

11.5 Adverbs, Nouns, and Verbs Derived from Adjectives

In learning a KANJI you may first have associated it with some particular part of speech in English and then later found that the same character can be used to form another part of speech. For example, the KANJI 熱 associated with the noun "heat" can be used to form the verb 熱する (to heat). From the KANJI 動 associated with the verb 動く (to move) we get the noun 動き (motion) and the adjective 動きやすい (moves easily). In this section we show that KANJI normally associated with adjectives can be used to make adverbs, nouns, and verbs. Awareness of the multiple uses of KANJI will be helpful to you in vocabulary building.

a. Formation of Adverbs

We have already pointed out in Section 9.5c that adverbs can be formed from adjectives in the following way:

i-adjectives: replace い by く
na-adjectives: replace な by に

For example:

quick	速い	quickly	速く
good	よい	well	よく
strong	強い	strongly	強く
mathematical	数学的な	mathematically	数学的に

Remember that よく sometimes has the meaning of "often," as in よく使われる, "[It] is often used."

b. Formation of Nouns

It is possible to convert i- and na-adjectives to abstract nouns by replacing the い or な by the ending さ.

high	高い	height	高さ
long	長い	length	長さ
heavy	重い	weight	重さ
large	大きい	size	大きさ
important	重要な	importance	重要さ

Infrequently nouns are formed by the suffix み. For example, 重み means a "(statistical) weight" in statistics and statistical mechanics.

The following example illustrates the extent to which word-building can proceed: 近い "near" (adjective); 近づく "to come near" (verb); 近づきやすい "which approaches easily" (adjective); 近づきやすさ "ease of approach" (noun).

In addition to the use of suffixes to make nouns from adjectives, nouns are generated in some cases by a juxtaposition of the KANJI representing two adjectives with opposite meanings.

large	大きい	[おおきい]			
small	小さい	[ちいさい]	size	大小	[ダイショウ]
many	多い	[おおい]			
few	少ない	[すくない]	number	多少	[タショウ]
long	長い	[ながい]			
short	短い	[みじかい]	length	長短	[チョウタン]
strong	強い	[つよい]			
weak	弱い	[よわい]	strength	強弱	[キョウジャク]

Sometimes the meanings of the nouns above will be the combination of ideas in the two KANJI: 強弱 "strength and weakness"; 正負 [セイフ] "plus and minus; positive and negative."

c. Formation of Verbs

As we pointed out in Section 9.5b, the く form of the adjective can be combined with the verbs なる and する to form verbs.

strong	強い	to become strong	強くなる
		to make strong, strengthen	強くする
red	赤い	to become red	赤くなる
		to make red	赤くする
white	白い	to become white	白くなる
		to make white, whiten	白くする
narrow	細い	to become narrow	細くなる
		to make narrow	細くする

In addition there are many adjectives whose KANJI are used for verb stems with the same KUN readings. For example:

strong	強い	to strengthen	強める
		to be strengthened	強まる
near	近い	to approach	近づく
correct	正しい	to correct	正す

11.6 Adjectives Derived from Other Parts of Speech

In this section you will learn to recognize some adjectives that are formed by the addition of ような, そうな, and らしい to various kinds of words. All three of these mean something like "having the appearance of," "looking like," or "seeming to be."

The first of these appears very frequently in technical Japanese, the second seldom, and the third very rarely.

a. Uses of よう

    You have already encountered よう in a number of example sentences and know that it can often be translated by "way" or "manner." In Chapter 6 you learned このような (this kind of), そのような (that kind of), このように (in this way, thus), and そのように (in that way).

    An adjectival phrase formed by a noun+の, a sentence-terminal verb, or a sentence-terminal adjective can be followed by ような, which then means "like" or "of the sort that" or "such as."

Gは運動量、エネルギー、質量、エンタルピーのような示量的性質の単位質量あたりの量とする。
Gは<u>ウンドウリョウ</u>、エネルギー、<u>シツリョウ</u>、エンタルピーのような<u>シリョウテキセイシツ</u>の<u>タンイシツリョウ</u>あたりの<u>リョウ</u>とする。
We let G be a quantity per unit mass for an extensive property like momentum, energy, mass, and enthalpy.

酸素、水素のような気体についてはpV = RTを使ってもよい結果が得られる。
<u>サンソ</u>、<u>スイソ</u>のような<u>キタイ</u>についてはpV = RTを<u>つか</u>ってもよい<u>ケッカ</u>が<u>え</u>られる。
For gases like oxygen and hydrogen, even if you use pV = RT, you can get good results.

    In adverbial expressions formed with ように the latter may mean "as," "like," or "in a manner such that ...." One example of each of these is given:

以上でのべたように赤外線スペクトルはよく使われる。
<u>イジョウ</u>でのべたように<u>セキガイセンスペクトル</u>はよく<u>つか</u>われる。
As we discussed above, infrared spectra are often used.

この化合物は強酸のように反応する。
この<u>カゴウブツ</u>は<u>キョウサン</u>のように<u>ハンノウ</u>する。
This chemical compound reacts like a strong acid.

この実験においてはモノマーを重合させないように加熱しなければならない。
この<u>ジッケン</u>においてはモノマーを<u>ジュウゴウ</u>させないように<u>カネツ</u>しなければならない。
In this experiment we must heat the monomer in such a way that we do not cause polymerization.

    Occasionally you will come upon the potential verb 見える (can be seen) in the combination ...ように見える meaning "It appears that ...." Note the following two sentences:

水の中にあわが見える。
<u>みず</u>の<u>なか</u>にあわが<u>み</u>える。
Bubbles can be seen in the water.

水の中にあわがあるように見える。
みずのなかにあわがあるようにみえる。
There appear to be bubbles in the water.

Two other constructions involving よう are ...ようにする (to ensure that ...) and ...ようになる (to turn out that ...); the latter construction may imply a gradually occurring change. Here are several sentences to illustrate these constructions.

プロセスを変えて強アルカリを使わないようにした。
プロセスをかえてキョウアルカリをつかわないようにした。
We changed the process to ensure that we did not use strong alkali.

ゴムとして合成高分子を使うようになってきた。
ゴムとしてゴウセイコウブンシをつかうようになってきた。
Synthetic polymers came to be used as rubber.

In addition, と同じように is used in comparisons of equality.

リン酸は塩酸と同じように強酸である。
リンサンはエンサンとおなじようにキョウサンである。
Phosphoric acid is a strong acid like hydrochloric acid.

b. そうな

Here そう is an ending that is added to the xi-base of verbs and to the stems of adjectives (the stem being what is left when the い or な of an i- or na-adjective has been removed). There are two irregular forms: from よい we get よさそうな, and from ない we get なさそうな. Some examples of these forms in phrases are

測れそうな量	[はかれそうなリョウ]	a quantity that appears to be measurable
熱そうなシリンダ	[あつそうなシリンダ]	a cylinder that appears to be hot
水平そうな面	[スイヘイそうなメン]	a surface that appears to be horizontal

The adverbial form can also be used with 見える, as in この面は水平そうに見える (this surface appears to be horizontal).

c. らしい

This word can be added to sentence-terminal verbs and adjectives, to nouns, and even to noun+particle phrases. The combinations thus made are sometimes called "semblative adjectives"; they are i-adjectives and can be inflected as such (e.g., ...らしくない, ...らしかった).

熱いらしいシリンダにさわらない方がよい。
あついらしいシリンダにさわらないホウがよい。
It is better not to touch a cylinder that appears to be hot.

この実験では重合が起こらなかったらしい。
この<u>ジッケン</u>では<u>ジュウゴウ</u>が<u>おこ</u>らなかったらしい。
In this experiment it appears that polymerization did not occur.

ADDITIONAL VOCABULARY FOR EXERCISES

のぞく		to remove
...かどうか		whether or not ...
verb+につれて		along with+gerund
よりよくなる		to become better, improve
ととのう		to be well ordered
となり合う	となりあう	to adjoin
やすい		inexpensive
どの方向においても	どのホウコウにおいても	in any direction
verb+はずである		should+verb
正しくいえば	ただしくいえば	speaking (more) exactly
したい {from する}		to want to do
ぐるぐる		round and round, in circles
まわる	【回る】	to revolve, rotate, spin
うつる	【移る】	to change (position, state)
中間的(な)	チュウカンテキ(な)	intermediate
あてる	【当てる】	to strike

11-21

EXERCISES

Ex 11.1 Matching Japanese and English words and technical terms

(a) Relational words

以下(　)　　1. after
以外(　)　　2. before
以後(　)　　3. front
以上(　)　　4. front face
以前(　)　　5. less than
以内(　)　　6. more than
後部(　)　　7. other than
後面(　)　　8. rear
最近(　)　　9. rear face
前部(　)　　10. recently
前面(　)　　11. within

(b) Technical terms

加速器(　)　　1. accelerator
強酸(　)　　2. change of state
強電解質(　)　　3. counter
計数器(　)　　4. equation
状態変化(　)　　5. evaporator
状態量(　)　　6. infrared rays
蒸気機関(　)　　7. inner quantum number
蒸発器(　)　　8. internal stress
周期関数(　)　　9. periodic function
周期表(　)　　10. periodic table
正多面体(　)　　11. platinum
赤外線(　)　　12. red light
赤色光(　)　　13. regular polyhedron
不対電子(　)　　14. state quantity
方程式(　)　　15. steam engine
内部応力(　)　　16. strong acid
内量子数(　)　　17. strong electrolyte
白金(　)　　18. unpaired electron
白色光(　)　　19. white heat
白熱(　)　　20. white light

Ex 11.2 Matching Japanese technical terms and definitions

外積( )　　　　　　1. 1gの液体を同じ温度の蒸気にするために必要な熱量。
蒸気圧( )　　　　　2. タングステンなどの金属[キンゾク＝metal]線を電流
状態図( )　　　　　　で加熱するとき発光する光。
蒸発( )　　　　　　3. ＜または＞を用いて、表される関係式。
蒸発熱( )　　　　　4. ある物質について外力(重力など)の場によるエネルギ
赤熱( )　　　　　　　ーをのぞいた全エネルギー量。
内部エネルギー( )　5. 物質の気相、液相、固相の関係を表すもの。
白熱光( )　　　　　6. 500℃前後の温度に加熱すること。
不等式( )　　　　　7. 光をおのおのの色に分けてスペクトル[spectrum,spec-
分光器( )　　　　　　tra] を得るもの。
　　　　　　　　　　8. ある温度での蒸気の圧力。
　　　　　　　　　　9. 液体表面から液体分子が飛び出て[from とびでる＝to
　　　　　　　　　　　fly out]、気体になること。
　　　　　　　　　10. 二つのベクトルX、Yからつくられるベクトル X×Y。

Ex 11.3 Converting active voice to passive

Translate the following sentences. Then convert from active voice to passive and again translate.

Example:　蒸発熱を測定した。　　We measured the heat of vaporization.
　　　　　蒸発熱が測定された。　The heat of vaporization was measured.

1. 方程式を解いた。
　　方程式＿解＿＿＿。
2. 塩化水素酸を注ぐ。
　　塩化水素酸＿注＿＿＿。
3. この方法を用いた。
　　この方法＿用い＿＿＿。
4. 定数Aを定めた。
　　定数A＿定め＿＿＿。
5. 白金を加えた。
　　白金＿加え＿＿＿。
6. 赤外線を使った。
　　赤外線＿使＿＿＿。
7. このような状態式を得る。
　　このような状態式＿得＿＿＿。
8. 強酸のpHを水酸化物を加えることにより上げた。
　　強酸のpH＿水酸化物を加えることにより上げ＿＿＿。

11-23

9. 重要な結果を得た。
   重要な結果__得__ __ __。
10. 振動の周期を変えた。
    振動の周期__変え__ __ __。
11. cgs単位でこの表を表した。
    この表__cgs単位で表__ __ __。
12. 光学においてホイヘンスの原理を学んだ。
    光学においてホイヘンスの原理__学__ __ __。
13. この周期関数を積分した。
    この周期関数__積分__ __ __。
14. 式(2)はNavier-Stokesの式とよんでいる。
    式(2)はNavier-Stokesの式とよ__ __ __いる。
15. Fourierはこの式を発見した。
    この式はFourier__ __ __ __発見__ __ __。

Ex 11.4 Translate the following sentences

1. シリンダ[cylinder]の中でピストン[piston]を前後に運動させることができる。
2. 内圧が外圧より10気圧ほど高くなる場合、容器[ヨウキ＝container]の強さはテストされる必要がある。
3. 近赤外線は赤外線に近ければ近い程見えなくなるかどうかは、実験せずにはわからない。
4. 白色光は単色光ではなく、多重の単色光より成る光である。
5. 振動する質点は振動数が高ければ高い程、周期の中点における速さが増加する。
6. CGS単位において、1ダインは1グラムの質量に1センチ/セコンド²の加速度を得させる力として定められている。
7. 体積一定で水を蒸発させる場合、温度を高くすればするほど得られる水蒸気の蒸気圧が高くなる。
8. スペースシャトル[space shuttle]の無重力状態では、シャトルの速度による遠心力[エンシンリョク＝centrifugal force]はシャトルの重力に方向が正反対で、大きさが相等しい。
9. 最小作用の原理はポテンシャルエネルギーVがq̇を含まなくて、運動エネルギーTがq̇の二次式の場合は

$$\delta \int_{t_0}^{t_1} 2T dt = 0$$

となる。

10. 電子対を作っていない電子を不対電子という。不対電子をもっている原子は電子対をもつものより反応性が高くて、不安定[フアンテイ = unstable]である。

Ex 11.5 Read the following essays for comprehension

1. CGS単位において長さは10mm[ミリメートル]以上になれば、cm[センチメートル]で表され、100[ヒャク]cm以上になれば、m[メートル]で表される。以前に10cm以上1m以下の長さはdm[デシメートル]で表されたこともあったが、もう大分前にdmという単位は使われなくなった。

2. 物体を熱して温度を十分に[ジュウブンに = sufficiently]上げると、まず赤熱状態になるが、次に赤色以外の光線が強くなるにつれて、光線が白色に近づき、これを白熱状態という。これは1000[(イッ)セン]°C以上に熱した場合に見られる状態である。

3. 元素の周期性が発見された後、元素の性質の理解がよりよくなって、周期表が作られた。例えば、周期表の第一[ダイイチ = first]周期は水素とヘリウムの2元素から成り、第二[ダイニ = second]周期はリチウムからネオンまでの8[ハチ]元素を含んでいる。

4. 多面体の中で最もととのったものは正多面体である。正多面体では次の関係がある。ある正多面体の各面[カクメン = each plane]の重心をとり、となり合っている面の重心を線分でつなぐと、その線分からできる多面体も正多面体となる。例えば、正6[ロク]面体をそのようにすればその中で正8[ハチ]面体ができる。また正8面体の中で正6面体ができる。

5. 水溶液から水を蒸発させるために蒸発器が使用される。最もよく使われるのは水蒸気加熱多管式蒸発器である。加熱用水蒸気の温度は高ければ高いほど蒸発能力[ノウリョク = ability]が大きいが、最も多く使われる水蒸気の温度は加熱用水蒸気の最高温度程{N.B.ほど}高くはなくて、それより大分低い[ひくい = low]。なぜならば、最もやすい加熱用水蒸気は一度水蒸気原動機に用いられた廃蒸気[ハイジョウキ = exhaust steam]であるからである。

6. 以上にのべたように、どの方向においても同じ性質を示す等方性の物質の状態は二つの変数、すなわち状態量できまる。したがって、体積をV、圧力をp、温度をTとすれば、このような等方性物質では$f(p, V, T) = 0$という関係がある。このような式を物質の状態式という。エネルギーも物質の状態によってきまるので、そのエネルギーは二つの状態量の関数であるはずである。このエネルギーをUとすれば、UはU(V, P)、あるいはU(V, T)などの関

11-25

数となる。このように状態によってきまるエネルギーは物質の運動エネルギーと位置エネルギーから分けて、物質の内部エネルギーとよばれている。状態AとBでの内部エネルギーをそれぞれU_aとU_bとし、物質の状態がAからBに変化する場合に外部から仕事[シごと＝work]Wと熱量Qが得られたとすれば、熱力学の第一[ダイイチ＝first]法則は$U_a - U_b = W + Q$で表される。

7．水素原子よりは炭素原子の方が重く、酸素原子はさらに重い。原子が大きい程重さも大きい。白金は金より重い。物体の重さを小さくするためには重さの小さい、正しくいえば比重の小さい物質を使えばよい。物質に含まれている原子の重さが小さく、その数が少ない程比重は小さくなる。水素は全元素中で最も重さが小さい。これより重さの小さい元素はあり得ない。

8．鉄[テツ＝iron]を熱して温度を上げていくと、500℃以下ではほとんど不変であるが、温度が600℃前後になると色が赤く変わる。強く熱してさらに温度を上げると1000℃内外で色が白くなる。これは周期運動している電子が大きなエネルギーを得るからで、1000℃以上の高温になると最後に状態変化が起って蒸気になってしまう。

Ex 11.6 Translate the following essay

　日光[ニッコウ＝sunlight]は白色であるが、赤外線からX線までいろいろな光を含んでいる。この内最も振動数の小さい赤外線は振動数が4×10^{14}ヘルツ以下で、1800年[ネン＝year] F.W. Herschelにより、強い熱作用をもつ熱線として発見されたが、1835年[ネン] A.Ampereはこれが光線であることを示した。振動数がこの程度に小さくなると人間には見えない。赤外線スペクトル、とくに振動数が2×10^{14}ヘルツ前後の近赤外部は大部分振動スペクトルである。

　分子の固有振動数は分子の成り立ち方によって違うので、赤外スペクトルは物質によって違う。この性質により、赤外スペクトルは化合物を正しく同定したいときに用いる。赤外線分光器にはエシェレット[echellete]格子[コウシ＝grating]が用いられている。

　日光[ニッコウ]に最も近い光を実験的に作り出すためにはシンクロトロン[synchrotron]を用いればよい。すなわち、まず電子に光の速度近くの速さでぐるぐるまわる周期運動をさせ、電子の速度を上げていくと、このような光が得られるのである。水から水蒸気にうつる中間的状態などは、このようなシンクロトロンで得られた光から不要の部分をのぞいて後、これを分子にあててしらべられている。

TRANSLATIONS

Ex 11.4 Sentences

1. It is possible to cause the piston to move back and forth in the cylinder.
2. When the internal pressure becomes as much as 10 atmospheres higher than the external pressure, it is necessary that test be performed on the strength of the container.
3. It cannot be known, without experiments, whether or not the near infrared rays become more invisible the closer they come to the infrared rays.
4. White light is not monochromatic light; it is light that consists of a multiplicity of monochromatic light [waves].
5. The higher the frequency of a vibrating mass point, the more the velocity at the midpoint of its period increases.
6. In CGS units one dyne is established as the force that imparts to a mass of 1 gram {lit.: causes it to receive} an acceleration of 1 cm/sec^2.
7. When we vaporize water {lit.: cause it to vaporize} at constant volume, the higher we make the temperature the higher (becomes) the pressure of the vapor obtained.
8. In the weightless state of the space shuttle, the centrifugal force due to the shuttle's velocity is directly opposite to the weight of the shuttle and equal [to it] in magnitude.
9. When the potential energy V does not include $\dot{q}$ and the kinetic energy T is a second-order equation in $\dot{q}$, the principle of least action is

$$\delta \int_{t_0}^{t_1} 2Tdt = 0.$$

10. An electron that is not forming an electron pair is called an unpaired electron. Atoms containing an unpaired electron have a higher reactivity than those that have [only] electron pairs, and they are stable.

Ex 11.6 Essay

Sunlight is white light, but it contains various [frequencies] of light from infrared rays to X-rays. Among these [rays] those infrared rays having the smallest frequencies have frequencies less than 4×10^{14} hertz, and these were discovered in 1800 by F. W. Herschel as "heat rays" having strong heating effects; but Ampere showed in 1835 that these are light rays. When frequencies become small to this extent, they are not visible to human beings. The infrared spectrum, especially that part of the near infrared around 2×10^{14}, is primarily a vibration spectrum.

11-27

The characteristic frequencies of a molecule differ depending upon the way the molecule is put together; therefore, the infrared spectrum differs depending on the substance. When we want to identify a compound correctly, we use the infrared spectrum, [which] depends on these properties {i.e., the characteristic frequencies}. In infrared spectrometers echellete gratings are used.

We may use a synchrotron in order to create light experimentally that is as close as possible to sunlight. That is, first we cause electrons to move round and round in circles with periodic motion at a speed close to the velocity of light; then if we keep on increasing the velocity of the electrons, we can obtain this kind of light. In [investigating] intermediate states such as water changing to water vapor, we [cause] the light from the synchrotron, after removing the unnecessary part of it, to strike the molecules and then [the intermediate states] are examined.

移	イ	moving, transferring
	うつ(す)	to move, transfer
	うつ(る)	to move (to a place)

陰	イン	negative; shade

過	カ	excess; going through
	す(ごす)	to spend time, go through
	す(ぎる)	to elapse; to go through
	-す(ぎる)	to over(do), be too ...

核	カク	nucleus, core

球	キュウ	sphere, bulb
	たま	sphere, ball

空	クウ	air, space
	そら	sky, heavens

形	ケイ	shape, form
	-かた; -がた	shape, form
	かたち	shape, form

構	コウ	construction, structure

地	ジ; チ	earth, ground
	つち	earth, ground

磁	ジ	magnetism

織	シキ; ショク	weaving
	お(る)	to weave

射	シャ	shooting

消	ショウ	extinguishing
	け(す)	to extinguish, put out
	き(える)	to go out, disappear

植	ショク	planting
	う(える)	to plant; to raise
	う(わる)	to be planted

組	ソ	assembling
	く(む)	to assemble
	-くみ	set, class {counter}

伝	デン	transmission
	つた(える)	to transmit
	つた(わる)	to be transmitted

放	ホウ	releasing
	はな(す)	to let go, release

胞	ホウ	sac, case

陽	ヨウ	positive; sun

粒	リュウ	grain; drop
	つぶ	grain; drop

移

移行する	イコウする	to shift (to)
移相器	イソウキ	phase shifter
移動度	イドウド	mobility
移動単位数	イドウタンイスウ	number of transfer units, NTU
物質移動	ブッシツイドウ	mass transfer
熱移動係数	ネツイドウケイスウ	heat transfer coefficient

陰

陰イオン	インイオン	negative ion, anion
陰電気	インデンキ	negative electricity
陰電子	インデンシ	negative electron
陰性元素	インセイゲンソ	electronegative element
陰生植物	インセイショクブツ	shade plant
陰関数	インカンスウ	implicit function

過

過程	カテイ	process
過電圧	カデンアツ	over-voltage
過熱蒸気	カネツジョウキ	superheated vapor
過熱液体	カネツエキタイ	superheated liquid
過酸化物	カサンカブツ	peroxide
過酸化水素	カサンカスイソ	hydrogen peroxide
強過ぎる	つよすぎる	to be too strong
使い過ぎる	つかいすぎる	to use too much

核

原子核	ゲンシカク	atomic nucleus
核子	カクシ	nucleon
核磁子	カクジシ	nuclear magneton
核内力	カクナイリョク	intranuclear force
核外電子	カクガイデンシ	extranuclear electron
核反応	カクハンノウ	nuclear reaction
核酸	カクサン	nucleic acid
核液	カクエキ	karyolymph {biol}
核質	カクシツ	karyoplasm {biol}; nucleoplasm
細胞核	サイボウカク	cell nucleus
核タンパク質	カクタンパクシツ	nucleoprotein

球

地球	チキュウ	the earth
電球	デンキュウ	light bulb
球形-	キュウケイ	spherical
球面	キュウメン	spherical surface
球状タンパク質	キュウジョウタンパクシツ	globular protein

空

空間	クウカン	space
空気	クウキ	air
空中電気	クウチュウデンキ	atmospheric electricity
空中放電	クウチュウホウデン	atmospheric discharge
空中線	クウチュウセン	antenna {also アンテナ}

形

形状	ケイジョウ	shape
無定形	ムテイケイ	amorphous
変形	ヘンケイ	deformation
長方形	チョウホウケイ	rectangle
正方形	セイホウケイ	square
線形-	センケイ	linear
形態学	ケイタイガク	morphology
形成する	ケイセイする	to form
原形質	ゲンケイシツ	protoplasm

構

構成する	コウセイする	to form, constitute
機構	キコウ	mechanism

地

地球	チキュウ	the earth
地面	ジメン	(the) ground, earth's surface
地上の	チジョウの	terrestrial
地理学	チリガク	geography
地下結実	チカケツジツ	geocarpy
地磁気	チジキ	geomagnetism
地質学	チシツガク	geology

磁

磁化	ジカ	magnetization
磁場	ジば	magnetic field
磁石	ジシャク	magnet

電磁石	デンジシャク	electromagnet
磁気テープ	ジキテープ	magnetic tape
電磁気	デンジキ	electromagnetism
磁力線	ジリョクセン	line of magnetic force
磁気量子数	ジキリョウシスウ	magnetic quantum number
核磁気-	カクジキ	nuclear magnetic

織

組織	ソシキ	tissue {biol}; organization; texture
組織学	ソシキガク	histology
組織分化	ソシキブンカ	histodifferentiation
組織細胞	ソシキサイボウ	tissue cell
織機	ショッキ	loom, weaving machine
織物	おりもの	woven fabric

射

射出成形	シャシュツセイケイ	injection molding
注射	チュウシャ	injection
注射器	チュウシャキ	syringe
放射-	ホウシャ	radiation, radiant
放射線	ホウシャセン	radiation
放射度	ホウシャド	radiation intensity
放射性同位元素	ホウシャセイドウイゲンソ	radioactive isotope
入射線	ニュウシャセン	incident ray
反射線	ハンシャセン	reflected ray
反射	ハンシャ	reflex

消

消化	ショウカ	digestion {biol}
消化管	ショウカカン	alimentary canal
消磁	ショウジ	demagnetization

植

植物	ショクブツ	plant, vegetation
植物学	ショクブツガク	botany
植物生理学	ショクブツセイリガク	plant physiology
植物性-	ショクブツセイ	vegetative
陽生植物	ヨウセイショクブツ	sun plant
陰生植物	インセイショクブツ	shade plant
移植	イショク	graft, transplant

組

組織	ソシキ	tissue {biol}; organization; texture
組織学	ソシキガク	histology
組織分化	ソシキブンカ	histodifferentiation
組織形成	ソシキケイセイ	histogenesis
組み合わせ	くみあわせ	combination
組み立て	くみたて	assembling
一組; 二組	ひとくみ; ふたくみ	one set; two sets

伝

伝熱係数	デンネツケイスウ	heat transfer coefficient
伝熱面積	デンネツメンセキ	heating surface area
伝熱管	デンネツカン	heat exchanger tube

放

放射-	ホウシャ	radiation, radiant
放射性-	ホウシャセイ	radioactive
放射線	ホウシャセン	radiation
放射度	ホウシャド	radiation intensity
放出	ホウシュツ	emission
放熱器	ホウネツキ	radiator
放物線	ホウブツセン	parabola

胞

細胞	サイボウ	cell
細胞学	サイボウガク	cytology
細胞核	サイボウカク	cell nucleus
細胞質	サイボウシツ	cytoplasm
細胞液	サイボウエキ	cell sap
液胞	エキホウ	vacuole
小胞	ショウホウ	vesicle
胞子	ホウシ	spore
胞子体	ホウシタイ	sporophyte
胞子形成	ホウシケイセイ	sporulation

陽

陽イオン	ヨウイオン	positive ion, cation
陽電気	ヨウデンキ	positive electricity
陽子	ヨウシ	proton
陽電子	ヨウデンシ	positron
陽性元素	ヨウセイゲンソ	electropositive element
陽関数	ヨウカンスウ	explicit function

陽生植物	ヨウセイショクブツ	sun plant
太陽	タイヨウ	sun

粒

粒子	リュウシ	particle; corpuscle
粒子線	リュウシセン	corpuscular beam
素粒子	ソリュウシ	elementary particle
反粒子	ハンリュウシ	anti-particle
粒度	リュウド	grain size
粒状-	リュウジョウ	granular
粒状組織	リュウジョウソシキ	granular texture

12 Tentative Forms; Miscellaneous Expressions

In this chapter we begin with the "tentative" forms for verbs and adjectives. The tentative occurs with moderate frequency in technical Japanese, but it has no direct counterpart in English. Next we discuss a standard construction involving the tentative followed by とする, and also summarize some other important constructions involving the particle と.

After that we show how interrogative words can be combined with the particles か and も to form several sets of expressions in a systematic way. Then we conclude by giving you some more noun-following expressions and verb-following expressions. These presentations are continuations of Sections 8.4 and 8.6.

12.1 The Tentative Form of Verbs (おう)

The tentative is made by adding う to the xo-base of xu-verbs and to the yo-base of ru-verbs. For xu-verbs the xo-base is obtained by replacing the last syllable of the dictionary form, a HIRAGANA symbol belonging to the う column, by the corresponding HIRAGANA symbol from the お column. For ru-verbs the yo-base is found by replacing る of the dictionary form by よ.

Some illustrations of the tentative forms for verbs are as follows:

	Present Affirmative	Tentative Affirmative
ru-verbs		
to see	見る	見よう
to consider	考える	考えよう
xu-verbs		
to express	いい表す	いい表そう
to say	いう	いおう
to move	移る	移ろう
to hold	もつ	もとう
to solve	解く	解こう
to connect	つなぐ	つなごう
to tie	結ぶ	結ぼう
to stack	積む	積もう
Irregular verbs		
to go	行く	行こう
to be	ある	あろう
to do	する	しよう！
to come	くる	こよう！

There are two main uses of the tentative: (a) When a tentative form of a verb involving a human action occurs at the end of a sentence, it can be translated as "Let us ...," "We shall ...," or "We are going to ...." For example, ...考えよう corresponds to the standard textbook phrase "Let us consider ...."

実験により定められた係数を表に示そう。
ジッケンによりさだめられたケイスウをヒョウにしめそう。
Let us show the experimentally determined coefficients in a table.

粒子の加速について次のように考えてみよう。
リュウシのカソクについてつぎのようにかんがえてみよう。
We shall try thinking about the acceleration of the particles in the following way.

次に流体力学における単振動の例をあげよう。
つぎにリュウタイリキガクにおけるタンシンドウのレイをあげよう。
Next let us give an example of simple harmonic motion in fluid dynamics.

この式の解をもとめるために、上でのべた方法にしたがおう。
このシキのカイをもとめるために、うえでのべたホウホウにしたがおう。
In order to get a solution of this equation, let us follow the method discussed above. {*Note:* The terminal verb is the tentative of 従う[したがう], "to follow, obey"}

このことが原子を形成する核外電子についても成り立つかどうかを見てゆこう。
このことがゲンシをケイセイするカクガイデンシについてもなりたつかどうかをみてゆこう。
We shall proceed to see whether or not this idea is valid also for the outer-shell electrons that make up the atom.

(b) For all other verbs (that is, those not involving a human action) and for adjectives, the phrase containing the tentative conveys the idea of some hesitation, uncertainty, vagueness, or conjecture. In English this corresponds to inserting a word like "probably," "possibly," or "perhaps" into the sentence. For example, 液相であろう means "It is probably the liquid phase." Sometimes the tentative form is used just to make the sentence seem somewhat less blunt or less dogmatic and may be omitted in translation; this is particularly true of sentences ending with ...のであろう. There are also occasions when the tentative form is used as a future tense and should be translated that way in English.

この二つの関数は単振動の方程式とどのような関係にあるのであろうか。
このふたつのカンスウはタンシンドウのホウテイシキとどのようなカンケイにあるのであろうか。

In what way might these two functions be related to the equations of simple harmonic motion?

上の例を見ると、この方程式の解き方はすぐにわかるであろう。
うえのレイをみると、このホウテイシキのときかたはすぐにわかるであろう。

If you look at the example above, you may quickly see the way to solve this equation.

さらに分子間力を考えにいれれば、この方程式はもっと解きにくくなろう。
さらにブンシカンリョクをかんがえにいれれば、このホウテイシキはもっとときにくくなろう。

Furthermore, if we take intermolecular forces into account, this equation (probably) will become more difficult to solve.

さて、流体力学の目的はなんであろうか。流体中を運動する物体にはどういう力がはたらくかをあきらかにするのが流体力学の最大の目的であるといえよう。
さて、リュウタイリキガクのモクテキはなんであろうか。リュウタイチュウをウンドウするブッタイにはどういうちからがはたらくかをあきらかにするのがリュウタイリキガクのサイダイのモクテキであるといえよう。

Now what [might we say] is the objective of fluid mechanics? We can probably say that the major objective of fluid mechanics is determining clearly what kinds of forces are acting on objects moving within a fluid.

In the last sentence いえよう is the tentative of the potential verb いえる, which comes from the verb いう (to say); hence いえよう means "we can probably say."

Sometimes the phrase であろう is shortened to だろう, and one will occasionally encounter constructions such as

	Tentative Affirmative		Tentative Negative	
Present	動くだろう	probably moves	動かないだろう	probably does not move
Past	動いただろう	probably moved	動かなかっただろう	probably did not move

In technical writing these abbreviated forms occur less frequently than the more formal expressions 動くであろう, 動かないであろう, etc.

12-9

それならばそのような運動はどんな関数で表したらよいだろうか。
それならばそのような<u>ウンドウ</u>はどんな<u>カンスウ</u>で<u>あらわ</u>したらよいだろうか。
If that is the case, then with what kind of function can we best describe that kind of motion?

12.2 The Tentative Form of Adjectives (かろう)

For i-adjectives the tentative is formed by dropping the terminal い and adding かろう. For na- and no-adjectives the terminal particles are replaced by であろう.

	Present Affirmative	Tentative Affirmative
i-adjectives		
non-existent	ない	なかろう
high	高い	高かろう
good	よい	よかろう
hot	熱い	熱かろう
equal	等しい	等しかろう
na- and no-adjectives		
important	重要である	重要であろう
constant	一定である	一定であろう
same	同じである	同じであろう

The tentative forms for i-adjectives do not occur very often. These forms are translated as なかろう, "is perhaps nonexistent," 高かろう, "is probably high," and so on.

この流れを表すのに球面調和関数を用いてもよかろう。
この<u>ながれ</u>を<u>あらわ</u>すのに<u>キュウメンチョウワカンスウ</u>を<u>もちい</u>てもよかろう。
Perhaps we may use (surface) spherical harmonics to describe this flow.

このためには粒子の加速度を測定する必要はなかろう。
このためには<u>リュウシ</u>の<u>カソクド</u>を<u>ソクテイ</u>する<u>ヒツヨウ</u>はなかろう。
For this it is probably not necessary to determine the acceleration of the particle.

In sentences like these some authors would prefer to use よいだろう and ないだろう. Negative forms and other tenses can be made similarly.

	Tentative Affirmative		Tentative Negative	
Present	強いだろう	is probably strong	強くないだろう	is probably not strong
Past	強かっただろう	was probably strong	強くなかっただろう	was probably not strong

Since だろう is a shortened form of であろう one may also encounter 強いであろう, 強くないであろう, and so on.

12.3 The Tentative plus とする and Other Constructions with と

In Chapter 6 you learned that と between two nouns means "and," and that と at the end of a clause may be translated as "if" or "when(ever)." In this section we summarize a number of constructions involving the particle と. We begin with one that involves the tentative form of verbs.

a. The Tentative plus とする

　　When the tentative is followed by the particle と and the verb する, the resulting phrase may have one of two possible meanings: (a) it may convey the notion that an action is about to begin, or (b) it may convey the idea that an attempt is made to do something, sometimes with the understanding that the attempt is unsuccessful.

反応が起ころうとするとき、圧力が上がる。
ハンノウがおころうとするとき、アツリョクがあがる。
When the reaction is about to occur, the pressure rises.

この実験において球が運動しようとすれば、流体の速度を増加させる。
このジッケンにおいてキュウがウンドウしようとすれば、リュウタイのソクドをゾウカさ
　　　せる。
In this experiment when the sphere is about to move, we increase the fluid velocity.

細胞の大きさを測定しようとした。
サイボウのおおきさをソクテイしようとした。
They tried to measure the size of the cell.

液体をちぢめようとすると、気体に比べてちぢめにくいことがわかる。
エキタイをちぢめようとすると、キタイにくらべてちぢめにくいことがわかる。
When we try to compress liquids, we find that they are difficult to compress compared to gases.

b. Expressions Involving ...という, ...とよぶ, *etc.*

　　When と precedes verbs like いう (to say), 知る[しる] (to know), 考える (to think), わかる (to understand), or 書く[かく] (to write) — or the passive or potential verbs derived from them — it is translated as "that" after a declarative statement, or as "why" after a question.

ニュートン力学により地球はなぜ球形ではないかということがわかった。
ニュートンリキガクによりチキュウはなぜキュウケイではないかということがわかった。
From Newtonian mechanics we know why the earth is not spherical.

電磁気の原理はわかりにくいといわれている。
デンジキのゲンリはわかりにくいといわれている。
It is said that the principles of electromagnetism are hard to understand.

粒子加速器の実験はますます重要になるであろうと考えられている。
リュウシカソクキのジッケンはますますジュウヨウになるであろうとかんがえられている。
It is thought that particle accelerator experiments will become increasingly important.

When a clause is followed by ということ, the latter means "the fact that."

細胞が原形質を含むということが知られている。
サイボウがゲンケイシツをふくむということがしられている。
It is known that cells contain protoplasm. {Lit.: The fact that cells contain protoplasm is known.}

The expression Aというのは (sometimes shortened to Aとは) means literally "the thing we call A." It is used in both the spoken and written language to focus attention on the noun "A," and may often be ignored in the English translation.

等速直線運動というのは速度が一定の運動のことである。
トウソクチョクセンウンドウというのはソクドがイッテイのウンドウのことである。
Uniform linear motion is motion at constant velocity.

Earlier you learned that AをBという means "A is called B." Instead of the verb いう (to say, call), other verbs are sometimes used, such as 呼ぶ[よぶ] (to call) or 名付ける[なづける] (to call, name); this last verb is made up of the noun 名[な] (name) and 付ける[つける] (to attach). Sometimes the corresponding passive verbs are used.

水素原子核は陽子とも呼ばれる。
スイソゲンシカクはヨウシともよばれる。
The hydrogen-atom nucleus is also called a proton.

このような植物を陰性植物という。
このようなショクブツをインセイショクブツという。
This kind of plant is called a shade plant.

電子・陽子・中性子のような粒子は素粒子と名付けられた。
デンシ・ヨウシ・チュウセイシのようなリュウシはソリュウシとなづけられた。
Particles like electrons, protons, and neutrons are called elementary (fundamental) particles.

c. Expressions Involving ...とする
In technical writing the expressions AをBとする and AをBとおく are ways to say "We let (concept or item) A be (represented by symbol) B."

f(x,y)の増分をΔfとおく。
f(x,y)のゾウブンをΔfとおく。
We let the increment in f(x,y) be Δf.

zの実数部をxとする。
zのジッスウブをxとする。
We let the real part of z be x.

When a verb or adjective precedes とする, the meaning of とする is "we suppose that."

水素原子と塩素原子との間にはたらく力は強さkのばねの力と同じように考えられるとし
　　　よう。
<u>スイソゲンシ</u>と<u>エンソゲンシ</u>との<u>あいだ</u>にはたらく<u>ちから</u>は<u>つよさ</u>kの<u>ばね</u>の<u>ちから</u>と<u>おな</u>
　　　じように<u>かんがえ</u>られるとしよう。
Let us suppose that the force acting between the hydrogen atom and the chlorine atom can be thought
　　　of as similiar to the force in a spring with strength k.

d. Expressions with ...となる

　　　The expression AはBとなる is synonymous with AはBになる and means "A
becomes B; A turns into B; A turns out to be B."

これらの原子は放射線により陽イオンとなる。
これらの<u>ゲンシ</u>は<u>ホウシャセン</u>により<u>ヨウイオン</u>となる。
By irradiation these atoms become positive ions.

e. と *in Expressions of Identity and Difference*

　　　In expressions of identity and difference と corresponds to "as," "to," and
"from" in English: ...と同じである (is the same as ...); ...と同一である (is identical
to ...); ...と違う (is different from ...); ...と異なる (differs from ...).

陽電子が電子と違うのは、陽性の電気をもつことである。
<u>ヨウデンシ</u>が<u>デンシ</u>と<u>ちが</u>うのは、<u>ヨウセイ</u>の<u>デンキ</u>をもつことである。
Positrons differ from electrons in that they have a positive charge.

アルファ粒子はヘリウム原子核と同一である。
アルファ<u>リュウシ</u>はヘリウム<u>ゲンシカク</u>と<u>ドウイツ</u>である。
Alpha particles are identical to helium-atom nuclei.

Note also the expression ...と同時に, "at the same time as ...."

　　　We hope that this summary of constructions involving the particle と will help
you remember the many different ways that と is used and how to translate it. All of
these expressions are quite common.

12.4 Interrogative Words with the Particles か and も

　　　When interrogative words are followed by the particle か they acquire an
"indefinite" meaning. Thus だれか means "someone," だれかに means "to someone," だれかの means "someone's." If the indefinite word is a topic or an object of
a verb, the particles は and を are usually omitted after the particle か; if it is a subject,
sometimes が is omitted. These interrogative words plus か occur only in affirmative
statements.

　　　When interrogative words are followed by the particle も, they take on a
"comprehensive" meaning; they are wholly inclusive with an affirmative verb and
wholly exclusive with a negative verb. For example, いつもできる means "It is
always possible," and だれもしらない, "No one knows." Other particles may be

used with も, but must precede it, as in だれにも; however, は, が, and を are not used with も. The following list summarizes the expressions with か and も:

Interrogative	Interrogative+か	Interrogative+も with Affirmative Verb	Negative Verb
だれ	だれか	...	だれも
who	someone		no one
どちら	どちらか	どちらも	どちらも
which of two	either of two	both	neither
どれ	どれか	どれも	どれも
which one	one of them	all, any	none, not any
どこ	どこか	どこも	どこも
where	somewhere	everywhere	nowhere
いくら	いくらか	いくらも	いくらも
how much	some amount	ever so much	not much
いくつ	いくつか	いくつも	いくつも
how many	several	ever so many	not many
いつ	いつか	いつも	いつも
when	sometime	always	never
いずれ	いずれか	いずれも	いずれも
which one	one of them	all, both	neither, none
なに	なにか	...	なにも
what	something		nothing
どの+noun	...	どの+noun+も	どの+noun+も
which+noun		every+noun	no+noun

Here are some sentences illustrating the use of a few of these combinations.

加熱過程においてはいつもこのような熱伝管を使う。
カネツカテイにおいてはいつもこのようなネツデンカンをつかう。
We always use this kind of heat exchanger tube in the heating process.

以前この重合プロセスではだれも過酸化水素を使ったことがなかった。
イゼンこのジュウゴウプロセスではだれもカサンカスイソをつかったことがなかった。
In this polymerization process no one had previously used hydrogen peroxide.

ラジウム原子はいつも放射線を放射している。
ラジウムゲンシはいつもホウシャセンをホウシャしている。
Radium atoms are always emitting radioactivity.

その振動はいくつかの単振動を重ね合わせたものである。
そのシンドウはいくつかのタンシンドウをかさねあわせたものである。
That oscillatory motion is the result of superposing several simple harmonic motions.

圧力はピストンの変位とともにいつまでも振動する。
アツリョクはピストンのヘンイとともにいつまでもシンドウする。
The pressure oscillates indefinitely along with the displacement of the piston.

ここで生体高分子のいくつかのいちじるしい性質についてのべることにする。
ここでセイタイコウブンシのいくつかのいちじるしいセイシツについてのべることにする。
Here we propose to discuss several of the remarkable properties of biopolymers.

トレーサー実験においては、いつも放射性元素が使われる。
トレーサージッケンにおいては、いつもホウシャセイゲンソがつかわれる。
In tracer experiments radioisotopes are always used.

In addition, the combination "interrogative+connective+も" also contains the idea of an all-inclusive meaning, as illustrated by the following sentences:

どの細胞を見ても、核が見える。
どのサイボウをみても、カクがみえる。
No matter which cell you look at, a nucleus is visible.

どのような溶液を用いても、流量は測定しやすいことがわかる。
どのようなヨウエキをもちいても、リュウリョウはソクテイしやすいことがわかる。
No matter what kinds of solutions we use, we know that the amount of flow is easy to measure.

Note also that the interrogatives followed by でも have an all-inclusive meaning:

だれでも	no matter who, any one at all
いつでも	no matter when, any time at all
なんでも	no matter what, anything at all

Finally, we illustrate how the indefinite phrases (interrogative+か) are used in relative clauses. Note the word order in the following pairs of sentences:

a. Indefinite phrase+predicate {no relative clause}
b. Indefinite phrase+relative clause+noun+predicate.

だれかがこの実験を行った。
だれかがこのジッケンをおこなった。
Someone performed this experiment.

だれかこの実験を行った人が溶液の酸性を知るだろう。
だれかこのジッケンをおこなったひとがヨウエキのサンセイをしるだろう。
Someone who has performed this experiment will probably know the acidity of the solution.

空気中のなにかが組織と反応する。
クウキチュウのなにかがソシキとハンノウする。
Something in the atmosphere reacts with the tissue.

空気中になにか組織と反応するものがある。
クウキチュウになにかソシキとハンノウするものがある。
There is something in the air that reacts with the tissue.

12.5 More Noun-Following Expressions

In Section 8.4 you learned a number of noun-following expressions. In this section we give some additional noun-following expressions that are common in technical writing. First we list them and then illustrate their use. Those marked with # are now often written with HIRAGANA. Those in the second group appear only at the end of a clause.

First Group

...に沿って	# [にそって]	along
...の代わりに	# [のかわりに]	instead of, in place of
...のほかに		other than; in addition to
...当たり	# [あたり]	per
...にもかかわらず		in spite of, notwithstanding
...によらず		independent of, regardless of
...に関せず	[にかんせず]	regardless of
...に関する限り	[にかんするかぎり]	as far as ... is concerned
...ばかりではなく...も		not only ... but also
...のみではなく...も		not only ... but also
...のみならず...も		not only ... but also
...に限らず	[にかぎらず]	not only ... but also
...とともに		with, along with
...に伴って	# [にともなって]	with, along with
...に従って	# [にしたがって]	following, in accordance with
...に基づいて	# [にもとづいて]	on the basis of
...に際して	# [にさいして]	on the occasion of, at the time of
...なしに		without
...なしで		without

Second Group

...に違いない	[にちがいない]	is certainly
...に過ぎない	# [にすぎない]	is just, is simply
...にほかならない		is just, is nothing other than

The noun-following expressions in the first group function as simple or compound postpositions, and those in the second group function as predicates.

式(2)は式(1)においてx,yをa,bで置きかえたものにすぎない。
シキ(2)はシキ(1)においてx,yをa,bでおきかえたものにすぎない。
Equation (2) is just Equation (1) with x,y replaced by a,b.

放物線にそって動くとき関数f(x,y)はあまり変化しない。
ホウブツセンにそってうごくときカンスウf(x,y)はあまりヘンカしない。
As we go along the parabola, we see that f(x,y) does not change much.

その粒子は中性子に違いない。
そのリュウシはチュウセイシにちがいない。
That particle is certainly a neutron.

この方程式においては速度vのかわりに運動量pを用いる。
このホウテイシキにおいてはソクドvのかわりにウンドウリョウpをもちいる。
In this equation we use the momentum **p** instead of the velocity **v**.

単位時間あたりの速度の変化は加速度とよばれる。
タンイジカンあたりのソクドのヘンカはカソクドとよばれる。
The change in velocity per unit time is called the acceleration.

気体の状態式は、分子間力にもとづいて理解できる。
キタイのジョウタイシキは、ブンシカンリョクにもとづいてリカイできる。
The equation of state of gases can be understood on the basis of intermolecular forces.

ここでf(x)はBessel関数にほかならない。
ここでf(x)はBesselカンスウにほかならない。
Here f(x) is nothing other than a Bessel function.

発熱反応にさいして温度が上がる。
ハツネツハンノウにさいしてオンドがあがる。
When an exothermic reaction occurs, the temperature increases.

高原らの方法にしたがって実験を行った。
たかはららのホウホウにしたがってジッケンをおこなった。
We performed the experiment following the method of Takahara et al.

気体にかぎらず液体も圧縮することができる。
キタイにかぎらずエキタイもアッシュクすることができる。
Not only gases but also liquids can be compressed.

12.6 More Verb-Following Expressions

In Section 8.6 you learned some verb-following expressions involving こと and の. Here we give you a few more verb-following expressions and illustrate their use. The two expressions marked with & are used when amplifying some previous statement. Those marked with # are often written with HIRAGANA. Constructions in the first group are used at the end of a sentence or independent clause; those in the second group correspond to subordinating conjunctions at the end of a clause.

First Group

...ようになる		to come about that
...ようにする		to see to it that
...はずである		we (have good reason to) expect that
...からである	&	that's because
...訳である	&# [わけである]	the reason is, it means that
...訳にはいかない	# [わけにはいかない]	it cannot be that
...かも知れない	# [かもしれない]	it may be that; perhaps
...に違いない	[にちがいない]	it is certain that
...に過ぎない	# [にすぎない]	we do not do more than
...とは限らない	[とはかぎらない]	it is not necessarily true that

12-17

...際(に)	# [さい(に)]	when
...限り	[かぎり]	as long as
...にもかかわらず		in spite of the fact that, even though
...かどうか		whether or not
...代わりに	# [かわりに]	instead of
...のみならず...も		not only ... but also
...ばかりでなく...も		not only ... but also
...というように		in such a manner that
...上に(も)	[うえに(も)]	(also) for ...ing
...上で (with present verb)	[うえで]	in order to, for the sake of
...上で (with past verb)	[うえで]	after
...に従って	# [にしたがって]	(according) as
...とともに		along with ...ing
...に伴って	# [にともなって]	along with ...ing
...ほか(に)		in addition to ...ing
...ことなく		without ...ing

The following sentences illustrate the use of some of the above verb-following expressions:

流体の中の応力は流体の運動状態によってきまるはずである。
リュウタイのなかのオウリョクはリュウタイのウンドウジョウタイによってきまるはずである。
We expect that the stress in the fluid will be determined by the state of flow of the fluid.

原子と分子がいかに気体を構成するかについての見方によって、気体の性質を明らかにすることができるはずである。
ゲンシとブンシがいかにキタイをコウセイするかについてのみかたによって、キタイのセイシツをあきらかにすることができるはずである。
We should be able to elucidate the properties of gases by considering how atoms and molecules constitute a gas.

気体の温度があまり変化しないかぎり、式(2)が用いられる。
キタイのオンドがあまりヘンカしないかぎり、シキ(2)がもちいられる。
As long as the gas temperature does not change too much, Equation (2) can be used.

ボンベに酸素が入っているかどうかはまだ知らない。
ボンベにサンソがはいっているかどうかはまだしらない。
We do not yet know whether or not oxygen is in the (gas) cylinder.

過酸化物によってモノマー重合がよく起こるにもかかわらず、この場合には起こらない。
カサンカブツによってモノマージュウゴウがよくおこるにもかかわらず、このばあいにはおこらない。
Even though polymerization of monomers occurs readily due to peroxides, with this monomer it does not (occur).

原子や分子の運動を解くにはニュートン力学を用いるわけにはいかず、量子力学を用いな
　　ければならない。
ゲンシやブンシのウンドウをとくにはニュートンリキガクをもちいるわけにはいかず、リョ
　　ウシリキガクをもちいなければならない。
To solve the motion of atoms and molecules, we cannot use Newtonian mechanics; we must use
　　quantum mechanics.

周期運動であるかぎり、どのような運動も、単振動を重ね合わせて表すことができる。
シュウキウンドウであるかぎり、どのようなウンドウも、タンシンドウをかさねあわせて
　　あらわすことができる。
We can describe any kind of motion, as long as it is periodic, by superposing simple harmonic motions.

どの細胞も原形質を含むに違いない。
どのサイボウもゲンケイシツをふくむにちがいない。
It is certain that every cell contains protoplasm.

この原理は光にかぎらず、物質の周期運動を理解する上にもやくだつ。
このゲンリはひかりにかぎらず、ブッシツのシュウキウンドウをリカイするうえにもやく
　　だつ。
This principle is helpful for understanding not only light, but also the periodic motions of matter.

この化合物はアルコールに溶けるのみならず、水にも溶ける。
このカゴウブツはアルコールにとけるのみならず、みずにもとける。
This compound not only dissolves in alcohol, but also in water.

積分方程式を解くかわりに、高原は違った方法を用いた。
セキブンホウテイシキをとくかわりに、たかはらはちがったホウホウをもちいた。
Instead of solving the integral equation, Takahara used a different method.

ガスの中に水蒸気があったにもかかわらず反応速度を測定することができた。
ガスのなかにスイジョウキがあったにもかかわらずハンノウソクドをソクテイすることが
　　できた。
In spite of the fact that water vapor was present in the gas, they were able to measure the reaction
　　velocity.

ADDITIONAL VOCABULARY FOR EXERCISES

うける	【受ける】	to receive
単位体	タンイタイ	unit (simple body)
みたす		to fill (up)
しめる		to occupy {space, location}
計器	ケイキ	measuring device
あまる		to be in excess
ペプチド		peptides
アミノ酸	アミノサン	amino acids
さかんにする		to make active; to invigorate
いちじるしい		marked, striking
かなり		rather
はっきり		clearly
マッハ数	マッハスウ	Mach number
形態形成	ケイタイケイセイ	morphogenesis
ただ		only, merely
化石	カセキ	fossil
とり入れる	とりいれる	to adopt
どのようにして		{same as どのように}
なす		to do, make, perform

EXERCISES

Ex 12.1 Matching Japanese and English technical terms

(a) Shapes and contours

球形-( )	1. amorphous
球状-( )	2. deformation
球面( )	3. globular
正方形( )	4. rectangle
線形-( )	5. linear
長方形( )	6. parabola
変形( )	7. spherical
放物線( )	8. spherical surface
無定形-( )	9. square

(b) Cells: structures and substances

液胞( )	1. cell nucleus
核酸( )	2. cell sap
原形質( )	3. cytoplasm
細胞液( )	4. nucleic acid
細胞核( )	5. protoplasm
細胞質( )	6. spore
組織( )	7. sporophyte
胞子( )	8. tissue
胞子体( )	9. vacuole

(c) Implements

移相器( )	1. antenna
空中線( )	2. electromagnet
磁気テープ( )	3. heat exchanger tube
注射器( )	4. light bulb
電球( )	5. magnetic tape
電磁石( )	6. phase shifter
伝熱管( )	7. radiation pyrometer
放射高温計( )	8. syringe

(d) Fields of study

形態学( )	1. botany
細胞学( )	2. cytology
組織学( )	3. electromagnetism
地質学( )	4. geography
地理学( )	5. geology
植物学( )	6. histology
植物生理学( )	7. morphology
電磁気学( )	8. plant physiology

(e) Nuclear physics

陰電子( )	1. anti-particle
核外電子( )	2. atomic nucleus
核子( )	3. extranuclear electron
核磁子( )	4. fundamental particle
核内力( )	5. intranuclear force
核反応( )	6. negatron
原子核( )	7. nuclear reaction
素粒子( )	8. nucleon
反粒子( )	9. nuclear magneton
陽子( )	10. positron
陽電子( )	11. proton

(f) Electricity and magnetism

過電圧( )	1. atmospheric discharge
空中放電( )	2. corpuscular beam
地磁気( )	3. demagnetization
磁化( )	4. electromagnetism
磁場( )	5. geomagnetism
磁力線( )	6. line of magnetic force
消磁( )	7. magnetic field
電磁気( )	8. magnetization
放射線( )	9. over-voltage
放射度( )	10. radiation
粒子線( )	11. radiation intensity

Ex 12.2 Comparing terminal verb and adjective forms

(a) In each of the following sentences, change the terminal verb to the tentative form and then translate the sentence.

 1. この線形方程式を解く。
 2. 次の関数を積分してみる。
 3. ガラス管の中の液体を流す。
 4. シリンダを運動させる。
 5. 電圧を測定する。
 6. ヨウ化カリウムの溶解度を測定しておく。
 7. Pauliの原理を考える。
 8. 粒子の加速度をａとする。
 9. ワイヤ[wire]を振動させる。
10.　アンモニアの入ったフラスコと塩化水素の入ったフラスコをつなぐ。

(b) Each set of sentences has three versions of the terminal verb or adjective. Translate each version.

```
                    解きにくい。
1. この方程式は解きにくくない。
                    解きにくいであろう。
```

```
                    わかりやすい。
2. この解法はわかるであろう。
                    わからないであろう。
```

```
                    用いた。
3. サイン関数を用いたかもしれない。
                    用いたであろう。
```

```
                    必要はない。
4. 分子量をしる必要があろう。
                    必要はなかろう。
```

```
                    測定しなければならない。
5. 電流を測定しなくてもよいであろう。
                    測定すればよい。
```

使うほうがよい。

6. 分光光度計を使ったであろう。
　　　　　　　　　使ったかもしれない。

　　　　　考える。
7. 陽イオンの反応を考えよう。
　　　　　　　　考えただろう。

　　　　固定した。
8. シリンダを固定してみよう。
　　　　　　固定しなかっただろう。

　　　　Lとする。
9. 伝熱管の長さをLとしよう。
　　　　　　Lとしただろう。

　　　　　　　　のべた。
10. 原子核の近くの電磁場についてのべよう。
　　　　　　　　　のべたであろう。

Ex 12.3 Matching Japanese technical terms and definitions

(a) Biology

核酸( )　　　　1. 体が細長いもの。

原形質( )　　　2. 細胞を構成する核質以外の部分のこと。

細胞( )　　　　3. 細胞の中にある重要な球のような形をしたもの。

細胞核( )　　　4. 生物体の細胞中にある重要な生体高分子物質。

細胞質( )　　　5. 生物体を構成する最小単位体。

線形動物( )　　6. 生物体の細胞を構成する主[シュ = main]成分。

組織( )　　　　7. 胞子から地下で生成された石炭。

胞子炭( )　　　8. 多細胞生物において、形態的、機能[キノウ = function]的
　　　　　　　　　に同一の細胞の集まり[あつまり = collection]。

(b) Physics and chemistry

核磁子( )　　　　　1. X線、γ線、粒子線などを放出するもの。
過酸化物( )　　　　2. 各点[カクテン＝each point]における接線[セッセン＝
原子核( )　　　　　　tangent]の方向がその点における磁場の方向をしめす曲線
磁場( )　　　　　　　[キョクセン＝curve]。
磁力線( )　　　　　3. 原子核の磁気モーメントを表す量子力学的単位。
地磁気( )　　　　　4. 原子の中央[チュウオウ＝center]にあり、まわりの電子と
電磁力( )　　　　　　で原子を構成するもの。
放射性物質( )　　　5. 原子、分子、イオン、電子などの物質粒子の高速度の流
無定形炭素( )　　　　れ。
陽子( )　　　　　　6. 磁石としての地球の性質とそれの作る磁場のこと。
陽電子( )　　　　　7. 磁石または電流によって作られる磁力があらわれる空間。
粒子線( )　　　　　8. 磁場において電流が流れている導体[ドウタイ＝
　　　　　　　　　　　conductor]を置いたときその導体[ドウタイ]のうける力。
　　　　　　　　　　9. 水素原子の核と同じで、中性子と結合して原子核を構成
　　　　　　　　　　　する素粒子。
　　　　　　　　　　10. その同素体のうち、はっきりした結晶[ケッショウ＝
　　　　　　　　　　　crystal]性を示さないもの。
　　　　　　　　　　11. 電子と同じ質量をもち、量として電子と同じプラスの電
　　　　　　　　　　　気量をもつ素粒子。
　　　　　　　　　　12. 分子中に －O－O－ の酸素結合をもつ酸化物。

Ex 12.4 Translate the following sentences

1. 細胞は生物体を構成する最小単位体で、細胞核とそのまわりの細胞質か
　 ら成り立っている。
2. 液胞は細胞に見られる小空間で、中は水溶液でみたされ、生長した植物
　 細胞の大部分をしめる。
3. 陰性植物は陰地で生きて成長する植物で、同化量が少ないため生長量も
　 少なく、大きくならない。
4. 放射性同位元素は安定[アンテイ＝stable]同位体と同じ化学的性質をも
　 つので、生物体中での物質移動をしらべるのに利用されており[from リ
　 ョウする＝to use]、この場合これをトレーサー[tracer]とよんでいる。
5. 球面で光線が反射する場合、入射光線と反射光線の方向の間の関係は平
　 面で反射する場合と同一である。
6. 移相とは位相を変化させることであり、移相器とは位相を変化させるも
　 のである。
7. 放射伝熱において高温物体はその温度に応じて熱を表面から放射する。
8. 放射高温度計とは高温物体から発する放射エネルギーの量を測りその温
　 度を定める計器である。

12-24

Ex 12.5 Read the following essays for comprehension

1. 水素原子と酸素原子とが化合して水の分子となるとき、あまったエネルギーが熱となって放出される。核子が結合して原子核を作るときも、同じように、結合エネルギーが放出される。例えば中性子を水にあてると、水素の原子核すなわち陽子がこれを受け入れて[from うけいれる = to receive]重陽子を作る場合結合エネルギーは放射線として放出される。

2. 消化管ではいろいろなホルモンが作られる。これら消化管ホルモンは、胃[イ = stomach]や腸[チョウ = intestines]の中にどういう物質が入ってきたかによって、それに応じたはたらきをする。例えばたんぱく質の分解物(ペプチド、アミノ酸)があると、ガストリン[gastrin]が出て、胃液[イエキ = gastric juice]を分泌[ブンピツ = secretion]させて、胃[イ]や腸[チョウ]の運動をさかんにする。

3. 気体、溶液、固体などの中でイオン、電子、コロイド粒子などの荷電[カデン = charged]粒子が電場により力を受ける[うける = to receive]とき、その平均[ヘイキン = average]の移動速度vと電場Eとの関係v = μEで定義[テイギ =definition]される係数μを移動度という。この比例関係はμEがあまり大きくないときに成り立ち、等方性物質ではμはスカラー定数である。

4. 地表近くの温度は気温の変化にともなって、たえず変化している。しかし地下20-30mより深く[from ふかい = deep]なると、気温とは無関係に、温度は深さ[ふかさ]とともに増していく。そして熱は温度のより高いところから流れるので、地球内部から地表に向かって熱が流れると考えられてきた。したがってこのような流れによって、地球表面の単位面積あたり、単位時間中に運ばれる熱量を測定することが多くの地方で行われた。その結果、地球内部からの熱の流れはどこでも同じ、1cm²、1秒間[ビョウカン = second]あたり1.5×10cal程度であることがわかった。

5. 植物の細胞の運動には細胞の壁[かべ = wall]にそって原形質がいつも一つの方向に流れているのがある。これを原形質流動とよんでいる。その速さは1秒間[ビョウカン]に0.015-0.1mmである。動物の細胞ではこのようないちじるしい原形質流動は見られないが、ある種[シュ = kind]の細胞ではかなりはっきり見ることができる。その中で最もよく知られている[from しる = to know]のはアメーバで、その運動は原形質の流れによって起こる。原形質はゲル[gel]の状態となっているが、それが流動性のあるゾル[sol]の状態となって、ある方向に流れるのである。

6. 飛行機[ヒコウキ = airplane]が高速で飛ぶ[とぶ = to fly]とき、機体のまわりの空気は高温になる。一部の熱は周囲[シュウイ = surroundings]の空気に

12-25

伝わるが、残り[from のこる = to remain]は機体表面を加熱する。これは空力加熱とよばれ、空気の絶対[ゼッタイ = absolute]温度はマッハ数の2乗[ジョウ = power]に比例して高くなる。例えば、高空をマッハ2で飛ぶ[とぶ]ときには150℃ぐらいになる。

Ex 12.6 Translate the following essay

　地球上には多くの違った生物が生きている。例えば、陰性植物と陽性植物とがある。生物の違いはどのようにして生じるのであろうか。どの生物も発生の過程においては一つの細胞から出発するが、数多くのステップを通って[from とおる = to pass through]分化が行われる。このことは動物でも植物でも、また人でもアヒル[duck]でも同じように起こる現象[ゲンショウ = phenomenon]である。

　人とアヒルの発生を比べると、人間でも一人一人の形態形成の初期[ショキ = beginning stage]には水かき[webfoot]の組織があるが、その細胞が消えてしまうのである。消えなければ水かきになってしまう。水かきのあるアヒルは、この間の細胞が消えない。ただそれだけの違いである。

　最近の分子生物学ではデオキシリボ核酸(DNA)をしらべて重要な知見[チケン = knowledge]が得られることが多い。例えば、コンドル[condor]はワシ[eagle]タカ[hawk]目[モク = order]ということになっていたが、ある人がそのDNAをしらべたところコウノトリ[white stork]に近いことが分かった。形の上ではワシやタカに近いが、いままでの考え方は間違いであった。

　化石のDNAをしらべれば、生物がどのように移り変わってきたかが分かる。生物が発生してからいままでになにが起こったかをDNAが伝えているのである。分子線・放射線等種々[シュジュ = various]の粒子線測定、核磁気測定等の物理学の方面で用いられてきた方法をとり入れて重大な発見がなされている。

TRANSLATIONS

Ex 12.4 Sentences

1. Cells are the smallest units that constitute organisms, and they are made up of a nucleus and its surrounding cytoplasm.
2. Vacuoles are small spaces seen in cells; they are filled with aqueous solutions and occupy the greater part of mature plant cells.
3. Shade plants are plants that live and grow in shady places; because their rates of assimilation are small, their growth rates are also small, and they do not become large.

4. Radioactive isotopes have the same chemical properties as stable isotopes; therefore, they are used to examine the transport of a substance within organisms, in which case they are called tracers.

5. When a light ray is reflected at a spherical surface, the relation between the directions of the incident ray and the reflected ray is identical to that when [a light ray] is reflected at a plane surface.

6. Causing a change in phase is (called) a phase shift, and a phase shifter is the instrument that brings about the change [in phase].

7. In radiant heat transfer a high temperature body radiates heat from its surface depending on its temperature.

8. A radiation pyrometer is a (measuring) device that measures the amount of radiant heat emitted from a high temperature body and determines the temperature [of that body].

Ex 12.6 Essay

Many different organisms are living on the earth. For example, there are shade plants and sun plants. How do the differences among organisms arise? In the process of its development, every organism emerges from a single cell and, in being differentiated, passes through numerous steps. The same phenomenon occurs for both plants and animals, and also for both human beings and ducks.

If we compare the development of human beings and ducks, we find that, at the beginning of every single person's morphogenesis, even a human being has tissue for webfeet; however, those cells completely disappear. If they did not disappear, they would end up as webfeet. For webfooted ducks these cells do not disappear. That (alone) is the sole difference.

In molecular biology in recent times, much important knowledge has been obtained by investigating deoxyribonucleic acids. For example, condors have been [placed] in the order of eagles and hawks, but some people have found, when studying DNA, that [condors] are close to white storks. In form [they] are close to eagles and hawks, but the idea [held] up to now [about their order] was mistaken.

If we study fossilized DNA, we can learn how organisms came to change. DNA is informing us what happened to organisms from their genesis to the present. Important discoveries are being made by the adoption of methods that [first] came to be used in the domain of physics, e.g., various corpuscular beam measurements, such as [those using] molecular beams and radiation (beams) and measurements with nuclear magnetism.

CHAPTER 13 　第十三章　[ダイジュウサンショウ]

割	カツ	split, division
	わり	rate; tenths
	わ(る)	to divide

基	キ	foundation; radical {chem}
	もと	basis
	もと(づく)	to be based (on)

求	キュウ	seeking; finding
	もと(める)	to seek; to find
	もと(まる)	to be obtained

及	キュウ	attainment
	およ(ぼす)	to exert (force)
	およ(ぶ)	to attain, reach
	およ(び)	and, as well as

吸	キュウ	inhalation
	す(う)	to suck, inhale

極	キョク	extremity, pole
	きわ(める)	to master
	きわ(めて)	extremely

工	-ク	worker
	コウ	manufacturing

自	シ; ジ	oneself
	みずか(ら)	by itself, oneself

受	ジュ	receiving
	う(ける)	to receive, accept

述	ジュツ	statement, discussion
	の(べる)	to state, discuss

所	ショ; ジョ	place
	ショ-	that which
	ところ	place

常	ジョウ	normal, usual
	つね(に)	always, continually

説	セツ	explanation
	-セツ	theory of
	と(く)	to explain

造	ゾウ	construction, structure

他	タ	other
	タ(の)	the other
	(その)タ	etc.

代	ダイ	substitution
	-ダイ	era; fee
	か(わる)	to replace
	か(わりに)	instead of

知	チ	knowledge
	し(る) {xu}	to know

値	チ	value
	あたい	value

調	チョウ	investigation; tone
	しら(べる)	to investigate

通	ツウ	passing through
	とお(す)	to admit, let pass
	とお(る)	to go through
	とお(りに)	in the manner, way

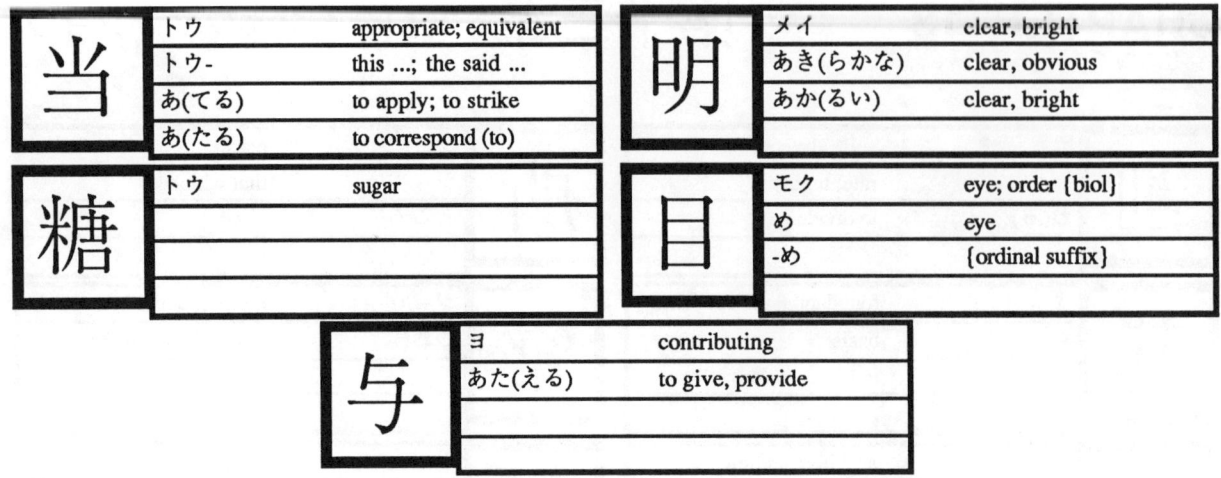

当	トウ	appropriate; equivalent
	トウ-	this ...; the said ...
	あ(てる)	to apply; to strike
	あ(たる)	to correspond (to)

明	メイ	clear, bright
	あき(らかな)	clear, obvious
	あか(るい)	clear, bright

糖	トウ	sugar

目	モク	eye; order {biol}
	め	eye
	-め	{ordinal suffix}

与	ヨ	contributing
	あた(える)	to give, provide

VOCABULARY

割

割合	わりあい	proportion, rate
割り当てる	わりあてる	to allocate
一割	イチわり	10%, one-tenth
分割	ブンカツ	division, partition
割球	カッキュウ	blastomere

基

塩基	エンキ	base
アルキル基	アルキルキ	alkyl group
基質	キシツ	substrate

求

求核反応	キュウカクハンノウ	nucleophilic reaction
求電子反応	キュウデンシハンノウ	electrophilic reaction
要求	ヨウキュウ	demand

及

及ぼし合う	およぼしあう	to exert (force) on each other

吸

吸熱	キュウネツ	endothermic
吸水	キュウスイ	water absorption
吸光度	キュウコウド	absorbance
吸光係数	キュウコウケイスウ	extinction coefficient

極

電極	デンキョク	electrode
陰極	インキョク	cathode
陽極	ヨウキョク	anode
分極	ブンキョク	polarization
極小の	キョクショウの	minimum, smallest
極大の	キョクダイの	maximum, greatest
極細胞	キョクサイボウ	polar cell
極性分子	キョクセイブンシ	polar molecule

工

工学	コウガク	engineering
化学工学	カガクコウガク	chemical engineering
工程	コウテイ	process
工場	コウば; コウジョウ	factory
人工の	ジンコウの	artificial, man-made
大工	ダイク	carpenter

自

自動的な	ジドウテキな	automatic
自動酸化	ジドウサンカ	auto-oxidation
自分	ジブン	oneself
自然	シゼン	nature

受

受動的な	ジュドウテキな	passive
電子受容体	デンシジュヨウタイ	electron acceptor
軸受(け)	ジクうけ	bearing

述

後述の	コウジュツの	as stated later
前述の	ゼンジュツの	as stated earlier
上述の	ジョウジュツの	as stated above

所

所長	ショチョウ	head {of an office, factory, or institute}
場所	ばショ	location, place
所要の	ショヨウの	required {lit.: that which is needed}
発電所	ハツデンショ	power plant

常

常温	ジョウオン	room temperature
常圧コンデンサー	ジョウアツコンデンサー	atmospheric condenser
常磁性	ジョウジセイ	paramagnetism
常用対数	ジョウヨウタイスウ	common logarithm
定常-	テイジョウ	constant, steady
通常	ツウジョウ	normally, usually

説

説明	セツメイ	explanation
解説	カイセツ	interpretation
地動説	チドウセツ	Copernican theory

造

構造	コウゾウ	structure
構造式	コウゾウシキ	structural formula
造粒	ゾウリュウ	granulation
造果器	ゾウカキ	carpogonium

他

他方	タホウ	the other side
他形	タケイ	allotriomorphic
他植	タショク	allogamy

代

代表的な	ダイヒョウテキな	representative
代数関数	ダイスウカンスウ	algebraic function
代入する	ダイニュウする	to substitute {math}
近代化	キンダイカ	modernization
石器時代	セッキジダイ	the Stone Age

知

知見	チケン	information, knowledge
知的な	チテキな	intelligent

値

極大値	キョクダイチ	(local) maximum value
最大値	サイダイチ	(global) maximum value
固有値	コユウチ	eigenvalue
測定値	ソクテイチ	measured value
実験値	ジッケンチ	experimental value
物性値	ブッセイチ	values of physical properties

調

調光器	チョウコウキ	dimmer
調色	チョウショク	toning
調速機	チョウソクキ	governor {mech engr}

通

通過	ツウカ	transit (through)
通常-	ツウジョウ	normal, usual
通気圧	ツウキアツ	ventilating pressure
通気組織	ツウキソシキ	aerenchyma
交通	コウツウ	traffic
二通り(に)	ふたとおり(に)	(in) two ways

当

当量	トウリョウ	equivalent
当量点	トウリョウテン	equivalence point
相当長さ	ソウトウながさ	equivalent length
相当する	ソウトウする	to correspond (to)
当所	トウショ	this place

糖

糖化	トウカ	saccharification
果糖	カトウ	fructose
ブドウ糖	ブドウトウ	D-glucose, grape sugar
ショ糖	ショトウ	sucrose

明

説明	セツメイ	explanation
明度	メイド	brightness
明反応	メイハンノウ	light reaction {biol}
明解な	メイカイな	lucid, clear
明白な	メイハクな	clear, evident
明示する	メイジする	to clarify

目

目的	モクテキ	purpose, objective, goal
目的ルーチン	モクテキルーチン	object routine {comp sci}
目的成分	モクテキセイブン	specified component
目次	モクジ	(table of) contents

与

関与する	カンヨする	to be involved, participate

13

Other Verb and Adjective Forms

13.1 The Representative Form of Verbs (たり) and Adjectives (かったり)
13.2 The Desiderative Adjectives (たい)
13.3 The Imperative Form of Verbs
13.4 The Verb Suffixes べき, ながら, and つつ
13.5 Polite and Honorific Forms Used in Instruction Manuals

The first four sections of this chapter treat a variety of verb and adjective forms and verb suffixes. We include here various inflected forms that you will encounter only occasionally. Though they are of minor importance in technical translation, you must still be able to recognize and understand them. Our discussion of them will be brief.

The last section of the chapter is optional if you plan to read scientific texts only. If, however, you read instruction manuals, advertisements, announcements, and certain other types of texts, you will need to recognize and translate the various "polite" and "honorific" forms that appear there.

13.1 The Representative Form of Verbs (たり) and Adjectives (かったり)

The "representative" form (also sometimes called the "alternative," the "frequentative," or the "enumerative") is very easy to obtain: for both verbs and adjectives, り is added to the past-tense form (either affirmative or negative). There are no exceptions. Thus the representative form always ends in たり or だり.

	Present Affirmative	Representative Affirmative	Representative Negative
ru-verbs			
to see	見る	見たり	見なかったり
to receive	受ける	受けたり	受けなかったり
xu-verbs			
to release	放す	放したり	放さなかったり
to stand	立つ	立ったり	立たなかったり
to pass through	通る	通ったり	通らなかったり
to inhale	吸う	吸ったり	吸わなかったり
to be based on	基づく	基づいたり	基づかなかったり
to pour	注ぐ	注いだり	注がなかったり
to contain	含む	含んだり	含まなかったり
to tie	結ぶ	結んだり	結ばなかったり
Irregular verbs			
to go	行く	行ったり	行かなかったり
to come	くる	きたり	こなかったり
to do	する	したり	しなかったり
i-adjectives			
large	大きい	大きかったり	大きくなかったり
thin, narrow	細い	細かったり	細くなかったり
na-adjectives			
necessary	必要である	必要であったり	必要でなかったり

Representative forms usually appear in pairs and the second one is almost always followed by the verb する or one of its inflected forms. Therefore, a typical construction will contain ...たり...たりする, which gives an enumeration of representative actions (or states) occurring simultaneously or alternatively, with the listing not necessarily complete. Occasionally only one たり form appears (followed by する), in which case one of a number of possible actions or states is being mentioned. Sometimes three or more たり forms appear. The ...たり...たりする construction for verbs and adjectives may be regarded as the analog of the ...や...や... construction for nouns, where a representative listing is given.

空気中の二酸化炭素の量は多くなったり少なくなったりするが、ほぼ一定である。
クウキチュウのニサンカタンソのリョウはおおくなったりすくなくなったりするが、ほぼ
イッテイである。
The quantity of carbon dioxide in the atmosphere does vary somewhat {lit.: it becomes more or it becomes less}, but it is approximately constant.

この場所では植物は光を受けたり受けなかったりする。
このばショではショクブツはひかりをうけたりうけなかったりする。
At this location the plants sometimes receive light and sometimes do not.

この大学では高分子反応を学んだり、高分子の性質を調べたりする。
このダイガクではコウブンシハンノウをまなんだり、コウブンシのセイシツをしらべたり
　　　する。

At this university they study polymer chemical reactions, investigate polymer properties, etc.

原形質の中では、物質が分解されたり、物質が合成されたり、熱や電気が発生したりする。
ゲンケイシツのなかでは、ブッシツがブンカイされたり、ブッシツがゴウセイされたり、
　　　ネツやデンキがハッセイしたりする。

Within the protoplasm, materials are decomposed and synthesized, and heat and electricity are produced.

13.2 The Desiderative Adjectives (たい)

The "desiderative" is an i-adjective obtained by adding たい to the xi-base of an xu-verb or to the stem of an ru-verb.

	Present Affirmative	Desiderative Affirmative	Desiderative Negative
ru-verbs			
to use	用いる	用いたい	用いたくない
to investigate	調べる	調べたい	調べたくない
xu-verbs			
to show	示す	示したい	示したくない
to stand	立つ	立ちたい	立ちたくない
to know	知る	知りたい	知りたくない
to follow, obey	したがう	したがいたい	したがいたくない
to move	動く	動きたい	動きたくない
to connect	つなぐ	つなぎたい	つなぎたくない
to tie	結ぶ	結びたい	結びたくない
Irregular verbs			
to go	行く	行きたい	行きたくない
to come	くる	きたい	きたくない
to do	する	したい	したくない

The desiderative means "wants to do (something)" or "desires to do (something)"; the thing desired is designated by を (or in some instances by が). Thus, 酸素を吸いたい means "He wants to inhale oxygen." In scientific writing the desiderative appears infrequently and then mainly in standard expressions such as ...を説明したい "We wish to explain ...," ...を調べたい "We wish to investigate ...," and the like.

13-8

The desiderative is an i-adjective and can be further inflected.

	Affirmative	Negative
Present	測定したい we want to measure	測定したくない we do not want to measure
Past	測定したかった we wanted to measure	測定したくなかった we did not want to measure
Provisional	測定したければ if we want to measure	測定したくなければ if we do not want to measure
Connective	測定したくて we want to measure and ...	測定したくなくて we do not want to measure and ...

Here are a few sentences using the desiderative forms.

いまこの実験の目的を説明したい。
いまこの<u>ジッケン</u>の<u>モクテキ</u>を<u>セツメイ</u>したい。
We now wish to explain the objective of this experiment.

次に陰極における化学反応を調べたい。
<u>つぎ</u>に<u>インキョク</u>における<u>カガクハンノウ</u>を<u>しら</u>べたい。
Next we want to investigate the chemical reactions occurring at the cathode.

力学では物体の重心の位置を知りたくなる場合がよくある。
<u>リキガク</u>では<u>ブッタイ</u>の<u>ジュウシン</u>の<u>イチ</u>を<u>し</u>りたくなる<u>ばあい</u>がよくある。
In mechanics it is frequently the case that we want to know the position of the center of gravity of a
　　body.

次の例には解がつけられているが、それを見る前に自らこころみられたい。
<u>つぎ</u>の<u>レイ</u>には<u>カイ</u>がつけられているが、それを<u>み</u>る<u>まえ</u>にみずからこころみられたい。
In the next example the solution is attached, but before you look at it, we want you to try [solving
　　it] by yourself.

In the last sentence こころみる is the verb "to try" or "to test"; the corresponding
passive verb is こころみられる, from which we get the desiderative adjective ここ
ろみられたい. This is an example of the "honorific passive" that you encountered in
Section 11.1. Therefore こころみられたい means "We want you to try [solving it]."
　　Some further uses of the desiderative of the honorific passive are the following
standard expressions (which contain KANJI that you do not yet know):

第一章を参照されたい。
<u>ダイイッショウ</u>を<u>サンショウ</u>されたい。
(We wish you to) consult Chapter 1.

第二節を参照されたい。
<u>ザイニセツ</u>を<u>サンショウ</u>されたい。
(We want you to) refer to Section 2.

付録に留意されたい。
フロクにリュウイされたい。
(We want you to) take note of the Appendix.

13.3 The Imperative Form of Verbs

About the only place that you will encounter the imperative in technical writing is in the problems and laboratory experiments in textbooks where the reader is told to perform certain operations or procedures. The imperative is a very brusque form, and is inappropriate for use in polite conversation.

The imperative form for xu-verbs is identical to the xe-base, which is obtained by replacing the final syllable of the dictionary form by the corresponding syllable from the え column. The imperative for ru-verbs is identical to the yo-base obtained by adding よ to the stem.

	Present Affirmative	Imperative
xu-verbs		
to express	表す	表せ
to hold	もつ	もて
to make	作る	作れ
to inhale	吸う	吸え
to put, set	置く	置け
to pour	注ぐ	注げ
to tie	結ぶ	結べ
to cut, carve	きざむ	きざめ
ru-verbs		
to see	見る	見よ
to obtain	求める	求めよ
Irregular verbs		
to do	する	せよ！
to come	くる	こい！

(The imperative for くる will never arise in technical Japanese but is included for completeness.) Here are a few sentences that illustrate the imperative forms.

ハロゲンのうち、フッ素だけが示す性質の例を上げよ。
ハロゲンのうち、フッソだけがしめすセイシツのレイをあげよ。
Give an example of a property, which, among the halogens, only fluorine exhibits.

これらのショ糖溶液の蒸気圧を求めてみよ。
これらのショトウヨウエキのジョウキアツをもとめてみよ。
Try determining the vapor pressure of these sucrose solutions.

単原子気体の化学ポテンシャルをTとpとの関数として表せ。
タンゲンシキタイのカガクポテンシャルをTとpとのカンスウとしてあらわせ。
Express the chemical potential for monatomic gases as a function of T and p.

13-10

この実験を始める前に、すべての反応物と生成物の物性値を調べよ。
このジッケンをはじめるまえに、すべてのハンノウブツとセイセイブツのブッセイチをし
らべよ。
Before starting this experiment look up the physical property values of all the reactants and products.

水とエチルアルコールの溶液の比重を測定せよ。
みずとエチルアルコールのヨウエキのヒジュウをソクテイせよ。
Measure the specific gravity of the solutions of water and ethyl alcohol.

以上の実験を他のアルコールと水の溶液について行え。
イジョウのジッケンをタのアルコールとみずのヨウエキについておこなえ。
Perform the above experiment for other alcohol-water solutions.

Occasionally when authors refer the reader to another chapter they may write 第二章
を見よ[ダイニショウをみよ] instead of 第二章を参照されたい[ダイニショウ
をサンショウされたい] as mentioned in the foregoing section.

13.4 The Verb Suffixes べき, ながら, and つつ

In this section we discuss several verb suffixes that occur occasionally in
technical writing. They are easy to recognize, posing no serious problems even for the
beginner.

a. The Suffix べき

This suffix is added to the dictionary form of the verb; for the verb する we find
both するべき and すべき in technical writing. The suffix べき expresses obligation
and is generally translated by "must, have to, ought to." The verb with the べき suffix
is an adjective and may occur directly before a noun, or it may be followed by some
inflected form of である; in this regard it is similar to the adjective 同じ. Here are a
few sentences that illustrate the use of べき.

f(x)は積分すべき関数である。
f(x)はセキブンすべきカンスウである。
f(x) is the function we have to integrate.

陽極反応を調べるべきであろう。
ヨウキョクハンノウをしらべるべきであろう。
We shall probably have to investigate the anode reaction.

さて、流体の運動を調べるさいにまず考えるべきことは、どんな量が求まれば流れの状態
がわかったといえるかということである。
さて、リュウタイのウンドウをしらべるさいにまずかんがえるべきことは、どんなリョウ
がもとまればながれのジョウタイがわかったといえるかということである。
Now when we investigate the motion of fluids, we ought to consider first what kinds of quantities must
be sought in order for us to be able to say that we understand the state of the flow.

The suffix べき also has a negative form べからず which you may occasionally see on signs in laboratories. For example, 立ち入るべからず means "You must not enter."

b. The Suffix ながら

This suffix is added to the xi-base of xu-verbs and to the stem of ru-verbs. It has two meanings: a durative sense of "at the same time as, while," and a concessive sense of "even though." The durative meaning is the one you will most often encounter. The first sentence below illustrates the durative meaning, and the second the concessive meaning.

果糖溶液を熱しながら、その体積変化を測定する。
カトウヨウエキをネッしながら、そのタイセキヘンカをソクテイする。
While heating the fructose solution we measure its volume change.

高分子溶液は蒸気圧についてのRaoultの法則からいちじるしくはずれたり、大変高い粘性
をもったりする。しかも溶液でありながら剛性などを示すのである。
コウブンシヨウエキはジョウキアツについてのRaoultのホウソクからいちじるしくはずれ
たり、タイヘンたかいネンセイをもったりする。しかもヨウエキでありながら、ゴ
ウセイなどをしめすのである。
Polymer solutions deviate remarkably from Raoult's law for vapor pressure and have very high
viscosity. Furthermore, even though they are solutions, they exhibit rigidity, etc. {*Note:* both
粘性 and 粘度 are used for "viscosity"; 剛性 means "rigidity."}

c. The Suffix つつ

This suffix is also added to the xi-base of xu-verbs and to the stem of ru-verbs. It is synonymous with ながら, again with the durative meaning occurring more frequently. In addition, it may be followed by a form of the verb ある, and this construction is a literary equivalent of the ...ている progressive form.

溶液を加熱しつつ、ブドウ糖を溶かす。
ヨウエキをカネツしつつ、ブドウトウをとかす。
We dissolve the grape sugar (D-glucose) while we are heating the solution.

化学反応においては温度や圧力の変化が見えなくても分子レベルでは反応は起こりつつあ
る。
カガクハンノウにおいてはオンドやアツリョクのヘンカがみえなくてもブンシレベルでは
ハンノウはおこりつつある。
In a chemical reaction, even though changes in temperature and pressure are not seen, a reaction is
occurring at the molecular level.

13.5 Polite and Honorific Forms Used in Instruction Manuals

All the verb and adjective forms you have thus far learned are in the "plain style." However, in instruction manuals, computer software descriptions, equipment advertisements, professional society announcements, transcripts of public lectures, and some scientific essays, you will encounter the "polite style" and the "honorific style." Here we describe some of the salient features of these other styles.

a. The Polite Style

To go from the plain style to the polite style one replaces the plain forms of verbs or adjectives at the end of a sentence by the corresponding polite forms. We now show you how the polite forms of verbs and adjectives are obtained.

The polite form of an xu-verb is obtained by adding ます to the xi-base of the verb; for ru-verbs, ます is added to the stem of the verb. Here we compare the "plain" and "polite" forms of the verb 示す, showing how the ます ending is inflected.

	Affirmative		Negative	
	Plain	Polite	Plain	Polite
Present	示す	示します	示さない	示しません
Past	示した	示しました	示さなかった	示しませんでした
Conditional	示したら	示しましたら		
Tentative	示そう	示しましょう		
Connective	示して	示しまして		
Progressive	示している	示しています	示していない	示していません
Passive	示される	示されます	示されない	示されません

Although the ます ending ends in す, its inflections are not always the same as those of xu-verbs ending in す, as you can see by comparing the endings of 示す and 示します in the list above. In the polite style, instead of using an imperative form, one makes a request by using the て form followed by 下さい[ください], the imperative of 下さる[くださる] "to give." Hence 示して下さい means "Please show me."

The verb ある has the polite form あります. The copula である and its polite equivalent であります mean "is, are," and call for special attention. Both the plain and polite affirmative forms can be shortened as shown here:

	Plain (Affirmative)		Polite (Affirmative)	
	Unabbreviated	Abbreviated	Unabbreviated	Abbreviated
Present	である	だ	であります	です
Past	であった	だった	でありました	でした
Conditional	であったら	だったら	でありましたら	でしたら
Tentative	であろう	だろう	でありましょう	でしょう
Provisional	であれば	なら(ば)		
Conjunctive	であり	で		

In technical writing employing the plain style the abbreviated forms are seldom used. As we pointed out in Section 12.2, だろう is sometimes used with adjectives; and in Section 10.4 we discussed the use of なら(ば). On the other hand, in the polite conversational style it is the abbreviated forms that are almost always used: the plain abbreviated forms at the ends of subordinate clauses, and the polite abbreviated forms at the ends of sentences. Note, however, that the negative forms are not shortened.

	Plain (Negative)	Polite (Negative)
Present	で(は)ない	で(は)ありません
Past	で(は)なかった	で(は)ありませんでした

At the end of a sentence i-adjectives are put into the polite form as follows:

	Affirmative		Negative	
	Plain	Polite	Plain	Polite
Present	長い	長いです	長くない	長くありません
Past	長かった	長かったです	長くなかった	長くありませんでした
Tentative	長いだろう	長いでしょう	長くないだろう	長くないでしょう

For na- and no-adjectives at the end of a sentence, である is changed to です, as explained above.

We now give some examples of sentences in the polite form. These contain a few KANJI unfamiliar to you.

3.5インチのディスクを使います。
3.5インチのディスクをつかいます。
We use a 3.5" disk.

次にこの日本語ワードプロセッサの基本的な操作方法を説明します。
つぎにこのニホンゴワードプロセッサのキホンテキなソウサホウホウをセツメイします。
Next we explain the basic operating methods for this Japanese word processor.

スペースバーはキーボード上の細長いバーです。
スペースバーはキーボードジョウのほそながいバーです。
The space bar is the long, narrow bar on the keyboard.

この方法については、26-27ページを参照してください。
このホウホウについては、26-27ページをサンショウしてください。
With regard to this method, please refer to pp. 26-27.

スペースバーは細長いですが、tabキーは細長くありません。
スペースバーはほそながいですが、tabキーはほそながくありません。
The space bar is long and narrow, but the tab key is not.

The polite style, with ます forms at the ends of sentences and plain forms at the ends of subordinate clauses, is the style taught in most elementary conversational grammars, since it provides an acceptable level of politeness for non-Japanese in the beginning stages of conversation. If, however, one wants to be able to function in a wide variety of situations and be sensitive to the rules of Japanese etiquette, one must also be thoroughly familiar with the differences between men's and women's speech patterns as well as with the honorific style.

b. *The Honorific Style*

The use of KEIGO (敬語[ケイゴ]), honorific language, in spoken Japanese is a very large and complicated topic. Here we are concerned only with the kind of honorific language that is used between a member of the "we" group and a member of the "you" group, as exemplified by the following:

"we"	"you"
Authors of an instruction manual	Readers of an instruction manual
Suppliers of a service	Users of a service
Editors of a journal	Authors or readers of a journal
Officers of a technical organization	Members of a technical organization
Manufacturers of equipment	Potential purchasers of equipment

In such situations the writers ("we") feel some deference toward the readers ("you") and sometimes use honorific language. We restrict ourselves here to just those honorific forms used by the sort of writers listed above in communicating with their readers. You are already aware of one kind of honorific language from Section 11.1, where you learned that the passive verb can be used as an active verb in an honorific sense. Here we discuss other honorific forms.

In honorific language the prefixes お and ご (which are the KUN and ON readings of the KANJI 御, introduced in Chapter 16) are often used before nouns and adjectives. These prefixes have no meaning and need not be translated; they just impart a more polite feeling to the sentence. Usually (but not always) the prefix お is used with the KUN reading of the following KANJI, and ご with the ON reading.

The verb あります is replaced by ございます. The most important inflected forms of ございます are given here.

	Affirmative		Negative	
Present	あります	ございます	ありません	ございません
Past	ありました	ございました	ありませんでした	ございませんでした
Conditional	ありましたら	ございましたら		

Similarly, in honorific writing でございます corresponds to です in the polite style.

The honorific prefixes お and ご can be used systematically for creating "exalted" and "humble" verbs; the exalted verbs are used to refer to the actions of the reader, the customer, or the user, whereas the humble verbs are used to refer to the actions of the writer, the manufacturer, or the provider. These verbs are formed as follows: for ordinary verbs the conjunctive form is prefixed by お, and for the KANGO+する verbs the KANGO is prefixed by ご. Then to form exalted expressions one adds either

13-15

になります or なさいます; to form humble expressions one adds either します or いたします. The following table illustrates the formation of the various honorific forms in the present tense:

		Ordinary Verbs [おくる] to send		KANGO+する Verbs [レンラクする] to contact
Plain		送る		連絡する
Polite		送ります		連絡します
Honorific passive		送られます		連絡されます
Exalted		お送りになります		ご連絡になります
	or	お送りなさいます	or	ご連絡なさいます
Humble		お送りします		ご連絡します
	or	お送りいたします	or	ご連絡いたします

Hence, if one wants to discuss the actions of the readers (in the "you" column above) it is proper to say お送りになります (you send us) and ご連絡になります (you contact us); on the other hand, to describe the actions of the writers (in the "we" column above) it is appropriate to write お送りいたします (we send you) and ご連絡いたします (we contact you). In the same vein, polite requests are formed as follows: お送りください (please send us), and ご連絡ください (please contact us).

Corresponding to some verbs there are special exalted and humble verbs.

	Ordinary Verbs Plain	Polite	Honorific Verbs in Polite Form Exalted	Humble
to do	する	します	なさいます	いたします
to be	いる	います	いらっしゃいます	おります
to say	いう	いいます	おっしゃいます	申[もう]します
to see	見る	見ます	ご覧[ゴラン]になります	拝見[ハイケン]します

Note that おります comes from the verb おる, which was mentioned in Section 9.4 in connection with its conjunctive form おり.

The following five honorific verbs belong to a separate conjugation (the xaru-verbs) and differ from the る verbs of the xu-type in the formation of the imperative and the ます forms:

	Plain Present	Polite Present	Plain Imperative
to be	いらっしゃる	いらっしゃいます	いらっしゃい
to be	ござる	ございます	...
to do	なさる	なさいます	なさい
to say	おっしゃる	おっしゃいます	...
to give	下さる	下さいます	下さい

The honorific verbs for "to be," ござる and いらっしゃる, correspond to the ordinary verbs ある and いる.

13-16

We now give some sentences to illustrate the honorific style.

トラブルが発生した場合は、まずお電話などで御連絡ください。
トラブルがハッセイしたばあいは、まずおデンワなどでゴレンラクください。
In case trouble arises, first of all please contact us by phone or by other means.

ご不明な点がございましたら御遠慮なくお問い合わせください。
ごフメイなテンがございましたらゴエンリョなくおといあわせください。
If any points are obscure, please do not hesitate to inquire. {*Note:*御遠慮なく is a standard expression
    meaning "without hesitation"; also 御遠慮ください means "please refrain from."}

ディスクが壊れた場合などは、とりあえず代替ディスクをお送りすることもできます。
ディスクがこわれたばあいなどは、とりあえずダイタイディスクをおおくりすることもで
    きます。
If the disk is broken or otherwise damaged, we can (even) send you a substitute disk at once.

乱丁、落丁の場合には、マニュアルをお取り替えいたします。
ランチョウ、ラクチョウのばあいには、マニュアルをおとりかえいたします。
In case of out-of-order or missing pages, we will replace the manual.

アルキル基	アルキルキ	alkyl group
とりのぞく		to remove
のこる		to remain
受けとる	うけとる	to accept
はじまる		to begin (*v.i.*)
ともなう		to accompany
ひずみ		strain, deformation
それほど		that much, to that extent
できるだけ		as much as possible
積む	つむ	to stow aboard; to pile up
上空	ジョウクウ	upper atmosphere
とりつける		to attach
のせる		to place {at rest on something}
ずれる		to slip out of place
でたらめの		random, haphazard
すっかり		completely
ふつうの		usual
そろう		to be in order; to be arranged
そろい方	そろいかた	the ordering; arrangement
さける		to avoid
押す	おす	to push
クリヤーされる		is cleared
さえぎる {xu}		to interrupt
やり直す	やりなおす	to redo
増え過ぎる	ふえすぎる	to increase excessively
すべく		ought to do; intended for
有無	ウム; ユウム	presence
解き明かす	ときあかす	to clarify
サイン		signal

EXERCISES

Ex 13.1 Matching Japanese and English technical terms

割球( )　　　1. allogamy　　　工程( )　　　1. (table of) contents
極核( )　　　2. allotriomorphic　交通( )　　　2. equivalent (amount)
造果器( )　　3. blastomere　　　工場( )　　　3. factory
造粒( )　　　4. carpogonium　　常態( )　　　4. normal state
他形( )　　　5. governor　　　相当( )　　　5. (industrial) process
他植( )　　　6. granulation　　通過( )　　　6. proportion
調色( )　　　7. polarization　　通常( )　　　7. traffic
調速器( )　　8. polar nucleus　目次( )　　　8. transit (through)
分極( )　　　9. toning　　　割合( )　　　9. usual

Ex 13.2 Matching Japanese technical terms and definitions

アルキル基( )　1. パラフィン炭化水素分子から水素原子一つをとりのぞい
塩基( )　　　　てのこる原子団[ゲンシダン = atomic group]。
果糖( )　　2. 原子、分子、イオンなどのうち、電子を受けとりやすい
自動酸化( )　　もの。
電子受容体( )　3. 分子内に固定的に双極子[ソウキョクシ=dipole]をもつも
糖化( )　　　の。
明反応( )　　4. 水溶液中で解離[カイリ = dissociation]し、水酸イオンを
有極分子( )　　生じる物質。
　　　　5. 光が関係する生体反応の一つで、光量子が色素に吸収[キュ
　　　　ウシュウ = absorption]されてからすぐに起きる反応。
　　　　6. デンプン[starch]などの多糖物質が酵素[コウソ = enzyme]
　　　　または酸の作用で加水分解されて糖となる反応。
　　　　7. 代表的な単糖で果実にあり、ショ糖とデンプンの加水分
　　　　解でも得られるもの。
　　　　8. 空気中の酸素で常温で起こる酸化。

13-19

Ex 13.3 Matching subjects and predicates

目的成分の割合を得るためにその量を全量で( )　　　1. ではない。
明るい場所の光度は明るくない場所のより( )　　　　2. 述べた。
求心力は直線運動に関する力( )　　　　　　　　　　3. わかりやすい。
工学的な方法によって人工物質を( )　　　　　　　　4. 割る。
このことについて以上に( )　　　　　　　　　　　　5. 要求した。
このことについて以下に( )　　　　　　　　　　　　6. 述べる。
明白な説明は( )　　　　　　　　　　　　　　　　　7. 高い。
明白でない解説は( )　　　　　　　　　　　　　　　8. 要らない。
所長がたんぱく質の実験のために要する物質を( )　　9. 作る。
人が自分で作動させる調光器には自動的な機構は( ) 10. わかりにくい。

Ex 13.4 Translate the following sentences
(For sentences 12 and 13 study Section 13.5.)

1. アミラーゼ[amylase]の作用によってデンプンがマルトース[maltose]に変わる場合デンプンをアミラーゼに対する基質とよぶ。
2. 求核試薬[シヤク =reagent]によって起こるイオン反応を求核反応といい、ハロゲン化アルキルのアルカリによる加水分解反応がその一例である。
3. 求電子試薬[シヤク]によって起こる反応を求電子反応といい、ハロゲン陽イオンまたはプロトンの付加[フカ = addition]ではじまる[to begin]2重結合へのハロゲンまたはハロゲン化水素の付加[フカ]反応はその一例である。
4. 最大値は実数値をとる関数がとる値のうち最も大きい値である。ただし、これは極大値とは必ずしも一致[イッチ = coincidence]しない。
5. 構造式は分子内での各[かく = each]原子の結合状態を元素記号[キゴウ = symbol]と結合記号[キゴウ]で表した化学式である。
6. 熱の放出がともなう化学反応を発熱反応といい、熱の吸収[キュウシュウ = absorption]がともなうものを吸熱反応という。
7. 電極反応において1クーロンの電気量が電極相と溶液相の界面[カイメン = interface]を通過することにより、析出[セキシュツ = precipitation]または溶解する原子または原子団[ダン = group]の量を電気化学当量という。
8. 物質が外部磁場と同じ向きに磁化され、かつ磁場の向きが反対になれば磁化もまたそれとともに変化する物性を常磁性という。
9. 体のたんぱく質の所要量は過剰[カジョウ = excess]を心配する[シンパイする = to be concerned]よりは欠乏[ケツボウ = deficiency]を心配[シンパイ]する方がよいという立場からきめてある。
10. 成形時に生じる応力がある程度大きくなれば成形後のこるひずみが大きくなるが、応力がそれほど大きくなるはずはない。
11. (1)式を(2)式に代入すれば、最後の結果が得られるはずである。

13-20

12. コンピュータをワード・プロセッサとして使うためにしたがうべき操作[ソウサ = operational]方法がマニュアルに説明してあります。

13. かな入力の場合は、かたかなを入力したいとき、Optionキーを押して[from おす = to push]ください。

Ex 13.5 Read the following essays for comprehension

1. マイクロ波[ハ = wave]は直線的に伝わるため、できるだけ高い地点から電波[デンパ = radio wave]を出せばよい。そのため送信[ソウシン = transmitting]機や受信[ジュシン = receiving]機を積んだ人工衛星[エイセイ = satellite]を打ち上げて[from うちあげる = to launch]これを中継局[チュウケイキョク = relay station]として使う。

　赤道[セキドウ = equator]上空約[ヤク = about]36,000kmの高さに打ち上げられた衛星[エイセイ]は、地球を1周する公転[コウテン = revolution]周期が地球の自転[ジテン = rotation]周期に等しく、地球からは静止[セイシ = stationary]したように見える。このような衛星[エイセイ]を静止衛星[セイシエイセイ]とよんでいるが、常に一定の位置に見えるため、アンテナの向きが固定できて、マイクロ波[ハ]の送受信[ソウジュシン = transmitting and receiving]がしやすくなる。

2. いわゆる単振り子はおもりの大きさが小さくて、質点と見なしてよい振り子である。ここではおもりの大きさが無視[ムシ = neglect]できないような振り子について考えよう。剛体[ゴウタイ = rigid body]に一つの刃形支点[はがたシテン = knife-edge]をとりつけ、これをかたい水平面の上にのせ、刃形支点[はがたシテン]の位置がずれないようにして振らせたのが実体振り子といわれるものである。

　このような振り子の周期に対して次の式が成り立つ。

$$T = 2\pi[I/Mgh]^{1/2}$$

ただし、ここでIは剛体[ゴウタイ]の慣性[カンセイ = inertia]モーメント、hは剛体の重心から刃形支点[はがたシテン]までの長さである。この式を単振り子の場合に比べてみると、糸[いと = string]の長さLに相当するものがI/Mhとなっている。この量を相当単振り子の長さという。

3. 常磁性体を磁場の中に入れると、磁場の向きに磁化されるが、その磁気は常磁性体に含まれる磁性的な原子、イオン、または分子のもつ磁気モーメントから生じる。

　磁性的な原子、イオンなどが物質の中にあっても、それらの磁気モーメントが熱運動のため向きが全くでたらめであれば、全体としては打ち消し合って[from うちけしあう = to cancel each other]しまい、外には磁気があらわ

れない。ここに外から磁場をかけると、個々の[ココの = each]原子的磁石
は、その向きに平行になろうとする。もしすべての原子の磁気モーメント
がすっかり平行になれば、強い磁石ができるのであるが、ふつうの常磁性
体に、ふつうの強さの磁場をかけたのでは、原子の磁気モーメントのそろ
い方は、不完全[フカンゼン = incomplete]なので、弱い[よわい = weak]磁石
にしかならない。

　そろい方は、外からの磁場の強さHに比例するので、磁化の強さMはHに
比例することになる。一方、Hが同じならば、温度が高いほど原子磁気モー
メントがそろいにくくなるので、Mは小さくなる。

4.　アミノ酸配列[ハイレツ = arrangement]は、そのたんぱく質の形と作用を
決定する[ケッテイする = to determine]最も重要な因子[インシ = factor]であ
る。これをたんぱく質の1次構造とよぶ。1953年[ネン = year]にイギリスの
生化学者[セイカガクシャ = biochemist]サンガー[Sanger]はたんぱく質ホルモ
ンであるインシュリン[insulin]の１次構造を決定[ケッテイ]したが、それ以
後多くの生化学者[セイカガクシャ]によって１次構造が明らかになったたん
ぱく質は1000種[シュ = varieties]以上になった。

　大部分のたんぱく質は、アミノ酸だけがペプチド[peptide]結合で長く連絡
[レンラク = connection]したものであるが、さまざまな生理的役割[ヤクわり
= roles]を果たすために、アミノ酸以外の成分をポリペプチド[polypeptide]錯
体[サクタイ = complex]に共有[キョウユウ = covalent]結合しているたんぱく
質もある。その代表的な例は糖たんぱく質であり、例えばトレオニン残基
[ザンキ = residue]の-OH基にN-グリコシド[glycoside]結合でできた糖錯[トウ
サク = sugar complex]はその一つである。細胞から分泌[ブンピツ = secretion]
されるたんぱく質はほとんど糖たんぱく質[glycoprotein]であるから、糖質は
分泌[ブンピツ]機構に関与していると考えられる。

Ex 13.6 Read the following excerpts from a solar calculator manual

1.　ご注意[ごチュウイ = please note]
　計算機[ケイサンキ = calculator]は精密な[セイミツな = precise]電子部品[ブ
ヒン = parts]で構成されておりますので急激な[キュウゲキな = sudden]温度
変化や強いショック[jolt, shock]をさけてください。高温、低温[テイオン =
low temperature]およびホコリ[dust]の多い場所での使用はさけてください。
落としたり、[from おとす = to drop]ぶつけたり[from ぶつける = to strike
against something]など強い力を与えないでください。

2.　オールクリヤー[all clear]キーーACとクリヤー[clear]キーーC/CE
　ACキー: ご使用の場合はこのキーを押して[from おす]から計算[ケイサン
= calculation]をはじめて[from はじめる = to begin]ください。計算[ケイサン]

中にこのキーを押す[おす]とメモリーを含む全ての内容[ナイヨウ=contents]がクリヤーされますので、ご注意[ごチュウイ]ください。

C/CEキー:置数キーを押したあと押すと表示されている数値がクリヤーされます。2回[ニカイ = twice]押すと、メモリーをのぞく全ての内容[ナイヨウ]がクリヤーされます。

3. 電源[デンゲン = power source]について、ご使用上のお願い[おねがい = our request (of you)]。

太陽電池[タイヨウデンチ = solar cell]にあたる光の状態により、表示が意味[イミ = meaning]のない数値となるときがありますが、故障[コショウ = breakdown]ではありません。ACキーを押したあと"0"と表示すれば正常ですから計算[ケイサン]にとりかかって[from とりかかる = to commence]ください。

計算[ケイサン]中に太陽電池[タイヨウデンチ]にあたる光がさえぎられたりしますと、表示内容[ナイヨウ]およびメモリーの内容[ナイヨウ]がかわることがありますが、ACキーを押したのち計算[ケイサン]を最初[サイショ = the beginning]からやりなおしてください。

光の不十分な[フジュウブンな = inadequate]ところでは表示が薄く[from うすい = faint]なり、応答[オウトウ = response]が遅く[from おそい = slow]なりますので、当商品[トウショウヒン = this merchandise]の太陽電池に光ができるだけ直角[チョッカク = at right angles]になるようにしてご使用ください。

Ex 13.7 Translate the following essay

植物は常に空気中の二酸化炭素を吸い入れたり、空気中に酸素を放出したりしている。このとき、植物の体内では光合成反応が起こって、糖とか、ヌクレオチド[nucleotide]とか、ATPとかで代表される生体構成成分が作り出されている。すなわち、植物の体内には生きるために必要な物質を作る工場があるわけである。通常、光エネルギーの値が高ければ高い程、光合成速度は大きくなるが、日[ひ = sun]の当たる所に生えている大木[タイボク = large tree]では光の量が増え過ぎると光合成速度の増加の割合を少なくすべく調速機構が作動する。すなわち、植物は日光[ニッコウ = sunlight]が強過ぎるからといってその場所から日光[ニッコウ]の作用の及ばない日陰[ひかげ = shade]を求めて他の場所へ移り動きたくても自分で動くことはできないが、その作用を少なくすることはできるのである。

これに反して、日陰[ひかげ]に生えている地表面の植物は極めて小量の光を受けても光合成反応が起きるような構造に成っている。一方、人間の目は植物のように光をエネルギーとして用いることはできないが、光の有無は分かる。植物も光の有無を知るべき機構をもっているかどうかということについては長い間説明が与えられなかったが、植物にはクロロフィル[chlorophyll]のような基本[キホン=fundamental]構造をもったフィトクローム[phytochrome]という物質があって、光があると自らこれに対応せよというサインを出すことが最近解き明かされた。すなわち、植物は上述のように光をエネルギーとして使用しながらサインとしても用いているのである。

TRANSLATIONS

Ex 13.4 Sentences

1. When starch changes to maltose by the action of amylase, starch is called the substrate for amylase.
2. Ionic reactions that occur due to nucleophilic reagents are called nucleophilic reactions; one example (of that) is the hydrolysis (reaction) of alkyl halides due to alkalis.
3. Ionic reactions that occur due to electrophilic reagents are called electrophilic reactions; one example is the addition reaction of a halogen or a hydrogen halide to a double bond, a reaction that begins with the addition of a halogen cation or a proton.
4. The global maximum value is the greatest value among the values taken by a real number function. However, it does not necessarily coincide with local maximum values.
5. A structural formula is a chemical formula that shows the bonding state of each atom in the molecule by means of symbols for the elements and for bonds.
6. Reactions accompanied by the emission of heat are called exothermic reactions; those accompanied by absorption are called endothermic (reactions).
7. The electrochemical equivalent is the amount of an atom or group of atoms that is precipitated or dissolved in an electrode reaction due to the transfer of 1 coulomb of electricity through the interface between the electrode phase and the solution phase.
8. Paramagnetism is the property of a substance [whereby] it is magnetized in the same direction as an external magnetic field and, moreover, if the direction of the magnetic field is reversed, the [direction of its] magnetism also changes together with it.
9. The amounts of proteins required for the body are determined from the point of view that it is better to be concerned about deficiencies rather than (to be concerned) about excesses.
10. If the stresses generated during molding become [so] large that they [reach] a certain amount, the strains that remain after molding become great; however, the stresses are not expected to become that large.
11. If [you] substitute equation (1) into equation (2), then [you] should obtain the final result.

12. The methods that must be followed for using a computer as a word processor are explained in the manual.
13. When inputting KANA, please push the option key when you want to input KATAKANA.

Ex 13.7 Essay

Plants are always breathing in atmospheric carbon dioxide and releasing oxygen to the atmosphere. During this time, photosynthesis reactions are occurring within the body of the plant, and components for structuring the organism, represented by such [chemicals] as sugars, nucleotides, and ATP, are being produced. That is, there is a "factory" within the body of the plant [where] substances necessary for life are produced. Usually, the higher the value of the sun's energy the greater the rate of photosynthesis. However, for large trees growing in places where the sun[light] strikes, if the amount of light increases excessively, a rate-controlling mechanism operates that is intended to reduce the rate of increase of the velocity of the photosynthesis. In other words, the plant cannot move by itself — even if it "wanted" to change its place and seek for shade beyond reach of the sun's action, "saying" that the sunlight is too strong — but it can decrease the action [of the sun's energy].

By contrast, plants that grow in shade on the earth's surface are so structured that photosynthesis reactions occur even when they receive small quantities of light. Although the human eye cannot use light as an energy source as plants do, [the eye] is aware of the presence of light. Whether or not plants also have a mechanism intended to detect the presence of light is [a topic] concerning which no explanation had been given for a long time. However, it has recently been made clear that [plants] have a substance known as phytochrome, which contains a fundamental structure akin to chlorophyll, and that if there is light, [the phytochrome] spontaneously sends to [the plant] a [command] signal "Respond!" That is, while using light as an energy source as described above, plants also use it as a signal.

回	カイ	rotation
	-カイ	{counter for times}
	まわ(す)	to rotate
	まわ(る)	to rotate, revolve

各	カク	each
	おのおの(の)	each

角	カク	angle, corner
	かど	corner, edge
	つの	horn {of an animal}

曲	キョク	curving; bending
	ま(げる)	to bend
	ま(がる)	to be curved; to be bent

径	ケイ	diameter

限	ゲン	limit, restriction
	かぎ(り)	limit; bound
	かぎ(る) {xu}	to be limited

個	コ	individual
	-コ	{counter for objects}

三	サン	three
	み	three
	み(つ); み(っつ)	three

種	シュ	kind; seed; species {biol}
	たね	seed, kernel

接	セツ	touching, contacting
	セツ(する)	to touch, contact

第	ダイ-	{ordinal prefix}

導	ドウ	conducting; guiding
	みちび(く)	to lead; to derive

倍	バイ	double
	-バイ	times, -fold

半	ハン	half, semi-, hemi-
	なか(ば)	half; halfway; middle

微	ビ	minute, micro-

約	ヤク	summary; promise
	ヤク-	approximately

率	リツ	rate; percentage

両	リョウ	both

類	ルイ	type, variety

路	ロ	route, path

回

三回	サンカイ	three times
回分法	カイブンホウ	batch process
回反	カイハン	rotatory inversion {chem}
回線	カイセン	(telephone) circuit
時計回り	とケイまわり	clockwise

各

各回	カッカイ	each time
各部	カクブ	each part
各個	カッコ	each one
各(々)の	おのおのの	each

角

三角形	サンカクケイ	triangle
角運動量	カクウンドウリョウ	angular momentum
内角	ナイカク	interior angle
外角	ガイカク	exterior angle
角振動数	カクシンドウスウ	circular frequency
角質	カクシツ	keratin

曲

曲線	キョクセン	curve, curved line
曲率	キョクリツ	curvature
曲率半径	キョクリツハンケイ	radius of curvature
曲率中心	キョクリツチュウシン	center of curvature
曲面	キョクメン	curved surface

径

直径	チョッケイ	diameter
半径	ハンケイ	radius
径路	ケイロ	path {e.g., of a chemical reaction}

限

無限の	ムゲンの	infinite
無限小の	ムゲンショウの	infinitesimal
極限	キョクゲン	limit
有限の	ユウゲンの	finite

個

個々の	ココの	each
個々に	ココに	one by one
個人用	コジンヨウ	for personal use
個体	コタイ	individual {biol}
個体性	コタイセイ	individuality
個体発生	コタイハッセイ	ontogeny
三個	サンコ	three {e.g., atoms}

三

三角形	サンカクケイ	triangle
三角関数	サンカクカンスウ	trigonometric function
三次元	サンジゲン	three-dimensional
三次反応	サンジハンノウ	third-order reaction
三重結合	サンジュウケツゴウ	triple bond
三重点	サンジュウテン	triple point
三原色説	サンゲンショクセツ	theory of three primary colors
三相交流	サンソウコウリュウ	three-phase (alternating) current
三塩基酸	サンエンキサン	tribasic acid
三極管	サンキョクカン	triode

種

種類	シュルイ	kind, variety
種々の	シュジュの	various
種子	シュシ	seed
種子植物	シュシショクブツ	spermatophyte
種物	たねもの	seeds

接

接点	セッテン	point of tangency
接線	セッセン	tangent (line)
接線加速度	セッセンカソクド	tangential acceleration
接線応力	セッセンオウリョク	shear stress
直接の	チョクセツの	direct
間接の	カンセツの	indirect
接合子	セツゴウシ	zygote
接近する	セッキンする	to approach, come near
近接する	キンセツする	to be adjacent, contiguous

第

| 第一- | ダイイチ | first, primary |
| 第二- | ダイニ | second, secondary |

第三-	ダイサン	third, tertiary
次第に	シダイに {N.B. rdg. of 次}	gradually
第一種の	ダイイッシュの	of the first kind

導

導管	ドウカン	conduit
導体	ドウタイ	conductor
半導体	ハンドウタイ	semiconductor
電気伝導率	デンキデンドウリツ	electrical conductivity
熱伝導率	ネツデンドウリツ	thermal conductivity
導関数	ドウカンスウ	derivative {math}
三次導関数	サンジドウカンスウ	third-order derivative {math}
導出する	ドウシュツする	to derive
導入する	ドウニュウする	to introduce
導き出す	みちびきだす	to derive, lead out
導き入れる	みちびきいれる	to lead into

倍

三倍	サンバイ	three times, three-fold
数倍	スウバイ	several times
倍率	バイリツ	magnification
倍数比例	バイスウヒレイ	multiple proportions
倍周器	バイシュウキ	frequency multiplier
倍加時間	バイカジカン	doubling time
倍数性	バイスウセイ	polyploidy
二倍体	ニバイタイ	diploid

半

半分	ハンブン	half
半径	ハンケイ	radius
半球	ハンキュウ	hemisphere
半微量-	ハンビリョウ	semimicro- {chem}
半導体	ハンドウタイ	semiconductor

微

微分	ビブン	differential {math}
微分学	ビブンガク	differential calculus
微生物	ビセイブツ	microorganism
微生物学	ビセイブツガク	microbiology
微粒子	ビリュウシ	minute particle
微量-	ビリョウ	micro- {chem}
微量元素	ビリョウゲンソ	trace element

約

約分する	ヤクブンする	to reduce a fraction
約数	ヤクスウ	divisor
要約	ヨウヤク	summary

率

熱伝導率	ネツデンドウリツ	thermal conductivity
電気伝導率	デンキデンドウリツ	electrical conductivity
曲率	キョクリツ	curvature

両

両方	リョウホウ	both
両性-	リョウセイ	amphoteric {chem}; bisexual {biol}
両生類	リョウセイルイ	amphibia
両電極	リョウデンキョク	both electrodes
両種	リョウシュ	both kinds

類

人類	ジンルイ	humankind
人類学	ジンルイガク	anthropology
種類	シュルイ	kind, variety
両生類	リョウセイルイ	amphibia
塩類	エンルイ	salts

路

回路	カイロ	circuit
径路	ケイロ	path {e.g., of a chemical reaction}

14 Mathematical Terminology

This chapter deals with numbers and related mathematical topics. In technical Japanese, numbers are usually written with arabic numerals, so that you seldom need to know how to read numbers written in KANJI. In this chapter we concentrate on those aspects of numbers and mathematics that are needed for scientific translation.

We begin by showing how numbers are written with KANJI. Even though arabic numbers are widely used, the KANJI for numbers will occasionally appear, primarily in the JUKUGO for some technical terms, and we give some examples of these. Then we offer a short discussion of special suffixes called counters, which are appended to numbers in Japanese. Following this, we summarize some of the other number words, such as ordinal numbers, which are formed by means of prefixes and suffixes. After that we list a few expressions that are used to indicate approximate quantities, and conclude with some mathematical terms of interest to scientists and engineers.

14.1 The KANJI Used for Numbers

Except for 一, 二, and 三 the KANJI for numbers are not frequent in scientific texts, and therefore we have not included them among the 365 KANJI to be memorized. Trusting in your natural curiosity about number systems, we expect you will learn the KANJI for 4 through 9 and those for the first four powers of 10. (These KANJI will not be underlined.) You will find it interesting that the Japanese number system, taken over from the Chinese, is based on powers of 10^4, not powers of 10^3 as in the West.

a. KANJI for the Numbers 1 through 10

Japanese has two systems for writing numbers for the first ten integers: a primary system using mostly ON readings and a secondary system using KUN readings.

Arabic Numerals	Primary System			Secondary System	
1	一	[イチ]		一つ	[ひとつ]
2	二	[ニ]		二つ	[ふたつ]
3	三	[サン]		三つ	[みっつ]
4	四	[シ]	[よ・よん]	四つ	[よっつ]
5	五	[ゴ]		五つ	[いつつ]
6	六	[ロク]		六つ	[むっつ]
7	七	[シチ]	[なな]	七つ	[ななつ]
8	八	[ハチ]		八つ	[やっつ]
9	九	[キュウ・ク]		九つ	[ここのつ]
10	十	[ジュウ]		十	[とお]

The primary system is used when reciting the numbers from 1 to 10 with their ON readings. The primary system is also used in combination with most counters (see Section 14.3), although for 4 and 7 the KUN readings are usually used. The secondary system is used for counting objects for which there are no counters. In addition, a few counters are added to the stem of the secondary numbers, that is, the secondary number without the final つ or っつ: for example, ひと in ひとつ, ふた in ふたつ, み in みっつ.

b. KANJI for Powers of Ten

The KANJI for the first four powers of 10, and then for the powers of 10^4 after that, are

10		十	[ジュウ]	ten
10^2		百	[ヒャク]	one hundred
10^3		千	[セン]	one thousand
10^4		万	[マン]	ten thousand
10^8	$(10^4)^2$	億	[オク]	one hundred million
10^{12}	$(10^4)^3$	兆	[チョウ]	one trillion
10^{16}	$(10^4)^4$	京	[ケイ]	ten quadrillion

Infinity is 無限大[ムゲンダイ], meaning "large without limit."

c. Compound Numbers

For integers above 10 the number of each power of 10 precedes the KANJI for that power; for example 358 is 三百五十八 or "3-hundreds 5-tens 8." In writing page numbers, however, each KANJI simply replaces the corresponding arabic numeral, so that 358 is 三五八; a circle ○ (called 丸[まる]) is used for zero, even though there is a KANJI for zero (零[レイ]).

14-7

Arabic Numerals	Number in KANJI		Page Numbers
15	十五	[ジュウゴ]	一五
20	二十	[ニジュウ]	二〇
36	三十六	[サンジュウロク]	三六
98	九十八	[キュウジュウハチ]	九八
103	百三	[ヒャクサン]	一〇三
247	二百四十七	[ニヒャクよんジュウなな]	二四七
1992	千九百九十二	[センキュウヒャクキュウジュウニ]	一九九二
25000	二万五千	[ニマンゴセン]	...
10^5	十万	[ジュウマン]	...
10^6	百万	[ヒャクマン]	...
10^7	一千万	[イッセンマン]	...
10^8	一億	[イチオク]	...

In the readings for compound numbers, phonetic changes sometimes occur. In addition, the readings for 4, 7, and 9 offer options. The following readings are always acceptable:

11	ジュウイチ	10	ジュウ	100	ヒャク	1000	セン
12	ジュウニ	20	ニジュウ	200	ニヒャク	2000	ニセン
13	ジュウサン	30	サンジュウ	300	サンビャク	3000	サンゼン
14	ジュウよん*	40	よんジュウ*	400	よんヒャク	4000	よんセン
15	ジュウゴ	50	ゴジュウ	500	ゴヒャク	5000	ゴセン
16	ジュウロク	60	ロクジュウ	600	ロッピャク	6000	ロクセン
17	ジュウなな*	70	ななジュウ*	700	ななヒャク*	7000	ななセン*
18	ジュウハチ	80	ハチジュウ	800	ハッピャク	8000	ハッセン
19	ジュウク#	90	キュウジュウ	900	キュウヒャク	9000	キュウセン

Note the phonetic changes that occur in the underlined entries. For the entries marked with an asterisk, よん may be replaced by シ, or なな may be replaced by シチ; in the entry marked with #, ク may be replaced by キュウ.

d. Fractions and Decimals

Scientists and engineers normally read decimals (小数[ショウスウ]) as follows, with 点 indicating the decimal point.

0.256   零点二五六   [レイテンニゴロク]

Fractions (分数[ブンスウ]) are pronounced by giving the denominator (分母 [ブンボ]) before the numerator (分子[ブンシ]).

2/3   三分の二   [サンブンのニ]
7/12   十二分の七   [ジュウニブンのなな]

One-half is usually written 半分[ハンブン] rather than 二分の一.

14.2 Numbers Used in Technical Terms

You will encounter the KANJI for numbers mainly in JUKUGO for technical terms in which the numbers are an integral part of the terms. Usually the meaning of the KANJI will be clear. We illustrate by giving some JUKUGO involving the first ten integers, as well as the KANJI for zero (零[レイ]) and one-half (半[ハン]).

一次コイル	[イチジコイル]	primary coil
一酸化炭素	[イッサンカタンソ]	carbon monoxide
二分子反応	[ニブンシハンノウ]	bimolecular reaction
二量体	[ニリョウタイ]	dimer
三次元	[サンジゲン]	three dimensions
三角形	[サンカクケイ]	triangle
三角関数	[サンカクカンスウ]	trigonometric function
三塩基酸	[サンエンキサン]	tribasic acid
四面体	[シメンタイ]	tetrahedron
四極子	[シキョクシ]	quadrupole
五塩化ヒ素	[ゴエンカヒソ]	arsenic pentachloride
五酸化リン	[ゴサンカリン]	phosphorous pentoxide
六フッ化ウラン	[ロクフッカウラン]	uranium hexafluoride
六角形	[ロッカクケイ]	hexagon
七色	[なないろ]	prismatic colors
八面体	[ハチメンタイ]	octahedron
九角形	[キュウカッケイ]	nonagon
十進法	[ジッシンホウ]	decimal system
百分率	[ヒャクブンリツ]	percentage
零点	[レイテン]	zero point
零ベクトル	[レイベクトル]	zero vector
半径	[ハンケイ]	radius
半球	[ハンキュウ]	hemisphere
半導体	[ハンドウタイ]	semiconductor

The KANJI for powers of 10 form combinations with the KANJI 数 to make the following rather common words:

数十	[スウジュウ]	several tens
数百	[スウヒャク]	several hundred(s)
数千	[スウセン]	several thousand(s)
数万	[スウマン]	several ten-thousand(s)

In addition to these KANJI for numbers, several other KANJI function as numbers in some JUKUGO. For example, for "1" 単[タン] (single, simple) or the combination 単一[タンイツ] is sometimes used. Similarly, for "2," the KANJI 両 [リョウ] (both) or 双[ソウ] (double) is used. Occasionally the KANJI 対[ツイ] (pair) appears. Furthermore, the KANJI 多[タ] (many) means "poly," and 多重[タジュウ] "multi-" or "multiple." Here are some technical terms that contain these "number substitutes."

単色光	[タンショクコウ]	monochromatic light
単量体	[タンリョウタイ]	monomer
単一積分	[タンイツセキブン]	single integral
単一層	[タンイツソウ]	monolayer
両性イオン	[リョウセイイオン]	zwitterion
両凸レンズ	[リョウトツレンズ]	biconvex lens
両凹レンズ	[リョウオウレンズ]	biconcave lens
双極子	[ソウキョクシ]	dipole
双曲線	[ソウキョクセン]	hyperbola
双曲線関数	[ソウキョクセンカンスウ]	hyperbolic function
熱電対	[ネツデンツイ]	thermocouple
電子対	[デンシツイ]	electron pair
多面体	[タメンタイ]	polyhedron
多糖類	[タトウルイ]	polysaccharide
多重極放射	[タジュウキョクホウシャ]	multipole radiation
多重周期運動	[タジュウシュウキウンドウ]	multiple periodic motion

Note the KANJI 凸[トツ] and 凹[オウ] for "convex" and "concave" here. They are so graphic that you will recognize them the next time you see them. They also form the JUKUGO 凸凹[でこぼこ] meaning "bumpy."

Remember that the KANJI for "1" (一) frequently means "the same" in JUKUGO. Some of these words contain KANJI you have not learned.

一様の	[イチヨウの]	uniform
一定の	[イッテイの]	constant
一般化	[イッパンカ]	generalization
一致	[イッチ]	agreement
同一の	[ドウイツの]	identical
統一の	[トウイツの]	unified
均一の	[キンイツの]	homogeneous

Note the pronunciation of the KANJI 一 in these last three words.

14.3 Numbers with Units and Counters

Numbers precede units just as in English. Usually the numbers are written with arabic numerals rather than with KANJI.

3メートル	[サンメートル]	3 meters
3.5グラム	[サンテンゴグラム]	3.5 grams
2秒	[ニビョウ]	2 seconds
15m/秒	[ジュウゴメートルパービョウ]	15 meters per second

Several suffixes and words similarly combine with numbers.

3度	[サンド]	3 times
5回	[ゴカイ]	5 times
2種類	[ニシュルイ]	2 kinds
63ページ	[ロクジュウサンページ]	63 pages, page 63

The word ページ is sometimes written with the KANJI 頁.

In counting objects in English we usually give the number and then the name of the object: 5 beakers, 10 molecules, 5 electrons. However, for some objects we interpose a "counter": 3 bars of soap, 2 slices of bread, 60 head of cattle. In Japanese this way is more prevalent, and therefore you must know some of the more common counters and their use.

We list here for reference the counters you will most often see in technical Japanese.

KANJI	Reading	Used for Counting
個	[コ]	a variety of objects, including particles, molecules, atoms, electrons, photons, cells, and protozoans
本	[ホン]	elongated objects such as rods, wires, and chains
枚	[マイ]	flat objects, such as sheets of aluminum foil, and metal plates
台	[ダイ]	vehicles and large machines
冊	[サツ]	books, journals, magazines
匹	[ヒキ]	small animals (dogs, cats, mice)
頭	[トウ]	large animals (cows, horses, bears)
羽	[ワ]	birds and rabbits

These counters are combined with the primary numbers, sometimes with phonetic changes, as described at the end of this section. In technical writing the counters usually appear as follows:

3個の原子	[サンコのゲンシ]	3 atoms
2個のアメーバ	[ニコのアメーバ]	2 amoebas
N個のすべての分子	[Nコのすべての分子]	all N molecules
3個のアルファ粒子	[サンコのアルファリュウシ]	3 alpha particles
5匹のイヌ	[ゴヒキのイヌ]	5 dogs
2枚の凸レンズ	[ニマイのトツレンズ]	2 convex lenses
4枚の凹レンズ	[よんマイのオウレンズ]	4 concave lenses
2枚の平板	[ニマイのヘイバン]	2 flat plates
1枚の球面	[イチマイのキュウメン]	1 spherical surface

In each case the KANJI immediately after the arabic numeral is the counter, and it usually need not be translated into English. Some counters combine with the stems of the secondary numbers. The most important of these are 組[くみ] meaning "class, group" and けた meaning "digit."

一組	[ひとくみ]	1 group	ひとけた		1 digit
二組	[ふたくみ]	2 groups	ふたけた		2 digits
三組	[みくみ]	3 groups	みけた		3 digits

Many Japanese switch over to the primary system at some point, so you may well hear 五組 pronounced as ゴくみ, for example.

    For things with no appropriate counter the "secondary numbers" are used; you might think of つ as a sort of "generalized counter." The secondary numbers are usually written in KANJI, but you will sometimes see 1つ, 2つ, etc., as well.

二つの物体	[ふたつのブッタイ]	2 bodies
三つの磁石	[みっつのジシャク]	3 magnets
四つのコンデンサー	[よっつのコンデンサー]	4 condensers
3つの曲線	[みっつのキョクセン]	3 curves

The rules for writing the primary and secondary numbers are flexible and you may well encounter

2本の平行光線	[ニホンのヘイコウコウセン]	2 parallel light rays
二つの平行光線	[ふたつのヘイコウコウセン]	
4個の水素原子	[よんこのスイソゲンシ]	4 hydrogen atoms
四つの水素原子	[よっつのスイソゲンシ]	
8個の細胞	[ハッコのサイボウ]	8 cells {biol}
八つの細胞	[やっつのサイボウ]	

In fact, you may even find both usages on the same page of text.

    The order "number+counter+の+noun" given above is the usual sequence in scientific writing. However, you will see other word-orders from time to time. For example, the following are virtually synonymous for "[they] used (the) 2 condensers":

2個のコンデンサーを使った	[ニコのコンデンサーをつかった]
コンデンサーを2個使った	[コンデンサーをニコつかった]
コンデンサー2個を使った	[コンデンサーニコをつかった]

Similar comments apply to other quantity words, such as すべて, meaning "all." For example, you will see both すべての分子は... and 分子はすべて....

    Note the following constructions involving the demonstratives:

この一つの実験	[このひとつのジッケン]	this 1 experiment
その1個の分子	[そのイッコのブンシ]	that 1 molecule
この一組の方程式	[このひとくみのホウテイシキ]	this 1 set of equations
これら二つの方法	[これらふたつのホウホウ]	these 2 methods
それら3種の内	[それらサンシュのうち]	among those 3 kinds

14-12

これら二組の方程式	[これらふたくみのホウテイシキ]			these 2 sets of equations	
これら両方	[これらリョウホウ]			both of these	

Note that これら and それら appear here (not これらの and それらの).

We conclude this discussion on counters by noting that phonetic changes take place when numbers combine with counters. The following list illustrates the kinds of changes that occur:

	Flat Objects	Long Objects	Round Objects	Minutes	People
	枚[マイ]	本[ホン]	個[コ]	分[フン]	人[ニン]
一	イチマイ	イッポン	イッコ	イップン	ひとり！
二	ニマイ	ニホン	ニコ	ニフン	ふたり！
三	サンマイ	サンボン	サンコ	サンプン	サンニン
四	よ(ん)マイ	よんホン	よんコ	よんプン	よニン
五	ゴマイ	ゴホン	ゴコ	ゴフン	ゴニン
六	ロクマイ	ロッポン	ロッコ	ロップン	ロクニン
七	ななマイ	ななホン	ななコ	ななフン	ななニン (シチニン)
八	ハチマイ	ハッポン	ハッコ	ハップン	ハチニン
九	キュウマイ	キュウホン	キュウコ	キュウフン	キュウニン (クニン)
十	ジュウマイ	ジュッポン	ジュッコ	ジュップン	ジュウニン
何	なんマイ	なんボン	なんコ	なんプン	なんニン

The underlined entries have phonetic changes. In the entries for 7, シチ may be used instead of なな; in the entries for 10, either ジュ or ジ may precede ッ. It should be noted that 十分 is pronounced ジュップン or ジップン if it means "10 minutes"; however, if it means "sufficient," it must be read ジュウブン. The row labeled with 何[なん] corresponds to "how many?" Alternatively one may use 幾[いく] instead of 何 with some counters.

We now give some sentences in which numbers and counters are used.

1個のU-235原子核が分解するとき、2個以上の中性子を放出する。
1コのU-235ゲンシカクがブンカイするとき、2コイジョウのチュウセイシをホウシュツする。
When a U-235 atomic nucleus disintegrates, 2 or more neutrons are emitted. {Note that the expression 2個以上 means "2 or more" and not "more than 2."}

核酸は細胞の中に多量に見られる酸性の高分子物質でリボ核酸(RNA)とデオキシリボ核酸 (DNA)の2種類がある。
カクサンはサイボウのなかにタリョウにみられるサンセイのコウブンシブッシツでリボカ クサン(RNA)とデオキシリボカクサン(DNA)の2シュルイがある。
Nucleic acids are acidic macromolecular substances that are seen in large quantities inside cells; the 2 kinds are ribonucleic acid (RNA) and deoxyribonucleic acid (DNA).

DNAに含まれ.ている4つの塩基の割合に関して、どの生物からとったDNAでもグアニンの
量とシトシンの量、およびアデニンの量とチミンの量が等しいことがわかった。
DNAにふくまれている4つのエンキのわりあいにカンして、どのセイブツからとったDNA
でもグアニンのリョウとシトシンのリョウ、およびアデニンのリョウとチミンのリョ
ウがひとしいことがわかった。
With regard to the proportions of the 4 bases that are contained in DNA, we know that the quantities
of guanine and cytosine and the quantities of adenine and thymine are equal for the DNA taken
from any living thing.

これら二組の方程式を連立に解けば、次のように解が得られる。
これらふたくみのホウテイシキをレンリツにとけば、つぎのようにカイがえられる。
If we solve these 2 sets of equations simultaneously, the solution is obtained as follows.

不活性の元素の電子配置としては、ヘリウムでは電子が2個だけあり、その他のものでは最
外殻に8個の電子がある。
フカッセイのゲンソのデンシハイチとしては、ヘリウムではデンシが2コだけあり、そのタ
のものではサイガイカクに8コのデンシがある。
With regard to the arrangement of the electrons in the inert elements, in helium there are only 2 electrons
in the outermost shell, but in the others there are 8.

Note also that, although 個 is the usual counter for molecules (分子), the word 分子
itself may specify the number of molecules. Hence you will sometimes come across

2分子の水　　　　　［ニブンシのみず］　　　　　　2 molecules of water
3分子の二酸化炭素　［サンブンシのニサンカタンソ］　3 molecules of carbon dioxide

Here is a sentence illustrating this use.

水素2分子が酸素1分子と反応すると2分子の水が生成する。
スイソ2ブンシがサンソ1ブンシとハンノウすると2ブンシのみずがセイセイする。
When 2 molcules of hydrogen react with 1 molecule of oxygen, 2 molecules of water are produced.

14.4 Numbers with Prefixes and Suffixes

Ordinal numbers can be written by using the prefix 第[ダイ] with the primary
numbers. Thus, 第一[ダイイチ], 第二[ダイニ], 第三[ダイサン], etc., mean "first,
second, third," etc. You will encounter these ordinal numbers in several ways in
technical Japanese: (a) an author in enumerating a sequence of steps or arguments may
preface each item by 第一に..., 第二に..., 第三に..., meaning "in the first place ...,
in the second place ..., in the third place ..."; (b) the ordinal numbers may be followed
directly by a noun, as in 第四周期[ダイよんシュウキ] "fourth period {of the
periodic table}" and 第十四章[ダイジュウよんショウ] "Chapter 14."

周期表の第6周期と第7周期に属する元素はたくさんある。
シュウキヒョウのダイ6シュウキとダイ7シュウキにゾクするゲンソはたくさんある。
There are many elements belonging to the sixth and seventh periods of the periodic table.

Another way to write ordinal numbers is by adding the suffix 目[め] to any primary number+counter combination or to the secondary numbers: 3枚目[サンマイめ] "the third (flat object)," 5本目[ゴホンめ] "the fifth (long object)," and 二つ目 [ふたつめ] "the second one." Ordinals may also be written with the general counter 番[バン], which means "number," and 目. Thus 一番[イチバン] means "No.1" and 一番目[イチバンめ] "the first"; 二番[ニバン] means "No.2" and 二番目[ニバン め] "the second," and so on.

四番目の殻の中の電子が一つぬけて、外の殻へ移っていく。
よ(ん)バンめのカクのなかのデンシがひとつぬけて、そとのカクへうつっていく。
One electron escapes from (within) the fourth shell and moves to an outer shell.

The suffix 倍[バイ] means "times" (in the sense of multiples), so that we have 2倍 [ニバイ] "twice," 3倍[サンバイ] "3 times," and so on. Strictly speaking, this suffix is added only to the primary numbers.

Van der Waalsの状態式において，bは分子体積の4倍である。
Van der Waalsのジョウタイシキにおいて、bはブンシタイセキの4バイである。
In the van der Waals equation of state, b is 4 times the volume of the molecules.

The suffix ずつ can be added either to a primary number+counter or to a secondary number. It indicates a distributive meaning, with English translations of "each, apiece, at a time."

水素分子では、二つの水素原子が電子を1個ずつ出し合い、それら二つの電子が電子対を形成する。
スイソブンシでは、ふたつのスイソゲンシがデンシを1コずつだしあい、それらふたつのデンシがデンシツイをケイセイする。
In the hydrogen molecule the 2 hydrogen atoms each contribute {lit.: offer each other} 1 electron, and those 2 electrons form an electron pair.

単結合がイオン結合でなければ、各原子が電子を1個ずつ出して結合をなす。
タンケツゴウがイオンケツゴウでなければ、カクゲンシがデンシを1コずつだしてケツゴウをなす。
If a single bond is not ionic, then each atom contributes 1 electron to form the bond.

There are two number-following expressions that have somewhat similar meanings. The expression ごとに indicates "every, at an interval of." For example, 三時間ごとに means "every three hours." The expression おきに is often synonymous with ごとに, but strictly speaking means "regularly skipping, setting aside." This latter meaning is particularly appropriate for the number 1: 一人おきに[ひとり おきに] "every other person," 一台おきに[イチダイおきに] "every other vehicle."

メンデレーエフは元素をその原子量にしたがって並べ、8個目ごとに性質のよく似た元素があることを発見したのである。

メンデレーエフはゲンソをそのゲンシリョウにしたがってならべ、8コめごとにセイシツのよくにたゲンソがあることをハッケンしたのである。

Mendeleev lined up the elements according to their atomic masses and discovered that every eighth element has similar properties. {似る[にる] means "to resemble."}

In addition, the prefix 毎[マイ] means "every." It is most often used with time words: 毎時[マイジ] "every hour, per hour"; 毎秒[マイビョウ] "every second, per second." Also the prefix 各[カク] means "each," as in 各点で[カクテンで] "at each point." The same KANJI can also be used to make the word 各々[おのおの], which, when followed by the particle の, also means "each": 各々の実験で[おのおのの ジッケンで] "in each experiment."

14.5 Approximate Numbers

In technical writing it is often necessary to indicate that a number is approximate. This may be done either by placing a word before the number or after it. The three most common words placed before the number are 約[ヤク], ほぼ, and およそ.

約100g	[ヤクヒャクグラム]	about 100 g
ほぼ250cm	[ほぼニヒャクゴジュッセンチ]	(very) nearly 250 cm
およそ75km	[およそななジュウゴキロ(メートル)]	approximately 75 km

The three words placed after the number — ぐらい, ばかり, and ほど — all mean "about (that amount)," but they are not wholly synonymous.

5人ぐらい	[ゴニンぐらい]	about 5 people
3時間ばかり	[サンジカンばかり]	(only) about 3 hours
20秒ほど	[ニジュウビョウほど]	about (as much as) 20 seconds

In technical writing the expression ...(の)程度[...(の)テイド] is the equivalent of the much-used English expression "of the order of."

この測定は、100万程度の分子量にかぎられることがある。

このソクテイは、100マンテイドのブンシリョウにかぎられることがある。

In these measurements the molecular weights are sometimes restricted of the order of 1,000,000.

この電子波の波長は2πaの程度で、電子の運動量の大きさはほぼh/2πaである。

このデンシハのハチョウは2πaのテイドで、デンシのウンドウリョウのおおきさはほぼh/2πaである。

The wave length of this electron wave is of the order $2\pi a$, and the magnitude of the electron momentum is about $h/2\pi a$.

ゴム管(長さ約15cm)を用いてもよい。
ゴムカン(ながさヤク15cm)をもちいてもよい。
You may use a rubber tube (about 15 cm in length).

μ-中間子の質量は電子の質量の約二百倍である。
μ-チュウカンシのシツリョウはデンシのシツリョウのヤクニヒャクバイである。
The mass of the μ-meson is about 200 times that of the electron.

Still another way to indicate approximate numbers is by juxtaposition of two adjacent integers.

二、三時間	[ニサンジカン]	2 or 3 hours
五、六個の光子	[ゴロッコのコウシ]	5 or 6 photons
三、四百倍	[サンよんヒャクバイ]	3 or 4 hundred times

Several words may be used to specify that a number is not approximate. The word 丁度 [チョウド] means "exactly" when it precedes a number. The word だけ (which usually means "only") means "just" or "exactly" when it follows a specific number.

ナトリウムとエチルアルコールの反応によって発生する水素の量は、エチルアルコール分子中の水素のちょうど1/6である。
ナトリウムとエチルアルコールのハンノウによってハッセイするスイソのリョウは、エチルアルコールブンシチュウのスイソのちょうど1/6である。
The quantity of hydrogen generated from ethyl alcohol by means of reaction with sodium is exactly equal to 1/6 of the hydrogen in the ethyl alcohol molecules.

円周上の周期的な運動において、角度は周期Tの間に、ラジアン単位で2πだけ増す。
エンシュウジョウのシュウキテキなウンドウにおいて、カクドはシュウキTのあいだにラジアンタンイで2πだけます。
In circular periodic motion, the angle increases by just 2π radians during a period T.

14.6 Some Mathematical Expressions

There are many elementary mathematical terms that are used frequently in physics, chemistry, biology, and engineering. You have learned the KANJI for writing some of these, but others will not be familiar to you. This material is included primarily for reference and need not be memorized for use in later chapters.

The verbs corresponding to the four basic arithmetic operations (加減乗除[カゲンジョウジョ]), along with the terms for the results of these basic operations, are

たす	to add	和	[ワ]	sum
ひく	to subtract	差	[サ]	difference
かける	to multiply	積	[セキ]	product
割る [わる]	to divide	商	[ショウ]	quotient

Powers and roots have general expressions, but there are also special expressions for the numbers 2 and 3.

xの平方	[xのヘイホウ]	x^2
xの自乗	[xのジジョウ]	
xの立方	[xのリッポウ]	x^3
xの三乗	[xのサンジョウ]	
xのn乗	[xのnジョウ]	x^n
xの平方根	[xのヘイホウコン]	$x^{1/2}$
xの自乗根	[xのジジョウコン]	
xの立方根	[xのリッポウコン]	$x^{1/3}$
xの三乗根	[xのサンジョウコン]	
xのn乗根	[xのnジョウコン]	$x^{1/n}$

Some other operations are

xの階乗	[xのカイジョウ]	$x!$
xの常用対数	[xのジョウヨウタイスウ]	$\log_{10} x$
xの自然対数	[xのシゼンタイスウ]	$\log_e x$
aを底とするxの対数	[aをテイとするxのタイスウ]	$\log_a x$

The trigonometric functions 三角関数[サンカクカンスウ] are

xの正弦	[xのセイゲン]	or サインx	$\sin x$
xの余弦	[xのヨゲン]	or コサインx	$\cos x$
xの正接	[xのセイセツ]	or タンジェントx	$\tan x$
xの余接	[xのヨセツ]	or コタンジェントx	$\cot x$
xの正割	[xのセイカツ]	or セカントx	$\sec x$
xの余割	[xのヨカツ]	or コセカントx	$\csc x$

The inverse trigonometric functions 逆三角関数[ギャクサンカクカンスウ] are obtained by prefixing 逆[ギャク] to the names of the trigonometric functions above. Similarly the hyperbolic functions 双曲線関数[ソウキョクセンカンスウ] are obtained by prefixing 双曲線[ソウキョクセン] to the various trigonometric functions.

The names of the most familiar "del" operations are

sの勾配	[sのコウバイ]	or グラジエントs	grad s
vの発散	[vのハッサン]	or ダイバージェンスv	div v
vの回転	[vのカイテン]	or カールv	curl v

The verbs for differentiation and integration are

微分する	[ビブンする]	to differentiate
積分する	[セキブンする]	to integrate

In addition we have

一次導関数	[イチジドウカンスウ]	first-order derivative
二次導関数	[ニジドウカンスウ]	second-order derivative
単積分	[タンセキブン]	single integral
二重積分	[ニジュウセキブン]	double integral
常微分方程式	[ジョウビブンホウテイシキ]	ordinary differential equation
偏微分方程式	[ヘンビブンホウテイシキ]	partial differential equation

A matrix is referred to as 行列[ギョウレツ], which is made up of the KANJI 行[ギョウ] "row," and 列[レツ] "column." The following are important words relevant to matrices:

対称行列	[タイショウギョウレツ]	symmetric matrix
対角行列	[タイカクギョウレツ]	diagonal matrix
正方行列	[セイホウギョウレツ]	square matrix
単位行列	[タンイギョウレツ]	unit matrix
逆行列	[ギャクギョウレツ]	inverse matrix
転置行列	[テンチギョウレツ]	transposed matrix
行列式	[ギョウレツシキ]	determinant (of a matrix)

Some common plane geometrical figures are

円	[エン]	circle
楕円	[ダエン]	ellipse
三角形	[サンカクケイ]	triangle
正三角形	[セイサンカクケイ]	equilateral triangle
直角三角形	[チョッカクサンカクケイ]	right triangle
正方形	[セイホウケイ]	square
長方形	[チョウホウケイ]	rectangle
平行四辺形	[ヘイコウシヘンケイ]	parallelogram

Some names for solid geometrical objects are

球	[キュウ]	sphere
楕円体	[ダエンタイ]	ellipsoid
(直)円柱	[(チョク)エンチュウ]	(right) circular cylinder
角柱	[カクチュウ]	prism
円錐	[エンスイ]	circular cone
角錐	[カクスイ]	pyramid
平行六面体	[ヘイコウロクメンタイ]	parallclcpipcd

14-19

The three most important coordinate systems are

直交座標	[チョッコウザヒョウ]	rectangular coordinates
円柱座標	[エンチュウザヒョウ]	cylindrical coordinates
球座標	[キュウザヒョウ]	spherical coordinates

Curvilinear coordinates are called 曲線座標 [キョクセンザヒョウ].
And finally we give a few miscellaneous terms.

べき指数	[べきシスウ]	exponent
べき級数	[べきキュウスウ]	power series
無限級数	[ムゲンキュウスウ]	infinite series
有限級数	[ユウゲンキュウスウ]	finite series
複素数	[フクソスウ]	complex number
実数	[ジッスウ]	real number
虚数	[キョスウ]	imaginary number
既知数	[キチスウ]	known (quantity)
未知数	[ミチスウ]	unknown (quantity)
展開	[テンカイ]	expansion
計算	[ケイサン]	calculation
演算子	[エンザンシ]	operator
因子	[インシ]	factor
記号	[キゴウ]	symbol
符号	[フゴウ]	sign
添え字	[そえジ]	index, suffix
項	[コウ]	term {in an equation}
公式	[コウシキ]	formula
x軸	[xジク]	x-axis
横軸	[よこジク]	horizontal axis
縦軸	[たてジク]	vertical axis
近似	[キンジ]	approximation
絶対値	[ゼッタイチ]	absolute value
代数方程式	[ダイスウホウテイシキ]	algebraic equation
幾何学	[キカガク]	geometry
三角法	[サンカクホウ]	trigonometry

ADDITIONAL VOCABULARY FOR EXERCISES

かこむ		to enclose
えがく		to draw
ネジ		screw
素反応	ソハンノウ	elementary reaction
多重線	タジュウセン	multiplet
しばしば		frequently
まとめる		to bring together
書き表す	かきあらわす	to express {in writing}
実部	ジツブ	real part
相となる	あいとなる	adjacent
そのまま		as it is
極形式	キョクケイシキ	polar form
一方では	イッポウでは	on the one hand
-著	チョ	(written) by
はさむ		to sandwich (something) between
すむ		to get by with
...ともなって生ずる	ともなってショウずる	generated along with ...
もどる		to return

EXERCISES

Ex 14.1 Insert the numbers that match the correct results of multiplication

Numbers	その三倍	その十倍	Results of Multiplication	
三	( )	( )	1. 五分の三	11. 百八十
九	( )	( )	2. 一	12. 四百
十	( )	( )	3. 三分の十	13. 六百
千	( )	( )	4. 二	14. 二千百
四十	( )	( )	5. 九	15. 三千
六十	( )	( )	6. 二十七	16. 七千
七百	( )	( )	7. 三十	17. 一万
十万	( )	( )	8. 九十	18. 三十万
三分の一	( )	( )	9. 百	19. 百万
五分の一	( )	( )	10. 百二十	

Ex 14.2 Matching Japanese and English technical terms

Japanese	English
三行目( )	1. triple point
三重点( )	2. third period of the periodic table
三次元( )	3. the third method
第三の方法( )	4. at 3 atmospheres
三本のばね( )	5. the third law of thermodynamics
3つの平面( )	6. triple bond
3個の細胞( )	7. 3 simple pendulums
三番目の質点( )	8. 3 or more mass points
第三次導関数( )	9. the third mass point
三回微分する( )	10. to differentiate 3 times
三番目の部分( )	11. 3 dimensions
3気圧のもとで( )	12. the third part
3つの単振り子( )	13. the third derivative
3個以上の質点( )	14. 3 times the mass of the electron
電子の質量の三倍( )	15. the third row
3個の塩素原子( )	16. 3 springs
3本の平行光線( )	17. 3 planes
周期表の第三周期( )	18. 3 cells
熱力学第三法則( )	19. 3 chlorine atoms
三重結合( )	20. 3 parallel light rays

Ex 14.3 Matching Japanese technical terms and definitions

熱伝導（　）
熱伝導率（　）
倍加時間（　）
接平面（　）
半導体（　）
三角形（　）
二分子反応（　）
角運動量（　）
両性化合物（　）
倍率（　）

1. 0°Kの低温[テイオン＝low temperature]に近づくと、絶縁体[ゼツエンタイ＝insulator]になり、高温では導体になるSi、Geなどのようなもの。
2. 酸性と塩基性との両方の性質をもつ化合物。
3. 物体内部の等温面に垂直[スイチョク＝perpendicular]に流れる単位面積単位時間あたりの熱量と、この方向における温度勾配[コウバイ＝gradient]との比。
4. 2つの分子(原子、イオンの場合も含む)の間の素反応。
5. 3つの直線でかこまれた平面図形[ズケイ＝figure]。
6. 幾何光学[キカコウガク＝geometric optics]において鏡[かがみ＝mirror]やレンズによって物体の像[ゾウ＝image]ができる場合、像[ゾウ]の大きさと物体の大きさとの比。
7. 原点に対する質点の位置ベクトルとその質点の運動量とのベクトル積。
8. 物体内で熱が高温部から低温[テイオン]部へ流れる場合、物体を構成する分子の運動によって熱が伝わる現象[ゲンショウ＝phenomenon]。
9. 動物体の大きさ(主[シュ]として体重)が出生時の二倍になるまでに要する時間。
10. 曲面上の1点を通ってえがかれる曲線に接線をひく場合その接線のすべてがなす平面。

Ex 14.4 Translate the following sentences

1. 二つの水素原子が電子を1個ずつ出し合い、それら二つの電子が1対になり、その電子対が二つの水素原子核の間に共有[キョウユウ＝covalent]結合をなすことによって水素の分子ができる。
2. 質点の角運動量は質点の位置ベクトルrとその質点の運動量pとのベクトル積であり、その大きさはrp sin θである。ただし、θはrとpとがなす角である。その方向はrとpの両方に垂直[スイチョク＝perpendicular]で向きはrをpへ回すとき右[みぎ＝right-handed]ネジが進む向きとして定義[テイギ＝definition]されている。
3. 曲線上の1点Pとその近傍の[キンボウの＝neighboring]同じ曲線上の点P′を結ぶ直線をつくるとき、P′をPに無限に近づけた極限として得られる直線を接線という。
4. 三相交流は周波数[シュウハスウ＝frequency]が相等しく位相が120°ずつ異なった[from ことなる＝to differ]三つの相からなる交流である。

14-23

5. 三重結合は分子内の2個の原子が3本[ボン]の原子結合で結ばれる結合である。

6. 有機化合物において第三炭素原子とはほかの3個の炭素原子と結合した炭素原子である。例えば$(CH_3)_3CH$の$\underline{C}$がこれである。第四炭素原子とはほかの4個の炭素原子と結合して、それ以外の原子とは結合していない炭素原子である。例えば$\underline{C}(CH_3)_4$の$\underline{C}$がこれである。

7. 四極子とは大きさが等しく向きが反対の双極子[ソウキョクシ=dipole]2個がきわめて接近しているものである。

8. 多重線は多重項[コウ=term]にもとづいて現われる[あらわれる]近接したスペクトル線の1組をいう。その本数[ホンスウ=number of lines]にしたがって二重線、三重線とよぶ。

9. 二つの整数[セイスウ=integers]A、BについてA=BCとなる整数[セイスウ]Cがあるとき、AはBの倍数、BはAの約数であるという。

10. 一般に[イッパンに=in general]二曲線の交点におけるそれら二曲線の交角とはその交点におけるそれぞれの曲線の接線間の交角をいう。

11. 倍数体は二組以上のゲノムをもった個体をいう。体細胞はふつう二倍体(2nで表す)であるが、ゲノムが重複[ジュウフク=duplication]して三倍体(3n)四倍体(4n)となることがある。

12. 微生物は大きさが大体0.1mm以下で、単細胞であるか、多細胞であっても細胞間の形態的分化がほとんどないものである。

Ex 14.5 Read the following essays for comprehension

1. 2種の元素A、Bが化合して2種以上の化合物ができることがある。このとき各化合物におけるAの一定量に対するBの量は簡単な[カンタンな=simple]整数[セイスウ]の比になっているという事実[ジジツ=fact]を表明したものを倍数比例の法則という。この法則はJ. Daltonによってその原子説と同時(1802)に発表され、その後において実験的に確認[カクニン=confirm]されたものである。したがってこの法則はしばしば原子説に対するもっとも有力な実験的支持[シジ=support]とみなされる。

2. 集積[シュウセキ=integrated]回路とはいくつかの素子をまとめ、配線[ハイセン=wiring]も含めて一つの基板[キバン=substrate]の上に作成し、一つの部品[ブヒン=part]として使えるようにしたものである。ICともよばれ、素子ごとの容器[ヨウキ=container]が不要で、素子ごとの接続[セツゾク=connection]のためのピン、コネクターなどの部品[ブヒン]も不要なことから、かなり複雑な[フクザツな=complicated]回路をきわめて小型[こがた=small size]に作ることができる。トランジスタが小さくでき、配線[ハイセン]も細かく短く[from みじかい=short]できるため、小電力、高速となる。

3. 一定の力**f**がはたらいて物体が**s**方向に変位したときに、この力がなした仕事[シごと = work]はfs cos θとして定義[テイギ]される。ただしθは力**f**の作用線とその作用点の変位**s**の方向とのなす角である。スカラー積として書き表せば**f**·**s**となる。大きさも方向も変化する力**f**がはたらき、物体が曲線PQにそって運動する場合には、径路PQを多数の微小変位Δ**s**に区分[クブン =division]し、それぞれの変位Δ**s**の間は**f**の大きさも方向も一定とみなして、PQの間で力**f**のなす仕事[シごと]は

$$\lim_{\Delta s \to 0} \sum f \Delta s \cos \theta = \int fds \cos \theta = \int \mathbf{f} \cdot d\mathbf{s}$$

で与えられる。これはいわゆる線積分である。

4. 複素[フクソ = complex]変数の指数[シスウ = exponent]関数

　虚数[キョスウ = imaginary number]単位 i(i² = −1)を含んで

$$z = x + iy \quad (x, y は実数)$$

の形にあらわされる数を複素[フクソ]数といい、xを実部、yを虚部[キョブ = imaginary part]という。実部が0である複素数を純[ジュン = pure]虚数[キョスウ]という。複素数の加減乗除[カゲンジョウジョ = the four arithmetic operations]は、i² = −1に注意[チュウイ = attention]すれば通常の2項式[ニコウシキ = binomial expression]と同じにおこなわれる。
　複素数 z = x + iy に対して、虚部の符号[フゴウ = sign]を変えたもの z = x - iy をzに共役[キョウヤク = conjugate]な複素数といい、z*であらわす。たがいに共役[キョウヤク]な二つの複素数の積 z * z = x² + y² は実数である。その正の平方根[コン = root] (x² + y²)^{1/2} を、複素数 z または z* の絶対[ゼッタイ = absolute]値といい、|z|であらわす。
　実数を一直線上の点に対応させることができるように、複素数を一平面上の点に対応させることができる。すなわち、一平面上にたがいに直交するx軸[ジク = axis]とy軸[ジク]とを定め、座標[ザヒョウ = coordinates] (x,y)の点と複素数x + iyとを対応させればよい。この平面を複素平面といい、このx軸を実軸といい、y軸を虚軸という。
　たがいに共役な二つの複素数は、実軸に関して対称な[タイショウな=symmetrical]二点であらわされる。絶対[ゼッタイ]値|z|は、原点0と点zを結ぶ線分の長さに等しい。また-zは、原点に関しzと点対称[タイショウ]なる点に対応する(図A.1)。

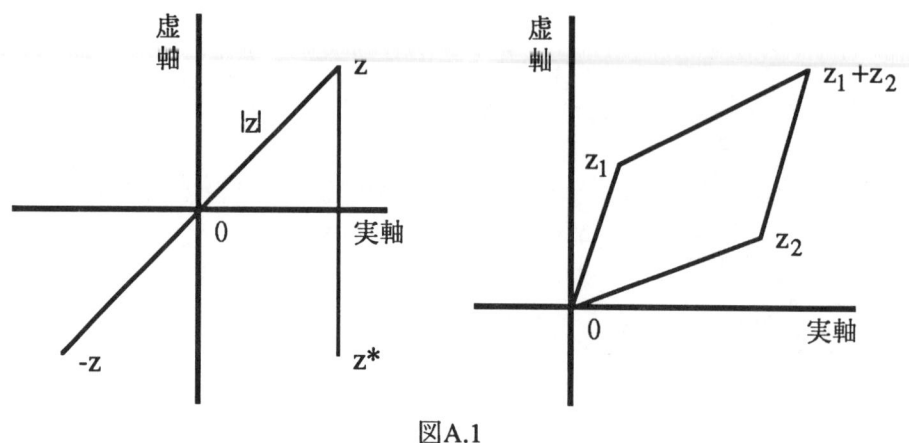

　　点 z_1 および z_2 を知って点 $(z_1 + z_2)$ を求めるには線分$0z_1$と$0z_2$とを相となる二辺[ニヘン = two sides]とする平行四辺形[ヘイコウシヘンケイ = parallelogram]の0に対する頂点[チョウテン = vertex]をとればよい。

　　実数xの関数 f(x) を拡張[カクチョウ = extension]して、複素数zの関数 f(z) を考えることができる。特[トク]に重要なものは指数[シスウ]関数 exp z である。実変数について成立する加法定理

$$\exp (x_1 + x_2) = (\exp x_1)(\exp x_2) \tag{1}$$

と展開[テンカイ = expansion]式

$$\exp x = 1 + x + (x^2/2!) + \cdots \tag{2}$$

がそのまま成立するように、exp x の意味[イミ = meaning]を定めようとすれば、まず

$$\exp z = \exp (x + iy) = (\exp x)(\exp iy) \tag{3}$$

としなければならない。ここにexp xは既知の[キチの = known]実関数である。exp iyを定めるために展開[テンカイ]式を利用すれば

$$\begin{aligned}
\exp iy &= 1 + iy - (y^2/2!) - i(y^3/3!) + \cdots \\
&= [1 - (y^2/2!) + \cdots] + i[y - (y^3/3!) + \cdots] \\
&= \cos y + i \sin y
\end{aligned} \tag{4}$$

となる。このことから、複素変数の指数関数はつぎのように定義[テイギ]される。

$$\exp (x + iy) = (\exp x)(\cos y + i \sin y) \tag{5}$$

(5)より明らかなように

$$\exp 2\pi i = \cos 2\pi + i \sin 2\pi = 1 \qquad (6)$$

したがって任意[ニンイ = arbitrary]のzに対してつねに

$$\exp (z + 2\pi i) = \exp z \qquad (7)$$

さらに、nを任意の整数[セイスウ = integer]として

$$\exp (z + 2n\pi i) = \exp z \qquad (8)$$

Adapted from pp. 224-228 of 木原太郎著, 『化学物理入門』, 岩波書店, 1978.

Ex 14.6 Translate the following essay

　一般に[イッパンに]金属[キンゾク = metal]の電気伝導率は温度、圧力、金属[キンゾク]の種類によって違うが、$\Omega^{-1} \cdot m^{-1}$単位で表して常温で約10^6程度である。ケルビン温度に反比例し、0°Kに近ずくと極めて大きくなる。電流は本質的に[ホンシツテキに = essentially]電子の流れであり、0°K近くの極低温[テイオン = low temperature]では電子も運動しなくなって電気は流れなくなるというのはニュートン力学の考えかたであったが、電子がもつ波動性[ハドウセイ = wave characteristics]のため運動は消えず、電子が2個ずつペアを組んで対になって活発に[カッパツに = actively]運動するためこのようなことが起こるのである。また、このような極低温[テイオン]では不導体を導体ではさんだトンネル接合で両導体の間に電流を流しても不導体には電圧が現われない[from あらわれる]。すなわち、電気伝導率が極めて大きくなったのである。
　電気伝導率が大きい回路に電流を流す場合には高い電圧を必要としないので電力が少なくてすむ。このような回路に電流を流して磁場を作り、そこでコイルを回せば、微小電力で動く電動機が得られる。しかしながら、このためには、第一に、導線の温度を0°K近くまで下げなければならない。第二に、このような温度で発生する熱を放出させるには、例えば4°Kで1W当たり約500-1000倍程度の動力が必要になる。第三に、電流にともなって生ずる磁場の強さがある極限より大きくなると常伝導にもどって電気伝導率が小さくなってしまう。そこで、できるだけ高い温度で電気伝導率が極めて大きくなる物質を見つけなければならない。
　各種酸化物の配合[ハイゴウ = arrangement]によって多角的に実験した結果、液化ネオン温度より60度も高い温度で使用できるものが発見された。もし常温で使用できるものが発見されれば、水素原子中10^{-8}cmの曲率半径の円形[エンケイ = circle]に電流が流れているのと同じ状態をマクロなスケールで見ることができるのである。

Ex 14.4   Sentences

1. A hydrogen molecule is produced by the formation of a covalent bond between the nuclei of two hydrogen atoms, [each] having given to the other one electron, these two electrons making an electron pair.

2. The angular momentum of a mass point is the vector product of the position vector **r** and the momentum vector **p** of the mass point; its magnitude is rp sin θ. Here θ is the angle made by **r** and **p**. The direction of the angular momentum is defined as the direction, perpendicular to both **r** and **p**, in which a right-handed screw advances when **r** is rotated towards **p**.

3. A tangent is the straight line obtained as the limit when a straight line joins a point P on a curve with a neighboring point P' on the same curve, and point P' approaches infinitely near to point P.

4. Three-phase alternating current is the (alternating) current that consists of three phases of currents that have equal frequencies and differ [successively] in phase by 120°.

5. A triple bond is the bond formed by three atomic bonds between two atoms in a molecule.

6. A tertiary carbon (atom) in an organic compound is the carbon atom that is bonded to three other carbon atoms. For example, the $\underline{C}$ in $(CH_3)_3\underline{C}H$ is [one of] these. A quarternary carbon (atom) is a carbon atom that is bonded to four other carbon atoms and not bound to any other atoms. For example, the $\underline{C}$ in $\underline{C}(CH_3)_4$ is [one of] these.

7. A quadrupole is [a charge distribution] where two dipoles of equal magnitude but opposite direction are extremely close.

8. A multiplet is a group of closely adjacent spectral lines that appear based on a multiplet term. They are called doublets and triplets based on the number of lines.

9. When, for two integers A and B, there is an integer C such that A = BC, then A is called a multiple of B, and B a divisor of A.

10. In general, the angle of intersection of two curves at their point of intersection is the angle of intersection between their respective tangents to the curves at that point.

11. A polyploid is an individual that has two or more sets of genomes. A somatic cell is usually a diploid, (expressed by 2n), but with duplication of the genomes there are cases where it may become a triploid (3n) or a tetraploid (4n).

12. A microorganism has a size of 0.1mm or less; it is unicellular or, if multicellular, has almost no morphological differentiation among its cells.

In general, the electric conductivities of metals differ depending on the temperature, pressure, and the type of metal; at room temperature they are about the order 10^6 when expressed in units $\Omega^{-1} \cdot m^{-1}$. They are inversely proportional to the Kelvin temperature and become extremely large as [the temperature] approaches $0°K$. Electric current is essentially a flow of electrons; [in] the Newtonian way of thinking [it was] thought that even electrons would cease to move and electricity cease to flow at extremely low temperatures near $0°K$. However, owing to the wave characteristics that electrons have, their motion does not disappear. This type of thing happens because electrons join in pairs to form doublets that move actively. Moreover, at such extremely low temperatures as these, electric potential does not occur in a non-conductor even if a current is passed through the two conductors that sandwich the non-conductor in a tunnel connection. That is, [its] electric conductivity has become extremely large.

When [we] pass an electric current through a circuit having a large conductivity, [we] do not need a high voltage, and thus can get by with a small [amount] of electric power. If [we] produce a magnetic field by passing current through this kind of circuit and rotate a coil within it, [we] can obtain an electric motor that runs with a minute [amount] of electric power. However, in order [to do] this, we must first lower the temperature of the conducting wires to close to $0°K$. Second, in order to remove the heat generated at these temperatures, power is necessary, e.g., on the order of 500-1000 fold per 1w [of heat removed] at $4°K$. Third, the electric conductivity [of the circuit] will return to normal conductivity, attaining some small final value, if the intensity of the magnetic field generated along with the current becomes larger than a certain limit. Thus, we must find substances whose electric conductivities become extremely large at as high a temperature as possible.

As a result of experimenting in various ways with each type of oxide arrangement, a substance has been discovered that can be used at temperatures as much as 60 degrees higher than the temperature of liquid neon. If a substance is discovered that can be used at room temperature, then we will be able to see on the macro-scale the same condition as when a current is flowing in a circle with radius of curvature 10^{-8}cm within the hydrogen atom.

亜	ア	sub-; -ous {acids}

異	イ	difference, hetero-
	こと(なる)	to differ, vary

鉛	エン	lead
	なまり	lead

銀	ギン	silver

酢	サク	acetic
	す	vinegar

脂	シ	fat
	あぶら	fat, grease

臭	シュウ	odor, stench
	くさ(い)	foul smelling

集	シュウ	collecting
	あつ(める)	to gather, collect
	あつ(まる)	to assemble, converge

硝	ショウ	nitric

進	シン	advancing
	すす(む)	to progress

析	セキ	dividing; analyzing

属	ゾク	belonging to;
		genus {biol}
	ゾク(する)	to belong to

族	ゾク	family {biol}, group

窒	チツ	suffocation

鉄	テツ	iron

銅	ドウ	copper

配	ハイ	distribution
	くば(る)	to distribute

利	リ	benefit, gain

硫	リュウ	sulfur

料	リョウ	materials; fee

亜

亜種	アシュ	subspecies
亜属	アゾク	subgenus
亜族	アゾク	subgroup {in the periodic table}
亜硫酸	アリュウサン	sulfurous acid
亜硝酸	アショウサン	nitrous acid
亜塩素酸	アエンソサン	chlorous acid
次亜塩素酸	ジアエンソサン	hypochlorous acid
亜鉛	アエン	zinc

異

異常の	イジョウの	abnormal
異性体	イセイタイ	isomer
異種	イシュ	different kind, species, variety
異方性	イホウセイ	anisotropy
異数性	イスウセイ	heteroploidy
異数体	イスウタイ	heteroploid
異化	イカ	catabolism, dissimilation
異質細胞	イシツサイボウ	heterocyst
異形胞子	イケイホウシ	heterospore

鉛

炭酸鉛	タンサンなまり	lead carbonate
二酸化鉛	ニサンカなまり	lead dioxide
亜鉛	アエン	zinc
鉛直線	エンチョクセン	vertical line

銀

水銀	スイギン	mercury
硝酸銀	ショウサンギン	silver nitrate
硝酸水銀	ショウサンスイギン	mercury nitrate
水銀電極	スイギンデンキョク	mercury electrode
塩化第一水銀	エンカダイイチスイギン	mercurous chloride

酢

酢酸	サクサン	acetic acid
酢酸亜鉛	サクサンアエン	zinc acetate
酢酸鉛	サクサンなまり	lead acetate
酢酸銅	サクサンドウ	copper acetate

脂

脂質	シシツ	lipid
類脂質	ルイシシツ	lipoid
色素類脂質	シキソルイシシツ	lipochrome

集

集中する	シュウチュウする	to focus, center on
集計する	シュウケイする	to sum up, to total
集約的な	シュウヤクテキな	intensive
集積回路	シュウセキカイロ	integrated circuit
集光器	シュウコウキ	optical condenser
集合状態	シュウゴウジョウタイ	state of aggregation
集合	シュウゴウ	set {math}
部分集合	ブブンシュウゴウ	subset
全体集合	ゼンタイシュウゴウ	universal set

臭

臭素	シュウソ	bromine
臭化銀	シュウカギン	silver bromide
臭気	シュウキ	bad odor
無臭の	ムシュウの	odorless

硝

硝酸	ショウサン	nitric acid
硝酸銅	ショウサンドウ	copper nitrate
亜硝酸	アショウサン	nitrous acid
硝石	ショウセキ	niter, potassium nitrate
硝化作用	ショウカサヨウ	nitrification

進

進化する	シンカする	to evolve
人類の進化	ジンルイのシンカ	evolution of humankind
十進法	ジ(ュ)ッシンホウ	decimal notation
二進化十進法	ニシンカジ(ュ)ッシンホウ	binary-coded decimal notation
二進回路	ニシンカイロ	binary circuit
二進計数器	ニシンケイスウキ	binary counter
進行	シンコウ	progress, advance

析

析出	セキシュツ	precipitation
析出電位	セキシュツデンイ	deposition potential
解析	カイセキ	analysis {math}

分析	ブンセキ	analysis {chem}
定性分析	テイセイブンセキ	qualitative analysis
定量分析	テイリョウブンセキ	quantitative analysis

属

金属	キンゾク	metal
半金属	ハンキンゾク	metalloid
属性	ゾクセイ	attribute {biol}

族

第一族	ダイイチゾク	first group {in the periodic table}
亜族	アゾク	subgroup {in the periodic table}
種族	シュゾク	stellar population {astronomy}
同族体	ドウゾクタイ	homolog {chem}

窒

窒素	チッソ	nitrogen
窒素固定	チッソコテイ	nitrogen fixation
窒素同化作用	チッソドウカサヨウ	nitrogen assimilation
窒素族元素	チッソゾクゲンソ	nitrogen family elements
窒化物	チッカブツ	nitrides
二酸化窒素	ニサンカチッソ	nitrogen dioxide

鉄

地下鉄	チカテツ	subway
水酸化鉄	スイサンカテツ	iron hydroxide
鉄線	テッセン	iron wire
鉄心	テッシン	iron core
鉄板	テッパン	iron plate
鉄族元素	テツゾクゲンソ	iron family elements
鉄合金	テツゴウキン	ferroalloys

銅

銅線	ドウセン	copper wire
銅合金	ドウゴウキン	copper alloys
硫酸銅	リュウサンドウ	copper sulfate
塩化第二銅	エンカダイニドウ	cupric chloride

配

配電変電所	ハイデンヘンデンショ	distributing substation
配置	ハイチ	arrangement, configuration
配管	ハイカン	piping
配線	ハイセン	wiring

配向	ハイコウ	orientation
配位子	ハイイシ	ligand
配位子場	ハイイシば	ligand field
配位結合	ハイイケツゴウ	coordination bond
配位説	ハイイセツ	coordination theory
分配	ブンパイ	allotment, distribution
分配関数	ブンパイカンスウ	partition function

利

利用	リヨウ	utilization
利用する	リヨウする	to use
利点	リテン	advantage
有利な	ユウリな	useful
電圧利得	デンアツリトク	voltage gain

硫

加硫	カリュウ	vulcanization
硫酸	リュウサン	sulfuric acid
硫酸基	リュウサンキ	sulfonic group
硫酸亜鉛	リュウサンアエン	zinc sulfate
硫化亜鉛	リュウカアエン	zinc sulfide
硫化第一鉄	リュウカダイイチテツ	ferrous sulfide

料

料金	リョウキン	rate, charge, fee
電気料金	デンキリョウキン	electric rates
原料	ゲンリョウ	raw materials
材料	ザイリョウ	material

15 Chemical Nomenclature

You have already encountered some chemical terms in previous chapters: in Chapter 3, the names of the elements that are GAIRAIGO and written in KATAKANA; in later chapters, the names of some of the elements that are written using KANJI (炭素, 酸素, 水素, and 塩素); some binary compounds (二酸化炭素 and 塩化水素); and some acids and their salts (炭酸 and 炭酸カリウム). In this chapter we want to discuss chemical nomenclature in a systematic fashion.

We begin by summarizing the nomenclature for the chemical elements. With the KANJI given in this lesson you are now able to read the names of all the elements. Then we discuss the main rules for naming inorganic compounds, organic compounds, and biochemical compounds. Clearly, translations of chemical terms must be extremely accurate, since the slightest misinterpretation could have serious consequences.

15.1 The Elements

To write the names of all the chemical elements, in addition to KATAKANA one needs only 14 KANJI, and with this lesson you will know all of these. The presentation here is designed to facilitate the learning of the names of the elements by grouping them according to the types of written symbols that are used, the nature of the elements, and the extent to which they can be recognized from English.

a. Metals Written with One or Two KANJI

Au	金	[キン]	gold		Pt	白金	[ハッキン]	platinum
Ag	銀	[ギン]	silver		Hg	水銀	[スイギン]	mercury
Pb	鉛	[なまり]	lead		Zn	亜鉛	[アエン]	zinc
Fe	鉄	[テツ]	iron					
Cu	銅	[ドウ]	copper					

Note the use of the KUN reading for Pb. This reading is used in most lead compounds. Also note that platinum is white gold, mercury is watery silver, and zinc is pseudo-lead.

b. Nonmetals Written with KANJI or KANA Followed by 素[ソ] (element)

H	水素	[スイソ]	hydrogen		B	ホウ素	boron
C	炭素	[タンソ]	carbon		Si	ケイ素	silicon
N	窒素	[チッソ]	nitrogen		As	ヒ素	arsenic
O	酸素	[サンソ]	oxygen				

The names for the four main elements of organic chemistry correspond to the Dutch words: H [*waterstof* (water substance)], C [*koolstof* (coal substance)], N [*stikstof* (suffocating substance)], O [*zuurstof* (acid substance)]. KANA are used in the names for B, Si, and As in place of KANJI which are no longer in use.

In addition, four of the halogens are written with KANJI or KANA followed by 素, but astatine, the most recently discovered one, is written with KATAKANA.

Cl	塩素	[エンソ]	chlorine		F	フッ素	fluorine
Br	臭素	[シュウソ]	bromine		I	ヨウ素	iodine
					At	アスタチン	astatine

In the names for fluorine and iodine, KANA are used in lieu of KANJI that are no longer in common use.

c. Elements Formerly Written with KANJI, But Now Written with KANA, and Not Recognizable from European Languages

P	リン	phosphorous
S	イオウ	sulfur
Sn	スズ	tin

The word for sulfur is not usually written with KANJI (硫黄[イオウ]), since the reading イ for 硫 is regarded as irregular; normally, 硫 is read as リュウ as in 硫酸 [リュウサン] (sulfuric acid). Since the KANJI 黄 (yellow) occurs rather commonly, the JUKUGO 硫黄 may possibly come back into general use.

d. Elements Recognizable from Dutch or German (we list here the German names)

Na	ナトリウム	Natrium	sodium
K	カリウム	Kalium	potassium
Mn	マンガン	Mangan	manganese
Sb	アンチモン	Antimon	antimony
Ti	チタン	Titan*	titanium
Cr	クロム	Chrom*	chromium
Se	セレン	Selen*	selenium
Nb	ニオブ	Niob*	niobium
Te	テルル	Tellur*	tellurium
Mo	モリブデン	Molybdän*	molybdenum
Ta	タンタル	Tantal**	tantalum
La	ランタン	Lanthan**	lanthanum
Nd	ネオジム	Neodym*	neodymium
Pr	プラセオジム	Praseodym*	praseodymium
U	ウラン	Uran*	uranium

Elements marked with * (**) are missing the -ium (-um) as used in English. The last element (U) is the only actinide that does not end in ウム, and the three previous entries (La, Nd, Pr) are the only lanthanides that do not end in ウム. As we mentioned in Chapters 2 and 3, elements ending in ウム are pronounced as though they were written with the ending ユーム.

e. Noble Gases Recognizable from English

He	ヘリウム	helium	Kr	クリプトン	krypton
Ne	ネオン	neon	Xe	キセノン	xenon
Ar	アルゴン	argon	Ra	ラドン	radon

f. Metals Not Ending in ウム Recognizable from English

W	タングステン	tungsten	Bi	ビスマス	bismuth
Ni	ニッケル	nickel	Co	コバルト	cobalt

g. Metals Ending in ウム Recognizable from English

Li	リチウム	lithium	Ru	ルテニウム	ruthenium
Be	ベリリウム	beryllium	Rh	ロジウム	rhodium
Mg	マグネシウム	magnesium	Pd	パラジウム	palladium
Al	アルミニウム	aluminum	Cd	カドミウム	cadmium
Ca	カルシウム	calcium	In	インジウム	indium
Sc	スカンジウム	scandium	Cs	セシウム	cesium
V	バナジウム	vanadium	Ba	バリウム	barium
Ga	ガリウム	gallium	Hf	ハフニウム	hafnium
Ge	ゲルマニウム	germanium	Re	レニウム	rhenium
Rb	ルビジウム	rubidium	Os	オスミウム	osmium

Sr	ストロンチウム	strontium	Ir	イリジウム	iridium
Y	イットリウム	yttrium	Tl	タリウム	thallium
Zr	ジルコニウム	zirconium	Po	ポロニウム	polonium
Tc	テクネチウム	technicium	Fr	フランシウム	francium
Ra	ラジウム	radium			

h. Lanthanides Ending in ウム Recognizable from English

Ce	セリウム	cerium	Dy	ジスプロシウム	dysprosium
Pm	プロメチウム	promethium	Ho	ホルミウム	holmium
Sm	サマリウム	samarium	Er	エルビウム	erbium
Eu	ユーロピウム	europium	Tm	ツリウム	thulium
Gd	ガドリニウム	gadolinium	Yb	イッテルビウム	ytterbium
Tb	テルビウム	terbium	Lu	ルテチウム	lutetium

Note that "europium" is written ユーロピウム, whereas "Europe" is written ヨーロッパ.

i. Actinides Ending in ウム Recognizable from English

Ac	アクチニウム	actinium	Bk	バークリウム	berkelium
Th	トリウム	thorium	Cf	カリホルニウム	californium
Pa	プロトアクチニウム	protoactinium	Es	アインスタイニウム	einsteinium
Np	ネプツニウム	neptunium	Fm	フェルミウム	fermium
Pu	プルトニウム	plutonium	Md	メンデレビウム	mendelevium
Am	アメリシウム	americium	No	ノーベリウム	nobelium
Cm	キュリウム	curium	Lr	ローレンシウム	lawrencium

15.2 Binary Compounds

Binary compounds have names in Japanese that correspond to their chemical formulas, as they do in English. However, the order in which the elements or groups are named is the reverse of the order in the formula, as is true also in French. This is because the character 化 that indicates chemical combination comes after the name of the negative combining element. This perhaps derives from the fact that generic binary compounds — carbides, oxides, hydrides, chlorides — are described in terms of the negative element and thus are written as follows in Japanese:

炭化物	carbides	酸化物	oxides
水素化物	hydrides	塩化物	chlorides

Note that the word for hydride differs from the other -ides. (The word for hydrate originally was 水化物; now it is 水和物.) With the elements you learn in this chapter, you can now add the following to this list:

15-9

窒化物	nitrides	臭化物	bromides
ホウ化物	borides	ヒ化物	arsenides
リン化物	phosphides		

It is the same with functional groups that have KATAKANA names.

シアン化物	cyanides	アジ化物	azides

Apart from the reversal of the order of the components in a binary compound, Japanese names follow closely those in English. If only one compound is formed from the combining pair, the name gives no indication of the numbers of combining units, as is true in English.

NaCN	シアン化ナトリウム	sodium cyanide
$Ca(CN)_2$	シアン化カルシウム	calcium cyanide

When several compounds are formed and the number of atoms of the positive element does not change, only the number for the negative element is *traditionally* given, just as in English.

P_2O_3	三酸化リン	phosphorus trioxide
P_2O_5	五酸化リン	phosphorus pentoxide

The reason we emphasize *traditionally* is that the Japanese Chemical Society continually revises Japanese nomenclature in keeping with changes in the Rules of the International Union of Pure and Applied Chemistry (IUPAC). IUPAC recommends that P_2O_3 be called diphosphorus trioxide but, just as some American chemists choose to continue the traditional name phosphorus trioxide, in Japan the traditional name 三酸化リン will probably continue for the present. If a change is made, it might be to 六酸化四リン, which corresponds to P_4O_6.

When several binary compounds are formed and the positive element is the one that differs in valence, the numbers of atoms for both elements are given except when there is a single atom of the positive element. Some oxides of nitrogen offer the best example.

N_2O	一酸化二窒素	dinitrogen monoxide
NO	一酸化窒素	nitrogen monoxide
NO_2	二酸化窒素	nitrogen dioxide
N_2O_5	五酸化二窒素	nitrogen pentoxide

For some compounds the numbers representing the different constituent elements may appear together at the very beginning of the compound name instead of each appearing singly before the element whose number of atoms it represents. For example, you will find

Fe₃O₄	四三酸化鉄	triiron tetroxide
Fe₂O₃	三二酸化鉄	iron sesquioxide

There is another variation in the Japanese system of binary nomenclature. Compounds that form pairs designated in English as "-ous" and "-ic" (e.g., mercurous and mercuric chlorides, and stannous and stannic oxides) are treated differently. They are identified as the first (-ous) and the second (-ic) as follows:

HgCl	塩化第一水銀	mercurous chloride
HgCl₂	塩化第二水銀	mercuric chloride
SnO	酸化第一スズ	stannous oxide
SnO₂	酸化第二スズ	stannic oxide

You may also find them written in the style recommended by IUPAC.

HgCl	塩化水銀(I)	mercury(I) chloride
HgCl₂	塩化水銀(II)	mercury(II) chloride
SnO	酸化スズ(II)	tin(II) oxide
SnO₂	酸化スズ(IV)	tin(IV) oxide

Occasionally, the character 亜 is used as a prefix to designate the -ous form (e.g., 亜酸化窒素 for N₂O). However, the use of this character as a prefix for -ous is far more prominent in the naming of salts.

15.3 Bases, Acids, and Salts

The generic chemical categories of bases, acids, and salts are designated by the KANJI 塩基, 酸, and 塩. (The word for "base," 塩基, means literally "salt radical.")

a. Bases 塩基

The names of hydroxides follow the pattern for binary compounds with the hydroxyl radical 水酸 as the negative component; they do not include the generic word for base.

Ca(OH)₂	水酸化カルシウム	calcium hydroxide
KOH	水酸化カリウム	potassium hydroxide
NH₄OH	水酸化アンモニウム	ammonium hydroxide

Chemical names that include the word "basic," such as basic oxide, do include the word for base.

塩基性酸化物	basic oxide

Chemical names which contain the word "alkali," however, contain the GAIRAIGO アルカリ.

アルカリ金属   alkali metals

b. Acids 酸

Acids are designated by the suffix 酸, which you recognize as the KANJI used to name oxygen 酸素. With the KANJI and chemical elements introduced in this lesson, you can now read the names of strong acids, such as

HCl	塩酸	hydrochloric acid	HNO_3	硝酸	nitric acid
H_2SO_4	硫酸	sulfuric acid	H_3PO_4	リン酸	phosphoric acid

and the names of weak acids, such as

CH_3COOH	酢酸	acetic acid	H_3BO_3	ホウ酸	boric acid

Note that hydrochloric acid is an anomaly here. It does not contain oxygen, as the other acids do. The acid of chlorine that contains oxygen and is comparable chemically to the strong acids above is named

$HClO_3$	塩素酸	chloric acid

In all the nomenclature rules that follow (i.e., the rules for naming the -ous, hypo-, and per- acids) this anomaly in the naming of the acids of chlorine persists: namely, the KANJI 素 for "element" precedes the KANJI 酸 for "acid." This is also true for the acids of bromine and iodine.

The Japanese names of the "-ous" acids are formed by adding the prefix 亜 to their corresponding "-ic" names.

H_2SO_3	亜硫酸	sulfurous acid	HNO_2	亜硝酸	nitrous acid

The names of acids beginning with "hypo-" begin with the prefix 次亜.

H_3PO_2	次亜リン酸	hypophosphorous acid

And the names beginning with "per-" begin with the prefix 過.

H_5IO_6	過ヨウ素酸	periodic acid

The four acids of chlorine and oxygen illustrate this gradation in composition by means of prefixes very well.

$HClO$	次亜塩素酸	hypochlorous acid	$HClO_3$	塩素酸	chloric acid
$HClO_2$	亜塩素酸	chlorous acid	$HClO_4$	過塩素酸	perchloric acid

15-12

c. Salts 塩

As indicated earlier, the generic word for salt is 塩. Thus, the generic names for the salts of particular acids have this ending in common.

硫酸塩	sulfates	硝酸塩	nitrates
亜硫酸塩	sulfites	亜硝酸塩	nitrites

In the names of specific salts, the metal or positive ion of the hydroxide replaces the character for salt.

NH_4NO_3	硝酸アンモニウム	ammonium nitrate
$PbSO_4$	硫酸鉛	lead sulfate

In IUPAC nomenclature the sulfates of lead are written in Japanese as

$PbSO_4$	硫酸鉛(II)	lead(II) sulfate
$Pb(SO_4)_2$	硫酸鉛(IV)	lead(IV) sulfate

The salts of hydrochloric acid are an exception to these rules. They are named according to the rules for binary compounds. Silver chloride is written 塩化銀, not 塩酸銀. Moreover, be aware of the distinction between sulfides and sulfates, both of which use the character 硫. Sulfides are named according to the rules for binary compounds, e.g., mercury sulfide is 硫化水銀, and sulfates by the rules for salts, e.g., mercury sulfate is 硫酸水銀. Consider the following examples:

KBr	臭化カリウム	potassium bromide
$KBrO_3$	臭素酸カリウム	potassium bromate
KCl	塩化カリウム	potassium chloride
$KClO_3$	塩素酸カリウム	potassium chlorate
K_2S	硫化カリウム	potassium sulfide
K_2SO_4	硫酸カリウム	potassium sulfate

Japanese nomenclature for acids and salts has traditionally shared the rule found in naming binary compounds, namely, the use of first and second, 第一 and 第二, to distinguish between "-ous" and "-ic." Thus, chloroplatinous and chloroplatinic acids have previously been named 第一, 第二塩化白金酸. However, in the latest Japanese nomenclature it is recommended that the naming of the salts of these acids correspond to the IUPAC nomenclature of tetrachloroplatinate(II) and hexachloroplatinate(IV).

テトラクロロ白金(II)酸塩	ヘキサクロロ白金(IV)酸塩

Thus, Japanese chemical nomenclature does not stand still. The Japanese Chemical Society continually revises the recommended nomenclature in keeping with changes in IUPAC rules. For example, it recently recommended a change in nomenclature for phosphorous and hypophosphorous acids from 亜リン酸 and 次亜リン

酸 to ホスホン酸 and ホスフィン酸 in keeping with the IUPAC changes to phosphonic acid and phosphinic acid.

A good example of how Japanese nomenclature has changed with international nomenclature is found in the changes that have occurred in naming salts that internationally were first prefixed with "bi-," e.g., bisulfates and bicarbonates. Initially, Japanese nomenclature used the prefix 重, which has as one of its meanings "to double." Thus, bisulfates and bicarbonates were named 重硫酸塩 and 重炭酸塩, and a specific salt such as sodium bisulfite was named 重亜硫酸ナトリウム. However, with improvements in international nomenclature, such as the designation of sodium bisulfite as sodium hydrogen sulfite, Japanese nomenclature followed suit, introducing hydrogen into the name; thus 重亜硫酸ナトリウム became 亜硫酸水素ナトリウム. Japanese chemical dictionaries continue to include the old entries, identify them as older or colloquial terms, and refer you to the most recent chemical name. As in the case of the change from 亜リン酸 to ホスホン酸 mentioned above, these changes often introduce Japanese GAIRAIGO names in place of the names of the chemical elements. This is especially true with coordination compounds.

15.4 Coordination Compounds

The Japanese name for coordination compounds is 配位化合物. It contains the base for the Japanese word for ligands (配位子), elements and groups of elements that form coordination bonds with some central element. The Japanese names for the ligands are for the most part written in KATAKANA. Note that therefore the Japanese names of the elements as ligands differ from their names as elements more than the English names do. Compare, for example, the names for hydrogen and the halogens.

H	ヒドリド	hydrido	水素	hydrogen
F	フルオロ	fluoro	フッ素	fluorine
Cl	クロロ	chloro	塩素	chlorine
Br	ブロモ	bromo	臭素	bromine
I	ヨード	iodo	ヨウ素	iodine

Here are the names of the other ligand elements and the ligand groups.

O	オキソ	oxo	NH_3	アンミン	ammine
O_2	ペルオキソ	peroxo	NO	ニトロシル	nitrosyl
H_2O	アクア	aqua	NO_2	ニトロ	nitro
HO	ヒドロキソ	hydroxo	NO_3	ニトラト	nitrato
S	チオ, スルフィド	thio, sulfido	PO_4	ホスファト	phosphato
HS	メルカプト	mercapto	CO	カルボニル	carbonyl
SO_2	二酸化硫黄	sulfur dioxide	CS	チオカルボニル	thiocarbonyl
SO_4	スルファト	sulfato	CN	シアノ	cyano
N	ニトリド	nitrido	SCN	チオシアナト	thiocynato
N_3	アジド	azido	CO_3	カルボナト	carbonato
NH_2	アミド	amido			

15-14

In English, the name for the ionic form of a ligand may differ from the name of the ligand. For example, the English name amido for the ligand NH_2 changes to aminyl for the positive ion. This is also true in Japanese nomenclature; the Japanese name correspondingly changes from アミド to アミニル. For the ligand NO_2 there are two ionic names in English: nitroyl and nitryl. The corresponding Japanese names are ニトロイル and ニトリル.

The names of coordination compounds usually follow the same pattern as those of binary compounds, namely, the reverse of the chemical formula.

$Ni(CO)_4$	テトラカルボニルニッケル	tetracarbonyl nickel
$Fe(CO)_5$	ペンタカルボニル鉄	pentacarbonyl iron
$NOHSO_4$	硫酸水素ニトロシル	nitrosyl hydrogensulfate

It is interesting that in the case of the two carbonyls the current English name also is the reverse of the chemical formula. For many compounds the Japanese name has exactly the same order as the English name.

$CoH(CO)_4$	ヒドリドテトラカルボニルコバルト	hydridotetracarbonyl cobalt
HBF_4	テトラフルオロホウ酸	tetrafluoroboric acid

In summary, the names of coordination compounds are primarily written with KATAKANA, and the order of the names often follows the pattern for binary compounds, i.e., reversing the order of the formula. For newer or more complicated compounds, the names have the same order as the names in English, and neither name strictly follows the formula. In Japanese nomenclature for organic compounds, KATAKANA are even more prominent, and the parallel order of KATAKANA Japanese chemical names with their English counterparts more prevalent.

15.5 Organic Compounds

a. Comparisons with Inorganic Nomenclature

Although most Japanese organic nomenclature follows the order of English nomenclature and uses GAIRAIGO to identify the constituent elements and radicals, some simple compounds are named in the order and style of inorganic ones. For example, the names of the alkyl halides follow the pattern of binary inorganic compounds.

CH_3F	フッ化メチル	methyl fluoride	C_2H_5Br	臭化エチル	ethyl bromide
CH_3Cl	塩化メチル	methyl chloride	C_3H_7I	ヨウ化プロピル	propyl iodide

Moreover, the names of acids again end with the suffix 酸, and 酸 also appears within the names of their salts.

マロン酸	malonic acid	マレイン酸	maleic acid
マロン酸ジメチル	dimethyl malonate	マレイン酸グリコール	glycol maleate

Most names of organic acids are GAIRAIGO written in KATAKANA as above, but a few are written in KANJI.

酢酸	サクサン	acetic acid	安息香酸	アンソクコウサン	benzoic acid
没食子酸	ボッショクシサン	gallic acid			

Some acids that were formerly written with KANJI are now written in KATAKANA because the KANJI have been discontinued (a type of change that you have already encountered with the elements).

リンゴ酸	malic acid	ギ酸	formic acid

The KATAKANA word リンゴ in malic acid stands for "apple"; the name came from the German *Apfelsäure.* The KATAKANA ギ in formic acid stands for "ant"; the name came from the German *Ameisensäure.*

But apart from these exceptions, the Japanese names for organic compounds bear close resemblance to their Western counterparts and are written in KATAKANA.

ベンゾキノン	benzoquinone	ベンゾトリクロリド	benzotrichloride
ベンゾピレン	benzopyrene	ベンゾフェノン	benzophenone

English speakers should remember, however, that the long pre-eminence of German chemistry led to a German origin for many GAIRAIGO, as with マレイン酸 for the German *Maleinsäure* (maleic acid) above.

b. Names for Radicals in KATAKANA

The Japanese names for constituent radicals remain far more consistent in the names of organic compounds than do the English names. English names will sometimes omit one of the two vowels that appear in succession when two constituent radicals are joined. Thus, the "amide" of "acetic acid" is not named "acetoamide," as it would logically be, since it represents the combination of the aceto and amide groups, but "acetamide," with one vowel dropped. The Japanese name アセトアミド retains both the name of the aceto group アセト and the name of the amide group アミド. Other examples are "paraminosalicylic acid" and "benzanthracene," which drop the 'a' from "amino" and the 'o' from "benzo." The Japanese names retain the full names of the radicals: パラアミノサリチル酸 and ベンゾアントラセン.

However, this is not necessarily the case for Japanese names that represent radicals which consist of the joining of two simpler radicals. For example, the Japanese name for "hydro" is ヒドロ and for "oxy" オキシ, but the name for their combination "hydroxy" is ヒドロキシ and *not* ヒドロオキシ. Other examples of the name of a

Japanese radical not retaining the exact names of its two component radicals are the following:

アゾ	azo	チオ	thio
オキシ	oxy	オキソ	oxo
アゾキシ	azoxy	チオキソ	thioxo

But usually, as in Western names, the names of the two radicals remain distinct because their joint name does not contain successive vowels.

クロロ	chloro	ヒドロ	hydro
ホルミル	formyl	ペロキシ	peroxy
クロロホルミル	chloroformyl	ヒドロペロキシ	hydroperoxy

On the following pages you will find the Japanese names and the corresponding English names for many important organic radicals. The list is not exhaustive. For example, in English $CONH_2$ is called "carbamoyl" at the beginning of a name but "carboxamide" at the end. The list gives the Japanese equivalent for "carbamoyl," カルバモイル, but not for "carboxamide" カルボキサミド.

A	アセトニル	acetonyl	アニリノ	anilino
	アセトキシ	acetoxy	アニソイル	anisoyl
	アセチル	acetyl	アニシル	anisyl
	アクリロイル	acryloyl	アントロイル	anthroyl
	アジポイル	adipoyl	アジド	azido
	アリル	allyl	アゾ	azo
	アミジノ	amidino	アゾキシ	azoxy
	アミノ	amino		
B	ベンズアミド	benzamido	ビフェニリル	biphenylyl
	ベンズヒドリル	benzhydryl	ブタノイル	butanoyl
	ベンゾイル	benzoyl	ブトキシ	butoxy
	ベンジル	benzyl	ブチリル	butyryl
	ベンジリデン	benzylidene		
C	カルバモイル	carbamoyl	シアナト	cyanato
	カルボニル	carbonyl	シアノ	cyano
	カルボキシ	carboxy	シクロヘキセニル	cyclohexenyl
	シンナモイル	cinnamoyl	シクロヘキシル	cyclohexyl
	シンナミル	cinnamyl	シクロヘキシリデン	cyclohexylidene
	クメニル	cumenyl	シクロペンチル	cyclopentyl
D	デシル	decyl	ジオキシ	dioxy
	ジアゾ	diazo	ドデカノイル	dodecanoyl

15-17

E	エポキシ	epoxy	エチリジン	ethylidyne
	エトキシ	ethoxy	エチニル	ethynyl
	エチリデン	ethylidene		

F	ホルミル	formyl	フルフリル	furfuryl

G	グルタリル	glutaryl	グアニジノ	guanidino

H	ヘプチル	heptyl	ヒドラゾ	hydrazo
	ヘキサノイル	hexanoyl	ヒドラゾノ	hydrazono
	ヘキシル	hexyl	ヒドロペロキシ	hydroperoxy
	ヒドラジノ	hydrazino	ヒドロキシ	hydroxy

I	イミノ	imino	ヨウジル	iodyl
	ヨウドシル	iodosyl	イソ	iso

L	ラウロイル	lauroyl		

M	マロニル	malonyl	メシル	mesyl
	メルカプト	mercapto	メトキシ	methoxy
	メシチル	mesityl	メチリジン	methylidyne

N	ナフトイル	naphthoyl	ニトロ	nitro
	ナフチル	naphthyl	ニトロソ	nitroso
	ニトリロ	nitrilo	ノニル	nonyl

O	オクタノイル	octanoyl	オキサリル	oxalyl
	オクチル	octyl	オキソ	oxo
	オレオイル	oleoyl	オキシ	oxy
	オキサロ	oxalo		

P	パルミトイル	palmitoyl	ピペリジノ	piperidino
	ペンテニル	pentenyl	ピペリジル	piperidyl
	ペンチル	pentyl	ピバロイル	pivaloyl
	フェナシル	phenacyl	プロパルギル	propargyl
	フェナントリル	phenanthryl	プロペニル	propenyl
	フェネチル	phenethyl	プロピオニル	propionyl
	フェノキシ	phenoxy	プロポキシ	propoxy
	フェニル	phenyl	プロピリデン	propylidene
	フェニレン	phenylene	ピリジル	pyridyl
	フタロイル	phthaloyl	ピロリル	pyrrolyl
	ピクリル	picryl	ピルボイル	pyruvoyl

Q	キノリル	quinolyl		

S	サリチル	salicyl	スクシニル	succinyl
	サリチリデン	salicylidene	スルファモイル	sulfamoyl
	サリチロイル	salicyloyl	スルフィノ	sulfino
	ステアロイル	stearoyl	スルフィニル	sulfinyl
	スチリル	styryl	スルホ	sulfo
	スベロイル	suberoyl	スルホニル	sulfonyl
T	テノイル	thenoyl	トルイジノ	toluidino
	テニル	thenyl	トルオイル	toluoyl
	チエニル	thienyl	トリル	tolyl
	チオ	thio	トシル	tosyl
	チオキソ	thioxo	トリチル	trityl
U	ウンデシル	undecyl	ウレイレン	ureylene
	ウレイド	ureido		
V	バレリル	valeryl	ビニレン	vinylene
	ビニル	vinyl	ビニリデン	vinylidene
X	キシリジノ	xylidino	キシリル	xylyl

Although the Japanese names of organic compounds do retain the exact names of their constituent radicals, you will not find it easy to decipher the string of KATAKANA that appear in the name of a complicated compound such as tricarbonylcyclobutadiene-iron(0), トリカルボニルシクロブタジエン 鉄(0). Such strings can become exceptionally long in biochemical nomenclature, where the compound deoxyribodipyrimidine photolyase is デオキシリボジ ピリミジンホトリアーゼ. Fortunately, the International Union of Biochemistry has established symbols to represent the constituent parts of many compounds as well as rules for expressing their combinations, saving chemists everywhere from the task of deciphering long strings of letters better designed for ordinary words than for chemical names.

15.6 Biochemical Compounds

Probably the most distinctive feature of biochemical compounds is that they often consist of chains of interlinked components in proteins, nucleic acids, polysaccharides, and fats. As we just noted, the International Union of Biochemistry has established symbols to represent constituent groups as well as rules for expressing their chemical combinations. For example, there are new symbolic representations for the structures of polysaccharide molecules. Maltose is Glc$p$a 1-4Glc, where p indicates the pyranose ring, a the anomer, and Glc glucose. Since in English it is 4-(a-glucopyranosyl) glucose and in Japanese it is 4-(a-グルコピラノシル)グルコース, quite obviously representation by the symbols and rules of this nomenclature is clearer and more compact.

Teaching those symbols and rules lies beyond the scope of this book, and we will introduce only the Japanese names for the international symbols that designate the chemical components: the amino acids, the major bases and nucleosides of RNA, and the monosaccharides and their derivatives.

Symbols		アミノ酸	Amino Acid	Symbols		アミノ酸	Amino Acid
Asn	N	アスパラギン	aspargine	Tyr	Y	チロシン	tyrosine
Asp	D	アスパラギン酸	aspartic acid	Trp	W	トリプトファン	tryptophan
Ala	A	アラニン	alanine	Thr	T	トレオニン	threonine
Arg	R	アルギニン	arginine	Val	V	バリン	valine
Ile	I	イソロイシン	isoleucine	Pro	P	プロリン	proline
Gly	G	グリシン	glycine	His	H	ヒスチジン	histidine
Gln	Q	グルタミン	glutamine	Phe	F	フェニルアラニン	phenylalanine
Glu	E	グルタミン酸	glutamic acid	Met	M	メチオニン	methionine
Cys	C	システイン	cysteine	Lys	K	リシン	lysine
Ser	S	セリン	serine	Leu	L	ロイシン	leucine

RNA (リボ核酸)を構成する塩基とヌクレオシド				
Bases and Nucleosides That Constitute RNA (Ribonucleic Acid)				
	塩基	Base	ヌクレオシド	Nucleoside
R	プリン塩基	purine	プリンリボヌクレオシド	purine ribonucleoside
A	アデニン	adenine	アデノシン	adenosine
G	グアニン	guanine	グアノシン	guanosine
Y	ピリミジン塩基	pyrimidine	ピリミジンリボヌクレオシド	pyrimidine ribonucleoside
U	ウラシル	uracil	ウリジン	uridine
C	シトシン	cytosine	シチジン	cytidine
T	チミン	thymine	リボシルチミン	ribosylthymine

単糖及びその誘導体[ユウドウタイ]					
Monosaccharides and Their Derivatives					
単糖		ウロン酸		アミノ酸	
Monosaccharide		Uronic Acid		Amino Acid	
グルコース		グルクロン酸		グルコサミン	
glucose	Glc	glucuronic acid	GlcUA	glucosamine	GlcN
ガラクトース		ガラクツロン酸		ガラクトサミン	
galactose	Gal	galacturonic acid	GalUA	galactosamine	GalN
マンノース		マンヌロン酸		マンノサミン	
mannose	Man	Mannuronic acid	ManUA	mannosamine	ManN

Finally, we want to take brief note of the names of some of the fatty acids that serve as the building blocks of lipids. (With the KANJI in this lesson you can read the KANGO for lipid, 脂質. However, you will not be able to read the KANGO for fatty acid, 脂肪酸[シボウサン], until Chapter 19.) As in English nomenclature, technical Japanese has both a common and a systematic name for each fatty acid. Because the systematic names for fatty acids having double bonds require symbols not commonly known, we will give only the names of some of the saturated fatty acids in animals. The numbers in the left column give the number of carbon atoms.

	Common Names		Systematic Names	
12	lauric acid	ラウリン酸	dodecanoic acid	ドデカン酸
14	myristic acid	ミリスチン酸	tetradecanoic acid	テトラデカン酸
16	palmitic acid	パルミチン酸	hexadecanoic acid	ヘキサデカン酸
18	stearic acid	ステアリン酸	octadecanoic acid	オクタデカン酸
20	arachi(di)c acid	アラキ(ジ)ン酸	eicosanoic acid	エイコサン酸
22	behenic acid	ベヘン酸	docosanoic acid	ドコサン酸
24	lignoceric acid	リグノセリン酸	tetracosanoic acid	テトラコサン酸

ADDITIONAL VOCABULARY FOR EXERCISES

下位-	カイ	sub-
ひずむ		to constrain
かこむ	【囲む】	to surround
主として	シュとして	primarily
糖たんぱく質	トウたんぱくシツ	glycoprotein
無性の	ムセイの	asexual
やはり		of course
...よりなる		{same as ...からなる}
しか+negative verb		only+affirmative verb
亜鉛鉄板	アエンテッパン	galvanized iron plate
(に)まさる		to be superior (to)
おかす		to attack
ぬる	【塗る】	to paint
すべり面	すべりメン	slip plane
もろい		brittle
単体のままで	タンタイのままで	{lit.: just as it is a single substance}
まれな		rare
かたまり		a block
成形加工	セイケイカコウ	forming operations
ひずみ		strain
さまたげる		to hinder
析出物	セキシュツブツ	precipitates {for hardening metals}
核タンパク質	カクタンパクシツ	nucleoprotein
わずか+number		only+number
...から分かれる	からわかれる	to separate from ...
-間に	カンに	among

EXERCISES

Ex 15.1 Matching Japanese and English technical terms

(a) Words with prefixes

亜鉛( )	1. different species
亜硝酸塩( )	2. heterocyst
亜属( )	3. heteroploid
亜族( )	4. heteroploidy
亜硫酸塩( )	5. heterospore
異形胞子( )	6. isomer
異質細胞( )	7. isomerism
異種( )	8. nitrites
異数性( )	9. piping
異数体( )	10. subgenus
異性( )	11. subgroup
異性体( )	12. sulfites
配管( )	13. wiring
配線( )	14. zinc

(b) Inorganic compounds

塩化カリウム( )	1. copper hydroxide
塩化水銀( )	2. copper sulfide
塩化鉄( )	3. hydrogen phosphide
塩素酸カリウム( )	4. iron phosphate
シアン化水銀( )	5. iron chloride
臭化ケイ素( )	6. lead hydroxide
臭化窒素( )	7. lead nitrate
臭素酸カリウム( )	8. lead sulfate
硝酸鉛( )	9. mercury chloride
水酸化銅( )	10. mercury cyanide
水酸化鉛( )	11. nitrogen bromide
フッ化銀( )	12. potassium bromate
ヨウ化銀( )	13. potassium chlorate
ヨウ素酸カリウム( )	14. potassium chloride
硫化亜鉛( )	15. potassium iodate
硫化銅( )	16. silicon bromide
硫酸亜鉛( )	17. silver fluoride
硫酸鉛( )	18. silver iodide
リン酸鉄( )	19. zinc sulfate
リン化水素( )	20. zinc sulfide

Ex 15.2 Matching Japanese technical terms and definitions

亜種( )　　　　　　　1. 生物分類学上、属をさらに小さい種の群[グン = group]
亜属( )　　　　　　　　　に分けたもの。
異化( )　　　　　　　2. 物質の性質が方向によって異なること。
異方性( )　　　　　　3. 有機物質がエネルギーの放出とともに化学的に分解し
鉛直線( )　　　　　　　　て、簡単[カンタン = simple]な物質になること。
硝化作用( )　　　　　4. 地中のアンモニアがバクテリアによって亜硝酸塩、さ
窒素同化作用( )　　　　　らに硝酸塩に変えられる作用。
分析( )　　　　　　　5. 物質の化学成分や組成を知るための操作[ソウサ =
脂質( )　　　　　　　　　operations]。
　　　　　　　　　　　6. 種の下位分類。
　　　　　　　　　　　7. 一般[イッパン = general]に水に溶けにくく、有機溶媒
　　　　　　　　　　　　　[ヨウバイ = solvent]に溶けやすい、生体に存在[ソンザ
　　　　　　　　　　　　　イ = existence]する「あぶら」状の物質。
　　　　　　　　　　　8. 生物が種々の窒素化合物からタンパク質、核酸等を合
　　　　　　　　　　　　　成する作用。
　　　　　　　　　　　9. 重力の方向をしめすもの。

Ex 15.3 Translate the following sentences

1. 第6周期と第7周期にはIII族a亜族に属する元素がたくさんあり、周期表
   に全部書き込む[かきこむ = to write in]ことができないので、これは取
   り出して[from とりだす = to remove]別に[ベツに = separately]示してあ
   る。

2. 配位は中心原子またはイオンのまわりにいくつかの原子、イオンなどが
   集まることで、配位数は中心となる原子またはイオンに直接配位してい
   る原子またはイオンの数である。たとえば塩化ナトリウムの固体におい
   てNa^+の配位数は6である。

3. 微量元素とは生元素の中で微量にしか必要でないもので、一般に[イッ
   パンに]生物の生理において酸素の活性[カッセイ = activity]に関与する。

4. 異性体とは同一の分子式をもちながら構造の違いによって化学的・物理
   的性質に相違のある2種以上の化合物である。エチルアルコールとメチ
   ルエーテルがその一例である。

5. 無水酢酸は酢酸2分子から水1分子がとれた化合物で、これを水に加える
   と分解し再び[ふたたび = again]酢酸2分子になる。

6. 10進法は0から9までの10種類の数字[スウジ = numerals]を使ってすべて
   の実数を表す方式である。

7. 2進化10進法は10進法の各10進数字[スウジ]を2進法で表す方式である。
   したがって、10進数字[スウジ]1けたあたりに4ビットが必要である。

8. 地磁気の水平分力と鉛直分力の分布図[ブンプズ = distribution diagram]を見ると、それらの分力が極大値を示す位置がわかる。

9. 滴下[テキカ = dropping]電極は水銀電極の一形態で、ポーラログラフィーの電極として重要である。

10. 硫酸鉛(IV)は水中では加水分解して酸化鉛(IV)になりやすい。

11. 硫化スズ(II)は層状[ソウジョウ = layer]構造をもち、Snは6個のSでひずんだ8面体状にかこまれているが、1つの3角面を占める[しめる = to occupy]3個のSがSnに強く結合している。

12. 硝酸鉄(III)は六、九水和物[スイワブツ = hydrate]があり、いずれも熱すると水および酸化窒素を失い[from うしなう = to lose]、酸化鉄(III)となる。

13. 臭化亜鉛の結晶[ケッショウ = crystal]構造において各Znは4個のBrで4面体状にかこまれているが、気体状では分子が直線状でZn-Brとなる。

14. ヨウ素酸塩の内には水溶性のものが多いが、アルカリ金属塩の水への溶解度は塩素酸塩、臭素酸塩より小さい。

Ex 15.4 Read the following essays for comprehension

1. クロロトリフルオロエチレン$CF_2 = CFCl$は無色でエチレンのような臭気のある気体である。主[シュ]として、1,1,2-トリクロロ-1,2,2-トリフルオロエタンCCl_2FCClF_2(フレオン113)をアルコール中で亜鉛および小量の塩化亜鉛とともに加熱し脱塩素[ダツエンソ = dechlorination]して製造[セイゾウ = manufacture]する。ハロゲン、ハロゲン化水素、四塩化炭素、二塩化硫黄[イオウ = sulfur]、アルコールなどは2重結合に付加[フカ = addition]する。また$CF_2 = CFH$や$CF_2 = CFCN$の合成の原料となる。

Note: クロロトリフルオロエチレン remains the subject throughout this essay.

2. アミノ酸のみよりなるタンパク質を単純[タンジュン = simple]タンパク質といい、それ以外のもの（補欠分子族[ホケツブンシゾク = prosthetic group]）を含むとき複合[フクゴウ = conjugated]タンパク質という。複合[フクゴウ]タンパク質には核タンパク質、糖タンパク質などがある。タンパク質の種類はほとんど無限といってもよい程である。一種の生物に見いだされるタンパク質の種類もどれ程あるか正確に[セイカクに = exactly]はわからないが、生物の種が違えば一般に[イッパンに = generally]タンパク質は異なる。しかしこの多種多様性[タシュタヨウセイ = diversity, variety]を構成しているアミノ酸はいずれも共通の[キョウツウの = common]わずか20種に限られている。この20の順列[ジュンレツ = permutation]の違いによって、動物、植物、微生物に見いだされる無数のタンパク質ができるのである。これは長い間の進化の結果である。

3. 現在の[ゲンザイの = present]生物で見られるように、あらゆる生物はそれぞれの種という個体の集まりとなって存在[ソンザイ = existence]している。同じ種に属する雄・雌[おす・めす = male and female]の個体は生殖[セイショク = reproduction]によって、やはりその種に属する子を生む。同じように無性生殖[セイショク]の場合でも、生じた子は同一の種に属する。こうして種は継続[ケイゾク = continuance]されていく。反面、進化が起こるには、一つの種が変化して新しい[あたらしい = new]種になるか、あるいは一つの種から分かれて新しい[あたらしい]種が生じなければならない。このように新しい[あたらしい]種の形成は進化の仕組み[しくみ = mechanism]の根本[コンポン = root, source]である。ダーウィンが進化の原理をつくったとき、その本[ホン = book]の表題[ヒョウダイ = title]を「種の起原」とした。

4. 集合Sに属するものaをSの元または要素という。元の数が有限であるものを有限集合、無限であるものを無限集合という。元の数がないものも一種の集合と考えて空集合とよぶ。集合Sの任意の[ニンイの = arbitrary]2元aとbに対し、Sの1つの元cが対応づけられているとき、この対応づけを算法[サンポウ = law of composition]という。cをa,bの結合とよび、abまたはa + bなどで表す。abを積とよび、その場合の算法[サンポウ]を乗法[ジョウホウ = multiplication]という。a + bを和[ワ = sum]とよび、その場合の算法[サンポウ]を加法という。これらの言葉[ことば = words]は一般に[イッパンに]は初等[ショトウ = elementary]数学と異なる意味[いみ = meaning]に用いられる。

5. すべての細胞は核酸をもっている。それだけでも核酸が生体の本質的な[ホンシツテキな = fundamental]成分であることは理解される。核酸は塩基:糖:リン酸が1:1:1のモル比で含まれる高分子化合物である。塩基、糖、リン酸の各1モルずつから成り立つものをモノヌクレオチドというから、核酸はポリヌクレオチドである。モノヌクレオチドを適当な[テキトウな = appropriate]方法で分解するとヌクレオチドといわれる塩基・糖化合物、糖リン酸エステルが得られるが、塩基とリン酸のみよりなる化合物は得られない。したがって、そのモノヌクレオチドは塩基・糖・リン酸、ポリヌクレオチドは(塩基・糖・リン酸)nと考えられる。

　核酸中のリン酸は解離基[カイリキ = dissociation radical]を一つしかもっていないので、核酸中ではリン酸が二つの糖として、2-デオキシ-D-リボースをもつものと、D-リボースをもつものとがある。前者[ゼンシャ = former]をデオキシリボ核酸(DNA)、後者[コウシャ = latter]をリボ核酸(RNA)という。また主な[おもな = chief, important]塩基としてはDNAにはアデニン(A)、グアニン(G)、シトシン(C) (ある場合には5-メチルシトシン、5-ヒドロキシルメチルシトシン)、チミン(T)があり、RNAにはアデニン、グアニン、シトシン、ウラシル(U)がある。

　DNAでは一般に[イッパンに]グアニンとシトシンの含量が等しくアデニンとチミンの含量が等しい。またDNA構造のX線の結果などにもとづいてWatsonとCrickはDNAではGとC、AとTとが互いに[たがいに =mutually]対になって二本の[ニホンの]ポリヌクレオチド鎖[サ = chain]が二重フセンを作っているという構造模型[モケイ =model]を提出[テイシュツ =proposal]した。この構造はその後多くの物理化学的または生物学的現象[ゲンショウ=phenom-ena]をよく説明することが示された。

6．二つの成分金属が比較的[ヒカクテキ=relatively]簡単な[カンタンな =simple]原子数の割合で結合しており、個々の成分金属と違った結晶[ケッショウ = crystal]構造をもちながら成分金属と違った性質を示す合金を金属化合物という。CuZn、Cu_3Al、Fe_3Cなどはその例である。H_2Oのような通常の化合物にある原子価[ゲンシカ = atomic valence]の関係は金属化合物ではそのまま当てはまらない。

　一般に[イッパンに]原子価[ゲンシカ]は原子の価電子[カデンシ = valence electrons]の数できまり、例えば、銅Cuは1、亜鉛Znは2、アルミニウムAlは3、スズSnは4である。金属化合物ではふつうの原子価[ゲンシカ]の価電子[カデンシ]数と原子数の比が一定になる一群[イチグン = one group]の化合物がある。例えば、CuZnは価電子数の合計が1＋2＝3、原子数は2で、その比は3/2になる。Cu_3Alもこの比を計算すると3/2になる。これをヒューム・ロザリー (Hume-Rothery) の規則[キソク = rule]という。このような金属化合物は、みな同じ結晶[ケッショウ]構造をもち、性質も似通っていて[from にかよう = to resemble]、電子化合物とよぶ。

　これ以外に二種類の金属化合物がある。その一つは配位多面体化合物といい、最密な[サイミツな = densest]原子配列[ハイレツ]をもつ化合物で、配位数12-16の多面体が基本[キホン]構造となる。他の一つは電気化学的化合物といい、電気化学的に陽性および陰性な金属、半金属間にできる化合物である。GaAs、CdSなどがその例である。

Ex 15.5 Translate the following essay

　鉄は元素周期表上第VIII族に属する白色無臭の金属元素で、地球上にアルミニウムの次に多くある。得やすい上に強いので、構造物を作るために最も多く利用されている。この点からいえば、鉄は人類にとって最も重要な金属であるということができるであろう。通常、酸化第二鉄として得られる原料を一酸化炭素と高温で反応させて作る。鉄は強度において銅、アルミニウムにまさるが、電気伝導率では銀、銅に及ばず銅の5分の1に過ぎない。

　鉄は酸化されやすいが、窒素とは化合しない。酢酸、塩酸、硫酸、硝酸等の酸類におかされやすいので、亜鉛鉄板[テッパン = iron plate]にしたりペンキ[paint]をぬったりして用いる。鉄の結晶形[ケッショウケイ = crystal-line form]は体心立方で、面心立方である銅、銀に比べればすべり面が少ない。すなわち、銅、銀よりはもろい。

鉄は単体のままで用いることはまれで、多くの場合、炭素を含んだ鋼[コウ = steel]として使う。鋼[コウ]は高温に加熱し、2本[ホン]のロールの間を通したり、かたい合金のかたまりにあなを設けた[from もうける = to provide]ダイを通したりして、目的の形状にして使用する。このような成形加工が与える変形によって金属組織の集合状態に変化が生じ、異方性が現われる[あらわれる = to appear, arise]。鋼を1000℃以上に熱して後、水中に入れて速やかに[すみやかに]常温まで温度を下げると異常に強くなる。マルテンサイトの生成によってひずみの進行がさまたげられ、変形に対する抗力[コウリョク = resisting force]が増大したからである。このほか、析出物等を利用して鋼の強化が行なわれている。

TRANSLATIONS

Ex 15.3 Sentences

1. There are many elements that belong to Group III Subgroup a in the 6th and 7th periods [of the periodic table] and not all of them can be written in [the table]; therefore they are taken out and shown separately.

2. Coordination is the name for the clustering of several atoms or ions around a central atom or ion; the coordination number is the number of atoms or ions that are directly coordinated with the central atom or ion. For example, the coordination number of Na^+ in solid sodium chloride is 6.

3. Trace elements are those bioelements that are necessary only in micro-quantities; they are generally involved in the activity of oxygen in the physiology of organisms.

4. Isomers are compounds of two or more varieties that, although they have identical molecular formulas, have differences in their chemical and physical properties due to different [molecular] structures. [The isomer pair of] ethyl alchohol and methyl ether is an example.

5. Acetic acid anhydride is the compound [obtained] when one molecule of water is removed from two molecules of acetic acid; if it is added to water, it decomposes and again forms two molecules of acetic acid.

6. The decimal system is a method for expressing all real numbers by using 10 kinds of numerals from 0 to 9.

7. The binary decimal system is a method for expressing each of the 10 decimal numerals within the decimal system by means of the binary system. Consequently, 4 bits are necessary per decimal (numeral) digit.

8. If we look at a diagram [showing] the horizontal and vertical force components of the earth's magnetism, we can see the locations where these components show maxima.

15-27

9. A dropping electrode is one type of mercury electrode and is important as the electrode [used] in polarography.

10. Lead(IV) sulfate readily hydrolyzes in water to form lead(IV) oxide.

11. Tin(II) sulfide has a layered construction, [each] Sn being surrounded by an octahedral shape constrained by 6 atoms of S; the 3 (atoms of) S that occupy one of the triangular planes are strongly bound with the Sn.

12. Iron(III) nitrate has hydrates of 6 and 9 (molecules of water), and if either one is heated, [it] loses water and nitrogen oxide and forms iron(III) oxide.

13. In the crystal structure of zinc bromide, each Zn is surrounded by a tetrahedral shape of 4 [atoms of] Br, but in its gaseous state the molecules take on the linear shape of Zn-Br.

14. Among iodates, a great many are water soluble, but the solubility of the alkaline metal [iodate] salts is less than that of chlorates and bromates.

Ex 15.5 Essay

Iron is a white, odorless metallic element that belongs to Group VIII in the periodic table of the elements; it is the [most] plentiful [metal] on the earth next to aluminum. In addition to being easy to obtain, it is strong and therefore used most widely to build structures. From this point of view we can perhaps say that iron is the most important metal for humankind. Usually we produce iron by reacting the raw material, obtained as ferric oxide, with carbon monoxide at high temperatures. Iron is superior to copper and aluminum in its strength, but it does not match silver and copper in its electrical conductivity, [its conductivity] being merely one-fifth [that] of copper.

Iron is easily oxidized, but it does not combine with nitrogen. Because it is easily attacked by acids such as acetic, hydrochloric, sulfuric, and nitric, we make it into galvanized iron plate or paint it [before] using it. The crystalline form of iron is body-centered cubic, and it has fewer slip planes compared to copper and silver, which are face-centered cubic. That is, it is more brittle than copper and silver.

It is rare to use iron by itself; in many cases we use it as steel, which contains carbon. We use steel in specified forms, made by heating it to high temperatures and then passing it through two rolls or through dies, which are blocks of hard alloys having holes within them. Because of the deformations that these kinds of forming operations give [to the steel], changes occur in the metallography of [its] aggregate state, and anisotropy arises. If, after heating the steel above 1000°C, we thrust it into water and quickly lower its temperature to ordinary temperatures, it becomes extraordinarily strong. That is because the development of strain is hindered by the formation of martensite, and the force resisting deformation is increased. In addition to this [method], the strengthening of steel is done by using [hardening] precipitates and other things.

| 影 | エイ | shadow |
| | かげ | shadow, shade |

| 環 | カン | ring, circle |

| 観 | カン | observation |

| 技 | ギ | art, skill |

| 究 | キュウ | investigating |

| 距 | キョ | distance |

| 御 | ギョ | governing, managing |
| | ゴ-; お- | {honorific prefix} |

| 境 | キョウ | boundary |
| | さかい | boundary |

| 響 | キョウ | echo |
| | ひび(く) | to sound, resound |

| 業 | ギョウ | business |

| 件 | ケン | case, matter |

| 研 | ケン | polishing, sharpening |

| 現 | ゲン | actual, current |
| | あらわ(れる) | to appear, be manifest |

| 号 | ゴウ | number; announcement |

| 在 | ザイ | existence |

| 察 | サツ | perceiving, knowing |

| 産 | サン | product |
| | う(む) | to give birth |

| 仕 | シ | doing; serving |

| 事 | ジ | thing, fact |
| | こと | thing, fact |

日	ジツ; ニチ	day
	ひ	sun
	-か	{counter for days}

術	ジュツ	art, technique
準	ジュン	level; aim
象	ショウ	image, shape
	ゾウ	elephant
条	ジョウ	item, article
情	ジョウ	circumstances, state of things
信	シン	trust, belief
制	セイ	controlling, regulating
続	ゾク	continuing
	つづ(く)	to continue
存	ソン; ゾン	existence
	ゾン(じる)	to know
題	ダイ	title, topic
特	トク	special
	トク(に)	in particular
標	ヒョウ	mark, sign
別	ベツ	other
	わか(れる)	to part from
報	ホウ	report
飽	ホウ	satiation
本	ホン	origin, base; book
	-ホン	{counter for long objects}
	ホン-	this
	もと	origin, base
問	モン	inquiry
	と(う)	to ask
	と(い)	question
離	リ	separation
	はな(れる)	to separate
連	レン	connecting
	つら(なる)	to be connected
和	ワ	sum; peace
	ワ-	Japan, Japanese

影響	エイキョウ	influence
環境	カンキョウ	environment
観察	カンサツ	observation
技術	ギジュツ	technology
距離	キョリ	distance
研究	ケンキュウ	research
現象	ゲンショウ	phenomenon
産業	サンギョウ	industry
仕事	シごと	work, job
条件	ジョウケン	condition
情報	ジョウホウ	information
信号	シンゴウ	signal
制御	セイギョ	control
存在	ソンザイ	existence
特別-	トクベツ	special
日本	ニッポン; ニホン	Japan
標準	ヒョウジュン	standard
飽和	ホウワ	saturation
問題	モンダイ	problem, issue
連続	レンゾク	continuity

環

環状の	カンジョウの	ring-shaped; cyclic
環状線	カンジョウセン	beltline {highway}
環状接続	カンジョウセツゾク	ring connection {elec engr}
環状構造	カンジョウコウゾウ	cyclic structure
環式の	カンシキの	cyclic
環式化合物	カンシキカゴウブツ	cyclic compound {chem}
一環の	イッカンの	monocyclic {botany}
円環	エンカン	annular ring

観

観測	カンソク	observation
観点	カンテン	viewpoint
外観	ガイカン	appearance
直観	チョッカン	intuition
主観的な	シュカンテキな	subjective
客観的な	キャッカンテキな	objective

境

境界	キョウカイ	boundary
無人(の)境	ムジン(の)キョウ	uninhabited region
境地	キョウチ	state, condition

業

水産業	スイサンギョウ	marine industry
工業	コウギョウ	industry
事業	ジギョウ	business
作業	サギョウ	work, operation

件

件数	ケンスウ	number of cases, items

現

現代の	ゲンダイの	present, current
現在の	ゲンザイの	present, current
現状(の)	ゲンジョウ(の)	current state (of)
発現	ハツゲン	manifestation
表現する	ヒョウゲンする	to express
実現する	ジツゲンする	to implement

在

実在の	ジツザイの	actual, real
在外研究	ザイガイケンキュウ	research abroad

察

考察する	コウサツする	to consider, contemplate

産

生産	セイサン	production
産出	サンシュツ	output
産物	サンブツ	product(s)

仕

仕方	シかた	means, method, procedure
仕様	シヨウ	specifications
仕組(み)	シくみ	contrivance, mechanism
仕上げる	シあげる	to finish, complete

事

事実	ジジツ	fact
事態	ジタイ	situation
出来事	できごと	occurrence, incident

日

日光	ニッコウ	sunlight
日常の	ニチジョウの	ordinary
日中の	ニッチュウの	daytime
本日	ホンジツ	today
明日	ミョウニチ {N.B. reading of 明}	tomorrow

準

標準化	ヒョウジュンカ	standardization
水準	スイジュン	standard, level
基準	キジュン	standard, criterion

象

事象	ジショウ	phenomenon
対象	タイショウ	object, subject {of study}
気象学	キショウガク	meteorology

信

通信	ツウシン	communication
電信	デンシン	telegraph

16-5

制

制振	セイシン	damping
制振器	セイシンキ	damper

続

接続	セツゾク	connection, junction
接続器	セツゾクキ	connector

存

保存	ホゾン	conservation
生存	セイゾン	survival
現存する	ゲンゾンする	to exist

題

表題	ヒョウダイ	title, heading
題目	ダイモク	title, heading, subject
出題	シュツダイ	proposing a question

特

特定の	トクテイの	specific
特異的な	トクイテキな	specific, singular
特異性	トクイセイ	specificity, singularity
特異点	トクイテン	unique point, singular point
特性	トクセイ	characteristics

標

目標	モクヒョウ	goal, objective

別

分別-	ブンベツ	fractional
類別	ルイベツ	classification
別表	ベッピョウ	attached table
別解	ベッカイ	alternative solution

飽

過飽和	カホウワ	supersaturation

本

基本の	キホンの	fundamental
見本	みホン	sample, specimen
本質的な	ホンシツテキな	essential

問
学問	ガクモン	field of study
質問	シツモン	question

離
離間距離	リカンキョリ	clearance
分離する	ブンリする	to separate

連
連結	レンケツ	coupling, connection
関連する	カンレンする	to be associated with
連成振動	レンセイシンドウ	coupled oscillation

和
調和分析	チョウワブンセキ	harmonic analysis
代数和	ダイスウワ	algebraic sum
中和	チュウワ	neutralization
和合性	ワゴウセイ	compatibility

16 Vocabulary Building and Translation Examples, I

Beginning with this chapter, the emphasis shifts to the development of translation and reading skills. This chapter and the next chapter will focus on translation skills, the final three chapters on readings skills. As before, each chapter will introduce important KANJI and vocabulary.

This chapter features 20 JUKUGO that appear in many texts, both technical and nontechnical. We strongly recommend that you become thoroughly familiar with the 20 JUKUGO presented, as you will find that they will enrich your reading vocabulary substantially. The 40 KANJI making up these JUKUGO are all high-frequency characters and form many other JUKUGO in addition to the 20 that are introduced at the beginning of the chapter.

In Chapter 17 you will learn 25 KANJI that we selected especially because they form many JUKUGO with KANJI learned in earlier chapters; these JUKUGO are important in many different disciplines. Chapters 18, 19, and 20 each introduce 25 more KANJI, these being for the most part chosen to emphasize characters important in physics, chemistry, and the bio-sciences; accordingly the reading selections are chosen primarily from these three fields.

EXERCISES

Ex 16.I Matching exercises

Write out the pronunciation of the Japanese words in KANA and then match them with their English equivalents. Each of the 20 JUKUGO featured in the KANJI list is included in these matching exercises.

(a)

自動制御( )	1. automatic control
影響関数( )	2. clearance
移動現象( )	3. cytology research institute
産業組織( )	4. environmental problem
細胞学研究所( )	5. industrial organization
離間距離( )	6. influence function
技術水準( )	7. many-body problem
過飽和溶液( )	8. supersaturated solution
多体問題( )	9. technical level
環境問題( )	10. transport phenomena

(b)

信号発生器( )	1. continuum mechanics
仕事当量( )	2. direct observation
標準電極電位( )	3. existence theorem
連続体力学( )	4. extra-heavy pipe
最大情報量( )	5. Japan Science Council
必要十分条件( )	6. maximum amount of information
直接観察( )	7. mechanical equivalent (of heat)
存在定理( )	8. necessary and sufficient condition
特別重量管( )	9. signal generator
日本学術会議[カイギ]( )	10. standard electrode potential

Ex 16.2 Sentence completion exercise

Select the correct JUKUGO to fill in the blanks and then translate the sentences.

1. ここに問題点が＿ ＿する。 　　　　　[存在、特別、信号]
2. 環境は＿ ＿になっている。 　　　　　[産業、信号、問題]
3. 工作物の見本を＿ ＿した。 　　　　　[問題、観察、存在]
4. 重要な＿ ＿成果が発表された。 　　　[研究、距離、標準]
5. 磁場の強さを＿ ＿した。 　　　　　　[問題、制御、連続]
6. すべての＿ ＿を説明できる。 　　　　[現象、存在、連続]
7. 工業＿ ＿化が進められている。 　　　[特別、標準、電流]

8. ＿＿な技術を用いる。　　　　　　　[特別、影響、距離]

9. 液体を＿＿体と見なす。　　　　　　[存在、連続、技術]

10. ロボットは＿＿をする。　　　　　　[仕事、飽和、特別]

Ex 16.3 Matching exercise for adjectives

本日の(　)　　　　　　　1. actual

日本の(　)　　　　　　　2. characteristic

日中の(　)　　　　　　　3. contemporary

日常の(　)　　　　　　　4. daytime

特定の(　)　　　　　　　5. everyday, ordinary

特性の(　)　　　　　　　6. finishing

特別な(　)　　　　　　　7. foreign, abroad

特異の(　)　　　　　　　8. Japanese

別々の(　)　　　　　　　9. present, current

現在の(　)　　　　　　　10. ring-shaped

現代の(　)　　　　　　　11. separate

環状の(　)　　　　　　　12. special

実在の(　)　　　　　　　13. specific

在外の(　)　　　　　　　14. today's

仕上げの(　)　　　　　　15. unique, singular

Ex 16.4 Sentence build-up exercises

Read each sentence aloud and then translate it.

(a)

1. ニュートン力学が当てはまる。

2. ニュートン力学が当てはまらない場合がある。

3. ニュートン力学が当てはまらない場合があることを示した。

4. ニュートン力学はすべての現象を説明できる。

5. ニュートン力学はすべての現象を説明できると考えられていた。

6. 当時までニュートン力学はすべての現象を説明できると考えられていた。

7. 当時まですべての現象を説明できると考えられていたニュートン力学が
当てはまらない場合があることを示した。

(b)

1. ベンゼンは炭化水素化合物である。

2. ベンゼンは正6角形の環式炭化水素化合物である。

3. 有機化合物ベンゼンは正6角形の環式炭化水素化合物である。

4. ベンゼンは環状構造をもつ。

5. ベンゼンが環状構造をもつことはドイツのケクレが見いだした。

6. 有機化合物ベンゼンは正6角形の環式炭化水素化合物で、環状構造をもつことはドイツのアウグスト・ケクレが見いだした。

(c)
1. 有限要素法を用いる場合が多い。
2. 有限要素法を用いる場合が少なくない。
3. 大気の運動を解析する。
4. 気象学において大気の運動を解析する。
5. 気象学において大気の運動を解析するために有限要素法を用いる。
6. 気象学において大気の運動を解析するために有限要素法を用いる場合が少なくない。

(d)
1. プラスチックは分解する。
2. プラスチックは地中で分解する。
3. プラスチックの研究が行われている。
4. 地中で分解するプラスチックの研究が行われている。
5. この実態に対応して、地中で分解するプラスチックの研究が行われている。

TRANSLATION EXAMPLES

Read the following paragraphs for comprehension. Then read the English translation. If you misunderstood any points in the Japanese text go back and re-examine the pertinent sentences in detail, reviewing the grammar if need be. Further careful study of these texts and translations will help you in developing translation techniques.

Translation 1

ある量が飽和状態以上に増加した状態を過飽和といい、溶液がその温度における溶解度に相当する量以上の溶質を含むとき、すなわち過飽和溶液や、蒸気がその温度における飽和蒸気圧以上の圧力をもつ場合、すなわち過飽和蒸気などがある。

A state where a certain quantity has increased beyond the saturated state is called supersaturated: when a solution contains more solute than the amount corresponding to the solubility at its temperature (that is, a supersaturated solution); when a vapor has a pressure above the saturated vapor pressure at its temperature (that is, a supersaturated vapor); and so on.

Note
Line 3: Remember that や indicates an incomplete listing, which is further reinforced by など found in Line 4.

Translation 2

　与えられた仕様[ショウ＝specifications]通りに仕上げた工作物の見本を観察した結果、仕様には不合理な点があることが見つけられた。

　　As a result of inspecting samples of the manufactured articles finished in accordance with the given specifications, it was found that there are inconsistencies in the specifications.

Notes

Line 1: In compound verbs 仕 means "to do"; 上げる as the second element of a compound verb implies completion of an action.

Line 2: 結果 following a verb means "as a result of ...ing."

Line 2: The は in 仕様には puts greater emphasis on what follows.

Translation 3

　生物の内ほとんどすべてのものは、酸素がないと生存できない。地球上で酸素は、単体として空気中に、化合物として地中に、実在の元素の内最も多く存在し、その量は、地球およびその周囲[シュウイ＝surroundings]の大気の全量の半分に及んでいる。

　　Among living things, almost none can survive if there is no oxygen. On earth oxygen is the most plentiful of the naturally occurring elements — as a simple substance in the air, and in compounds within the earth; its quantity amounts to half of the total quantity [of elements] in the earth and its surrounding atmosphere.

Notes

Line 1: すべてのものは...生存できない is literally "all of them cannot survive"; but "None can survive" is a more appropriate English translation. もの here means 生物.

Line 1: 地球上で has the same meaning as 地球の上; another example of this construction is 空気中に in Line 2.

Line 2: 実在の literally means "actually existing," but here an appropriate translation is "naturally occurring."

Line 3: The first その＝of it＝of the oxygen, and the second その＝of it＝of the earth.

Translation 4

　東京[トウキョウ＝Tokyo]における日中の交通騒音[ソウオン＝noise]は環境基準に及ばず、特に環状線の中での騒音[ソウオン]が問題になっている。交通量の多い路上各所に観測点をおいて騒音測定が行われている。最近特に関心のもたれている問題は、生活[セイカツ＝life]環境における音[おと＝sound]の利用や、オフィス空間における音環境といった問題である。

　　Daytime traffic noise in Tokyo does not meet environmental standards; in particular, the noise within the beltline has become a problem. Noise measurements are being made at observation points placed at various locations along streets with heavy traffic. Recently of particular concern are problems such as the use of sound in people's living environment and the sound environs in office spaces.

Notes
Line 3: 交通量の多い路上各所: Keep in mind that in modifying clauses の is often used instead of が to mark the subject of the verb. See Section 7.3 regarding the use of 多い before a noun.
Line 3: 観察点をおいて is in the active voice and means "[traffic engineers] have placed ..., and"; we chose to use the passive voice, "[which have been] placed," in the absence of an explicit subject.
Line 4: 関心のもたれている問題: Here is another の marking the subject in a modifying clause in which the verb もたれる is the passive of もつ, "to have." This clause is literally "problems [for which] concern is had" or "problems [in which] interest is taken."

Translation 5

移行する	イコウする	to shift to

　二つ以上の振動系[ケイ＝system]が連結されている場合、各振動系[ケイ]が影響を及ぼし合っていると連成振動が観察される。全体の系の固有振動数は各振動系の固有振動数とは異なり、また各振動系の間にエネルギーの交換[コウカン＝exchange]が行われて、振動の大きい状態が振動系の間を移行していく現象も見られる。

　When two or more oscillating systems are connected, if each oscillating system exerts an influence on the others, coupled oscillations are observed. The characteristic frequency of the entire system differs from the characteristic frequency of each oscillating system, and energy exchanges take place among the individual oscillating systems; the phenomenon in which states having large oscillations continually shift among the oscillating systems is also observed.

Notes
Line 1: 二つ以上 = two or more (*not* more than two).
Line 4: In long sentences with several clauses ending in conjunctives and/or connectives, it is often convenient in translation to split the sentence up into two or more main clauses joined by semicolons, as we have done here.
Lines 4-5: 移行していく: Since the -ていく construction implies continued action, we use the word "continually" in the translation.

Translation 6

重なり合う	かさなりあう	to be superposed
でき事	できごと	event
相反する	あいハンする	to be contrary (to each other)
消し合う	けしあう	to cancel each other

　電磁気学においては、等量の正および負[フ＝negative]の電気の位置が重なり合い、外部に電気の影響が全く現われない時、正負[フ]の電気は中和したというが、化学では、酸と塩基が反応することを中和という。日常のでき事では、相反する事象が同時に起こって、それぞれの影響が消し合う時にも用いられる。

　In electromagnetism, when the positions of equal quantities of positive and negative electricity are superposed and the effects of the electricity do not appear externally at all, we say that the positive and negative electric [charges] have neutralized [each other], whereas in chemistry we call the reaction of an acid and a base neutralization. In everyday events, when contrary phenomena occur at the same time and their respective impacts cancel each other, [the word neutralization] is also used.

Notes
Lines 1-2: 重なり合う is literally "to pile up on each other"; the 合う in compound verbs usually contains the meaning of reciprocal action (see Section 9.6); in line 4 we also have 消し合う meaning "to cancel each other."
Line 2: 正負: When the KANJI for two opposing ideas are juxtaposed, "and" has to be inserted in the English translation.
Line 5: Often the subject of a Japanese clause or sentence is not explicitly stated, and it has to be supplied in English. Here the implied subject of 用いられる is 中和, and we have included this in our English translation.

Translation 7

　表題から明らかなように、本日の発表の主な[おもな = principal]題目は、そこにある水産物をいかにしてとるかという水産業に関するものではなくて、水の中にいかにして産物を産出させるかという質問に答える[こたえる = to respond]ものである。明日の水産業は、このように、現在の工業に近い形態をとるものと信ずる。

As is clear from the title, the main subject of today's presentation is not the one regarding the fishing industry — how can we catch the marine life that is out there [in the ocean] — but the one that responds to the question: how can we manufacture marine products in water? We believe that tomorrow's marine industry will thus be one that takes on a form similar to today's [manufacturing] industry.

Notes
Line 1: The KANJI 本 is used as a prefix with several meanings: (a) "here, the current, the ... in question," and here 本日 means "this day, today"; (b) "main, principal," as in 本線, "main line": (c) "real" as in 本物[ホンもの], "the real thing."
Line 2: ...いかにしてとるかという...もの can be understood as follows: いかにして = how; とる = to take; か is the question-marking particle; という highlights the previous question phrase so that something further can be done with it; and the word もの here stands for the word 題目 (subject) and is translated as "one." Hence the entire phrase means "the subject of how we catch ...."

Translation 8

| 曲がりはり | まがりはり | curved beam |
| 解かりやすい | わかりやすい | easy to understand |

　円環[エンカン = circular ring]の応力解析は、曲がりはりの問題として解くこともできるが、ここでは別解としてチモシェンコの本に出ている方法を用いた解を示そう。この解法の方が直観的で解かりやすい。しかし、円環[エンカン]に関する問題は出題しないことにする。

The stress analysis in a circular ring can also be solved [by regarding it] as a curved beam problem, but here we shall show a solution in which [we] used a method that appears as an alternative solution in Timoshenko's book. This solution is more intuitive and easy to understand. However, we will not give any problems related to circular rings [on exams].

Notes
Line 2: 別解 will not be found in most dictionaries. It is an abbreviation for 別の解法. Such abbreviations are not uncommon in written Japanese, and only experience can help you to interpret such words.
Line 3: The word わかる (to understand) is now normally written in HIRAGANA. However, it is sometimes written using KANJI, and there are three possibilities: 分かる, 解かる, and 判かる. You may encounter these from time to time.

Translation 9
その後　　　　　　　　そのゴ　　　　　　　　　　　after that

　ラザフォードは金のフォイルに放射能[ホウシャノウ = radioactivity]から出てくるアルファ線を当てる実験中、原子核を発見した。その後、ラザフォードの研究室[ケンキュウシツ =laboratory]からは、無人の境を行くように、原子核に関する多くの重要な研究成果が発表された。

Rutherford discovered the atomic nucleus during experiments in which he made alpha-rays coming from radioactivity impinge on a gold foil. After that many important research results concerning atomic nuclei were reported by Rutherford's laboratory — like [reports from those] going through virgin territory.

Notes
Line 3: 研究室 [ケンキュウシツ] means "research rooms." 石原の研究室 is best translated as "[Professor] Ishihara's laboratories" or sometimes "[Professor] Ishihara's research group"; it is often abbreviated 石原研. The term 研究所 is "research institute."
Line 3: 無人の境 is literally "a region with no people," and hence we translate it as "virgin territory." The particle を used with 行く indicates motion through a region.

Translation 10
いっそうの　　　　　　　【一層の】　　　　　　　　further
進める　　　　　　　　　すすめる　　　　　　　　　to stimulate, promote, hasten

　技術水準のいっそうの向上、先端[センタン = (ultra-)advanced]技術の発展[ハッテン = development]、高度情報化社会[シャカイ = society]の進展[シンテン = evolution]などの変化に対応した工業標準化が、関連する産業の間で進められている。

Industrial standardization is being stimulated among related industries in response to changes such as the further improvements in technical level, developments in advanced technologies, and the evolution of a highly informationalized society.

16-15

きっかけ　　　　　　　　　　　　　　　　　　　　start, beginning
形態をととのえる　ケイタイをととのえる　　to take shape

　無線通信を発明したイタリアのマルコーニは、25馬力[バリキ＝horsepower]のエンジンで交流発電機を動かし、変圧器で20,000ボルトの高電圧を作り、放電させて、アメリカとイギリスの間3500キロメートルの距離の通信を実現した。このことがきっかけとなって、電信機等関連する機器が作り始められ[from はじめる＝to begin]、無線通信工学という学問ができ、電信事業が形態をととのえたのである。

　　Marconi of Italy, who invented wireless communication, drove an alternating current generator by means of a 25 hp engine, then produced a high voltage of 20,000 volts with a transformer and discharged the electricity, [whereby] he achieved radio communication over a distance of 3500 km between America and England. With this accomplishment as the start, instruments connected with telegraphic equipment began to be made, the (academic) discipline of radio-communication engineering developed, and the electrical communications industry took shape.

Notes
Line 4: Read 等 as など.
Line 5: 無線通信工学という学問 is literally "the discipline that [we] call radio-communication engineering."
Line 5: Keep in mind that できる can mean "to be formed, to be made, to come into existence, to be produced."

Translation 12

あてはまる　　　　　【当てはまる】　　　　　　to be applicable, be valid
いたる　　　　　　　【至る】　　　　　　　　　to reach, arrive at

　アインシュタインは光量子の理論[リロン＝theory]、ブラウン運動の理論[リロン]に続いて特殊[トクシュ＝special]相対性理論を発表し、当時まですべての現象を説明できると考えられていたニュートン力学があてはまらない場合があることを示し、質量とエネルギーの等価性[トウカセイ＝equivalence]を導いた。さらに、重力の理論を含むものに拡張する[カクチョウする＝to expand]ことが必要であると考える境地にいたり、一般[イッパン＝general]相対性理論を作り、そのいっそうの発展[ハッテン＝development]に力を注いだ。

　　Immediately following his theory of light quanta and theory of Brownian motion, Einstein published his theory of special relativity; [there he] showed that there are cases for which Newtonian mechanics, which until then had been thought to explain all phenomena, is not valid, and he derived the equivalence of mass and energy. Furthermore, reaching the stage where he considered it necessary to expand [his theory] to one that includes a theory of gravitation, he created the general theory of relativity and poured his energies into its further development.

Notes
Line 2: 当時 means "the time in question," either in the past (as in this paragraph) or in the future.
Line 6: いたり is the conjunctive form of the verb 至る[いたる] and not the representative form of いる.

Translation 13

まず	【先ず】	(at) first, to begin with
あつさ	【厚さ】	thickness
とりのぞく	【取り除く】	to remove

　有機化合物ベンゼンは正6角形の環式炭化水素化合物で、環状構造をもつことはドイツの化学者[カガクシャ = chemist]アウグスト・ケクレが見いだした。その後、X線解析などによる解明は行われたが、分子の形状を直接観察することはできなかった。著者[チョシャ = the author]はIBM研究所で在外研究中、まず真空[シンクウ = vacuum]中で金属ロジウムの表面から数原子のあつさの部分をとりのぞいて新生面[シンセイメン = newly formed surface]を作りそこへベンゼンを吸着させ[from キュウチャクする = to adsorb]、さらに、一酸化炭素を加えてベンゼンの動きを制御するという特別な技術を用いて、トンネル顕微鏡[ケンビキョウ = microscope]で分子形状を直接観察した。ベンゼン分子1個の大きさは5/100,000,000 cmであることがわかった。

The organic chemical compound benzene is a regular hexagonal, ring-shaped hydrocarbon; the German chemist August Kekulé discovered that it has a ring-shaped structure. After that, elucidation [of the structure] was accomplished by X-ray and other analyses, but it was not possible to observe directly the shape of the molecule. The author, during research abroad at the IBM Research Laboratories, first removed a portion several atoms thick from a rhodium surface in a vacuum and, onto the newly formed surface thus made, caused benzene to be adsorbed. Then, using a special technique of adding carbon monoxide to the benzene for controlling its motion, he observed directly the molecular shape with a tunneling microscope. [The author] learned that the size of 1 molecule of benzene is 5×10^{-8} cm.

Notes
Line 1: で here is short for であり; it is not the particle で.
Line 2: The ending 者 is a standard suffix to indicate the practitioner of a discipline; 物理学者 is "a physicist."
Line 2: The centered dot (・) is used to separate the first and last names written in KATAKANA.

わるい	【悪い】	bad, adverse
とどく	【届く】	to reach
回しおわる	まわしおわる	to finish turning
とりいれる	【取り入れる】	to take in
くみ上げる	【汲み上げる】	to pump up

　環境にわるい影響を与えることなく産業用エネルギーを得る方法の一つとして、海[うみ＝sea]の水の温度の違いを利用した発電がある。海洋[カイヨウ＝ocean]において、太陽[タイヨウ＝the sun]に加熱される表面近くの水と日光のとどかない所の水とでは、温度に大きな違いがあることを利用して電気を得るものである。まず、海[うみ]の表面近くの温水によってアンモニアなどの液体を蒸発させ、その蒸気圧でタービン発電機を回し、回しおわったガスは温度の低い[ひくい＝low]水で液化させ、リサイクルするという仕組みになっている。最近、太平洋[タイヘイヨウ＝Pacific Ocean]に作られた最大出力100キロワットの実験プラントでは、30℃程度の表面温度に対し、これより20℃以上低い[ひくい]温度の水をとり入れるため、表面下580メートルの距離の所から直径75センチ、全長945メートルのポリエチレン管で連続的に水をくみ上げている。

One method for obtaining energy for industrial use without having adverse effects on the environment is the generation of electrical power by using differences in water temperature in the sea. We obtain the electrical power [by] using the large temperature difference between the ocean water near the surface heated by the sun and the water where sunlight does not reach. First we vaporize a liquid such as ammonia by means of the warm water near the surface of the sea, and then turn the turbine generator by means of its vapor pressure; we [then] liquefy the gas that has finished turning [the turbine] with the low-temperature water; [thus] it is a mechanism that recycles [the ammonia]. At an experimental plant (that was) recently constructed on the Pacific Ocean with a maximum output of 100 kw, they are pumping up water continuously through a polyethylene pipe 75 cm in diameter and 945 m in total length from a place 580 m below the surface, in order to take in water more than 20°C colder than [water at] the surface temperature (about 30°C).

Notes
Line 3: 近くの水 = water in the vicinity (of); the く-forms of a few adjectives function as nouns.
Line 4: The の in 日光のとどかない marks the subject of the verb in the relative clause.
Line 4: Three particles appear in succession: とでは; can you explain the function of each?
Line 7: ガスは...: This は marks the topic of the sentence; however, this topic is actually the object of the verb 液化させ. Beware of thinking that a noun marked with は is always the subject of the corresponding English sentence.
Line 7: The の in 温度の低い水 marks the subject in the relative clause, "water whose temperature is low."

大いに	おおいに	greatly
向上する	コウジョウする	to improve
あらかじめ		previously
くりかえす	【繰り返す】	to repeat
のぞましい	【望ましい】	desired, hoped for
受け入れる	うけいれる	to receive

　日本では現在、産業用ロボットは、自動車[ジドウシャ = automobile]を初め[はじめ = beginning]とする多くの方面で、生産ラインの自動化のために使われ、生産性を大いに向上している。これらの産業用ロボットのほとんどすべてのものは、ティーチング・プレイバック方式で動作している。ロボットの動作はすべて、あらかじめ基本として与えておかなければならない。このように与えられた情報がくりかえし用いられて、一つの作業を行うことになる。環境条件、作業対象の状態が変化していても、ロボットは全くこのことを理解できず、あらかじめ示された基本的動作をくりかえすのみであり、作業としてのぞましい結果が得られず、ここに問題点が存在する。ロボットが仕事をしながら外部からの信号を受け入れることのできるようなセンサーをもつことが必要なのである。

　　In Japan at present industrial-use robots are used for automating production lines in many fields, with automobiles as the first, and are greatly improving productivity. Nearly all these industrial-use robots operate in the teaching-playback mode. As the basis [for automating], all the robot actions must be assigned beforehand. The information thus given is repeatedly used, and the result is that the robot performs [that] one task. Even if the state of the surrounding conditions or the object of the task changes, the robots, being wholly unable to understand these changes, only repeat the basic operation (that they were) previously shown; the desired results of the task are [thus] not attained, and here problems exist. [Thus] it is necessary for the robot to have a sensor (of the kind) that can receive external signals while doing [its] work.

Notes
Line 1: You probably won't find 産業用 in a dictionary; 用 is a common suffix meaning "for use in."
Lines 4-5: Note in these lines the two uses of すべて: すべての noun, and noun はすべて.
Lines 5-6: 与えておかなければならない means "we have to give (for subsequent use)"; the idea expressed by the auxiliary verb おく does not need to be translated here.
Lines 10-11: このようなセンサー means "this kind of sensor"; 受け入れることのできるようなセンサー is then "a sensor (of the kind) that can receive." Here の marks the subject of できる.

16-19

Translation 16

少なからず...	すくなからず	is not infrequent, and ...
常に	つねに	always
調和分析する	チョウワブンセキする	to perform harmonic analysis; to Fourier-analyze

　気象学において大気の運動を解析するために有限要素法を用いる場合が少なからず存在する。気象学の対象は主として[シュとして＝basically]連続体であるが、これを有限個の小部分、すなわち要素に分割し、要素の特性を近似[キンジ＝approximation]する数学的モデル、すなわち要素方程式を作り、それを組み合わせて全体の方程式を作って解く。周期関数はすべて調和分析し、三角関数の代数和として表現する。異相間の境界面[キョウカイメン＝boundary surface]などでは特異点が存在するので、特別な計算[ケイサン＝calculation]の仕方が用いられる。理論[リロン＝theoretical]計算の結果は常に観測結果と比べてみることが必要である。

In meteorology, situations in which we use the finite-element method to analyze atmospheric motions are not infrequent; the object of study in meteorology [the atmosphere], is basically a continuum, but we divide it into a finite number of small parts (i.e., elements), construct a mathematical model (i.e., the finite-element equations) that approximates the characteristics of the elements, then combine [them] to form the equation for the whole [system] and solve. We subject all the periodic functions to harmonic analysis and express them as an algebraic sum of trigonometric functions. Because singular points exist on the boundary surfaces between the phases (and elsewhere), special calculation methods are used. It is always necessary to see how the results of the theoretical calculations compare with the observed results.

Notes

Line 1:　要素 is an element in electrical and mechanical circuits as well as an element in the finite-element method; surface and volume elements in mathematics are 表面素 and 体積素, respectively. Keep in mind that 元素 is an element in chemistry.

Line 2:　少なからず is the negative conjunctive of the adjective 少ない, borrowed from the literary style; it is formed by adding からず to the stem of the adjective.

Lines 5-6:　In 周期関数はすべて調和分析し、the は marks the topic, but 周期関数 has to be regarded as the object of 調和分析し.

Line 9:　比べてみる means "we compare (and see what happens)"; we have translated it as "[we] see how ... compare" to give the implication of the auxiliary みる.

わたる		to spread, extend, range
むつかしい	(or むずかしい)	difficult
うめる	【埋める】	to bury
この度	このたび	recently
でんぷん	(or デンプン)	starch
<u>混</u>ぜ合わせる	まぜあわせる	to mix (together)
ごく		extremely
ありふれた		abundant
元の	もとの	original
もどる	【戻る】	to return, revert

　プラスチックの利用は多方面にわたっているが、使用後の分解がむつかしく、大半は地中にうめられて、そのままの形で<u>保存</u>[ホゾン＝preservation]されているのが事実である。その量は加速度的に増加していて、<u>環境汚染</u>[オセン＝pollution]の原<u>因</u>[ゲンイン＝cause]の一つになっている。この実態に対応して、地中で分解するプラスチックの研究が行われている。この度<u>開発</u>[カイハツ＝development]されたシート状プラスチックは、でんぷんのような<u>天然</u>[テンネン＝natural]高分子多糖類の溶液を数種まぜ合わせ、水分を蒸発させて作ったもので、地中にいるごくありふれた<u>細菌</u>[サイキン＝bacteria]によって分解され、はやければ二、三<u>箇月</u>[ニサンカゲツ＝two or three months]で元の高分子多糖類にもどり、全く<u>公害</u>[コウガイ＝pollution]を発生しない。

　The use of plastics has spread into many fields; however, the fact is that after being used they do not decompose readily, and that most of them are buried in the ground and are preserved there in their original form. Their volume is increasing at an accelerated pace and has become one of the causes of environmental pollution. In response to this situation, research is underway on plastics that will decompose in the ground. A recently developed plastic sheeting is a material made by mixing together several kinds of solutions of natural macromolecular starchlike polysaccharides and then evaporating off the moisture. It is decomposed by bacteria that are very abundant in the earth and reverts to its original macromolecular polysaccharides in as quickly as two or three months; it generates absolutely no pollution.

Notes
Line 2: The noun まま means something like "original condition" or "current state" or "present form." そのまま is often translated as "as it is" or "as it was."
Line 8: ごく is sometimes written as 極(く) with the same KANJI as in 極めて[きわめて].
Line 9: 三月[サンガツ] is "March," but "(a period of) three months" is 三箇月[サンカゲツ], also written as 三ヶ月, 三ヵ月, or 三か月. The last of these, 三か月, is regarded as the best current usage.

Translation 18

ヒト		human beings
科、属、種	カ、ゾク、シュ	family; genus; species
にる	【似る】	to resemble
さえ		even

　生物としてのヒトは、別表に示すように、ヒト科[カ＝family]ヒト属ヒト種に属するが、その進化において、他の動物には見られない種としての特異性がある。現存するヒトはすべて同種であるが、属を同じくするものはいない。種や属は、形態などの外観上の特徴[トクチョウ＝characteristics]から類別するが、本質的には生殖[セイショク＝reproduction]細胞の和合性、すなわち交配の可能性[カノウセイ＝possibility]、つまり子が生まれるかどうかで定まる。交配によって子が生まれ、その子にも交配能力[ノウリョク＝capability]があれば同種である。一代の交配は可能[カノウ]であるが、その子に交配能力が無い時は同属ではあるが異種である。科が違うと、いくら形などが同じようでも交配が不可能[フカノウ＝impossibility]である。形態、その他の点でヒトと最もよくにているチンパンジーやゴリラは、ヒトとは科さえ異なるのである。

　　　As we show in a separate table, human beings, considered as biological creatures, belong to the family Hominidae, the genus *Homo*, and the species *sapiens*; in their evolution as a species they have special characteristics that are not seen in other animals. All existing human beings are of the same species, and no [other] species belong to the same genus. We classify genus and species from the characteristics of external appearance, such as form and shape, but essentially they are determined by the compatibility of reproductive cells, that is, the possibility of mating — or, in other words, whether or not offspring can be born. If an offspring is born by mating, and if there is mating capability in that offspring, then [those that mated] are of the same species. When mating is possible in one generation but there is no mating capability in the offspring, then [those that mated] are of the same genus but of different species. When the families are different, then no matter how similar their form may be, mating is impossible. Chimpanzees and gorillas, which most nearly resemble human beings in form and in other aspects, differ from human beings even in family.

Notes
Line 1: 生物としてのヒト "humans (considered) as biological creatures": the としての construction occurs two more times in this paragraph.
Line 3: ヒトは同種である illustrates that AはBである does not always mean "A is B." Here the idea is that "A is a member of the group of B" or "A belongs to B."
Lines 3-4: 属を同じくするものはいない: A literal translation of this would be "There exist no species whose genus we can make the same [as that of humans]"; note that 同じくなる = "to become similar" and 同じくする = "to make (something) similar, to cause (something) to be similar."
Line 9: 交配能力が無い時: Note that ない is often written as 無い.
Line 12: When the particle さえ follows a noun, the particles が, を, and は are normally dropped. Here が has been omitted, and 科 is understood to be the subject of the verb 異なる.

きりかえ	【切り替え】	switching
はさむ		to put between
さえぎる {xu}	【遮る】	to cut off
くぐりぬける		to slip through

コンピュータは演算[エンザン＝operation]を二進法で行うから、論理回路[ロンリカイロ＝logical circuit]のオン、オフのきりかえ速度が速いほど演算[エンザン]速度も速くなる。ジョセフソン素子は超[チョウ＝super]伝導の原理を利用して、このスイッチングを極めて速く行うもので、超[チョウ]高速コンピュータ用の超高速論理[ロンリ＝logic]素子として、研究されてきた。

イギリスのブライアン・ジョセフソンが発見したその原理は次のようである。フィルム状の絶縁体[ゼツエンタイ＝insulator]を二つの高温超伝導体でサンドイッチ状にはさむ。常温では絶縁体[ゼツエンタイ]にさえぎられて、電流は流れない。

この回路を臨界[リンカイ＝critical]温度以下にすると、二つの高温超伝導体は超伝導状態になる。するとトンネル効果[コウカ＝effect]によって、電子が超伝導体から超伝導体へ、絶縁フィルムをくぐりぬけるようにして通過するため、電流が流れるようになる。

しかし、この回路は周りの磁場の強さが臨界[リンカイ]磁場になると超伝導作用を失う[うしなう＝lose]。また、回路に流れる電流が臨界電流密度[ミツド＝density]以上になると超伝導作用を失う[うしなう]。すなわち、磁場の強さ、電流密度[ミツド]を制御してオン、オフのきりかえを行うことができ、これが超高速で行える。

これまでの実験では、スイッチングに要する時間が3.3ピコ秒[ビョウ＝second]で、シリコン素子を用いたスイッチング速度の100倍以上になる。その上、高温超伝導体接点間の離間距離が極めて短い[みじかい＝short]ので、素子全体の大きさを小さくすることもできるという利点も生ずる。

Computers perform their operations in the binary system; therefore the quicker the on-off switching speed of the logic circuits, the faster their speed of operation becomes. The Josephson element is a device that utilizes the principle of superconductivity and performs the switching extremely quickly. It has become the object of research as a super-high-speed element for use in super-high-speed computers.

The principle discovered by Brian Josephson of England is as follows: We sandwich an insulating film between two high-temperature superconductors. At normal temperatures [the two] are cut off by the insulator, and current does not flow.

If we put this circuit below the critical temperature, the two high-temperature superconductors go into a superconducting state. The electrons pass from one superconducting material to the other by the tunnel effect, as though they slip through the insulating film, and an electric current flows.

16-23

However, if the intensity of the surrounding magnetic field reaches the critical magnetic field, this circuit loses its superconducting function. Moreover, if the electric current flowing in the circuit exceeds the critical current density, it loses its superconducting function. That is, by controlling the intensity of the magnetic field and the electric current density, we can actuate on-off switching and can do it at super-high speed.

In the experiments done thus far, the time interval needed for switching is 3.3 picoseconds, more than 100 times the switching velocity when using silicon elements. In addition, the clearance between the contact points of the high-temperature superconductors is extremely small, and thus there arises the extra advantage of being able to reduce the overall size of the element as well.

Note
Lines 22-23: In the very last sentence the entire clause 素子全体...という modifies 利点.

安	アン	secure, safe, quiet
	やす(い)	cheap, inexpensive

械	カイ	machine

開	カイ	opening
	あ(ける), あ(く)	to open
	ひら(く)	to open
	ひら(ける)	to open

換	カン	exchanging
	か(える)	to exchange; to convert

記	キ	inscription, record

型	ケイ	model, type, pattern
	かた	model, type, mold
	-がた	model, type

検	ケン	investigation

減	ゲン	decreasing
	へ(らす)	to decrease
	へ(る) {xu}	to decrease

効	コウ	effect
	き(く)	to be effective

散	サン	scattering
	ち(る) {xu}	to scatter

算	サン	calculation

者	シャ	person
	もの	person

処	ショ	managing, dealing with

晶	ショウ	crystal

設	セツ	installing, setting up
	もう(ける)	to establish, set up

然	ゼン; ネン	state; nature

装	ソウ	equipment

低	テイ	low
	ひく(い)	low

適	テキ	proper, suitable
	テキ(する)	to be suitable

転	テン	revolution, turning
	ころ(がる)	to roll, tumble

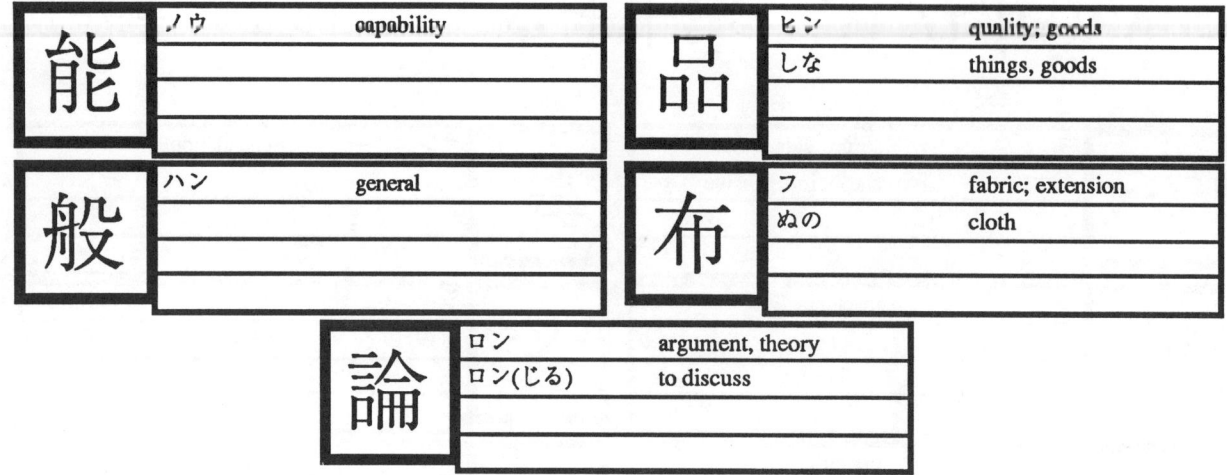

能	ノウ	capability

品	ヒン	quality; goods
	しな	things, goods

般	ハン	general

布	フ	fabric; extension
	ぬの	cloth

論	ロン	argument, theory
	ロン(じる)	to discuss

VOCABULARY

安

安定な	アンテイな	stable
不安定な	フアンテイな	unstable
安全	アンゼン	safety
安全第一	アンゼンダイイチ	safety first
目安	めやす	standard, aim

械

機械	キカイ	machine
器械	キカイ	appliance, instrument

開

開環重合	カイカンジュウゴウ	ring-opening polymerization
開放サイクル	カイホウサイクル	open cycle
開発	カイハツ	development
開場する	カイジョウする	to open {e.g., a facility}
開路	カイロ	open circuit

換

変換	ヘンカン	conversion
交換	コウカン	exchange
換気	カンキ	ventilation
換算表	カンサンヒョウ	conversion table
組(み)換えDNA	くみかえDNA	recombinant DNA

記

記号	キゴウ	symbol
記述	キジュツ	description
記事	キジ	(newspaper) article
記入する	キニュウする	to fill out, make an entry

型

大型の	おおがたの	large-sized
中型の	チュウがたの	medium-sized
小型の	こがたの	small-sized
型式	ケイシキ	model, type
標準型	ヒョウジュンがた	standard type; normal mode

検

検出	ケンシュツ	detection
検定	ケンテイ	(qualifying) test; calibration
検定器	ケンテイキ	calibration instrument
検流計	ケンリュウケイ	galvanometer

減

減少	ゲンショウ	decrease, reduction
減速機	ゲンソクキ	speed reducer
加減-	カゲン	adjustable
半減期	ハンゲンキ	half-life

効

効率	コウリツ	efficiency
効用	コウヨウ	utility
効果	コウカ	effect
光電効果	コウデンコウカ	photoelectric effect
実効の	ジッコウの	effective
効力	コウリョク	effectiveness

散

分散	ブンサン	dispersion
発散する	ハッサンする	to diverge
放散	ホウサン	dispersion
散水機	サンスイキ	sprinkler
散在する	サンザイする	to lie scattered
散光	サンコウ	scattered light
散布	サンプ	sprinkling, spraying

算

計算	ケイサン	calculation
計算器	ケイサンキ	calculator
計算機	ケイサンキ	computer
算術	サンジュツ	arithmetic
割り算	わりザン	division

者

学者	ガクシャ	scholar
化学者	カガクシャ	chemist
後者	コウシャ	latter {for persons and things}
前者	ゼンシャ	former {for persons and things}

処

処理する	ショリする	to process
処理-	ショリ	treated
処理水	ショリスイ	treated water
処置	ショチ	treatment, handling
情報処理	ジョウホウショリ	information processing

晶

結晶	ケッショウ	crystal
結晶化	ケッショウカ	crystallization
水晶	スイショウ	quartz
液晶	エキショウ	liquid crystal

設

設立する	セツリツする	to establish
設計	セッケイ	design, plan
設計応力	セッケイオウリョク	design stress
設定機構	セッテイキコウ	setting mechanism
設置する	セッチする	to install, set up
開設する	カイセツする	to inaugurate

然

自然	シゼン	nature
天然の	テンネンの	natural
当然の	トウゼンの	just, proper
必然的な	ヒツゼンテキな	inevitable

装

| 装置 | ソウチ | device, apparatus |
| ディスク装置 | ディスクソウチ | (computer) disk drive |

低

高低	コウテイ	height
最低の	サイテイの	lowest
低気圧	テイキアツ	a low {meteorology}
低下させる	テイカさせる	to lower, decrease
低分子量	テイブンシリョウ	low molecular weight
低圧	テイアツ	low pressure
低速	テイソク	low speed
低減する	テイゲンする	to diminish
低温	テイオン	low temperature

適

適当な	テキトウな	proper, suitable
最適-	サイテキ	optimum, optimal
適用コード	テキヨウコード	applicable code
適応制御	テキオウセイギョ	adaptive control

転

反転	ハンテン	inversion; reversal
回転	カイテン	rotation
運転	ウンテン	operating, running
自転	ジテン	rotation
地球の自転	チキュウのジテン	rotation of the earth
転位	テンイ	(crystal) dislocation
転移	テンイ	(phase) transition; (gene) transposition
転動体	テンドウタイ	rolling element

能

能率	ノウリツ	efficiency
能力	ノウリョク	capability, capacity
能動-	ノウドウ	active
能動回路	ノウドウカイロ	active circuit
知能	チノウ	intelligence
性能	セイノウ	performance
機能	キノウ	function
放射能	ホウシャノウ	radioactivity

般

一般の	イッパンの	general
一般化する	イッパンカする	to generalize
全般的に	ゼンパンテキに	generally, on the whole

品

品質	ヒンシツ	quality
品質管理	ヒンシツカンリ	quality control
品物	しなもの	goods
品位の(低い)	ヒンイの(ひくい)	(low) grade
(高)品位	(コウ)ヒンイ	(high) grade
部品	ブヒン	components, parts
部分品	ブブンヒン	components, parts
少品種	ショウヒンシュ	small-variety (type)
多品種	タヒンシュ	multi-product (type)

布

配布する	ハイフする	to distribute
分布	ブンプ	distribution
分布曲線	ブンプキョクセン	distribution curve
速度分布	ソクドブンプ	velocity distribution
不織布	フショクフ	nonwoven fabric

論

論理学	ロンリガク	logic
論理的な	ロンリテキな	logical
結論	ケツロン	conclusion
理論	リロン	theory
確率過程理論	カクリツカテイリロン	theory of stochastic process
量子論	リョウシロン	quantum theory

17   Vocabulary Building and Translation Examples, II

Read the following paragraphs aloud several times and seek to understand the text as you go along. Compare your understanding of the texts with the translations given, and review any grammar points that you have not mastered.

TRANSLATION EXAMPLES

Translation 1

　環状化合物の開環によって重合体を得る重合法を開環重合という。全般的にはイオン反応で、放射線による固相重合で結晶性高分子を与えるものもある。

The polymerization technique in which we obtain a polymer by means of the ring-opening of ring-shaped compounds is called ring-opening polymerization. Generally [these] are ionic reactions. Some give crystalline polymers in solid-phase polymerizations that are induced by radiation.

Notes
Line 2: The first で that appears here is the shortened form of the connective であって.
Line 2: もの here stands for "ring-opening polymerizations"; hence ...を与えるものもある means literally "There are ring-opening polymerizations that give ...."

Translation 2

配向　　　　　　　　ハイコウ　　　　　　　　　orientation

　高分子の加工プロセスに液晶状態を利用すると、配向を制御することによって高強度のファイバーが得られる。ケブラーはその一例で、高い比強度が要求される使用に対して効果的である。

If we use the liquid-crystalline state in processing polymers, we can obtain high-strength fibers by controlling the [polymer] orientation. Kevlar is one example of [such fibers], and it is effective in uses where high specific strengths are required.

Translation 3

さす　　　　　　　　　　【指す】　　　　　　　　　　to indicate

　大気中で周りより気圧の低い所を低気圧という。標準気圧以下をさすのではなく、周りの気圧との相対的な気圧の高低を表す。低気圧は大気中に不安定な波動[ハドウ＝wave]が生じた時に発生する。

A place in the atmosphere where pressure is lower than in its surroundings is called a low. Lows do not indicate pressures that are below the standard pressure; they indicate the height of the pressure relative to the surrounding pressures. Lows develop when unstable waves have arisen in the atmosphere.

Translation 4

織機	ショッキ	loom
はり合わせる	はりあわせる	to stick together
とかし合わせる	とかしあわせる	to fuse together
たがいに接合する	たがいにセツゴウする	to join with each other

　織機を使わずに各種のファイバーのウェブを機械的、化学的、熱的あるいはそれらの組み合わせによって処理し、構成ファイバーをはり合わせたりとかし合わせたりして、たがいに接合して作った布を不織布という。その構造は織物とは全く異なっている。

What we call nonwoven fabrics are fabrics made without using a loom; they are made by processing each kind of fiber-web mechanically, chemically, thermally, or by a combination of these, [such that] the constituent fibers are stuck or fused together, [thereby] joining them with each other. The structure [of the resulting material] differs completely from that of woven fabrics.

Translation 5

　工程管理の目標は、最少の費用[ヒヨウ＝cost]、最少の人員[ジンイン＝personnel]、機械、資材[シザイ＝material]で最大の効果と能力を発揮し[ハッキする＝toexhibit]、最少の期間内に目的とする品物を作り出すことである。

The objective of process management is to produce specified goods within a minimum time period, [in ways] that exhibit maximum effectiveness and capability with minimum costs and minimum personnel, machinery, and materials.

Translation 6

もっぱら   exclusively

　一般の直流発電機としてもっぱら利用されている他励[タレイ ＝ separately excited]発電機は、電圧変動率が小さく、励磁[レイジ ＝ excitation]を変えることにより任意の[ニンイの ＝ arbitrary]安定な電圧が得られる。起電力は励磁[レイジ]電流とともに増加するという開路特性を示す。

　　　　The separately excited generator, which is exclusively used as the general dc generator, has a small degree of voltage fluctuation, and by varying the excitation we can obtain an arbitrary, stable voltage. Its electromotive force shows the open-circuit characteristic of increasing with the excitation current.

Translation 7

作業者   サギョウシャ   worker
てまち   waiting

　流れ作業においては、速い工程の作業者がおそい工程の作業者にテンポを合わせるために、多少のてまちをすることになり、能率が低下する。したがって、作業者のてまち時間の減少、すなわち工程別の時間の不均衡[フキンコウ ＝ imbalance]を少なくすることが最も重要である。

　　　　In an assembly line, because workers in a fast process match their tempo to that of workers in a slow process, they spend some [time] waiting, and efficiency decreases. Consequently, reduction of waiting time of workers, i.e., decreasing the imbalance among the times for each of the separate processes, is most important.

Note
Line 3: 工程別の時間 has the same meaning as それぞれの工程の時間. Note that here -別 is used as a suffix meaning "separated according to"; hence, "the time [needed] for each separate process."

Translation 8

きり出す   きりだす   to cut out
分周する   ブンシュウする   to decompose into frequencies
発振波   ハッシンハ   (generated) oscillating wave

　圧電振動子の一種に水晶振動子がある。水晶の結晶から一定の方位にきり出したもので、通常板状[いたジョウ ＝ plate-shaped]である。固有振動数の共振[キョウシン ＝ resonance]を利用して安定な発振周波数[ハッシンシュウハスウ ＝ oscillation frequency]を得る水晶発振器に用いられる。発振波を分周して1kHz程度以下にし電気的時間信号を発生させたものが水晶時計で、極めて小型にすることもできる。

　　　　A quartz oscillator is one kind of piezoelectric oscillator. It is cut out from a crystal of quartz in a fixed orientation and is usually plate-shaped. It is used in the quartz oscillator that utilizes the resonance of the characteristic frequencies to obtain a stable oscillation frequency. The quartz watch is a device that decomposes an oscillating wave into frequencies of the order of 1 KHz or less and generates an electric time signal; also it can be made extremely compact.

Note
Line 2: 板状 may be read いたジョウ or バンジョウ.

Translation 9

　ころがり軸受け[ジクうけ＝bearings]はラジアル荷重[カジュウ＝load]を受けるラジアル軸受け[ジクうけ]と、アキシアル荷重[カジュウ]をうけるスラスト軸受けとに大別される。また、転動体の種類によってたま軸受け[たまジクうけ＝ball bearing]、ころ軸受け[ころジクうけ＝roller bearing]に分けられ、さらに、転動体の内部構造によって分離形と非[ヒ＝non-]分離形がある。目的に応じて、適当な形式のものを使用する。

Rolling bearings are divided broadly into radial bearings, which bear a radial load, and thrust bearings, which bear an axial load. They are again divided into ball bearings and roller bearings according to the type of rolling element, and further into separable and nonseparable bearings, depending on the internal structure of the rolling element. [We] use that type of bearing appropriate to [our] purpose.

Notes
Line 1:　ころがり軸受け may be written using the KANJI 転 of this chapter: 転がり軸受け.
Line 1:　Note that 軸[ジク] means both "axle" and "axis"; hence x-軸 is the x-axis.
Lines 1-2:　Here we have 受ける and うける in the same sentence.

Translation 10

受動-	ジュドウ	passive

　電気回路は、レジスタンス、コンダクタンス、インダクタンスなどの受動素子だけから構成され、増幅器[ゾウフクキ＝amplifier]などのエネルギーを出す能動素子を含まない受動回路と、トランジスター、電池[デンチ＝battery]などの電力供給源[キョウキュウゲン＝sources]を内部に含む能動回路に分類される。

Electrical circuits are classified [as follows]: passive circuits, which are made up of only passive elements such as resistances, conductances, and inductances, and contain no energy-producing active elements such as amplifiers; and active circuits, which contain within them electric power sources, such as transistors and batteries.

Translation 11

配布する	ハイフする	to distribute, spread out
集中する	シュウチュウする	to concentrate

振動系[ケイ = system]において、質量、ダンパーなどが連続的に配布され、数個所[カショ = location]に集中していると見なし得ないとき、これを分布定数系[ケイ]といい、振動方程式は時間および空間座標[ザヒョウ = co-ordinate]に関する偏微分[ヘンビブン = partial differential]方程式となる。

In a vibrating system, when such [elements] as masses and dampers are distributed continuously and cannot be regarded as concentrated at several locations, this [system] is called a distributed parameter system, and the vibration equation is a partial differential equation in time and space coordinates.

Notes
Line 1: Another word for ダンパー (damper) is ダシュポット (dashpot), the latter being more common in viscoelasticity.
Line 2: 個所[カショ] contains 個 with the irregular reading カ. For counting places 箇所, か所, カ所, and ヶ所, all pronounced カショ, are used; here ヶ is an alternate form for 箇. Current usage seems to prefer か所.

Translation 12

...をはじめ	【を初め】	including ...
まもる		to protect

人間をはじめ生物では、外部から入ってきたウイルスなどの異物に対して抗体[コウタイ = antibody]が形成されて生体をまもる。この抗体[コウタイ]分子の種類は極めて多い。多数の抗体分子が遺伝子[イデンシ = gene]転移によって形成される機構が最近になって明らかにされ、多方面の応用が考えられている。

In living beings, including humans, antibodies are formed against foreign bodies such as viruses, which have entered from outside, and thus protect the organism. The varieties of antibody molecules are extremely numerous. Mechanisms by which many of the antibody molecules are formed by means of gene transposition have recently been clarified, and applications in many fields are being considered.

Notes
Line 1: Be sure to pronounce 人間 as ニンゲン.
Line 1: 入ってくる means "enter, come in."

Translation 13

ひん度	ヒンド	frequency (of use)
できるだけ...		as ... as possible
きり換える	きりかえる	to replace
のぞむ		to desire

日本では、機械工学で使用ひん度の多い重量キログラム毎[マイ = per]平方センチメートル、重量キログラム毎[マイ]平方ミリメートルなどは、できるだけはやくパスカルを用いた単位にきり換えることがのぞまれている。

17-11

このような重力単位を用いた場合には、SIとの換算表をつけることが要求されている。

In Japan it is desired to replace as soon as possible the [kilogram] weight [units] such as kgf/cm² and kgf/mm², frequently used in mechanical engineering, by units that use pascals. When these kinds of gravitational units are used, attaching a conversion table for SI is required.

Note
Lines 2-3: できるだけはやく＝できるだけ早く. Note that there are two adjectives pronounced the same: 速い meaning "rapid, quick" and 早い meaning "early, soon."

Translation 14

わずかな		slight
くりかえす		to repeat
速やかな	すみやかな	rapid, quick

性質の類似した[ルイジした＝similar]構成成分からなる混合物[コンゴウブツ＝mixture]から各成分を分離するために、わずかな溶解度の違いを利用して、結晶化と溶解をくりかえし行う操作[ソウサ＝operation]を分別結晶という。高圧を用いて、特定の成分を速やかに分別結晶する方法が最近開発され、工業的に用いられている。

Fractional crystallization is an operation that utilizes slight differences in solubility in order to separate, by repeated crystallization and dissolution, each component from a mixture consisting of components similar in properties. A method of doing fractional crystallization of specific components rapidly by using high pressure has recently been developed and is being used industrially.

Translation 15

とめる	【止める】	to turn off, stop
きる	【切る】	to cut (off)

等方加圧装置の型式によっては、電気式安全装置が用いられる。圧力計で検出した作用圧力を電気信号に変換し、高圧バルブを開いて、常用の圧力以下に低下させたり、場合によっては、ポンプの運転をとめたり、ヒーターの加熱電源[デンゲン＝electrical heating source]をきって、圧力を下げる。

Electrical safety devices are in use for certain types of isostatic pressing equipment. We transform the working pressure, as detected by a pressure gauge, into an electric signal. We then open the high-pressure valve and lower the pressure below the usual value, or at times we stop (the operation of) the pump; we then cut off the electrical heat source to the heater and decrease the pressure.

Translation 16

しかしながら		however
各論	カクロン	a discussion of details
当然	トウゼン	natural

　エネルギー問題の半永久的[エイキュウテキ = permanent]解決策[カイケツサク = solution]として原子エネルギーの利用に反対する人はいない。しかしながら、それでは原子力発電所をどこに設置するかという各論になると、自分の近くでもよいという人はいない。原子力発電の安全性が証明[ショウメイ = proof]されていないことの当然の結果である。

　　No one is against the use of atomic energy as a semipermanent solution to the energy problem. However, when it then comes down to a discussion of details as to where to locate an atomic energy power station, no one will say that it is all right [to build it] in his own neighborhood. [This] is a natural consequence of the fact that the safety of atomic energy generation has not been proven.

Translation 17

へだてる		to separate

　直流検流計の原理は、可動[カドウ = movable]コイル形電流計と同じで、その感度[カンド = sensitivity]は1mへだてたスケール上での光点の動きによる。交流検流計は可動[カドウ]コイル形電流計の可動部分の慣性[カンセイ = inertia]モーメントを小さくし、使用周波数[シュウハスウ = frequency]に共振[キョウシン = resonance]して感度[カンド]を上げるようにしたものである。

　　The principle of the dc galvanometer is the same as that of the movable-coil-type ammeter, and its sensitivity depends on the motion of a light point on a scale 1 meter distant from it. The ac galvanometer is a meter whose sensitivity has been raised by reducing the moment of inertia of the movable part of the movable-coil-type ammeter [so that] it resonates at the working frequency.

Note
Line 3: コイル形 = coil-type. Both 形 (form, shape(d)) and 型 (model, type) appear as suffixes, with somewhat overlapping meanings. Both KANJI used as suffixes are pronounced ケイ or がた; for example, 球形[キュウケイ] and 星形[ほしがた] "star-shaped."

Translation 18

物理面	ブツリメン	physical domain
直す	なおす	to change, correct

　ラプラス変換を用いると、常微分方程式は代数方程式に変換されるので、割り算のような算術計算で解を求めることができる。しかしながら、得られた解は元の物理面の変数で記述されていないので、ラプラス逆[ギャク =

inverse]変換によって物理面の変数に直さなければならない。この目的のためには、ラプラス逆[ギャク]変換表を利用するのがよい。

Since, when we use the Laplace transform, an ordinary differential equation is transformed into an algebraic equation, we can get a solution by arithmetic calculations such as division. However, because the solution obtained is not expressed in the variables of the original physical domain, we must change to the variables of the physical domain by means of the inverse Laplace transform. For this purpose, it is convenient to use a table of inverse Laplace transforms.

Translation 19
CADPASは計算機支援[シエン = aided]高分子データベースシステムで、高分子に関する文献[ブンケン = literature]、高分子物性のファクト、図[ズ = figure]、表からカラーイメージまで、高分子の研究開発に必要なデータを、日本高分子素材[ソザイ = material]センターで集めたものである。

CADPAS is a computer-aided polymer data base system at the Japan Polymer Materials Center (Liberta), and it is one that brings together data necessary for polymer research and development — from literature on polymers, facts about polymer properties, figures, and tables, to color images.

Notes
Line 1: Strictly speaking 高分子 means "macromolecule," whereas 重合体 means "polymer." In English this distinction has become blurred, and polymer is now often used for the more general term "macromolecule."
Line 3: 研究開発 (= 研究と開発) is Japanese for "research and development."

Translation 20
とり入れる   とりいれる   to take in

ある種の物質は塩類の水溶液中でそのイオンが溶液中に出て、溶液中のイオンが物質の中にとり入れられる。この現象をイオン交換といい、このような物質をイオン交換体という。イオン交換体を用いて物質を分離する技術をイオン交換分離といい、イオン交換体としては、イオン交換樹脂[ジュシ = resin]が最も多く用いられている。

For certain classes of substances in [contact with] aqueous solutions of salts, their ions come out into the solution, and the ions in the solution are taken up by the substance. This phenomenon is called ion exchange, and these kinds of substances are called ion exchangers. The technique of separating materials by using ion exchangers is called ion-exchange separation, and ion-exchange resins are most frequently used as ion exchangers.

Translation 21

発表	ハッピョウ	announcement, publication
がん		cancer
正常化	セイジョウカ	normalization
組み込む	くみこむ	to insert {lit.: to build into}
もどる	【戻る】	to return

　理化学研究所の分子生物学者の発表によれば、がん細胞正常化に効力のある遺伝子[イデンシ＝gene]が発見された。遺伝子[イデンシ]を正常細胞から分離して、がん細胞に組み込むという処置を行ったところ100,000個中7個の細胞が正常な細胞にもどった。この遺伝子の構造は、184個のアミノ酸からなるたんぱく質を作っていることがわかった。

　　　According to an announcement by the molecular biologists at the Institute of Physical and Chemical Research, a gene has been discovered that is effective in the normalization of cancer cells. When they carried out a procedure that isolated [these] genes from normal cells and [then] inserted them into cancer cells, 7 out of 100,000 cells reverted to normal cells. They learned that the structure of this gene is that of a protein made up of 184 amino acids.

Notes
Lines 1-2:　The の in 効力のある is the subject marker in a subordinate clause.
Line 3:　ところ means both "location in space" and "point in time"; when ところ occurs at the end of a clause, it means "when."
Line 3:　行った might be read いった or おこなった; the latter is correct here.

Translation 22

　遺伝病[イデンビョウ＝hereditary disease]の治療[チリョウ＝treatment]のために、外から正常な遺伝子[イデンシ＝gene]を組みこむ方法が、アメリカのミシガン大学で開発された。遺伝子[イデンシ]組換えの方法を用いて、正常な遺伝子をウイルスの遺伝子に組みこみ、このウイルスに感染させて[from カンセンする＝to be infected]、その組換えDNAを組みこむのである。

　　　For the treatment of hereditary diseases, a method of inserting a normal gene from another [person] has been developed at the University of Michigan in America. Using the method of gene recombination, they inserted the normal gene into a viral gene and then inserted [the resulting] recombinant DNA [into the patient] by infecting [him] with this virus.

Notes
Line 2:　アメリカ is used both for "America" and for "USA." USA is correctly translated as アメリカ合衆国[ガッシュウコク].
Line 4:　このウイルスに: Keep in mind that the agent in a causative construction is usually designated by に, and note that the object of the action is understood to be "the patient."

Translation 23

　本研究は、大型電子計算機のディスク装置内で磁気ディスクが高速回転する時に、ディスクに引きずられて[from ひきずる = to drag]発生する回転流れによるディスク振動の特性を解明するために、空気中高速回転と水中低速回転とでレイノルズ数を等価[トウカ = equivalence]にして水中で低速回転する一重ディスクと二重ディスクの流れによる振動特性を実験的に明らかにすることを目的としている。

　　　　This research has as its goal to clarify experimentally the vibrational characteristics resulting from the flow around single and double disks rotating at low speeds in water; [in doing this] we make the Reynolds number for the low-speed rotation in water equivalent to that for high-speed rotation in air. [This experiment is being done] in order to elucidate the characteristics of the disk vibration that depends on the radial flow [of air] that arises from its being dragged by the disk when the magnetic disk in the disk drive of a large electronic computer rotates with a very high speed.

Notes
Line 1: 本研究 is a more formal way of saying この研究.
Line 5: 一重[イチジュウ] is "single," and 二重 is "double."

Translation 24

ふたたび　　　　　　　　【再び】　　　　　　　　　　again
おくりかえす　　　　　　　　　　　　　　　　　　　to return, send back

　ガスタービンにおいて、排気[ハイキ = exhaust gas]を大気中に放出しないで、冷却器[レイキャクキ = cooler]で低温にして、ふたたび圧縮器[アッシュクキ = compressor]におくりかえして使用する方式を密閉[ミッペイ = closed]サイクルという。これに対して、タービンで仕事をした排気[ハイキ]を大気中に放出してしまう形式を開放サイクルという。

　　　　In gas turbines, the type [of cycle] in which we do not discharge the exhaust gases into the atmosphere [but instead] lower their temperature in a cooler and return them again to the compressor and use them is called a closed cycle. In contrast to this, the type [of cycle] in which we discharge to the atmosphere the exhaust gases that have performed work in the turbine is called an open cycle.

Translation 25

このたび　　　　　　　　【この度】　　　　　　　　recently
...にすぐれる　　　　　　　　　　　　　　　　　　to excel in ...
ひろい　　　　　　　　　　【広い】　　　　　　　　wide, broad

　このたび開発されたスーパーグラファイトは、単結晶と同等の物性を有する、大面積シート状グラファイトで、耐熱性[タイネツセイ = heat resistant]高分子のフィルムを、2500°C以上の温度で焼成して[from ショウセイする = to fire]作る。高い電気伝導性と熱伝導性をもち、環境安定性にすぐれ

ている。電子・機械工業用にひろい効用があり、放射線装置、光学部品など の使用に最も適している。

The recently developed super-graphite is a large-area, sheet-shaped graphite that has properties the same as [those of] a single crystal, and we make it by firing a heat-resistant polymer film at a temperature of 2500°C or more. It has high electrical and thermal conductivities and is excellent in its environmental stability. It has wide utility in the electronic and machine industries, being most suitable for use in radiation equipment, optical components, and the like.

Translation 26
電流の中では、交流は直流と異なって、一定の周期をもって、その大きさおよび方向が時間とともに変化するので、交流の大きさを表すには、必然的に自乗[ジジョウ = square]の時間的平均値[ヘイキンチ = average value]の平方根[ヘイホウコン = square root]か、絶対値[ゼッタイチ = absolute value]の時間的平均値[ヘイキンチ]を用いなければならない。前者を実効値、後者を平均値といい、実効値は平均値より常に大きい。

With regard to electric currents, alternating current differs from direct current in that it has a fixed period, and its magnitude and direction vary with time. Therefore, in order to indicate the magnitude of the alternating current, we must use either the square root of the time average of the square [of the electric current vector] or the time-averaged value of the absolute value [of the electric current vector]. The former is called the effective value, and the latter the average value; the effective value is always larger than the average value.

Note
Lines 2-3: 必然的に ("necessarily") here alerts the reader to an upcoming verb, ending in なければ ならない, and need not be translated.

Translation 27
かきこむ	【書き込む】	to write in, enter
どれだけ多くの	どれだけおおくの	how many
集積技術	シュウセキギジュツ	integrated-circuit technology

コンピュータを使用するとき、入力したプログラムやデータはRAMにかきこまれる。メモやノートに記入するように、コンピュータはRAMにかきこんでおくのである。したがって、どれだけ多くの情報をRAMにかきこむことができるかは、コンピュータの性能を定める重要な要素の一つである。最近では集積技術の進歩[シンポ = progress]によって、大容量のRAMチップが次々に実用化している。

When we use a computer, the program or data that we input is entered into the RAM. Just as we make entries in a memo[pad] or notebook, the computer enters and stores [the input] into the RAM. Therefore how many [bits] of information the computer can enter into the RAM is one of the important factors that determine its performance. Recently, because of progress in integrated-circuit technology, very large capacity RAM chips have been put to practical use one after another.

Notes
Lines 2-3:　かきこんでおく means "enters for future use"; we have translated this as "enters and stores."
Lines 3-4:　どれだけ...できるか is followed by は to indicate that the entire question is the topic of the sentence.

Translation 28

たたく		to hit, strike
所要時間	ショヨウジカン	the time required

　農業[ノウギョウ = agriculture]用に、ひろい範囲[ハンイ = range]にわたって散水するために用いられる大型の散水機では、加圧用ポンプによって高圧水をノズルから噴射[フンシャ = jet]し、噴射[フンシャ]水流がスプリングつきの反動レバーをたたいて本体を動かし、一定方向に回転させる。 散水量は通常毎[マイ = per]分5-400リットル、散水直径は5-60メートル、1回転の所要時間は30秒[ビョウ = second]-2分である。

　　　Large-scale sprinklers in agriculture, used for sprinkling over a broad range, eject high-pressure water from a nozzle by means of a pressurized pump; the water jet hits a spring-loaded reaction lever and moves the main body [of the sprinkler], [and] makes it rotate in a fixed direction. The quantity of sprinkled water is usually 5 to 400 liters per minute, the diameter of the sprinkled water [area] is 5 to 60 meters, and the time for 1 revolution is 30 seconds to 2 minutes.

Note
Line 4:　The suffix 付き[つき] means something like "equipped with, with ... attached." Here we have a lever "equipped with a spring"; hence, "spring-loaded" seems an appropriate translation.

Translation 29

つり上げる	つりあげる	to suspend
たわみ形	たわみがた	deflection-type

　材料試験機[ザイリョウシケンキ = materials-testing machine]で計量する荷重[カジュウ = load]の許容誤差[キョヨウゴサ = allowable error]は±1.0%以内でなければならない。 その精度検査[セイドケンサ = accuracy test]には材料試験機[ザイリョウシケンキ]用荷重[カジュウ]検定器を用いる。 1tf以下の荷重にはおもりをつり下げ、50tf-10kgfの荷重にはたわみ形検定器を、500tf-1tfの荷重には容積[ヨウセキ = volume]検定器を用いる。

　　　The allowable error for the load measured by a materials-testing machine must be within ±1.0%. In the accuracy test [of the machine] we use load calibration instruments [specific] for use with materials-testing machines. For loads of 1 tf or less we suspend weights, for loads between 50 tf and 10 kgf we use deflection-type calibration instruments, and for loads between 500 tf and 1 tf we use volume-calibration instruments.

Translation 30

あざやかに		clearly, vividly
つつむ	【包む】	to wrap, envelop

　流体の流れの温度分布は、コレステリック液晶からの散光が、温度によってあざやかに色を変えることを利用して、可視化[カシカ = visualization]することができる。液晶をゼラチンのフィルムにつつんでカプセル状にしたものを液体中に分散して懸濁液[ケンダクエキ = suspension]を、フィルム状の光で照明[ショウメイ = illumination]することにより、任意の[ニンイの = arbitrary]断面[ダンメン = cross-section]内の温度分布を可視化[カシカ]することができる。

　　We can produce a visualization of the temperature distribution within a fluid flow, using the fact that the scattered light from cholesteric liquid crystals clearly changes color depending on the temperature. By encapsulating the liquid crystals within a film of gelatin, dispersing them throughout the liquid, and then illuminating the suspension with a thin plane of light, we can produce a visualization of the temperature distribution at an arbitrary cross-section.

Notes
Line 1: The は after the first phrase marks a topic; it is the object of 可視化する at the end of the clause. The comma after は alerts the reader to the fact that the relevant verb is much later in the sentence.
Line 4: フィルム状の光 is literally "a film-shaped [beam of] light," and a free translation is "a thin plane of light."

Translation 31

まじきり		partition
むつかしい	(or むずかしい)	difficult
大きくとる	おおきくとる	to make large

　最近の大きなビルでは、コアとよばれる中心部にいろいろな設備[セツビ = equipment]を集めるコアシステムが用いられている場合が多い。中心部にエレベーター、電気配線、換気用ダクトなどを集めておく。この中心部のコアに耐震壁[タイシンヘキ = earthquake-proof walls]を用いておけば、それ以外のところには、構造力学的にむつかしい問題がなくなるので、窓[まど = window]を大きくとったり、移動まじきりなどを効果的に使うことができる。

　　In contemporary large buildings, [builders] often use a core system in which they bring together a variety of equipment in the central part, called the core. In the central part they assemble elevators, electric wiring, ventilation ducts, and so on. If they use earthquake-proof walls in this central part — the core — then difficult structural mechanical problems at other places disappear. Therefore, they are able to do such things as making the windows large and using movable partitions effectively.

Notes
Line 1:　ビル is shortened from ビルディング; note that ビール is "beer."
Line 3:　集めておく = we assemble (for subsequent use). Normally in English we do not express the idea embodied in the auxiliary verb おく; the same applies in Line 4 with 用いておけば.
Line 3:　The particle の indicates apposition, and is sometimes translated as "i.e.,""known as," or "called"; for example, here この中心部のコア means the "central part, known as the core." Another example would be ともだちの井上先生[ともだちのいのうえセンセイ] "[my] friend (whose name is) Professor Inoue."
Line 4:　In 耐震壁, the first KANJI is a common prefix equivalent to the English suffix "proof." The second KANJI is one of the characters in 地震[ジシン] "earthquake."
Line 6:　大きくとったり = "we do such things as take." Note that in this case the verb する is omitted after the representative form of the verb.
Line 6:　If you cannot find まじきり in your dictionary you might try to piece together the meaning from the component parts; if you think the component parts are まじ and きり you will not have much success. When written in KANJI this word is 間仕切り, from which it is easier to see that it is made up of 間[ま] (space) and 仕切り (from the verb 仕切る[しきる] (to partition), an xu-verb).

Translation 32

…にはじまって		starting with …
あきる		to lose interest in
でき上がる	できあがる	to be completed
さきがけ		forerunner
こういう		this kind of
組みこみ	くみこみ	installation

　自動車[ジドウシャ = automobile]産業では、フォードにはじまってもともと少品種大量生産方式がとられた。ところが、それでは個性が無いというのでユーザーにあきられる。そこで同一の生産ラインを流しながら、でき上がった車[くるま = car]は違っているという生産方法を導入し始めた[from しはじめる = to begin doing]。FMSのさきがけである。これが現在一般に行われている多品種大量生産である。こういう生産ラインを効率的に運転するには特別な品質管理が必要である。すなわち、ライン中への自動検出装置の組みこみである。

In the automobile industry, originally starting with Ford, the method of small-variety mass production was adopted. However, [the cars] then have no individuality, and buyers lose interest in them. Thus [the companies] began introducing production methods in which the finished cars differed, even though they were running on identical production lines. This was the forerunner of FMS, which is the multiple-variety mass production generally being practiced today. To run this kind of production line efficiently, special quality control is needed, that is, the incorporation of on-line automatic detection equipment.

17-20

Notes

Line 2: Note that ところが is "but, however," whereas ところで means "by the way, incidentally." Some authors fail to follow this usage, thus blurring the distinction between the two phrases.

Lines 2-3: In 個性が無いというので the particle の is the nominalizer (like こと) and で is the connective of である, literally "The fact is that there is no individuality, and ...."

Translation 33

自発的に　　　　　　　　ジハツテキに　　　　　　　　　　spontaneously

　物質から全く自発的に放射線が放出される性質を放射能という。物質を構成する原子核の状態の変化にともなってエネルギーが放出されるので、放射能は核種に固有の性質である。自然に存在する物質でもこのような能力をもっているものがあるが、核反応等人工的に作られた物質の放射能を人工放射能という。放射性元素の原子は放射線を出して違った元素の原子に変換する。全体の原子の半分が変換してしまうまでの時間は元素の種類ごとに一定で、これをその元素の半減期という。

The property of radiation being emitted from substances completely spontaneously is called radioactivity. Because energy is emitted along with changes in the states of the atomic nuclei that make up the substances, radioactivity is a characteristic property of a nuclear species. Among materials that exist naturally, some have this kind of capability, and the radioactivity of substances made artificially, as in nuclear reactions, is called artificial radioactivity. The atoms of radioactive elements emit radioactive rays and are transmuted into atoms of different elements. The time for one-half of all the atoms to transmute is a constant for each kind of element, and this is called the half-life of that element.

Notes

Line 4: 核反応等: 等 at the end of a string of KANJI is almost always read など.

Line 6: In 変換してしまう the auxiliary verb しまう merely indicates that the action is completed.

Line 6: 原子...まで means "until half the atoms change." This clause modifies 時間 as indicated by the particle の.

Translation 34

ひろく　　　　　　　　【広く】　　　　　　　　　　　　widely

　本日の新聞[シンブン = newspaper]の記事によれば、日本では超[チョウ = super]高温材料[ザイリョウ = material]の開発を目的として、超[チョウ]高温材料[ザイリョウ = material]センターを設立するための準備[ジュンビ = preparation]が開始された[from カイシする = to commence]。超高温材料は、超々[チョウチョウ = hyper]音速航空機[コウクウキ = aircraft]や宇宙[ウチュウ = outerspace]機器などにひろく応用されるもので、最低1500℃から2000℃までのものと、2000℃以上のものとに分けて、2箇所[ニカショ = 2 places]に研究所が作られる。

17-21

According to an article in today's newspaper, preparations have commenced in Japan for establishment of a super-high-temperature materials center, with the objective of developing super-high-temperature materials. Super-high-temperature materials are (those that are) widely applied in hypersonic aircraft, outer-space instruments, and the like. Research institutes are being constructed at two locations, divided [as follows]: one for materials [for use] from a low of 1500°C up to 2000°C, the other for materials [for use] above 2000°C.

Notes
Lines 2-3: The clause 超高温材料センターを設立するため modifies 準備 as indicated by the particle の.
Line 5: 宇宙 means "cosmos" or "(outer) space." Hence, 宇宙線 means "cosmic rays."
Line 7: 2箇所[ニカショ] is sometimes written as 2個所 with the same pronunciation.

Translation 35

一環	イッカン	one step
ゆがむ		to distort
はやめる	【早める】	to hasten

　光通信の超大容量[チョウタイヨウリョウ = super-large capacity]化を進める一環として、超[チョウ = super]高速光パルスの波形[ハケイ = wave form]をフェムト秒[ビョウ = second]の精度[セイド = accuracy]で測定できる器械が開発された。光の波形[ハケイ]の測定精度[セイド]を一ケタ以上も向上させたことで、電送[デンソウ = electrical transmission]中に波形のゆがまない光源[コウゲン = light source]の開発がはやめられる。この器械は、ヨウ素酸リチウムを利用し、基準光にヘリウム・ネオン・レーザー光を用いている。

As one step in advancing the super-large-capacitization of optical communications, an instrument has been developed with which one can measure the wave form of a super-high-velocity light pulse with an accuracy of femtoseconds. [We] have improved by as much as one digit or more the accuracy of the light wave-form measurements and have hastened the development of a light source for which the wave form is not distorted during electrical transmission. The instrument utilizes lithium iodate and uses a helium-neon laser light as the standardizing light [source].

Note
Line 4: 一ケタ以上も[ひとけたイジョウも] means "as much as one digit or more"; 以上 means "or more," and も is best translated by "as much as."

Translation 36

ことば	【言葉】	language, words
あいまいな		vague
おそい	【遅い】	late

ファジー理論では、ことばによるあいまいな表現を的確に[テキカクに＝accurately]評価[ヒョウカ＝evaluation]し、判断[ハンダン＝judgment]や制御に利用する。例えば、品物の品質について、品位の高いもの、品位の低いものとか、速度が速いかおそいかとか、流量が減少するとか増加するとか、高品位の鉄と低品位の鉄といった表現を基にして、論理演算[エンザン＝operation]を行い、最適の結論を導く。このような方法を用いるとコンピュータの処理速度は必然的に極めて大きくなる。

In fuzzy theory we evaluate accurately expressions that are vague owing to the language, and use [them] for [making] judgments, in [exercising] control, and the like; for example, with regard to the quality of goods, we take as the basis the expressions for whether quality is high or low, whether speed is fast or slow, whether flow rate is increasing or decreasing, whether iron is high or low grade, and [then] perform logical operations and derive optimal conclusions. If we use these kinds of methods, the processing speed of computers inevitably becomes extremely large.

Notes
Lines 3-5: 品物...鉄といった modifies 表現. Hence, a literal translation would be something like "expressions in which [someone] has said that ...."
Line 4: とか is a conjunction ("and") that joins together two or more actions, states, or items in an incomplete listing.

Translation 37

通りぬける	とおりぬける	to pass through
ぶつかる		to collide
やや		moderately, fairly, rather
...にあたる		to agree with ...

　一般にニュートリノとして知られている素粒子は、地球も通りぬける性質がある。地下約1000メートルに設置された約3000トンの水タンクを中心とする大型の実験装置を用いて、地中を通りぬけてきたニュートリノが水中に散在する素粒子にぶつかったために起こる現象を観測した。この一年半[イチネンハン＝a year-and-a-half]の間に約450日分のデータをコンピュータ処理したところ、装置の機能で検出できるやや高いエネルギーのニュートリノ計約50個についてデータが得られた。この結果は理論的な計算値の約45％にあたると結論された。

The elementary particle generally known as the neutrino has the property of passing even through the earth. Using a large-scale experimental apparatus consisting mainly of a water tank of about 3000 tons located about 1000 m underground, [scientists] measured the phenomena that occur because neutrinos that have passed through the earth collided with elementary particles dispersed in the water. When they computer-processed some 450 days' worth of data taken during this year and one-half, they obtained data on a total of about 50 neutrinos, having the moderately high energies that they could detect with the capabilities of [their] equipment. It was concluded that the above figure was about 45% of the theoretically calculated value.

Notes
Line 2:　水タンク should be read みずタンク.
Line 5:　日分 is read ニチブン; the suffix 分 means something like "amount allotted for, amount sufficient for, amount corresponding to."
Line 7:　計 preceding a number means "altogether, in all, a total of." For example, 計3万円 means "a total of ¥30,000."

Translation 38

　橋かけ[はしかけ = cross-linked]全芳香族[ホウコウゾク = aromatic]ポリアミドを素材[ソザイ = material]とする脱塩層[ダツエンソウ = demineralization layer]と、これを一体的に支持する[シジする = to support]ポリスルホン支持層[シジソウ = support layer]、ポリエステル基材[キザイ = substrate]の3層[ソウ = layer]構造を有する複合膜[フクゴウマク = compound membrane]を使用した低圧逆浸透膜[ギャクシントウマク = reverse-osmosis membrane]エレメントが開発された。水処理用で、これによる処理水は超純[チョウジュン=ultra-pure]水として電子工業用に使用される。また、ボイラー用水用にも適している。

A low-pressure reverse-osmosis membrane element has been developed that uses a compound membrane having a three-layer structure: (i) a demineralization layer with a cross-linked wholly aromatic polyamide as its material, (ii) a polysulfone support layer that supports this [layer] as a single body, and (iii) a polyester substrate. It is used for water treatment, and the water processed by it is used as ultra-pure water in the electronics industry. It is also suitable for use [in treating] water used in boilers.

Translation 39

数多く	かずおおく	in large numbers
いままで	【今まで】	up to now
...の存在下	のソンザイカ	in the presence of ...
まとめ上げる	まとめあげる	to collect

　一般に加工熱処理のように相転移が関連している現象は工業的に数多く存在し、セラミックス、アモルファス合金等の例に見られるように、その重要性はますます増加している。ところがこれらの問題に関するいままでの研究は、それぞれの現象を個別に考察したものがほとんどであり、相変態の存在下における固体力学という観点から全般的に解析した、金属学者、化学者、物理学者、技術者の組織的研究が要求されている。本解説は問題の本質を明示し、関連する研究の現状と動向を記述したもので、ウィスコンシン大学における在外研究期間中にまとめ上げられたものである。

In general, phenomena related to phase transitions, as in thermomechanical treatment, are numerous in industry, and their importance is steadily increasing, as is seen in examples such as ceramics and amorphous alloys. However, almost all the research related to these problems up to now has considered each phenomenon individually, and what is needed is organized research — by metallurgists, chemists, physicists, and technologists — that analyzes [these phenomena] globally from the viewpoint of the mechanics of solids when phase transformations are present. This analysis will clarify the essence of the problem and discuss the current state and trends in related research, [based on material] collected during a period of research abroad at the University of Wisconsin.

Notes
Line 2: Keep in mind that 等, as the last in a string of KANJI, is read など.
Lines 5-6: Note that the clause ending with the verb 解析した modifies 組織的研究.
Line 7: 現状 is short for 現在の状態.
Line 8: In the compound verb まとめ上げる, the verb 上げる indicates that the action is completed.

Translation 40

ゆれる		to sway, shake
ゆれ		swaying, shaking
うち消す	うちけす	to eliminate
つり上げる	つりあげる	to suspend
おさえる		to suppress, curb

　近く開設されるビジネスパーク内に設置されるクリスタルタワーのために設計された制振装置では、振り子の原理を応用して、ビルがゆれる時にビルと反対の方向に振り子がゆれ、ビル全体のゆれをうち消し、ビルのゆれを一定限度内に設定する設定機構がある。ビルの最上部に約80トンの空調用タンクを5-6個つり上げ、このタンクを振り子にしてビルのゆれをおさえる。この制振装置により、最上部でのゆれをいままでの半分にすることができる。このため、ビルの構造設計における設計応力も低減することができた。クリスタルタワーは<u>来年</u>[ライネン＝next year]開場する。

In the vibration-control equipment designed for the Crystal Tower set up in the soon-to-open Business Park, [the designers] applied the principle of the pendulum. When the building sways the pendulum sways in a direction opposite to [the motion of] the building and eliminates the swaying of the building as a whole. This mechanism maintains the building sway within fixed limits. In the topmost part of the building five or six tanks of about 80 tons, used for air conditioning, have been suspended, and these tanks serve as pendulums and curb the sway of the building. By means of this vibration-control equipment, [designers] were able to make the sway at the top part one-half of the previous [amount]. Because of this, they could also lower the design stresses in the structural design of the building. Crystal Tower will open next year.

Translation 41

はじめて	【初めて】	for the first time
たがいに他の周り	たがいに夕のまわり	around each other

　地球の回転をはじめてニュートン力学の対象として論じたのはスイスの数理学者オイラーである。オイラーは、回転する楕円体[ダエンタイ＝ellipsoid]の短軸[タンジク＝minor axis]がその自転軸[ジテンジク＝axis of rotation]と一致[イッチ＝coincidence]していないとき、自転軸[ジテンジク]と短軸[タンジク]はたがいに他の周りに一定な周期で円錐[エンスイ＝cone]運動することを明らかにした。地球の円錐[エンスイ]運動の周期は300日程度と計算された。その後、アメリカのアマチュア天文学者[テンモンガクシャ＝astronomer]チャンドラーは、約430日の周期をもつ緯度[イド＝latitude]変化を観測した。理論計算の結果、周期が300日ではなく430日であったのは、地球が剛体[ゴウタイ＝rigid body]ではなく弾性体[ダンセイタイ＝elastic body]であるためと結論された。

The Swiss mathematician Euler was the first to discuss the rotation of the earth as a subject in Newtonian mechanics. Euler made it clear that when the minor axis of a rotating ellipsoid does not coincide with the axis of rotation, the axis of rotation and the minor axis execute a conical motion around each other with a fixed period. The period of the conical motion of the earth was calculated to be of the order of 300 days. Later the American amateur astronomer Chandler measured a latitude change that has a period of about 430 days. It was concluded — as a result of theoretical calculations — that the period was 430 days and not 300 because the earth is not a rigid body but an elastic body.

Notes
Line 2: 楕円 (ellipse) is now usually written だ円.
Line 3: The opposite of 短軸 is 長軸[チョウジク] (major axis).
Line 6: 300日 is read サンビャクニチ.
Line 11: ため (because) refers back to the clause 周期が...であったのは.

Translation 42

時代	ジダイ	era
過ぎる	すぎる	to pass by
つきとめる		to ascertain
ただ一つ	ただひとつ	one single
当面は	トウメンは	at present

人工知能の研究においては、コンピュータが論理学の法則にしたがって論理的に推論[スイロン＝deduction]する能力を開発するという時代は過ぎ、現在では人工知能用に多くの知識[チシキ＝knowledge]を蓄積する[チクセキする＝to store]ことが最も要求されている。

一例を上げると、物質の化学構造をつきとめるための人工知能システムとして開発されたデンドラルの場合、一般の化学分析のデータだけなら15,000,000通りもの構造が考えられる物質でも、質量分析や磁気測定に関する知識[チシキ]などを組み合わせてコンピュータに考えさせると、ただ一つの物質を同定した。

当面は蓄積する[チクセキする]知識の件数を100,000のけたにのせることが目的である。

In research on artificial intelligence the era in which we developed the capability of computers to make logical deductions in accordance with the laws of logic has ended. At present what is needed most of all is the storing of much information for use in artificial intelligence.

To give one example, [consider] the case of DENDRAL, which was developed as an artificial intelligence system for ascertaining the chemical structure of substances. Even with substances for which as many as 15,000,000 [chemical] structures can be considered if there are only analytical chemical data, if we supplement [the data] with knowledge from mass spectrometry and magnetic and other measurements, and then have the computer consider [all the facts], it identifies one single substance.

As for now, the goal is to increase the number of items of knowledge that we store to the order of 100,000.

Notes
Lines 6-7:   The 通り in 15,000,000通りもの構造 is a counter for ways of doing things, and も is best translated by "as many as."
Line 10:   当面は has about the same meaning as 現在では "for now, at the present time."

Translation 43

できる限り	できるかぎり	as much as possible
みたす		to fill
きりかく		to notch

2サイクル機関ではバルブがないため、吸入、排気[ハイキ＝exhaust]の行程はピストンの作用とガスの流れによらなければならない。新しい[あたらしい＝fresh]混合気[コンゴウキ＝gas mixture]が燃焼室[ネンショウシツ＝combustion chamber]に流入すると同時に燃焼[ネンショウ＝combustion]ガスを燃焼室[ネンショウシツ]からできる限り排気[ハイキ]させ、燃焼室を新しい[あたらしい]混合気[コンゴウキ]でみたす。この行程を掃気[ソウキ＝scavenging]といって、2サイクル機関の性能を定める最も重要なものである。

対流掃気[ソウキ]法は、反転掃気法の一種で、ピストンの一部をきりかいて新しい混合気の通路としたもので、新しい混合気はシリンダー壁面[ヘキメン = wall surface]にそって上昇し[from ジョウショウする = rise]、上部で反転する。燃焼[ネンショウ]ガスは対流により排出する。

Because there are no valves in a two-cycle engine, the intake and exhaust strokes must depend on the action of the piston and the flow of the gas. At the same time that a fresh gas mixture flows into the combustion chamber, the burned gases are exhausted from the combustion chamber as much as possible, and it is filled with a fresh gas mixture. This stroke is called scavenging, and it is the most important one for determining the performance of a two-cycle engine.

Convection scavenging is one form of reversed scavenging. A part of the piston is notched to make a path for the fresh gas mixture; the fresh gas mixture rises along the surface of the cylinder wall, and reverses its direction of flow in the upper part. The burned gases are exhausted by convection.

Translation 44

うすい	【薄い】	thin
たちまち		suddenly
生かす	いかす	to make good use of
はずれる	【外れる】	to deviate, slip off

物質はどこまでうすい旋削[センサク = lathe turning]ができるか、という研究のため、銅の試験片[シケンペン = test piece]を10cm/secの速さで旋削[センサク]し、刃物[はもの = cutting tool]に加わる力を測定した。切り込み[きりこみ = depth of cut]が4-10ミクロン程度なら150kgf/mm²位であったが、2ミクロン位からたちまち大きくなり、0.5ミクロン程度で約3倍の500kgf/mm²近くになった。

結晶粒が集まってできた金属などの場合、100ミクロン程度の切り込み[きりこみ]では、結晶粒の境界[キョウカイ = boundary]にそって分離が起きる。切り込みが10ミクロン程度になると、結晶中の転位を生かしながら、旋削が進む。ところが、切り込みが1ミクロンくらいになると、転位間の距離と同程度になるため、転位を生かしながら分離を進めることがむつかしく、転位からはずれることが多くなる。これが旋削力増大の原因[ゲンイン =cause]である。

In order to research [the question] of how thinly we can turn materials on a lathe, we machined a copper test piece at a speed of 10 cm/sec, and measured the force supplied to the cutting tool. At a cutting depth of the order of 4-10 microns, [the force] was about 150 kgf/mm²; below about 2 microns it suddenly became larger, and at about 0.5 microns it came close to 500 kgf/mm², about three times as large.

At a cutting depth of the order of 100 microns, for metals or other materials formed by the agglomeration of crystalline grains, separation occurs along the boundaries of the crystalline grains. If the cutting depth becomes of the order of 10 microns, the lathe-turning makes good use of the dislocations within the crystals as it proceeds. If the cutting depth becomes about 1 micron, however, it is now of the same order of magnitude as the distance between dislocations. Therefore, it is difficult for the separation [of the metal] to proceed by making good use of the dislocations, and slippages from [the dislocations] become frequent. This is the cause of the increase in the lathe-turning force.

Translation 45

ならべる	【並べる】	to align, line up
ひずみ		strain, deformation
かねそなえる	【兼ね備える】	to combine
われわれ		we

　高分子鎖[サ＝chain]中に大きな双極子[ソウキョクシ＝dipole]モーメントを有する原子や原子団[ダン＝group]を導入し、これを同一方向にならべるように高次構造制御を行うと、高分子圧電体を作成することができる。圧電体は力を加えると電圧が発生し、逆[ギャク＝converse]に交流電圧を加えると周期的ひずみを生ずる。したがって、これらの性質を利用すると、マイクロホンやスピーカーに応用することが可能[カノウ＝possibility]になる。

　導電性材料[ザイリョウ＝material]は通常光を反射したり、吸収[キュウシュウ＝absorption]するため、不透明[トウメイ＝transparent]である。しかし、光と作用し合うキャリヤの数や、その移動度を加減すると、透明性[トウメイセイ＝transparency]と電導性をかねそなえた材料[ザイリョウ]を合成することが可能[カノウ]になる。われわれは、ピロールを気相重合することによって透明[トウメイ]導電性が発現することを見いだした。これによって、ポリフッ化ビニリデン圧電フィルム上にポリピロールを重合して、透明薄膜[ハクマク＝thin membrane]スピーカーを作成した。

If we introduce atoms or groups of atoms with large dipole moments into a polymer chain, and if we control the high-order structure so as to line up the dipoles in the same direction, we can produce a polymer piezoelectric material. If we impose a force on a piezoelectric material a voltage is produced; and conversely, if we impose an alternating current, a periodic strain is generated. Therefore, by using these properties, it becomes possible to use [polymers] for microphones and speakers.

Because conducting materials ordinarily reflect and absorb light, they are nontransparent. However, if we adjust the number of light-sensitive carriers and their mobility, it becomes possible to synthesize materials that combine transparency and electrical conductivity. We have discovered that, by the gas-phase polymerization of pyrrole, the properties of transparency and conductivity emerge. By polymerizing polypyrrole on a piezoelectric film of polyfluorovinylidene with this [technique], we produced a transparent thin-membrane speaker.

結びつく	むすびつく	to be attached
つける	【付ける】	to tag, attach
ひろく	【広く】	widely
やすい	【安い】	cheap
かるい	【軽い】	light {in weight}
ふせぐ	【防ぐ】	to shut out, protect against
こわす	【壊す】	to destroy

　フロンガスは、炭化水素に塩素とフッ素が結合した有機化合物で、結びつくフッ素などの数によってF11、F12といった記号がつけられた、いくつかの種類がある。地表では人体に直接の毒性[ドクセイ = toxicity]がなく、化学的にも安定しているので、クーラー、ヒートポンプの冷媒[レイバイ = refrigerant]、スプレー製品[セイヒン = product]、半導体、プリント基盤[キバン = (printed)-circuit board]など電子部品の洗浄剤[センジョウザイ = clean-ing agent]、発泡スチロール[ハッポウスチロール = Styrofoam]製造[セイゾウ =manufacture]などにひろく使われ、これ以上使いやすい製品[セイヒン]はないという意味[イミ = meaning]で、「究極の洗浄剤[センジョウザイ]」ともよばれている。

　問題は、空気よりかるいため、地表で放散されたフロンガスが成層圏[セイソウケン = stratosphere]まで上がり、太陽[タイヨウ = sun]からの過度の紫外線[シガイセン = ultraviolet rays]をふせいでいるオゾン層[ソウ = layer]を光化学反応でこわし、その結果、地表に注ぐ紫外線[シガイセン]が増加することである。

　このため、F11、F12、F113、F114、F115の5種類のフロンガスに対して規制[キセイ = regulation]の処置がとられている。これら規制[キセイ]対象のフロンガスの代替品[ダイタイヒン = substitute]として、クロロジフルオロメタン、ジクロロトリフルオロエタン、クロロテトラフルオロエタンなどが考えられている。

The Freon gases are organic compounds in which chlorine and fluorine are combined with a hydrocarbon. There are several kinds of [Freons], to which the symbols F11, F12, etc., have been assigned, depending on the number of attached fluorine or other atoms. Because on (the surface of) earth they are not directly toxic to human beings and (in addition) are chemically stable, they are widely used for such things as refrigerants in air-conditioners and heat pumps, spray products, Styrofoam manufacture, and cleaning agents for electrical parts such as semiconductor printed-circuit boards; they are even referred to as "ultimate cleansing agents," meaning that there are no commercial products that are easier to use than these [Freons].

The problem is that because they are lighter than air, the Freon gases dispersed at the surface of the earth rise up to the stratosphere and by photochemical reactions destroy the ozone layer that shuts out the excessive ultraviolet rays from the sun, and as a result the ultraviolet rays that pour down on the earth increase.

Because of this, regulatory measures are now being taken against five kinds of Freons, F11, F12, F113, F114, and F115. As substitutes for these Freon gases, subject to regulation, chlorodifluoromethane, dichlorotrifluoroethane, chlorotetra-fluoroethane, and other compounds are being considered.

Notes

Line 1: フロン is sometimes written as フレオン.

Line 7: 発泡[ハッポウ] means literally "produce bubbles." Note that スチロール (styrene) comes from the German *Styrol.*

音	オン	sound
	おと	sound

送	ソウ	transmitting
	おく(る)	to send, transmit

確	カク	certain
	たし(かめる)	to confirm, make certain
	たし(かな)	certain, sure

帯	タイ	band, zone, belt
	お(びる)	to put a band around;
		to take on (a color)

屈	クツ	bending (over)

達	タツ	attainment
	タッ(する)	to attain, reach

系	ケイ	system

端	タン	tip, end
	はし	tip, end

抗	コウ	opposite; anti-

断	ダン	cutting off
	た(つ)	to cut off
	ことわ(る)	to give notice, warn

縮	シュク	shrinking
	ちぢ(める)	to compress
	ちぢ(まる)	to shrink
	ちぢ(まない)	incompressible

抵	テイ	resistance

静	ジョウ; セイ	silent, quiet
	しず(かな)	silent, quiet

統	トウ	governing; lineage

図	ズ; ト	diagram, drawing
	はか(る)	to devise

粘	ネン	viscous
	ねば(る)	to be sticky

折	セツ	folding, bending
	お(る)	to fold, bend

波	ハ	wave
	なみ	wave

層	ソウ	layer

板	ハン; バン	plate, board
	いた	plate, board

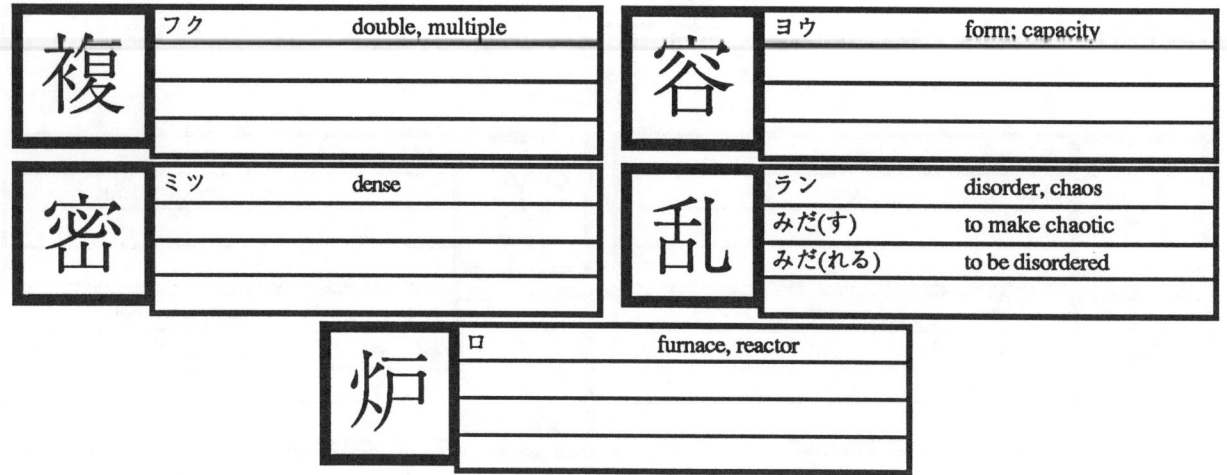

複	フク	double, multiple

容	ヨウ	form; capacity

密	ミツ	dense

乱	ラン	disorder, chaos
	みだ(す)	to make chaotic
	みだ(れる)	to be disordered

炉	ロ	furnace, reactor

VOCABULARY

音

音波	オンパ	sound wave
音圧	オンアツ	sound pressure
音速	オンソク	speed of sound
亜音速	アオンソク	subsonic speed
音子	オンシ	phonon
音素	オンソ	phoneme
音程	オンテイ	musical interval
全音	ゼンオン	whole tone
半音	ハンオン	half tone
音色	ねいろ {N.B. ね, not おと}	(sound) timbre
音の高さ	おとのたかさ	pitch
音響抵抗	オンキョウテイコウ	acoustic resistance
音響結合	オンキョウケツゴウ	acoustic coupling

確

確立する	カクリツする	to establish
確率	カクリツ	probability
確率関数	カクリツカンスウ	probability function
確率分布	カクリツブンプ	probability distribution
確率過程	カクリツカテイ	stochastic process
事前確率	ジゼンカクリツ	a priori probability
事後確率	ジゴカクリツ	a posteriori probability
確実性	カクジツセイ	certainty, reliability
正確な	セイカクな	exact

屈

屈折	クッセツ	refraction
屈曲性ポリマー	クッキョクセイポリマー	flexible polymer
屈性	クッセイ	tropism
光屈性	ひかりクッセイ	phototropism
化学屈性	カガククッセイ	chemotropism

系

太陽系	タイヨウケイ	solar system
単位系	タンイケイ	system of units
体系	タイケイ	system
断熱体系	ダンネツタイケイ	adiabatic system
反応系	ハンノウケイ	reaction system
質点系	シッテンケイ	mass-point system
帯系	タイケイ	band system {spectroscopy}
系統的に	ケイトウテキに	systematically

抗

抵抗	テイコウ	resistance, drag
粘性抵抗	ネンセイテイコウ	viscous drag
抵抗係数	テイコウケイスウ	drag coefficient
抵抗接地系統	テイコウセッチケイトウ	resistance-grounded (neutral) system
抗原	コウゲン	antigen
抗体	コウタイ	antibody
異性抗体	イセイコウタイ	heterogenetic antibody

縮

圧縮	アッシュク	compression
圧縮性流体	アッシュクセイリュウタイ	compressible fluid
縮合重合体	シュクゴウジュウゴウタイ	condensation polymer
重縮合	ジュウシュクゴウ	condensation polymerization
縮合環	シュクゴウカン	condensed ring
縮図	シュクズ	reduced figure

静

静圧	セイアツ	static pressure
静水圧	セイスイアツ	hydrostatic pressure
静磁場	セイジば	static magnetic field
静電位	セイデンイ	electrostatic potential
静止質量	セイシツリョウ	rest mass

図

図形	ズケイ	figure
図式	ズシキ	graph
図解	ズカイ	explanatory diagram
図示する	ズシする	to illustrate
管理図	カンリズ	control chart
平面図形	ヘイメンズケイ	plane figure
線図	センズ	line drawing

折

回折	カイセツ	diffraction
屈折率	クッセツリツ	index of refraction
屈折波	クッセツハ	refracted wave
屈折角	クッセツカク	angle of refraction

層

層流	ソウリュウ	laminar flow
層位学	ソウイガク	stratigraphy {geol}
層状の	ソウジョウの	stratified
二重層	ニジュウソウ	double layer
単分子層	タンブンシソウ	monomolecular layer
積層成形	セキソウセイケイ	laminate molding
石炭層	セキタンソウ	coal seam
断層	ダンソウ	fault {geol}
地層	チソウ	stratum

送

送り出す	おくりだす	to send out
送信機	ソウシンキ	transmitter
送信所	ソウシンショ	transmitting station
送信する	ソウシンする	to transmit
送受信波	ソウジュシンハ	transceived waves
伝送回線	デンソウカイセン	transmission line
伝送(線)路	デンソウ(セン)ロ	transmission line
伝送特性	デンソウトクセイ	transmission characteristics
放送	ホウソウ	broadcasting {radio or TV}

帯

帯水層	タイスイソウ	aquifer
帯電	タイデン	electrification
帯電体	タイデンタイ	charged body
帯状の	タイジョウの	belt-shaped, zonal

| 極光帯 | キョクコウタイ | auroral zone |
| 熱帯 | ネッタイ | tropics |

達

達成する	タッセイする	to achieve
発達する	ハッタツする	to develop
伝達する	デンタツする	to transmit
伝達関数	デンタツカンスウ	transfer function {process control}
熱伝達係数	ネツデンタツケイスウ	heat transfer coefficient

端

端子	タンシ	terminal
端子板	タンシバン	terminal assembly
端子電圧	タンシデンアツ	terminal voltage
端面図	タンメンズ	end view
両端	リョウタン	both ends
極端	キョクタン	extremity

断

断熱-	ダンネツ	adiabatic
断熱変化	ダンネツヘンカ	adiabatic change
断熱消磁	ダンネツショウジ	adiabatic demagnetization
断面積	ダンメンセキ	cross-sectional area
断面図	ダンメンズ	cross-sectional drawing
断層面	ダンソウメン	fault plane
断続的な	ダンゾクテキな	intermittent
中断する	チュウダンする	to interrupt

抵

電気抵抗	デンキテイコウ	electrical resistance
抵抗率	テイコウリツ	resistivity
抵抗温度計	テイコウオンドケイ	resistance thermometer
抵抗成分	テイコウセイブン	resistive component
抵抗素子	テイコウソシ	resistor element
抵抗器	テイコウキ	resistor
抵抗体	テイコウタイ	resistor

統

統計力学	トウケイリキガク	statistical mechanics
統計法則	トウケイホウソク	statistical law
統一場理論	トウイツばリロン	unified-field theory
系統学	ケイトウガク	systematics
数理統計学	スウリトウケイガク	mathematical statistics

粘

粘性	ネンセイ	viscosity
粘度	ネンド	viscosity
粘性流体	ネンセイリュウタイ	viscous fluid
粘液	ネンエキ	mucilage {biol}
粘液層	ネンエキソウ	slime layer
粘液酸	ネンエキサン	mucic acid
動粘性率	ドウネンセイリツ	coefficient of kinematic viscosity

波

波長	ハチョウ	wave length
波動関数	ハドウカンスウ	wave function
波動論	ハドウロン	wave theory
波動力学	ハドウリキガク	wave mechanics
波形	ハケイ	wave form
波数	ハスウ	wave number
周波数	シュウハスウ	frequency
導波管	ドウハカン	wave guide
電波	デンパ	radio wave
電磁波	デンジハ	electromagnetic wave
一次波	イチジハ	primary wave
二次波	ニジハ	secondary wave
球面波	キュウメンハ	spherical wave
反射波	ハンシャハ	reflected wave
津波	つなみ	tsunami, tidal wave

板

平板	ヘイバン	flat plate
銅板	ドウバン	copper plate
半波長板	ハンハチョウバン	half-wave plate
接地板	セッチバン	grounded plate
板金加工	バンキンカコウ	sheet metal working
合板	ゴウハン	plywood
積層板	セキソウバン	laminate
基板	キバン	substrate
板状の	バンジョウの; いたジョウの	plate-shaped

複

複塩	フクエン	double salt
複屈折	フククッセツ	double refraction, birefringence
複素数	フクソスウ	complex number
複合波	フクゴウハ	composite wave

複分解	フクブンカイ	double decomposition
複合タンパク質	フクゴウタンパクシツ	conjugated protein

密

密度	ミツド	density
密接な	ミッセツな	close, near
密集する	ミッシュウする	to crowd together
密生する	ミッセイする	to grow thickly

容

容積	ヨウセキ	volume, capacity
容量分析	ヨウリョウブンセキ	volumetric analysis
容量	ヨウリョウ	capacity
熱容量	ネツヨウリョウ	heat capacity
電気容量	デンキヨウリョウ	capacitance
(圧力)容器	(アツリョク)ヨウキ	(pressure) vessel

乱

乱流	ランリュウ	turbulent flow
乱数	ランスウ	random number
乱反射	ランハンシャ	diffuse reflection
散乱	サンラン	scattering
光散乱	ひかりサンラン	light scattering
小角散乱	ショウカクサンラン	small-angle scattering

炉

原子炉	ゲンシロ	nuclear reactor
熱中性子炉	ネッチュウセイシロ	thermal (neutron) reactor
炉心	ロシン	reactor core
高炉	コウロ	blast furnace
反射炉	ハンシャロ	reverberatory furnace
平炉	ヘイロ	open-hearth furnace
電気炉	デンキロ	electric furnace
抵抗炉	テイコウロ	resistance furnace

Ex 18.3

導電率	ドウデンリツ	electrical conductivity, conductance
中空-	チュウクウ	hollow
単位長	タンイチョウ	unit length
位相	イソウ	phase
形式	ケイシキ	form
標的	ヒョウテキ	target

Ex 18.4

おもに	【主に】	primarily, mainly
多糖体	タトウタイ	polysaccharide
接地する	セッチする	to ground {elec}
粒径	リュウケイ	particle-diameter
入射する	ニュウシャする	to be incident
相対論的な	ソウタイロンテキな	relativistic
導線	ドウセン	lead wire
成形	セイケイ	molding
多数	タスウ	large number

Ex 18.5

発する	ハッする	to arise
対地高度	タイチコウド	elevation
受信する	ジュシンする	to receive
無線-	ムセン	wireless, radio
下地	したジ	base, foundation
流路	リュウロ	passage, channel
たもつ		to maintain
こえる		to go beyond, surpass
重率	ジュウリツ	weight

Ex 18.6(1)

適用する	テキヨウする	to apply
直進する	チョクシンする	to propagate linearly
前進する	ゼンシンする	to advance
前方	ゼンポウ	front
後方	コウホウ	back
出発(点)	シュッパツ(テン)	(point of) departure

Ex 18.6(2)

かつては		previously
流線形-	リュウセンケイ	streamlined

機関	キカン	engine
出現	シュツゲン	emergence
ひろがる	【広がる】	to broaden, widen

Ex 18.6(3)

ばく大な	ばくダイな	huge, enormous
とうてい {+ neg}		not at all, not nearly
実測	ジッソク	actual measurements
量的な	リョウテキな	quantitative
日常生活	ニチジョウセイカツ	daily life
極微の	キョクビの	(ultra)microscopic
たいせつな	【大切な】	important
実体の	ジッタイの	real
たとえ...あろうと 　なかろうと		whether it is or is not ...
微細な	ビサイな	minute, tiny
構成要素	コウセイヨウソ	component {lit.: constituent element}
全体的に	ゼンタイテキに	overall
物質観	ブッシツカン	image of [the nature of] matter
見地	ケンチ	point of view

18 Vocabulary Building and Readings in Physics

EXERCISES

Ex 18.1 Look-alike KANJI

Beginning with this lesson, you will have an exercise involving pairs of KANJI that have a common feature and thus might be confused. For each pair, numbered (1) and (2), you will be given two other KANJI, each of which will form a meaningful JUKUGO with only one of the given KANJI. You are to indicate the appropriate KANJI by writing its number, then to give the pronunciation of the resulting JUKUGO in KANA along with its English meaning.

Example:

(1) 層 (2) 増	(2)加 ゾウカ increase	(1)流 ソウリュウ laminar flow

1. (1) 続 (2) 統	連( )	系( )
2. (1) 低 (2) 抵	( )抗	( )温
3. (1) 倍 (2) 部	( )分	( )数
4. (1) 容 (2) 溶	( )積	( )液
5. (1) 反 (2) 板	( )金	( )対
6. (1) 析 (2) 折	回( )	分( )
7. (1) 系 (2) 係	無関( )	単位( )
8. (1) 出 (2) 屈	( )力	( )折
9. (1) 能 (2) 態	状( )	( )率
10.(1) 伝 (2) 転	( )達	( )位
11.(1) 時 (2) 特	( )間	( )別
12.(1) 表 (2) 素	元( )	周期( )
13.(1) 胞 (2) 飽	( )和	( )子
14.(1) 陽 (2) 場	( )子	磁( )
15.(1) 流 (2) 硫	( )体	( )酸
16.(1) 速 (2) 連	( )続	( )度

18-10

Ex 18.2 Matching Japanese and English technical terms

(a) Equipment and materials

原子炉( )　　1. nuclear reactor
高炉( )　　　2. blast furnace
合板( )　　　3. flat plate
接地板( )　　4. grounded plate
送信機( )　　5. laminate
積層板( )　　6. open-hearth furnace
送信所( )　　7. plywood
反射炉( )　　8. reverberatory furnace
平板( )　　　9. transmitter
平炉( )　　10. transmitting station

(b) Waves and sound

音圧( )　　　1. acoustic
音響( )　　　2. composite wave
音色( )　　　3. electromagnetic wave
音素( )　　　4. musical interval
音程( )　　　5. phoneme
音波( )　　　6. sound pressure
電磁波( )　　7. sound wave
波面( )　　　8. timbre
波長( )　　　9. wave length
複合波( )　10. wave surface

(c) Figures, systems, and zones

極光帯( )　　1. auroral zone
極端( )　　　2. band system
縮図( )　　　3. cross-sectional drawing
図形( )　　　4. line drawing
図式( )　　　5. end view
線図( )　　　6. extremity
帯系( )　　　7. figure
体系( )　　　8. graph
端面図( )　　9. reduced figure
断面図( )　10. system

(d) Words with common suffixes

化学屈性( ) 1. capacitance
光屈性( )　2. chemotropism
石炭層( )　3. coal seam
層流( )　　4. complex number
電気容量( ) 5. heat capacity
熱容量( )　6. laminar flow
粘液層( )　7. phototropism
複素数( )　8. random number
乱数( )　　9. slime layer
乱流( )　　10. turbulent flow

Ex 18.3 Matching Japanese technical terms and definitions

(a) Wave-related concepts

亜音速( )　　1. 導電率の高い中空導管からなるマイクロ波の伝送路。
音子( )　　　2. 波において、単位長の間に同じ状態がくりかえされる数。
音程( )　　　3. 流体の速度がその流体を伝わる音波の速度より遅い[おそい
小角散乱( )　　 = slow]場合の流れ。
導波管( )　　4. 波上で同一位相にあるとなり合った二点の間の距離。
波数( )　　　5. 電子を物質の波として見なす量子力学の1形式。
波長( )　　　6. 単色X線の物質による散乱で、とくに3°くらいまでの小さい
波動力学( )　　 散乱角で生ずるもの。
　　　　　　　7. 2音の高さの関係を示す量で、2音の周波数比で表すもの。
　　　　　　　8. 結晶中の電子と結晶格子[コウシ = lattice]イオンとの相互[ソ
　　　　　　　　 ウゴ = mutual]作用によって起こる結晶格子[コウシ]振動を
　　　　　　　　 量子化したもの。

(b) Physical and chemical terms

断面積( )　　1. 絶縁[ゼツエン = insulation]された導体に電気量Qを与えたと
重縮合( )　　 き、導体の電位がVだけ高くなった場合、Q/Vの量。
帯電( )　　　2. 岩石[ガンセキ = rock]や地層が破壊[ハカイ = fracture]されて
断層( )　　　 生じる不連続面。
抵抗比( )　　3. 物体に電荷[デンカ = electric charge]を帯びさせること、また
粘性抵抗( )　　 電荷[デンカ]をもった状態。
電気容量( )　4. 粘性流体中を物体が速さUで動くとき、物体にはたらく抵抗
密度( )　　　 のうちUに比例する一つの部分。
複分解( )　　5. 交流に対する抵抗と直流に対する抵抗の割合。
　　　　　　　6. 1つの量が空間、面または線の上に分布しているとき、微小
　　　　　　　　 部分に含まれる量の体積、面積または長さに対する比。
　　　　　　　7. 粒子の衝突[ショウトツ = collision]がおこる確率を標的の面
　　　　　　　　 積として表す量。
　　　　　　　8. 2種の化合物が成分を交換して、違った2種の化合物を生ずる
　　　　　　　　 反応。
　　　　　　　9. 縮合しながら重合する反応。

Ex 18.4 Translate the following sentences

1. 抗原とは生体を刺激[シゲキ = stimulus]し、特異な抗体をつくらせるも
   とになる物質である。おもにタンパク質であるが、多糖体、リン脂質な
   どもある。

2. 抵抗接地系統とは中性点が抵抗を通じて接地されている電力方式である。

3. 光散乱法とは光散乱を利用して高分子、コロイド粒子、バクテリアなどの微粒子の大きさ(分子量)、形、粒径分布、溶媒[ヨウバイ = solvent]や溶質の濃度[ノウド = concentration]などを測定する方法である。

4. 伝送特性は電力、信号、情報などを伝送線路を通して伝送する場合、入力端子と出力端子の所での電圧、電流などの減衰量[ゲンスイリョウ = attenuation]、位相量などを周波数あるいは時間に対して示した伝送路の特性である。

5. 複屈折とは光学的に異方性の物質に光が入射して、互いに[たがいに = mutually]垂直な[スイチョクな = perpendicular]直線偏光[ヘンコウ = polarized light]が二通りに屈折する現象である。

6. 非[ヒ = non-]圧縮性流体とは、密度は変化しないと考えてもよいような流体であり、ふつう液体はこう考えてよいが、場合によっては気体をこう扱う[あつかう = to treat]ことがある。

7. 静止[セイシ = rest]質量とは、相対論的力学で質量の定義[テイギ = definition]に速度によって変化する値を用いるとき速度0の場合の質量でニュートン力学の質量と同じものである。

8. 質点系とはいくつかの質点からなる系であるが、一般の連続体も質点系からの極限として考えることができる。

9. 断熱消磁とは液体ヘリウムによって低温(0.3°K以下の低温)を得る方法であり、常磁性体を等温で磁化した後、断熱状態で磁場をのぞく。

10. 端子板の一種には電気機械の導線と外部回路との接続点に設ける小型端子多数を合成樹脂[ジュシ = resin]の成形で集合固定したものがある。

11. 音響結合とは、一つの電話[デンワ = telephone]系に他の電話[デンワ]系を接続するのに直接電気回路を接続することなく、一方の電話系の電話機[デンワキ = telephone]の送話器[ソウワキ = transmitter]と受話器[ジュワキ = receiver]に対し、音波を介して[from カイする = through the medium of]他方の電話系の受話器[ジュワキ]と送話器[ソウワキ]に結合することである。

12. 高さと大きさが同じ音でも、人の耳[みみ = ear]には違った音と感じられる[from かんじる = to sense]場合には音色が違うという。音色は音のスペクトルや波形、音圧およびそれらの時間的変化などに関係がある。

13. 変数が不連続的である場合に変数のとりうる値の確率を、また連続的なときは確率密度を、この変数の関数として見なす場合それを確率関数という。

14. 容器の壁[かべ = wall]に作用する気体の圧力は、壁[かべ]1m² あたり毎秒[マイビョウ = every second]10^{28}個にも及ぶ多数の分子が数百m/sの速さで衝突[ショウトツ = collision]する衝撃[ショウゲキ = impulse]の平均[ヘイキン = average]結果である。

15. 信号伝送要素の入力、出力をそれぞれx(t)、y(t)とし、それぞれのラプラス変換をX(s)、Y(s)としたとき、Y(s)/X(s)の比を伝達関数という。

Ex 18.5 Read the following short essays for comprehension

1．抵抗炉とは抵抗体を電流が通るとき発するジュール熱を利用する電気炉である。加熱すべきものを抵抗体とするものと、特別の抵抗体(ニクロム線、白金など)を用いるものとがある。前者は直接抵抗加熱方式といい、後者は間接抵抗加熱方式という。

Adapted from p. 526 of 『電気用語辞典』, コロナ社, 1982.

2．航空機[コウクウキ = aircraft]が安全に飛行[ヒコウ = flying]するために電波はよく利用される。例えば、電波高度計がある。この高度計によって航空機[コウクウキ]が自己の[ジコの = its own]対地高度を知るために、地上へ向けて電波を送信し、その地表面からの反射波を受信し、送受信波の時間差[サ = difference]から、対地高度を求めることができる。また無線航空局[コウクウキョク = navigation station]が電波の直進性、定速性を利用して、航空機を目的地に導く、いわゆる無線航法[ムセンコウホウ = radio navigation]方式がある。

Adapted from ibid., pp. 568, 809.

3．半導体集積回路などを形成するために、回路素子を組み立てる下地となる板状の物体を基板という。基板材料[ザイリョウ = materials]としてはガラス、アルミナ、セラミック、シリコーンなどの絶縁物[ゼツエンブツ = insulating substance]あるいは半導体が使われる。

Adapted from ibid., p. 148.

4．流体の流れの状態は、一般に流速を次第にあげていくと、層流から乱流へ移っていく。流れの状態は流体の種類、流路の大きさなどの条件により異なるが、いわゆるレノルズ数Reはそのような相違に無関係な無次元の数であり、流れが層流であるか乱流であるか大体の区別[クベツ = distinction]をつけることができる。すなわち、流速、流体の種類が異なっていても、Reが等しければ流れの状態に変わりはないから、レノルズ数は流れを分類するためにきわめて重要である。この数は円管[エンカン = cylindrical pipe]内の流れが層流から乱流へ遷移[センイ = transition]する条件を記述するパラメーターとしてレノルズが導入した(1879)。すなわち、円管[エンカン]に水を流すとき、流れのレノルズ数Re = dU/v(dは円管の直径、Uは平均[ヘイキン = average]流速 = 流量/断面積、vは動粘性率)が大体2100よりも小さければ、管内の流れは規則的に[キソクテキに =regularly]流線をたもち、Reが2100をこえると、流れは時間的に複雑な[フクザツな = complicated]変動を行なって乱れた状態になる。

5．熱力学的重率とは、統計力学的系において巨視的[キョシテキ = macro-scopic]状態変数の値を定めてある状態を指定[シテイ =designation]するとき、この条件のもとに許される[from ゆるす = to allow]微視的[ビシテキ = micro-scopic]状態の数、すなわち、量子力学的固有状態の数をいう。この数はその巨視的[キョシテキ]状態の統計学的重率を与え、その対数はボルツマンの原理により、エントロピーに比例する。

Adapted from p. 955 of 『理化学辞典』, 第四版, 岩波書店, 1987.

Ex 18.6 Read the following longer essays for comprehension

1．ホイヘンス(C. Huygens)は波動論の立場から光の伝搬[デンパン = propa-gation]の機構を説明するために、次のような原理を解説した。ある瞬間[シュンカン = instant]の波面上のすべての点は、新しい[あたらしい = new]波の源[みなもと = origin]となって、球面波を送り出す。短[タン = short]時間たった後の波面は、これらの球面波つまり2次波の包絡[ホウラク = envelope]面として求まる。

　図6.1(a)は、点0から生じた球面波の伝搬[デンパン]の仕方が、ホイヘンスの原理によっていかに与えられるかを示している。ある瞬間[シュンカン]の波面が球面S₁であったとすると、S₁上の各点から生じた2次波の包絡[ホウラク]面は、次の瞬間の波面であるS₂になっている。ホイヘンスはこの原理によって光の反射・屈折の現象を説明したし、また、この原理は光に限らず一般の波の性質を理解する上にも役立つ[ヤクだつ = to be helpful]。しかし、図6.1(a)の球面波が穴[あな = hole]のあいた衝立[ついたて = partition]にあたった場合にこれを適用すると、図6.1(b)のように、波は直進して幾何学的な[キカガクテキな = geometrical]影をつくる。つまり、回折は起こらないことになってしまう。また、図6.1では2次波の波面を前方だけに限ったが、球面波とする以上2次波はあらゆる方向へ一様に[イチヨウに = uniformly]伝搬しなければならない。そうすると、前進する波と同時に後退[コウタイ = retro-gression]する波も生じてしまう。もちろんこのような後退[コウタイ]波は存在しない。

　これらの欠点[ケッテン = defect]を取り除く[とりのぞく = to remove]ために、フレネル(A. J. Fresnel)は、(i) 2次波は球面波ではあるが前方で強く後方で弱い[よわい = weak]こと、(ii) このような2次波が重なり合って、すなわち干渉[カンショウ = interference]して新しい[あたらしい]波面ができることを仮定[カテイ　=hypothesis]した。後にキルヒホッフ(G. R. Kirchhoff)は、波動方程式から出発してフレネルのこの考え方に数学的に厳密な[ゲンミツな = rigorous]形式を与えた。

　このホイヘンス-フレネルの原理は次のようにいい表せる。光源[コウゲン = light source]Oから発した光が任意の[ニンイの = any]点Pでつくる波動は、図6.2のように、OとPの間に設定した1つの面Sから生じたすべての2次波(球

面波)がPまで伝搬し、干渉[カンショウ]した結果として求められ.る。ただし、Oから S 上の各点まで達した1次波とそこから生じる2次波の位相は互いに[たがいに = mutually]等しく、振幅[シンプク = amplitude]は互いに[たがいに]比例する。上に述べたように、正確には2次波の振幅[シンプク]は方向によって異なるが、ほぼ1方向へ進む2次波のみとして取り扱って[from とりあつかう = to treat]、この相異を考えなくてもよい。この原理は光の研究から得られたものであるが、光に限らず一般の波の性質を理解するのに有用である。

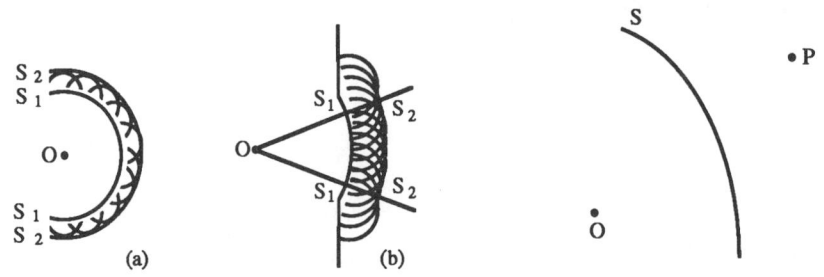

図 6.1　ホイヘンスの原理　　　　　図 6.2　光源と観測点

Adapted from pp. 166-167 of 寺沢徳雄著,『振動と波動』, 岩波書店, 1983.

2. 流体力学の最大の応用分野[ブンヤ = field]の1つである航空力学[コウクウリキガク = aerodynamics]では、かつては空気を縮まない完全[カンゼン = perfect]流体としてとり扱う[とりあつかう]のがふつうであった。翼[つばさ = wings]や胴体[ドウタイ = hull]のような流線形物体を対象とするかぎり、許される[from ゆるす = to permit]のはもちろんであるが、空気を縮まない流体と仮定[カテイ = hypothesis]してもよいのはなぜであろう。流速がおそければ流れの中の流速変化は小さく、したがって、ベルヌーイの定理により圧力変化も小さい。それゆえ密度変化も小さいから、これを無視する[ムシする = to neglect]ことが許される。これはすなわち縮まない流体を考えることにほかならない。ところが、ジェット機関の出現とともに飛行機[ヒコウキ = airplane]の速度向上はいちじるしく、密度変化を無視[ムシ]することが許されなくなってきた。

　静止[セイシ = stationary]流体の中の1点Oに乱れが与えられると、それによって生じた圧力および密度の変化は、Oを中心とする球面状の音波としてひろがっていく(図a)。いまOが一定速度Uで進行しているとすると、音速cと速度Uとの大小関係によって2通りのばあいができる。$U < c$では音波は全空間に伝わるが(図b)、$U > c$のばあいには音源[オンゲン = sound source]の影響はOを頂点[チョウテン = vertex]とする円錐[エンスイ = cone]状の領域[リョウイキ = region]の内部に限られる(図c)。このため、流速Uと音速cの大小によって流れの様子[ヨウス = behavior]が非常に[ヒジョウに = very]ちがうので、$U < c$を亜音速流れ、$U > c$を超音速[チョウオンソク = supersonic]流れといって区別[クベツ]する。

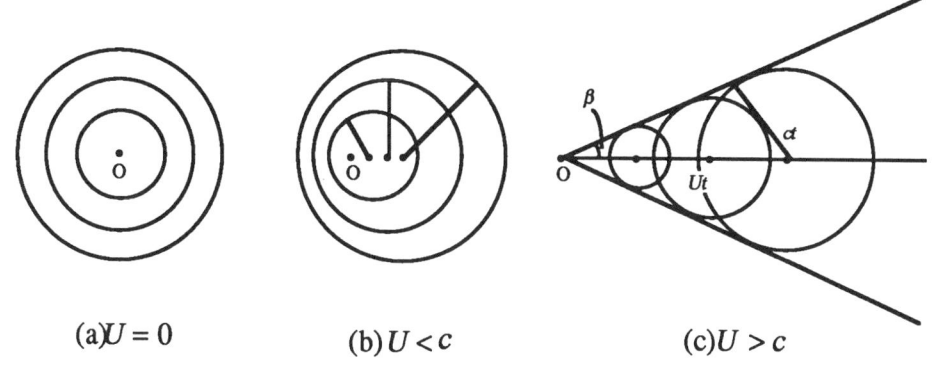

(a)$U = 0$　　　　(b)$U < c$　　　　(c)$U > c$

Adapted from pp. 164-165 of 今井功著，『流体力学』, 岩波書店, 1970.

3. 　　　　　ボルツマン統計力学とギブス統計力学

　気体をばく大な数の分子の集団[シュウダン = group]と見るとき、個々の分子の力学を追求[ツイキュウ = pursuit]することは複雑[フクザツ]すぎて、とうてい不可能[フカノウ = impossible]である。しかし、平均[ヘイキン]的な性質を集団[シュウダン]全体として考えることはできよう。たとえば、分子が容器の壁[かべ]に衝突していると仮定して、その壁の単位表面積当たりに受ける力の平均を、その気体の圧力と定義[テイギ = definition]することができる。ボルツマンは、分子の質量、速度、1グラム中の分子数などをあらかじめ仮定して、ある温度における気体の圧力を分子の運動速度から求めたり、また、分子運動とそのような速度を持つ分子の数のスペクトルを計算したりして、その結果が実測の量的関係を矛盾[ムジュン =contradiction]なく説明できることを示した。

　このようにして、日常生活[セイカツ = life]で定義できる量を、極微の分子の世界[セカイ = world]の力学に確率的・平均的な考え方を付加[フカ = addition]して導くことが統計力学の出発点となった。さらに、無数の粒子の集団の中では、粒子の衝突が絶えず[from たえる = to end]起こって、最後にはある平衡[ヘイコウ = equilibrium]の状態に達するという考えもたいせつな意味[イミ = meaning]をもつようになった。

　ボルツマンはさらに確率論の考え方を導入して、分子という微視的[ビシテキ = microscopic]世界[セカイ]の実体の力学から、熱という巨視的世界の現象の経験[ケイケン = experience]事実を導く統計力学の基礎[キソ = foundation]をつくった。ボルツマンは、理想[リソウ = ideal]気体のように互いに相互[ソウゴ=mutual]作用のない分子の一つ一つを確率的なものと見て、気体分子全体の集合を実在的な統計的集団と見なす立場をとった。ギブスはこのボルツマンの統計力学を一般化して、考えている系全体を(たとえ分子間に相互[ソウゴ]作用があろうとなかろうと)一つの確率的対象として取り扱うように拡張[カクチョウ = extension]した。こうしてギブスは一般的な古典[コテン =classical]統計力学の基礎[キソ]を設立した。統計力学の発展[ハッ

テン－development]は、物体が微細な構成要素の目に見えない<u>無秩序</u>[チツジョ＝order]運動によって全体的には<u>秩序</u>[チツジョ]を<u>保</u>って[from たもつ＝to maintain]いることを示し、物質観がニュートン力学から<u>一歩</u>[イッポ＝one step]<u>新</u>しい[あたらしい]見地に進んだということができる。

Adapted from pp. 199-200 of 湯川秀樹著,『物理講義』,講談社, 1977.

TRANSLATIONS

Ex 18.4 Sentences

1. Antigens are substances that stimulate organisms and [thereby] become the sources for causing [the organisms] to make specific antibodies. They are chiefly proteins, but [they] also [include] polysaccharides and phospholipids.
2. A resistance-grounded system is a type of electric power [system] in which the neutral point is grounded via a resistance.
3. Light-scattering methods are those using the scattering of light to measure such [quantities] as solvent and solute concentrations, and sizes (molecular weights), shapes, and particle-diameter distributions for minute particles such as polymers, colloids, and bacteria.
4. Transmission characteristics are the characteristics of transmission lines when [electricity] is sent as (electric) power, signals, and information via [these] transmission lines; [they] show various quantities versus frequency or time, such as the attenuation and phase quantities for voltage and current at the input and output terminals.
5. Double refraction is the phenomenon [in which] a light [beam] is incident on an optically anisotropic substance, and the mutually perpendicular linear polarized light [within the beam] refracts in two ways.
6. An incompressible fluid is one whose density may be thought of as unchanging. Usually, we may consider liquids in this [way] and, in some cases, we [may] treat gases in this [manner].
7. When we use time-dependent quantities in the definition of mass in relativistic dynamics, the rest mass is the mass at zero velocity; it is the same (quantity) as the mass in Newtonian mechanics.
8. A mass-point system is a system that consists of many mass points, but even a general continuum can be thought of as the limit [obtained] from a mass-point system.

9. Adiabatic demagnetization is a method [for] obtaining low temperatures, temperatures as low as 0.3°K or less, using liquid helium; [it is done] under adiabatic conditions [by] removing a magnetic field from a paramagnetic body after isothermally magnetizing it.

10. One kind of terminal board is that in which a large number of small terminals, which are provided for the contact points between the leads to an electrical machine and [its] external circuits, are assembled and fixed [to the board] by means of a synthetic resin molding.

11. Acoustic coupling is not the coupling of one telephone system to another telephone system by directly connecting the electrical circuits. It couples the transmitter and receiver of the one telephone with the receiver and transmitter of the other telephone respectively through the medium of sound waves.

12. When sounds, though having the same pitch and magnitude, are sensed as different (sounds) by the human ear, we say their timbre differs. Timbre is related to the sound spectrum, the wave shape, and the acoustic pressure, as well as to their changes with time.

13. When the probability of a value that a variable can take for a discontinuous variable, or the probability density for a continuous one, is considered [to be] a function of the variable, it is called a probability function.

14. The pressure that a gas exerts on the walls of [its] container is the average result of impulses [when] large numbers of molecules, reaching as high as 10^{28} per second per $1\,m^2$ of wall, collide[with the wall] at speeds of several hundred m/s.

15. When we let the input and output of the signal transmission elements be x(t) and y(t) respectively, and their (respective) Laplace transforms be X(s) and Y(s), [then] the ratio Y(s)/X(s) is called the transfer function.

CHAPTER 19　第十九章　[ダイジュウキュウショウ]

可	カ -	-ible, -able

| 価 | カ | value |
| | あたい | value |

| 界 | カイ | world; field {phys} |

| 活 | カツ | life, activity |

| 逆 | ギャク | contrary, reverse, inverse |

| 共 | キョウ | common |
| | (と)とも(に) | together with |

| 互 | ゴ | mutual, each other |
| | たが(いの) | mutual, reciprocal |

| 鉱 | コウ | mineral |

| 鋼 | コウ | steel |
| | はがね | steel |

| 香 | コウ | fragrance, aroma |
| | かお(り) | fragrance, aroma |

混	コン	mixing
	ま(ぜる)	to mix
	ま(ざる)	to be mixed
	ま(じる) {xu}	to be blended

| 材 | ザイ | material |

| 剤 | ザイ | drug; agent |

| 錯 | サク | complex; mixed |

試	シ	trial, test
	ため(す)	to try, test
	こころ(みる)	to try, attempt

| 製 | セイ | manufacturing |

| 遷 | セン | transferring location |

| 超 | チョウ - | super-, ultra, trans-, hyper- |

| 濃 | ノウ | concentrated |
| | こ(い) | concentrated |

| 非 | ヒ - | {negative prefix} |

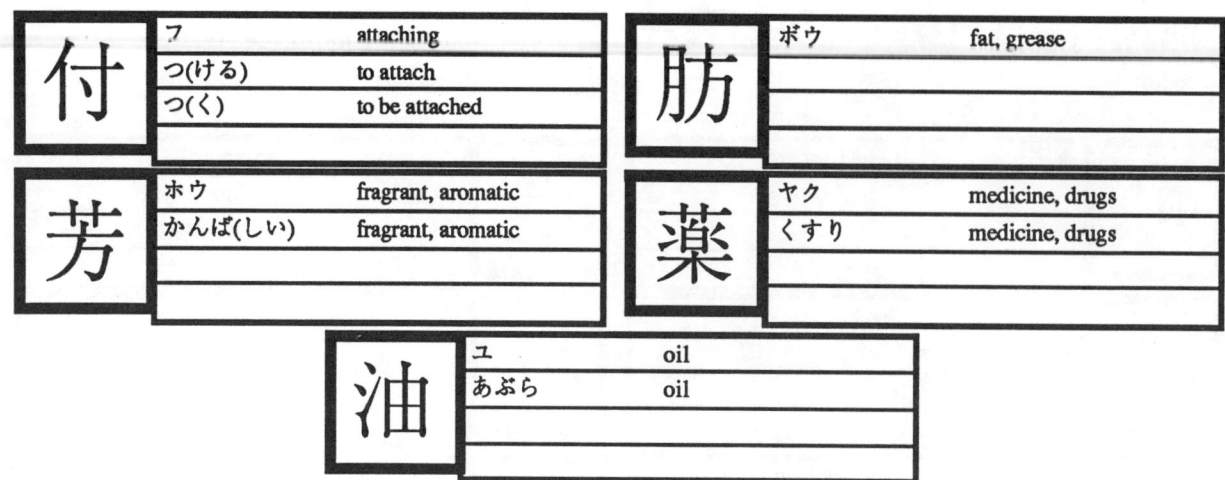

付	フ	attaching
	つ(ける)	to attach
	つ(く)	to be attached

| 肪 | ボウ | fat, grease |
| | | |

芳	ホウ	fragrant, aromatic
	かんば(しい)	fragrant, aromatic

薬	ヤク	medicine, drugs
	くすり	medicine, drugs

油	ユ	oil
	あぶら	oil

VOCABULARY

可

(不)可能な	(フ)カノウな	(im)possible
(不)可逆的な	(フ)カギャクテキな	(ir)reversible
可動な	カドウな	movable
可動接点	カドウセッテン	traveling contact
可溶性の	カヨウセイの	soluble
可変抵抗器	カヘンテイコウキ	rheostat
適用可能性	テキヨウカノウセイ	applicability

価

価値	カチ	value
原子価	ゲンシカ	valence
価電子	カデンシ	valence electron
価電子帯	カデンシカイ	valence band
一価金属	イッカキンゾク	monovalent metal
一価関数	イッカカンスウ	single-valued function

界

境界条件	キョウカイジョウケン	boundary condition
界磁石	カイジシャク	field magnet
界磁極	カイジキョク	field pole
界磁鉄心	カイジテッシン	field core
界磁制御	カイジセイギョ	field control
電界強度地図	デンカイキョウドチズ	(electric) field-strength map
動物界	ドウブツカイ	animal kingdom

植物界	ショクブツカイ	plant kingdom
界面	カイメン	interface
界面動電位	カイメンドウデンイ	electrokinetic potential
界面活性剤	カイメンカッセイザイ	surfactant
乱流境界層	ランリュウキョウカイソウ	turbulent (flow) boundary layer
層流境界層	ソウリュウキョウカイソウ	laminar (flow) boundary layer
業界	ギョウカイ	(the world of) industry

活

生活環	セイカツカン	life cycle
活動度	カツドウド	activity {thermo}
活性中心	カッセイチュウシン	active site
活性化	カッセイカ	activation
不活性な	フカッセイな	inert

逆

可逆過程	カギャクカテイ	reversible process
可逆反応	カギャクハンノウ	reversible reaction
逆数	ギャクスウ	reciprocal (number)
逆比	ギャクヒ	inverse ratio
逆三角関数	ギャクサンカクカンスウ	inverse trigonometric function
逆流	ギャクリュウ	backward flow
逆方向	ギャクホウコウ	opposite direction
逆行運動	ギャッコウウンドウ	retrograde motion
逆転層	ギャクテンソウ	inversion layer

共

共有する	キョウユウする	to share
共有結合	キョウユウケツゴウ	covalent bond
共重合	キョウジュウゴウ	copolymerization
共線の	キョウセンの	collinear
共生	キョウセイ	symbiosis
共晶点	キョウショウテン	eutectic point
共析晶	キョウセキショウ	eutectoid
共振	キョウシン	resonance
共振子	キョウシンシ	resonator
共通イオン効果	キョウツウイオンコウカ	common ion effect
共同研究	キョウドウケンキュウ	collaborative research
共変; 反変	キョウヘン; ハンヘン	covariant; contravariant

互

相互の	ソウゴの	mutual, reciprocal
交互に	コウゴに	alternately
相互作用	ソウゴサヨウ	interaction
相互通信	ソウゴツウシン	two-way communication
相互関係	ソウゴカンケイ	correlation
互変異性	ゴヘンイセイ	tautomerism
互換性	ゴカンセイ	interchangeability
互換性組み立て	ゴカンセイくみたて	interchangeable assembly

鉱

鉄鉱	テッコウ	iron ore
鉱物	コウブツ	mineral
鉱石	コウセキ	ore
鉱層	コウソウ	ore bed, seam

鋼

鋼鉄	コウテツ	steel
鋼鉄管	コウテツカン	steel tubing
鋼鉄製の	コウテツセイの	made of steel
合金鋼	ゴウキンコウ	alloy steel
炭素鋼	タンソコウ	carbon steel

香

芳香化	ホウコウカ	aromatization
芳香油	ホウコウユ	fragrant oil
芳香族の	ホウコウゾクの	aromatic
芳香族化合物	ホウコウゾクカゴウブツ	aromatic compound
芳香族炭化水素基	ホウコウゾクタンカスイソキ	aromatic hydrocarbon group
安息香酸	アンソクコウサン	benzoic acid

混

混合物	コンゴウブツ	mixture
混和性	コンワセイ	miscibility
混晶	コンショウ	mixed crystal
混信	コンシン	(radio) interference
混圧タービン	コンアツタービン	mixed-pressure turbine
混乱	コンラン	disorder
混成軌道	コンセイキドウ	hybridized orbital
混じり合う	まじりあう	to be mixed together

材

材料	ザイリョウ	materials
材料力学	ザイリョウリキガク	strength of materials
材料試験	ザイリョウシケン	materials testing
複合材料	フクゴウザイリョウ	composite materials
鋼鉄材	コウテツザイ	steel materials
吸音材	キュウオンザイ	sound-absorbing materials

剤

安定剤	アンテイザイ	stabilizer
減極剤	ゲンキョクザイ	depolarizer
消極剤	ショウキョクザイ	depolarizer
表面活性剤	ヒョウメンカッセイザイ	surface-active agent
変性剤	ヘンセイザイ	denaturant
酸化剤	サンカザイ	oxidizing agent
固定剤	コテイザイ	fixative

錯

錯体	サクタイ	a complex {chem}
錯基	サクキ	complex radical
錯化合物	サクカゴウブツ	complex compound
錯塩	サクエン	complex salt
活性錯合体	カッセイサクゴウタイ	activated complex

試

試験	シケン	test
試験管	シケンカン	test tube
試験所	シケンジョ	experimental station
試験炉	シケンロ	test kiln, test reactor
試金	シキン	assay
試料	シリョウ	sample
試行	シコウ	trial
試運転	シウンテン	trial run

製

製品	セイヒン	manufactured goods
日本製	ニホンセイ	made in Japan
製鋼所	セイコウショ	steel mill
製鋼業	セイコウギョウ	steel industry
製作	セイサク	manufacture
製造	セイゾウ	manufacture

製造所	セイゾウショ	manufacturing facility
製図	セイズ	drafting

遷

遷移	センイ	succession {biol}
遷移元素	センイゲンソ	transition elements
遷移状態	センイジョウタイ	transition state
遷移確率	センイカクリツ	transition probability

超

超音波	チョウオンパ	ultrasonic waves
超音速	チョウオンソク	supersonic speed
超ウラン元素	チョウウランゲンソ	transuranium elements
超伝導体	チョウデンドウタイ	superconductor
超伝導磁石	チョウデンドウジシャク	superconducting magnet
超流動	チョウリュウドウ	superfluidity
超微細構造	チョウビサイコウゾウ	hyperfine structure

濃

濃度	ノウド	concentration
濃度分布	ノウドブンプ	concentration distribution
濃度分極	ノウドブンキョク	concentration polarization
濃硫酸	ノウリュウサン	concentrated sulfuric acid
濃縮ウラン	ノウシュクウラン	enriched uranium
濃縮機	ノウシュクキ	thickener
濃化油	ノウカユ	thickened oil

非

非常に	ヒジョウに	extremely, very
非線形の	ヒセンケイの	nonlinear
非圧縮性流体	ヒアッシュクセイリュウタイ	incompressible fluid
非金属	ヒキンゾク	nonmetal
非球面レンズ	ヒキュウメンレンズ	aspherical lens
非環状の	ヒカンジョウの	acyclic
非極性結合	ヒキョクセイケツゴウ	nonpolar bond
非水溶液	ヒスイヨウエキ	nonaqueous solution
非電解質	ヒデンカイシツ	nonelectrolyte
非可換体	ヒカカンタイ	noncommutative field {math}
非晶質の	ヒショウシツの	amorphous
非定常の	ヒテイジョウの	unsteady

付

付与する	フヨする	to grant, give
付加重合	フカジュウゴウ	addition polymerization
付加反応	フカハンノウ	addition reaction
重付加反応	ジュウフカハンノウ	polyaddition reaction
大学付属の	ダイガクフゾクの	university-affiliated
付近	フキン	vicinity
付録	フロク	appendix, supplement

芳

芳香族の	ホウコウゾクの	aromatic
芳香族環	ホウコウゾクカン	aromatic ring

肪

脂肪	シボウ	fat
脂肪酸	シボウサン	fatty acid
脂肪細胞	シボウサイボウ	fat cell
脂肪組織	シボウソシキ	fatty tissue
脂肪族の	シボウゾクの	aliphatic

薬

薬品	ヤクヒン	chemicals
薬品処理	ヤクヒンショリ	chemical treatment {of waste}
薬物	ヤクブツ	drugs
薬物学	ヤクブツガク	pharmacology
試薬	シヤク	chemical reagent
抗ヒスタミン薬	コウヒスタミンヤク	antihistamic agent

油

石油	セキユ	petroleum
石油化学薬品	セキユカガクヤクヒン	petrochemicals
油層	ユソウ	oil strata
油細胞	ユサイボウ	oil cell
油圧機械	ユアツキカイ	hydraulic machine
油溶性の	ユヨウセイの	oil soluble
油脂	ユシ	fats and oils

Ex 19.3

固溶体	コヨウタイ	solid solution
解離する	カイリする	to dissociate
つながる		to be connected, joined, linked
減極	ゲンキョク	depolarization
つぎつぎ	【次々】	successively, one after another
部位	ブイ	a part
どちら(で)も		either one

Ex 19.4

伝導帯	デンドウタイ	conduction band
すぐ下	すぐした	immediately below
原系	ゲンケイ	original system
同調する	ドウチョウする	to synchronize
水晶振動子	スイショウシンドウシ	quartz oscillator
...もつほか(に)		in addition to having ...
発光スペクトル	ハッコウスペクトル	emission spectra

Ex 19.5

-次数	ジスウ	order (of)
あてはまる		to be applicable
ただ		but
前端	ゼンタン	front end
下流	カリュウ	downstream
ごく		very, extremely
わずかの		few
たやすい		easy
どちらかの		whichever
ずらす		to shift

Ex 19.6(1)

中ほど	なかほど	the middle, halfway
ふくらむ		to swell (out), distend
くびれる		to be constricted

Ex 19.6(2)

関連づける	カンレンづける	to relate
気づく	キづく	to become aware of
静的な	セイテキな	static
動的な	ドウテキな	dynamic
ふるまい		behavior

ありさま		state, condition, sight
見当	ケントウ	conjecture
ふつうの		usually
たよる		to rely on, depend on
反発	ハンパツ	repulsion
反面	ハンメン	the reverse
置換体	チカンタイ	substitution product
それほど		to that extent
置換基	チカンキ	substituent
なげかける		to throw
当時	トウジ	in those days, then
とりくむ		to grapple with
注目する	チュウモクする	to notice
現実に	ゲンジツに	actually, in actuality

Ex 19.6(3)

熱間等方加圧	ネツカントウホウカアツ	hot isostatic pressing (HIP)
実用に	ジツヨウに	in practical use
代表する	ダイヒョウする	to represent
圧電磁器	アツデンジキ	piezoelectric ceramics
集積化	シュウセキカ	integration
対処する	タイショする	to cope with
実現	ジツゲン	implementation
極度に	キョクドに	extremely

19 Vocabulary Building and Readings in Chemistry

EXERCISES

Ex 19.1 Look-alike KANJI (see instructions in Ex 18.1)

#	(1)	(2)	中	右
1.	族	肪	脂( )	亜( )
2.	活	乱	( )性	( )流
3.	果	界	境( )	結( )
4.	制	製	( )品	( )御
5.	消	硝	( )酸	( )磁
6.	対	付	( )加	( )数
7.	験	検	試( )	( )出
8.	種	動	( )類	( )力
9.	集	進	( )化	( )合
10.	半	平	( )面	( )径
11.	他	地	( )球	( )方
12.	位	粒	( )子	( )置
13.	自	白	( )金	( )動
14.	現	観	( )象	( )察
15.	開	関	( )数	( )発
16.	品	晶	結( )	製( )
17.	在	布	分( )	存( )
18.	設	般	一( )	( )立
19.	形	型	大( )	変( )

Ex 19.2 Matching Japanese and English technical terms

(a) Elements and chemicals

安定剤( )　　1. chemicals
一価金属( )　2. complex radical
固定剤( )　　3. complex salt
錯塩( )　　　4. concentrated sulfuric acid
錯基( )　　　5. drugs
遷移金属( )　6. fixative
遷移元素( )　7. monovalent metal
濃硫酸( )　　8. stabilizer
薬物( )　　　9. transition element
薬品( )　　　10. transition metal

(b) Materials-related terms

鋼鉄材( )　　1. alloy steel
合金鋼( )　　2. composite materials
材料科学( )　3. experimental station
材料力学( )　4. materials science
試験所( )　　5. steel industry
試験炉( )　　6. steel making
製鋼( )　　　7. steel materials
製鋼業( )　　8. steel mill
製鋼所( )　　9. strength of materials
複合材料( )　10. test kiln

(c) Common KANGO as prefixes

界磁極( )　　　1. activated complex
界磁鉄心( )　　2. active site
活性錯合体( )　3. concentration distribution
活性中心( )　　4. concentration polarization
相互関係( )　　5. correlation
相互作用( )　　6. field core
超音速( )　　　7. field pole
超音波( )　　　8. interaction
濃度分極( )　　9. ultrasonic wave
濃度分布( )　　10. supersonic speed

(d) Modifiers

可逆の( )　　1. collinear
可動の( )　　2. disordered
可変の( )　　3. mixed
逆行の( )　　4. movable
共線の( )　　5. retrograde
共生の( )　　6. reversible
混合の( )　　7. symbiotic
混乱の( )　　8. superconducting
超伝導の( )　9. superfluid
超流動の( )　10. variable

(e) Words with the negative prefix 非

非圧縮性の( )　　1. acyclic
非可換体( )　　　2. amorphous magnetic material
非環状の( )　　　3. incompressible
非極性の( )　　　4. nonelectrolyte
非金属( )　　　　5. noncommutative field
非晶質磁性体( )　6. noncrystalline semiconductor
非晶質半導体( )　7. nonlinear
非線形の( )　　　8. nonmetal
非定常の( )　　　9. nonpolar
非電解質( )　　　10. unsteady

Fx 19.3 Matching Japanese technical terms and definitions

(a) Terms that define substances

界面活性剤( )　　1. 固溶体から同時に析出する2種またはそれ以上の異なる結
共析晶( )　　　　　晶の混合物。
鋼( )　　　　　　2. 水溶液中でイオンに解離しない物質。
鉱層( )　　　　　3. 二つ以上の環が二つ以上の原子を共有してつながってい
金属混晶( )　　　　る環式化合物。
消極剤( )　　　　4. 2層またはそれ以上の材料を結合して製作された製品。
縮合環( )　　　　5. 小量で界面または表面の性質を変化させる物質。
積層板( )　　　　6. たとえば、銅とニッケルのようにあらゆる割合でつくる
炭素鋼( )　　　　　結晶。
非電解質( )　　　7. Fe-C系の合金でC濃度が約2%(重量)以下のもの。
　　　　　　　　　8. 炭素だけを合金元素として含む鋼。
　　　　　　　　　9. 減極を目的として用いる物質。
　　　　　　　　10. 特定元素またはその化合物の地殻[チカク = earth's crust]
　　　　　　　　　における異常濃集体。

(b) Chemical-related terms

活性中心( )　　　1. 石油系炭化水素から芳香族の炭化水素をつくる反応。
共有結合( )　　　2. 二重結合をもつ単量体が二重結合の一方を離してつぎつ
原子価( )　　　　　ぎつながり、高分子になる反応。
試金( )　　　　　3. 同種または異種の二個以上の化合物が直接結合して別の
互変異性( )　　　　種類の分子を生成する反応。
脂肪酸( )　　　　4. ある元素の原子が他の原子と単結合をいくつ作れるかを
付加重合( )　　　　表す数。
付加反応( )　　　5. 酵素[コウソ = enzyme]タンパク質分子中において、基質
芳香族化( )　　　　が特異的に結合し、触媒[ショクバイ = catalyst]を受ける
濃縮ウラン( )　　　部位。
　　　　　　　　　6. 二つの原子が 二個の電子を共有することによって安定化
　　　　　　　　　し、結合すること。
　　　　　　　　　7. 鉱石、金属、合金などの定量分析。
　　　　　　　　　8. 天然[テンネン = natural]ウランに比べ、ウラン235の量を
　　　　　　　　　多くしたウラン元素。
　　　　　　　　　9. Rがアルキル基を示すときRCOOHで表されるカルボン酸。
　　　　　　　　10. ある化合物が2種の異性体として存在し、条件によって
　　　　　　　　　どちらにでもなるような現象。

Ex 19.4 Translate the following sentences

1. 価電子帯とは特定の原子核に束縛[ソクバク＝bound]されている価電子が属するエネルギー帯である。半導体及び絶縁体[ゼツエンタイ＝insulator]の場合は伝導帯のすぐ下のエネルギー帯をいう。

2. 活性錯合体とは、化学反応で素反応の進行につれて反応系が原系の状態から生成系の状態に向かって原子配置を変える経過[ケイカ＝course]の中で、ギブズ・エネルギー(定圧)あるいはヘルムホルツ・エネルギー(定積)の最も高い状態(遷移状態)、またはその状態における反応系をいう。

3. 共振子とはある振動電流の周波数に同調して電気的にまたは機械的に振動する電気回路素子で、水晶振動子などは一種の共振子である。

4. 抗ヒスタミン薬とは、生体内に広く[from ひろい＝wide]存在し、アレルギー反応に重要な役割[ヤクわり＝role]をもつほか、種々の生理作用を有する生体内アミン、ヒスタミンに対して桔抗[キッコウ＝antagonism]作用を示す薬物である。

5. 複塩はたとえば2種以上の塩が結合した形の$KCl + MgCl_2 \rightarrow KCl \cdot MgCl_2$のような塩で、溶かすとそれぞれのイオンになり、$[MgCl_3]^-$というような錯イオンはできない。錯イオンができれば錯体である。

6. ポアッソン分布において1回の試行である事象が起こる確率がp、起こらない確率がq = (1 – p)であるとすると、この試行をN回くりかえしたとき、その事象がその中でn回起こる確率WN(n)は次の式で与えられる。

$$WN(n) = \{N!/n! (N-n)!\}p^n (1-p)^{N-n}$$

7. 超微細構造は、原子による光の吸収[キュウシュウ＝absorption]または発光スペクトル線の微細構造に現われるさらに細かい構造で、電子の磁気モーメントの1/1000程度に小さい原子核の磁気モーメントの作用によって生じる。

8. ある薬物の濃度と、それによって起こされた反応の強さとの間の関係は各薬物に固有の関係であり、濃度・反応曲線として示される。

9. 界磁制御とは直流電流機の回転速度を制御する方式の一つで、端子電圧を一定に保ち[from たもつ＝to maintain]、界磁電流を変えて行うものである。

10. 芳香族ポリアミドは主鎖[シュサ＝main chain]に芳香族環をもつポリアミドで、芳香族のジアミンとジカルボン酸クロリドから界面重縮合や低温溶液重縮合により合成される。

11. 時間的に進行するある物理的過程に対し、時間の向きを反転させたその逆過程が物理的に可能であるとき、その過程は可逆であるという。

12. 遷移確率とは原子・分子などの系(一般的に量子力学系)が、電磁場のような外からの小さな作用を受けて、ある定常状態から他の定常状態へ一定の時間内に遷移する割合をいう。

Ex 19.5 Read the following short essays for comprehension

1．反応速度は温度の<u>上昇</u>[ジョウショウ＝rise]と共に増大する。速度係数k
の温度Tによる変化はアレニウス[Arrhenius]の式

d ln k/d ln T＝E/RT

で表される。ここでEはアレニウスの活性化エネルギーであり、反応速度の
温度変化から求められ、遷移状態論における活性化エンタルピーΔH‡とΔH‡
＝E‐nRTの関係にある(nは反応次数、溶液反応ではn＝1)。遷移状態論にお
ける活性化<u>自由</u>[ジユウ＝free]エネルギーを活性化エネルギーとよぶことが
ある。反応が進行するために与えられなければならないエネルギーである
が、<u>触媒</u>[ショクバイ]や<u>酵素</u>[コウソ]はこれを小さくすることにより反応を
<u>促進</u>[ソクシン＝acceleration]する。

Adapted from p. 258 of 『生化学辞典』, 東京化学同人, 1984.

2．水や空気のような粘性の小さい流体では、粘性を<u>無視</u>[ムシ＝neglect]し
た完全流体の理論が大体あてはまる。ただ物体表面の近くでは、速度<u>勾</u>配
[コウバイ＝gradient]、したがって<u>渦度</u>[うずド＝vorticity]が大きく、粘性が
<u>無視</u>[ムシ]できない。粘性の小さい流体ではこのような<u>領域</u>[リョウイキ＝
region]がきわめて<u>薄</u>く[from うすい＝thin]、境界層とよばれる。たとえば速
度Uの<u>一様</u>な[イチヨウな＝uniform]流れの中に、流れに平行に平板をおく
と、板の前端からxだけ下流では境界層の<u>厚</u>さ[あつさ＝thickness]はδ＝√νx/U
の程度である。νは動粘性率で、空気ではν ＝0.15cm²/s、U＝10m/s、x＝
10cmとすればδ＝0.04cmとなる。

Adapted from p. 305 of 『理化学辞典』, 第四版, 岩波書店, 1987.

3．ごくわずかに正の過電圧を加えると、電極反応がたやすく酸化方向R→
0＋neに進行して酸化電流が流れ、逆に過電圧をわずかに<u>負</u>[フ＝negative]に
すると、電極反応が容<u>易</u>に[ヨウイに＝easily]<u>還元</u>[カンゲン＝reduction]方向
0＋ne→Rに進行して<u>還元</u>[カンゲン]電流が流れるような電極を可逆電極と
いう。電極反応の交換電流が大きいものほど可逆電極としての性質を示す。
これに対し、交換電流が小さく、電極反応をどちらかの方向に進行させる
のに大きな過電圧を必要とする電極を不可逆電極という。

Adapted from ibid., p. 212.

4．重付加とは高分子生成反応の一つである。化合物ROHやRNHなどがHと
<u>残部</u>[ザンブ＝remainder]にわかれ、2重結合をもつ化合物または環式化合物
に付加する反応を素反応としている。この反応は以下に述べるように、連

鎖[レンサ = chain]重合の一つである付加重合とは全く異なる反応であり、外国[ガイコク = foreign (Western) countries]ではほとんど使われない用語[ヨウゴ = (technical) term]であることに注意[チュウイ = attention]する必要がある。重付加反応の多くは重縮合反応と同様な[ドウヨウな = similar]逐次[チクジ = consecutive]反応で、数平均[スウヘイキン = number average]分子量、分子分布は重縮合と同様[ドウヨウ]になる。重縮合の場合と異なり低分子量化合物の脱離[ダツリ = elimination]がないので、これをのぞく必要がない。しかし、反応が平衡[ヘイコウ = equilibrium]している場合、平衡[ヘイコウ]をずらして生成高分子の分子量を高めるというようなことはできない。

Adapted from ibid., p. 587.

Ex 19.6 Read the following longer essays for comprehension

1. H_2に限らずN_2、F_2、HF、C_2H_2、CO_2などの多くの線形分子は軸対称[ジクタイショウ = axial symmetry]の電子状態、すなわち分子軸[ジク = axis]のまわりの全軌道[キドウ = orbit]角運動量がゼロの状態にある。

　HFではH原子の1s軌道[キドウ]とF原子の2p軌道とが電子対によって共有され、F_2では両原子の$2p_\sigma$軌道が共有される。またN_2では、両原子の$2p_\sigma$軌道、$2p_\pi$軌道がおのおのの電子対結合を作ると考えられる。

　図に、N_2、F_2の電子雲[デンシウン = electron cloud]の密度分布を描く[えがく = to draw]。分子の形はN_2では中ほどがふくらみ、F_2では中ほどがくびれていることに注意[チュウイ = attention]すべきであろう。

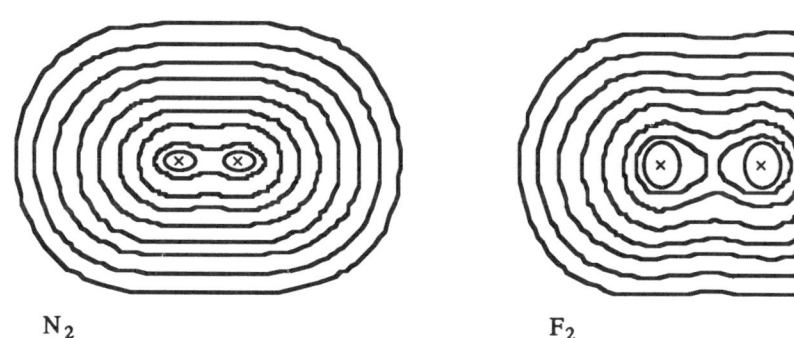

N₂   F₂

　ベリリウムBeの基底[キテイ = ground]状態は$1s^2 2s^2$の電子配置をもつ閉殻[ヘイカク = closed shell]構造である。この原子が不活性でないのは2s電子1個が容易に[ヨウイに = easily]2p軌道に昇る[のぼる = to climb]ことができ、両方のスピンの向きが自由[ジユウ]になるからである。実際[ジッサイ = actually]、塩化ベリリウム$BeCl_2$に見られるようにBeの原子価は2である。この分子Cl-Be-Clは直線形で左右対称[サユウタイショウ = right-left symmetry]である。このことはBeの2s、$2p_\sigma$両軌道[キドウ]の混成を考えることによって理解される。

Adapted from pp. 87-89 of 木原太郎著, 『化学物理入門』, 岩波書店, 1978.

2.   This essay is adapted from the address by 福井謙一[フクイ ケンイチ] upon the occasion of his receiving the Nobel Prize for chemistry in 1981. Since it is written in the polite style, you may wish to review Section 13.6. The English words in parentheses are from the original text.

　有機電子説においては、酸、塩基や酸化、還元[カンゲン]などのような化学的な概念[ガイネン = concept]が、古く[ふるく = long ago]から便利に[ベンリに = conveniently]使われてきました。さらに、電子をもっと中心において考えた概念[ガイネン]として、求電子性と求核性(electrophilicity and nucleophilicity)、あるいは電子供与体[キョウヨタイ]と電子受容体(electron donor and acceptor)という用語[ヨウゴ = (technical) term]がありますが、これらはいずれも互いに対になった相対的な概念であります。

　これらの概念は、電子密度あるいは電荷[デンカ = electric charge]といったものの大きさと定量的に関連づけることができることに気づかれるでしょう。電子説においては、分子の静的・動的なふるまいを電子効果(electronic effect)という用語がありますが、その根底[コンテイ = foundation]にあるのも、分子内の電子の空間的な分布という概念にほかならなかったのです。

　これら分子内の電荷[デンカ]分布のありさまは、有機化学の経験[ケイケン = experience]によって、原子の電気陰性度(electronegativity)の概念などを使って、ある程度、見当を付けることができます。しかし、また同時に、それは電子分布の物理的な測定や量子論に基づく理論計算などによって基礎[キソ = foundation]づけられ、定量化され、そして支持[シジ = support]されました。

　分子内の電子分布や電荷 ── これらはどちらを用いても結果は変わりませんが ── はふつう分子内のそれぞれの原子や結合ごとに、そこに存在する電子の総数[ソウスウ = total number](これは一般に整数[セイスウ = integral number]ではない)を用いて表され、それはかなり実在的な意味[イミ = meaning]をもつものとして、経験[ケイケン = empirical]化学者にも容易に[ヨウイに = readily]受け入れられた概念でした。したがって、化学者はさまざまの現象の説明や理解に際[サイ]して、電子密度を基本的な概念として用いました。とくに、化学の研究を押し進めて[from おしすすめる = to expedite, push forward]いくために、ふつう、われわれは経験[ケイケン]を通じての類推[ルイスイ = analogy]にたよることが多いのですが、電子密度はその類推[ルイスイ]における基本的な概念として非常に効果的に広く[from ひろい]用いられました。

　電子密度の大小を判断[ハンダン = judgment]の基準にとるときは、電子密度によって生じる静電的な安定化あるいは反発というものを考えます。したがって、求電子試薬が分子内の電子密度の大きい場所を攻撃[コウゲキ = attack]しやすい反面、求核試薬の反応は電子密度の小さい場所に起こりやすいと考えるのが妥当[ダトウ=appropriate]でしょう。事実、ウィーランド(Wheland)とポーリング(Pauling)は、このような考え方によって置換ベンゼンにお

ける芳香族置換の配向性についての説明をはじめ、さらに多くの化学反応の起こり方をも同様に[ドウヨウに = similarly]理論的に説明することができたのです。

　しかしながら、古く[ふるく]から知られていた単純な[タンジュンな = simple]反応の一つ、すなわちナフタレンの求電子置換反応の、たとえばニトロ化のような反応で、なぜ優先的に[ユウセンテキに = preferentially]置換体ができるかという問題に答える[こたえる = to answer]のはそれほど容易なことではありませんでした。なぜなら、このような置換基をもたない芳香族炭化水素の多くは、求電子試薬も求核試薬も同じ場所に反応するからです。このことは電子密度が万能[バンノウ = omnipotent]有機反応性理論に、疑問[ギモン = doubt]をなげかけるものでした。

　私[わたし]は当時としては少し違った考え方でこの問題にとりくみました。それは、原子と原子とから分子ができる場合に、主な[おもな = primary]役割[ヤクわり = role]を演ずる[エンずる = to play]のが原子価電子であるという考え方に注目して、芳香族炭化水素の電子のうちエネルギーの最も高い軌道を占有して[センユウする = to occupy]いる電子だけの分布を求めてみるというものでした。この試みは予想[ヨソウ = anticipation]以上の成功[セイコウ = success]を収め、求電子試薬が現実に攻撃[コウゲキ]する場所と、図1に示したようにこれらの特別な電子の密度の大きい場所(site)との間に完全な[カンゼンな= perfect]一致[イッチ = agreement]が得られました。

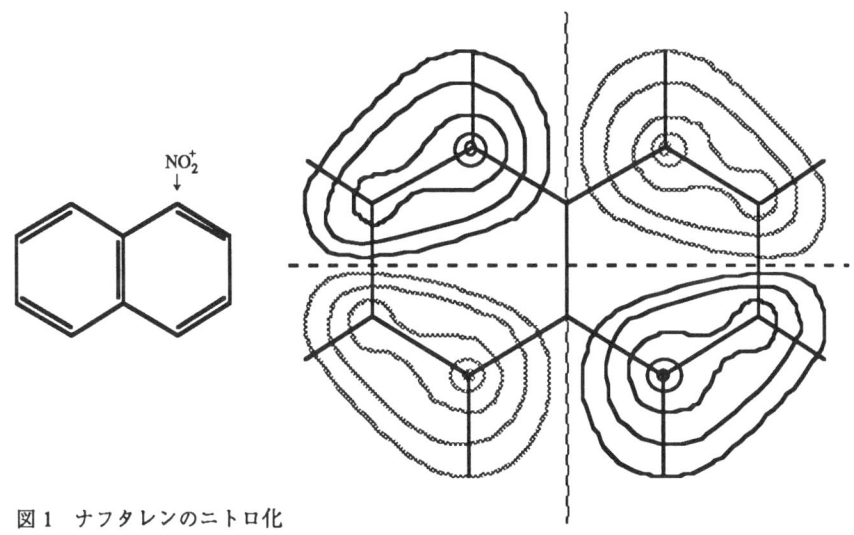

図1　ナフタレンのニトロ化

Adapted from pp. 130-132 of 福井謙一著, 山邊時雄編, 『化学と私』, 化学同人, 1982.

3.

HIP	hot isostatic pressing
PZT	lead-based zirconate titanates
PLZT	lead-based lanthanum-doped zirconate titanates
チタン酸ジルコン酸鉛	lead zirconate titanates
La置換の	lanthanum-doped

　機能性セラミックスとは、電磁気的機能、光学的機能、化学的機能、生物的機能などを指す[さす = to indicate]が、熱間等方加圧(HIP)成形あるいはホットプレス技術を用いてセラミックスの機能性を高めて実用に供されて[from キョウする = to offer]いるセラミックスでは電磁気的機能、光学的機能を有するセラミックス、いわゆる電子セラミックスについての例が多く、他の機能分野[ブンヤ = field]についてはむしろこれからの発展[ハッテン = development]が期待[キタイ = expectation]されているといってもよい。そこでここにおいては、とくにわが国[わがくに = our nation]において、その生産技術が進行したところのフェライトとよばれている磁性材料、チタン酸ジルコン酸鉛磁器に代表される圧電磁器(PZT)、及び電気光学材料として注目されているLa置換のPZT(PLZT)などについてHIP技術を説明する。

　磁性セラミックス、誘電[ユウデン = dielectric]セラミックスは現在ではセラミックス業界全体の発展[ハッテン]によりもたらされた原料精製[セイセイ = refining]技術、粉体[フンタイ = powder]処理技術、焼結[ショウケツ = sintering]技術の高度化により焼結[ショウケツ]体のもつ不足[フソク = deficiency]、不安定性などに改良[カイリョウ = improvements]が加えられ、一段[イチダン = one notch]と性能が向上してきている。さらに電子機器の精密[セイミツ = precision]化、集積化の流れの中で電子材料に対し、よりミクロなスケールでの高度化が要求され、セラミックスには付きものであった空孔[クウコウ = voids]ももはや許されなく[from ゆるす = to allow]なってきた分野[ブンヤ]が出現してきた。これに対処するためには、原料から焼結に至る[いたる = to reach]全般の革新[カクシン = innovation]が必要となってきた。ここで焼結技術に関していえば、空孔[クウコウ]を「完全」[カンゼン = complete]になくするというようなことは、大気圧中の通常の焼結技術だけでは実現がむずかしい。そこでホットプレス技術が導入され、より完全[カンゼン]な機能性セラミックスの実現へと努力[ドリョク = effort]が重ねられ、実際の[ジッサイノ=actual]生産において適用されるようになった。しかし通常のホットプレスはダイ、パンチの高温強度の問題、生産性の問題などはもちろんであるが、電磁気的機能などを求めるセラミックスにおいては、定められた成分以外の不純物[フジュンブツ = impurities]の混入を極度に嫌う[きらう=to abhor]場合が多く、ダイ、パンチおよび圧力伝達媒体[バイタイ = medium]からの汚染[オセン=contamination]は致命的[チメイテキ = lethal]とな

る。そこで以下にフェライトおよび<u>誘電</u>[ユウデン]セラミックスの場合についてのHIP技術、およびそれによって付与された特性について説明する。

Adapted from pp. 216-217 of 小泉光恵・西原正夫編著, 『等方加圧技術』, 日刊工業新聞社, 1988.

TRANSLATIONS

Ex 19.4 Sentences

1. A valence band is the energy band that belongs to the valence electrons which are bound to a specific atomic nucleus. In semiconductors and insulators, it refers to the energy band immediately below the conduction band.

2. In a chemical reaction, an activated complex is the state (transition state) of maximum Gibbs energy (constant pressure) or Helmholtz energy (constant volume) — or the reaction system at that state — [attained] during the course of change of atomic arrangements as the reaction system proceeds, via its elementary reactions, from the state of the original system to the state of the product system.

3. A resonator is an element in an electric circuit that oscillates, either electrically or mechanically, with the same frequency as a certain oscillating current; quartz oscillators are one type of resonator.

4. Antihistamines are chemicals widely present throughout the body that, in addition to having an important role in allergic reactions, exhibit antagonistic actions toward amines and histamines, which have various physiological actions within the body of the organism.

5. Double salts are salts like $KCl + MgCl_2 \rightarrow KCl \cdot MgCl_2$, for example, which have the form in which two or more [simple] salts are combined; when they are dissolved, they turn into their respective ions. However, complex ions such as $[MgCl_3]^-$ are not formed. If complex ions are formed, [the substance] is [known as] a complex.

6. In Poisson's distribution, if we let p be the probability that an event will occur in a single trial and $q = (1 - p)$ the probability that it will not occur, then when these trials are repeated N times, the probability WN(n) that the event occurs n times within [N trials] is given by the following equation:

$$WN(n) = \{N!/n!(N - n)!\}p^n(1 - p)^{N - n}$$

7. Hyperfine structure is the more detailed structure that appears in the fine structure of the lines in atomic absorption and emission spectra; it arises from the action of magnetic moments in the small atomic nucleus of the order of 1/1000th the magnetic moment of electrons.

8. The relation between the concentration of a certain drug and the strength of the reaction caused by it is a relation characteristic of each drug and is expressed as the curve of concentration vs. reaction [strength].

9. Field control is one system for controlling the rotational speed of a direct current motor; it operates by changing the field current (while) maintaining a constant terminal voltage.

10. Aromatic polyamides are polyamides that have an aromatic ring on their main chain; they are synthesized from aromatic diamines and dicarboxylic chlorides by means of interfacial or low-temperature solution condensation polymerization.

11. For a certain physical process that progresses with time, when the process [obtained] by reversing the direction of time is physically possible, we say that the process is reversible.

12. For a system [of particles] such as atoms and molecules (in general a quantum mechanical system), the transition probability is the rate of transition from one stationary state to another within a fixed period of time when [the system] receives a small external action, such as [one] from an electromagnetic field.

遺	イ	bequeathing

	ショク	propagating, increasing
殖	ふ(やす)	to propagate, increase
	ふ(える)	to propagate, increase

黄	オウ; コウ	yellow
	き	yellow

触	ショク	touching
	ふ(れる)	to touch

官	カン	organ {biol}; government

神	シン	spirit; gods

菌	キン	bacteria, fungi

精	セイ	precision, refinement; details; semen; spirit

経	ケイ	longitude; experience
	た(つ)	to elapse {time}
	...(を)へ(て)	via ...

染	セン	dyeing, staining
	そ(める)	to dye, stain
	そ(まる)	to be dyed, stained

血	ケツ	blood
	ち	blood

着	チャク	arriving
	つ(く)	to arrive, contact

酵	コウ	fermentation

透	トウ	transparent

差	サ	difference
	さ(す)	to offer

突	トツ	sudden; thrusting
	つ(く)	to thrust

再	サイ	again, re-
	ふたた(び)	again, a second time

燃	ネン	burning
	も(やす)	to burn
	も(える)	to burn

収	シュウ	taking in, collecting
	おさ(める)	to obtain, gather

媒	バイ	medium

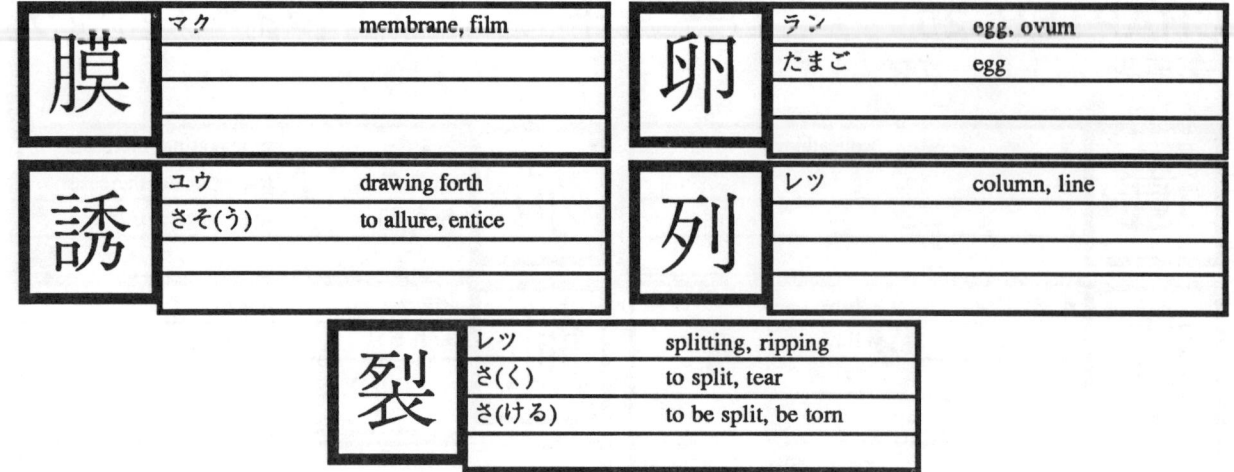

膜	マク	membrane, film
卵	ラン	egg, ovum
	たまご	egg
誘	ユウ	drawing forth
	さそ(う)	to allure, entice
列	レツ	column, line
裂	レツ	splitting, ripping
	さ(く)	to split, tear
	さ(ける)	to be split, be torn

VOCABULARY

遺

遺伝	イデン	heredity
遺伝学	イデンガク	genetics
遺伝子	イデンシ	gene
遺伝子分析	イデンシブンセキ	gene analysis
(複)対立遺伝子	(フク)タイリツイデンシ	(multiple) alleles

黄

硫黄	いオウ {N.B. irregular reading of 硫}	sulfur
黄鉄鉱	オウテッコウ	(iron) pyrite
黄銅	オウドウ	brass
黄銅鉱	オウドウコウ	chalcopyrite
黄色	きいろ	yellow
黄道	コウドウ	ecliptic
卵黄	ランオウ	egg yolk
卵黄細胞	ランオウサイボウ	egg yolk cell
卵黄膜	ランオウマク	vitelline membrane

官

器官	キカン	organ {biol}
器官系	キカンケイ	organ system
器官原基	キカンゲンキ	organ primordium
細胞(小)器官	サイボウ(ショウ)キカン	(cell) organelle
生殖器官	セイショクキカン	reproductive organ

| 消化器官 | ショウカキカン | digestive organ |
| 官能基 | カンノウキ | functional group {chem} |

菌

細菌	サイキン	bacteria
溶原菌	ヨウゲンキン	lysogenic bacteria
細菌学	サイキンガク	bacteriology
菌学	キンガク	mycology
菌類	キンルイ	fungi
菌核	キンカク	sclerotium
大腸菌	ダイチョウキン	*E. coli*

経

経過	ケイカ	passage {of time}
経験	ケイケン	experience
経験式	ケイケンシキ	empirical formula
経度	ケイド	longitude
経差	ケイサ	difference in longitude
(反応)経路	(ハンノウ)ケイロ	(reaction) path, (reaction) route
神経	シンケイ	nerve

血

血液	ケツエキ	blood
血圧	ケツアツ	blood pressure
血管	ケッカン	blood vessel
血糖	ケットウ	blood sugar
血液移送	ケツエキイソウ	blood transfusion
血色素	ケッシキソ	hemoglobin
血液色素	ケツエキシキソ	hemochrome
白血球	ハッケッキュウ	leucocyte
赤血球	セッケッキュウ	erythrocyte
出血	シュッケツ	hemorrhage

酵

酵素	コウソ	enzyme
透過酵素	トウカコウソ	permease
消化酵素	ショウカコウソ	digestive enzyme
酵素活性	コウソカッセイ	enzymatic activity
酵素の活性化	コウソのカッセイカ	activation of enzyme
発酵	ハッコウ	fermentation

差

差異	サイ	difference, disparity
差分方程式	サブンホウテイシキ	difference equation
差分法	サブンホウ	calculus of finite differences
差動変圧器	サドウヘンアツキ	differential transformer
示差熱分析	シサネツブンセキ	differential thermal analysis
電位差	デンイサ	potential difference
光行差	コウコウサ	aberration of light
色収差	いろシュウサ	chromatic aberration

再

再生結晶	サイセイケッショウ	regenerated crystal
再結晶	サイケッショウ	recrystallization
再結合	サイケツゴウ	recombination
再現精度	サイゲンセイド	reproducibility
再現性	サイゲンセイ	reproducibility
再処理	サイショリ	reprocessing
再使用	サイショウ	reuse, reusing
再生産曲線	サイセイサンキョクセン	reproduction curve
再利用する	サイリヨウする	to reuse

収

吸収	キュウシュウ	absorption
吸収剤	キュウシュウザイ	absorbent
吸収帯	キュウシュウタイ	absorption band
収率	シュウリツ	yield
収量	シュウリョウ	yield
収縮	シュウシュク	contraction
収縮期血圧	シュウシュクキケツアツ	systolic blood pressure
収着	シュウチャク	sorption
収差	シュウサ	aberration
収集	シュウシュウ	collection
回収する	カイシュウする	to recover

殖

生殖	セイショク	reproduction
生殖原細胞	セイショクゲンサイボウ	gonium
生殖器	セイショクキ	genital organ
生殖周期	セイショクシュウキ	reproductive cycle
生殖不能	セイショクフノウ	sterility
有性生殖	ユウセイセイショク	sexual reproduction

無性生殖	ムセイセイショク	asexual reproduction
増殖	ゾウショク	propagation, multiplication
増殖炉	ゾウショクロ	breeder reactor

触

触媒作用	ショクバイサヨウ	catalysis
接触分解	セッショクブンカイ	catalytic cracking
接触酸化	セッショクサンカ	catalytic oxidation
接触法	セッショクホウ	contact process
接触抵抗	セッショクテイコウ	contact resistance
接触角	セッショクカク	angle of contact
触角	ショッカク	antenna {biol}
小触角	ショウショッカク	small antenna
前触角	ゼンショッカク	anterior antenna

神

神経	シンケイ	nerve
神経系	シンケイケイ	nervous system
神経細管	シンケイサイカン	neural tubule
神経細胞	シンケイサイボウ	neuron
反射神経	ハンシャシンケイ	reflexes
精神安定剤	セイシンアンテイザイ	tranquilizer

精

精神	セイシン	mind, spirit
精子	セイシ	spermatozoon
精子形成	セイシケイセイ	spermatogenesis
精子進入	セイシシンニュウ	semination
精液	セイエキ	semen
精液糖	セイエキトウ	seminal sugar
受精	ジュセイ	fertilization
精製する	セイセイする	to refine
精製油	セイセイユ	refined oil
単離精製	タンリセイセイ	isolation purification
精白糖	セイハクトウ	refined sugar
精密な	セイミツな	precise
精密機械	セイミツキカイ	precision machinery
精油所	セイユショ	oil refinery

染

染料	センリョウ	dyestuff
染着性	センチャクセイ	dyeing affinity

染色	センショク	dyeing
染色法	センショクホウ	staining technique
染色体	センショクタイ	chromosome
染色体地図	センショクタイチズ	chromosome map
染色体異常	センショクタイイジョウ	chromosomal aberration
染色体の組み換え	センショクタイのくみかえ	recombination of chromosomes
(非)染色質	(ヒ)センショクシツ	(a)chromatin
細胞染色	サイボウセンショク	staining of bacteria
倍数染色体	バイスウセンショクタイ	diploid
半数染色体	ハンスウセンショクタイ	haploid
異常染色体	イジョウセンショクタイ	heterochromosome

着

着色	チャクショク	coloring
着色剤	チャクショクザイ	coloring agent
着目する	チャクモクする	to give attention to
着水する	チャクスイする	to land on water
着生植物	チャクセイショクブツ	epiphyte
接着剤	セッチャクザイ	adhesive
付着	フチャク	adhesion
吸着	キュウチャク	adsorption
粘着テープ	ネンチャクテープ	sticky tape

透

透過性	トウカセイ	permeability
透過X線	トウカXセン	penetrating X-rays
透過波	トウカハ	transmitted wave
透過率	トウカリツ	transmissivity
透磁率	トウジリツ	magnetic permeability
透析(法)	トウセキ(ホウ)	dialysis (method)
透明の	トウメイの	transparent
半透明の	ハントウメイの	translucent
不透明な	フトウメイな	opaque
半透-	ハントウ	semipermeable

突

突然の	トツゼンの	sudden
突然変異	トツゼンヘンイ	mutation
突然変異体	トツゼンヘンイタイ	mutant
突然変異細胞	トツゼンヘンイサイボウ	mutant cell
突然変異原	トツゼンヘンイゲン	mutagen

| 突起 | トッキ | protrusion, projection |
| 衝突 | ショウトツ | collision |

燃

燃料	ネンリョウ	fuel
燃料要素	ネンリョウヨウソ	fuel element
燃料集合体	ネンリョウシュウゴウタイ	fuel assembly
核燃料	カクネンリョウ	nuclear fuel
内燃機関	ナイネンキカン	internal combustion engine
可燃性の	カネンセイの	combustible

媒

触媒	ショクバイ	catalyst
媒染染料	バイセンセンリョウ	mordant dye
媒質	バイシツ	medium
溶媒	ヨウバイ	solvent
媒精	バイセイ	insemination

膜

膜電位	マクデンイ	membrane potential
膜小胞	マクショウホウ	membrane vesicle
半透膜	ハントウマク	semipermeable membrane
粘膜	ネンマク	mucous membrane
両性膜	リョウセイマク	amphoteric membrane
油膜	ユマク	oil film
薄膜	ハクマク; うすマク	film, thin membrane
生体膜	セイタイマク	biomembrane

誘

誘電体	ユウデンタイ	dielectric
誘電率	ユウデンリツ	dielectric constant
誘電分極	ユウデンブンキョク	induced polarization
誘電起電力	ユウデンキデンリョク	induced electromotive force
誘導	ユウドウ	induction
誘導電界	ユウドウデンカイ	induced electric field
誘導加速器	ユウドウカソクキ	induction accelerator
誘導性酵素	ユウドウセイコウソ	inducible enzyme
誘導体	ユウドウタイ	derivative {chem}
誘導物質	ユウドウブッシツ	inducing substance
誘導放射能	ユウドウホウシャノウ	induced radioactivity
誘発する	ユウハツする	to induce

卵

受精卵	ジュセイラン	fertilized egg
産卵期	サンランキ	spawning (season)
卵割	ランカツ	cleavage
卵白	ランパク	albumen
卵黄	ランオウ	yolk
卵形成	ランケイセイ	oogenesis
卵管	ランカン	oviduct
卵胞子	ランホウシ	oospore

列

行列	ギョウレツ	matrix {math}
行列式	ギョウレツシキ	determinant
配列	ハイレツ	arrangement, array
再配列	サイハイレツ	rearrangement

裂

核分裂	カクブンレツ	nuclear fission
細胞分裂	サイボウブンレツ	cell division
減数分裂	ゲンスウブンレツ	meiosis
分裂生殖	ブンレツセイショク	reproduction by division
分裂組織	ブンレツソシキ	meristem {botany}
分裂子	ブンレツシ	oidiospore
分裂菌類	ブンレツキンルイ	schizomycete

ADDITIONAL VOCABULARY FOR EXERCISES

Ex 20.3

ひきあう		to attract each other
形質	ケイシツ	character
形質発現	ケイシツハツゲン	phenotypic expression
...を異にする	をことにする	to differ in ...
分化	ブンカ	differentiation

Ex 20.4

両者の	リョウシャの	both
一体	イッタイ	a (single) unit
求心性	キュウシンセイ	afferent
しつくす {compound verb: する+つくす}		to do completely

Ex 20.5

せきつい		backbone, spine
体細胞	タイサイボウ	somatic cell
生体電位	セイタイデンイ	biopotential
温和な	オンワな	mild
立体特異性	リッタイトクイセイ	stereospecificity
限定する	ゲンテイする	to limit, restrict
多糖類	タトウルイ	polysaccharides
形態	ケイタイ	configuration

Ex 20.6

活性化剤	カッセイカザイ	activation agent
差しつかえない	さしつかえない	there is no reason not to ...
混同する	コンドウする	to mix up, confuse
非特異的な	ヒトクイテキな	unspecific
...むしろ		rather than ...
共存する	キョウゾンする	to coexist
ないし		or
置換	チカン	substitution
調製	チョウセイ	preparation
外表層	ガイヒョウソウ	outer-surface layer
所在する	ショザイする	to be located at, situated at
大腸	ダイチョウ	large intestine
生成能	セイセイノウ	ability to generate
物質交代	ブッシツコウタイ	metabolism

20 Vocabulary Building and Readings in Biology and Biochemistry

EXERCISES

Ex 20.1 Look-alike KANJI (see instructions in Ex 18.1)

1. (1) 然 (2) 燃	自( )	( )料
2. (1) 装 (2) 裂	分( )	( )置
3. (1) 則 (2) 測	法( )	観( )
4. (1) 透 (2) 誘	半( )明	( )電体
5. (1) 列 (2) 例	行( )	比( )
6. (1) 官 (2) 管	器( )	鉄( )
7. (1) 突 (2) 空	( )然	( )気
8. (1) 経 (2) 径	直( )	神( )
9. (1) 酵 (2) 酢	( )酸	( )素
10.(1) 着 (2) 差	付( )	( )異
11.(1) 異 (2) 黄	硫( )	( )常
12.(1) 情 (2) 静	( )圧	( )報
13.(1) 植 (2) 殖	( )物	生( )
14.(1) 固 (2) 個	( )定	( )人用
15.(1) 生 (2) 性	( )産	( )質
16.(1) 目 (2) 自	( )的	( )然
17.(1) 含 (2) 合	( )有	重( )
18.(1) 精 (2) 積	受( )	体( )
19.(1) 積 (2) 種	( )類	( )層

Ex 20.2 Matching Japanese and English technical terms

(a) Terms involving reproduction

減数分裂( )	1. cell division
細胞分裂( )	2. cleavage nucleus
受精波( )	3. cleavage plane
受精卵( )	4. fertilized egg
媒精( )	5. fertilization wave
卵黄核( )	6. insemination
卵黄球( )	7. meiosis
卵黄膜( )	8. oogenesis
卵割核( )	9. oogonium
卵割面( )	10. yolk nucleus
卵形成( )	11. yolk sphere
卵原細胞( )	12. vitteline membrane

(b) Terms involving genetics

異常染色体( )	1. alleles
遺伝( )	2. chromosome
遺伝学( )	3. chromosome map
遺伝子( )	4. gene
遺伝子分析( )	5. gene analysis
染色体( )	6. genetics
染色体地図( )	7. heredity
対立遺伝子( )	8. heterochromosome
突然変異( )	9. mutagen
突然変異原( )	10. mutant
突然変異細胞( )	11. mutant cell
突然変異体( )	12. mutation

(c) Terms involving the blood

血液移送( )	1. blood sugar
血液色素( )	2. blood transfusion
血管( )	3. blood vessel
血色素( )	4. erythrocyte
血糖( )	5. hemochrome
出血( )	6. hemoglobin
赤血球( )	7. hemorrhage
白血球( )	8. leucocyte

(d) Terms involving bacteria and fungi

菌核( )	1. bacteria
菌学( )	2. bacteriology
菌類( )	3. fungi
細菌( )	4. lysogenic bacteria
細菌学( )	5. mycology
分裂子( )	6. oidiospore
分裂菌類( )	7. schizomycete
溶原菌( )	8. sclerotium

(e) Terms involving the nerves and the mind

安定剤( )	1. nervous system
神経系( )	2. neuron
神経細管( )	3. neuroreceptor
神経細胞( )	4. neurotransmitter
神経受容体( )	5. neural tube
神経伝達物質( )	6. psychometrics
精神異常発現性物質( )	7. psychoneurosis
精神神経症[ショウ = illness]( )	8. psychotogen
精神測定( )	9. schizophrenia
精神分裂病[ビョウ = illness]( )	10. tranquilizer

Ex 20.3 Matching Japanese technical terms and definitions

(a) Physical sciences

官能基( )   1. 変位電流は通すが導電電流に対しては高い抵抗を示すもの。
再現性( )   2. 自らは反応の前後に変化がなく、ある化学反応の速さを変化
色収差( )   させるために反応系に加えられる少量の物質。
触媒( )   3. 酸化バナジウム触媒などを用いて、二酸化硫黄を三酸化硫黄
接触法( )   へ酸化する方法。
透過性( )   4. 半透膜を用い、コロイド溶液中の電解質などの低分子溶質を
透析( )   とりのぞく操作[ソウサ = operations]。
半透性( )   5. 固体中を液体またはガス体が透過する性質。
付着( )   6. 膜が溶液中の一部の成分は通すが、他は通さない場合の性質。
誘電体( )   7. 化合物が異なっても本質的には同じ反応性を示す有機化合物
       の分子構造の中の原子団[ダン = group]。
       8. ある実験の結果と同じ条件下で再び実験を行ったときの結果
       との差の程度。
       9. 波長による屈折率の相違すなわち分散によって起こる収差。
    10. 異種の2物質が接触したとき互いにひきあう現象。

(b) Biological sciences

遺伝子分析( )   1. 個体群[グン = group]における密度と次世代[セダイ =
再生産曲線( )   generation]への増殖の関係を示すもの。
細胞器官( )   2. ある形質の遺伝について、その遺伝子の数、染色体上
精子進入( )   の場所などを決定[ケッテイ = decision]すること。
突然変異原( )   3. 同一遺伝子座[ザ = locus]にあって形質発現に対する作
突然変異体( )   用を少しずつ異にする一群[グン]の遺伝子。
媒精( )   4. 突然変異した遺伝子をもつ個体または細胞。
複対立遺伝子( ) 5. 器官原基または組織の分化が誘導によって起こされる
誘導性酵素( )   ときにはたらくと考えられる物質。
誘導物質( )   6. 突然変異を誘発するような物理的または化学的作用を
       有するもの。
       7. 細胞に特定の誘導物質を加えることによって、合成の
       速度が増加する酵素。
       8. 精子と卵が同じ液体の媒質中におかれたとき、受精が
       行われること。
       9. 原形質の一部が特殊[トクシュ = special]に分化し、一定
       の機能をもつ有機的単位となった細胞内の構造。
    10. 精子が受精にさいして卵に入りこむこと。

Ex 20.4 Translate the following sentences

1. 試料と基準物質(測定温度範囲[ハンイ = range]内で熱的異常を示さない物質)を一定の温度上昇[ジョウショウ = rise]率で加熱し、両者の間に生じる温度差から試料の熱的性質を解析する方法を示差熱分析という。

2. 燃料集合体とは、原子炉内外への核燃料の出し入れに際し、一体となった燃料要素の集合である。

3. 一般の化学反応はいくつかの素反応から構成されている複合反応であるが、各素反応の配列と順序[ジュンジョ = order]をふくむ反応の経路と、さらに各素反応の速度の相対的大小関係や律速段階[リッソクダンカイ = rate-controlling step]などの知見を総合して[from ソウゴウする = to synthesize]反応構成という。

4. 第一触角とは甲殻類[コウカクルイ = crustacea]の2対の触角のうち、前方の1対で、第二対(第二触角)に比べて小形の場合が多いので小触角または前触角ともよぶ。

5. 溶液を構成する一成分を溶媒、他の成分を溶質といい、液体と固体、または液体と気体からなる溶液では液体成分を溶媒、液体と液体では多量のほうを一般に溶媒という。

6. 生物学では反射という言葉[ことば=word]は光学における場合と全く違った意味[イミ = meaning]で使われているが、それは生体の受容器に内・外から刺激[シゲキ = stimuli]が与えられ、発生した求心性インパルスが反射神経系を経て遠心性[エンシンセイ =efferent]インパルスに変換され、意識[イシキ = consciousness]作用の関与なしに、ある器官に特定的な反応を誘発することである。

7. 生物体内において生体物質は常に合成されると同時に分解されているが、ある生体物質を完全に[カンゼンに = completely]分解しつくさないで、途中の[トチュウの = intermediate]段階[ダンカイ = stage]で回収し、再利用するような反応をサルベージ合成(salvage synthesis)という。

8. 普通の[フツウの = usual]細胞分裂は同じ細胞2個が生ずる均等[キントウ =equal]分裂であるが、分化を伴う[ともなう]場合は質的、量的に表現形質の異なった細胞を生ずる不均等[キントウ]分裂となることがあり、たとえばマウスのリンパ球の場合は遺伝子配列の異なった細胞が生ずることが知られている。

Ex 20.5 Read the following short essays for comprehension

1. 透過酵素とは能動輸送[ユソウ = transport]のうち、比較的[ヒカクテキ = comparatively]少数のタンパク質で構成されている輸送系[ユソウケイ =transport system]を示す。パーミアゼ、ペルミアーゼなどともよばれる。物質を膜の外部から内部へ透過させる働き[はたらき = work]をもつ。物質に対して特異性をもつこと、飽和の見られること、阻害剤[ソガイザイ = inhibitor]

の存在することなど酵素に似た[from にる = to resemble]面があるので、酵素様[ヨウ = kind of]の名[な = name]でよばれるが、物質が化学的に変化するわけではない。そのためキャリヤーとよばれることが多い。

Adapted from p. 858 of 『生化学辞典』, 化学同人, 1984.

2. ヘモグロビンとはせきつい動物[vertebrates]のすべて、および若干の[ジャッカンの = a few of]無せきつい動物[invertebrates]の血液に含まれる色素蛋白質[タンパクシツ]で、グロビンとヘムとから成る。酸素との結合能力が強く、空気中の酸素分圧により容易に[ヨウイに = easily]酸素化されて、ヘム1分子と酸素1分子とが特殊な[トクシュな]結合(酸素付加)をして酸素ヘモグロビンとなるが、酸素分圧が低下すれば、また容易に[ヨウイに]酸素を放出してデオキシ型に戻る[もどる = to return]性質をもち、血中の酸素運搬体[ウンパンタイ = carrier]として重要な役割[ヤクわり = role]を果たしている。ヘモグロビンは複合蛋白質のうちでは分離精製による結晶化が容易な[ヨウイな=easy]ものであって、蛋白化学的に最もよく研究されたものの一つである。

Adapted from p. 1186 of 『生物学辞典』, 岩波書店, 1983.

3. 染色体数は各生物種に固有で生物の種類により一定である。たとえばソラマメ[broad bean]では12本(6対)、ニワトリ[chicken]は78本(39対)、人間では46本(23対)などである。染色体の数と形はそれぞれ、生物種の重要な遺伝的な特徴[トクチョウ= distinctive feature]である。体細胞では形の等しい二組の染色体からできている。一組は母方[ははかた = mother's side]から他の一組は父方[ちちかた = father's side]から由来した[from ユライする = to originate (in)]もので、これを全数(2n)で表し、生殖細胞の染色体数は半数(n)で表される。

Adapted from ibid., p. 712.

4. 膜電位とは一般には膜によって隔てられた[from へだてる = to separate]溶液の間に発生する電位差である。細胞やミトコンドリアなど細胞小器官は生体膜に包まれており[from つつむ = to wrap]、その内外の間に見られる生体電位はこの種の電位と考えられる。二つの電解質溶液を膜で仕切り[from シきる = to partition]、その一側[イチがわ = one side]に膜を透過しない粒子を含ませると、その影響によって電解質の両側[リョウがわ = both sides]分布が変化し、ドナンの膜平衡[ヘイコウ = equilibrium]が成立すれば、膜の両側[リョウがわ]にドナンの膜電位が成立する。このような不透性の粒子が存在せず、単に濃度の異なる電解質が仕切られている[from シきる]だけでも、陽イオンと陰イオンの膜を通る速さが異なる場合には電位差が発生する。

両側に0.1Nと0.01NのKClを入れた場合に発生する膜電位は、膜の特性を示すものとして標準膜電位差といわれ、最大58 mVに達する。

Adapted from ibid., p. 1242.

5．生体内の種々の反応の触媒となる酵素は、常温、常圧という温和な条件下での優れた[from すぐれる = to be excellent]触媒作用や、基質に対する選択性[センタクセイ = selectivity]、反応の立体特異性など、通常の化学触媒の成し得ない利点を有している。反面、熱、強酸、強アルカリ、有機溶媒などに対して不安定であるためその利用が限定され、また反応終了[シュウリョウ = completion]後、溶液状態から活性な酵素を回収して再利用することは非常にむずかしい。

Adapted from p. 6 of 『バイオテクノロジー』, 化学工学協会編, 槙書店, 1986.

6．微生物の細胞は細胞膜の外側[そとがわ = outside]に多糖類を主[シュ = main]成分とする細胞壁[ヘキ = wall]をもっており、これは細胞の形態を特徴づける[トクチョウづける = to characterize]と共に、外部との間で、浸透圧[シントウアツ = osmotic pressure]のバランスをたもつ役割[ヤクわり = role]を果たしている。そこで、この細胞壁[ヘキ]を溶解酵素などによって除去する[ジョキョする = to remove]とプロトプラスト[protoplast]とよばれる裸[はだか = bare]の細胞が得られる。この細胞は外壁を欠く[かく = to lack]ことにより球状の形態を有し、浸透圧[シントウアツ]感受性[カンジュセイ = sensitivity]であるため、プロトプラストをうかべた[from うかべる = to float]溶液に浸透圧安定剤を加えなければ破裂して[from ハレツする = to burst]溶解してしまう。

Adapted from ibid., p. 62.

Ex 20.6 Read the following longer essays for comprehension

1．酵素の活性化は酵素活性の上昇[ジョウショウ]である。酵素活性がない状態からある状態に変換するに際[サイ]して、その前後で酵素タンパク質分子に化学修飾[シュウショク = modification]が見られる場合は、正しくは酵素の活性化とはよばずに酵素前駆体[ゼンクタイ = precursor]の活性化とよぶべきである。チモーゲンの活性化(activation of zymogen)はその典型例[テンケイレイ = typical example]である。これに対して、ある酵素活性の測定に際して、特定の金属イオンやSH[スルフヒドリル = sulfhydryl]還元剤[カンゲンザイ = reducing agent]の添加[テンカ = addition]により活性上昇がみられるならば、それは酵素活性の賦活[フカツ](stimulation of enzyme activity)であり、簡単[カンタン = simple]には酵素が活性化されたという。また、いわゆるアロステリック[allosteric]活性化剤(正のモジュレーター)が酸素分子に相

20-15

互作用をもったために酵素活性が上昇した場合も、酵素の活性化とよんで差しつかえない。しかし、活性化(activation)という用語[ヨウゴ＝technical term]はチモーゲンの活性化という異なった現象の記述用語[ヨウゴ]とまぎらわしい[to be confused with]ので、混同しないように注意[チュウイ＝attention]して使用する必要がある。酵素の活性化は、温度、pH、溶媒のイオン強度など非特異的な因子[インシ＝factor]によってもたらされる[from もたらす＝to cause]ほかに、その酵素に特異的な因子[インシ]によってひき起こされる。特定の金属イオンや補酵素[ホコウソ＝coenzyme]などの補因子[ホインシ＝cofactor]のほかに、人為的な[ジンイテキな＝artificial]活性化の例としては、活性に必須[ヒッス＝essential]のSH基を保護[ホゴ＝protection]する目的で反応系に添加[テンカ]されるシステイン[cysteine]や2-メルカプトエタノール[2-mercaptoethanol]などをあげることができる。これらの薬剤は、本来[ホンライ＝original]天然の[テンネンの＝natural]酵素が保有していた[from ホユウする＝to possess]因子ではないので、活性化剤というにふさわしい[appropriate]。活性化剤の活性化機構は、補酵素[ホコウソ]を含む補因子[ホインシ]やアロステリック活性化剤の場合を除いて[from のぞく＝to exclude]は、むしろ明らかでない場合が多い。ある添加物が見かけの活性化を与えた場合でも、その仕組みが酵素失活[シッカツ＝loss of activity]の防止作用[ボウシサヨウ＝inhibiting action]にある場合もある。また、粗[ソ＝crude]酵素標品[commercial product]を用いて実験している時に、ある添加物で観察される活性化現象は、当該[トウガイ＝the said]酵素そのものの活性化ではなくて、その酵素標品に共存する阻害物質[ソガイブッシツ＝inhibiting substance]の除去[ジョキョ]ないし阻害物質[ソガイブッシツ]との解離または置換にすぎない場合もあるので注意[チュウイ]を要する。ある添加物で真の[シンの＝true]活性化がみられた場合には、それが本来の[ホンライの]補因子(補酵素を含む)であるかどうかを明らかにし、また、阻害物質についてするのと同様の[ドウヨウの＝same kind of]反応動力学的解析を行って、活性化剤定数(K_a)を求め、活性化機構を研究する。

Adapted from pp. 451-452 of 『生化学辞典』.

2.　　　　　　　　酸化発酵と電子伝達系

　　上に述べた酸化発酵の酵素は、スフェロプラスト[spheroplast]から調製した膜小胞と反転膜小胞について活性やイムノブロットを調べることで、いずれも細胞膜の外表層に所在していることがわかっている。だから、酸化発酵では大量の基質は細胞に入ることなく、ペリプラズム[periplasmic]側[がわ＝side]だけで酸化されて、大量の生産物を蓄積[チクセキ＝accumulation]する。このとき、図に示すように、基質の脱水素[ダッスイソ＝dehydrogenation]で生じた電子は細胞膜中の電子伝達鎖[サ＝chain]に渡され[from わたす＝to transfer]、最終的[サイシュウテキ＝ultimate]には末端[マッタン＝terminal]酸化酵素の働き[はたらき]で酸素と結合して水になる。そのようにいうと簡単に[カンタンに = simply]聞こえる[きこえる = to sound]が、そのディテールはどうか、となると難しい[むずかしい = difficult]。

　脱水素[ダッスイソ]酵素と末端[マッタン]酸化酵素の単離精製については上に述べた。残る[のこる = to remain]問題は電子伝達鎖[サ]の詳細[ショウサイ = details]である。脱水素酵素から電子が渡される[from わたす = to transfer]成分は何[なに = what]か、末端酸化酵素に電子を渡すのは何[なに]か、1つの電子伝達鎖が酸化発酵とエネルギー生成の両方に機能しているのか、それとも電子伝達鎖は2つに分岐[ブンキ = branch]してそれぞれの機能を分担している[from ブンタンする = to carry]のか、それらについて調べた成果を紹介したい[from ショウカイする = to introduce]。

酢酸菌のグルコースあるいはアルコール酸化系の再構成

　酢酸菌のグルコース酸化系の再構成は、大腸菌[ダイチョウキン = *E. coli*]の場合と同様に[ドウヨウに = similarly]、グルコースデヒドロゲナーゼ[glucose dehydrogenase]を初め[ハジメ = beginning]から混合ミセル[micelle]中に加える。酢酸菌の場合にはオクチルグルコシド[octyl glucoside]希釈[キシャク = dilution]法よりも透析法のほうが再構成の効率がよい。アルコール酸化系は先に[さきに = previously]リン脂質とQ10とcytochrome *o*から成るプロテオリボソーム[proteoribosome]を作っておいて、アルコールデヒドロゲナーゼを後から加えることでも再構成することができる。2つの脱水素酵素の疎水性の[ソスイセイの = hydrophobic]違いによるものだろう。

　再構成系は図4に示すように、大腸菌[ダイチョウキン]のときと同様[ドウヨウ]、脱水素酵素とQ10とcytochrome *o*の3成分だけから成る。

　H^+の電気化学的勾配[コウバイ = gradient]はこの図に示しているようにして形成される。すなわち、脱水素酵素によって基質からぬきだされた[from ぬきだす = to remove]H^+と電子が、ユビキノン[ubiquinone]を介して[from カイする = by means of] cytochrome *o*に渡される。H^+と電子はcytochrome *o*の分子内で分離し、H^+だけが外側[そとがわ]に放出されるとともに、電子は逆に内側[うちがわ = inside]に運ばれ、H^+と反応して水を形成する。このとき、陽電荷[カ = charge]が外側に移動し、負[フ = negative]電荷[カ]が内側[うちがわ]に移動するために、内部に負[フ]の電位を生じるし、また、H^+が外側に放出され内側のH^+が消費[ショウヒ = consumption]されるために内部がアルカリ性となる。膜電位とpH勾配[コウバイ]は、疎水性[ソスイセイ]の蛍光[ケイコウ = fluorescent]色素であるカーボシアニンとダンシルグリシンがそれぞれ膜小胞内に取り込まれる[from とりこむ = to take within]ために生じる消光から測定できる。このように、*G. suboxydans*のcytochrome*o*はユビキノールオキシダーゼとしてはたらき、エネルギー生成能をもっている。

末端[マッタン＝terminal]酸化酵素のところで生成するエネルギーとして、グルコース酸化系では190 mV、アルコール酸化系では260 mVの電位差が観察された。このプロテオリボソームの物質交代回転も細胞膜のそれと同等であった。

　　このように、大腸菌と*Gluconobacter*についてはエネルギーを作るほうの電子伝達鎖は解明できた。

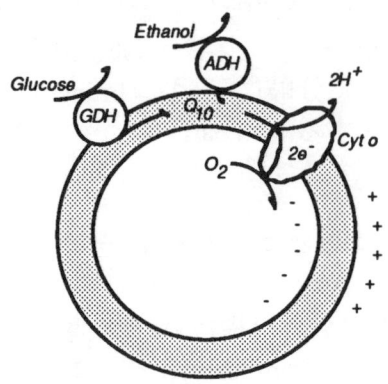

図4　*Gluconobacter*のグルコースとアルコールの酸化系を再構成したプロテ
　　　オリボソーム(模式図)
　　　　　GDH: グルコース脱水素酵素。
　　　　　ADH: アルコール脱水素酵素。
　　　　　Cyt *o*: チトクロム *o*。

Adapted from pp. 6-7 of 『酢酸菌の生化学的研究』, 飴山實著, 日本農芸化学会誌, 第62巻, 第8号, 昭和63年, 8月.

TRANSLATIONS

Ex 20.4 Sentences

1. Differential thermal analysis is a method for analyzing the thermal properties of a sample from the temperature differences that arise between the sample and a standard substance (a substance that does not exhibit thermal abnormalities within the temperature range of the measurements) when both are heated at a constant rate of rising temperature.

2. A fuel assembly is an assembly of fuel elements to form a single unit [and to function as one] when nuclear fuel is inserted into and removed from a nuclear reactor.

3. General chemical reactions are compound reactions consisting of several elementary reactions, and the reaction mechanism is the synthesis of information such as [the following]: the path of the reactions, including the arrangement and order of the individual elementary reactions; the relation between the relative magnitudes of the velocities of the individual elementary reactions and their rate-controlling steps.

4. The first antenna [pair] of a crustacean is the anterior pair of its two pairs of antennas; they are called the anterior antennas or, because they are frequently small in comparison to the second antenna [pair], the small antennas.

5. Of the components that constitute a solution, one is called the solvent, the other the solute; for solutions made from liquids and solids, or from liquids and gases, the liquid component is (called) the solvent; for those made from liquids and liquids, it is generally the one [that is present] in a larger quantity.

6. In biology the word HANSHA is used with a meaning completely different from that in (the case of) optics; it is the process that induces a specific reaction in a certain organ, without involving conscious action, when the receptors of the organism are given a stimulus from within or without, and the afferent impulses [thus] generated are converted to efferent impulses via the reflex system.

7. The biosubstances in the body of an organism are continually being synthesized and at the same time being broken down, but some biosubstances are not completely broken down. [These] are recovered at an intermediate stage, and the [chemical] reactions in which they are used are called salvage syntheses.

8. The usual cell division is equal division in which two similar cells are generated; but when [cell division] accompanies differentiation, it becomes unequal division in which cells having qualitatively and quantitatively different expressive characteristics are generated; for example, it is known that cells having different genetic arrangements arise in the (case of) differentiation of lymphocytes in mice.

Appendix **A**   Table of Verb Forms

The table summarizes the verb forms that can be generated for the two major classes of verbs, the xu-verbs and the ru-verbs. It also includes the four irregular verbs. In Japanese the xu-verbs are called GODAN verbs, and the ru-verbs are referred to as ICHIDAN verbs.

A.1 Stems, Bases, and Endings

The stem of a verb is obtained by removing the final syllable of the dictionary form.

Dictionary Form		Stem	
示す	[しめす]	示	[しめ]
定まる	[さだまる]	定ま	[さだま]
定める	[さだめる]	定め	[さだめ]
間違う	[まちがう]	間違	[まちが]
及ぼし合う	[およぼしあう]	及ぼし合	[およぼしあ]
見る	[みる]	見	[み]
出る	[でる]	出	[で]

The stem is the unchanging part of the verb; that is, it remains constant throughout all inflected forms. The verbs する and くる are irregular because their stems are variable.

Various bases of a verb are formed by adding one, two, or no HIRAGANA symbols to the stem. Most of the table is concerned with showing how the bases are formed for the xu- and ru-verbs. The verbs ある and 行く are each irregular in one base.

The endings are syllables that are added to the various bases in order to generate the inflected forms of the verbs. The endings are given at the bottom of the chart, along with the corresponding names of the inflected forms. The endings are to be added to the bases in the columns directly above them. For example, the negative of 示す is obtained by adding the ending ない to the base form 示さ to give 示さない. The negative of 定める is obtained by adding the same ending, ない, to the base form 定め to give 定めない. Note that this table is so arranged that *all* verbs have the same set of endings, these being added to the various bases. These bases then play a key role in the verb conjugations and they are obtained from the dictionary form of the verb by well-defined algorithms.

A.2 Classification of Verbs

In this book we divide the verbs into six classes: xu-verbs, irregular xu-verbs, ru-verbs, irregular ru-verbs, the verb "masu," and the xaru-verbs. The first four classes are found in technical Japanese and are included in the table; the other two classes are found in instruction manuals and in some other types of writing, as discussed in Chapter 13.

a. The xu-Verbs

In the dictionary form (the present tense) these verbs end in a syllable of the u-column of the KANA table (see Chapter 4); we designate such syllables by 'xu', where the 'x' stands for a consonant (k, g, s, ts, n, b, m, or r) or no consonant at all. Specifically, 'xu' can stand for う, く, ぐ, す, つ, ぬ, ぶ, む, or る. The xu-verbs have five bases consisting of the stem plus the KANA symbols for xa, xi, xu, xe, and xo, as well as a "modified xi-base" shown at the right of the table. There is one irregularity in the bases for verbs whose dictionary form ends in う: the xa-base ends in わ, not あ! For the xu-verbs the only base that is difficult to learn is the "modified xi-base."

b. Irregular xu-Verbs

This class contains two verbs for each of which one base is irregular: (1) the modified xi-base of 行く is 行っ (*not* 行い, as one might expect for an xu-verb whose dictionary form ends in く); (2) the verb ある does *not* have an xa-base あら, as one might expect for an xu-verb ending in る. The negative of the verb ある is the adjective ない, which may be found in the table in Appendix B.

c. The ru-Verbs

The dictionary forms of these verbs end in 'xiru' or 'xeru' — that is, they end in る, and the next-to-last syllable must be one from the い or え column of the HIRAGANA table. Note in the table that the bases for the ru-verbs are formed quite differently from those for the xu-verbs. Note particularly that some bases are identical to the verb stem. Most verbs ending in "xiru" and "xeru" are ru-verbs and are inflected like 用いる and 定める, but a few are inflected like xu-verbs that end in 'ru' such as 作る; the most important of these in technical Japanese are

A-2

入る	[はいる]	to enter		減る	[へる]	to decrease
要る	[いる]	to need		照る	[てる]	to shine
知る	[しる]	to know		帰る	[かえる]	to return
限る	[かぎる]	to limit		滑る	[すべる]	to slip
散る	[ちる]	to scatter		練る	[ねる]	to knead
切る	[きる]	to cut		捻る	[ひねる]	to turn, twist
走る	[はしる]	to run		湿る	[しめる]	to be(come) damp
遮る	[さえぎる]	to obstruct		茂る	[しげる]	to grow thickly, luxuriantly
陥る	[おちいる]	to fall into				
握る	[にぎる]	to grasp				
混じる	[まじる]	to mingle				
仕切る	[しきる]	to partition				

d. Irregular ru-Verbs

This class contains only the two variable stem verbs, くる and する. These verbs occur with very high frequency.

e. The Verb "masu"

The verb ます is attached to the xi-base to form polite verbs. See Chapter 13 for a discussion of ます as well as of です (a contraction of であります). The conjugation of ます is different from that of an xu-verb ending in す.

f. The xaru-Verbs

There are five verbs in this group, which we list here along with their polite (ます) forms, the latter being formed from an irregular xi-base that ends in い instead of り.

下さる	[くださる]	下さいます	to give
おっしゃる		おっしゃいます	to say
なさる		なさいます	to do
いらっしゃる		いらっしゃいます	to be, go, come
ござる		ございます	to be

These verbs are discussed in Chapter 13.

Japanese Verbs: Stems, Bases, and Endings

xu

Stems	Bases → xa-Base (Stem+xa)	xi-Base (Stem+xi)	DICTIONARY FORM xu-Base (Stem+xu)	xe-Base (Stem+xe)	xo-Base (Stem+xo)	Modified xi-Base
REGULAR						
shimesu 示 [しめ]	示さ	示し	示す	示せ	示そ	示し
tatsu 立 [た]	立た	立ち	立つ	立て	立と	立っ
tsukuru 作 [つく]	作ら	作り	作る	作れ	作ろ	作っ
tsukau 使 [つか]	使わ !	使い	使う	使え	使お	使っ
tsuku 付 [つ]	付か	付き	付く	付け	付こ	付い
sosogu 注 [そそ]	注が	注ぎ	注ぐ	注げ	注ご	注い
musubu 結 [むす]	結ば	結び	結ぶ	結べ	結ぼ	結ん
fukumu 含 [ふく]	含ま	含み	含む	含め	含も	含ん
shinu 死 [し]	死な	死に	死ぬ	死ね	死の	死ん
IRREGULAR						
iku 行 [い]	行か …!	行き	行く	行け	行こ	行っ !
aru あ [り]	…!	あり	ある	あれ	あろ	あっ

ru

Stems	Bases → ra-Base (Stem+ra)	sa-Base (Stem+sa)	Stem	ru-Base (Stem+ru)	re-Base (Stem+re)	rare-Base (Stem+rare)	yo-Base (Stem+yo)	yo-Base (Stem+yo)	xo-Base yo-Base (Stem+yo)	Modified Stem
REGULAR										
mochiiru 用い [もちい]	用いら	用いさせ	用い	用いる	用いれ	用いられ	用いよ	用いよ	用いよ	用い
sadameru 定め [さだめ]	定めら	定めさせ	定め	定める	定めれ	定められ	定めよ	定めよ	定めよ	定め
IRREGULAR										
kuru variable	こさ	こさせ	き	くる	くれ	こられ	こい	こい	こよ	き
suru variable	させ	させ	し	する	すれ	…	せよ	せよ	しよ	し

Endings to add to bases for all verbs →

	Neg	NC	Pass	Caus	C	D	Pol	Other	P	Ger	Other	Prov	Pot	Imp	Ten
	ない	ず	れる	せる	…	たい	ます	ながら / つつ / やすい# / にくい / そうな*	…	…	こと / らしい# / ようだ*	ば	る	…	う

Terminology used in this book (chapter numbers in parentheses) →

Neg	Negative (7) #
NC	Negative Conjunctive (9)
Pass	Passive (11) $
Caus	Causative (11) $
C	Conjunctive (9)
D	Desiderative (13) #
Pol	Polite (13) &
	Other (11, 13)
P	Present (7)
Ger	Gerund (8)
	Other (11, 13)
Prov	Provisional (10)
Pot	Potential (11) $
Imp	Imperative (13)
Ten	Tentative (12)

Terminology (continued) →

- Past (8)
- Conditional (10)
- Representative (13)
- Past Tentative (⋯)
- Connective (9)
- Progressive (9) $

Past	Conditional	Representative	Past Tentative	Connective	Progressive
だ	だら	だろ	で	でいる	でいる
た	たら	たろう	て	ている	ている

Appendix **B** Table of Adjective Forms

The table provides an overview of the principal inflected forms of the two types of adjectives: i-adjectives, and na- and no-adjectives. These forms are obtained by adding endings to the stems of the adjectives, which are given in the second column.

B.1 The i-Adjectives

The i-adjectives (sometimes called "true adjectives" or "verbal adjectives") are characterized by the ending い in the dictionary form; the stem is formed by dropping the い. In the table three kinds of i-adjectives are included: (a) the regular i-adjectives, further classified according to their endings (-xai, -xii, -xui, and -xoi), all of which are inflected according to a single pattern; (b) the verb forms that are i-adjectives; (c) the i-adjectives of size and quantity that show irregularities in their attributive forms (indicated by "!").

B.2 The na- and no-Adjectives

The na-adjectives (sometimes called "quasi-adjectives," "adjectival nouns," or "nominal adjectives") are characterized by the ending な in the dictionary form; the stem is formed by dropping the な. In the table we also include the no-adjectives (sometimes called "quasi-adjectival nouns" or "precopular nouns"), since their inflections are very similar to those of the na-adjectives. The irregular adjective 同じ is also included, with its irregularities marked by "!"

B.3 The Endings

The endings for i-adjectives are given across the top of the table, and those for the na- and no-adjectives are given in the middle. At the bottom we give "further endings," in three boxes labeled *, #, and &; these can be added to the inflected forms of all adjectives directly above the corresponding symbols in the chart. For example, in the third column from the right, 熱かった is the past form of the i-adjective 熱い, and 熱かったら and 熱かったり are the conditional and representative forms; also 重要であった is the past form of the na-adjective 重要な and 重要であったら and 重要であったり are the conditional and representative forms.

B-1

Japanese Adjectives: Stems and Endings

i

	Stems		い	...	な/の		く	に	くて	ければ	かった	かろう	さ
REGULAR													
takai	高	[たか]	高い				高く		高くて	高ければ	高かった	高かろう	高さ
hitoshii	等し	[ひとし]	等しい				等しく		等しくて	等しければ	等しかった	等しかろう	等しさ
atsui	熱	[あつ]	熱い				熱く		熱くて	熱ければ	熱かった	熱かろう	熱さ
omoi	重	[おも]	重い				重く		重くて	重ければ	重かった	重かろう	重さ
VERB FORMS													
nai	な	[な]	ない				なく		なくて	なければ	なかった	なかろう	な…
shimesanai	示さな	[しめさな]	示さない				示さなく		示さなくて	示さなければ	示さなかった	示さなかろう	示さ…
shimeshitai	示した	[しめした]	示したい				示したく		示したくて	示したければ	示したかった	示したかろう	示した…
IRREGULAR													
ookii	大き	[おおき]	大きい		大きな!		大きく		大きくて	大きければ	大きかった	大きかろう	大きさ
chiisai	小さ	[ちいさ]	小さい		小さな!		小さく		小さくて	小さければ	小さかった	小さかろう	小ささ
ooi	多	[おお]	多い		多くの!		多く		多くて	多ければ	多かった	多かろう	多さ
sukunai	少な	[すくな]	少ない		…!		少なく		少なくて	少なければ	少なかった	少なかろう	少な…

na/no

	Stems		な/の	である	*	な/の	#	で(ある)	に	で	であれば	であった	であろう	さ
REGULAR														
juuyoo na	重要	[ジュウヨウ]	重要な	重要である		重要な		重要で(あり)	重要に	重要で(あって)	重要であれば	重要であった	重要であろう	重要さ
muyoo no	無用	[ムヨウ]	無用の	無用である		無用な		無用で(あり)	無用に	無用で(あって)	無用であれば	無用であった	無用であろう	無用さ
IRREGULAR														
onaji	同じ	[おなじ]	同じ!	同じである		同じ!		同じで	同じに	同じで(であって)	同じであれば	同じであった	同じであろう	…

	DF	Trm	*	Attr	#	Conj	Adv	Conn	Prov	P	&	Ten	Noun

Terminology used in this book (chapter numbers in parentheses) →

DF	Dictionary Form (7)
Trm	Terminal (end of clause) (7)
Attr	Attributive (before noun) (7)
#	Conjunctive (9)
	Adverbial (9)
	Connective (9)
Prov	Provisional (10)
P	Past (8)
Ten	Tentative (12)
Noun	Noun (11)
&	Conditional (10)
	Representative (13)

* **! Note irregularity**

Further endings for all adjectives →

#	Terminal (polite) (13)	です
	Tentative (12)	だろう
	Provisional (10)	なら(ば)
	Semblative (11)	らしい

*	Negative (7)	(は)ない
	Negative (polite) (13)	(は)ありません

Appendix C
Additional KANJI Frequent in Technical Japanese

Here we list 135 additional important KANJI, compiled mainly by using several KANJI frequency tabulations. Some of these KANJI are frequent because they form nontechnical words that are common in technical reading, such as the KANJI 意, which appears in 意味, "meaning," 注意, "caution," and 意見, "opinion." Others are frequent because they form technical words that are common to several disciplines; for example, the KANJI 凝, which appears in 凝固, "solidification, coagulation," and in 凝縮, "condensation."

However, frequency was not the only basis for our choices. Some KANJI are included because of their obvious importance in a given field; for example, 星, "star" is clearly essential in astronomy, as are 火, "fire," 木, "wood," and 土, "earth" for 火星, "Mars," 木星, "Jupiter," and 土星, "Saturn." A few KANJI are included in order to provide the "opposite" for KANJI among the 365 in the main body of the book: for example, 短, "short" is included as a complement to 長, "long," 軽, "light" as a complement to 重, "heavy."

The KANJI are listed by ON reading in the 五十音 order. For KANJI having a transitive-intransitive pair, only the transitive verb is given. The JUKUGO in the list are for the most part ones that can be formed from KANJI in the list of 365 and those in this list of 135. For the few exceptions, the KANA pronunciations are underlined. Parentheses are used when a JUKUGO contains a word that may be replaced with other words. Thus, 遠心(分離機), "centrifugal (separator)," illustrates a use of 遠. We might also have used 遠心(力), "centrifugal (force)."

C-1

依	イ	depending on; intact
	(に)よ(る)	to depend (on)
	(温度)依存性	(temperature) dependence
	(オンド)イゾンセイ	
	依然として	still now, as before
	イゼンとして	

囲	イ	enclosure
	かこ(む)	to surround
	範囲	extent, range, scope
	ハンイ	
	周囲	periphery; surroundings
	シュウイ	

維	イ	rope
	(合成)繊維	(synthetic) fiber
	(ゴウセイ)センイ	
	維持する	to maintain
	イジする	

意	イ	intention; idea
	注意	caution
	チュウイ	
	意見	opinion
	イケン	

域	イキ	region
	地域	region, zone
	チイキ	
	流域	drainage basin
	リュウイキ	

因	イン	cause; factor
	因子	factor {math}
	インシ	
	原因	cause; origin
	ゲンイン	

引	イン	pulling, attraction
	ひ(く)	to pull, attract
	引力	attractive force
	インリョク	
	引張り(応力)	tensile (stress)
	ひっぱり(オウリョク)	

衛	エイ	protection
	(人工)衛星	(artificial) satellite
	(ジンコウ)エイセイ	
	衛生	hygiene, sanitation
	エイセイ	

円	エン	circle; yen (¥)
	まる(い)	round
	円振動	circular vibration
	エンシンドウ	
	円周	circumference
	エンシュウ	

遠	エン	distant
	とお(い)	distant
	遠日点	aphelion
	エンジツテン	
	遠心(分離機)	centrifugal (separator)
	エンシン(ブンリキ)	

汚	オ	pollution; filth
	よご(す)	to pollute, make dirty
	汚染	pollution; contamination
	オセン	
	汚臭	foul odor
	オシュウ	

仮	カ	provisional
	仮定	assumption
	カテイ	
	仮説	hypothesis
	カセツ	

火	カ	fire
	ひ	fire
	火星	Mars
	カセイ	
	点火	ignition
	テンカ	

科	カ	branch; department
	-カ	family {biol}
	(自然)科学	(natural) sciences
	(シゼン)カガク	
	工学科	engineering department
	コウガクカ	

荷	カ	load
	に	load
	荷重(曲線)	load (curve)
	カジュウ(キョクセン)	
	荷受人/荷送人	consignee/shipper
	にうけニン/におくりニン	

画	ガ; カク	picture, drawing
	画面(表示)	screen (display)
	ガメン(ヒョウジ)	
	計画	plan
	ケイカク	

壊	カイ	destruction
	こわ(す)	to destroy
	破壊	destruction
	ハカイ	
	壊血病	scurvy
	カイケツビョウ	

改	カイ	renewing, revising
	あらた(める)	to modify, renew
	改造	rebuilding
	カイゾウ	
	改正	revision
	カイセイ	

海	カイ	sea
	うみ	sea
	日本海	The Sea of Japan
	ニホンカイ	
	海産物	marine products
	カイサンブツ	

害	ガイ	damage; harm
	(産業)公害	(industrial) pollution
	(サンギョウ)コウガイ	
	有害な	harmful
	ユウガイな	

概	ガイ	general situation
	概念	concept
	ガイネン	
	概要	summary, outline
	ガイヨウ	

拡	カク	spreading, expanding
	ひろ(げる)	to spread out, broaden
	拡大率	magnifying power
	カクダイリツ	
	拡散(係数)	diffusion (coefficient)
	カクサン(ケイスウ)	

格	カク; コウ	frame; standard
	格子	lattice; grating
	コウシ	
	規格化(条件)	normalization (condition)
	キカクカ(ジョウケン)	

較	カク	comparison
	比較的な	comparative
	ヒカクテキな	
	比較する	to compare
	ヒカクする	

完	カン	completion
	完全な	complete, perfect
	カンゼンな	
	完成する	to complete
	カンセイする	

感	カン	feeling, sensation
	感染(細菌)	infectious (bacteria)
	カンセン(サイキン)	
	感(光)度	(photo)sensitivity
	カン(コウ)ド	

緩	カン	relaxing; mitigating
	緩和(時間)	relaxation (time)
	カンワ(ジカン)	
	緩衝(液)	buffer (solution)
	カンショウ(エキ)	

還	カン	returning
	還元(剤)	reducing (agent) {chem}
	カンゲン(ザイ)	
	還流(比)	reflux (ratio)
	カンリュウ(ヒ)	

陥	カン	caving in
	おちい(る) {xu}	to fall into
	(格子)欠陥	(lattice) defect
	(コウシ)ケッカン	
	陥入	invagination {zool}
	カンニュウ	

希	キ	rare; dilute
	希薄溶液	dilute solution
	キハクヨウエキ	
	希土類元素	rare earth elements
	キドルイゲンソ	

規	キ	standard
	日本工業規格　JIS*	
	* {JIS = Japanese Industrial Standards}	
	ニホンコウギョウキカク	
	不規則信号	random signal
	フキソクシンゴウ	

義	ギ	significance
	定義	definition
	テイギ	
	意義	meaning
	イギ	

却	キャク	(doing) completely
	冷却(装置)	cooling (system)
	レイキャク(ソウチ)	
	焼却炉	incinerator
	ショウキャクロ	

鏡	-キョウ	-scope; mirror
	かがみ	mirror
	(電子)顕微鏡	(electron) microscope
	(デンシ)ケンビキョウ	
	(反射)望遠鏡	(reflecting) telescope
	(ハンシャ)ボウエンキョウ	

凝	ギョウ	freezing, congealing
	凝固	solidification, coagulation
	ギョウコ	
	凝縮	condensation
	ギョウシュク	

均	キン	average; equal
	平均(値)	average (value)
	ヘイキン(チ)	
	均一(系)	homogeneous (system)
	キンイツ(ケイ)	

区	ク	division, section
	区別	differentiation
	クベツ	
	区分	classification
	クブン	

具	グ	tool
	道具, 工具	tool
	ドウグ, コウグ	
	具体的な	concrete
	グタイテキな	

群	グン	group
	むれ	herd, flock
	(可換)群	(commutative) group
	(カカン)グン	
	群体	colony {biol}
	グンタイ	

軽	ケイ	light (of weight)
	かる(い)	light (of weight)
	軽金属	light metal
	ケイキンゾク	
	軽量材	lighter-weight materials
	ケイリョウザイ	

欠	ケツ	lacking; absent
	か(く)	to lack, fail in
	欠点	defect
	ケッテン	
	間欠(荷重)	intermittent (load)
	カンケツ(カジュウ)	

決	ケツ	decision
	き(める)	to decide
	決定(制御)	decision (control)
	ケッテイ(セイギョ)	
	解決する	to solve
	カイケツする	

顕	ケン	disclosing, appearing
	顕色染料	developed color {chem}
	ケンショクセンリョウ	
	顕微(操作)	micro(manipulation)
	ケンビ(ソウサ)	

源	ゲン	source, origin
	光源/音源	light source/sound source
	コウゲン/オンゲン	
	天然資源	natural resources
	テンネンシゲン	

誤	ゴ	mistake, error
	あやま(り)	mistake, error
	誤差(関数)	error (function)
	ゴサ(カンスウ)	
	誤り(検出方式)	error (detecting system)
	あやまり(ケンシュツホウシキ)	

公	コウ	formal, public
	公式	formula
	コウシキ	
	公理(系)	(system of) axioms
	コウリ(ケイ)	

厚	コウ	thick
	あつ(い)	thick
	濃厚溶液	concentrated solution
	ノウコウヨウエキ	
	厚板	thick board
	あついた	

衡	コウ	balance beam, scales
	(化学)平衡	(chemical) equilibrium
	(カガク)ヘイコウ	
	均衡点	balance point
	キンコウテン	

査	サ	investigating
	検査	inspection
	ケンサ	
	調査(中)	(under) investigation
	チョウサ(チュウ)	

鎖	サ	chain
	くさり	chain
	連鎖反応	chain reaction
	レンサハンノウ	
	鎖状構造	chain structure
	サジョウコウゾウ	

座	ザ	seat
	(極)座標	(polar) coordinates
	(キョク)ザヒョウ	
	遺伝子座	gene locus
	イデンシザ	

雑	ザツ	mixing; miscellany
	複雑な	complicated, intricate
	フクザツな	
	雑種(形成)	hybrid(ization) {biol}
	ザッシュ(ケイセイ)	

指	シ	indicating, pointing
	さ(す)	to indicate, point
	指数関数	exponential function
	シスウカンスウ	
	指示薬	indicator {chem}
	シジヤク	

止	シ	halting, stopping
	と(める)	to halt, stop
	静止(質量)	rest (mass)
	セイシ(シツリョウ)	
	中止する	to stop, shut down
	チュウシする	

視	シ	seeing
	微視的な	microscopic
	ビシテキな	
	可視光線	visible light ray
	カシコウセン	

似	ジ	resembling
	に(る)	to resemble
	類似	similarity, resemblance
	ルイジ	
	近似(値)	approximate (value)
	キンジ(チ)	

持	ジ	holding; maintaining
	も(つ)	to hold; to maintain
	保持する	to maintain, preserve
	ホジする	
	持続(振動)	sustained (vibration)
	ジゾク(シンドウ)	

取	シュ	taking
	と(る)	to take, seize
	取消キー	cancel key {on keyboard}
	とりけしキー	
	取り除く	to remove, take away
	とりのぞく	

識	シキ	knowing
	知識	knowledge
	チシキ	
	標識(遺伝子)	marker (gene)
	ヒョウシキ(イデンシ)	

純	ジュン	purity
	単純(気化器)	simple (carburetor)
	タンジュン(キカキ)	
	純系	pure line {genetics}
	ジュンケイ	

軸	ジク	axle, axis
	軸受(け)	bearing
	ジクうけ	
	軸方向(応力)	axial (stress)
	ジクホウコウ(オウリョク)	

初	ショ	beginning
	はじ(め)	beginning
	最初の	the first
	サイショの	
	初期(条件)	initial (condition)
	ショキ(ジョウケン)	

写	シャ	copying, duplicating
	うつ(す)	to copy, duplicate
	写真	photograph
	シャシン	
	複写する	to duplicate, (photo)copy
	フクシャする	

除	ジョ	division
	のぞ(く)	to remove, exclude
	加減乗除	the four operations (+ - × +)
	カゲンジョウジョ	
	除数/被除数	divisor/dividend
	ジョスウ/ヒジョスウ	

車	シャ	vehicle, wheel
	くるま	vehicle
	自動車	automobile
	ジドウシャ	
	車両	vehicles, rolling stock
	シャリョウ	

衝	ショウ	collision
	(非弾性)衝突	(inelastic) collision
	(ヒダンセイ)ショウトツ	
	衝動タービン	impulse turbine
	ショウドウタービン	

弱	ジャク	weak
	よわ(い)	weak
	弱電解質	weak electrolyte
	ジャクデンカイシツ	
	弱塩基	weak base
	ジャクエンキ	

焼	ショウ	burning
	や(く)	to burn
	燃焼	combustion
	ネンショウ	
	焼結	sintering
	ショウケツ	

主	シュ	principle, main
	おも(な)	chief, main
	主として	principally
	シュとして	
	主軸	principal axis
	シュジク	

照	ショウ	illuminating
	てら(す)	to illuminate
	照明(工学)	illumination (engineering)
	ショウメイ(コウガク)	
	照射	irradiation
	ショウシャ	

称	ショウ	admiration
	対称(軸)	(axis of) symmetry
	タイショウ(ジク)	
	相称	symmetry {biol}
	ソウショウ	

乗	ジョウ	power, multiplication
	ジョウ(じる)	to multiply {math}
	二乗/三乗	square/cube {math}
	ニジョウ/サンジョウ	
	乗法群	multiplicative group
	ジョウホウグン	

食	ショク	eating
	た(べる)	to eat
	食品(加工)	food (processing)
	ショクヒン(カコウ)	
	日食	solar eclipse
	ニッショク	

真	シン	truth, reality
	ま	truth, reality
	真空	vacuum
	シンクウ	
	真上	directly above
	まうえ	

新	シン	new
	あたら(しい)	new
	新薬	new medicine
	シンヤク	
	新製品	new manufactured article
	シンセイヒン	

推	スイ	inferring; impelling
	推進(効率)	propulsion (efficiency)
	スイシン(コウリツ)	
	推測する	to infer
	スイソクする	

星	セイ	star
	ほし	star
	水星/金星	Mercury/Venus
	スイセイ/キンセイ	
	変光星	variable star
	ヘンコウセイ	

整	セイ	arranging in order
	ととの(える)	to put in order
	整数	integer
	セイスウ	
	整流器	rectifier
	セイリュウキ	

切	セツ	cutting
	き(る) {xu}	to cut
	適切な	appropriate, pertinent
	テキセツな	
	切換(発振器)	change-over (oscillator)
	きりかえ(ハッシンキ)	

節	セツ	temperate, restraining
	ふし	joint
	調節する	to adjust, regulate
	チョウセツする	
	節約する	to economize
	セツヤクする	

繊	セン	fine, slender
	繊維(光学)	fiber (optics)
	センイ(コウガク)	
	繊毛	cilia
	センモウ	

礎	ソ	cornerstone
	基礎	basis, foundation
	キソ	
	基礎(方程式)	fundamental (equations)
	キソ(ホウテイシキ)	

双	ソウ	a pair; a set
	双曲線(関数)	hyperbolic (function)
	ソウキョクセン(カンスウ)	
	(磁気)双極子	(magnetic) dipole
	(ジキ)ソウキョクシ	

操	ソウ	steering, operating
	(単位)操作	(unit) operation(s)
	(タンイ)ソウサ	
	操業(短縮)	plant operation (cut back)
	ソウギョウ(タンシュク)	

総	ソウ	all; general
	総計	total amount
	ソウケイ	
	総和公式	summation formula
	ソウワコウシキ	

像	ゾウ	image
	鏡像	mirror image
	キョウゾウ	
	実像	real image
	ジツゾウ	

側	ソク	side
	がわ	side
	側鎖	side chain
	ソクサ	
	外側	outside, exterior
	そとがわ	

損	ソン	loss, damage
	そこ(なう)	to harm, injure
	損失(係数)	loss (factor)
	ソンシツ(ケイスウ)	
	損害	damage
	ソンガイ	

太	タイ	fat, big
	ふと(い)	fat, big
	太陽(視差)	solar (parallax)
	タイヨウ(シサ)	
	太陽(雑音)	solar (noise)
	タイヨウ(ザツオン)	

耐	タイ	-resistant
	た(える)	to endure
	耐火(材)	fireproof (material)
	タイカ(ザイ)	
	耐食(鋼)	corrosion-resistant (steel)
	タイショク(コウ)	

脱	ダツ	removing
	ダツ-	de-, dis-
	脱塩	desalting
	ダツエン	
	脱水素	dehydrogenation
	ダッスイソ	

短	タン	short
	みじか(い)	short
	楕円の短軸	minor axis of ellipse
	ダエンのタンジク	
	短波(受信)	short wave (reception)
	タンパ(ジュシン)	

弾	ダン	bullet; rebound
	(粘)弾性	(visco)elasticity
	(ネン)ダンセイ	
	弾道学	ballistics
	ダンドウガク	

抽	チュウ	extracting
	抽出	extraction {chem}
	チュウシュツ	
	抽象的な	abstract
	チュウショウテキな	

張	チョウ	stretching
	は(る)	to stretch
	(表面)張力	(surface) tension
	(ヒョウメン)チョウリョク	
	拡張	expansion, enlargement
	カクチョウ	

天	テン	sky, heavens
	天体(力学)	celestial (mechanics)
	テンタイ(リキガク)	
	天然(繊維)	natural (fiber)
	テンネン(センイ)	

展	テン	expanding
	展開	expansion {math}
	テンカイ	
	発展	development, growth
	ハッテン	

添	テン	adding to
	そ(える)	to attach, append
	添加剤	additive {chem}
	テンカザイ	
	添(え)字	index, suffix {math}
	そえジ	

土	ト；ド	earth, ground
	つち	earth, ground
	土星の環	the rings of Saturn
	ドセイのカン	
	土地(利用)	land (use)
	トチ(リヨウ)	

道	ドウ	road; course; way
	みち	path {math}
	尿道	urethra
	ニョウドウ	
	高速道路	express highway
	コウソクドウロ	

毒	ドク	poison
	触媒毒	catalyst poison
	ショクバイドク	
	(抗)毒素	(anti)toxin
	(コウ)ドクソ	

乳	ニュウ	milk
	乳糖	lactose
	ニュウトウ	
	乳製品	dairy products
	ニュウセイヒン	

尿	ニョウ	urine
	尿素(回路)	urea (cycle)
	ニョウソ(カイロ)	
	尿検査	urinalysis
	ニョウケンサ	

認	ニン	recognition; approving
	みと(める)	to recognize; to approve
	確認	confirmation, check
	カクニン	
	認識	recognition
	ニンシキ	

農	ノウ	agriculture
	(機械化)農業	(mechanized) agriculture
	(キカイカ)ノウギョウ	
	農薬	agricultural chemicals
	ノウヤク	

破	ハ	breaking; tearing
	やぶ(る)	to break; to tear
	破裂圧	bursting pressure
	ハレツアツ	
	破線	dashed line, broken line
	ハセン	

廃	ハイ	waste; outdated
	廃熱(管理)	waste heat (management)
	ハイネツ(カンリ)	
	(工場)廃水	(industrial) waste water
	(コウジョウ)ハイスイ	

排	ハイ	expelling
	排気(行程)	exhaust (stroke)
	ハイキ(コウテイ)	
	排除(体積)	excluded (volume)
	ハイジョ(タイセキ)	

薄	ハク	thin; dilute
	うす(い)	thin
	薄膜	thin film; thin membrane
	ハクマク	
	薄積層板	thin laminate
	ハクセキソウバン	

範	ハン	limit; model
	範囲	range, scope
	ハンイ	
	模範(農場)	model (farm)
	モハン(ノウジョウ)	

被	ヒ	receiving
	ヒ-	{passive prefix}
	被害(査定)	damage (assessment)
	ヒガイ(サテイ)	
	被変調(波)	modulated (wave)
	ヒヘンチョウ(ハ)	

備	ビ	provision
	そな(える)	to provide; to equip
	設備/装備	equipment
	セツビ/ソウビ	
	準備	preparation
	ジュンビ	

病	ビョウ	sickness
	やまい	illness
	糖尿病	diabetes
	トウニョウビョウ	
	伝染病	contagious disease
	デンセンビョウ	

負	フ	burdened; negative
	お(う)	to bear (a burden)
	負荷(特性)	load (characteristics)
	フカ(トクセイ)	
	負の(無限大)	negative (infinity)
	フの(ムゲンダイ)	

幅	フク	width
	はば	width
	振幅(変調)	amplitude (modulation)
	シンプク(ヘンチョウ)	
	道路幅	width of street
	ドウロはば	

沸	フツ	boiling
	わ(かす)	to boil
	(真)沸点	(true) boiling point
	(シン)フッテン	
	沸騰	boiling
	フットウ	

粉	フン	powder, dust
	こな	flour; powder
	粉乳	powdered milk
	フンニュウ	
	粉状化	pulverization
	フンジョウカ	

壁	ヘキ	wall
	かべ	wall
	管壁	pipe wall
	カンペキ	
	壁効果	wall effect
	かべコウカ	

偏	ヘン	one-sided, biased
	ヘン-	partial {math}
	偏光	polarized light
	ヘンコウ	
	偏微分	partial differential
	ヘンビブン	

保	ホ	preserve, maintain
	たも(つ)	to preserve, maintain
	保存の法則	conservation law {phys}
	ホゾンのホウソク	
	保存法	method of preservation
	ホゾンホウ	

模	ボ; モ	model, pattern
	規模	scale
	キボ	
	模型	model
	モケイ	

望	ボウ	commanding (a view)
	のぞ(ましい)	desirable
	(太陽)望遠鏡	(solar) telescope
	(タイヨウ)ボウエンキョウ	
	展望鏡	periscope
	テンボウキョウ	

防	ボウ	prevention; defense
	ふせ(ぐ)	to prevent; to protect
	予防(法)	preventative (measure)
	ヨボウ(ホウ)	
	公害防止の	for pollution control
	コウガイボウシの	

木	ボク; モク	wood; tree
	き	wood; tree
	土木工学	civil engineering
	ドボクコウガク	
	木星の衛星	the moons of Jupiter
	モクセイのエイセイ	

味	ミ	taste
	あじ	taste
	意味	meaning
	イミ	
	酸味	acid taste, sourness
	サンミ	

鳴	メイ	making a sound
	な(く)	to chirp
	共鳴器	resonator
	キョウメイキ	
	鳴管	syrinx {zool}
	メイカン	

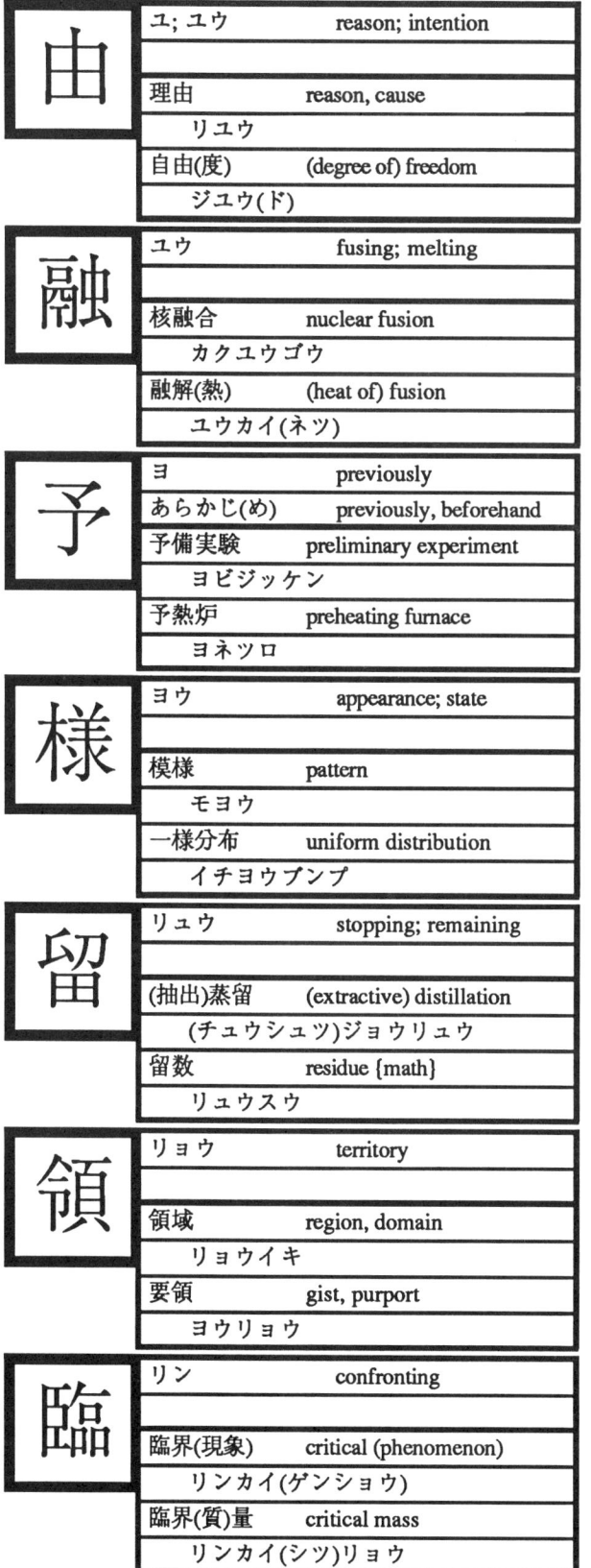

由	ユ; ユウ	reason; intention
	理由 リユウ	reason, cause
	自由(度) ジユウ(ド)	(degree of) freedom

融	ユウ	fusing; melting
	核融合 カクユウゴウ	nuclear fusion
	融解(熱) ユウカイ(ネツ)	(heat of) fusion

予	ヨ	previously
	あらかじ(め)	previously, beforehand
	予備実験 ヨビジッケン	preliminary experiment
	予熱炉 ヨネツロ	preheating furnace

様	ヨウ	appearance; state
	模様 モヨウ	pattern
	一様分布 イチヨウブンプ	uniform distribution

留	リュウ	stopping; remaining
	(抽出)蒸留 (チュウシュツ)ジョウリュウ	(extractive) distillation
	留数 リュウスウ	residue {math}

領	リョウ	territory
	領域 リョウイキ	region, domain
	要領 ヨウリョウ	gist, purport

臨	リン	confronting
	臨界(現象) リンカイ(ゲンショウ)	critical (phenomenon)
	臨界(質)量 リンカイ(シツ)リョウ	critical mass

励	レイ	encouragement
	励起(状態) レイキ(ジョウタイ)	excited (state)
	自励 ジレイ	self-excitation

冷	レイ	cold, cool
	ひ(やす)	to cool, refrigerate
	冷却(器) レイキャク(キ)	cooling (machine)
	冷間(加工) レイカン(カコウ)	cold (working)

KANJI Charts

一	子	人	方
行	示	水	面
金	石	大	用
見	小	二	力
高	生	入	立

液	間	体	比
温	気	中	物
下	原	定	分
化	固	度	変
学	上	動	例

関 少 的 表
含 素 等 無
係 多 同 有
酸 炭 熱 要
重 注 必 流

圧 合 性 電
違 式 成 発
応 質 積 反
験 実 速 法
元 数 対 量

位	計	時	則
運	結	色	単
解	向	出	部
管	細	心	溶
機	使	全	理

塩 光 振 置

果 考 線 長

加 作 相 直

起 次 増 点

交 場 測 平

以 近 蒸 程
外 後 正 得
器 最 赤 内
期 周 前 白
強 状 態 不

移 空 織 伝

陰 形 射 放

過 構 消 胞

核 地 植 陽

球 磁 組 粒

割 極 所 代
基 工 常 知
求 自 説 値
及 受 造 調
吸 述 他 通

当	回	限	第
糖	各	個	導
明	角	三	倍
目	曲	種	半
与	径	接	微

約 亜 脂 析

率 異 臭 属

両 鉛 集 族

類 銀 硝 窒

路 酢 進 鉄

銅　影　距　件

配　環　御　研

利　観　境　現

硫　技　響　号

料　究　業　在

察	術	信	特
産	準	制	標
仕	象	続	別
事	条	存	報
日	情	題	飽

本　安　型　算

問　械　検　者

離　開　減　処

連　換　効　晶

和　記　散　設

然	能	音	縮
装	般	確	静
低	品	屈	図
適	布	系	折
転	論	抗	層

共　混　製　付

互　材　遷　芳

鉱　剤　超　肪

鋼　錯　濃　薬

香　試　非　油

遺	血	殖	着
黄	酵	触	透
官	差	神	突
菌	再	精	燃
経	収	染	媒

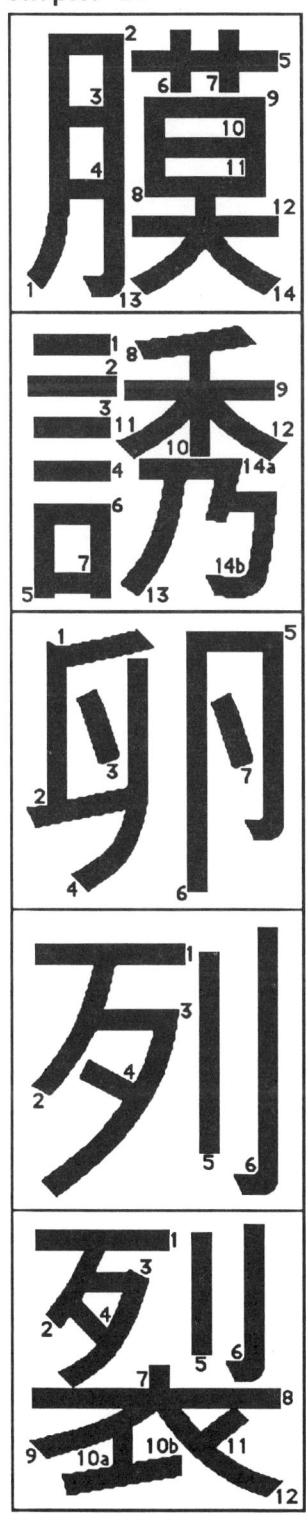

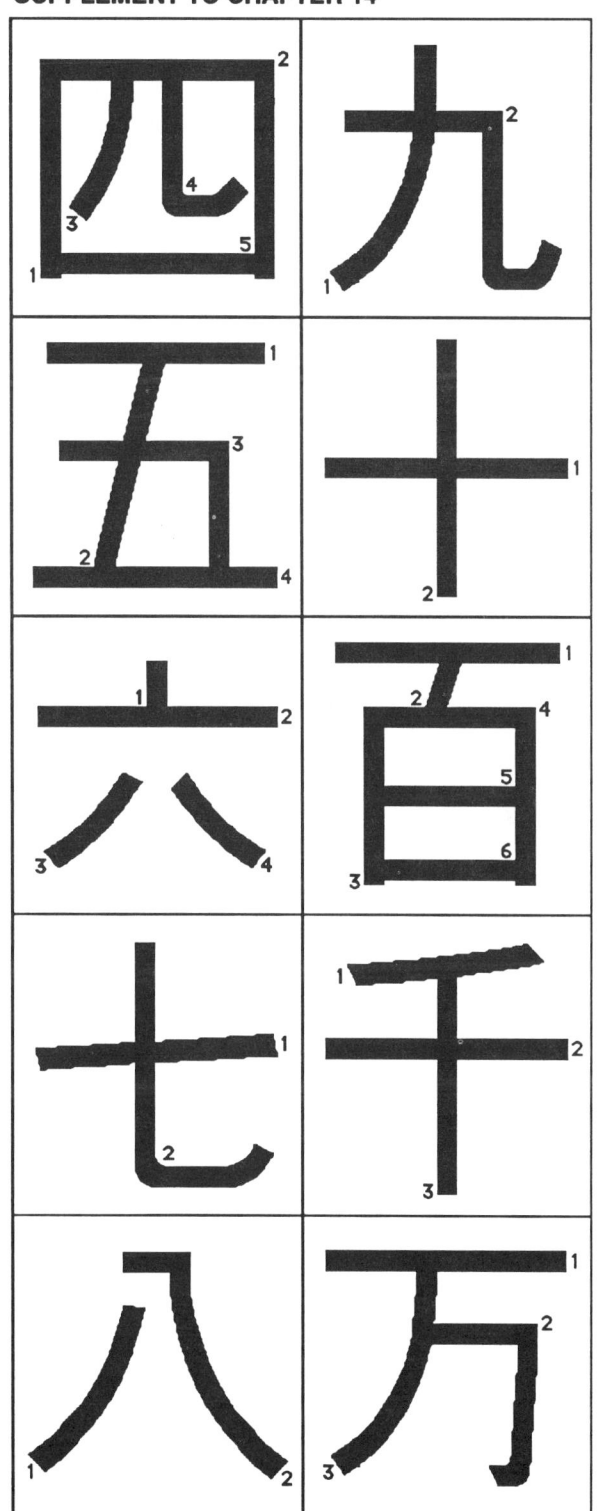

KANJI Listed by Stroke Count with "ON" Readings

1 STROKE
一　イチ, イツ

2 STROKES
人　ジン, ニン
二　ニ
入　ニュウ
力　リキ, リョク

3 STROKES
下　カ, ゲ
及　キュウ
工　ク, コウ
三　サン
子　シ
小　ショウ
上　ジョウ
大　タイ, ダイ
与　ヨ

4 STROKES
化　カ
元　ゲン
互　ゴ
日　ジツ, ニチ
収　シュウ
少　ショウ
心　シン
水　スイ
中　チュウ
内　ナイ
反　ハン
比　ヒ
不　フ

分　フン, ブン
方　ホウ

5 STROKES
圧　アツ
以　イ
可　カ
加　カ
外　ガイ
号　ゴウ
仕　シ
示　シ, ジ
石　シャク, セキ
出　シュツ
処　ショ
生　ショウ, セイ
正　セイ
他　タ
代　ダイ
白　ハク
半　ハン
必　ヒツ
付　フ
布　フ
平　ヘイ
本　ホン
目　モク
用　ヨウ
立　リツ

6 STROKES
安　アン
回　カイ
各　カク

気　キ
吸　キュウ
共　キョウ
行　ギョウ, コウ
曲　キョク
血　ケツ
件　ケン
向　コウ
交　コウ
光　コウ
考　コウ
合　ゴウ
再　サイ
在　ザイ
自　シ, ジ
次　ジ
地　ジ, チ
式　シキ
色　シキ, ショク
成　セイ
全　ゼン
存　ソン, ゾン
多　タ
伝　デン
当　トウ
同　ドウ
有　ユウ
両　リョウ
列　レツ

7 STROKES
亜　ア
位　イ
応　オウ

角　カク
含　ガン
技　ギ
求　キュウ
究　キュウ
近　キン
系　ケイ
形　ケイ
見　ケン
抗　コウ
作　サ, サク
材　ザイ
条　ジョウ
状　ジョウ
図　ズ, ト
赤　セキ
折　セツ
体　タイ
対　タイ, ツイ
低　テイ
別　ベツ
芳　ホウ
乱　ラン
卵　ラン
利　リ

8 STROKES
果　カ
価　カ
学　ガク
官　カン
金　キン
空　クウ
屈　クツ

径 ケイ
固 コ
効 コウ
使 シ
事 ジ
実 ジツ
者 シャ
受 ジュ
周 シュウ
述 ジュツ
所 ショ, ジョ
制 セイ
性 セイ
析 セキ
知 チ
注 チュウ
長 チョウ
直 チョク
定 テイ
抵 テイ
的 テキ
突 トツ
波 ハ
板 ハン, バン
非 ヒ
表 ヒョウ
物 ブツ
放 ホウ
法 ホウ
肪 ボウ
明 メイ
油 ユ
例 レイ
炉 ロ
和 ワ

9 STROKES
音 オン
界 カイ
活 カツ
逆 ギャク
係 ケイ
型 ケイ
計 ケイ
研 ケン
限 ゲン
後 ゴ, コウ
香 コウ
臭 シュウ

重 ジュウ
信 シン
神 シン
染 セン
前 ゼン
相 ソウ
送 ソウ
則 ソク
単 タン
炭 タン
点 テン
度 ド
発 ハツ
品 ヒン
変 ヘン
胞 ホウ
面 メン
約 ヤク
要 ヨウ

10 STROKES
核 カク
記 キ
起 キ
原 ゲン
個 コ
高 コウ
差 サ
剤 ザイ
脂 シ
時 ジ
射 シャ
消 ショウ
振 シン
素 ソ
造 ゾウ
速 ソク
帯 タイ
値 チ
通 ツウ
透 トウ
特 トク
能 ノウ
配 ハイ
倍 バイ
般 ハン
容 ヨウ
流 リュウ
料 リョウ

連 レン

11 STROKES
異 イ
移 イ
陰 イン
液 エキ
黄 オウ, コウ
械 カイ
基 キ
球 キュウ
距 キョ
御 ギョ, ゴ
強 キョウ
菌 キン
経 ケイ
現 ゲン
混 コン
細 サイ
産 サン
術 ジュツ
常 ジョウ
情 ジョウ
進 シン
接 セツ
設 セツ
組 ソ
族 ゾク
第 ダイ
断 ダン
窒 チツ
転 テン
動 ドウ
得 トク
粘 ネン
部 ブ
密 ミツ
問 モン
理 リ
率 リツ
粒 リュウ

12 STROKES
運 ウン
温 オン
過 カ
開 カイ
割 カツ
換 カン

間 カン
期 キ
結 ケツ
検 ケン
減 ゲン
最 サイ
酢 サク
散 サン
集 シュウ
晶 ショウ
硝 ショウ
象 ショウ, ゾウ
場 ジョウ
植 ショク
殖 ショク
然 ゼン, ネン
装 ソウ
測 ソク
属 ゾク
達 タツ
着 チャク
超 チョウ
程 テイ
等 トウ
統 トウ
媒 バイ
報 ホウ
無 ム
陽 ヨウ
硫 リュウ
量 リョウ
裂 レツ
路 ロ

13 STROKES
違 イ
塩 エン
鉛 エン
解 カイ
業 ギョウ
極 キョク
鉱 コウ
試 シ
準 ジュン
蒸 ジョウ
触 ショク
数 スウ
続 ゾク
置 チ

鉄	テツ		錯	サク
電	デン		積	セキ
微	ビ		糖	トウ
飽	ホウ		燃	ネン
溶	ヨウ		濃	ノウ
			薬	ヤク

14 STROKES

管	カン
関	カン
境	キョウ
銀	ギン
構	コウ
酵	コウ
察	サツ
算	サン
酸	サン
磁	ジ
種	シュ
静	ジョウ, セイ
精	セイ
製	セイ
説	セツ
層	ソウ
増	ゾウ
態	タイ
端	タン
適	テキ
銅	ドウ
複	フク
膜	マク
誘	ユウ

15 STROKES

遺	イ
影	エイ
確	カク
器	キ
質	シツ
線	セン
遷	セン
調	チョウ
導	ドウ
熱	ネツ
標	ヒョウ
論	ロン

16 STROKES

機	キ
鋼	コウ

17 STROKES

環	カン
縮	シュク

18 STROKES

観	カン
験	ケン
織	シキ, ショク
題	ダイ
離	リ
類	ルイ

20 STROKES

響	キョウ

KANJI Vocabulary List

This list gives the 365 KANJI taught in this book by the most frequent ON reading in the 五十音 order and their JUKUGO. For KANJI entries having the same ON reading the order is by stroke count. Each KANJI entry includes the ON and KUN readings and meanings given for that KANJI in the chapter where it was introduced, the transitive verbs always preceding the intransitive. JUKUGO having KUN readings come immediately thereafter, followed by the JUKUGO having ON readings, which constitute the vast majority of words in the vocabulary. They are listed under the KANJI that appears first in the JUKUGO. Thus, 固体 is listed under 固 and not under 体. The JUKUGO under a given KANJI are in the 五十音 order of the ON reading of the second KANJI. Thus, 固体 comes before 固定. If the second KANJI has the same ON reading as other second KANJI under a given first KANJI, they are ordered first by the number of strokes and then, if necessary, by radical number. Thus, 確立 comes before 確率. At the end of the list is a table of the 365 KANJI by stroke count with ON readings in 五十音 order under each stroke entry.

KANJI	PRONUNCIATION	MEANING	CHAPTER
ア			
●亜	ア	sub-; -ous {acids}	15
亜塩素酸	アエンソサン	chlorous acid	15
亜鉛	アエン	zinc	15
亜鉛鉄板	アエンテッパン	galvanized iron plate	15
亜音速	アオンソク	subsonic speed	18
亜種	アシュ	subspecies	15
亜硝酸	アショウサン	nitrous acid	15
亜族	アゾク	subgroup {in the periodic table}	15

ア

亜属	アゾク	subgenus	15
亜硫酸	アリュウサン	sulfurous acid	15
●圧	アツ	pressure	8
圧縮	アッシュク	compression	18
圧縮性流体	アッシュクセイリュウタイ	compressible fluid	18
圧電-	アツデン	piezoelectric	8
圧電磁器	アツデンジキ	piezoelectric ceramics	19
圧力	アツリョク	pressure	8
圧力計	アツリョクケイ	pressure meter	9
圧力容器	アツリョクヨウキ	pressure vessel	18
●安	アン	secure, safe, quiet	17
安い	やすい	cheap, inexpensive	17
安全	アンゼン	safety	17
安全第一	アンゼンダイイチ	safety first	17
安息香酸	アンソクコウサン	benzoic acid	19
安定な	アンテイな	stable	17
安定剤	アンテイザイ	stabilizer	19

イ

●以	イ	from; than	11
以下: (これ)～	(これ)イカ	equal to or less than (this); below	11
以外: (これ)～	(これ)イガイ	other than (this)	11
以後: (これ)～	(これ)イゴ	after (this)	11
以上: (これ)～	(これ)イジョウ	equal to or more than (this); above	11
以前: (これ)～	(これ)イゼン	before (this)	11
以内: (これ)～	(これ)イナイ	within (this)	11
●位	イ	rank; place; position	9
位	くらい	approximately	9
位相	イソウ	phase	18
位相速度	イソウソクド	phase velocity	10
位置	イチ	location	10
位置エネルギー	イチエネルギー	potential energy	10
位置ベクトル	イチベクトル	position vector	10
●異	イ	difference, hetero-	15
異なる	ことなる	to differ, vary	9
異化	イカ	catabolism, dissimilation	15
異形胞子	イケイホウシ	heterospore	15
異質細胞	イシツサイボウ	heterocyst	15
異種	イシュ	different kind, species, variety	15
異常の	イジョウの	abnormal	15
異常染色体	イジョウセンショクタイ	heterochromosome	20
異数性	イスウセイ	heteroploidy	15
異数体	イスウタイ	heteroploid	15
異性抗体	イセイコウタイ	heterogenetic antibody	18
異性体	イセイタイ	isomer	15
異方性	イホウセイ	anisotropy	15

●移	イ	moving, transferring	12
移す	うつす	to move, transfer	12
移る	うつる	to move (to a place)	12
移行する	イコウする	to shift (to)	12
移植	イショク	graft, transplant	12
移相	イソウ	phase shift(ing)	18
移相器	イソウキ	phase shifter	12
移動単位数	イドウタンイスウ	number of transfer units, NTU	12
移動度	イドウド	mobility	12
●違	イ	difference	8
違い	ちがい	difference	8
違う	ちがう	to differ, vary	8
違法キャラクタ	イホウキャラクタ	illegal character	8
●遺	イ	bequeathing	20
遺伝	イデン	heredity	20
遺伝学	イデンガク	genetics	20
遺伝子	イデンシ	gene	20
遺伝子分析	イデンシブンセキ	gene analysis	20
●一	イチ	one	5
一	イツ	one; same	5
一組	ひとくみ	one set	12
一つ	ひとつ	one	5
一人	ひとり	one person	5
一価関数	イッカカンスウ	single-valued function	19
一価金属	イッカキンゾク	monovalent metal	19
一割	イチわり	10%, one-tenth	13
一環の	イッカンの	monocyclic, one step	16
一気圧	イチキアツ	one atmosphere	8
一見する	イッケンする	to glance	5
一酸化炭素	イッサンカタンソ	carbon monoxide	7
一次波	イチジハ	primary wave	18
一体	イッタイ	a (single) unit	20
一対	イッツイ	(a) pair, couple	8
一定の	イッテイの	constant	6
一定温度	イッテイオンド	constant temperature	6
一度	イチド	one degree; one time	6
一般に	イッパンに	generally, in general	4
一般の	イッパンの	general	17
一般化する	イッパンカする	to generalize	17
一部	イチブ	one part	9
一分間	イップンカン	one minute	6
一平方キロ	イチヘイホウキロ	one square kilometer	10
一方	イッポウ	one side, way; however	4
●陰	イン	negative; shade	12
陰イオン	インイオン	negative ion, anion	12
陰関数	インカンスウ	implicit function	12

イン

陰極	インキョク	cathode	13
陰生植物	インセイショクブツ	shade plant	12
陰性元素	インセイゲンソ	electronegative element	12
陰電気	インデンキ	negative electricity	12
陰電子	インデンシ	negative electron	12

ウ

●運	ウン	transporting	9
運ぶ	はこぶ	to carry	9
運び出す	はこびだす	to carry out	9
運転	ウンテン	operating, running	17
運動	ウンドウ	motion	9
運動量	ウンドウリョウ	momentum	9

エ

●影	エイ	shadow	16
影	かげ	shadow, shade	16
影響	エイキョウ	influence	16
●液	エキ	liquid	6
液化	エキカ	liquefaction	6
液晶	エキショウ	liquid crystal	17
液相	エキソウ	liquid phase	10
液体	エキタイ	liquid	6
液胞	エキホウ	vacuole	12
液面	エキメン	liquid surface	6
●塩	エン	salt	10
塩	しお	salt	10
塩化ナトリウム	エンカナトリウム	sodium chloride	10
塩化水素	エンカスイソ	hydrogen chloride	10
塩化第一水銀	エンカダイイチスイギン	mercurous chloride	15
塩化第二銅	エンカダイニドウ	cupric chloride	15
塩化物	エンカブツ	chloride	10
塩基	エンキ	base	13
塩酸	エンサン	hydrochloric acid	10
塩素	エンソ	chlorine	10
塩素化	エンソカ	chlorination	10
塩素酸塩	エンソサンエン	chlorate	10
塩素水	エンソスイ	chlorine water	10
塩類	エンルイ	salts	14
●鉛	エン	lead	15
鉛	なまり	lead	15
鉛直線	エンチョクセン	vertical line	15

オ

●応	オウ	responding	8
応じる	オウじる	to respond (to)	8

力

応用数学	オウヨウスウガク	applied mathematics	8
応用力学	オウヨウリキガク	applied mechanics	8
応力	オウリョク	stress	8
●黄	オウ; コウ	yellow	20
黄	き	yellow	20
黄色	きいろ	yellow	20
黄鉄鉱	オウテッコウ	(iron) pyrite	20
黄道	コウドウ	ecliptic	20
黄銅	オウドウ	brass	20
黄銅鉱	オウドウコウ	chalcopyrite	20
●音	オン	sound	18
音	おと	sound	18
音の高さ	おとのたかさ	pitch	18
音色	ねいろ	(sound) timbre	18
音圧	オンアツ	sound pressure	18
音響-	オンキョウ	acoustic	18
音響結合	オンキョウケツゴウ	acoustic coupling	18
音響抵抗	オンキョウテイコウ	acoustic resistance	18
音子	オンシ	phonon	18
音素	オンソ	phoneme	18
音速	オンソク	speed of sound	18
音程	オンテイ	musical interval	18
音波	オンパ	sound wave	18
●温	オン	warmth, heat	6
温度	オンド	temperature	6
温度計	オンドケイ	thermometer	9
温和な	オンワな	mild	20

力

●下	カ; ゲ	below; down	6
下	した	lower part, bottom	6
-下(に)	した(に)	beneath	6
-下(で)	もと(で)	under, at	6
下る	くだる	to go down	6
下げる	さげる	to hang, lower	6
下がる	さがる	to sag, go lower	6
下向き	したむき	downward	9
下位-	カイ	sub-	15
下地	したジ	base, foundation	18
下等な	カトウな	lower (plant, animal)	9
下方	カホウ	lower region	7
下流	カリュウ	downstream	19
●化	カ	conversion, transformation	6
-化	カ	-ization, -cation, -tion	6
化学	カガク	chemistry	6
化学屈性	カガククッセイ	chemotropism	18

K-5

カ

化学工学	カガクコウガク	chemical engineering	13
化学式	カガクシキ	chemical formula	8
化学者	カガクシャ	chemist	17
化学上	カガクジョウ	from the chemical point of view	6
化学的な	カガクテキな	chemical	7
化合物	カゴウブツ	chemical compound	8
化石	カセキ	fossil	12
●可	カ	-ible, -able	19
可逆過程	カギャクカテイ	reversible process	19
可逆的な	カギャクテキな	reversible	19
可逆反応	カギャクハンノウ	reversible reaction	19
可動な	カドウな	movable	19
可動接点	カドウセッテン	traveling contact	19
可燃性の	カネンセイの	combustible	20
可能な	カノウな	possible	19
可変の	カヘンの	variable	19
可変抵抗器	カヘンテイコウキ	rheostat	19
可溶性の	カヨウセイの	soluble	19
●加	カ	addition, increase	10
加える	くわえる	to add, include	10
加わる	くわわる	to increase	10
加圧する	カアツする	to pressurize	10
加減-	カゲン	adjustable	17
加工する	カコウする	to process, treat, work upon	10
加水分解	カスイブンカイ	hydrolysis	10
加速器	カソクキ	accelerator	11
加速電圧	カソクデンアツ	accelerating voltage	10
加速度	カソクド	acceleration	10
加熱する	カネツする	to heat	10
加硫	カリュウ	vulcanization	15
●果	カ	fruit	10
果たす	はたす	to accomplish	10
果実	カジツ	fruit	10
果実学	カジツガク	carpology	10
果糖	カトウ	fructose	13
●価	カ	value	19
価	あたい	value	19
価値	カチ	value	19
価電子	カデンシ	valence electron	19
価電子帯	カデンシタイ	valence band	19
●過	カ	excess; going through	12
過ごす	すごす	to spend (time), go through	12
過ぎる	すぎる	to elapse; to go through	12
-過ぎる	すぎる	to over(do), be too ...	9
過酸化水素	カサンカスイソ	hydrogen peroxide	12
過酸化物	カサンカブツ	peroxide	12

過程	カテイ	process	12
過電圧	カデンアツ	over-voltage	12
過熱液体	カネツエキタイ	superheated liquid	12
過熱蒸気	カネツジョウキ	superheated vapor	12
過飽和	カホウワ	supersaturation	16
●回	カイ	rotation	14
-回	カイ	{counter for times}	14
回す	まわす	to rotate	14
回る	まわる	to rotate, revolve	11
回収する	カイシュウする	to recover	20
回折	カイセツ	diffraction	18
回線	カイセン	(telephone) circuit	14
回転	カイテン	rotation	17
回反	カイハン	rotatory inversion {chem}	14
回分法	カイブンホウ	batch process	14
回路	カイロ	circuit	14
●界	カイ	world; field {phys}	19
界磁石	カイジシャク	field magnet	19
界磁制御	カイジセイギョ	field control	19
界磁鉄心	カイジテッシン	field core	19
界面	カイメン	interface	19
界面活性剤	カイメンカッセイザイ	surfactant	19
界面動電位	カイメンドウデンイ	electrokinetic potential	19
●械	カイ	machine	17
●開	カイ	opening	17
開く	あく	to open	17
開ける	あける	to open	17
開く	ひらく	to open	17
開ける	ひらける	to open	17
開環重合	カイカンジュウゴウ	ring-opening polymerization	17
開場する	カイジョウする	to open {e.g., a facility}	17
開設する	カイセツする	to inaugurate	17
開発	カイハツ	development	17
開放サイクル	カイホウサイクル	open cycle	17
開路	カイロ	open circuit	17
●解	カイ	dismantling; analysis	9
解く	とく	to untie; to solve	9
解き明かす	ときあかす	to clarify	13
解重合	カイジュウゴウ	depolymerization	9
解析	カイセキ	analysis {math}	15
解説	カイセツ	interpretation	13
解離する	カイリする	to dissociate	19
●外	ガイ	outer, external	11
外	そと	outside, exterior	11
外の	ほかの	another, different	11
外: の〜に	のほかに	other than	11

外れる	はずれる	to deviate, slip off	17
外圧	ガイアツ	external pressure	11
外角	ガイカク	exterior angle	14
外観	ガイカン	appearance	16
外積	ガイセキ	outer product, vector product	11
外表層	ガイヒョウソウ	outer-surface layer	20
外部-	ガイブ	external	11
外面	ガイメン	outer surface	11
外力	ガイリョク	external force	11
●各	カク	each	14
各	おの,おのおの	each	14
各(々)の	おのおのの	each	7
各回	カッカイ	each time	14
各個	カッコ	each one	14
各点	カクテン	each point	18
各部	カクブ	each part	14
各論	カクロン	a discussion of details	17
●角	カク	angle, corner	14
角	かど	corner, edge	14
角	つの	horn {of an animal}	14
角運動量	カクウンドウリョウ	angular momentum	14
角質	カクシツ	keratin	14
角振動数	カクシンドウスウ	circular frequency	14
●核	カク	nucleus, core	12
核タンパク質	カクタンパクシツ	nucleoprotein	12
核液	カクエキ	karyolymph {biol}; nucleoplasm	12
核外電子	カクガイデンシ	extranuclear electron	12
核酸	カクサン	nucleic acid	12
核子	カクシ	nucleon	12
核磁気-	カクジキ	nuclear magnetic	12
核磁子	カクジシ	nuclear magneton	12
核質	カクシツ	karyoplasm {biol}	12
核内力	カクナイリョク	intranuclear force	12
核燃料	カクネンリョウ	nuclear fuel	20
核反応	カクハンノウ	nuclear reaction	12
核分裂	カクブンレツ	nuclear fission	20
●確	カク	certain	18
確かめる	たしかめる	to confirm, make certain	18
確かな	たしかな	certain, sure	18
確かに	たしかに	to be sure, undoubtedly	4
確実性	カクジツセイ	certainty, reliability	18
確立する	カクリツする	to establish	18
確率	カクリツ	probability	18
確率過程	カクリツカテイ	stochastic process	18
確率過程理論	カクリツカテイリロン	theory of stochastic process	17
確率関数	カクリツカンスウ	probability function	18

確率分布	カクリツブンプ	probability distribution	18
●学	ガク	learning	6
-学	ガク	science (of)	6
-学では	ガクでは	in the field of ...	6
学ぶ	まなぶ	to learn, study	6
学者	ガクシャ	scholar	17
-学部	ガクブ	college of {e.g. engineering}	9
学問	ガクモン	field of study	16
●活	カツ	life, activity	19
活性化	カッセイカ	activation	19
活性化剤	カッセイカザイ	activation agent	20
活性錯合体	カッセイサクゴウタイ	activated complex	19
活性中心	カッセイチュウシン	active site	19
活動電位度	カツドウデンイド	action potential	19
活動度	カツドウド	activity {thermo}	19
●割	カツ	split, division	13
割	わり	rate; tenths	13
割る	わる	to divide	13
割合	わりあい	proportion, rate	13
割り算	わりサン	division	17
割り当てる	わりあてる	to allocate	13
割球	カッキュウ	blastomere	13
●官	カン	organ {biol}; government	20
官能基	カンノウキ	functional group {chem}	20
●換	カン	exchanging	17
換える	かえる	to exchange; to convert	17
換気	カンキ	ventilation	17
換算表	カンサンヒョウ	conversion table	17
●間	カン	interval, space, between	6
間	あいだ	interval, space, between	6
間違い	まちがい	mistake, error	8
間違う	まちがう	to be in error	10
間接の	カンセツの	indirect	14
●管	カン	governing; tube, pipe	9
管	くだ	pipe	9
管状の	カンジョウの	tubular	11
管状反応器	カンジョウハンノウキ	tubular reactor	11
管理	カンリ	management, control	9
管理図	カンリズ	control chart	18
●関	カン	connection	7
関係	カンケイ	relation	7
関心を持つ	カンシンをもつ	to have concern	9
関数	カンスウ	function	8
関与する	カンヨする	to be involved, participate	13
関連する	カンレンする	to be associated with	16
関連づける	カンレンづける	to relate	19

カン

●環	カン	ring, circle	16
環境	カンキョウ	environment	16
環式の	カンシキの	cyclic	16
環式化合物	カンシキカゴウブツ	cyclic compound {chem}	16
環状の	カンジョウの	ring-shaped, cyclic	16
環状構造	カンジョウコウゾウ	cyclic structure	16
環状接続	カンジョウセツゾク	ring connection {elec engr}	16
環状線	カンジョウセン	beltline {highway}	16
●観	カン	appearance	16
観察	カンサツ	observation	16
観測	カンソク	observation	16
観測者	カンソクシャ	observer	20
観点	カンテン	viewpoint	16
●含	ガン	containing	7
含む	ふくむ	to contain, include	7
含水の	ガンスイの	hydrated, hydrous	7
含水量	ガンスイリョウ	water content	8
含有する	ガンユウする	to contain	7

キ

●気	キ	air, gas	6
気づく	キづく	to become aware of	19
気圧計	キアツケイ	barometer	9
気化	キカ	vaporization	6
気象学	キショウガク	meteorology	16
気相	キソウ	vapor phase	10
気体	キタイ	gas	6
●記	キ	inscription, record	17
記号	キゴウ	symbol	17
記事	キジ	(newspaper) article	17
記述	キジュツ	description	17
記入する	キニュウする	to fill out, make an entry	17
●起	キ	occurring; initiating	10
起こす	おこす	to generate, initiate	10
起こる	おこる	to happen, occur	10
起重機	キジュウキ	crane	10
起振力	キシンリョク	vibromotive force	10
起電力	キデンリョク	electromotive force	10
起動力	キドウリョク	motive power	10
●基	キ	foundation; radical {chem}	13
基	もと	basis	13
基づく	もとづく	to be based (on)	13
基質	キシツ	substrate	13
基準	キジュン	standard, critcrion	16
基板	キバン	substrate	18
基本の	キホンの	fundamental	16

●期	キ	period, term	11
期間	キカン	period of time	11
●器	キ	instrument; container	11
器械	キカイ	appliance, instrument	17
器官	キカン	organ {biol}	20
器官系	キカンケイ	organ system	20
器官原基	キカンゲンキ	organ primordium	20
●機	キ	machine	9
機械	キカイ	machine	17
機関	キカン	engine	9
機構	キコウ	mechanism	12
機能	キノウ	function	17
●技	ギ	art, skill	16
技術	ギジュツ	technology	16
●逆	ギャク	contrary, reverse, inverse	19
逆行の	ギャッコウの	retrograde	19
逆行運動	ギャッコウウンドウ	retrograde motion	19
逆三角関数	ギャクサンカクカンスウ	inverse trigonometric function	19
逆数	ギャクスウ	reciprocal (number)	19
逆転層	ギャクテンソウ	inversion layer	19
逆比	ギャクヒ	inverse ratio	19
逆方向	ギャクホウコウ	opposite direction	19
逆流	ギャクリュウ	backward flow	19
●及	キュウ	attainment	13
及ぶ	およぶ	to attain, reach	13
及び	および	and, as well as	6
及ぼす	およぼす	to exert (force)	10
及ぼし合う	およぼしあう	to exert (force) on each other	13
●吸	キュウ	inhalation	13
吸う	すう	to breath, suck	4
吸音材	キュウオンザイ	sound-absorbing materials	19
吸光係数	キュウコウケイスウ	extinction coefficient	13
吸光度	キュウコウド	absorbance	13
吸収	キュウシュウ	absorption	20
吸収剤	キュウシュウザイ	absorbent	20
吸収帯	キュウシュウタイ	absorption band	20
吸水	キュウスイ	water absorption	13
吸着	キュウチャク	adsorption	20
吸熱	キュウネツ	endothermic	13
●求	キュウ	seeking; finding	13
求める	もとめる	to seek; to find	13
求まる	もとまる	to be obtained	13
求核反応	キュウカクハンノウ	nucleophilic reaction	13
求心性	キュウシンセイ	afferent	20
求電子反応	キュウデンシハンノウ	electrophilic reaction	13
●究	キュウ	investigating	16

キュウ

●球	キュウ	sphere, bulb	12
球	たま	sphere, ball	12
球形-	キュウケイ	spherical	12
球状タンパク質	キュウジョウタンパクシツ	globular protein	12
球面	キュウメン	spherical surface	12
球面波	キュウメンハ	spherical wave	18
●距	キョ	distance	16
距離	キョリ	distance	16
●御	ギョ	governing, managing	16
御-	ゴ,お	{honorific prefix}	16
●共	キョウ	common	19
共: と～に	とともに	together with	19
共重合	キョウジュウゴウ	copolymerization	19
共晶点	キョウショウテン	eutectic point	19
共振	キョウシン	resonance	19
共振子	キョウシンシ	resonator	19
共生	キョウセイ	symbiosis	19
共析晶	キョウセキショウ	eutectoid	19
共線の	キョウセンの	collinear	19
共存する	キョウゾンする	to coexist	20
共通イオン効果	キョウツウイオンコウカ	common ion effect	19
共同研究	キョウドウケンキュウ	collaborative research	19
共変	キョウヘン	covariant	19
共有する	キョウユウする	to share	19
共有結合	キョウユウケツゴウ	covalent bond	19
●強	キョウ	strength	11
強い	つよい	strong	11
強さ	つよさ	strength	11
強過ぎる	つよすぎる	to be too strong	12
強酸	キョウサン	strong acid	11
強電解質	キョウデンカイシツ	strong electrolyte	11
強度	キョウド	strength	11
●境	キョウ	boundary	16
境	さかい	boundary	16
境界	キョウカイ	boundary	16
境界条件	キョウカイジョウケン	boundary condition	19
境地	キョウチ	state, condition	16
●響	キョウ	echo	16
●行	ギョウ	line; row	5
行	コウ	acting	5
行う	おこなう	to do, perform	5
行く	いく; ゆく	to go	4
行程	コウテイ	stroke {of a piston}	11
行動	コウドウ	behavior	6
行列	ギョウレツ	matrix {math}	20
行列式	ギョウレツシキ	determinant	20

●業	ギョウ	business	16
業界	ギョウカイ	(the world of) industry	19
●曲	キョク	curving; bending	14
曲げる	まげる	to bend	14
曲がる	まがる	to be curved; to be bent	14
曲線	キョクセン	curve, curved line	14
曲面	キョクメン	curved surface	14
曲率	キョクリツ	curvature	14
曲率中心	キョクリツチュウシン	center of curvature	14
曲率半径	キョクリツハンケイ	radius of curvature	14
●極	キョク	extremity, pole	13
極	ゴク	very, extremely	16
極める	きわめる	to master	13
極めて	きわめて	extremely	13
極形式	キョクケイシキ	polar form	14
極限	キョクゲン	limit	14
極光帯	キョクコウタイ	auroral zone	18
極細胞	キョクサイボウ	polar cell	13
極小の	キョクショウの	minimum, smallest	13
極性分子	キョクセイブンシ	polar molecule	13
極大の	キョクダイの	maximum, greatest	13
極大値	キョクダイチ	(local) maximum value	13
極端	キョクタン	extremity	18
極度に	キョクドに	extremely	19
極微の	キョクビの	(ultra)microscopic	18
●近	キン	near, close	11
近い	ちかい	near, close	11
近々	ちかぢか	in the near future	4
近赤外線	キンセキガイセン	near infrared rays	11
近接する	キンセツする	to be adjacent, contiguous	14
近代化	キンダイカ	modernization	13
●金	キン	gold; metal	5
金	かね	money; metal	5
金メッキ	キンメッキ	gold plate	5
金属	キンゾク	metal	15
●菌	キン	bacteria, fungi	20
菌核	キンカク	sclerotium	20
菌学	キンガク	mycology	20
菌類	キンルイ	fungi	20
●銀	ギン	silver	15

ク

●空	クウ	air, space	12
空	そら	sky, heavens	12
空間	クウカン	space	12
空気	クウキ	air	12

クウ

空中線	クウチュウセン	antenna {also アンテナ}	12
空中電気	クウチュウデンキ	atmospheric electricity	12
空中放電	クウチュウホウデン	atmospheric discharge	12
●屈	クツ	bending (over)	18
屈曲性ポリマー	クッキョクセイポリマー	flexible polymer	18
屈性	クッセイ	tropism	18
屈折	クッセツ	refraction	18
屈折角	クッセツカク	angle of refraction	18
屈折波	クッセツハ	refracted wave	18
屈折率	クッセツリツ	index of refraction	18

ケ

●系	ケイ	system	18
系統学	ケイトウガク	systematics	18
系統的に	ケイトウテキに	systematically	18
●形	ケイ	shape, form	12
-形	かた; がた	shape, form	12
形	かたち	shape, form	12
形式	ケイシキ	form	18
形質	ケイシツ	character	20
形質発現	ケイシツハツゲン	phenotypic expression	20
形状	ケイジョウ	shape	12
形成する	ケイセイする	to form	12
形態	ケイタイ	configuration	20
形態学	ケイタイガク	morphology	12
形態形成	ケイタイケイセイ	morphogenesis	12
●径	ケイ	diameter	14
径路	ケイロ	path {e.g., of a chemical reaction}	14
●係	ケイ	connection	7
係数	ケイスウ	coefficient	8
●型	ケイ	model, type, pattern	17
型	かた	model, type, mold	17
-型	がた	model, type	17
型式	ケイシキ	model, type	17
●計	ケイ	plan; measure	9
-計	ケイ	meter	9
計る	はかる	to measure	9
計器	ケイキ	measuring device	12
計算	ケイサン	calculation	17
計算器	ケイサンキ	calculator	17
計算機	ケイサンキ	computer	17
計数器	ケイスウキ	counter	11
●経	ケイ	longitude; experience	20
経つ	たつ	to elapse {time}	20
-経て: -を～	をへて	via ...	20
経過	ケイカ	passage {of time}	20

経験	ケイケン	experience	20
経験式	ケイケンシキ	empirical formula	20
経差	ケイサ	difference in longitude	20
経度	ケイド	longitude	20
経路	ケイロ	path	20
●血	ケツ	blood	20
血	ち	blood	4
血圧	ケツアツ	blood pressure	20
血液	ケツエキ	blood	20
血液移送	ケツエキイソウ	blood transfusion	20
血液色素	ケツエキシキソ	hemochrome	20
血管	ケッカン	blood vessel	9
血色素	ケッシキソ	hemoglobin	20
血糖	ケットウ	blood sugar	20
●結	ケツ	binding; concluding	9
結び	むすび	conclusion	9
結ぶ	むすぶ	to tie, bind; to conclude	9
結びつく	むすびつく	to be attached	17
結果	ケッカ	result	10
結果を得る	ケッカをえる	to obtain results	11
結合	ケツゴウ	bond {chem}	9
結合水	ケツゴウスイ	bound water	9
結合性電子	ケツゴウセイデンシ	bonding electron	9
結晶	ケッショウ	crystal	17
結晶化	ケッショウカ	crystallization	17
結論	ケツロン	conclusion	17
●件	ケン	case, matter	16
件数	ケンスウ	number of cases, items	16
●見	ケン	seeing, viewing	5
見る	みる	to see	5
見える	みえる	to be visible	5
見なす	みなす	to regard ... as	5
見かけ上の	みかけジョウの	apparent	6
見出す	みいだす	to discover, find	9
見方	みかた	point of view	5
見本	みホン	sample, specimen	16
見地	ケンチ	point of view	18
見当	ケントウ	conjecture	19
●研	ケン	polishing, sharpening	16
研究	ケンキュウ	research	16
●検	ケン	investigation	17
検出	ケンシュツ	detection	17
検定	ケンテイ	(qualifying) test; calibration	17
検定器	ケンテイキ	calibration instrument	17
検流計	ケンリュウケイ	galvanometer	17
●験	ケン	testing	8

ゲン

●元	ゲン	source, origin	8
元	もと	source, origin	8
元々	もともと	originally, in the past	4
元素	ゲンソ	element {chem}	7
●限	ゲン	limit, restriction	14
限り	かぎり	limit; bound	14
限る {xu}	かぎる	to be limited	14
限定する	ゲンテイする	to limit, restrict	20
●原	ゲン	original, proto-	6
原	はら	field	6
原系	ゲンケイ	original system	19
原形質	ゲンケイシツ	protoplasm	12
原子	ゲンシ	atom	5
原子価	ゲンシカ	valence	19
原子核	ゲンシカク	atomic nucleus	12
原子動力	ゲンシドウリョク	atomic power	6
原子量	ゲンシリョウ	atomic weight	8
原子力	ゲンシリョク	atomic power	5
原子炉	ゲンシロ	nuclear reactor	18
原色	ゲンショク	primary color	9
原生動物	ゲンセイドウブツ	protozoan	6
原則	ゲンソク	principle	9
原点	ゲンテン	origin (of coordinates)	10
原理	ゲンリ	principle	9
原料	ゲンリョウ	raw materials	15
●減	ゲン	decreasing	17
減らす	へらす	to decrease	17
減る {xu}	へる	to decrease	17
減極	ゲンキョク	depolarization	19
減極剤	ゲンキョクザイ	depolarizer	19
減少	ゲンショウ	decrease, reduction	17
減数分裂	ゲンスウブンレツ	meiosis	20
減速器	ゲンソクキ	speed reducer	17
●現	ゲン	actual, current	16
現われる	あらわれる	to appear, be manifest	16
現在の	ゲンザイの	present, current	16
現実に	ゲンジツに	actually, in actuality	19
現象	ゲンショウ	phenomenon	16
現状(の)	ゲンジョウ(の)	current state (of)	16
現存する	ゲンゾンする	to exist	16
現代の	ゲンダイの	present, current	16

コ

●固	コ	solid; firm	6
固める	かためる	to harden	6
固まる	かたまる	to harden	6

固化	コカ	solidification	6
固相	コソウ	solid phase	10
固体	コタイ	solid	6
固定-	コテイ	fixed	6
固定剤	コテイザイ	fixative	19
固定子	コテイシ	stator {elec engr}	6
固有-	コユウ	characteristic, eigen-	7
固有値	コユウチ	eigenvalue	13
固溶体	コウヨウタイ	solid solution	19
●個	コ	individual	14
-個	コ	{counter for objects}	14
個々に	ココに	one by one	14
個々の	ココの	each	14
個人用	コジンヨウ	for personal use	14
個体	コタイ	individual {biol}	14
個体性	コタイセイ	individuality	14
個体発生	コタイハッセイ	ontogeny	14
●互	ゴ	mutual, each other	19
互い(の)	たがい(の)	mutual, reciprocal	19
互換性	ゴカンセイ	interchangeability	19
互換性組み立て	ゴカンセイくみたて	interchangeable assembly	19
互変異性	ゴヘンイセイ	tautomerism	19
●後	ゴ,コウ	behind; after	11
後で	あとで	after	11
後に	のちに	after	11
後ろ	うしろ	behind	11
後者	コウシャ	latter {for persons and things}	17
後述の	コウジュツの	as stated later	13
後部	コウブ	back (part)	11
後方	コウホウ	back	18
後面	コウメン	rear face	11
後流	コウリュウ	backwash, wake	11
●工	コウ	manufacturing	13
-工	ク	worker	13
工学	コウガク	engineering	13
工業	コウギョウ	industry	16
工場	コウば; コウジョウ	factory	13
工程	コウテイ	process	13
●向	コウ	direction	9
向き	むき	direction	9
向く	むく	to turn toward	9
向かう	むかう	to face toward	9
向上	コウジョウ	improvement	9
向心力	コウシンリョク	centripetal force	9
●交	コウ	intersecting; exchanging	10
交わる	まじわる	to intersect	10

コウ

交換	コウカン	exchange	17
交互に	コウゴに	alternately	19
交通	コウツウ	traffic	13
交点	コウテン	point of intersection, node	10
交流	コウリュウ	alternating current	10
●光	コウ	light	10
光	ひかり	light	10
光る	ひかる	to shine, glitter	10
光屈性	ひかりクッセイ	phototropism	18
光高温計	ひかりコウオンケイ	optical pyrometer	10
光散乱	ひかりサンラン	light scattering	18
光化学的な	コウカガクテキな	photochemical	10
光学	コウガク	optics	10
光学的高温計	コウガクテキコウオンケイ	optical pyrometer	10
光起電力	コウキデンリョク	photoelectromotive force	10
光行差	コウコウサ	aberration of light	20
光合成	コウゴウセイ	photosynthesis	10
光子	コウシ	photon	10
光線	コウセン	light ray	10
光速度	コウソクド	velocity of light	10
光電管	コウデンカン	photoelectric tube	10
光電気	コウデンキ	photoelectricity	10
光電効果	コウデンコウカ	photoelectric effect	17
光電子	コウデンシ	photoelectron	10
光度	コウド	luminous intensity	10
光分解	コウブンカイ	photolysis	10
●考	コウ	thought, consideration	10
考える	かんがえる	to think, consider	10
考え直す	かんがえなおす	to rethink	10
考えに入れる	かんがえにいれる	to take into consideration	10
考え方	かんがえかた	way of thinking	10
考察する	コウサツする	to consider, contemplate	16
●抗	コウ	opposite; anti-	18
抗ヒスタミン薬	コウヒスタミンヤク	antihistamic agent	19
抗原	コウゲン	antigen	18
抗体	コウタイ	antibody	18
●効	コウ	effect	17
効く	きく	to be effective	17
効果	コウカ	effect	17
効用	コウヨウ	utility	17
効率	コウリツ	efficiency	17
効力	コウリョク	effectiveness	17
●香	コウ	fragrance, aroma	19
香り	かおり	fragrance, aroma	19
●高	コウ	tall, high	5
高い	たかい	tall	5

高さ	たかさ	height	5
高圧	コウアツ	high pressure	8
高温	コウオン	high temperature	6
高速度	コウソクド	high velocity	8
高大な	コウダイな	grand, impressive	5
高低	コウテイ	height	17
高度計	コウドケイ	altimeter	9
高熱	コウネツ	high fever	7
高熱-	コウネツ	pyro-	7
高分子	コウブンシ	macromolecule	5
高炉	コウロ	blast furnace	18
●鉱	コウ	mineral	19
鉱石	コウセキ	ore	19
鉱層	コウソウ	ore bed, seam	19
鉱物	コウブツ	mineral	19
●構	コウ	construction, structure	12
構成する	コウセイする	to form, constitute	12
構成要素	コウセイヨウソ	component	18
構造	コウゾウ	structure	13
構造式	コウゾウシキ	structural formula	13
●酵	コウ	fermentation	20
酵素	コウソ	enzyme	19
酵素の活性化	コウソのカッセイカ	activation of enzyme	20
酵素活性	コウソカッセイ	enzymatic activity	20
●鋼	コウ	steel	19
鋼	はがね	steel	19
鋼鉄	コウテツ	steel	19
鋼鉄管	コウテツカン	steel tubing	19
鋼鉄材	コウテツザイ	steel materials	19
鋼鉄製の	コウテツセイの	made of steel	19
●号	ゴウ	number; announcement	16
●合	ゴウ	agreement; joining	8
合わせる	あわせる	to put together	8
合う	あう	to meet; to combine	8
合金	ゴウキン	alloy	8
合金鋼	ゴウキンコウ	alloy steel	19
合計	ゴウケイ	sum, total	9
合成	ゴウセイ	synthesis	8
合成化学	ゴウセイカガク	synthetic chemistry	8
合板	ゴウハン	plywood	18
合理的な	ゴウリテキな	rational	9
合力	ゴウリョク	resultant force	8
●混	コン	mixing	19
混ぜる	まぜる	to mix	4
混ざる	まざる	to be mixed	19
混じる {xu}	まじる	to be blended	19

コン

混圧タービン	コンアツタービン	mixed-pressure turbine	19
混合の	コンゴウの	mixed	19
混合物	コンゴウブツ	mixture	19
混晶	コンショウ	mixed crystal	19
混信	コンシン	(radio) interference	19
混成	コンセイ	hybridization	19
混成軌道	コンセイキドウ	hybridization orbital	19
混同する	コンドウする	to mix up, confuse	20
混乱	コンラン	disorder	19
混和性	コンワセイ	miscibility	19

サ

●作	サ; サク	making, building	10
作る	つくる	to make, build	4
作り出す	つくりだす	to produce	9
作り直す	つくりなおす	to remake, rebuild	10
作業	サギョウ	work, operation	16
作業者	サギョウシャ	worker	17
作動-	サドウ	working	10
作動させる	サドウさせる	to run, operate	10
作動シリンダ	サドウシリンダ	working cylinder	10
作物	サクモツ	crops	10
作用	サヨウ	action	10
作用-	サヨウ	working	10
作用高さ	サヨウたかさ	working depth	10
●差	サ	difference	20
差す	さす	to offer	20
差異	サイ	difference, disparity	20
差動変圧器	サドウヘンアツキ	differential transformer	20
差分方程式	サブンホウテイシキ	difference equation	20
差分法	サブンホウ	calculus of finite differences	20
●再	サイ	again, re-	20
再び	ふたたび	again, a second time	20
再結合	サイケツゴウ	recombination	20
再結晶	サイケッショウ	recrystallization	20
再現性	サイゲンセイ	reproducibility	20
再現精度	サイゲンセイド	reproducibility	20
再構成	サイコウセイ	reconstitution	20
再使用	サイシヨウ	reuse, reusing	20
再処理	サイショリ	reprocessing	20
再生	サイセイ	regeneration	20
再生結晶	サイセイケッショウ	regenerated crystal	20
再生産曲線	サイセイサンキョクセン	reproduction curve	20
再配列	サイハイレツ	rearrangement	20
再利用する	サイリヨウする	to reuse	20
●細	サイ	slender, fine	9

細い	ほそい	slender, narrow	9
細かい	こまかい	detailed, fine	9
細長い	ほそながい	long and slender	10
細菌	サイキン	bacteria	20
細菌学	サイキンガク	bacteriology	20
細部	サイブ	detail	9
細分する	サイブンする	to subdivide	9
細胞	サイボウ	cell	12
細胞液	サイボウエキ	cell sap	12
細胞核	サイボウカク	cell nucleus	12
細胞学	サイボウガク	cytology	12
細胞器官	サイボウキカン	(cell) organelle	20
細胞質	サイボウシツ	cytoplasm	12
細胞小器官	サイボウショウキカン	(cell) organelle	20
細胞染色	サイボウセンショク	staining of bacteria	20
細胞分裂	サイボウブンレツ	cell division	20
●最	サイ	most, maximum	11
最も	もっとも	most	11
最近	サイキン	recently	11
最近の	サイキンの	most recent	11
最後の	サイゴの	last, final	11
最高の	サイコウの	highest	11
最小の	サイショウの	minimum	11
最大の	サイダイの	maximum	11
最大値	サイダイチ	(global) maximum value	13
最低の	サイテイの	lowest	17
最適-	サイテキ	optimum, optimal	17
●在	ザイ	existence	16
在外研究	ザイガイケンキュウ	research abroad	16
●材	ザイ	material	19
材料	ザイリョウ	materials	15
材料試験	ザイリョウシケン	materials testing	19
材料力学	ザイリョウリキガク	strength of materials	19
●剤	ザイ	drug; agent	19
●酢	サク	acetic	15
酢	す	vinegar	15
酢酸	サクサン	acetic acid	15
酢酸亜鉛	サクサンアエン	zinc acetate	15
酢酸鉛	サクサンなまり	lead acetate	15
酢酸銅	サクサンドウ	copper acetate	15
●錯	サク	complex; mixed	19
錯塩	サクエン	complex salt	19
錯化合物	サクカゴウブツ	complex compound	19
錯基	サクキ	complex radical	19
錯体	サクタイ	a complex {chem}	19
●察	サツ	perceiving, knowing	16

サン

●三	サン	three	14
三	み	three	14
三つ	みっつ; みつ	three	14
三塩基酸	サンエンキサン	tribasic acid	14
三回	サンカイ	three times	14
三角関数	サンカクカンスウ	trigonometric function	14
三角形	サンカクケイ	triangle	14
三極管	サンキョクカン	triode	14
三原色説	サンゲンショクセツ	theory of three primary colors	14
三個	サンコ	three {e.g., atoms}	14
三次元	サンジゲン	three-dimensional	14
三次導関数	サンジドウカンスウ	third-order derivative {math}	14
三次反応	サンジハンノウ	third-order reaction	14
三重結合	サンジュウケツゴウ	triple bond	14
三重点	サンジュウテン	triple point	14
三相交流	サンソウコウリュウ	three-phase current	14
三倍	サンバイ	three times, three-fold	14
●産	サン	product	16
産む	うむ	to give birth	16
産業	サンギョウ	industry	16
産出	サンシュツ	output	16
産物	サンブツ	product(s)	16
産卵期	サンランキ	spawning (season)	20
●散	サン	scattering	17
散る {xu}	ちる	to scatter	17
散光	サンコウ	scattered light	17
散在する	サンザイする	to lie scattered	17
散水機	サンスイキ	sprinkler	17
散布	サンプ	sprinkling, spraying	17
散乱	サンラン	scattering	18
●算	サン	calculation	17
算術	サンジュツ	arithmetic	17
●酸	サン	acid; oxygen	7
酸っぱい	すっぱい	sour	7
酸化	サンカ	oxidation	7
酸化剤	サンカザイ	oxidizing agent	19
酸化物	サンカブツ	oxide	7
酸性の	サンセイの	acidic	8
酸素	サンソ	oxygen	7

シ

●子	シ	child	5
-子	シ	small entity	5
子	こ	child	5
●仕	シ	doing, serving	16
仕上げる	シあげる	to finish, complete	16

仕方	シカタ	means, method, procedure	16
仕組(み)	シくみ	contrivance, mechanism	16
仕事	シごと	work, job	16
仕様	シヨウ	specifications	16
●示	シ; ジ	indication	5
示す	しめす	to show, indicate	5
示差熱分析	シサネツブンセキ	differential thermal analysis	20
示量変数	ジリョウヘンスウ	extensive variable	9
示力図	ジリョクズ	force diagram	5
●自	シ; ジ	oneself	13
自ら	みずから	by itself, oneself	13
自然	シゼン	nature	13
自転	ジテン	rotation	17
自動酸化	ジドウサンカ	auto-oxidation	13
自動的な	ジドウテキな	automatic	13
自発的な	ジハツテキな	spontaneous	17
自分	ジブン	oneself	13
●使	シ	use	9
使う	つかう	to use	9
使い方	つかいかた	way of using	9
使い過ぎる	つかいすぎる	to use too much	12
使用-	シヨウ	working	9
使用する	シヨウする	to use	9
使用温度	シヨウオンド	working temperature	9
使用法	シヨウホウ	(directions for) how to use	9
●脂	シ	fat	15
脂	あぶら	fat, grease	15
脂質	シシツ	lipid	15
脂肪	シボウ	fat	19
脂肪細胞	シボウサイボウ	fat cell	19
脂肪酸	シボウサン	fatty acid	19
脂肪組織	シボウソシキ	fatty tissue	19
脂肪族の	シボウゾクの	aliphatic	19
●試	シ	trial, test	19
試す	ためす	to try, test	19
試みる	こころみる	to try, attempt	19
試運転	シウンテン	trial run	19
試金	シキン	assay	19
試験	シケン	test	19
試験管	シケンカン	test tube	19
試験所	シケンジョ	experimental station	19
試験炉	シケンロ	test kiln, test reactor	19
試行	シコウ	trial	19
試薬	シヤク	chemical reagent	19
試料	シリョウ	sample	19
●次	ジ	order; next	10

ジ

次に	つぎに	next	4
次の	つぎの	next, the following	9
次ぐ	つぐ	to come after, follow	10
次々	つぎつぎ	successively, one after another	19
次亜塩素酸	ジアエンソサン	hypochlorous acid	15
次元	ジゲン	dimension	10
-次数	ジスウ	order (of)	19
次第に	シダイに	gradually	14
●地	ジ; チ	earth, ground	12
地	つち	earth, ground	12
地下結実	チカケツジツ	geocarpy	12
地下鉄	チカテツ	subway	15
地球	チキュウ	the earth	12
地球の自転	チキュウのジテン	rotation of the earth	17
地磁気	チジキ	geomagnetism	12
地質学	チシツガク	geology	12
地上の	チジョウの	terrestrial	12
地層	チソウ	stratum	18
地動説	チドウセツ	Copernican theory	12
地面	ジメン	(the) ground, earth's surface	12
地理学	チリガク	geography	12
●事	ジ	thing, fact	16
事	こと	thing, fact	16
事業	ジギョウ	business	16
事後確率	ジゴカクリツ	a posteriori probability	18
事実	ジジツ	fact	16
事象	ジショウ	phenomenon	16
事前確率	ジゼンカクリツ	a priori probability	18
事態	ジタイ	situation	16
●時	ジ	time; hour	9
時	とき	time; occasion	9
時々	ときどき	sometimes	9
時計	とケイ	clock, watch	9
時計回り	とケイまわり	clockwise	14
時計方向	とケイホウコウ	clockwise direction	9
時間	ジカン	time	9
時代	ジダイ	era	17
時定数	ジテイスウ	time constant	9
●磁	ジ	magnetism	12
磁化	ジカ	magnetization	12
磁気テープ	ジキテープ	magnetic tape	12
磁気量子数	ジキリョウシスウ	magnetic quantum number	12
磁場	ジば	magnetic field	12
磁石	ジシャク	magnet	12
磁力線	ジリョクセン	line of magnetic force	12
●式;-式	シキ	formula; equation	8

-式	シキ	style, type, mode	8
●色	シキ; ショク	color	9
色	いろ	color	7
色々な	いろいろな	various	6
色収差	いろシュウサ	chromatic aberration	20
色素	シキソ	pigment	9
色素類脂質	シキソルイシシツ	lipochrome	15
●織	シキ, ショク	weaving	12
織る	おる	to weave	12
織物	おりもの	woven fabric	12
織機	ショッキ	loom, weaving machine	12
●質	シツ	substance; quality; essence	8
質的な	シツテキな	qualitative	20
質点系	シッテンケイ	mass-point system	18
質問	シツモン	question	16
質量	シツリョウ	mass	8
質量数	シツリョウスウ	mass number	8
●日	ジツ; ニチ	day	16
日	ひ	sun; day	16
-日	か	{counter for days}	16
日光	ニッコウ	sunlight	16
日常の	ニチジョウの	ordinary	16
日常生活	ニチジョウセイカツ	daily life	18
日中の	ニッチュウの	daytime	16
日本	ニッポン; ニホン	Japan	16
日本製	ニホンセイ	made in Japan	19
●実	ジツ	true, real; fruit	8
実	み	fruit	8
実験	ジッケン	experiment	8
実験式	ジッケンシキ	empirical formula {chem}	8
実験値	ジッケンチ	experimental value	13
実現	ジツゲン	implementation	19
実現する	ジツゲンする	to implement	16
実効の	ジッコウの	effective	17
実在の	ジツザイの	actual, real	16
実数	ジッスウ	real number	8
実測	ジッソク	actual measurements	18
実体の	ジッタイの	real	18
実部	ジツブ	real part	14
実用に	ジツヨウに	in practical use	19
実用性	ジツヨウセイ	practicality	8
●者	シャ	person	17
者	もの	person	17
●射	シャ	shooting	12
射出成形	シャシュツセイケイ	injection molding	12
●石	シャク; セキ	rock, stone	5

石	いし	stone(s)	5
石けん	セッケン	soap	5
石けん水	セッケンスイ	soapy water	5
石器時代	セッキジダイ	the Stone Age	13
石炭	セキタン	coal	7
石炭酸	セキタンサン	phenol, carbolic acid	7
石炭層	セキタンソウ	coal seam	18
石油	セキユ	petroleum	19
石油化学薬品	セキユカガクヤクヒン	petrochemicals	19
●種	シュ	kind; seed; species {biol}	14
種	たね	seed, kernel	14
種物	たねもの	seeds	14
種子	シュシ	seed	14
種子植物	シュシショクブツ	spermatophyte	14
種々の	シュジュの	various	14
種族	シュゾク	stellar population {astronomy}	15
種類	シュルイ	kind, variety	14
●受	ジュ	receiving	13
受ける	うける	to receive, accept	12
受け取る	うけとる	to accept	13
受け入れる	うけいれる	to receive, accept	12
受信する	ジュシンする	to receive	18
受精	ジュセイ	fertilization	20
受精卵	ジュセイラン	fertilized egg	20
受動-	ジュドウ	passive	17
受動的な	ジュドウテキな	passive	13
●収	シュウ	taking in, collecting	20
収める	おさめる	to obtain, gather	20
収差	シュウサ	aberration	20
収集	シュウシュウ	collection	20
収縮	シュウシュク	contraction	20
収縮期血圧	シュウシュクキケツアツ	systolic blood pressure	20
収着	シュウチャク	sorption	20
収率	シュウリツ	yield	20
収量	シュウリョウ	yield	20
●周	シュウ	circuit, circumference	11
周り	まわり	circumference; surroundings	11
周期	シュウキ	cycle, period	11
周期運動	シュウキウンドウ	periodic motion	11
周期関数	シュウキカンスウ	periodic function	11
周期的な	シュウキテキな	periodic	11
周期表	シュウキヒョウ	periodic table	11
周期律表	シュウキリツヒョウ	periodic table	11
周波数	シュウハスウ	frequency	18
周波数分析	シュウハスウブンセキ	frequency analysis	18
●臭	シュウ	odor, stench	15

臭い	くさい	foul smelling	15
臭化銀	シュウカギン	silver bromide	15
臭気	シュウキ	bad odor	15
臭素	シュウソ	bromine	15
●集	シュウ	collecting	15
集める	あつめる	to gather, collect	15
集まる	あつまる	to assemble, converge	15
集計する	シュウケイする	to sum up, total	15
集光器	シュウコウキ	optical condenser	15
集合	シュウゴウ	set {math}	15
集合状態	シュウゴウジョウタイ	state of aggregation	15
集積化	シュウセキカ	integration	19
集積回路	シュウセキカイロ	integrated circuit	15
集積技術	シュウセキギジュツ	integrated-circuit technology	17
集中する	シュウチュウする	to focus, center on, concentrate	15
集約的な	シュウヤクテキな	intensive	15
●重	ジュウ	heavy; layered	7
重い	おもい	heavy	7
重さ	おもさ	weight	7
重ね合わせ	かさねあわせ	superposition	8
重ねる	かさねる	to pile up, layer	7
重なる	かさなる	to be piled up	7
重合体	ジュウゴウタイ	polymer	8
重縮合	ジュウシュクゴウ	condensation polymerization	18
重心	ジュウシン	center of gravity	9
重水	ジュウスイ	heavy water	7
重水素	ジュウスイソ	deuterium	7
重付加反応	ジュウフカハンノウ	polyaddition reaction	19
重要な	ジュウヨウな	important	7
重率	ジュウリツ	weight	18
重量	ジュウリョウ	weight	8
重力	ジュウリョク	gravity	7
●縮	シュク	shrinking	18
縮める	ちぢめる	to compress	18
縮まる	ちぢまる	to shrink	18
縮まない	ちぢまない	incompressible	4
縮合	シュクゴウ	condensation	18
縮合環	シュクゴウカン	condensing ring	18
縮合重合体	シュクゴウジュウゴウタイ	condensation polymer	18
縮図	シュクズ	reduced figure	18
●出	シュツ	sending out, going out	9
出す	だす	to send out, take out	9
出る	でる	to emerge, go out (from)	9
出入りする	でいりする	to go in and out	9
出来事	できごと	occurrence, incident	16
出血	シュッケツ	hemorrhage	20

出現	シュツゲン	emergence	18
出題	シュツダイ	proposing a question	16
出発	シュッパツ	departure	18
出発点	シュッパツテン	point of departure	18
出力	シュツリョク	output	9
●述	ジュツ	statement, dicussion	13
述べる	のべる	to state, discuss	13
●術	ジュツ	art, technique	16
●準	ジュン	level; aim	16
●処	ショ	managing, dealing with	17
処置	ショチ	treatment, handling	17
処理する	ショリする	to process	17
処理-	ショリ	treated	17
処理水	ショリスイ	treated water	17
●所	ショ; ジョ	place	13
所-	ショ	that which	13
所	ところ	place	13
所在する	ショザイする	to be located at, situated at	20
所長	ショチョウ	head {of an office, factory, or institute}	13
所要の	ショヨウの	required {lit.: that which is needed}	13
●小	ショウ	small	5
小-	こ	small	5
小さい	ちいさい	small	4
小さな	ちいさな	small	5
小型の	こがたの	small-sized	17
小角散乱	ショウカクサンラン	small-angle scattering	18
小触角	ショウショッカク	small antenna	20
小胞	ショウホウ	vesicle	12
●少	ショウ	few; small amount	7
少ない	すくない	few	7
少し	すこし	a little; slightly	7
少品種	ショウヒンシュ	small-variety (type)	17
少量	ショウリョウ	small amount	8
●消	ショウ	extinguishing	12
消す	けす	to extinguish, put out	12
消える	きえる	to go out, disappear	12
消化	ショウカ	digestion {biol}	12
消化管	ショウカカン	alimentary canal	12
消化器官	ショウカキカン	digestive organ	20
消化酵素	ショウカコウソ	digestive enzyme	20
消極剤	ショウキョクザイ	depolarizer	19
消磁	ショウジ	demagnetization	12
●晶	ショウ	crystal	17
●硝	ショウ	nitric	15
硝化作用	ショウカサヨウ	nitrification	15
硝酸	ショウサン	nitric acid	15

硝酸銀	ショウサンギン	silver nitrate	15
硝酸水銀	ショウサンスイギン	mercury nitrate	15
硝石	ショウセキ	niter, potassium nitrate	15
硝酸銅	ショウサンドウ	copper nitrate	15
●象	ショウ	image, shape	16
象	ゾウ	elephant	16
●上	ジョウ	over, up, above	6
-上	ジョウ	from view point of; on {a line, surface}	6
上	うえ	upper part, top	6
上(に)	うえ(に)	above	6
上げる	あげる	to raise, elevate	6
上がる	あがる	to rise, go up	6
上向き	うわむき	upward	9
上下	ジョウゲ	up and down	6
上空	ジョウクウ	upper atmosphere	13
上述の	ジョウジュツの	as stated above	13
上方	ジョウホウ	upper region	7
●条	ジョウ	item, article	16
条件	ジョウケン	condition	16
●状	ジョウ	condition, state	11
-状	ジョウ	-shape(d)	11
状態	ジョウタイ	state	11
状態変化	ジョウタイヘンカ	change of state	11
状態(方程)式	ジョウタイ(ホウテイ)シキ	equation of state	11
状態量	ジョウタイリョウ	state quantity	11
●常	ジョウ	normal, usual	13
常に	つねに	always, continually	13
常々	つねづね	usually	4
常圧コンデンサー	ジョウアツコンデンサー	atmospheric condenser	13
常温	ジョウオン	room temperature	13
常磁性	ジョウジセイ	paramagnetism	13
常用対数	ジョウヨウタイスウ	common logarithm	13
●情	ジョウ	circumstances, state of things	16
情報	ジョウホウ	information	16
情報処理	ジョウホウショリ	information processing	17
●場	ジョウ	place	10
場	ば	place; occasion	10
-場	ば	field {electric, force}	10
場合	ばあい	case, situation	4
場所	ばショ	location, place	13
●蒸	ジョウ	vapor; steam	11
蒸す	むす	to steam	11
蒸気圧	ジョウキアツ	vapor pressure	11
蒸気管	ジョウキカン	steam pipe	11
蒸気機関	ジョウキキカン	steam engine	11
蒸発	ジョウハツ	vaporization	11

ジョウ

蒸発器	ジョウハツキ	evaporator, vaporizer	11
蒸発熱	ジョウハツネツ	heat of vaporization	11
●植	ショク	planting	12
植える	うえる	to plant; to raise	12
植わる	うわる	to be planted	12
植物	ショクブツ	plant, vegetation	12
植物界	ショクブツカイ	plant kingdom	19
植物学	ショクブツガク	botany	12
植物生理学	ショクブツセイリガク	plant physiology	12
植物性-	ショクブツセイ	vegetative	12
●殖	ショク	propagating, increasing	20
殖やす	ふやす	to propagate {biol}, increase (in number)	20
殖える	ふえる	to propagate {biol}, increase (in number)	20
●触	ショク	touching	20
触れる	ふれる	to touch	20
触角	ショッカク	antenna {biol}	20
触媒	ショクバイ	catalyst	20
触媒作用	ショクバイサヨウ	catalysis	20
●心	シン	heart; mind	9
心	こころ	heart	9
心配する	シンパイする	to be concerned	13
心理学	シンリガク	psychology	9
●信	シン	trust, belief	16
信号	シンゴウ	signal	16
●神	シン	spirit; gods	20
神経	シンケイ	nerve	20
神経系	シンケイケイ	nervous system	20
神経細管	シンケイサイカン	neural tube	20
神経細胞	シンケイサイボウ	neuron	20
●振	シン	vibration	10
振る	ふる	to swing, vibrate	10
振り子	ふりこ	pendulum	10
振動	シンドウ	oscillation, vibration	10
振動子	シンドウシ	oscillator	10
振動数	シンドウスウ	frequency	10
振動量子数	シンドウリョウシスウ	vibrational quantum number	10
●進	シン	advancing	15
進む	すすむ	to progress	15
進化する	シンカする	to evolve	15
進行	シンコウ	progress, advance	15
進入	シンニュウ	entry	20
●人	ジン; ニン	person, people	5
人	ひと	person, people	5
人々	ひとびと	persons, people	6
人間	ニンゲン	human being(s)	6
人工の	ジンコウの	artificial, man-made	13

人力の	ジンリョクの	manual	5
人類	ジンルイ	humankind	14
人類の進化	ジンルイのシンカ	evolution of humankind	15
人類学	ジンルイガク	anthropology	14

ス

●図	ズ; ト	diagram, drawing	18
図る	はかる	to devise	18
図解	ズカイ	explanatory diagram	18
図形	ズケイ	figure	18
図示する	ズシする	to illustrate	18
図式	ズシキ	graph	18
●水	スイ	water	5
水	みず	water	5
水時計	みずどケイ	water clock	9
水圧	スイアツ	water pressure	8
水化物	スイカブツ	hydrate	6
水銀	スイギン	mercury	15
水銀電極	スイギンデンキョク	mercury electrode	15
水産業	スイサンギョウ	marine industry	16
水酸化ナトリウム	スイサンカナトリウム	sodium hydroxide	7
水酸化鉄	スイサンカテツ	iron hydroxide	15
水酸化物	スイサンカブツ	hydroxide	7
水準	スイジュン	standard, level	16
水晶	スイショウ	quartz	17
水晶振動子	スイショウシンドウシ	quartz oscillator	19
水蒸気	スイジョウキ	steam, water vapor	11
水生の	スイセイの	aquatic	5
水素	スイソ	hydrogen	7
水素化物	スイソカブツ	hydride	7
水分	スイブン	moisture	6
水平面	スイヘイメン	horizontal plane	10
水面	スイメン	water surface	5
水流ポンプ	スイリュウポンプ	aspirator	7
水力	スイリョク	water power	5
水力学	スイリキガク	hydraulics	6
●数	スウ	number	8
数	かず	number	8
数える	かぞえる	to count	8
数々の	かずかずの	several, numerous	8
数学	スウガク	mathematics	8
数係数	スウケイスウ	numerical coefficient	8
数度	スウド	several times	8
数倍	スウバイ	several times	14
数表	スウヒョウ	numerical table	8
数理統計学	スウリトウケイガク	mathematical statistics	18

スウ

数量的な	スウリョウテキな	quantitative, numerical	8

セ

●正	セイ	positive {+}; correct	11
正しい	ただしい	correct	11
正の電気	セイのデンキ	positive electricity	11
正確な	セイカクな	exact	18
正確に言えば	セイカクにいえば	if we state it (more) precisely	4
正常化	セイジョウカ	normalization	17
正数	セイスウ	a positive number	11
正多面体	セイタメンタイ	regular polyhedron	11
正反対の	セイハンタイの	directly opposite	11
正比例	セイヒレイ	direct proportion	11
正方形	セイホウケイ	square	12
●生	セイ; ショウ	life, existence	5
生む	うむ	to give birth	5
生かす	いかす	to give life, enliven	5
生きる	いきる	to live	5
生じる	ショウじる	to arise, be generated	5
生ずる	ショウずる	to arise, be generated	5
生化学	セイカガク	biochemistry	6
生活環	セイカツカン	life cycle	19
生産	セイサン	production	16
生殖	セイショク	reproduction	20
生殖器	セイショクキ	genital organs	20
生殖器官	セイショクキカン	reproductive organs	20
生殖原細胞	セイショクゲンサイボウ	gonium	20
生殖周期	セイショクシュウキ	reproductive cycle	20
生殖不能	セイショクフノウ	sterility	20
生成する	セイセイする	to generate	8
生成能	セイセイノウ	ability to generate	20
生成物	セイセイブツ	(reaction) products	8
生存	セイゾン	survival	16
生体	セイタイ	organism	6
生体電位	セイタイデンイ	biopotential	20
生体膜	セイタイマク	biomembrane	20
生体力学	セイタイリキガク	biomechanics	6
生態学	セイタイガク	ecology	11
生態的地位	セイタイテキチイ	ecological niche	11
生物	セイブツ	living thing, creature	6
生物学	セイブツガク	biology	6
生理学	セイリガク	physiology	9
●成	セイ	consisting of; turning into	8
成る	なる	to consist of; to turn into	8
成り立つ	なりたつ	to be valid; to consist of	8
成形	セイケイ	molding	18

成形加工	セイケイカコウ	forming operations	15
成長する	セイチョウする	to grow	10
成分	セイブン	component(s) {not meaning "part(s)"}	8
成立する	セイリツする	to be valid, hold true	8
●制	セイ	controlling, regulating	16
制御	セイギョ	control	16
制振	セイシン	damping	16
制振器	セイシンキ	damper	16
●性	セイ	property, characteristic	8
性質	セイシツ	property	8
性能	セイノウ	performance	17
●精	セイ	precision; refinement; details; semen	20
精液	セイエキ	semen	20
精液糖	セイエキトウ	seminal sugar	20
精子	セイシ	spermatozoon	20
精子形成	セイシケイセイ	spermatogenesis	20
精子進入	セイシシンニュウ	semination	20
精神	セイシン	mind, spirit	20
精神安定剤	セイシンアンテイザイ	tranquilizer	20
精製する	セイセイする	to refine	20
精製油	セイセイユ	refined oil	20
精白糖	セイハクトウ	refined sugar	20
精密	セイミツ	precision	19
精密な	セイミツな	precise	20
精密機械	セイミツキカイ	precision machinery	20
精油所	セイユショ	oil refinery	20
●製	セイ	manufacture	19
製鋼	セイコウ	steel making	19
製鋼業	セイコウギョウ	steel industry	19
製鋼所	セイコウショ	steel mill	19
製作	セイサク	manufacture	19
製図	セイズ	drafting	19
製造	セイゾウ	manufacture	19
製造所	セイゾウショ	manufacturing facility	19
製品	セイヒン	manufactured goods	19
●静	セイ；ジョウ	silent, quiet	18
静かな	しずかな	silent, quiet	18
静圧	セイアツ	static pressure	18
静止質量	セイシシツリョウ	rest mass	18
静磁場	セイジば	static magnetic field	18
静水圧	セイスイアツ	hydrostatic pressure	18
静的な	セイテキな	static	19
静電位	セイデンイ	electrostatic potential	18
●赤	セキ	red	11
赤い	あかい	red	11
赤外線	セキガイセン	infrared rays	11

セキ

赤血球	セッケッキュウ	erythrocyte	20
赤色光	セキショクコウ	red light	11
赤熱	セキネツ	red heat	11
●析	セキ	dividing; analyzing	15
析出	セキシュツ	precipitation	15
析出電位	セキシュツデンイ	deposition potential	15
析出物	セキシュツブツ	precipitates {for hardening metals}	15
●積	セキ	accumulation; product {math}	8
積もる	つもる	to accumulate	8
積む	つむ	to stow aboard; to pile up	13
積層成形	セキソウセイケイ	laminate molding	18
積層板	セキソウバン	laminate	18
積分	セキブン	integral	8
積分学	セキブンガク	integral calculus	8
積分法	セキブンホウ	integration	8
●折	セツ	folding, bending	18
折る	おる	to fold, bend	18
●接	セツ	touching, contacting	14
接する	セッする	to touch, contact	14
接近する	セッキンする	to approach, come near	14
接合子	セツゴウシ	zygote	14
接触角	セッショクカク	angle of contact	20
接触酸化	セッショクサンカ	catalytic oxidation	20
接触抵抗	セッショクテイコウ	contact resistance	20
接触分解	セッショクブンカイ	catalytic cracking	20
接触法	セッショクホウ	contact process	20
接線	セッセン	tangent (line)	14
接線応力	セッセンオウリョク	shear stress	14
接線加速度	セッセンカソクド	tangential acceleration	14
接続	セツゾク	connection, junction	16
接続器	セツゾクキ	connector	16
接地する	セッチする	to ground {elec}	18
接地板	セッチバン	grounded plate	18
接着剤	セッチャクザイ	adhesive	20
接点	セッテン	point of tangency	14
●設	セツ	installing, setting up	17
設ける	もうける	to establish, set up, equip	4
設計	セッケイ	design, plan	17
設計応力	セッケイオウリョク	design stress	17
設置する	セッチする	to install, set up	17
設定機構	セッテイキコウ	setting mechanism	17
設立する	セツリツする	to establish	17
●説	セツ	explanation	13
-説	セツ	theory of	13
説く	とく	to explain	13
説明	セツメイ	explanation	13

●染	セン	dyeing, staining	20
染める	そめる	to dye, stain	20
染まる	そまる	to be dyed, stained	20
染色	センショク	dyeing	20
染色質	センショクシツ	chromatin	20
染色体	センショクタイ	chromosome	20
染色体の組み換え	センショクタイのくみかえ	recombination of chromosomes	20
染色体異常	センショクタイイジョウ	chromosomal aberration	20
染色体地図	センショクタイチズ	chromosome map	20
染色法	センショクホウ	staining technique	20
染着性	センチャクセイ	dyeing affinity	20
染料	センリョウ	dyestuff	20
●線	セン	line; wire	10
線形-	センケイ	linear	12
線図	センズ	line drawing	18
線積分	センセキブン	line integral	10
線分	センブン	line segment	10
●遷	セン	transferring location	19
遷移	センイ	succession {biol}, transition	19
遷移確率	センイカクリツ	transition probability	19
遷移金属	センイキンゾク	transition metal	19
遷移元素	センイゲンソ	transition element	19
遷移状態	センイジョウタイ	transition state	19
●全	ゼン	all	9
全く	まったく	entirely	9
全て(の)	すべて(の)	all (of something)	9
全音	ゼンオン	whole tone	18
全色性の	ゼンショクセイの	panchromatic	9
全体では	ゼンタイでは	on the whole	4
全体の	ゼンタイの	all of	9
全体集合	ゼンタイシュウゴウ	universal set	15
全体的な	ゼンタイテキな	overall	18
全般の	ゼンパンの	general	19
全般的に	ゼンパンテキに	generally, on the whole	17
全部(の)	ゼンブ(の)	all (of)	9
●前	ゼン	front; before	11
前	まえ	front; before	11
-の前後に	のゼンゴに	before and after ...	11
前後に(動く)	ゼンゴに(うごく)	(to move) back and forth	11
前者	ゼンシャ	former {for persons and things}	17
前述の	ゼンジュツの	as stated earlier	13
前触角	ゼンショッカク	anterior antenna	20
前進する	ゼンシンする	to advance	18
前線	ゼンセン	(weather) front	11
前端	ゼンタン	front end	19
前部	ゼンブ	front (part)	11

ゼン

前方	ゼンポウ	front	18
前面	ゼンメン	front face	11
●然	ゼン,ネン	state; nature	17

ソ

●素	ソ	element; basic part	7
素子	ソシ	element {e.g., electronic}	7
素数	ソスウ	prime number	8
素反応	ソハンノウ	elementary reaction	14
素粒子	ソリュウシ	elementary particle	12
●組	ソ	assembling	12
-組	くみ	set, class {counter}	12
組む	くむ	to assemble	12
組み合わせ	くみあわせ	combination	12
組(み)換えDNA	くみかえDNA	recombinant DNA	17
組み立て	くみたて	assembling	12
組織	ソシキ	tissue {biol}; organization; texture	12
組織学	ソシキガク	histology	12
組織形成	ソシキケイセイ	histogenesis	12
組織細胞	ソシキサイボウ	tissue cell	12
組織分化	ソシキブンカ	histodifferentiation	12
●相	ソウ	phase	10
相-	あい	each other	10
相等しい	あいひとしい	to equal each other	10
相交わる	あいまじわる	to intersect each other	10
相違	ソウイ	difference	10
相違点	ソウイテン	points of difference	10
相互の	ソウゴの	mutual, reciprocal	19
相互関係	ソウゴカンケイ	correlation	19
相互作用	ソウゴサヨウ	interaction	19
相互通信	ソウゴツウシン	two-way communication	19
相関関係	ソウカンカンケイ	correlation	10
相対運動	ソウタイウンドウ	relative motion	10
相対性原理	ソウタイセイゲンリ	principle of relativity	10
相対論的な	ソウタイロンテキな	relativistic	18
相当する	ソウトウする	to correspond (to)	13
相当長さ	ソウトウながさ	equivalent length	13
相同の	ソウドウの	homologous	10
●送	ソウ	transmitting	18
送る	おくる	to send, transmit	4
送り出す	おくりだす	to send out	18
送受信波	ソウジュシンハ	transceived waves	18
送信する	ソウシンする	to transmit	18
送信機	ソウシンキ	transmitter	18
送信所	ソウシンショ	transmitting station	18
●装	ソウ	equipment	17

装置	ソウチ	device, apparatus	17
●層	ソウ	layer	18
層位学	ソウイガク	stratigraphy {geol}	18
層状の	ソウジョウの	stratified	18
層流	ソウリュウ	laminar flow	18
層流境界層	ソウリュウキョウカイソウ	laminar flow boundary layer	19
●造	ゾウ	construction, structure	13
造果器	ゾウカキ	carpogonium	13
造粒	ゾウリュウ	granulation	13
●増	ゾウ	increase	10
増やす	ふやす	to increase	10
増える	ふえる	to increase	10
増す	ます	to increase	10
増加	ゾウカ	increase	10
増殖	ゾウショク	propagation, multiplication	20
増殖炉	ゾウショクロ	breeder reactor	20
増大	ゾウダイ	increase	10
●則	ソク	rule, law	9
●速	ソク	speed	8
速い	はやい	fast, rapid	8
速やかに	すみやかに	quickly, immediately	8
速度	ソクド	velocity	8
速度計	ソクドケイ	speedometer	9
速度分布	ソクドブンプ	velocity distribution	17
●測	ソク	measurement	10
測る	はかる	to measure	10
測光単位	ソッコウタンイ	photometric unit	10
測色計	ソクショクケイ	colorimeter	10
測定	ソクテイ	measurement	10
測定値	ソクテイチ	measured value	13
測面計	ソクメンケイ	planimeter	10
測面法	ソクメンホウ	planimetry	10
測量学	ソクリョウガク	surveying	10
●族	ゾク	family {biol}, group	15
●属	ゾク	belonging to; genus {biol}	15
属する	ゾクする	to belong to	6
属性	ゾクセイ	attribute {biol}	15
●続	ゾク	continuing	16
続ける	つづける	to continue	4
続く	つづく	to continue	16
●存	ソン,ゾン	exist	16
存じる	ゾンじる	to know	16
存在	ソンザイ	existence	16

タ

●他	タ	other	13

タ

他の	タの	the other	13
他: その〜	そのタ	etc.	13
他形	タケイ	allotriomorphic	13
他植	タショク	allogamy	13
他方	タホウ	the other side	13
●多	タ	many; large amount	7
多-	タ	poly-, multiple	7
多い	おおい	many; frequent	4
多原子-	タゲンシ	polyatomic	7
多重の	タジュウの	multiple	7
多重線	タジュウセン	multiplet	14
多少の	タショウの	some	7
多数	タスウ	large number	18
多糖体	タトウタイ	polysaccharide	18
多糖類	タトウルイ	polysaccharides	14
多品種	タヒンシュ	multi-product (type)	17
多面体	タメンタイ	polyhedron	7
多量	タリョウ	large amount	8
●大	タイ; ダイ	large	5
大きい	おおきい	large	4
大きな	おおきな	large	5
大きさ	おおきさ	magnitude	5
大型の	おおがたの	large-sized	17
大水	おおみず	flooding	5
大学付属の	ダイガクフゾクの	university-affiliated	19
大気	タイキ	atmosphere	6
大気圧	タイキアツ	atmospheric pressure	8
大工	ダイク	carpenter	13
大小	ダイショウ	size	5
大切な	タイセツな	important	18
大体	ダイタイ	generally	6
大腸	ダイチョウ	large intestine	20
大腸菌	ダイチョウキン	*E. coli*	20
大部分	ダイブブン	the greater part	9
●体	タイ	(the) body, object	6
体	からだ	(the) body	6
体温	タイオン	body temperature	6
体系	タイケイ	system	18
体細胞	タイサイボウ	somatic cell	20
体積	タイセキ	volume	8
●対	タイ	contrasting, opposite	8
対	ツイ	pair, couple	8
対応する: -(に)〜	(に)タイオウする	to correspond (to)	8
対向流	タイコウリュウ	countercurrent flow	9
対処する	タイショする	to cope with	19
対象	タイショウ	object, subject {of study}	16

対数	タイスウ	logarithm	8
対地高度	タイチコウド	elevation	18
対物レンズ	タイブツレンズ	objective lens	8
対立遺伝子	タイリツイデンシ	alleles	20
対流	タイリュウ	convection current	8
●帯	タイ	band, zone, belt	18
帯びる	おびる	to put a band around, take on (a color)	18
帯系	タイケイ	band system {spectroscopy}	18
帯状の	タイジョウの	belt shaped, zonal	18
帯水層	タイスイソウ	aquifer	18
帯電	タイデン	electrification	18
帯電体	タイデンタイ	charged body	18
●態	タイ	condition, appearance	11
●代	ダイ	replacing	13
代わる	かわる	to replace	13
代わり:の〜に	のかわりに	instead of	13
代数関数	ダイスウカンスウ	algebraic function	13
代数和	ダイスウワ	algebraic sum	16
代入する	ダイニュウする	to substitute {math}	13
代表する	ダイヒョウする	to represent	19
代表的な	ダイヒョウテキな	representative	13
●第-	ダイ	{ordinal prefix}	14
第一-	ダイイチ	first, primary	14
第一種の	ダイイッシュの	of the first kind	14
第一族	ダイイチゾク	first group {in the periodic table}	15
第三-	ダイサン	third, tertiary	14
第二-	ダイニ	second, secondary	14
●題	ダイ	title, topic	16
題目	ダイモク	title, heading, subject	16
●達	タツ	attainment	18
達する	タッする	to attain, reach	18
達成する	タッセイする	to achieve	18
●単	タン	simple; single	9
単-	タン	mono-, single	9
単位	タンイ	unit	9
単位系	タンイケイ	system of units	18
単位体	タンイタイ	unit (simple body)	12
単位長	タンイチョウ	unit length	18
単一	タンイツ	single-	9
単原子分子	タンゲンシブンシ	monatomic molecule	9
単色の	タンショクの	monochromatic	9
単振り子	タンふりこ	simple pendulum	10
単体	タンタイ	simple substance	9
単動式	タンドウシキ	single action type	9
単分子層	タンブンシソウ	monomolecular layer	18
単離精製	タンリセイセイ	isolation purification	20

単量体	タンリョウタイ	monomer	9
●炭	タン	carbon	7
炭	すみ	charcoal	7
炭化	タンカ	carbonization	7
炭化水素	タンカスイソ	hydrocarbon	7
炭化物	タンカブツ	carbide	7
炭酸	タンサン	carbonic acid	7
炭酸鉛	タンサンなまり	lead carbonate	15
炭水化物	タンスイカブツ	carbohydrate	7
炭水素定量法	タンスイソテイリョウホウ	method of determining C and H	8
炭素	タンソ	carbon	7
炭素鋼	タンソコウ	carbon steel	19
●端	タン	tip, end	18
端	はし	tip, end	18
端子	タンシ	terminal	18
端子電圧	タンシデンアツ	terminal voltage	18
端子板	タンシバン	terminal assembly	18
端面図	タンメンズ	end view	18
●断	ダン	cutting off	18
断つ	たつ	to cut off	18
断る	ことわる	to give notice, warn	18
断層	ダンソウ	fault {geol}	18
断層面	ダンソウメン	fault plane	18
断続的な	ダンゾクテキな	intermittent	18
断熱-	ダンネツ	adiabatic	18
断熱消磁	ダンネツショウジ	adiabatic demagnetization	18
断熱体系	ダンネツタイケイ	adiabatic system	18
断熱変化	ダンネツヘンカ	adiabatic change	18
断面図	ダンメンズ	cross-sectional drawing	18
断面積	ダンメンセキ	cross-sectional area	18

チ

●知	チ	knowledge	13
知る {xu}	しる	to know	13
知見	チケン	information, knowledge	13
知的な	チテキな	intelligent	13
知能	チノウ	intelligence	17
●値	チ	value	13
値	あたい	value	13
●置	チ	place, location	10
置く	おく	to put, place	10
置換	チカン	substitution	20
置換基	チカンキ	substituent	19
置換体	チカンタイ	substitution product	19
●窒	チツ	suffocation	15
窒化物	チッカブツ	nitrides	15

窒素	チッソ	nitrogen	15
窒素固定	チッソコテイ	nitrogen fixation	15
窒素族元素	チッソゾクゲンソ	nitrogen family elements	15
窒素同化作用	チッソドウカサヨウ	nitrogen assimilation	15
●着	チャク	arriving	20
着く	つく	to arrive, contact	20
着色	チャクショク	coloring	20
着色剤	チャクショクザイ	coloring agent	20
着水する	チャクスイする	to land on water	20
着生植物	チャクセイショクブツ	epiphyte	20
着目する	チャクモクする	to give attention to	20
●中	チュウ	center, middle	6
-中	チュウ	within; during	6
中	なか	inside	6
中型の	チュウがたの	medium-sized	17
中間子	チュウカンシ	meson	6
中間体	チュウカンタイ	(an) intermediate {chem}	6
中空-	チュウクウ	hollow	18
中心	チュウシン	center	19
中心力	チュウシンリョク	central force	9
中性の	チュウセイの	neutral	8
中性子	チュウセイシ	neutron	8
中断する	チュウダンする	to interrupt	18
中点	チュウテン	mid-point	10
中立面	チュウリツメン	neutral plane	6
中和	チュウワ	neutralization	16
●注	チュウ	injection; pouring	7
注	チュウ	annotations; notes	7
注ぐ	そそぐ	to pour	7
注ぎ入れる	そそぎいれる	to pour into	7
注射	チュウシャ	injection	12
注射器	チュウシャキ	syringe	12
注入する	チュウニュウする	to pour into	7
注目する	チュウモクする	to notice	19
●長	チョウ	length	10
-長	チョウ	head (of)	10
長い	ながい	long	10
長さ	ながさ	length	10
長時間	チョウジカン	long time	10
長方形	チョウホウケイ	rectangle	12
●超	チョウ	super-, ultra-, trans-, hyper-	19
超ウラン元素	チョウウランゲンソ	transuranium elements	19
超音速	チョウオンソク	supersonic speed	19
超音波	チョウオンパ	ultrasonic wave	19
超伝導の	チョウデンドウの	superconducting	19
超伝導磁石	チョウデンドウジシャク	superconducting magnet	19

チョウ

超伝導体	チョウデンドウタイ	superconductor	19
超微細構造	チョウビサイコウゾウ	hyperfine structure	19
超流動	チョウリュウドウ	superfluidity	19
●調	チョウ	investigation; tone	13
調べる	しらべる	to investigate	13
調光器	チョウコウキ	dimmer	13
調色	チョウショク	toning	13
調製	チョウセイ	preparation	20
調速機	チョウソクキ	governor {mech engr}	13
調和分析	チョウワブンセキ	harmonic analysis	16
●直	チョク	straight; direct	10
直す	なおす	to mend; to correct	9
直る	なおる	to get well	10
直観	チョッカン	intuition	16
直径	チョッケイ	diameter	14
直結する	チョッケツする	to connect directly	10
直後に	チョクゴに	immediately after	11
直交する	チョッコウする	to intersect at right angles	10
直進する	チョクシンする	to propagate linearly	18
直接の	チョクセツの	direct	14
直線	チョクセン	straight line	10
直前に	チョクゼンに	immediately before	11
直流	チョクリュウ	direct current	10

ツ

●通	ツウ	passing through	13
通す	とおす	to admit, let pass	13
通る	とおる	to go through	12
通り	とおり	manner, way	4
-通りに	どおりに	in the manner, way	13
通過	ツウカ	transit (through)	13
通気圧	ツウキアツ	ventilating pressure	13
通気組織	ツウキソシキ	aerenchyma	13
通常-	ツウジョウ	normal, usual	13
通常	ツウジョウ	normally, usually	13
通信	ツウシン	communication	16

テ

●低	テイ	low	17
低い	ひくい	low	17
低圧	テイアツ	low pressure	17
低温	テイオン	low temperature	17
低下させる	テイカさせる	to lower, decrease	17
低気圧	テイキアツ	a low {meteorology}	17
低減する	テイゲンする	to diminish	17
低速	テイソク	low speed	17

低分子量	テイブンシリョウ	low molecular weight	17
●定	テイ	fixed, constant	6
定める	さだめる	to determine	6
定まる	さだまる	to be determined	6
定温-	テイオン	constant temperature	6
定式化する	テイシキカする	to formalize	8
定常-	テイジョウ	constant, steady	13
定数	テイスウ	constant	8
定性的な	テイセイテキな	qualitative	8
定性分析	テイセイブンセキ	qualitative analysis	15
定積分	テイセキブン	definite integral	8
定比例	テイヒレイ	fixed proportion	6
定理	テイリ	theorem	9
定量的な	テイリョウテキな	quantitative	8
定量分析	テイリョウブンセキ	quantitative analysis	15
●抵	テイ	resistance	18
抵抗	テイコウ	resistance, drag	18
抵抗温度計	テイコウオンドケイ	resistance thermometer	18
抵抗器	テイコウキ	resistor	18
抵抗係数	テイコウケイスウ	drag coefficient	18
抵抗成分	テイコウセイブン	resistive component	18
抵抗接地系統	テイコウセッチケイトウ	resistance-grounded (neutral) system	18
抵抗素子	テイコウソシ	resistor element	18
抵抗体	テイコウタイ	resistor	18
抵抗率	テイコウリツ	resistivity	18
抵抗炉	テイコウロ	resistance furnace	18
●程	テイ	extent	11
程	ほど	extent	11
程度	テイド	degree, extent	11
●的	テキ	target	7
-的な	テキな	{adjectival suffix}	7
●適	テキ	proper, suitable	17
適する	テキする	to be suitable	17
適応制御	テキオウセイギョ	adaptive control	17
適当な	テキトウな	proper, suitable	17
適用する	テキヨウする	to apply	18
適用コード	テキヨウコード	applicable code	17
適用可能性	テキヨウカノウセイ	applicability	19
●鉄	テツ	iron	15
鉄鉱	テッコウ	iron ore	19
鉄合金	テツゴウキン	ferroalloys	15
鉄心	テッシン	iron core	15
鉄線	テッセン	iron wire	15
鉄族元素	テツゾクゲンソ	iron family elements	15
鉄板	テッパン	iron plate	15
●点	テン	point; dot	10

点線	テンセン	dotted line	10
●転	テン	revolution, turning	17
転がる	ころがる	to roll, tumble	17
転位	テンイ	(crystal) dislocation	17
転移	テンイ	(phase) transition, (gene) transposition	17
転動体	テンドウタイ	rolling element	17
●伝	デン	transmission	12
伝える	つたえる	to transmit	12
伝わる	つたわる	to be transmitted	12
伝送回線	デンソウカイセン	transmission line	18
伝送線路	デンソウセンロ	transmission line	18
伝送特性	デンソウトクセイ	transmission characteristics	18
伝送路	デンソウロ	transmission line	18
伝達する	デンタツする	to transmit	18
伝達関数	デンタツカンスウ	transfer function {process control}	18
伝導帯	デンドウタイ	conduction band	19
伝熱管	デンネツカン	heat exchanger tube	12
伝熱係数	デンネツケイスウ	heat transfer coefficient	12
伝熱面積	デンネツメンセキ	heating surface area	12
●電	デン	electricity	8
電圧	デンアツ	voltage	8
電圧変成器	デンアツヘンセイキ	voltage transformer	11
電圧利得	デンアツリトク	voltage gain	15
電位	デンイ	electric potential	9
電位差	デンイサ	potential difference	20
電界強度地図	デンカイキョウドチズ	(electric) field-strength map	19
電解質	デンカイシツ	electrolyte	9
電気	デンキ	electricity	8
電気化学	デンキカガク	electrochemistry	8
電気抵抗	デンキテイコウ	electrical resistance	18
電気伝導率	デンキデンドウリツ	electrical conductivity	14
電気容量	デンキヨウリョウ	capacitance	18
電気料金	デンキリョウキン	electric rates	15
電気炉	デンキロ	electric furnace	18
電球	デンキュウ	light bulb	12
電極	デンキョク	electrode	13
電子	デンシ	electron	8
電子管	デンシカン	electron tube	9
電子計算器	デンシケイサンキ	electronic calculator	17
電子受容体	デンシジュヨウタイ	electron acceptor	13
電子素子	デンシソシ	electronic element	7
電子対	デンシツイ	electron pair	8
電磁気	デンジキ	electromagnetism	12
電磁石	デンジシャク	electromagnet	12
電磁波	デンジハ	electromagnetic wave	18
電場	デンば	electric field	10

電信	デンシン	telegraph	16
電線	デンセン	electric wire	10
電線管	デンセンカン	(electrical) conduit	10
電動(式)	デンドウ(シキ)	electrically-driven (type)	8
電波	デンパ	radio wave	18
電流	デンリュウ	electric current	8
電力	デンリョク	electric power	8

ト

●度	ド	degree, measure (of)	6
●当	トウ	appropriate; equivalent	13
当-	トウ	this ...; the said ...	13
当てる	あてる	to apply, strike	11
当たる	あたる	to correspond (to)	13
-当たり	あたり	per ...	7
当時	トウジ	in those days, then	19
当然の	トウゼンの	just, proper	17
当所	トウショ	this place	13
当面は	トウメンは	at present	17
当量	トウリョウ	equivalent	13
当量点	トウリョウテン	equivalence point	13
●透	トウ	transparent	20
透過X線	トウカエックスセン	penetrating X-rays	20
透過酵素	トウカコウソ	permease	20
透過性	トウカセイ	permeability	20
透過波	トウカハ	transmitted wave	20
透過率	トウカリツ	transmissivity	20
透磁率	トウジリツ	magnetic permeability	20
透析	トウセキ	dialysis	20
透析法	トウセキホウ	dialysis method	20
透明の	トウメイの	transparent	20
●等	トウ	grade; equal	7
等しい	ひとしい	equal	7
等	など	etc.	7
-等	ら	et al.	7
等ポテンシャル面	トウポテンシャルメン	equipotential surface	7
等圧-	トウアツ	isobaric	8
等圧変化	トウアツヘンカ	isobaric change	8
等温-	トウオン	isothermal	7
等式	トウシキ	equality	8
等速運動	トウソクウンドウ	uniform motion	9
等速度	トウソクド	uniform velocity	8
等分する	トウブンする	to divide equally	7
等方性の	トウホウセイの	isotropic	8
●統	トウ	governing; lineage	18
統一場理論	トウイツばリロン	unified field theory	18

トウ

統計法則	トウケイホウソク	statistical law	18
統計力学	トウケイリキガク	statistical mechanics	18
●糖	トウ	sugar	13
糖たんぱく質	トウたんぱくシツ	glycoprotein	15
糖化	トウカ	saccharification	13
●同	ドウ	same, identical	7
同じ	おなじ	the same	7
同位体	ドウイタイ	isotope	9
同一の	ドウイツの	identical	7
同時の	ドウジの	simultaneous	9
同素体	ドウソタイ	allotrope	7
同族体	ドウゾクタイ	homolog {chem}	15
同調する	ドウチョウする	to synchronize	19
同定	ドウテイ	identification	7
同等の	ドウトウの	equal	7
●動	ドウ	motion	6
動かす	うごかす	to move	6
動く	うごく	to move	6
動作-	ドウサ	working	10
動作時間	ドウサジカン	working time	10
動作電流	ドウサデンリュウ	working (operating) current	10
動作流体	ドウサリュウタイ	working fluid	10
動的な	ドウテキな	dynamic	19
動粘性率	ドウネンセイリツ	coefficient of kinematic viscosity	18
動物	ドウブツ	animal	6
動物界	ドウブツカイ	animal kingdom	19
動物学	ドウブツガク	zoology	6
動力	ドウリョク	power	6
動力学	ドウリキガク	dynamics	6
●銅	ドウ	copper	15
銅合金	ドウゴウキン	copper alloys	15
銅線	ドウセン	copper wire	15
銅板	ドウバン	copper plate	18
●導	ドウ	conducting; guiding	14
導く	みちびく	to lead; to derive	9
導き出す	みちびきだす	to derive, lead out	14
導き入れる	みちびきいれる	to lead into	14
導管	ドウカン	conduit	14
導関数	ドウカンスウ	derivative {math}	14
導出する	ドウシュツする	to derive	14
導線	ドウセン	lead wire	18
導体	ドウタイ	conductor	14
導電率	ドウデンリツ	electrical conductivity, conductance	18
導入する	ドウニュウする	to introduce	14
導波管	ドウハカン	wave guide	18
●特	トク	special	16

特に	トクに	in particular	4
特異性	トクイセイ	specificity, singularity	16
特異的な	トクイテキな	specific, singular	16
特異点	トクイテン	unique point, singular point	16
特性	トクセイ	characteristics	16
特定の	トクテイの	specific	16
特別-	トクベツ	special	16
●得	トク	benefit, profit	11
得る	える	to get, obtain, gain	11
-得る	うる	to be able to	11
-得ない	えない	to be unable to	11
●突	トツ	sudden; thrusting	20
突く	つく	to thrust	20
突起	トッキ	protrusion, projection	20
突然の	トツゼンの	sudden	20
突然変異	トツゼンヘンイ	mutation	20
突然変異原	トツゼンヘンイゲン	mutagen	20
突然変異細胞	トツゼンヘンイサイボウ	mutant cell	20
突然変異体	トツゼンヘンイタイ	mutant	20

ナ

●内	ナイ	inner, internal	11
内	うち	inside; among	11
内圧	ナイアツ	internal pressure	11
内角	ナイカク	interior angle	14
内積	ナイセキ	inner product, scalar product	11
内燃機関	ナイネンキカン	internal combustion engine	20
内部-	ナイブ	internal	11
内部エネルギー	ナイブエネルギー	internal energy	11
内部応力	ナイブオウリョク	internal stress	11
内面	ナイメン	inner surface	11
内量子数	ナイリョウシスウ	inner quantum number	11

二

●二	ニ	two	5
二組	ふたくみ	two sets	12
二つ	ふたつ	two	5
二通り(に)	ふたとおり(に)	(in) two ways	13
二人	ふたり	two people	5
二原子-	ニゲンシ	diatomic	5
二原子分子	ニゲンシブンシ	diatomic molecule	6
二酸化硫黄	ニサンカいオウ	sulfur dioxide	7
二酸化ケイ素	ニサンカケイソ	silicon dioxide	7
二酸化鉛	ニサンカなまり	lead dioxide	15
二酸化炭素	ニサンカタンソ	carbon dioxide	7
二酸化窒素	ニサンカチッソ	nitrogen dioxide	15

二

二次電子	ニジデンシ	secondary electron	10
二次波	ニジハ	secondary wave	18
二次反応	ニジハンノウ	second-order reaction	10
二重らせん	ニジュウらせん	double helix	7
二重結合	ニジュウケツゴウ	double bond	9
二重積分	ニジュウセキブン	double integral	8
二重層	ニジュウソウ	double layer	18
二進化十進法	ニシンカジッシンホウ	binary-coded decimal notation	15
二進回路	ニシンカイロ	binary circuit	15
二進計数器	ニシンケイスウキ	binary counter	15
二相流	ニソウリュウ	two-phase flow	10
二度	ニド	two degrees; two times	6
二倍体	ニバイタイ	diploid	14
二分の一	ニブンのイチ	one-half	9
●入	ニュウ	enter	5
入れる	いれる	to insert	5
入る {xu}	はいる	to enter	5
入る {xu}	いる	to enter	5
入射する	ニュウシャする	to be incident	18
入射線	ニュウシャセン	incident ray	12
入射波	ニュウシャハ	incident wave	20
入力する	ニュウリョクする	to input	5

ネ

●熱	ネツ	heat	7
熱-	ネツ	thermal, thermo-	7
熱する	ネッする	to heat (up)	7
熱い	あつい	hot	7
熱移動係数	ネツイドウケイスウ	heat transfer coefficient	12
熱応力	ネツオウリョク	thermal stress	8
熱間等方加圧	ネツカントウホウカアツ	hot isostatic pressing (HIP)	19
熱機関	ネツキカン	heat engine	9
熱帯	ネッタイ	tropics	18
熱中性子炉	ネツチュウセイシロ	thermal (neutron) reactor	18
熱伝達係数	ネツデンタツケイスウ	heat transfer coefficient	18
熱伝導率	ネツデンドウリツ	thermal conductivity	14
熱電対	ネツデンツイ	thermocouple	8
熱容量	ネツヨウリョウ	heat capacity	18
熱力学	ネツリキガク	thermodynamics	7
熱力学的な	ネツリキガクテキな	thermodynamic	7
●粘	ネン	viscous	18
粘る	ねばる	to be sticky	18
粘液	ネンエキ	mucilage {biol}	18
粘液酸	ネンエキサン	mucic acid	18
粘液層	ネンエキソウ	slime layer	18
粘性	ネンセイ	viscosity	18

粘性抵抗	ネンセイテイコウ	viscous drag	18
粘性流体	ネンセイリュウタイ	viscous fluid	18
粘着テープ	ネンチャクテープ	sticky tape	20
粘度	ネンド	viscosity	18
粘膜	ネンマク	mucous membrane	20
●燃	ネン	burning	20
燃やす	もやす	to burn	20
燃える	もえる	to burn	20
燃料	ネンリョウ	fuel	20
燃料集合体	ネンリョウシュウゴウタイ	fuel assembly	20
燃料要素	ネンリョウヨウソ	fuel element	20

ノ

●能	ノウ	capability	17
能動-	ノウドウ	active	17
能動回路	ノウドウカイロ	active circuit	17
能率	ノウリツ	efficiency	17
能力	ノウリョク	capability, capacity	17
●濃	ノウ	concentrated	19
濃い	こい	concentrated	19
濃化油	ノウカユ	thickened oil	19
濃縮ウラン	ノウシュクウラン	enriched uranium	19
濃縮機	ノウシュクキ	thickener	19
濃度	ノウド	concentration	19
濃度分極	ノウドブンキョク	concentration polarization	19
濃度分布	ノウドブンプ	concentration distribution	19
濃硫酸	ノウリュウサン	concentrated sulfuric acid	19

ハ

●波	ハ	wave	18
波	なみ	wave	18
波形	ハケイ	wave form	18
波数	ハスウ	wave number	18
波長	ハチョウ	wave length	18
波動-	ハドウ	wave	18
波動関数	ハドウカンスウ	wave function	18
波動力学	ハドウリキガク	wave mechanics	18
波動論	ハドウロン	wave theory	18
●配	ハイ	distribution	15
配る	くばる	to distribute	15
配位結合	ハイイケツゴウ	coordination bond	15
配位子	ハイイシ	ligand	15
配位子場	ハイイシば	ligand field	15
配位説	ハイイセツ	coordination theory	15
配管	ハイカン	piping	15
配向	ハイコウ	orientation	15

配線	ハイセン	wiring	15
配置	ハイチ	arrangement, configuration	15
配電変電所	ハイデンヘンデンショ	distributing substation	15
配布する	ハイフする	to distribute, spread out	17
配列	ハイレツ	arrangement, array	20
●倍	バイ	double	14
-倍	バイ	times, -fold	14
倍加時間	バイカジカン	doubling time	14
倍周期	バイシュウキ	frequency multiplier	14
倍数性	バイスウセイ	polyploidy	14
倍数染色体	バイスウセンショクタイ	diploid	20
倍数比例	バイスウヒレイ	multiple proportions	14
倍率	バイリツ	magnification	14
●媒	バイ	medium	20
媒質	バイシツ	medium	20
媒精	バイセイ	insemination	20
媒染染料	バイセンセンリョウ	mordant dye	20
●白	ハク	white	11
白い	しろい	white	11
白金	ハッキン	platinum	11
白血球	ハッケッキュウ	leucocyte	20
白色光	ハクショクコウ	white light	11
白熱	ハクネツ	white heat, incandescence	11
白熱光	ハクネツコウ	incandescent light	11
●発	ハツ	emerging; emanating	8
発する	ハッする	to arise	18
発見	ハッケン	discovery	8
発現	ハツゲン	manifestation	16
発光スペクトル	ハッコウスペクトル	emission spectra	19
発酵	ハッコウ	fermentation	20
発散する	ハッサンする	to diverge	17
発生する	ハッセイする	to arise, emerge	8
発生学	ハッセイガク	embryology	8
発達する	ハッタツする	to develop	18
発電	ハツデン	generation of electricity	8
発電子	ハツデンシ	armature	8
発電所	ハツデンショ	power plant	13
発熱反応	ハツネツハンノウ	exothermic reaction	8
発表	ハッピョウ	announcement, publication	17
●反	ハン	opposite	8
反応	ハンノウ	chemical reaction	8
反応系	ハンノウケイ	reaction system	18
反応経路	ハンノウケイロ	(reaction) path, (reaction) route	20
反応式	ハンノウシキ	reaction equation (formula)	8
反応性	ハンノウセイ	reactivity	8
反応速度	ハンノウソクド	rate of reaction	8

反応熱	ハンノウネツ	heat of reaction	8
反応物	ハンノウブツ	reactants	8
反作用	ハンサヨウ	reaction	10
反射	ハンシャ	reflex	12
反射神経	ハンシャシンケイ	reflexes	20
反射線	ハンシャセン	reflected ray	12
反射波	ハンシャハ	reflected wave	18
反射炉	ハンシャロ	reverberatory furnace	18
反対	ハンタイ	opposite	8
反対向き	ハンタイむき	opposite direction	9
反対力	ハンタイリョク	counterforce, opposing force	8
反転	ハンテン	inversion; reversal	17
反発	ハンパツ	repulsion	19
反発力	ハンパツリョク	repulsive force	8
反比例	ハンピレイ	inverse proportion	8
反変	ハンヘン	contravariant	19
反面	ハンメン	the reverse	19
反粒子	ハンリュウシ	anti-particle	12
●半	ハン	half, semi-, hemi-	14
半ば	なかば	half; halfway; middle	14
半音	ハンオン	half tone	18
半球	ハンキュウ	hemisphere	14
半金属	ハンキンゾク	metalloid	15
半径	ハンケイ	radius	14
半減期	ハンゲンキ	half-life	17
半数染色体	ハンスウセンショクタイ	haploid	20
半透-	ハントウ	semipermeable	20
半透膜	ハントウマク	semipermeable membrane	20
半透明の	ハントウメイの	translucent	20
半導体	ハンドウタイ	semiconductor	14
半波長板	ハンハチョウバン	half-wave plate	18
半微量-	ハンビリョウ	semimicro- {chem}	14
半分	ハンブン	half	14
●板	ハン; バン	plate, board	18
板	いた	plate, board	18
板金加工	バンキンカコウ	sheet metal working	18
板状の	いたジョウの; バンジョウの	plate-shaped	18
●般	ハン	general	17

ヒ

●比	ヒ	ratio; comparison	6
比-	ヒ	specific	6
比べる	くらべる	to compare	6
比強度	ヒキョウド	specific strength	11
比重	ヒジュウ	specific gravity	7
比重測定法	ヒジュウソクテイホウ	method for measuring specific gravity	10

ヒ

比熱	ヒネツ	specific heat	7
比例	ヒレイ	proportion	6
●非-	ヒ	{negative prefix}	19
非圧縮性流体	ヒアッシュクセイリュウタイ	incompressible fluid	19
非可換体	ヒカカンタイ	noncommutative field {math}	19
非環状の	ヒカンジョウの	acyclic	19
非球面レンズ	ヒキュウメンレンズ	aspherical lens	19
非極性結合	ヒキョクセイケツゴウ	nonpolar bond	19
非金属	ヒキンゾク	nonmetal	19
非晶質の	ヒショウシツの	amorphous, noncrystalline	19
非常に	ヒジョウに	extremely, very	19
非水溶液	ヒスイヨウエキ	nonaqueous solution	19
非染色質	ヒセンショクシツ	achromatin	20
非線形の	ヒセンケイの	nonlinear	19
非定常の	ヒテイジョウの	unsteady	19
非電解質	ヒデンカイシツ	nonelectrolyte	19
非特異的な	ヒトクイテキな	unspecific	20
●微	ビ	minute, micro-	14
微細な	ビサイな	minute, tiny	18
微生物	ビセイブツ	microorganism	14
微生物学	ビセイブツガク	microbiology	14
微分	ビブン	differential {math}	14
微分学	ビブンガク	differential calculus	14
微粒子	ビリュウシ	minute particle	14
微量-	ビリョウ	micro- {chem}	14
微量元素	ビリョウゲンソ	trace element	14
●必	ヒツ	certainty; necessity	7
必ず	かならず	necessarily	7
必ずしも...ない	かならずしも...ない	not necessarily	7
必然的な	ヒツゼンテキな	inevitable	17
必要な	ヒツヨウな	necessary	7
●表	ヒョウ	expressing, showing; table	7
-表	ヒョウ	table of ...	7
表す	あらわす	to express, show	7
表現する	ヒョウゲンする	to express	16
表現形質	ヒョウゲンケイシツ	expressive characteristic	20
表示する	ヒョウジする	to indicate, display	7
表題	ヒョウダイ	title, heading	16
表面	ヒョウメン	surface	7
表面活性剤	ヒョウメンカッセイザイ	surface-active agent	19
●標	ヒョウ	mark, sign	16
標準	ヒョウジュン	standard	16
標準化	ヒョウジュンカ	standardization	16
標準型	ヒョウジュンがた	standard type; normal mode	17
標的	ヒョウテキ	target	18
●品	ヒン	quality; goods	17

品	しな	things, goods	17
品物	しなもの	goods	17
品位	ヒンイ	grade	17
品質	ヒンシツ	quality	17
品質管理	ヒンシツカンリ	quality control	17

フ

●不	フ	{negative prefix}	11
不安定な	フアンテイな	unstable	17
不安定性	フアンテイセイ	instability	19
不可逆的な	フカギャクテキな	irreversible	19
不可能な	フカノウな	impossible	19
不活性な	フカッセイな	inert	19
不合理な	フゴウリな	illogical	11
不織布	フショクフ	nonwoven fabric	17
不対電子	フツイデンシ	unpaired electron	11
不透明な	フトウメイな	opaque	20
不等式	フトウシキ	inequality	11
不必要な	フヒツヨウな	unnecessary	11
不変な	フヘンな	unchangeable, constant	11
●付	フ	attaching	19
付ける	つける	to attach, tag	8
付く	つく	to be attached	19
付加	フカ	addition	19
付加重合	フカジュウゴウ	addition polymerization	19
付加反応	フカハンノウ	addition reaction	19
付近	フキン	vicinity	19
付着	フチャク	adhesion	20
付与する	フヨする	to grant, give	19
付録	フロク	appendix, supplement	19
●布	フ	fabric; extension	17
布	ぬの	cloth	17
●部	ブ	part	9
-部	ブ	department (of)	9
部位	ブイ	a part	19
部長	ブチョウ	department head; dean	10
部品	ブヒン	components, parts	17
部分	ブブン	part	9
部分モル量	ブブンモルリョウ	partial molar quantity	9
部分集合	ブブンシュウゴウ	subset	15
部分積分	ブブンセキブン	integration by parts	9
部分品	ブブンヒン	components, parts	17
●複	フク	double, multiple	18
複塩	フクエン	double salt	18
複屈折	フククッセツ	double refraction, birefringence	18
複合タンパク質	フクゴウタンパクシツ	conjugated protein	18

フク

複合材料	フクゴウザイリョウ	composite materials	19
複合波	フクゴウハ	composite wave	18
複素数	フクソスウ	complex number	18
複対立遺伝子	フクタイリツイデンシ	multiple alleles	20
複分解	フクブンカイ	double decomposition	18
●物	ブツ	thing, object	6
物	もの	thing, object	6
物質	ブッシツ	substance(s)	8
物質移動	ブッシツイドウ	mass transfer	12
物質観	ブッシツカン	image of [the nature of] matter	18
物質交代	ブッシツコウタイ	metabolism	20
物性値	ブッセイチ	values of physical properties	13
物体	ブッタイ	body; object	6
物理化学	ブツリカガク	physical chemistry	9
物理学	ブツリガク	physics	9
物理面	ブツリメン	physical domain	17
●分	フン	minute {of time}	6
分	ブン	dividing; fraction (of)	6
分ける	わける	to divide (in parts)	6
分かる	わかる	to understand, know	6
分圧	ブンアツ	partial pressure	8
分液ロート	ブンエキロート	separatory funnel	6
分化	ブンカ	differentiation	20
分解	ブンカイ	decomposition	9
分割	ブンカツ	division, partition	13
分極	ブンキョク	polarization	13
分光器	ブンコウキ	spectroscope	11
分散	ブンサン	dispersion	17
分子	ブンシ	molecule	5
分子間力	ブンシカンリョク	intermolecular force	6
分子式	ブンシシキ	molecular formula	8
分子量	ブンシリョウ	molecular weight	8
分周する	ブンシュウする	to decompose into frequencies	17
分析	ブンセキ	analysis {chem}	15
分配	ブンパイ	allotment, distribution	15
分配関数	ブンパイカンスウ	partition function	15
分布	ブンプ	distribution	17
分布曲線	ブンプキョクセン	distribution curve	17
分別-	ブンベツ	fractional	16
分離する	ブンリする	to separate	16
分力	ブンリョク	component of force	6
分裂菌類	ブンレツキンルイ	schizomycete	20
分裂子	ブンレツシ	oidiospore	20
分裂生殖	ブンレツセイショク	reproduction by division	20
分裂組織	ブンレツソシキ	meristem {botany}	20

ヘ

●平	ヘイ	horizontal; flat	10
平らな	たいらな	horizontal; flat	10
平たい	ひらたい	flat	10
平行な	ヘイコウな	parallel	10
平行線	ヘイコウセン	parallel lines	10
平板	ヘイバン	flat plate	18
平面	ヘイメン	plane surface	10
平面図形	ヘイメンズケイ	plane figure	18
平炉	ヘイロ	open-hearth furnace	18
●別	ベツ	other	16
別れる	わかれる	to part from	16
別解	ベッカイ	alternative solution	16
別表	ベッピョウ	attached table	16
●変	ヘン	change	6
変な	ヘンな	strange	6
変える	かえる	to change	6
変わる	かわる	to be changed	6
変位	ヘンイ	displacement	9
変化	ヘンカ	change	6
変換	ヘンカン	conversion	17
変形	ヘンケイ	deformation	12
変数	ヘンスウ	variable	8
変性剤	ヘンセイザイ	denaturant	19
変動	ヘンドウ	fluctuation, variation	6
変分学	ヘンブンガク	calculus of variations	6
変分法	ヘンブンホウ	calculus of variations	8

ホ

●方	ホウ	side, direction	5
-方	かた	way, style	5
方向	ホウコウ	direction	9
方式	ホウシキ	method, mode, system	8
方程式	ホウテイシキ	equation	11
方々	ホウボウ	all directions; everywhere	5
方法	ホウホウ	method	8
方面	ホウメン	field {e.g., of study}	5
●芳	ホウ	fragrant, aromatic	19
芳しい	かんばしい	fragrant, aromatic	19
芳香化	ホウコウカ	aromatization	19
芳香族-	ホウコウゾク-	aromatic	19
芳香族化合物	ホウコウゾクカゴウブツ	aromatic compound	19
芳香族環	ホウコウゾクカン	aromatic ring	19
芳香族炭化水素基	ホウコウゾクタンカスイソキ	aromatic hydrocarbon group	19
芳香油	ホウコウユ	fragrant oil	19
●放	ホウ	releasing	12

ホウ

放す	はなす	to let go, release	12
放散	ホウサン	dispersion	17
放射-	ホウシャ	radiation, radiant	12
放射性-	ホウシャセイ	radioactive	12
放射性同位元素	ホウシャセイドウイゲンソ	radioactive isotope	12
放射線	ホウシャセン	radiation	12
放射度	ホウシャド	radiation intensity	12
放射能	ホウシャノウ	radioactivity	17
放出	ホウシュツ	emission	12
放送	ホウソウ	broadcasting {radio or TV}	18
放熱器	ホウネツキ	radiator	12
放物線	ホウブツセン	parabola	12
●法	ホウ	law; method	8
-法	ホウ	method, method of	8
法線応力	ホウセンオウリョク	normal stress	10
法則	ホウソク	law	9
●胞	ホウ	sac, case	12
胞子	ホウシ	spore	12
胞子形成	ホウシケイセイ	sporulation	12
胞子体	ホウシタイ	sporophyte	12
●報	ホウ	report	16
●飽	ホウ	satiation	16
飽和	ホウワ	saturation	16
●肪	ボウ	fat, grease	19
●本	ホン	origin, base; book	16
本	もと	origin, base	16
本-	ホン	this	16
-本	ホン	{counter for long objects}	16
本質的な	ホンシツテキな	essential	16
本日	ホンジツ	today	16

マ

●膜	マク	membrane, film	20
膜小胞	マクショウホウ	membrane vesicle	20
膜電位	マクデンイ	membrane potential	20

ミ

●密	ミツ	dense	18
密集する	ミッシュウする	to crowd together	18
密生する	ミッセイする	to grow thickly	18
密接な	ミッセツな	close, near	18
密度	ミツド	density	18

ム

●無	ム	non-existence	7
無-	ム	{negative prefix}	7

無い	ない	is not; are none	7
無関係の	ムカンケイの	unrelated	7
無機的な	ムキテキな	inorganic	9
無限の	ムゲンの	infinite	14
無限小の	ムゲンショウの	infinitesimal	14
無次元	ムジゲン	dimensionless	10
無臭の	ムシュウの	odorless	15
無色の	ムショクの	colorless, achromatic	9
無人の境	ムジンのキョウ	uninhabited region	16
無水の	ムスイの	anhydrous	7
無水物	ムスイブツ	anhydride	7
無性の	ムセイの	asexual	15
無性生殖	ムセイセイショク	asexual reproduction	20
無線-	ムセン	wireless, radio	18
無定形	ムテイケイ	amorphous	12
無用の	ムヨウの	useless	7

メ

●明	メイ	clear, bright	13
明らかな	あきらかな	clear, obvious	13
明るい	あかるい	clear, bright	13
明解な	メイカイな	lucid, clear	13
明示する	メイジする	to clarify	13
明度	メイド	brightness	13
明日	ミョウニチ	tomorrow	16
明白な	メイハクな	clear, evident	13
明反応	メイハンノウ	light reaction {biol}	13
●面	メン	surface, plane	5
-面	メン	aspect(s) of	5
面	おもて	surface	5
面積	メンセキ	area	8

モ

●目	モク	eye; order {biol}	13
目	め	eye	13
-目	め	{ordinal suffix}	13
目安	めやす	standard, aim	17
目次	モクジ	(table of) contents	13
目的	モクテキ	purpose, objective, goal	13
目的ルーチン	モクテキルーチン	object routine {comp sci}	13
目的成分	モクテキセイブン	specified component	13
目標	モクヒョウ	goal, objective	16
●問	モン	inquiry	16
問う	とう	to ask	16
問い	とい	question	16
問題	モンダイ	problem, issue	16

ヤク

ヤ

●約	ヤク	summary; promise	14
約-	ヤク	approximately	14
約数	ヤクスウ	divisor	14
約分する	ヤクブンする	to reduce a fraction	14
●薬	ヤク	medicine, drugs	19
薬	くすり	medicine, drugs	19
薬剤	ヤクザイ	drugs	19
薬品	ヤクヒン	chemicals	19
薬品処理	ヤクヒンショリ	chemical treatment {of waste}	19
薬物	ヤクブツ	drugs	19
薬物学	ヤクブツガク	pharmacology	19

ユ

●油	ユ	oil	19
油	あぶら	oil	19
油圧機械	ユアツキカイ	hydraulic machine	19
油細胞	ユサイボウ	oil cell	19
油脂	ユシ	fats and oils	19
油層	ユソウ	oil strata	19
油膜	ユマク	oil film	20
油溶性の	ユヨウセイの	oil soluble	19
●有	ユウ	possession	7
有る	ある	to be, exist; to have	7
有機的な	ユウキテキな	organic	9
有限の	ユウゲンの	finite	14
有性生殖	ユウセイセイショク	sexual reproduction	20
有無	ウム; ユウム	presence	13
有用な	ユウヨウな	useful	7
有利な	ユウリな	useful	15
有理化単位	ユウリカタンイ	rationalized units	9
●誘	ユウ	drawing forth	20
誘う	さそう	to allure, entice	20
誘電起電力	ユウデンキデンリョク	induced electromotive force	20
誘電体	ユウデンタイ	dielectric	20
誘電分極	ユウデンブンキョク	induced polarization	20
誘電率	ユウデンリツ	dielectric constant	20
誘導	ユウドウ	induction	20
誘導加速器	ユウドウカソクキ	induction accelerator	20
誘導性酵素	ユウドウセイコウソ	inducible enzyme	20
誘導体	ユウドウタイ	derivative {chem}	20
誘導電界	ユウドウデンカイ	induced electric field	20
誘導物質	ユウドウブッシツ	inducing substance	20
誘導放射能	ユウドウホウシャノウ	induced radioactivity	20
誘発する	ユウハツする	to induce	20

ヨ

●与	ヨ	contributing	13
与える	あたえる	to give, provide	13
●用	ヨウ	use, utility	5
-用	ヨウ	for use in	5
用いる	もちいる	to use	4
-用水	ヨウスイ	water for use in	5
●要	ヨウ	necessity	7
要る {xu}	いる	to need, require	7
要求	ヨウキュウ	demand	13
要約	ヨウヤク	summary	14
●容	ヨウ	form; capacity	18
容器	ヨウキ	vessel	18
容積	ヨウセキ	volume, capacity	18
容量	ヨウリョウ	capacity	18
容量分析	ヨウリョウブンセキ	volumetric analysis	18
●陽	ヨウ	positive; sun	12
陽イオン	ヨウイオン	positive ion, cation	12
陽関数	ヨウカンスウ	explicit function	12
陽極	ヨウキョク	anode	13
陽子	ヨウシ	proton	12
陽生植物	ヨウセイショクブツ	sun plant	12
陽性元素	ヨウセイゲンソ	electropositive element	12
陽電気	ヨウデンキ	positive electricity	12
陽電子	ヨウデンシ	positron	12
●溶	ヨウ	melting, dissolving	9
溶かす	とかす	to melt, dissolve	9
溶ける	とける	to melt, dissolve	9
溶液	ヨウエキ	solution	9
溶解する	ヨウカイする	to dissolve	9
溶解酵素	ヨウカイコウソ	solution enzyme	20
溶解度	ヨウカイド	solubility	9
溶解度積	ヨウカイドセキ	solubility product	9
溶解熱	ヨウカイネツ	heat of solution	9
溶原化	ヨウゲンカ	lysogenization	20
溶原菌	ヨウゲンキン	lysogenic bacteria	20
溶原性の	ヨウゲンセイの	lysogenic	9
溶質	ヨウシツ	solute	9
溶出	ヨウシュツ	elution	9
溶出液	ヨウシュツエキ	effluent	9
溶媒	ヨウバイ	solvent	20

ラ

●卵	ラン	egg, ovum	20
卵	たまご	egg	20
卵黄	ランオウ	(egg) yolk	20

ラン

卵黄細胞	ランオウサイボウ	egg yolk cell	20
卵黄膜	ランオウマク	vitelline membrane	20
卵割	ランカツ	cleavage	20
卵管	ランカン	oviduct	20
卵形成	ランケイセイ	oogenesis	20
卵白	ランパク	albumen	20
卵胞子	ランホウシ	oospore	20
●乱	ラン	disorder, chaos	18
乱す	みだす	to make chaotic	18
乱れる	みだれる	to be disordered	18
乱数	ランスウ	random number	18
乱反射	ランハンシャ	diffuse reflection	18
乱流	ランリュウ	turbulent flow	18

リ

●利	リ	benefit, gain	15
利点	リテン	advantage	15
利用	リヨウ	utilization	15
利用する	リヨウする	to use	15
●理	リ	principle; reason	9
理化学	リカガク	the physical sciences	9
理解する	リカイする	to understand	9
理論	リロン	theory	17
●離	リ	separation	16
離れる	はなれる	to separate	16
離間距離	リカンキョリ	clearance	16
●立	リツ	standing upright	5
立てる	たてる	to set up, erect	5
立つ	たつ	to stand	5
立場	たちば	standpoint	10
立体化学	リッタイカガク	stereochemistry	6
立体特異性	リッタイトクイセイ	stereospecificity	20
立方-	リッポウ	cubic	5
立方体	リッポウタイ	cube	6
●率	リツ	rate; percentage	14
●流	リュウ	flowing; current	7
流れ	ながれ	flow	7
流す	ながす	to let flow; to flush	7
流れる	ながれる	to flow	7
流れ出る	ながれでる	to flow out	9
流線	リュウセン	streamline	10
流線形-	リュウセンケイ	streamlined	18
流速	リュウソク	flow velocity	8
流体	リュウタイ	fluid	7
流体力学	リュウタイリキガク	fluid mechanics	7
流量	リュウリョウ	flow	8

流量計	リュウリョウケイ	flow meter	9
流路	リュウロ	passage, channel	18
●粒	リュウ	grain; drop	12
粒	つぶ	grain; drop	12
粒径	リュウケイ	particle-diameter	18
粒子	リュウシ	particle; corpuscle	12
粒子線	リュウシセン	corpuscular beam	12
粒状-	リュウジョウ	granular	12
粒状組織	リュウジョウソシキ	granular texture	12
粒度	リュウド	grain size	12
●硫	リュウ	sulfur	15
硫黄	いオウ	sulfur	20
硫化亜鉛	リュウカアエン	zinc sulfide	15
硫化第一鉄	リュウカダイイチテツ	ferrous sulfide	15
硫酸	リュウサン	sulfuric acid	15
硫酸亜鉛	リュウサンアエン	zinc sulfate	15
硫酸基	リュウサンキ	sulfonic group	15
硫酸銅	リュウサンドウ	copper sulfate	15
●両	リョウ	both	14
両者の	リョウシャの	both	20
両種	リョウシュ	both kinds	14
両生類	リョウセイルイ	amphibia	14
両性-	リョウセイ	amphoteric {chem}; bisexual {biol}	14
両性膜	リョウセイマク	amphoteric membrane	20
両端	リョウタン	both ends	18
両電極	リョウデンキョク	both electrodes	14
両方	リョウホウ	both	14
●料	リョウ	materials; fee	15
料金	リョウキン	rate, charge, fee	15
●量	リョウ	quantity (of)	8
量る	はかる	to measure	8
量子化する	リョウシカする	to quantize	8
量子数	リョウシスウ	quantum number	8
量子力学	リョウシリキガク	quantum mechanics	8
量子論	リョウシロン	quantum theory	17
量的な	リョウテキな	quantitative	18
●力	リョク; リキ	force, power	5
力	ちから	force	5
力学	リキガク	mechanics	5
力学的な	リキガクテキな	mechanical	7
力場	リキば	force field	10

ル

●類	ルイ	type, variety	14
類脂質	ルイシシツ	lipoid	15
類別	ルイベツ	classification	16

レ

HIRAGANA Vocabulary List

This list includes all verbs, i-adjectives, noun- and verb-following expressions, sentence-initial words and phrases, and JUKUGO with KUN readings, plus a few ON words often written in HIRAGANA. They are listed in 五十音 order. Each entry is written in HIRAGANA, then with KANJI when applicable, followed by the English meaning, and the chapter in which the word first appeared. Note that the KANJI entry is given regardless of whether or not the word was written with KANJI in the text. Verbs are identified as intransitive with {自}, and as transitive with {他}; xu-verbs are marked with {xu}.

PRONUNCIATION	KANJI FORM	MEANING	CHAPTER
あ			
あい-	相-	each other	10
あいだ	間	interval, space, between	6
あいひとしい	相等しい	to equal each other	10
あいまいな		vague	7
あいまじわる {自}	相交わる	to intersect each other	10
あう {自}	合う	to meet; to combine	8
あかい	赤い	red	11
あがる {自}	上がる	to rise, go up	5
あかるい	明るい	clear, bright	13
あきらかな	明らかな	clear, obvious	13
あきる {自}	飽きる	to lose interest in	17
あく {自}	開く	to open	17
あける {他}	開ける	to open	17
あげる {他}	上げる	to raise, elevate	6
あざやかに	鮮やかに	clearly, vividly	17
あたい	値	value	13

あ

あたい	価	value	19
あたえる {他}	与える	to give, provide	13
あたらしい	新しい	new	18
-あたり	-当たり	per	7
あたる {自}	当たる	to correspond (to)	13
あつい	熱い	hot	7
あつい	厚い	thick	19
あつさ	厚さ	thickness	16
あつまる {自}	集まる	to assemble, converge	15
あつめる {他}	集める	to gather, collect	15
あてはまる {自}	当てはまる	to be applicable, be valid	16
あてる {他}	当てる	to apply; to strike	11
あと(で)	後(で)	after	11
あな	穴	hole	9
あぶら	脂	fat, grease	15
あぶら	油	oil	19
あまり...ない	余り...ない	are not very ...	7
あまる {自}	余る	to be in excess	12
あらかじめ	予め	previously	16
あらゆる		all, every	5
あらわす {他}	表す	to express, show	7
あらわれる {自}	現われる	to appear, manifest	10
ありさま	有様	state, condition, sight	19
ありふれた		abundant	16
ある {自}	有る	to be, exist; to have	4
ある	或る	a certain ...	7
あるいは	或いは	or	4
あわ	泡	bubble	5
あわせる {他}	合わせる	to put together	8

い

いいかえれば	言い換えれば	in other words	4
いう {他}	言う	to say	6
いう：-と〜ように		in such a manner that	12
いうまでもない	言うまでもない	it goes without saying	9
いうまでもなく	言うまでもなく	needless to say	4
いかす {他}	生かす	to give life, enliven	5
いかなるばあいにも	いかなる場合にも	in any case	7
いかに		how	112
いきる {自}	生きる	to live	5
いく {自}	行く	to go	4
いくつ	幾つ	how many	12
いくら	幾ら	how much, how many	6
いし	石	stone(s)	5
いずれ	何れ	which one	12
いずれにしても	何れにしても	in either case	4

いた	板	plate, board	18
いたる {自}	至る	to reach, arrive at	16
いちじるしい	著しい	marked, striking	12
いつ		when	12
いっぱんに	一般に	generally, in general	4
いっぽう	一方	however, on the other hand	4
いつも		always	6
いま	今	now	4
-いる {xu 自}	入る	to enter	5
いる {自}	居る	to be	6
いる {xu 自}	要る	to need, require	7
いれる {他}	入れる	to insert	5
いろ	色	color	9
いろいろな	色々な	various	6
いわゆる	所謂	so-called	7

う

うえ	上	upper part, top	6
-うえに	上に	in addition to the fact that, above	6
-うえに(も)	上に(も)	(also) for ...ing	12
-うえで	上で	in order to, for the sake of, after	12
うえる {他}	植える	to plant; to raise	12
うけいれる {他}	受け入れる	to receive, accept	12
うけとる {他}	受け取る	to accept	13
うける {他}	受ける	to receive	16
うごかす {他}	動かす	to move	6
うごく {自}	動く	to move	6
うしなう {他}	失う	to lose	8
うしろ	後ろ	behind	11
うすい	薄い	thin	17
うち	内	inside; among	11
うつす {他}	移す	to move, transfer	12
うつる {自}	移る	to move (to a place)	12
うむ {他}	生む	to give birth	5
うむ {他}	産む	to give birth	16
うめる {他}	埋める	to bury	16
-うる	-得る	to be able to	11
うわむき	上向き	upward	9
うわる {自}	植わる	to be planted	12

え

えがく {他}	描く	to draw	14
-えない	-得ない	not to be able to	11
える {他}	得る	to get, obtain, gain	11

お

お

お-	御-	{honorific prefix}	16
おいて: -に～		in, at, on, as for	8
おうじて: -に～	-に応じて	in response to	8
おうじる: -に～	-に応じる	in response to	8
おおい	多い	many; frequent	4
おおいに	大いに	greatly	16
おおがたの	大型の	large-sized	17
おおきい	大きい	large	4
おおきさ	大きさ	magnitude	5
おおきな	大きな	large	5
おおくの	多くの	many, frequent	4
おおみず	大水	flooding	5
おおよそ	大凡	roughly, approximately	6
おかす {他}	侵す	to attack	15
おく {他}	置く	to put, place	9
おくりかえす {他}	送り返す	to return, send back	17
おくりだす {他}	送り出す	to send out	18
おくる {他}	送る	to send, transmit	4
おける: -に～		in, at, on, as for	8
おこす {他}	起こす	to generate, initiate	10
おこなう {他}	行う	to do, perform	5
おこる {自}	起こる	to happen, occur	10
おさえる {他}	抑える	to suppress, curb	17
おさめる {他}	収める	to obtain, gather	20
おす	押す	to push	13
おそい	遅い	late	17
おちる {自}	落ちる	to fall	9
おと	音	sound	18
おとのたかさ	音の高さ	pitch	18
おなじ	同じ	the same	7
おのおのの	各々の,各の	each	6
おびる {他}	帯びる	to put a band around; to take on (a color)	18
おもい	重い	heavy	7
おもさ	重さ	weight	7
おもて	面	surface	5
おもな	主な	primary, main, chief	18
おもり		a (plumb) weight	10
およそ	凡そ	approximately	14
および	及び	and, as well as	6
およぶ {自}	及ぶ	to attain, reach	13
およぼしあう {他}	及ぼし合う	to exert (force) on each other	9
およぼしかえす {他}	及ぼし返す	to exert (a force) in return	10
およぼす {他}	及ぼす	to exert (force)	10
おりもの	織物	woven fabric	12
おる {自}	居る	to be	9

おる {他}	織る	to weave	12
おる {他}	折る	to fold, bend	18
おわる {自}	終わる	to finish (doing something)	9

か

か		{interrogative marker}	6
か		or	6
-か	-日	{counter for days}	16
が		{subject marker}	6
かえる {他}	変える	to change	6
かえる {他}	換える	to exchange; to convert	17
かおり	香り	fragrance, aroma	19
かかわらず: -にも〜		in spite of (the fact that), notwithstanding	12
かきあらわす {他}	書き表す	to express	14
かきこむ {他}	書き込む	to write in, enter	17
かぎらない: -とは〜	-とは限らない	it is not necessarily true that	12
かぎらず: -に〜	-に限らず	not only ... but also	12
かぎり	限り	limit; bound	14
-かぎり	-限り	as long as	12
かぎる {xu 他}	限る	to be limited	14
かげ	影	shadow, shade	16
かける {他}		to apply (pressure, voltage)	9
かける {他}	掛ける	to multiply	14
かこむ {他}	囲む	to surround, enclose	11
かさなりあう {自}	重なり合う	to be superposed	16
かさなる {自}	重なる	to be piled up	7
かさねあわせ	重ね合わせ	superposition	8
かさねる {他}	重ねる	to pile up, layer	7
かず	数	number	8
かずかずの	数々の	several, numerous	8
かぞえる {他}	数える	to count	8
かた	型	model, type, mold	17
-かた	-方	way, style	5
-かた	-形	shape, form	12
-がた	-形	shape, form	12
-がた	-型	model, type	17
かたち	形	shape, form	12
かたまり	塊	a clump, piece, block	6
かたまる {自}	固まる	to harden	6
かためる {他}	固める	to harden	6
かつ	且つ	moreover	4
かつては		previously	18
かど	角	corner, edge	14
かどうか		whether or not	6
かならず	必ず	necessarily	7
かならずしも...ない	必ずしも...ない	not necessarily	7

か

かなり		rather	12
かね	金	money; metal	5
かねそなえる {他}	兼ね備える	to combine	17
からだ	体	(the) body	6
からである		it is because	7
から		from	6
かるい	軽い	light {in weight}	17
がわ	側	side	20
かわり: -の〜に	-の代わりに	instead of, in place of	12
かわる {自}	変わる	to be changed	6
かわる {自}	代わる	to replace	13
がん	癌	cancer	17
かんがい		irrigation	5
かんがえかた	考え方	way of thinking	10
かんがえなおす {他}	考え直す	to rethink	10
かんがえにいれる {他}	考えに入れる	to take into consideration	10
かんがえる {他}	考える	to think, consider	10
かんして: -に〜	-に関して	about, as regards, with respect to	8
かんする: -に〜	-に関する	about, as regards, with respect to	8
かんするかぎり: -に〜	-に関する限り	as far as ... is concerned	12
かんせず: -に〜	-に関せず	regardless of	12
かんばしい	芳しい	fragrant, aromatic	19

き

き	黄	yellow	20
きいろ	黄色	yellow	20
きえる {自}	消える	to go out, disappear	12
きく {自}	効く	to be effective	17
きこえる {自}	聞こえる	to sound	20
きざむ {他}	刻む	to cut, carve	13
きっかけ		start, beginning	16
きまる {自}	決まる	to be determined	10
きらう {他}	嫌う	to abhor	19
きりかえ	切り替え {替＝換}	switching	16
きりかえる {他}	切り換える {換＝替}	to replace	17
きりかく {他}	切り欠く	to notch	17
きりだす {他}	切り出す	to cut out	17
きる {xu 他}	切る	to cut (off)	17
きわめて	極めて	extremely	13
きわめる {他}	極める	to master	13

く

くぐりぬける {自}	潜り抜ける	to slip through	16
くさい	臭い	foul smelling	15
くすり	薬	medicine, drugs	19
くだ	管	pipe	9

H-6

くだく	砕く	to crush	10
くだける	砕ける	to be crushed	10
くに	国	country, nation	19
くばる {他}	配る	to distribute	15
くびれる {自}		to be constricted	19
-くみ	-組	set, class {counter}	12
くみあげる {他}	くみ上げる	to pump in	16
くみあわせ	組み合わせ	combination	12
くみかえDNA	組(み)換えDNA	recombinant DNA	17
くみこみ	組み込み	installation	17
くみこむ {他}	組み込む	to insert {lit.: to build into}	17
くむ {他}	組む	to assemble	12
くらい	位	approximately	9
くらべて: -に～	-に比べて	as compared to	8
くらべる {他}	比べる	to compare	6
くらべる: -に～	-に比べる	as compared to	8
くりかえす {他}	繰り返す	to repeat	10
くる	来る	to come	8
ぐるぐる		round and round, in circles	11
くわえる {他}	加える	to add, include	10
くわしくいえば	詳しく言えば	strictly speaking	4
くわわる {自}	加わる	to increase	10

け

けしあう {他}	消し合う	to cancel each other	16
けす {他}	消す	to extinguish, put out	12

こ

こ	子	child	5
こ-	小-	small	5
ご-	御-	{honorific prefix}	16
こい	濃い	concentrated	19
こう		in this way	4
こうして		by doing this	4
こえる {自}	越える	to go beyond, surpass	18
こがたの	小型の	small-sized	17
ごく	極く	extremely, very	16
こころ	心	heart	9
こころみる {他}	試みる	to try, attempt	19
こたえる {自}	答える	to answer	19
こと	事	thing, fact	8
ことなく		without ...ing	12
ことなる {自}	異なる	to differ, vary	9
-ごとに	-毎に	every, every so many, at an interval of	14
ことば	言葉	language, words	17
ことわる {他}	断る	to give notice, warn	18

こ

この		this {adjective}	4
このたび	この度	recently	17
このため	この為	because of this	4
このとき	この時	for this situation	4
このばあい	この場合	in this case	4
このように	この様に	thus, in this way	4
このようにして	この様にして	by doing this	4
こまかい	細かい	detailed, fine	9
これ		this {pronoun}	4
これにはんし(て)	これに反し(て)	in contrast to this	4
ころがる {自}	転がる	to roll, tumble	17
こわす {他}	壊す	to destroy	17

さ

さい(に)	-際(に)	when	12
さいして: -に〜	-に際して	on the occasion of, at the time of	12
さえ		even	16
さえぎる {xu 他}	遮る	to interrupt, cut off	13
さかい	境	boundary	16
さがる {自}	下がる	to sag, go lower	6
さかんな	盛んな	active	12
さきがけ	先駆け	forerunner	17
さく {他}	裂く	to split, tear	20
さける {他}	避ける	to avoid	13
さける {自}	裂ける	to be split, be torn	20
さげる {他}	下げる	to hang, lower	6
さす {他}	指す	to indicate	17
さす {他}	差す	to offer	20
させる {他}		to cause {an action}	9
さそう {他}	誘う	to allure, entice	20
さだまる {自}	定まる	to be determined	6
さだめる {他}	定める	to determine	6
さて		well, now	4
さまざまな	様々な	various	7
さまたげる {他}	妨げる	to hinder	15
さらに	更に	further(more), again	4

し

しお	塩	salt	10
しか		only {when the verb is negative}	6
しかし(ながら)		however	4
しかも		furthermore	4
しきる {xu 他}	仕切る	to partition	20
しずかな	静かな	silent, quiet	18
した	下	lower part, bottom	6
した: -の〜	-の下に	beneath	6

したがう {他}	従う	to obey {an equation}; to follow {a method}	10
したがって	従って	therefore	4
したがって: -に～	-に従って	following, in accordance with, (according) as	12
したむき	下向き	downward	9
しつくす {他}		to do completely	20
して: -と～(の)	-として(の)	(considered) as	8
しな	品	things, goods	17
しなもの	品物	goods	17
しぬ {自}	死ぬ	to die	7
しばしば		frequently	14
しぼり	絞り	orifice	9
しぼる {他}	絞る	to narrow, contract in area	9
-しまう {他}		to complete {an action}	9
しめす {他}	示す	to show, indicate	5
しめる {他}	占める	to occupy {space, location}	12
しらべる {他}	調べる	to investigate	13
しる {xu 他}	知る	to know	13
しれない: -かも～	-かも知れない	it may be that; perhaps	12
しろい	白い	white	11

す

す	酢	vinegar	15
すう {他}	吸う	to breath, suck	4
すぎない: -に～	-に過ぎない	is just, is simply	12
すぎる {自}	過ぎる	to elapse; to go through	12
-すぎる	-過ぎる	to over(do), be too ...	12
すぐ		immediately	19
すくない	少ない	few	7
すぐれる {自}	優れる	to excel in ...	17
すこし	少し	a little; slightly	7
すごす {他}	過ごす	to spend (time), go through	12
すすむ {自}	進む	to progress	15
-ずつ		each, apiece, at a time	14
すっかり		completely	13
すっぱい	酸っぱい	sour	7
すでに	既に	previously	4
すなわち	即ち	that is (to say), in other words	4
すべき		ought to do; intended for	13
すべく		having to, needing to do	13
すべて	全て	all (of something)	6
すみ	炭	charcoal	7
すみやかに	速やかに	quickly; immediately	8
すむ {自}		to get by with	14
ずらす {他}		to shift	19
する {他}		to do	6
すると		if so	4

す

ずれる {自}		to slip out of place	13

せ

せいかくにいえば	正確に言えば	if we state it (more) precisely	4
せきつい	脊椎	backbone, spine	20
ぜんたいでは	全体では	on the whole	4

そ

そう		in that way	4
そうしたら		if so, then	4
そうして		and	4
そうすると		if so, then	4
そうすれば		if we do that	4
そうでないと		if that is not true	4
そこで		thereupon, accordingly	4
そして		and, then	4
そそぎいれる {他}	注ぎ入れる	to pour into	7
そそぐ {他}	注ぐ	to pour	4
そって: -に〜	-に沿って	along	12
そと	外	outside, exterior	11
そとがわ	外側	outside	20
その		that {adjective}	4
そのあいだ	その間	during that time (interval)	4
そのうえ	その上	moreover	4
そのけっか	その結果	as a result	4
そのさい	その際	in that situation	4
そのた	その他	etc.	13
そのため	その為	because of that	4
そのまま		as it is	14
そまる {自}	染まる	to be dyed, stained	20
そめる {他}	染める	to dye, stain	20
そら	空	sky, heavens	12
それ		that {pronoun}	4
それから		and then	4
それぞれ		respectively	7
それぞれの		several, each	7
それだから		therefore, accordingly	4
それで		thereupon, then	4
それでは		well then	4
それでも		but, be that as it may	4
それとも		or	4
それなのに		in spite of that, nevertheless	4
それなら		if so	4
それにしては		considering that	4
それにしても		even so, admitting that	4
それにはんして	それに反して	in contrast to that	4

それにもかかわらず		in spite of that, nevertheless	4
それほど	それ程	that much, to that extent	18
それゆえ	それ故	consequently, therefore	4
そろいかた	そろい方	the ordering; arrangement	13
そろう〔自〕		to be in order; to be arranged	13

た

たいおうして: -に～	-に対応して	corresponding to	8
たいおうする: -に～	-に対応する	corresponding to	8
たいして: -に～	-に対して	for, in, against	8
たいする: -に～	-に対する	for, in, against	8
たいせつな	大切な	important	18
たいらな	平らな	horizontal; flat	10
たえる〔自〕	絶える	to end	18
たかい	高い	tall	5
たがい(の)	互い(の)	mutual, reciprocal	19
たかさ	高さ	height	5
たくさん		many	6
だけ		only, just	6
だけで		only by (means of) ...	8
たしかな	確かな	certain, sure	18
たしかに	確かに	to be sure, undoubtedly	4
たしかめる〔他〕	確かめる	to confirm, make certain	18
たす〔他〕	足す	to add	5
だす〔他〕	出す	to send out, take out	9
ただ		only, merely, but	12
たたく〔他〕		to hit, strike	17
ただし	但し	provided that	4
ただしい	正しい	correct	11
たちば	立場	standpoint	10
たちまち		suddenly	17
たつ〔自〕	立つ	to stand	5
たつ〔他〕	断つ	to cut off	18
たつ〔自〕	経つ	to elapse (time)	20
たてる〔他〕	立てる	to set up, erect	5
たとえば	例えば	for example	4
たね	種	seed, kernel	14
たねもの	種物	seeds	14
たま	球	sphere, ball	12
たまご	卵	egg	20
ためす〔他〕	試す	to try, test	19
ために	-為に	in order to ...	18
たもつ〔他〕	保つ	to maintain	18
たやすい		easy	19
たよる〔自〕	頼る	to rely on, depend on	19
だれ		who	12

ち

ち -

ち	血	blood	4
ちいさい	小さい	small	4
ちいさな	小さな	small	5
ちかい	近い	near, close	9
ちがい	違い	difference	8
ちがいない: -に〜	-に違いない	is certainly	12
ちがう {自}	違う	to differ, vary	8
ちがう: -と〜	-と違う	unlike, differing from	8
ちかくに: -の〜	-の近くに	near, close	11
ちかぢか	近々	in the near future	4
ちがって: -と〜	-と違って	unlike, differing from	8
ちから	力	force	5
ちぢまない	縮まない	incompressible	18
ちぢまる {自}	縮まる	to shrink	18
ちぢめる {他}	縮める	to compress	18
ちる {xu 自}	散る	to scatter	17

つ

ついて: -に〜		as for, as regards, with respect to	8
つかいかた	使い方	way of using	9
つかう {他}	使う	to use	9
つぎつぎ	次々	successively, one after another	19
つきとめる {他}	突き止める	to ascertain	17
つぎに	次に	next	4
つぎの	次の	(the) next	8
つく {自}	付く	to be attached	19
つく {他}	突く	to thrust	20
つく {自}	着く	to arrive, contact	20
つぐ {自}	次ぐ	to come after, follow	10
つくす {他}	尽くす	to do something exhaustively	9
つくりだす {他}	作り出す	to produce	9
つくりなおす {他}	作り直す	to remake, rebuild	10
つくる {他}	作る	to make, build	4
つける {他}	付ける	to attach, tag	8
つたえる {他}	伝える	to transmit	12
つたわる {自}	伝わる	to be transmitted	12
つち	地	earth, ground	12
-つつ		at the same time as, while	13
つづく {自}	続く	to continue	16
つづける {他}	続ける	to continue	4
つつむ {他}	包む	to wrap, envelop	16
つながる {自}		to be connected, joined, linked	19
つなぐ {他}		to connect {wires}	8
つなみ	津波	tsunami, tidal wave	18
つねづね	常々	usually	4

つねに	常に	always, continually	13
つの	角	horn {of an animal}	14
つばさ	翼	wings	18
つぶ	粒	grain; drop	12
つまり	詰まり	in other words, put simply	4
つむ {自}	積む	to stow aboard	13
つもる {自}	積もる	to accumulate	8
つよい	強い	strong	11
つよさ	強さ	strength	11
つらなる {自}	連なる	to be connected	16
つりあげる {他}	つり上げる	to suspend	17
つるす {他}		to suspend	10
つれて: -に〜	-に連れて	in accordance with, as	8
つれる: -に〜	-に連れる	in accordance with, as	8

て

て	手	hand	4
で		in, at; by means of	6
でいりする {自}	出入りする	to go in and out	9
できあがる {自}	出来上がる	to be completed	17
できごと	出来事	occurrence, incident, event	16
できる {自}	出来る	to be possible, be do-able	7
できる: -ことが〜	ことが出来る	to be possible	7
でたらめの		random, haphazard	13
てづくり	手作り	hand-made	4
てまち	手待ち	waiting	17
でる {自}	出る	to emerge, go out (from)	9
でんぷん		starch	16

と

と		and; with	6
とい	問い	question	16
とう {他}	問う	to ask	16
どう		in what way	4
とうてい...ない		not at all, not nearly	18
とおい	遠い	far	4
とおす {他}	通す	to admit, let pass	13
とおり(に)	通り(に)	(in) the manner, way	4
とおりぬける {自}	通り抜ける	to pass through	17
とおる {自}	通る	to go through	12
とか		and	6
とかす {他}	溶かす	to melt; to dissolve	9
とき	時	time; occasion	9
ときあかす {他}	解き明かす	to clarify	13
ときどき	時々	sometimes	9
とく {他}	解く	to untie; to solve	9

と

とく {他}	説く	to explain	13
とくに	特に	in particular	4
とける {自}	溶ける	to melt; to dissolve	9
どこ		where	12
どこかで		at some place	10
ところ	所	place	13
ところが		but, however	4
ところで		incidentally, by the way	4
どちら		which {of several}	12
とどく {自}	届く	to reach	16
ととのう {自}	整う	to be well ordered	11
どの		which	12
とは		{abbreviation for というのは}	6
とめる {他}	止める	to turn off, stop	17
ともなう {自}	伴う	to accompany	13
ともなって: -に～	-に伴って	with, along with ...ing	12
とも: -と～に	-と共に	with, along with ...ing	12
とりあえず		at once	13
とりいれる {他}	取り入れる	to adopt, take in	12
とりくむ {自}	取り組む	to grapple with	19
とりつける {他}	取り付ける	to attach	13
とりのぞく {他}	取り除く	to remove	13
どれ		which one	12

な

な	名	name	12
ない	無い	is not, are none	7
ないし		or	20
なお	尚	further	4
なおす {他}	直す	to mend; to correct	9
なおる {自}	直る	to get well	10
なか	中	inside	6
なか: -の～に	-の中に	inside	6
ながい	長い	long	10
ながさ	長さ	length	10
ながす {他}	流す	to let flow; to flush	7
なかば	半ば	half; halfway; middle	14
なかほど	中ほど	the middle, halfway	19
-ながら		at the same time as, while	13
ながれ	流れ	flow	4
ながれでる {自}	流れ出る	to flow out	9
ながれる {自}	流れる	to flow	7
なげかける {他}	投げ掛ける	to throw	19
なしで		without	12
なしに		without	12
なす {他}		to do, make, perform	12

なぜ	何故	why	4
なぜかといえば	何故かと言えば	the reason is	4
なぜなら(ば)	何故なら(ば)	the reason is	4
なづける {他}	名付ける	to call, name	12
など	等	etc., and so on	6
なに	何	what	12
なまり	鉛	lead	15
なみ	波	wave	18
ならびに	並びに	and	6
ならべる {他}	並べる	to align, line up	17
なりたつ {自}	成り立つ	to be valid; to consist of	8
なる {自}	なる	to form, turn into, be	5
なる {自}	成る	to consist of; to turn into	8
なん	何	what	14
なんとなれば	何となれば	the reason is	4

に

に		in, on, at	6
-にくい		hard to ..., difficult to ...	9
にる {自}	似る	to resemble	14

ぬ

ぬの	布	cloth	17
ぬる {他}	塗る	to paint	15

ね

ねいろ	音色	(sound) timbre	18
ねばる {自}	粘る	to be sticky	18

の

の		of	6
のこる {自}	残る	to remain	13
のせる {他}		to place {at rest on something}	13
のぞく {他}	除く	to remove	11
のぞましい	望ましい	desired, hoped for	16
のぞむ {他}	望む	to desire	17
のち(に)	後(に)	after	11
のべる {他}	述べる	to state, discuss	13
のみ		only	6
のみではなく...も		not only ... but also	12
のみならず...も		not only ... but also	12

は

は		{topic marker}	6
ば	場	place; occasion	10
-ば	-場	field {electric, force}	10

は

ばあい	場合	case, occasion	4
ばあいによって	場合によって	depending on the situation	4
はいりこむ {自}	入り込む	to enter	20
はいる {xu 自}	入る	to enter	5
はがね	鋼	steel	19
ばかり		(only) about	14
ばかりではなく...も		not only ... but also	12
はかる {他}	量る,計る,測る	to measure	8
はかる {他}	図る	to devise	18
ばくだいな	莫大な	huge, enormous	18
はこびだす {他}	運び出す	to carry out	9
はこぶ {他}	運ぶ	to carry	9
はさむ {他}	挟む	to sandwich (something) between, put between	14
はし	端	tip, end	18
はじまる {自}	始まる	to begin	13
はじめ	初め	beginning	20
はじめて	初めて	for the first time	17
はじめに	初めに	first, at the start	4
はじめる {他}	始める	to begin	9
はず: -〜である	-筈である	should, we (have good reason to) expect that	11
はずれる {自}	外れる	to deviate, slip off	17
はだか	裸	bare	20
はたす {他}	果たす	to accomplish	10
はたらく {他}	働く	to work	9
はっきり		clearly	12
はな	鼻	nose	4
はなす {他}	放す	to let go, release	10
はなぢ	鼻血	nosebleed	4
はなれる {自}	離れる	to separate	16
ばね		spring	10
はやい	速い	fast, rapid	8
はやめる {他}	早める	to hasten	17
はら	原	field	6
はんして: -に〜	-に反して	in contrast to, contrary to	8
はんする: -に〜	-に反する	in contrast to, contrary to	8

ひ

ひ	日	sun	16
ひかり	光	light	10
ひかる {自}	光る	to shine, glitter	10
ひきあう {自}	引き合う	to attract each other	20
ひく {他}	引く	to subtract; to pull, attract	14
ひくい	低い	low	17
ひずみ	歪	strain, deformation	13
ひずむ {他}	歪む	to constrain	15
ひと	人	person, people	5

ひとくみ	一組	one set	12
ひとしい	等しい	equal	4
ひとつ	一つ	one	5
ひとびと	人々	persons, people	6
ひとり	一人	one person	5
ひびく {自}	響く	to sound, resound	16
ひらく {他 & 自}	開く	to open	17
ひらける {自}	開ける	to open	17
ひらたい	平たい	flat	10
ひろい	広い	wide, broad	17
ひろがる {自}	広がる	to broaden, widen	18

ふ

ふえる {自}	増える	to increase	10
ふえる {自}	殖える	to propagate {biol}, increase (in number)	20
ふくむ {他}	含む	to contain, include	5
ふくらむ {自}		to swell (out), distend	19
ふさわしい		to be proper	20
ふせぐ {他}	防ぐ	to shut out, protect against	17
ふたくみ	二組	two sets	12
ふたたび	再び	again, a second time	17
ふたつ	二つ	two	5
ふたとおり(に)	二通り(に)	(in) two ways	13
ふたり	二人	two people	5
ふつうの	普通の	usual	13
ぶつかる {自}		to collide	17
ふやす {他}	増やす	to increase	10
ふやす {他}	殖やす	to propagate {biol}, increase (in number)	20
ふる {他}	振る	to swing, vibrate	10
ふるい	古い	old	19
ふるまい	振る舞い	behavior	19
ふれる {自}	触れる	to touch	20

へ

へ		to, toward	6
-べき		must, have to, ought to	13
へだてる {他}	隔てる	to separate	17
へて: -を〜	-を経て	via ...	20
へらす {他}	減らす	to decrease	17
へる {xu 自}	減る	to decrease	17

ほ

ほか: -の〜に	-の外に	other than; in addition to (...ing)	11
ほかならない: -に〜		is just, is nothing other than	12
ほかの	外の	another, different	11
ほそい	細い	slender, narrow	9

ほ

ほそながい	細長い	long and slender	10
ほど	程	extent	11
ほとんど	殆ど	almost	6
ほぼ		(very) nearly	14

ま

まえ	前	front; before	11
まがる {自}	曲がる	to be curved; to be bent	14
まぎらわしい		confusing	20
まげる {他}	曲げる	to bend	14
まさる {自}		to be superior (to)	15
まざる {自}	混ざる	to be mixed	19
まじきり	間仕切り	partition	17
まじる {xu 自}	混じる	to be blended	14
まじわる {自}	交わる	to intersect	10
ます	升	a container {for measuring}	9
ます {他}	増す	to increase	10
まず	先ず	first (of all), (at) first, to begin with	4
まぜる {他}	混ぜる	to mix	4
また	又	moreover, and (in addition)	4
または	又は	or	4
まちがい	間違い	mistake, error	8
まちがう {自}	間違う	to be in error	10
まっすぐ		straight ahead	6
まったく	全く	entirely	9
まで		up (down) to, as far as	5
まとめる {他}		to bring together	14
まなぶ {他}	学ぶ	to learn, study	6
まもる {他}	守る	to protect	17
まれな		rare	15
まわしおわる {他}	回し終わる	to finish turning	16
まわす {他}	回す	to rotate	14
まわり	周り	circumference; surroundings	11
まわる {自}	回る	to rotate, revolve	11

み

み	実	fruit	8
み	三	three	14
みいだす {他}	見出す; 見いだす	to discover, find	9
みえる {自}	見える	to be visible	5
みかた	見方	point of view	5
みじかい	短い	short	11
みず	水	water	5
みずから	自ら	by itself, oneself	13
みたす {他}	満たす	to fill (up)	12
みだす {他}	乱す	to make chaotic	18

H-18

みだれる 〔自〕	乱れる	to be disordered	18
みちびきいれる 〔他〕	導き入れる	to lead into	14
みちびきだす 〔他〕	導き出す	to derive; to lead out	14
みちびく 〔他〕	導く	to lead; to derive	9
みつ	三つ	three	14
みっつ	三つ	three	14
みなす 〔他〕	見なす	to regard ... as	5
みなもと	源	origin	18
みみ	耳	ear	18
みる 〔他〕	見る	to see	5

む

むかう 〔自〕	向かう	to face toward	9
むき	向き	direction	9
むく 〔自〕	向く	to turn toward	9
むしろ		rather than ...	20
むす 〔他〕	蒸す	to steam	11
むずかしい	難しい	difficult	9
むすび	結び	conclusion	9
むすびつく 〔自〕	結びつく	to be attached	17
むすぶ 〔他〕	結ぶ	to tie, bind; to conclude	9
むつかしい	難しい	difficult	16

め

め	目	eye	13
-め	-目	{ordinal suffix}	13
めやす	目安	standard, aim	17

も

も		also, even	6
も...も		both ... and ...	6
もう		already	4
もうける 〔他〕	設ける	to establish, set up, equip	4
もえる 〔自〕	燃える	to burn	20
もし		if	4
もちいる 〔他〕	用いる	to use	4
もちろん	勿論	of course	4
もつ 〔他〕	持つ	to have	9
もっと		more	19
もっとも	最も	most	11
もっぱら	専ら	exclusively	17
もと	元	source, origin	8
もと	基	basis	13
もと	本	origin, base	16
もとづいて: -に～	-に基づいて	on the basis of	12
もとづく 〔自〕	基づく	to be based (on)	13

も

もとで	-下で	under, at	6
もとまる〔自〕	求まる	to be obtained	13
もとめる〔他〕	求める	to seek; to find	13
もともと	元々	originally, in the past	4
もどる〔自〕	戻る	to return, revert	14
もの	物	thing, object	5
もの	者	person	17
もやす〔他〕	燃やす	to burn	20
もろい		brittle	15
もろもろの	諸々の	various, all	7

や

や		and, or	6
やすい	安い	cheap, inexpensive	11
-やすい		easy to ...	9
やはり		after all, still, of course	4
やや		moderately, fairly, rather	17
やりなおす〔他〕	やり直す	to redo	13
やる〔他〕		to do	7

ゆ

ゆえに	故に	therefore	4
ゆがむ〔他〕		to distort	17
ゆく〔自〕	行く	to go	5
ゆるす〔他〕	許す	to allow, permit	18
ゆれ	揺れ	swaying, shaking	17
ゆれる〔自〕	揺れる	to sway, shake	17

よ

よい	良い	good	9
よう	様	way, manner	4
ようにする		to see to it that	12
ようになる		to come about that	12
よって		consequently, therefore	4
よって: -に〜		by (means of), on the basis of, due to	8
よぶ〔他〕	呼ぶ	to call	12
よらず: -に〜		independent of, regardless of	12
よる: -に〜		by (means of), on the basis of, due to	8
よわい	弱い	weak	11

ら

| -ら | -等 | et al. | 7 |
| -らしい | | -like, appears to be ... | 11 |

わ

| わがくに | 我が国 | our country, our nation | 7 |

をを

わかる {自}	分かる	to understand, know	6
わかれる {自}	別れる	to part from	16
わけ: -〜である	-訳である	the reason is, it means that	12
わけにはいかない	-訳にはいかない	it cannot be that	12
わける {他}	分ける	to divide (in parts)	6
わずかな	僅かな	slight	17
わずかの	僅かの	few	19
わたす {他}	渡す	to transfer	20
わたって: -に〜	-に渡って	(extending) over	8
わたる: -に〜	-に渡る	(extending) over	8
わたる {自}	渡る	to spread, extend, range	16
わり	割	rate; tenths	13
わりあい	割合	proportion, rate	13
わりあてる {他}	割り当てる	to allocate	13
わりサン	割り算	division	17
わる {他}	割る	to divide	13
わるい	悪い	bad	16
われわれ	我々	we	17

を

を		{object marker}	6

H-21

Subject Index

Entry locations are given by section for Chapters 1 through 15; that is, 15.3 means Chapter 15, Section 3. For Chapters 16 and 17 the entries refer to the Notes at the conclusion of the translation examples; that is, 16(14) means Chapter 16, Notes to Translation Example 14. In addition, App A means Appendix A, and Ex 4.7 means Exercise 4.7 of Chapter 4.